Steven Spielberg FAQ

Steven Spielberg FAQ

All That's Left to Know About the Films of Hollywood's Best Known Director

Barry Monush

APPLAUSE
THEATRE & CINEMA BOOKS
An Imprint of Hal Leonard LLC

Published in 2018 by Applause Theatre & Cinema Books
An Imprint of Hal Leonard LLC
7777 West Bluemound Road
Milwaukee, WI 53213

Trade Book Division Editorial Offices
33 Plymouth St., Montclair, NJ 07042

All photos are from the author's collection unless otherwise noted.

The FAQ series was conceived by Robert Rodriguez and developed with Stuart Shea.

Printed in the United States of America

Book design by Snow Creative

Library of Congress Cataloging-in-Publication Data
Names: Monush, Barry.
Title: Steven Spielberg FAQ : all that's left to know about the films of
  Hollywood's best known director / Barry Monush.
Other titles: Steven Spielberg frequently asked questions
Description: Milwaukee, WI : Applause Theater & Cinema Books, an imprint of
  Hal Leonard, LLC, 2018. | Series: The FAQ series | Includes
  bibliographical references and index.
Identifiers: LCCN 2017052708 | ISBN 9781495064739 (pbk.)
Subjects: LCSH: Spielberg, Steven, 1946—Criticism and interpretation.
Classification: LCC PN1998.3.S65 M66 2018 | DDC 791.4302/33092--dc23
LC record available at https://lccn.loc.gov/2017052708
ISBN 978-1-4950-6473-9

www.applausebooks.com

To James Sheridan

. . . always kind, always knowledgeable, always supportive

Contents

Introduction: A Lifetime of Spielberg   ix

Acknowledgments   xvii

1   Spielberg Through the Years: A Timeline of Pivotal Events from Steven Spielberg's Life and Career   1

2   Spielberg Sources: Literary and Real-Life Origins of Some of Steven Spielberg's Movies   17

3   Spielberg Directs for Television: His Fifteen Credits for the Small Screen   80

4   Spielberg on Location: Where Steven Spielberg Shot Each of His Films   105

5   Scripted by Spielberg: When the Director Received an Onscreen Writing Credit   170

6   Produced by Spielberg: From Amblin to DreamWorks and Beyond   189

7   Small-Screen Spielberg Productions: Producing for Television   240

8   Spielberg in Front of the Camera: When the Director Did Some "Acting" or Guest Starred as Himself   273

9   The Sound of Spielberg: The Important Use of Music in Steven Spielberg's Films, with a Special Nod to John Williams   284

10   Spielberg by the Numbers: How Spielberg's Films Have Performed at the Box Office   342

Bibliography   379

Index   381

Introduction
A Lifetime of Spielberg

B ecause your average citizen, even one who goes to the movies on a fairly regular basis, hasn't a vast knowledge of who is directing what, or might not even understand what precisely a director does, shorthand is required. For about forty years now, if you want to explain to someone what a filmmaker is, or find a quick example of a director, or sum up motion pictures in reference to someone working *behind* the camera, that shorthand has been "Steven Spielberg."

Steven Spielberg is, beyond a doubt, the most famous motion picture director of our time, the one with the unbeatable track record for box office success, the guy who has so thoroughly influenced the medium since the 1970s that he cannot help but be a polarizing figure. You can't become *that* famous and *that* rich and *that* creatively productive without rubbing *some* people the wrong way. Over the years I have heard him spoken of with awe and respect, reverence and pleasure, just as I have heard him dismissed as overrated and untalented, always with a certain degree of resentment, as if someone is not allowed to create movies and have that level of public awareness, clout, dominance, and endurance in an industry that customarily tosses everyone aside to make way for the next new thing. Steven Spielberg has been a force of nature from the time I started going to the movies on a regular basis, and I for one am *thrilled* to have experienced all but one of his movies in "real time."

I mark 1975 as the beginning of my moviegoing obsession, and that was the year that *Jaws* arrived on the scene and shook the very foundations of the motion picture industry, changing the concept of film distribution, not really for the better. For those too young to have been around in that era, popular films did not scorch the box office for a weekend or two and then peter out in a month's time, as most of them do now. Back then, distribution was *not* predominantly of the saturation kind, and therefore movies really did stick around for a reasonable amount of time, allowing pictures to have a resonance in popular culture that is all but absent today. Even though *Jaws* opened in what, at the time, was considered a "wide release," not every theater you passed on the highway or on your downtown main street was playing it. The multiplex was only just then beginning to blossom on the American landscape, so you had to search out a specific movie and make a little more effort to see it. This meant that popular films hopped around from cinema to cinema over the course of many months, making them very available for a substantial period for those who weren't accustomed to rushing out to see something on its opening weekend. *Jaws* didn't just come and go but was nothing less than phenomenal in its impact throughout the summer of that year. It continued to be a part of the cultural conversation into the fall and throughout holiday time and award season as well. And it prevailed for years and then decades to come because it not only entertained and terrified millions at the time, but it inspired generations of filmmakers and became a touchstone for an exciting degree of modern filmmaking that went beyond being a mere passing thrill but instead entered the consciousness in such a way that it could be thought of as an indelible form of motion picture folklore.

I must confess: at that time I was still of the age that the name of every director didn't always register with me, even those who helmed many of the movies I enjoyed. But I certainly knew that what I was watching that evening at the United Artists Cinema in Hazlet, New Jersey, back in late June of that year, was making a tremendous impact on me, and that most certainly had to do with the way it was directed. I filed away the name "Steven Spielberg" in my subconscious, so I was well aware of him being left out of that year's Oscar nominations in the directing category. This curious omission occurred despite the fact that *Jaws* did rate a Best Picture nomination and that everyone who followed such things really understood that without Spielberg's expertise this whole thing could have played with the same degree of enervation and dropped instantly into the same level of obscurity as Cornel Wilde's *Sharks' Treasure,* which had popped up on screens that same year. I didn't realize at the time that this was the first sign of what would become a lifetime of backlash.

But in the meantime, my Spielberg awareness arose. Later, that same year, when *The Sugarland Express* played on *NBC Saturday Night at the Movies,* I remember that the ads in *TV Guide* played up the fact that it was "From the Director of *Jaws.*" The actual listing for the movie led off with "Director Steven Spielberg (*Jaws*) made his theatrical film debut with . . ." Although I was well aware of this movie opening only the year before in cinemas, in my mind (and most everyone else's at the time) it was "a Goldie Hawn movie." It hadn't stuck around that long, but suddenly it had taken on a whole new level of interest because it was connected to "that *Jaws* guy" who had satisfied so much of the public with that superbly crafted shark movie. Soon, I came to realize that *Jaws* was not my first experience having seen something directed by Steven Spielberg because sometime in the early 1970s I had caught a showing of the *Night Gallery* pilot movie on WOR Channel 9, which included that memorably eerie segment with Joan Crawford as a nasty blind lady who pays to experience temporary sight with dire results. That, it turned out, was the very first thing Steven Spielberg had directed for television. Having enjoyed that as well as the commercial-ridden television presentation of *Sugarland,* I guess it was safe to say that I knew this fellow was nothing if not competent. *Highly* competent. Then *Close Encounters of the Third Kind* came along and upped the "wow" factor considerably.

Close Encounters (as it quickly became known to those who found it too time consuming to say the whole title) opened in 1977, which was, by a wide margin, the year of *Star Wars.* Although the two sci-fi movies could not have been farther apart in intention, there was much debate at the school I attended, Rutgers College, as to which was the better of the two fantasy epics. The general consensus weighed heavily in favor of George Lucas's rousing adventure, but I had a definite preference for Spielberg's film. This is no slight on *Star Wars*, which I enjoyed and still enjoy very much, but I always tend to react better to a science fiction story that has an earthly setting rather than one that takes place in a mythical world or another galaxy. *Close Encounters* tapped into a human element that made it very easy to relate to, even for someone like me who never once believed there were extraterrestrials out there trying to make contact with us. I found it thrilling, funny, mysterious, and finally awe inspiring. In Roy Neary's life, the spacemen had arrived. In my life, Steven Spielberg had arrived, and I knew that as long as I could fish a few bucks out of my pocket and find my way to a cinema, I would follow, with great curiosity and interest, whatever it was he had to offer.

Then came, as it must in every filmmaker's life, that inevitable pothole on the highway of success: *1941*. I was kept abreast of some of the developments of the making of this gigantic comedy because the brother of my Rutgers friend Larry Deutchman knew one of the writers of the picture, Bob Gale. Larry was very excited by the possibilities of the director of *Jaws* making his grand slapstick epic, much as Stanley Kramer had done with *It's a Mad Mad Mad Mad World*. But once *1941* opened, you couldn't stop reading the bad reviews, as each tried to top the other with gleeful proclamations that the man who had hit dual bullseyes with his last two movies was fallible after all and could deliver a dud with the best of them (or, rather, the worst of them).

This certainly did not deter me from experiencing it myself, and my friend Paul Larkins and I decided we would see *1941* when we journeyed to Hollywood for a vacation in January of 1980. The film was, after all, set in the movie capital, and, better yet, was playing at a theater I was always intrigued to visit, the Cinerama Dome (which had opened, coincidentally, with the premiere of *Mad Mad World*). Often referred to as a gigantic golf ball cut in half, this theater provided us with a dazzlingly loud Dolby Stereo sound system to such a degree that the extreme noise level of this incredibly strident movie nearly gave my friend and I headaches by the time it was all over. So, the naysayers were correct, Steven Spielberg *had* pretty much fallen flat on his face, and yet, damned if I still didn't come out impressed by the opulent production and the execution of one sequence that was pretty awesome for its sheer outrageousness: a Ferris wheel at an oceanfront amusement park being shot off its hinges by a Japanese sub and then rolling down the boardwalk like an oversized bicycle wheel before dunking into the water and sinking as its lights went out. Even a bad movie by a good filmmaker will get you to notice his flair off and on, and there were other details and moments in this picture that would stay in my mind long after my brain was done exploding from irritation overload.

The early 1980s brought the one-two punch of *Raiders of the Lost Ark* and *E.T. the Extra-Terrestrial*. Like *Close Encounters*, cinemagoers quickly shortened both these titles, and during the summer of 1981 and 1982, respectively, one was frequently asked if they had seen *Raiders* or what they thought of *E.T.* To say that these two movies entered the *Jaws* realm of pop culture phenomena is perhaps an understatement. Both easily dominated their summer seasons and became so spoken of, parodied, referenced, and embraced that there was no doubting that this marked the moment when Steven Spielberg went from a director admired by his industry peers and select cinemaniacs to a household name. This sort of thing was seldom done in the history of motion pictures. Cecil B. DeMille and Alfred Hitchcock managed it, but you couldn't walk up to your average citizen and mention the names of even those as highly publicized and revered as John Ford, Stanley Kubrick, or Billy Wilder and get instant recognition. I'm absolutely certain that Spielberg entered the modern-day consciousness at this unprecedented level because in the last thirty-five years I have never once seen someone react, regardless of age or social standing, with a puzzled look at the mention of his name.

With this degree of fame came an avalanche of opinions and assessments of Steven Spielberg's worth, not just in contemporary terms, but in the very history of cinema itself. He was now a "star director," and by expanding his industry involvement into the field of producing, his name was seemingly everywhere, so much so that many people who did not follow the movie scene as a favorite pastime assumed he was the director of such motion pictures as *Gremlins, Back to the Future,* and **batteries not included.* From this era onward he would never again escape extreme scrutiny and judgment on whatever he chose to direct, and because he had reached the Mount Olympus of filmmaking, select people expected a masterpiece every time or insisted on pigeon-holing him in regards to what genre or theme he was expected to tackle and how it was assumed he would approach it. Less successful filmmakers, or those who couldn't hope to attain his level of clout, turned on him. It was a classic case of jealousy: If he was so successful, why not me? Some made him jump through hoops never expected of other industry creators to prove his value.

This disgruntled manner was evident by the overreaction to the perceived darkness and excessive violence in *Indiana Jones and the Temple of Doom,* criticized by the very people who had no complaints about anything of a similar nature in the works of such filmmakers as Martin Scorsese and Sam Peckinpah. Because Spielberg had been pegged as a creator of works for a "family audience," getting gruesome or ugly was deemed unacceptable from him. Frankly, I have little patience for someone who doesn't see the humor in chilled monkey brains, but what was all too evident to me and to those not insistent on finding the bad wherever they could find it was that many chose not to notice just how exceedingly well directed this movie was. Spielberg had only to make a single false move in order to be taken to task by those dead set on exposing his faults, but in my eyes I continued to be astounded by his talents. One had only to see a similar adventure, *Romancing the Stone,* directed by his protégé Robert Zemeckis and released the same year as *Temple of Doom,* to realize how it was inferior in every department. Spielberg could take the pulp of a serial and elevate it with a daring sense of cinema that was a marvel to behold.

If this did not prove to me that Steven Spielberg was now held to the loftiest of expectations and was never going to win over certain detractors, *The Color Purple* did the trick. It is not very often that a movie this good is raked so mercilessly over the coals by those who insist on pointing to it as an example of Spielberg's worst excesses of a populist filmmaker. A lot of leverage is given to those who derided the picture at the time, but less so to those who championed it enthusiastically or to the audience, who turned it into the sort of box office smash that sadly, where straight dramas were concerned, had become less common in the 1980s.

My recollection of the year 1985 was that the best word of mouth that summer was for the Spielberg-produced *Back to the Future*, while the movie of the holiday season and the New Year that I heard the most positive comments on was undoubtedly *The Color Purple*. I myself was heartened to see how many people were pulled into this difficult story, one that many people might have not bothered to see at all had Steven Spielberg's name not been attached to it. He was one of its principal attractions, initially, but the satisfying nature of the picture itself soon had people buzzing and recommending it to others. History has instead decided to rewrite the story to make it appear as if this career highpoint was a serious error made by Spielberg, a filmmaker clearly out of his element, a Caucasian Jew who dared to helm a story about impoverished blacks, as if there was a color barrier for him and only him when it came to choosing material. (Compare this to the criticism that black director Bill Nunn received in 1993 for piloting *The Cemetery Club*, a story of three elderly Jewish white women—in fact, I don't recall any complaints, whatsoever, as well there shouldn't have been.) That Spielberg had already so clearly tapped into the humanity of his subjects on so many previous occasions seemed to not be considered a crucial factor in bringing this story to life onscreen. The book's author, Alice Walker, was pleased with his efforts, his cast spoke glowingly of him making this important tale accessible to mainstream audiences, the Directors Guild named him that year's winner, and the paying customers applauded it wildly. All filmmakers would give their proverbial right arms to make such a "misstep." But how did the industry reward Spielberg for his exemplary efforts, for showing that he could go outside of their restrictions set upon him and still make both an outstanding film and box office magic? They made sure that the eleven Oscar nominations the movie received did *not* include one for his direction. I don't think in the whole history of that venerable institution there had ever been made so firm a statement against someone's achievement that came off as a plain case of petulant resentment. To this day, I hear many speak glowingly of *The Color Purple* and few at all about the movie the Academy designated to take its place as the year's Best Picture winner, *Out of Africa*. Clearly, the work was and remains its own reward.

It seemed the camps were becoming vocally and seismically divided over the mighty Spielberg. He was gargantuan in presence; that household name designation comes with a backbreaking burden after all. To the celebrity-hungry world, his own degree of notoriety was beginning to overshadow his tremendous talent. Certain detractors could no longer see the superlative balance of thrills and humor in *Indiana Jones and the Last Crusade*; they wanted to know instead why he didn't surprise them again exactly the way he had when Indiana Jones was brand new, why they couldn't look at his movies anymore with that removal most people have toward directors. There was baggage aplenty now in most reviews. He was so disdained by some that when criticizing a particularly bad production from his Amblin Entertainment, *Harry and the Hendersons*, many reviews mentioned Spielberg's name (despite the fact that it does not even appear on the credits of this movie) more than they did the actual director, William Dear. It was as if he had personally been responsible for influencing an entire generation of filmmakers who hadn't the same degree of talent, showmanship, savvy, and personal vision when it came to making motion pictures. When he himself did indeed miss the goal, as he did with, say, *Hook*, there was rancor hurled in his direction of the sort less talented filmmakers never received. Curiously, while all kinds of terrible movies were still coming down the pike year after year, it was someone who still showed an incredible combination of craft, humanity, humor, heart, soul, commercial sense, and artistry who was receiving the louder knocks.

As if to exercise his full faculties to prove he wasn't down yet, Steven Spielberg accomplished what I consider to be one of the most astounding dual achievements in the history of film. In 1993 he gave us both the year's highest-grossing movie, *Jurassic Park*, and its most acclaimed and honored, *Schindler's List*, two pictures that could not have been further apart in tone and intention. The former was as rousingly entertaining as any fantasy adventure that had come before it, and one has only to see so much similar fare that has been presented in the twenty-four years since to appreciate all over again just how superbly suspenseful, awe-inspiring, and fun this movie remains. *Schindler* was the one that finally seemed to win over the skeptics who required nothing less than a miracle to snap them out of their anti-Spielberg stance. This movie *was* that miracle; so startlingly frank, so emotionally wrenching, so raw, so uncompromising was it that it took many by surprise. For those of us who always saw greatness, it was a vindication. Steven Spielberg had already found his place in film history, to be sure, but because of *Schindler's List* there was no longer the possibility of examining the impact of the medium without the inclusion of this accomplishment, without ranking its maker among the most important talents of the day. It was that significant, that instantly a classic.

This banner year reiterated what had been my belief for some time; that modern cinema would be a poorer place without the addition of Steven Spielberg. Just as movies would have been that much less interesting without the likes of Fred Astaire, Donald Duck, and sound, there is no doubting that some of my continuing obsession with modern motion pictures would be lessened had Mr. Spielberg not been able to join the Hollywood elite and show us what he could do behind a camera. I firmly believe that his love for film, his incisive depiction of the wonders of the world and the wonderment inherent in us all, his deeply optimistic belief in the best in human beings, his mastery to seduce you with the magical power of cinema, and his ability to get under our skin have made motion pictures that much more exciting for a vast public who, years ago, might have gone from having a fervent interest to a passing one.

I for one cannot imagine the cinema landscape without the anticipation of the next work of some of our most invaluable creators. I have decried the years that have gone by without some of our greatest filmmakers contributing a title to make moviegoing that much more exciting. This has most certainly been the case with Steven Spielberg, who, alas, would sometimes let two years or more pass between projects.

Working on this book has been such an absolute pleasure because it allowed me to take time out from the constant, ongoing rush of current-day movie viewing and sit back and revisit several Spielberg works that I had not seen since their original runs in cinemas. I can tell you that the experience has only had its positives. Although I still found certain efforts like *Hook* and *The Terminal* to be lacking, I was stirred to new feelings of respect for such movies as *Amistad* and *Munich*, which, despite their degree of acclaim and, for the latter, a Best Picture nomination from the Academy, deserve to be far better known and studied and absorbed all over again, so richly do they enlighten us on true events, provoking the deepest of feelings about injustice, retribution, freedom, and the necessity of compromise in a complex world. I know now that I didn't initially allow myself to take the entire journey into the unsettling world of *A.I. Artificial Intelligence*, only now understanding the full intention of its controversial last half hour. I saw once again how shattering the opening twenty-five minutes of *Saving Private Ryan* remain, as horrific a depiction of the abhorrent nature of war as any committed to celluloid. I am convinced that *Minority Report* and *War of the Worlds* are among the very best science fiction movies to be produced in the past twenty years; that *Lincoln* is the most intelligent depiction of the beloved sixteenth president that could have been hoped for; and that despite having no valid reason to exist outside of further revenue, both *The Lost World: Jurassic Park* and *Indiana Jones and the Kingdom of the Crystal Skull* remain more than watchable because of Spielberg's sure directorial hand.

There is so much to be grateful for in the works of Steven Spielberg; sequences, performances, and images have lodged themselves in my consciousness over the years, as is often the case with great filmmakers who are well aware that attention to detail can raise something to a higher, more personal, and more exciting level for audiences.

And just for the record, I reached a goal back in 2012 when the Film Forum in New York celebrated the hundredth anniversary of Universal Pictures with a screening series of some of the standout productions from that studio. Among the attractions was *The Sugarland Express*, so, in the midst of a torrential downpour, I made sure I made my way down to the cinema and saw the one Steven Spielberg movie I had missed seeing on the big screen. It was a pleasure to behold and well worth sitting in the theater watching it unfold the way it was meant to be seen, even while wearing wet socks. I felt privileged to be watching the origination of a filmmaker who would reach a level of accomplishment that sometimes seems no longer possible for the new crop of filmmakers to attain in the modern era of cinema. To have the opportunity to pay tribute to his career with this book is more than I could have wished for.

—*Barry Monush*

Acknowledgments

nce again, a tremendous degree of thanks to John Cerullo for the opportunity to take on this project in the first place. I'm so grateful that he believes I've got something worthwhile to say. Additional thanks to Marybeth Keating, Micah White, and the rest of the staff at Applause Books/Hal Leonard for all their help and understanding.

There are not enough words to express my appreciation for the show of support my partner Tom Lynch has given me, not only with this particular project but for every previous book and beyond. It is with Tom that I had the good fortune to see the bulk of Steven Spielberg's movies over the years, and I could not have asked for a better companion in this endeavor.

Much thanks to James Sheridan for his never wavering support and enthusiasm for my efforts on putting together this book. Everyone should have someone with so positive an attitude in their corner.

Thanks also to my colleague Rebecca Paller for being so gung ho on my doing this book as well; to Jim Howard for thoughtfully sending me a copy of the DVD of *The Color Purple* many years back; and to Brian Durnin for so frequently providing a bigger boat.

Thanks for assisting me in my research to Natalia Stysło from the Wroclaw Film Commission/Lower Silesian Film Fund; Amelia Newman from the Luton Hoo Estate; Tony Albarella for *The Season to be Wary*; Ray Morton, whose book *Close Encounters of the Third Kind: The Making of Steven Spielberg's Classic Film* was not only incredibly helpful but one of the best making-of books I have ever read and one I strongly recommend; *Amistad*'s own Robert Walsh; and Karolina Grysiak, Dział Nowych Mediów PR.

Steven Spielberg FAQ

Spielberg Through the Years

A Timeline of Pivotal Events from Steven Spielberg's Life and Career

1946: Steven Allan Spielberg is born at the Jewish Hospital in Cincinnati, Ohio, on December 18 to Arnold (b. February 6, 1917) and Leah Posner (b. January 12, 1920) Spielberg. (In the early years of his career, press releases and bios would lower Steven's age by one year, giving the impression that he was born in 1947 and therefore even more of a wunderkind.) Steven and his family live in the Avondale section of Cincinnati for the first two and a half years of his life.

1949: The Spielbergs move to Camden, New Jersey, in June. Steven's oldest sister, Anne, is born in Philadelphia.

1952: The Spielbergs move to Haddon Township, New Jersey, a suburb of Camden. While here, there are two more sisters added to the family: Susan (b. 1953) and Nancy (b. 1956).

1957: In February, the family is obliged to move again because of Arnold's job, this time ending up in Phoenix, Arizona. It is while living here that Steven becomes deeply interested in making movies, using his dad's 8 mm camera. Among those efforts are the nine-minute western spoof "The Last Gunfight" (1958); a fifteen-minute World War II tribute to flyers, "Fighter Squadron" (1960); and a longer, forty-minute effort covering the same genre, "Escape to Nowhere" (1962).

1964: Steven's 135-minute science fiction film *Firelight* has its premiere at the Phoenix Little Theatre on March 24, one day before the Spielberg family departs for their new home in San Jose, California. Later that year they move once again, to nearby Saratoga.

   During the summer, Spielberg works as an apprentice at the Universal Studios lot in Universal City.

1965: Spielberg graduates from Saratoga High School in Saratoga, California, on June 18. In September he begins attending California State College at Long Beach, majoring in English. Because of his contract with Universal, he drops out before graduating.

1968: Spielberg's twenty-two-minute short film "Amblin'" is premiered in the Los Angeles area at the Crest Theater in Westwood on December 18 (Steven's twenty-second birthday), as the added attraction on the bill with the Otto Preminger comedy *Skidoo*. It is this short that brings him to the attention of Sid Sheinberg, the Vice President of Production at Universal Television, who signs him to a contract in December.

1969: Spielberg's very first professional credit, directing Joan Crawford in the "Eyes" segment of Rod Serling's *Night Gallery* pilot movie, makes its television debut on November 8.

1970: The *Marcus Welby, M.D.* episode "The Daredevil Gesture," directed by Spielberg, is aired on March 17.

1971: Six television series with episodes directed by Spielberg air this year: *Night Gallery* ("Make Me Laugh," January 6); *The Name of the Game* ("LA 2017," January 15); *The Psychiatrist* ("The Private World of Martin Dalton," February 10); *The Psychiatrist* ("Par for the Course," March 10); *Columbo* ("Murder by the Book," September 15); and *Owen Marshall Counselor at Law* ("Eulogy for a Wide Receiver," September 30).

   ▪ Spielberg directs his first television movie, *Duel*, to critical acclaim. It airs on November 13. The following year it will be shown in theaters in Europe, with additional footage added.

1972: Spielberg's one early television credit done outside of Universal, the TV movie *Something Evil*, a CBS production, is shown on January 21.

1973: Steven Spielberg's first theatrical motion picture, *The Sugarland Express*, begins shooting in Texas on January 15, with Goldie Hawn, Ben Johnson, William Atherton, and Michael Sacks as the stars.

   ▪ The last television credit to bear Spielberg's name for some time, the pilot movie *Savage*, airs on March 31.

   ▪ The first theatrical motion picture to carry a credit for Steven Spielberg ("story by"), *Ace Eli and Rodger of the Skies*, opens in select theaters on April 11.

1974: Spielberg's feature film debut as director, *The Sugarland Express*, has its premiere in New York City on Sunday, March 31. That Friday, April 5, it will open in other areas throughout the country. For the most part favorably reviewed, it launches his career in motion pictures. It also marks the first time John Williams scores one of his films.

   ▪ At the Cannes Film Festival, *The Sugarland Express* wins the Best Screenplay Award, which Spielberg (as one of the credited story writers) shares with Hal Barwood and Matthew Robbins. Spielberg is also in the running for

Steven Spielberg directs Goldie Hawn on the set of his first theatrical feature, *The Sugarland Express*.

the coveted Palme d'Or, which is awarded to Francis Ford Coppola for *The Conversation*.

- That summer Spielberg directs the difficult Martha's Vineyard shoot of *Jaws*.

1975: *The Sugarland Express* receives a nomination from the Writers Guild of America, for Comedy Written Directly for the Screen.

- *Jaws* opens in 409 theaters in the United States on Friday, June 20. It becomes the highest-grossing motion picture released up to that time and firmly establishes Steven Spielberg as one of the hottest and most important new talents in the film industry.

1976: *Jaws* receives four Oscar nominations, including one for Best Picture. (Spielberg's omission in the directing category is the first of many award snubs over the years.) Best Picture is the only one of its nominations it does *not* win at the March 29 ceremony, with victories for Best Music – Original Dramatic Score, Best Film Editing, and Best Sound.

- Steven Spielberg receives his first nomination from the Directors Guild of America, for his work on *Jaws*.

1977: *Close Encounters of the Third Kind* has its premiere in New York City on November 16, 1977, at the Ziegfeld Theater. Its Los Angeles opening is two days later, at the Cinerama Dome. It becomes the highest-grossing movie in Columbia Pictures' history.

1978: *Close Encounters* receives eight Oscar nominations. For the first time, Spielberg is a nominee in the directing category. At the April 3 ceremony, the film wins for Best Cinematography and receives a Special Achievement Award for Sound Effects Editing. Spielberg loses in his category to Woody Allen (for *Annie Hall*).

- The Directors Guild of America nominates Spielberg for *Close Encounters of the Third Kind*; he is also nominated for a Golden Globe and by the British Academy of Film and Television Arts (BAFTA) in this category.

- Spielberg receives his second nomination from the Writers Guild of America, for his script of *Close Encounters*.

- The one award Spielberg receives for directing *Close Encounters* is the Saturn Award from the Academy of Science Fiction, Fantasy & Horror Films, in a tie with George Lucas (for *Star Wars*). Spielberg would receive additional directing awards from this organization for *Raiders of the Lost Ark*, *Jurassic Park*, *A.I. Artificial Intelligence*, and *Minority Report*, as well as being given a President's Award from them in 1994.

- Spielberg's first film on which he's credited as executive producer, *I Wanna Hold Your Hand*, opens on April 21.

1979: *1941*, Spielberg's slapstick comedy, debuts in wide release on Friday, December 14.

1980: *1941* receives three technical Oscar nominations but wins none.

- Spielberg appears on screen as a clerk in the John Landis comedy *The Blues Brothers* (debut: June 20).

- *Used Cars*, with Spielberg credited as executive producer, opens on July 11.

- A re-edited version of *Close Encounters of the Third Kind* referred to as "The Special Edition," which contains newly filmed footage and missing sequences shown in the original print, opens across the country in theaters on August 1.

1981: *Raiders of the Lost Ark* premieres on June 12. It becomes the year's highest-grossing movie and the biggest money earner in the history of Paramount Pictures.

- Amblin Entertainment, named after Spielberg's breakthrough short subject, is founded by Spielberg and producers Kathleen Kennedy and Frank Marshall.

- *Continental Divide*, with Spielberg listed as executive producer, opens on September 18; it is the first feature to carry an Amblin production credit of any kind.

1982: *Raiders of the Lost Ark* receives eight Oscar nominations, including those for Best Picture and Director. It is the winner in the categories of Best Special Visual Effects, Art Direction, Sound, and Film Editing. It also receives a special Oscar for Sound Effect Editing.

- Spielberg receives a Directors Guild nomination for *Raiders*.
- *Poltergeist*, with Spielberg credited as co-producer, co-screenplay writer, and story writer, debuts on June 4. There is much debate on how much of the movie was actually directed by Spielberg and how much by the credited director, Tobe Hooper. The film becomes one of the year's top box office hits.
- Spielberg's sixth theatrical credit as director, *E.T. the Extra-Terrestrial*, opens on June 11, 1982, and quickly turns into a box office phenomenon. By year's end it becomes the highest-grossing motion picture in history. With this and *Raiders*, Steven Spielberg has now become the best-known filmmaker in the world. It marks the first time he has a producer credit on a film he directed.

1983: *E.T.* receives nine Oscar nominations, including one for Spielberg as Best Director (his third nomination in this category), and one for Best Picture. It ends up winning four Academy Awards: Best Music, Best Effects – Visual Effects, Best Effects – Sound Effects Editing, and Best Sound.
- Spielberg receives his fourth nomination from the Directors Guild, for *E.T.*
- *E.T.* is named Best Picture at the Golden Globes and by the Los Angeles Film Critics Association. Spielberg is named Best Director by the National Society of Film Critics.
- *Twilight Zone: The Movie*, an omnibus movie with its second segment directed by Spielberg, opens on June 29. He is also listed as producer.

1984: The PBS documentary series *Strokes of Genius*, which includes uncredited direction by Steven Spielberg of the wraparound intros and outros featuring Dustin Hoffman, is aired in May.
- On May 16, Steven Spielberg and George Lucas have their handprints immortalized in cement in the forecourt of the Chinese Theater on Hollywood Boulevard.
- *Indiana Jones and the Temple of Doom* opens on May 23, 1984, in a record number of theaters. It is another box office smash, becoming the third highest-grossing film released that year. Some objections to its intense violence are credited in bringing about the new PG-13 rating.
- *Gremlins*, which Spielberg produced, opens on June 8. It becomes the fourth highest-grossing release of the year. Spielberg can be spotted briefly in the movie.

1985: At the March 25 ceremony, *Indiana Jones and the Temple of Doom* wins one of its two Oscar nominations, for Best Visual Effects.
- *The Goonies*, with a story credited to Spielberg (who is also executive producer), opens on June 7.
- Spielberg's first child (with actress Amy Irving), Max Samuel, is born in Los Angeles on June 13.
- *Back to the Future*, on which Spielberg served as executive producer, opens on July 1. It becomes the highest-grossing movie released that year.
- Spielberg appears on his first *Time* magazine cover (July 15), billed as "Magician of the Movies."

- *Amazing Stories*, created and produced by Steven Spielberg, debuts as a weekly series on NBC on September 29. Two episodes are directed by Spielberg: the premiere, "Ghost Train," and "The Mission" (November 3). During the first season, fourteen of the episodes have stories credited to Spielberg. One, "Vanessa in the Garden" (December 29), is scripted by him.
- Spielberg marries actress Amy Irving (born September 10, 1953, in Palo Alto, CA), on November 27, in Santa Fe, NM.
- Another executive producer credit for Spielberg, *Young Sherlock Holmes*, debuts on December 4.
- Spielberg's eighth film on which he is credited as director, *The Color Purple*, opens on December 18. It will become one of the five highest-grossing films of the year.

1986: *The Color Purple* receives eleven Oscar nominations, but Spielberg is skipped over in the Best Director category. He does receive a nomination, however, as one of the film's producers. The film ends up winning none of its nominations.

- For the first time, Spielberg wins the Directors Guild of America Award, for *The Color Purple*. He becomes the first director to receive this award and not be one of the five nominees at the Academy Awards.
- Steven Spielberg is given the BAFTA Fellowship lifetime achievement award "in recognition of outstanding achievement in the art forms of the moving image." He is only the second American-born recipient of this honor, following John Huston.
- Two more executive producer credits: *The Money Pit* (March 26) and Amblin's first animated feature, *An American Tail* (November 21), are released.
- Spielberg receives his first Emmy nomination, for his direction of "The Mission," but loses the award to Georg Stanford Brown (for *Cagney & Lacey*). It is his only Emmy nomination for directing thus far.
- *Amazing Stories* has its second season premiere on September 22. During this season, four of the episode stories are credited to Spielberg.

1987: At the March 30 Academy Awards ceremony, Spielberg is awarded the Irving G. Thalberg Memorial Award for his work as a producer.

- Executive Producer credits: *Innerspace* (July 1) and **batteries not included* (December 18) are released.
- Spielberg's tenth film as director, *Empire of the Sun*, debuts on December 9. For it, he is named Best Director by the National Board of Review, which also selects the film as Best Picture.

1988: *Empire of the Sun* receives six Oscar nominations (no wins).

- Spielberg is nominated by the Directors Guild of America for *Empire of the Sun*.
- Executive producer credits: *Who Framed Roger Rabbit* (June 22) and *The Land Before Time* (November 19). *Roger* becomes the second highest-grossing 1988 release.

- Theo, whom Kate Capshaw adopted and is later adopted by Steven Spielberg, is born.

1989:   Steven Spielberg and Amy Irving are divorced on February 2.
- The third installment in the intended trilogy, *Indiana Jones and the Last Crusade*, opens on May 24. It is another success, placing number two on the year's box office list.
- Executive producer credits: *Dad* (November 10) and *Back to the Future Part II* (November 22).
- The eleventh Spielberg directorial credit, *Always*, opens on December 22, marking the first time two of his theatrical efforts have been distributed in the same calendar year.

1990:   *Indiana Jones and the Last Crusade* receives three Oscar nominations, winning for Best Sound Effects Editing.
- Executive Producer credits: *Joe Versus the Volcano* (March 9), *Back to the Future Part III* (May 25), *Gremlins 2: The New Batch* (June 15), and *Arachnophobia* (July 18).
- Steven's first biological child with Kate Capshaw, Sasha Rebecca, is born in Los Angeles on May 14.
- Spielberg's first venture into producing an animated television series, *Tiny Toon Adventures*, premieres on September 7.
- With film producer Peter Samuelson, Spielberg establishes the Starbright Foundation to help children and teenagers suffering from life-threatening illnesses. This organization merges with Samuelson's other charity, the Starlight Children's Foundation.

1991:   When *Tiny Toon Adventures* is named Outstanding Animated Program at the Daytime Emmys (June 22), it brings executive producer Steven Spielberg his first award from the Academy of Television Arts & Sciences.
- Spielberg marries actress Kate Capshaw (born Kathleen Sue Nail in Forth Worth, Texas, on November 3, 1953) at his estate in East Hampton on Long Island, New York, on October 13.
- *An American Tail: Fievel Goes West*, produced by Spielberg, opens on November 22.
- Spielberg's thirteenth film as director, *Hook*, opens on December 11 and ends up ends up at Number 10 among that year's top box office releases.

1992:   *Hook* is nominated for five Oscars, winning none of them.
- Spielberg's son Sawyer Avery is born on March 10.
- *The Plucky Duck Show*, a spinoff of *Tiny Toon Adventures*, executive produced by Spielberg, premieres on Fox on September 19.

1993:   The first television movie produced by Spielberg, *Class of '61*, is aired on April 12.
- Spielberg wins another daytime Emmy Award for producing *Tiny Toon Adventures*.

- *Jurassic Park* is released on June 11, on 3,800 screens in North America, and becomes the highest-grossing movie of the year. Its worldwide grosses send it to the top of the box office charts, as it becomes another Spielberg record-breaker.
- Spielberg is given a special Golden Lion Career Award at the Venice Film Festival.
- Spielberg returns to primetime weekly television as executive producer of the sci-fi series *seaQuest DSV*, which debuts on September 12.

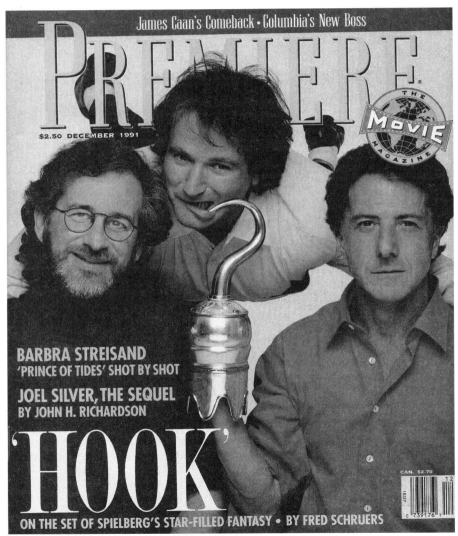

Spielberg joins his two stars, Robin Williams and Dustin Hoffman, on the cover of the movie-focused *Premiere* magazine.

- The animated *We're Back! A Dinosaur's Story*, from executive producer Steven Spielberg, opens on November 24.
- *Schindler's List* premieres on December 15 and brings Steven Spielberg the best reviews of his career.

1994: With the announcement of the Oscar nominations, Spielberg's two 1993 releases, *Jurassic Park* and *Schindler's List*, end up with fifteen nominations: three nods for the former and twelve for the latter (the most so far for any of Spielberg's directing credits). At the March 21 ceremony, *Jurassic* wins all three of its nominations: Best Sound, Best Sound Effects Editing, and Best Visual Effects. *Schindler* wins for Best Picture, Best Director, Best Writing – Based on Material Previously Produced or Published, Best Cinematography, Best Art Direction–Set Decoration, Best Film Editing, and Best Original Score. Spielberg comes home with his first two competitive Academy Awards (as producer and director).

- Spielberg wins Best Director awards for *Schindler's List* from the Directors Guild, Golden Globes, BAFTA, the New York Film Critics Circle, Boston Society of Film Critics, Chicago Film Critics Association, Kansas City Film Critics Circle, National Society of Film Critics, and the London Critics Circle (1995).
- *Schindler's List* is named the year's Best Picture from the Golden Globes, BAFTA, and Producers Guild.
- By the end of its run, *Schindler's List* becomes the ninth highest-grossing 1993 release.
- Spielberg establishes the Survivors of the Shoah Visual History Foundation in order to record the testimonies of Holocaust survivors.
- With the profits earned from *Schindler's List*, Spielberg establishes the Righteous Persons Foundation. It's mission, as stated on its website, is as follows: "For more than two decades, RPF has funded innovative approaches that help bridge the divide between people of different backgrounds; galvanize the power of the arts, media, and storytelling; preserve and make Jewish history and traditions accessible for generations to come; build on the Jewish values of justice to inspire social activism; and ensure that the moral lessons of the Holocaust are not forgotten." Profits from *Munich* and *Lincoln* were also turned over to the foundation.
- A live action version of the animated series *The Flintstones* premieres, presented by Steven Spiel*rock*.
- In partnership with former Walt Disney Studios chairman Jeffrey Katzenberg and record industry executive David Geffen, Steven Spielberg announces on October 14 that the trio will be starting their own studio, which eventually is named DreamWorks SKG.

1995: France's national film award, the César, bestows an honorary award upon Spielberg for his work; despite five nominations from this organization, he has never won an award from them in competition.

- Spielberg becomes the twenty-third recipient of the American Film Institute Life Achievement Award on March 2. Among those paying tribute are Tom

Hanks (host), Karen Allen, Christian Bale, Laura Dern, Richard Dreyfuss, Harrison Ford, Danny Glover, Whoopi Goldberg, John Goodman, Goldie Hawn, Amy Irving, Samuel L. Jackson, Ben Kingsley, George Lucas, Liam Neeson, Sam Neill, Roy Scheider, Henry Thomas, Dennis Weaver, and John Williams.

■ Executive producer credits: *Casper* (May 26) and *Balto* (December 22).

WEEKLY INTERNATIONAL EDITION

a BPi publication

64th year   March 22, 1994 $1.50 *(California)* $1.75 *(Elsewhere)* £2.40 *(U.K.)*

Oscar: 'Schindler'

7 nods to film; Spielberg finally is best director

● *Academy Awards coverage continues on page 6.*

By Anita M. Busch

"This is the best drink of water after the longest drought in my life," said Steven Spielberg, who, after two decades of feature filmmaking, won his first competitive honors from the Academy — including best picture and director for the gripping Holocaust drama "Schindler's List."

An appreciative Dorothy Chandler Pavilion audience jumped to its feet Monday night to honor Spielberg, whose films won 10 Oscars in all at the 66th annual Academy Awards — seven for "Schindler's List" and three for the phenomenally successful "Jurassic Park."

It was only eight years ago that the Academy of Motion Picture Arts & Sciences snubbed Spielberg when his film "The Color Purple" received 11 nominations but failed to earn him a director nom. "Schindler's List" also won for cinematography, editing, original score, art direction and adapted screenplay.

"There are 350,000 survivors of the Holocaust alive tonight," said Spielberg after the crowd finally

See **WINNERS** *on page 6*

Alex Berliner

A triumphant Anna Paquin radiates after winning best supporting actress kudos for "The Piano."

OSCARS BY PICTURE

Schindler's List	7
Jurassic Park	3
The Piano	3
Philadelphia	2
Belle Epoque	1
Mrs. Doubtfire	1
The Age of Innocence	1
The Fugitive	1

Tony Barnard

Steven Spielberg savors victory of awards for best director and film.

Spielberg: 'I have no resentment'

By Donna Parker

After some 20 years of making movies, Steven Spielberg became the man of the hour Monday night.

Gathering a total of 10 Oscars for "Schindler's List" and "Jurassic Park," the prolific filmmaker proved that the world's most commercially successful director could illuminate as well as entertain.

After four previous nominations, the 47-year-old helmsman finally broke the Oscar jinx with "Schindler's List," the Holocaust drama that earned him the best director Academy Award.

Spielberg said he had no ill will about waiting so long to receive the recognition — even though it was something he had dreamed about since making the highly regarded telefilm "Duel" in 1971.

"I have no resentment, I never have, but I'm not just saying that because I won tonight," he said. "I came here hopeful and it was a wonderful experience."

The irony of nabbing the coveted trophy from Hollywood's Academy for a film that was made on location in Poland, with foreign cast and crew, was not lost on the

See **SPIELBERG** *on page 12*

Oscar arrivals

Catch a glimpse of many of Hollywood's leading executive movers and shakers as they make their way into the big show. Pages 89-92.

BEST PERFORMANCE BY A CHAMPAGNE IN A SERIES OF CELEBRATORY TOASTS.

MOËT & CHANDON

It's front page news when Steven Spielberg finally gets some Oscars to call his own, as *Schindler's List* wins Best Director and Best Picture of 1993.

1996: Spielberg and Kate Capshaw's children they adopted together, Mikaela and Destry, are born.

- Spielberg receives the Peabody Award for presenting the documentary *Survivors of the Holocaust*, in association with Survivors of the Shoah Visual History Foundation.
- The year's second highest-grossing movie, *Twister* (May 10), is executive produced by Steven Spielberg.
- *Animaniacs* is named Outstanding Children's Animated Program at the Daytime Emmy Awards, making producer Spielberg a winner again.
- Spielberg receives his first Primetime Emmy Award as one of the producers of the animated special *A Pinky and the Brain Christmas*.

1997: At the Daytime Emmy Awards, *Freakazoid* wins Outstanding Special Class Animated Program, while *Animaniacs* wins Outstanding Children's Animated Program, bringing producer Spielberg two trophies.

- Spielberg's only directorial credit to date on a sequel to one of his movies, *The Lost World: Jurassic Park*, opens on May 23.
- His second directorial credit that year, *Amistad*, opens on December 10. The former is the third highest-grossing release of the year.
- Another box office smash, *Men in Black* (July 2), is a Spielberg executive producer credit.
- The first movie to be distributed by DreamWorks, *The Peacemaker* (starring George Clooney and Nicole Kidman), is released on September 26.

1998: *Amistad* receives four Oscar nominations (no wins). Spielberg is a Directors Guild and Golden Globe nominee for this film. *The Lost World* receives an Oscar nomination for its visual effects.

- Spielberg receives directing nominations for *Amistad* from the DGA and Golden Globes (which also nominates the film for best motion picture – drama).
- *Amistad* wins the Producers Guild of America's Vision Award.
- Spielberg is the executive producer on *Deep Impact* (May 9), *The Mask of Zorro* (July 17), and the documentary *The Last Days* (October 23).
- Steven Spielberg's eighteenth credit as director, *Saving Private Ryan*, opens on July 24. It becomes the highest-grossing movie released that year. It is the first Spielberg directorial credit to be released by DreamWorks (in partnership with Paramount Pictures).

1999: *Saving Private Ryan* receives eleven Oscar nominations including Best Picture. At the March 21 ceremony Steven Spielberg is given the Academy Award for Best Director for the second time in his career. Although the film loses Best Picture to *Shakespeare in Love*, it wins additional awards for Best Cinematography, Best Film Editing, Best Sound, and Best Sound Effects Editing.

- A Spielberg executive producer credit, *The Last Days*, wins the Academy Award for Best Documentary, Feature.

- For the third time Spielberg wins the Directors Guild of America Award, for *Saving Private Ryan*.
- Spielberg is also named Best Director for his work on *Saving Private Ryan* by the Golden Globes, Broadcast Film Critics Association, and the Dallas-Fort Worth Film Critics Association.
- Spielberg wins the Daytime Emmy as a producer on *Pinky and the Brain* when it is named Outstanding Special Class Animated Program.

Spielberg gives direction to Tom Hanks and Edward Burns on the set of *Saving Private Ryan*.

2000: Steven Spielberg receives a Lifetime Achievement Award from the Directors Guild of America at the organization's fifty-second annual event on March 11.

▦ This year it's *Pinky, Elmyra & the Brain* that earns Spielberg another Emmy, with the series being declared Outstanding Children's Animated Program.

2001: Steven Spielberg is given an honorary knighthood at the British Embassy in Washington DC "in recognition of his unique and outstanding contribution to international film, and in particular, his services to the entertainment industry of the United Kingdom." January 30.

▦ *A.I. Artificial Intelligence*, derived from a property developed by the late Stanley Kubrick, opens on June 29. It is Spielberg's nineteenth directorial movie credit and the first since *Close Encounters* on which he is credited for the writing the screenplay.

▦ For the third *Jurassic Park* movie (*III*), Spielberg is the executive producer.

2002: *A.I. Artificial Intelligence* receives two Oscar nominations but wins neither.

▦ *Minority Report* is released on June 21.

▦ Executive producer: *Men in Black II* (July 3).

▦ *Band of Brothers* is named Outstanding Miniseries at the Emmy Awards, bringing another trophy from the Television Academy to Spielberg, one of the program's producers.

▦ *Catch Me If You Can* is released on December 25. It becomes the eleventh highest-grossing 2002 release.

2003: Steven Spielberg receives a star—at 6801 Hollywood Blvd., near Highland—on the Hollywood Walk of Fame on January 10. Kate Capshaw, John Williams, and Stan Winston are among those in attendance at the ceremony.

▦ The Oscar nominations for 2002 include two for *Catch Me If You Can* and one for *Minority Report* (no wins).

▦ Spielberg is one of the Emmy Award winners for producing the year's Outstanding Miniseries, *Taken*.

2004: *The Terminal* is released on June 18.

2005: *War of the Worlds* debuts on June 29 and becomes the fourth highest-grossing movie released that year.

▦ *The Legend of Zorro* (October 28), with Spielberg as executive producer, and *Memoirs of a Geisha* (December 23), with Spielberg as producer, open.

▦ Spielberg's twenty-fourth directorial credit, *Munich*, opens on December 23.

2006: *Munich* receives five Oscar nominations, including Best Picture and Best Director. It is the seventh time a Spielberg movie is in the running for the top prize and his sixth mention from the Academy in the directing category. *War of the Worlds* receives three Oscar nominations. Neither film ends up winning anything.

▦ Spielberg receives additional nominations for his direction of *Munich* from the Directors Guild of America and the Golden Globes.

- *Monster House* opens (July 21) with Spielberg as an executive producer. It is one of the finalists at the Oscars for Animated Feature.
- Two World War II films directed by Clint Eastwood, *Flags of Our Fathers* and *Letters from Iwo Jima*, are produced by Steven Spielberg.
- On December 3, Steven Spielberg becomes one of the five recipients of the twenty-ninth annual Kennedy Center Honors for lifetime achievement in the performing arts. (The others honored that night are Zubin Mehta, Dolly Parton, Smokey Robinson, and Andrew Lloyd Webber).

2007: When *Letters from Iwo Jima* ends up as one of the year's five finalists for the Best Picture Oscar, it marks the first time Spielberg is in the running in this category for a movie he did *not* direct. The film loses the award to *The Departed*.
- Spielberg is an executive producer on the box office hit *Transformers* (July 3).
- Steven Spielberg's first grandchild, Luke Hudson Gavigan, is born on September 8 to Spielberg's stepdaughter, Jessica Capshaw.

2008: After a nineteen-year gap, Spielberg directs a fourth installment in the Indiana Jones adventure series, *Indiana Jones and the Kingdom of the Crystal Skull* (May 22). It becomes the third highest-grossing release of the year.
- A seven-minute film paying tribute to US veterans, *A Timeless Call*, directed by Steven Spielberg, premieres at the Democratic Convention in Denver, Colorado, on August 28.
- *Eagle Eye* (September 26) includes Spielberg as one of its executive producers.

2009: Steven Spielberg is given the Cecil B. DeMille Award, a lifetime achievement honor from the Hollywood Foreign Press, at the Golden Globes ceremony on January 11. This award had been postponed from the previous year because of a writers' strike.
- Executive producer: *Transformers: Revenge of the Fallen* (June 24) and *The Lovely Bones* (December 11).

2010: Spielberg is among the many producers to receive an Emmy Award for *The Pacific* when it is named Outstanding Miniseries.
- *Hereafter* (October 15) and the remake of *True Grit* (December 22) are executive produced by Spielberg. The latter is among the year's Best Picture Oscar nominees.

2011: Four executive producer credits: *Super 8* (June 10), *Transformers: Dark of the Moon* (June 29), *Cowboys & Aliens* (July 29), and *Real Steel* (October 7).
- For the first time, Spielberg directs a motion-capture film, *The Adventures of Tintin*, which is released on December 21.
- Only three days after *Tintin*'s debut, Spielberg's twenty-seventh motion picture credit as director, *War Horse*, premieres.

2012: *War Horse* is nominated for Oscars for Best Picture, Cinematography, Art Direction, Original Score, Sound Editing, and Sound Mixing. (It wins none of these.)

- *War Horse* is named Movie of the Year by the American Film Institute and earns a Golden Globe nomination for Best Picture—Drama.
- Spielberg is given a Lifetime Achievement Award in Motion Pictures from the Producers Guild. Previously, the Guild had named him Outstanding Producer in various categories for *Schindler's List*, *Amistad*, *Saving Private Ryan*, *Band of Brothers*, *The Pacific*, and *The Adventures of Tintin*.
- *Men in Black 3* (May 25) is executive produced by Spielberg.
- *Lincoln* is released on November 9 and ends up the thirteenth highest-grossing film to open that year.

2013: *Lincoln* ties with *Schindler's List* for most Oscar nominations for a Spielberg film when it receives twelve: Picture, Director, Actor (Daniel Day-Lewis), Supporting Actor (Tommy Lee Jones), Supporting Actress (Sally Field), Adapted Screenplay, Cinematography, Production Design, Costume Design, Original Score, Film Editing, and Sound Mixing. The film wins for Actor and Production Design. The former win marks the very first time Spielberg has directed an Academy Award winning performance (after nine previous acting nominations from his movies). Spielberg receives additional nominations for his direction of *Lincoln* from the DGA, Golden Globes, and the Broadcast Film Critics Association, among others. *Lincoln* is named Movie of the Year by the American Film Institute and receives Picture nominations from the Golden Globes, BAFTA, Australian Film Institute, Broadcast Film Critics Association, and Chicago Film Critics.

2014: *Transformers: Age of Extinction* (June 27) carries an executive producer credit for Spielberg; on *The Hundred-Foot Journey* (August 8) he is one of the producers.

2015: Spielberg is executive producer on the year's second highest-grossing release, *Jurassic World* (June 12).
- *Bridge of Spies* debuts on October 16.
- Steven Spielberg is given the nation's highest civilian honor, the Presidential Medal of Freedom, by Barack Obama on November 24. Although past recipients have included actors who have directed films, he is only the second full-time director since John Ford (in 1973) to receive the honor.

2016: *Bridge of Spies* becomes the tenth Steven Spielberg film to receive an Oscar nomination for Best Picture. It receives additional nominations for Supporting Actor (Mark Rylance), Original Screenplay, Original Score, Production Design, and Sound Mixing. Rylance becomes the second actor to win an Academy Award under Spielberg's direction. The American Film Institute names *Bridge of Spies* Movie of the Year. Spielberg receives nominations from BAFTA for directing and producing the film.
- Steven Spielberg's thirtieth motion picture as director, *The BFG*, opens on July 1.
- In July, Spielberg begins directing the science fiction adventure *Ready Player One*, based on the popular 2011 novel by Ernest Cline. Cline was enlisted to write the screenplay, along with Zak Penn. The film stars Tye Sheridan,

Steven Spielberg confers with stars Meryl Streep and Tom Hanks on the set of his 2017 film, *The Post.*

Olivia Cooke, Ben Mendelsohn, Mark Rylance, Simon Pegg, and T. J. Miller. The plan was for Warner Bros. to release the movie on March 30, 2018.

2017:   Leah Adler, Spielberg's mother, passes away at the age of ninety-seven at her Los Angeles home on February 21. Two weeks earlier, Steven's father, Arnold, had turned one hundred.

- *Five Came Back*, a documentary executive produced by Steven Spielberg and also featuring him as one of its on-camera commentators, is released in theatres on March 31, the same day it is made available on Netflix in three parts.
- Additional executive producer credits for Spielberg: the documentary *Finding Oscar* (April 14) and *Transformers: The Last Knight* (June 21).
- Spielberg begins filming *The Post*, starring Tom Hanks and Meryl Streep, in White Plains, New York, in late May. The drama, which is about the *Washington Post*'s challenge to publish the Pentagon Papers, is scripted by Liz Hannah and Josh Singer and also features Bruce Greenwood, David Cross, Bradley Whitford, Bob Odenkirk, Michael Stuhlbarg, Sarah Paulson, Tracy Letts, and Zach Woods. 20th Century Fox scheduled the opening for December 22, 2017, three months before *Ready Player One*, making this the first time two Spielberg directorial credits would debut out of order from when they were filmed.
- The National Board of Review Awards selects *The Post* for Best Picture, Best Actor (Tom Hanks), and Best Actress (Meryl Streep).

2

Spielberg Sources

T here are those who refuse to believe that filmmakers can ever adapt something from a previously published or established source and make it soar onscreen. Of course, nothing is further from the truth. There are countless motion pictures that are beloved, acclaimed works that have not only done their source material proud but have sometimes surpassed them to become the version of the story that most instantly comes to mind. While some of Steven Spielberg's best-loved movies were original ideas developed directly for the big screen (*Close Encounters of the Third Kind*, the Indiana Jones movies, *E.T.*, etc.), his films have more often than not been inspired by works of fiction and real-life incidents. And his track record for making something memorable from them shows far more hits than misses.

Here are the twenty-three Spielberg movies and two television assignments that used previously published stories or books, real life occurrences, theatrical creations, a television episode, and someone else's movie to inspire him to create his own work. Each summary gives examples of the changes, omissions, additions, and revisions that took place in the transfer from the original source to what appeared in the final version of Spielberg's movie.

Night Gallery: Eyes

Although there is no mention of it in the onscreen credits, two of the entries in the *Night Gallery* pilot—the final chapter, "Escape Route," and Spielberg's contribution, "Eyes"—were derived from previously published Rod Serling stories. These two (along with a third tale called "Color Scheme") made up a compilation Serling published (by Little, Brown) in September of 1967 under the umbrella title *The Season to Be Wary*. These three stories, in fact, started out as pieces of a script Serling had hoped to sell to the networks for an omnibus series in the vein of his classic *The Twilight Zone*, but his lack of success prompted him to revamp the pieces in the short story format. When he finally got Universal interested in the premise, he substituted "Color Scheme" with a different tale, "The Cemetery," and based them around the gimmick of paintings working their way into the plotlines.

His teleplay for "Eyes" was reworked considerably from its original form. The short story centered around a down-on-his-luck former boxer and his sleazy ex-manager, thereby giving it more than a passing resemblance to the vivid world of lost dreams and despair Serling had created in one of his most memorable works, "Requiem for a Heavyweight." Petrozella, the manager, is under pressure to pay off a $980 gambling debt and sees his one-time client, Indian Charlie Hatcher, as his means of escape. Ruthlessly, he cons the hapless, dim-witted Charlie into believing he'll be working as a bodyguard for a rich blind lady, Miss Claudia Menlo, when he knows that the real deal is for Charlie to sacrifice his eyes for cash so that the lady will have twelve hours of sight. To ensure that Charlie agrees to the deal, he schemes to have Miss Menlo pretend she has nearly been assaulted by the ex-pug, as Petrozella is aware that the prison time Charlie served for statutory rape haunts him to this day. For the television adaptation, these two characters were basically combined into a simpleminded schnook named Sidney Resnick; the gambling debt was retained as the motivation for him agreeing to the operation, but the debt balance was upped to $9,000; and the assault plot point was dropped altogether.

Also gone was Miss Menlo using blackmail to get her lawyer to consent to search for someone for her outrageous proposal, having brought up his shady dealings in the stock market as a way of ensuring his cooperation. The lawyer, renamed Packer from the "Parker" of the story, was around to get Resnick to sign some papers but was spared Menlo's diabolical wrath onscreen.

In Serling's ironic twist, the original story had a despondent Charlie hanging himself after signing the agreement, leaving Petrozella in the lurch. Knowing he still has the debt hanging over his head, the manager begrudgingly allows himself to be the proxy donor of Miss Menlo's sight.

Miss Menlo's monstrous behavior was still very much in evidence in the teleplay, as was her blackmailing Dr. Heatherton to go along with the operation, making her much more the focus of the piece, which wouldn't have been acceptable otherwise, once a star of Joan Crawford's stature was attached to the project.

The revamped "Eyes" now mercifully spared TV viewers of the two worst passages in the Serling original: Charlie having a hallucinatory conversation with his father's ghost (who ends up resembling Miss Menlo at one point!) before his suicide, and Petrozella's request to the nurse anesthetizing him for his operation to remove her clothing so that her "knockers" will be the last thing he sees. Even without these misguided moments, Steven Spielberg couldn't help in later years referring to Serling's script as "terrible."

Duel

Rather than conjuring up something from his imagination, Richard Matheson came up with the idea of an innocent motorist terrorized without motivation by a menacing truck because of a very specific incident that took place on a very specific date: November 22, 1963, the day of the Kennedy assassination. During an emotional drive heading from Simi Valley back to Los Angeles, following news of the tragic event, Matheson and his driving companion, writer Jerry Sohl, found themselves taunted by a reckless trucker whose insistence on tailgating at high speeds forced them to drive off the road into a turnabout to avoid possible harm. Matheson, who had contributed scripts to such series as *The Alfred Hitchcock Hour* and *The Twilight Zone*, instantly began thinking of his narrow escape as story material, and thought he could pitch the idea of man vs. truck as a potential television episode. He could not, however, seem to convince anyone that this seemingly limited concept could work even in that short a format. Therefore, another eight years passed before he fashioned the idea into a short story and published it, under the title *Duel*, in the April 1971 issue of *Playboy* (a magazine in which he had premiered several pieces previously, with this one being his last).

Among those who read and were impressed by the story were contracted Universal writer Steven Bochco, who brought the piece to the attention of producer George Eckstein. Although Bochco was clearly hoping for the job of adapter, once Eckstein convinced the studio to buy the story for the purpose of making it one of the television movie presentations for the upcoming season, he made it clear that Matheson was his only choice to bring his own tale to life. This required some convincing because, although Matheson had once pictured his idea as a possibility for series television, a fuller sized movie (one that would run approximately seventy-four minutes in length) seemed less easy to stretch and required extensive rethinking of his story.

In the meantime, Steven Spielberg's personal assistant at Universal had also caught wind of the story and decided it was right up her boss's alley. When the director realized the rights to the property were sitting right there at the very studio at which he worked, he eagerly made it known that he would like to take a crack at it. Inspired by the fact that Matheson's original work had no actual dialogue between anyone, he envisioned a tale told as a pure visual experience without any speaking. Although Eckstein was sold on the young filmmaker's enthusiasm, he knew that management would never greenlight a "silent" TV movie and encouraged Spielberg to come down to earth with at least that aspect of his vision. Once the property was his to guide, the director made sure that, if he couldn't make it wordless, he could at least scale down the amount of interior thoughts and asides the protagonist, David Mann (in the story he was given no first name), was given to speak.

Although the script of *Duel* would stay pretty close to the outline of the original story, there were plenty of additions, all of which further enhanced the suspense. Chief among these were scenes requiring Mann to actually engage in dialogue with others along the route of his ride of terror. Following the initial cat-and-mouse interplay between man and truck, Matheson added a sequence in which the nervous driver stops to get some gas, only to have the truck pull up on the other side of the pumps. This sequence created a tremendous amount of discomfort by having Mann be very close to the person who has just put him at risk but unsure of whether or not to make contact. It was during this moment that both the protagonist and the home viewers caught the closest thing to a glimpse of the tormentor: an arm at the steering wheel (seen from Mann's windshield before an overly solicitous service station attendant splashes it with water) and the man's cowboy boots (seen kicking the tires and providing a clue that will run Mann astray in a later scene). Rather than make a reference to an earlier, unseen incident as happened in the story, it was here that the exuberant attendant was able to point out the need for a new radiator hose, something Mann dismisses but later regrets.

The sequence most enhanced in the teleplay was the shaken Mann's stop at a roadside café, after his dash to outrun the truck has caused his car to hit a fence across from the eating establishment. In the movie, he is questioned by a concerned elderly man about his physical status after the abrupt stop, something that does not appear in the story. Also, Mann actually confronts a café patron he suspects might be the terrorizing road hog only to have the insulted man punch him and start a fight, which is halted by the restaurant's owner. This adds to the disorientation Mann is feeling when his attacker then leaves the café and takes off in an entirely different vehicle than the demon truck, which has been sitting parked in the lot. In the story, Mann has already started to drive off after his unnerving stop when he sees the truck depart the café grounds; this was revised so that the motorist is still inside the building when he sees the truck take off, making it very clear that no one in the café was the offending driver. In the story it is at this location that Mann decides to rest for a spell, in hopes of allowing the trucker to get farther ahead on his journey, a sequence relocated to a lot near a railroad track onscreen. Although it would have seemed unlikely to transfer Matheson's images of broken, rusted cars as victims of the trucker, the railroad scene in the movie does, in fact, allow for such imagery, as several discarded vehicles rest in the vicinity of where Mann has paused.

It is following the café scene that Matheson inserted another diversion to vary from the potential monotony of just keeping his hero in his car, having Mann stop off at another gas station, this one having an eccentric (and ominous) touch due to a "Snakerama" display of reptiles and spiders. It is here that Mann makes an attempt to contact the police while standing in a phone booth incongruously placed near the snake cages, only to have his enemy try to run him down, obliterating the booth and unleashing some of the offending critters when the trucker persists in circling his destructive vehicle through the display. This sequence gave the hapless Mann one more potential danger when a tarantula attaches itself to his leg, a startlingly black example of "if it's not one thing it's another" that added both tremendous menace and humor to the moment.

In order to give Mann another unsuccessful attempt to get someone to acknowledge his dilemma, for the teleplay Matheson wrote a variation on the moment where the truck parked in the road causes Mann to bring his vehicle to an abrupt halt at an angle, having the anxious driver flagging down an elderly couple, only to scare them off with his ravings and the threatening onslaught of the truck.

The finale was also altered in order to give the innocent driver his moment of glory in disposing of his nemesis. Rather than simply have the truck lose control and topple into a canyon in its latest effort to bring down his prey, as Matheson had concluded the story, Mann comes up with the idea to sacrifice his own vehicle. Aiming for a head-to-head collision only to bail out to safety, Mann knows full well that the truck will have no chance of slowing down before reaching the cliff the driver is fully aware is in back of him. This scene concluded not with an explosion, as would be expected from a truck marked "flammable," but with a slow-motion plunge ending with a sickening, monstrous crunch and groan sound that was borrowed, in a curious nod to the Universal sound effects library, from *The Creature from the Black Lagoon*. Although Universal executives felt cheated by not having a big blast to finish off the villain, Spielberg was insistent in allowing the confrontation to end with something a little less clichéd and predictable.

The Sugarland Express

So outlandish was the premise of Steven Spielberg's feature debut that it came as a surprise to many that it was based on a real incident, one that received less attention outside of its Texas setting than one might expect. At six o'clock in the morning on Friday, May 2, 1969, twenty-seven-year-old Department of Public Safety patrolman James Kenneth Crone, answering a distress call, arrived at the Jefferson County farmhouse of Robert Bauer only to be disarmed by Robert Dent. Twenty-two-year-old Dent, two weeks out of Angola State Farm Prison in Louisiana, and his twenty-one-year-old wife, Ila Fae, were on the run after a patrolman had tried to stop them while they were driving through Port Arthur, Texas. Because of his criminal record, Dent decided to flee rather than confront the police. After their car broke down in the town of Anahuac, the couple made it north to the farmhouse where they hit upon the idea of stealing a police car. With Crone as their captive, they drove toward Houston only to draw the attention of one state trooper after another. In short time, a caravan of a hundred or so vehicles ended up trailing the fugitives, who kept the law at a distance by holding firearms on their prisoner. Knowing the situation would put him right back in jail, Dent requested that the police allow him and his wife to at least visit Ila Fae's children from her previous marriage, a two-year-old boy and a one-year-old girl; he knew the chances of seeing them again were slim. The children were staying with Ila Fae's parents, Mr. and Mrs. Wilmer Halidy, at their home near Wheelock, about two hours northwest of Houston.

When the Dents arrived at their destination at the end of their 399-mile trek, Crone approached the house in the lead, with Ila Fae and Robert in tow, the latter pointing his shotgun at the captive patrolman. Unbeknownst to the couple, three lawmen (including FBI Special Agent Bob Wiatt and Robertson County Sheriff Sonny Elliott) were waiting in ambush inside the house and opened fire. Robert Dent received a shotgun blast to the face and two pistol shots in the arm. Ila Fae was captured and Crone escaped unharmed. Dent died an hour later at St. Joseph Hospital.

At Ila Fae's trial, where she was charged with stealing Crone's patrol car and pistol, her lawyer hoped to emphasize that only Robert Dent was a threat to the patrolman's life. Ila Fae was quoted at the time of her capture as saying: "We treated him very nicely. We never mistreated him and weren't going to." Crone testified that he was indeed worried that Mrs. Dent might harm him, as he recounted being left alone with her at one point and having her point her pistol directly in his face. Although Ila Fae ended up being sentenced to five years in prison, she only served five months. She passed away in 1992 in Livingston, Texas, while working as a dietician at a Holiday Inn. Crone stayed with the Department of Public Safety until 1978.

Spielberg knew there was a great movie in this bizarre tale, but he did not want to be restricted by an accurate telling of what happened, choosing instead to use the event as a launching point, allowing the tale to unfold in different directions. To this end, all of the principals had their names changed; the Dents became Clovis and Lou Jean Poplin, and the patrolman was now Maxwell Slide instead of Kenneth Crone. To ensure that the Poplins' goal was foolish, hopeless, and illegal from the get-go, the film script had the impatient Lou Jean goad her husband into breaking out of a pre-release center with only a few weeks to go before he will be legally set free. The Poplins were less calculated in commandeering their captive's vehicle, conning an elderly couple into giving them transport only to have the police stop them, which in turn prompts the fugitives to steal their hosts' car, causing Slide to give chase. It is when Slide catches up with them that Lou Jean manages to disarm him, tossing his weapon to her husband and thereby allowing them to take him hostage in his police car. Although the setting was still Texas, their destination was no longer Wheelock but Sugarland. This was not the actual Texan city called Sugar Land (two words) but a fictionalized version set near the Mexican border, thereby giving the Poplins a possible escape route. Their trek was also elongated, stretching overnight and therefore allowing for a respite at a used car lot near a drive-in movie theater.

Whereas the Dents wanted merely to see their two children before bargaining for a fifteen-minute head start with the understanding that they would release Crone, Lou Jean is under the misapprehension that they will not just visit but actually reclaim their one child (there was no mention in the screenplay of the character having been married before or having another child) from a foster couple who have taken charge of the baby. Seeing just how close the Poplins might get to their unobtainable goal before some inevitable turn of events put an end to their misguided dreams gave the plotline more suspense. To make Clovis that much more naïve and doomed, Spielberg's version of the story, at the climax, had the hapless husband approach the house unarmed, as Slide, well aware that something was amiss, stayed in the patrol car and ordered Lou Jean to get down to avoid harm.

Miraculously, despite the insistence on being a fictionalized version of the true story, *Sugarland* did the job of capturing the absurdist plight of these two criminals with both compassion and a dollop of satire on the fleeting nature of "celebrity" in America. There needn't be any future, more direct dramatization of the Dent story—Spielberg has already done the definitive take on it.

Jaws

For those only acquainted with the film version of *Jaws*, it is important to point out that in Peter Benchley's original novel, on which the movie is based, the character of Ellen Brody prefers Roquefort dressing on her salad, while Matt Hooper is partial to French, and that after a hard day of shark hunting, which includes watching Hooper be devoured by a giant fish, Chief Brody is content to settle down in front of the television set and watch Ginger Rogers in *Week-End at the Waldorf*. Such trivial details make it quite understandable that Steven Spielberg let it slip out to the press that he had strong reservations about the source material from which his breakthrough movie was made. Astutely pointing out that Benchley didn't write characters who were all that deep or likable, Spielberg told *Newsweek* that "you were rooting for the shark to eat the people—in alphabetical order."

Peter Benchley (whose father, Nathaniel, had authored *The Off-Islanders*, which was adapted into the Oscar-nominated comedy *The Russians Are Coming, the Russians Are Coming*) published *Jaws*, his first novel, while working as an associate editor at *Newsweek*. Having spent summers shark hunting in Nantucket with his dad, he penned a thriller about a giant shark feasting upon the inhabitants of a fictitious beachside community called Amity, and the end result initially tantalized readers as a book-of-the-month-club offering in the fall of 1973. By the time it was officially published by Doubleday in February of 1974, Universal had already snatched up the film rights, based on reading the galleys, for $175,000, which included $25,000 for Benchley's screenplay adaptation. *Jaws* debuted on the *New York Times* Best Seller list's Top 10 the week of March 10, 1974, and remained in the top five through the week of October 27. Despite its high status, strong competition for the number one position kept it from attaining that goal in its hardcover edition, with rival works—including Richard Adams's *Watership Down*, John le Carré's *Tinker, Tailor, Soldier, Spy*, and James Michener's *Centennial*—crowding *Jaws* out during that time.

When Bantam (paying a staggering $575,000 for the rights) published the paperback version the following year, *Jaws* finally made it to the top, reaching number one the week of February 23, 1975, and remaining there for a twelve-week stretch, which boded well for the upcoming movie.

Although Spielberg would work with Benchley, who had no previous screenwriting experience, in restructuring part of the script, it was clear that he needed someone else to polish it up. Playwright Howard Sackler, best known for both the stage and film adaptation of *The Great White Hope*, was hired to do some rewriting but asked for no credit. Instead, he ended up listed onscreen as one of the writers on the sequel, *Jaws 2*. Someone else was needed, basically to enhance the action scenes, dispose of pretty much all of Benchley's dialogue, and work closely with Steven Spielberg, on location, in coming up with new ideas when he needed them. This job went to Carl Gottlieb, an actor and a writer, whom Spielberg had known for several years. Interestingly enough, it was not thrillers or suspense with which Gottlieb had been associated when it came to writing, but television variety, with Gottlieb having worked on such shows as *The Smothers Brothers Comedy Hour* and the short-lived *Music Scene*, among others. Gottlieb would prove to be a godsend to the production, improving on Benchley in every way and bringing the story to a higher realm of believability and relatability for audiences. He would be forever pointed to as the real screenwriter on the project despite taking second billing to Benchley in the opening credits. For his outstanding work, he was also rewarded with a role in the picture as Amity's newspaper editor, Meadows, a part greatly diminished from the novel's counterpart.

The first line of business was disposing of Benchley's melodramatic subplot about Ellen Brody's restlessness with her life, which leads to a sexual dalliance with ichthyologist Matt Hooper in a motel. Indeed, throughout the first part of the book, Ellen has a larger role than shark hunter Quint, and her unhappy home life and subsequent adultery in no way adds to the fish business at hand, except to make her husband, Police Chief Brody, jealous and ill-tempered to the point of tedium. This makes for a tense trio aboard the *Orca* in the final chapters—the bickering and rancorous conversations between the shark hunters in no way engendering sympathy or much interest in the behavior of these thinly drawn characters. Spielberg and Gottlieb also wisely let Mr. Hooper survive his ocean descent inside the shark cage. In the book he is brutally chomped by the shark and given a violent sendoff by being thrashed about in his assailant's mouth while Brody and Quint watch. Onscreen he escapes the angry shark and hides down among the rocks until all is clear above.

Another subplot from the novel that only serves to add some pages to the manuscript and pull further focus from the killer fish involves Mayor Larry Vaughan, whose real estate business turns out to involve a shady alliance with the Mafia, who, following the shark attacks, are eager to cash in on plunging interest in Amity housing by buying up property for bargain prices. Although the cinematic Vaughan would remain far too focused on attracting summer business to the resort town and thereby be the one to blame for too many deaths, any suggestion of unlawful motivations was kept out of the screenplay. It wasn't necessary to bring in the mob because being a politician made him oily enough for most viewers to dislike him.

Further taking the pulpiness out of the storytelling, the screenplay did not give the doomed Chrissie and her drunken lover a chance to have sex on the beach before her brutal demise at the start of the story, thereby eliminating the cliché

Sheriff Brody (Roy Scheider) may look happy, but Matt Hooper (Richard Dreyfuss) knows they've caught the wrong shark in *Jaws*.

(which Hollywood was too often guilty of following) of "punishing" youth for an illicit dalliance. Also gone was the potentially laughable image of not only Officer Hendricks but of Brody and Chrissie's fling, Tom, *all* vomiting at the sight of her mangled remains on the beach; the scene of Brody having poor Mrs. Kintner, the mother of the boy killed by the shark while on his raft, given a shot and taken away by doctors, thereby almost callously dismissing her suffering as a nuisance; and most mercifully, an absurd scene in which, because of Brody's knowledge of Larry's Mafia connections, the Brody family cat has its neck broken by a thug in front of one of Brody's kids, prompting the incensed police chief to drag the kitty's corpse over to the Mayor's house and toss it at him.

While Benchley had Brody's deputy, Hendricks, describe another attack—this time on an old man—this was deemed a shark too far and eliminated in favor of a sequence that brought the terror much closer to home for Brody: his own son is nearly gobbled up by the predator in an estuary while boating with his friends. During this scene a hapless fellow trying to help becomes the next shark victim, graphically losing his leg before it sinks to the ocean floor. The script also put Brody on the beach, nervously anticipating trouble, when Alex Kintner is attacked, making for a much more exciting and personal response to the tragedy.

A town council gathering to decide how to destroy the seemingly unstoppable shark was given a spot much earlier in the movie version and had the great added touch of putting Quint there, memorably drawing attention from the bickering bunch by running his fingernails down a blackboard. In the book, he was initially little more than a vague figure, mentioned in passing for the most part until he was finally hired for the job. He and his prey would each end up making much more dramatic exits onscreen, both of which fit the excitement generated by Spielberg's direction; Quint is chomped by his nemesis, who is, in turn, dispatched explosively when he gets a tank of compressed air in his teeth. On the page, the shark called it quits by simply being harpooned repeatedly, dragging Quint down with him, in Captain Ahab fashion, when the latter ends up caught on one of the ropes. The entire "shark hunt" sequence onscreen was given considerably more tension by having the three men set out to sea and stay there, with no other characters, nor land, being seen by them for the remainder of the movie. Having them pull up anchor and go home each night after a fruitless quest, as Benchley depicted it, was something of a bummer that took away the sense of isolation and terror of an endeavor that seemed to have cordoned them off from regular society.

Benchley's frequently terrible dialogue between the confrontational characters was given a complete overhaul, making them seem less idiotic and one dimensional. Onscreen, Brody is a vulnerable man placed in an awkward position of power, having to confront the enemy on water, something he expresses no fondness for, thereby making him far more relatable and ultimately heroic, unlike his literary counterpart whose relentless sarcasm and seeming disdain for all around him keeps him at arm's length.

In the long run, the tremendous success of the movie kept Benchley's book climbing the sales charts, no matter how much it may have thrown moviegoers with its many differences from what appeared onscreen. It returned to the number one spot on the *New York Times* list of mass-market paperback best sellers on

July 6, 1975, only seventeen days after the movie's wide opening. It would remain in the top spot for the next ten weeks, making it by far *the* page-turner to curl up with on the beach that summer, while staying clear of the water.

1941

The last thing *1941* does is suggest anything akin to real life, but the inspiration for Spielberg's strident comedy did come from an actual incident.

Starting at about 7:15 p.m. on February 23, 1942, a Japanese submarine surfaced in the Santa Barbara Channel off the Southern California coast, directly across from the town of Ellwood, and fired some fifteen shells toward the mainland. One shell hit the pumping equipment of an oil derrick at the Bankline Oil Company refinery. Other missiles landed at nearby ranches, but there were no reported casualties or injuries. Navy planes quickly flew over the water, thereby causing the sub to retreat. A blackout was ordered, and all radio stations in the area went off the air until an all-clear was signaled after a four-hour-and-thirteen-minute stretch. This was the first recorded enemy attack on American soil since the Pearl Harbor invasion on December 7, 1941.

The attack clearly instilled panic in Southern California residents, and only two days later sirens heralded the appearance of a mysterious aircraft over the Los

Wild Bill (John Belushi) displays his aggressive nature towards the hapless Winowski (Ronnie McMillan) in *1941*.

Angeles-Long Beach Harbor area. Searchlights swept the night sky as antiaircraft guns fired thousands of rounds of ammunition upward at the phantom object to no avail. Another blackout was declared, lasting from 2:25 a.m. to 7:21 a.m. The aircraft went unidentified, although four years after *1941* hit theaters, the military concluded that it was most likely a weather balloon drifting off course. Despite there being no enemy assault, it was later reported that there were three civilians killed during the incident by friendly fire, while heart attacks claimed three others.

From these reports, writers Robert Zemeckis and Bob Gale (in collaboration with John Milius) came up with an exaggerated version of how the high-strung and all too gung ho American populace might react to such a brazen attack on US soil. Wanting to increase the paranoia and give it more urgency, the writers moved the time frame back to the week following the Pearl Harbor attack. The location was made more colorful by making Hollywood the principal setting, and placing the story in December meant that the sets could be decorated for the Christmas holidays. All of the silly folks on hand in Spielberg's version of the tale were fabricated and exaggerated for maximum impact, with the exception of Major General Joseph W. Stillwell (Robert Stack), the commanding officer of the 8th Division at Fort Ord, California, who was indeed reported to have taken in a showing of Disney's *Dumbo* while in Los Angeles in December of 1941. At the time of the actual "phantom aircraft" incident, however, the General was over in India, having been appointed commander of the American Army Force of the China-Burma-India Theater.

1941 also tossed in a version of the notorious Zoot Suit riots, a series of racially motivated attacks committed on Mexican Americans by angry servicemen who viewed the fanciful menswear, which consisted of a long coat with padded shoulders and high-waist trousers, as "unpatriotic." The actual riots had taken place in Los Angeles a year and a half after the events portrayed here onscreen, in May and June of 1943.

Twilight Zone: The Movie

Although he initially had another "remake" in mind for his contribution to the big screen revisit to *The Twilight Zone*, Steven Spielberg's enthusiasm for the whole concept was suddenly derailed by the tragic deaths of actor Vic Morrow and a pair of Vietnamese children on the set of director John Landis's segment. Months after the awful event, with pending lawsuits and legal complications clouding the whole project, Steven settled upon an update of "Kick the Can," a rather gentle episode from the series' third season, one that focused on a group of senior citizens and children and had no terror or violence to speak of.

The original version, which aired on CBS on February 9, 1962, was filled with familiar character faces rather than star names, with Ernest Truex, then a busy player mainly on the small screen (*The Ann Sothern Show, Pete and Gladys*), cast in the leading role. At the Sunnyvale Rest senior citizen's home, Charles Whitley (Truex) is the one resident not content to watch his autumn years slip away merely sitting around, staring into space, and waiting to die. Trying to rally his fellow housemates into playing the sort of games they enjoyed as kids, the old fellow instead finds himself facing possible isolation ward incarceration from the staff because of his unorthodox behavior and desire to deviate from the routine. Fantasy intervenes, allowing Whitley and most of his fellow residents to become the rambunctious children they once were, playing a game of kick the can on the Sunnyvale lawn. Pragmatic resident Ben Conroy (Russell Collins) is the only one not given a second chance at youth, but seeing the joy on display and feeling envious, he pleads with the now-young Whitley and the other children to take him away with them. Instead, he is left behind as the others run off.

Spielberg asked two former collaborators—*E.T.* scripter Melissa Mathison (working under the pseudonym "Josh Rogan") and *Duel* writer Richard Matheson—to give a spin on George Clayton Johnson's original teleplay. This time the rallying senior (now called "Mr. Bloom," played by Scatman Crothers) was more of a mysterious outsider, the possessor of magical powers, as he is the one who turns the other seniors into children while staying elderly himself. Whereas the teleplay had Charles Whitley be the one rejected by his own son at the story's outset, with the younger man informing his disappointed father that he would not be able to leave the rest home to visit his family yet *again*, the movie gave this story-line to the skeptical Conroy (Bill Quinn). The ending was drastically changed, as the seniors come to the realization that they do *not* want to be young again and relive so many painful memories, concluding that it is wiser to keep a youthful spirit than attempt to physically regain what you have lost. They return to their elderly state. Only a single senior, Mr. Agee (Murray Matheson), is not swayed, choosing to stay a child (Evan Richards). It is to him that a regretful Mr. Conroy pleads in vain to come with. At the conclusion, Conroy is seen hopefully kicking a can, while Bloom trots on over to yet another nearby rest home, no doubt to teach the same lesson.

The mysterious Mr. Bloom (Scatman Crothers) checks into another senior home to work his magic, as seen in Segment 2 from *Twilight Zone: The Movie*.

Presumably, Spielberg took this as an opportunity to make a statement against those who accused him of being a Peter Pan-sort who dwelled in a world of wonder and "immaturity" as far as his movie subjects were concerned. Although the revision of the ending might have given the update a justification for its existence, the presentation was soft and unmemorable, with Spielberg, in a rare instance, actually losing his grasp on one department he often excelled at, directing child actors, as many here came off as amateurish and too precocious by half. Scatman Crothers was a welcome bit of casting, however, and gave the sequence what little gravitas it possessed.

Of the three *Twilight Zone: The Movie* segments taken directly from the series, George Miller took a good episode ("Nightmare at 20,000 Feet") and made it even better; Joe Dante took a famous one ("It's a Good Life") and trashed it; and Spielberg went for a mild but pleasant offering but didn't add much to it at all.

The Color Purple

Of all the literary adaptations Steven Spielberg tackled, this was the toughest one, the book that came with the highest expectations and the greatest amount of pre-judgement baggage from fans and critics. Alice Walker's novel premiered in the summer of 1982 to mostly rave reviews. In April of the following year, *The Color Purple* was given the Pulitzer Prize for Fiction, making Walker the very first black woman to receive this honor. This kind of attention increased sales tremendously, with the paperback edition ending at number one on the Trade Paperback Best Seller list that same year. By autumn of 1984, the press announced that there were more than one million copies of the book in print after twenty-one printings. Warner Bros. had already purchased the rights to the novel with the team of Peter Guber and Jon Peters in charge of producing in partnership with musician Quincy Jones. Walker, who had no screenwriting experience, took a crack at a screenplay, but once Spielberg came aboard he rejected hers in favor of an adaptation by Dutch writer Menno Meyjes, who had gotten noticed in the industry by way of a script he wrote called "The Children's Crusade," which eventually, under the name *Lionheart*, made it to the screen as a production from actress Talia Shire's company and was released in very limited engagements two years *after* the movie of *The Color Purple* had debuted.

Walker's novel is made up entirely of letters, those written by its protagonist, Celie—who writes first to God and then to her sister Nettie in Africa—as well as those from Nettie to Celie. This letter format had been used on many occasions before, among the most celebrated being Bram Stoker's *Dracula*, Chonderlos de Laclos's *Les Liaisons Dangereuses*, and Bel Kaufman's *Up the Down Staircase*. The film script would keep several instances of the novel's correspondence, read in voiceover narration.

Spielberg lost the preconditioned naysayers almost instantly by giving the film a more hopeful, spirited tone right from the opening scene, with young Celie and her beloved sibling playing happily among a field of flowers, until it is made clear that the former is well along in her pregnancy, despite her age. Walker's book plunges readers directly into the grim reality of Celie's situation—being raped at age fourteen by the man she believed to be her father and bearing two children, which are immediately taken from their mother and presumed by her to have been killed somewhere in the woods. Celie's very casual recounting of these incestuous crimes sets a bleak, unsentimental tone that no doubt would have lost its share of

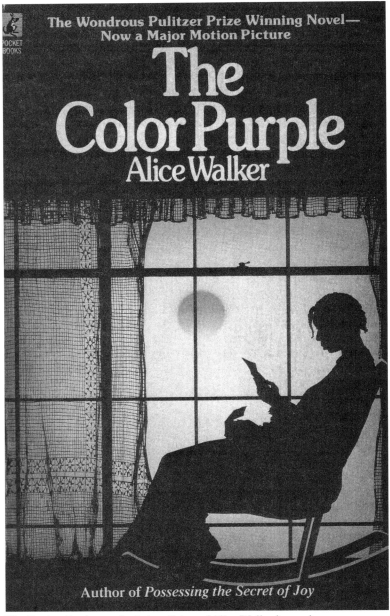

The Pocket Books movie tie-in edition of Alice Walker's novel.

viewers had this been the cinematic approach. Relentless unpleasantness is seldom the goal of commercial Hollywood properties looking to sell tickets. While Meyjes's script would not shy away from Celie's often dire situation, Spielberg was canny enough to realize that there is a way to depict extreme hardship, human cruelty, and misfortune onscreen without wallowing in it to the detriment of audience empathy.

Further darkening Celie's world is the fact that the previous wife of her brutish new husband, Mr. _____, and the mother of his brood of "rotten children," had been shot dead in front of her son, Harpo (who relates having nightmares of the incident), by a jealous lover. In another spirit-crushing incident, Celie's father yanks her out of school, insisting she is too dumb to get any value from it, and any further hope of being educated is derailed when a schoolteacher, Miss Beasley, decides not to change Celie's situation when she notices the girl is once again pregnant. Neither of these incidents are mentioned in the film script. Celie is able to receive some degree of instruction from her sister when Nettie comes to live with her and Mr.____, a sequence given a more memorable visual aspect onscreen by having Nettie adorn objects with signs on them, helping her sister to learn to iden-tify and spell them. Spielberg also gave the sisters' key moment of separation far more fire than had been evident in Walker's story, in which the girls part quietly, Nettie being glad to go to get away from Mr.____'s lewd intentions. Onscreen, the parting is nothing less than electrifying in its drama, as Mr.____ cruelly pulls the bawling siblings apart and tosses rocks at the hapless Nettie—an emotional high-point that became one of the film's most unforgettable, gut-wrenching moments.

Walker's narrative includes visits to Mr.____'s house by his two sisters, one of whom, Kate, tries to get the lazy Harpo to take up some of Celie's chores and buy her sister-in-law some nicer clothes. For her efforts, she is driven away in tears by her brother, but not before encouraging the timid Celie to put up a fight. There is also a drop-by by Mr.____'s oversized brother, Tobias, who is equally unhappy in his own marriage, although he believes Mr.____ has fared better. These family members were dropped from the screenplay altogether, with only Mr.____'s equally selfish father retained from the book.

Recreating the scene of pregnant Sofia's first introduction to the rude and uninviting Mr. ____, the script added a sublime moment not in the book that made it that much more effective, having Mr.____ coldly order his dutiful wife to bring him a different glass of lemonade because the first one "ain't cold enough," thereby prompting a reaction of disgust, pity, and disbelief from Sofia that spoke volumes. While it is made clear in the film that Sofia refused to take a subservient position to Harpo once they were married, any more than she had during their courtship, their domestic violence is kept offscreen; in the book, however, Celie is witness to one of their many knock-down, drag-out fights. When Sofia is unjustly tossed in jail for daring to fight back when the mayor had struck her, Walker depicts Celie, Mr.____, Harpo, and Shug actually visiting her at the penal facility. There is no such indication of contact with the outside world in the movie, making Sofia's plight come across as that much more solitary and demeaning. Depicting another heinous act of male cruelty, Walker has Squeak approach her uncle, the warden, in an effort to shorten Sofia's sentence, only to be viciously raped by him, another depressing moment that was dropped from the screen transfer.

Certainly the most controversial aspect of Spielberg's take on Walker's original story was his approach to the lesbianism that had been a key theme in Celie's relationship with Shug Avery. Although the film makes it clear that Celie was smitten by the outspoken, independent singer just from looking at her picture, Walker had made it quite clear that this was more than a mere infatuation or sisterly devotion; it was Shug and only Shug whom Celie loved in a romantic manner. The book includes an explicit moment of Shug encouraging Celie to strip and examine her naked body in front of her (the movie was intent on receiving a PG-13 rating, so there was no nudity of that nature) and then makes it clear that the pair had sex while their husbands were away from the house, something that would happen on a fairly regular basis from that point on in the story. Spielberg's version reduced this intimacy to a timid mouth-to-mouth kiss between the women (long before Shug's marriage to Grady), which left audiences with the impression that things might have gone no further than this. Many of the book's readers, gay or straight, had been greatly disappointed by this reluctance to go that extra step—a valid complaint. The love between the two women was, however, there to behold onscreen, minus the physical emphasis, despite the insistence of some disgruntled readers that there was *nothing* whatsoever to suggest a lesbian relationship in the movie.

Wanting to keep Celie the center of attention, Spielberg knew that there wasn't much point in recreating Nettie's accounts of life in Africa as thoroughly as Walker had done with her many letters on this topic. Nettie explains that she had gone to Africa to do missionary work along with Corrine and Steven, the couple who had raised Celie's children as their own. There, Corrine, in her illness, accused her husband and Nettie of being the actual biological parents of Adam and Olivia. There are vivid accounts of their village being destroyed by English rubber planters and of Adam's pursuit of Tashi, who submits herself to an African mutilation ritual for women. The portrait of poverty and the indifference of the locals toward the missionary's efforts makes life in Africa much of a mixed blessing, although it would come across as mostly a positive experience in the abbreviated version that showed up on screen. Among the many other details of Nettie's correspondence skipped in the screen transfer is her realization that the pictures in the Bible have led people to believe that all of those being written about were white. A further religious discussion, with Shug explaining to Celie that God is not some white man with a beard but something within each of us, is not included either.

Also gone is most of Squeak's storyline: her insistence that she no longer be called by her nickname but by her real name, Mary Agnes; her desire to follow in Shug's footsteps and become a singer; her eventual marriage to Shug's ex, Grady; and their move to Panama where they run a reefer plantation. Drugs play no part in the film version. Also missing is a visit to Celie's supposed father, who is revealed to be her stepfather, and his new, fifteen-year-old wife. Walker had Shug further break Celie's heart when she—insistent that she needs one last fling at this stage in her life—decides to take up with a nineteen-year-old flute player named Germaine. This too was eliminated in the screenplay, as was Mr._____ collecting seashells after Celie leaves him; a letter from the Department of Defense that leads them to believe Nettie's ship was sunk; and Celie's inheritance, including a store, where she hires Sofia to help wait on the black customers.

One of the most regrettable omissions involves a character that found no place in the film adaptation: the grownup Miss Eleanor Jane, the daughter of the mayor and Miss Millie, whom Sofia has been obliged to raise since being forced to work for these self-involved people. When Miss Eleanor Jane has her own baby, she expects Sofia to show it affection and concern, but Sofia lets her know, in no uncertain terms, that the child means *nothing* to her, and she expresses bitterness at having been ordered to become a servant to a family she never wanted anything to do with. The anger toward entire generations of white children—who were raised by black maids and nannies and who expected their demeaned employees to consider them the earth and sky while never showing any consideration whatsoever for *their* lives—had been stated by Walker pointedly and powerfully.

Walker had been accused by many reviewers and readers of painting an exceedingly negative view of males, which might account for the least convincing turn of events in the novel, when Mr.____ develops a conscience and begins speaking to Celie like a confidant and friend, putting his violent and insensitive past behind him. This all too abrupt about-face, almost glossing over the amount of physical and mental abuse inflicted upon this poor woman to the degree that it suddenly seemed less reprehensible, denied the character the reparation that he warranted in light of his behavior. Spielberg and Meyjes were far less forgiving of Mr.____ onscreen, making his change of heart more acceptable. His gesture of writing to the government to inquire about Nettie's whereabouts and insuring that she be reunited with Celie, a plot turn not in the novel, was written so that it is done on the sly, as his inability to do so openly would be a more believable action coming from someone so unwilling to show Celie any previous degree of appreciation, respect, or kindness. Indeed, Spielberg gave the climax of Walker's book the full throttle emotional effect—one that either confirmed his detractors' worst fears about his open sentimentality or that was one of the most gracefully beautiful endings of any film release in the 80s, or any decade. Mr.____ goes about his business of plowing the fields, seeing the reunion of the two sisters from afar and feeling a jolt of pride for a kindness that might or might not receive any thanks, as the sisters pick right up where they left off, sharing their bonding game of pat-a-cake silhouetted against the setting sun. The image of Mr.____ passing behind them suggests the possibility of a family at last, or perhaps one of which he will never really be a part.

Empire of the Sun

Born in 1930 in Shanghai, where his father had been sent from the United Kingdom to work, J. G. (James Graham) Ballard was clearly writing about his own experiences through the protagonist of young Jim in his 1984 novel *Empire of the Sun*. Atypical, this work veered from science fiction/fantasy, the genre in which Ballard specialized; his books in this field included *Crash*, *High Rise*, and *Hello America*. In many ways, *Empire* was the very best of all the books Steven Spielberg would end up using as source material for his films.

The one crucial aspect of Ballard's real-life story that was changed for his book was having Jim incarcerated in a prison camp for a three-year period *away* from his parents following the Japanese invasion of Shanghai. In fact, Ballard and his family were placed in the camp together. Having a small boy experience the horrors of wartime alone, coping with the alternately ruthless and hopeless behavior of the adults around him, made for a more effective statement on the destruction of innocence, the often devastating events on hand seen through the eyes of the

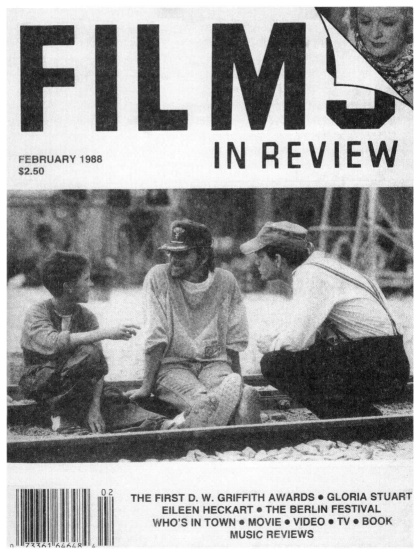

This cover of *Films in Review* magazine captures Steven Spielberg on the set of *Empire of the Sun* with two of his stars, Christian Bale and John Malkovich.

impressionably young. Although the character's last name was never specified in the book, Tom Stoppard's screenplay chose to use Ballard's middle name, Graham, as the fictional Jim's last name, thereby drawing an even closer parallel to the autobiographical nature of the piece.

The basic structure of how the events in the book unfolded was adhered to for the most part onscreen, but there was a good deal of alteration and rethinking, nonetheless, not to mention downplaying or avoidance of the more physically unpleasant results of the collapse of civility Ballard had written about. There had been a most disturbing but undeniably effective emphasis on human suffering, with descriptions of physical violence, decapitations, fly infestation, bodily deterioration from dwindling health, scarring and sores, excrement, and an abundance of corpses treated no better than debris discarded by the side of the road. Steven Spielberg figured a harrowing existence could be dramatized effectively without smearing the audience's faces in the unwatchable.

Jim's family chauffeur, Yang, although left a vague figure, was made less unsympathetic onscreen. In the book the driver is given to beating away beggars from the car with a leather riding crop, whereas onscreen Jim witnesses, from the vehicle, this insensitive act being done by the police. Jim's governess, Vera, a White Russian, is absent from the film; instead, Jim is given a Chinese employee whom he timidly reminds is obliged to listen to orders from him. This makes the scene (reprised from the book) in which Jim is slapped for questioning why a servant is looting furniture after the Japanese invasion more effective by having that very same Graham family employee, and not an anonymous worker, be the one to strike the boy.

While the reason behind the blast that knocks Jim from his hotel window is kept vague in the movie, Ballard explains that a British ship, *HMS Petrel*, has been shelled in the Shanghai harbor by the Japanese. This act leads directly to Jim being separated from his parents when his father goes to help rescue the wounded British sailors trying to get ashore. Hoping to help as well, Jim ends up being separated from his mother and finds himself eventually split from his father after they are hospitalized and the latter is taken away to the Hongkew prison camp before Jim can track him down. Stoppard's script merely had the family torn apart because of the chaotic stampede of fleeing citizens around them, as they try to escape on foot.

Jim's initial attempts to survive on his own took place onscreen exclusively at the vacated Graham house, whereas Ballard documented the boy exploring and taking up residence in various dwellings in the neighborhood and even spending an extended period of time living at the empty apartment of the Maxted family. Being chased relentlessly by a threating Chinese boy through the streets of Shanghai was retained, but the film version had the pursuer steal Jim's shoes before the hapless English lad is rescued by American profiteer Frank. Ballard had Jim first encountering Frank when the boy had rowed himself to a derelict freighter on the river and was, in turn, taken by Frank to the coal ship, where he and his fellow black marketer, Basie, had surreptitiously set up residence.

In the novel, Frank does not end up in the prison camp as he does in the film. The screenplay provides an extra tension (and further suggestions of his homosexual inclinations toward Basie) when he is temporarily displaced by Jim as Basie's flunky, with the boy actually taking up residence in the American dorm in the prison, causing extreme jealousy on Frank's part. The camp scenes in the book place more emphasis on Jim's relationships with Dr. Ransome and Mr. Maxted; give the couple with whom the boy shared living quarters, Mr. and Mrs. Phillips, an ailing six-year-old son; and feature destitute Chinese refugees trying desperately to get into the camp in order to obtain food and shelter but being denied access by the Japanese. The young kamikaze pilot is not encountered by Jim on the written page until our young hero returns to the Lunghua airfield after the camp evacuation, whereas their relationship commences earlier onscreen during Jim's incarceration. To add further poignancy to the Japanese lad's brutal death, the film script has him shot by Basie and his squad of bandits, who mistakenly believe he is threatening Jim with his sword, whereas his murder is committed anonymously in the book.

The novel has Jim bond with an increasingly feeble Mr. Maxted at the stadium on their forced march from the camp, with the boy lying near the older man on the field, only to awaken the next morning and find him dead. Stoppard wrote a similar scene for the movie, substituting Mrs. Phillips for Maxted; the lady gives up and agrees to pretend to be dead in order not to be marched any further, only to actually die.

The final scenes of the movie were given a considerable makeover from the book. In Ballard's version, Jim returns more than once to the prison camp. During his first trip back, he encounters fellow prisoners Tulloch and Price, who demand he take them to the stadium with the intention of looting the merchandise placed there. They are shot down in their efforts, and Jim ends up tagging along with Basie and his new band of scavengers. Once Jim has been returned home to Shanghai, the boy actually insists that his chauffeur drive him back to the prison camp, which is now occupied by British nationals. Jim's odd longing to once again experience his place of imprisonment, because of the sense of community and purpose he believed it had, was played down, and for the film he was instead given a reunion at a children's displacement camp with his parents.

Always

As early as 1980, when asked what prospective projects he had planned for the near future, Steven Spielberg would mention a remake of the 1943 MGM fantasy-drama *A Guy Named Joe*. This was a dream property for the director, who had grown fond of the movie due to television viewings while he was growing up. When he discovered that his *Jaws* and *Close Encounters* star Richard Dreyfuss shared his affection for the piece, Spielberg figured he also had his potential leading man, once the project finally came to fruition.

The original movie was very much a product of the patriotic cinema of World War II. In it, Spencer Tracy portrayed Pete Sandidge, an Air Force pilot stationed in the United Kingdom, whose tendency to be reckless during flight missions keeps his girlfriend, Dorinda Durston (Irene Dunne), herself a Ferry Command flier, in a constant state of anxiety. Dorinda hopes he will take up a safer job training upcoming pilots back in the States. To placate her, he agrees, but only under the condition that she herself transfer to ground duty. It is not to be. When a German aircraft carrier is spotted off the coast, Pete joins the mission only to be killed when he heroically bombs the vessel. Up in Heaven, Pete is commanded to return to earth and pass along his flight skills to the newer pilots. At the training base in Phoenix, Pete becomes the surrogate instructor to young Ted Randall (Van Johnson), getting through to him by an otherworldly thought process, although no one on Earth can actually see the deceased pilot. When Ted is assigned to a base in New Guinea, Pete is surprised to find that Dorinda is stationed there as well. When Dorinda and Pete begin to fall in love, Pete faces the difficult task of leaving behind his own feelings and helping the living fulfill theirs.

A prankish Pete (Richard Dreyfuss) tries the old "grease on the face" gag with his buddy Al (John Goodman) in *Always*.

Released in New York City at Christmastime in 1943, *A Guy Named Joe* was hardly a critic's favorite but quickly caught on with the public, who enjoyed its surprisingly smooth mix of romance and whimsy. It was directed by Victor Fleming, who had a firm grasp on the material. Frederick Hazlitt Brennan had adapted the original concept by Chandler Sprague and David Boehm into a sturdy tale of sacrifice and redemption, while Dalton Trumbo added some pungent dialogue, making the first portion of the story, which stressed the loving relationship between Pete and Dorinda, its strongest aspect. Because the picture had been delayed by a two-month shutdown when Van Johnson was badly injured in a car accident, MGM could not find a suitable house in the Los Angeles area in which to book it by year's end. As a result, it waited until March of 1944 to release it there (at Grauman's Chinese Theater, among others), where it continued its box office success. Sprague and Boehm ended up with an Oscar nomination the following year for their original story, as the film was treated as a 1944 release by the Academy.

Spielberg, knowing that the World War II setting was no longer necessary or relevant, had no intention of doing a direct remake. Instead, he wanted to make the concept of accepting the unfortunate loss of a loved one timeless by changing the backdrop altogether and setting it in the present. Keeping the flight theme, the characters now were aerial firefighters. Pete received a slight name change, becoming "Pete Sandich" instead of "Sandidge," and Ted Randall was now "Ted Baker," but Dorinda Durston and Al Yackey remained the same. Although there was a character named "Nails" on hand, having been the base commander played by James Gleason in the first film, he was given much less importance this time out (as portrayed by Ed Van Nuys). The heavenly former flyer who had advised Pete the first time around, "The General" (Lionel Barrymore), no longer needed to be military or male and became, quite delightfully, as it marked her return to motion pictures after an eight year absence, Audrey Hepburn, a serenely delicate, white sweatered advisor dubbed "Hap" (named, perhaps, in tribute to WWII Air Force General Henry "Hap" Arnold). Hap is the only heavenly host on hand this time; in *Joe*, Pete was also greeted up in the clouds by another deceased pilot, Dick Rumney (Barry Nelson), who would join him in his duties back on Earth. He was deemed unnecessary the second time around. While the original movie gave Van Johnson a brief interaction with a hostess—played by a dry Esther Williams in one of her first movie roles—*Always* added a character to pine for Ted in vain, Rachel, played by Marg Helgenberger, a redheaded lady who clumsily has a habit of letting her "Follow Me" cart get away from her.

Ted was brought into the story earlier for the remake, flying as part of a "birthday greetings" plane service and hanging around the sidelines at the airbase, and he is shown as being clearly smitten with Dorinda *before* Pete exits the Earth. In *A Guy Named Joe*, Pete first encounters his "assignment" at the Phoenix training camp, with Van Johnson not showing up until more than fifty minutes into the picture. Pete's tragic demise now came not because of a heroic gesture to stop an enemy (that would entail a deliberately evil blaze) but due to him risking his own life to ensure that the fire emanating from Al's plane is extinguished, thereby saving his pal. A nice touch.

In *Joe*, not only do Pete and Dorinda have a different song of their own than in *Always*—the 1928 standard "I'll Get By (As Long as I Have You)," (written by Fred E. Ahlert and Roy Turk, and originally introduced by Aileen Stanley)—but Dorinda herself sings it. Because Irene Dunne was a trained soprano and had sung many times onscreen, even in some of her non-musical assignments, audiences were not at all surprised to hear her chime in on the tune, sung while Al (Ward Bond) played the harmonica. Despite Spielberg's efforts to replace this song with "Always" for the remake (hence the new title), Irving Berlin's resistance to release the rights caused him to have to fall back on Jerome Kern and Otto Harbach's "Smoke Gets in Your Eyes," which worked just fine and made for a cheeky double meaning as well. Ironically, Irene Dunne had once sung this song onscreen as well, in the 1935 film of *Roberta*.

Carried over from the original film were occasional bits of dialogue. In *Joe*, when Pete arrived in Heaven he remarks to Dick Rumney, "Either I'm dead or I'm crazy," which prompts the response, "You're not crazy," thereby causing Pete to realize he is, in fact, deceased. In *Always*, this very same exchange was repeated by Pete and Hap, while Pete's final reflection on seeing Dorinda and Ted safe and happy together as he returns to the afterlife ("That's my girl. And that's my boy.") was kept as well. Pete's habit of plucking at his eyebrow was retained and even inherited by Ted this time out. Best of all, it was crucial to make sure that Dorinda once again flew the dangerous mission as a way of ensuring that her lover did not risk his life. This—putting a woman in a position that was considered suitable only for males in the eyes of many less enlightened people of the day (of either sex)—had been a wonderfully progressive touch on the part of the 1943 filmmakers. This time, for extra dramatic emphasis (alas, resulting in a miscalculated moment of corn on Spielberg's part), Pete finally appears temporarily visible to Dorinda when she's resigned herself to dying under the water, until he reaches out and pulls her to the surface.

Hook

The writing credit for *Hook* reads "Based upon the original stage play and books by J. M. Barrie," which is a safe way to cover all possible source materials. *Peter Pan*, after all, is a tale lodged in our subconscious to the point where most of us aren't all that certain where we first knew it or what precisely its origins are. Peter Pan, the character, wasn't even the star of his first depiction, showing up in chapters thirteen through eighteen of Barrie's 1902 novel *The Little White Bird*. Two years later, the author moved him front and center for the stage play *Peter Pan, or The Boy Who Wouldn't Grow Up*, which premiered on December 27, 1904, at London's Duke of York Theatre. (Strangely enough, Barrie initially considered calling it *The Great White Father*, a reference to the name bestowed upon Peter by the Indians grateful for him saving Tiger Lily.) For the first (but not the last) time, Peter was played by a grown woman, in this case thirty-seven-year-old Nina Boucicault—a curious practice considering Barrie's very deliberate celebration of young males. Gerald du Maurier took on the dual role of Captain Hook and Mr. Darling, a bit of Freudian casting which also became the norm in many revivals and adaptations of the piece.

Running for 145 performances (and becoming a revival staple in London for the next thirty Christmases), the play came to New York's Empire Theatre the following year, with thirty-two-year-old Maude Adams as Peter (the role she'd become most identified with) and Ernest Lawford as Hook/Darling. Proving even more popular than it had been in London, the show ran for 223 performances. Barrie continued to tinker with the play version off and on over the years and, knowing his creation of the boy who defiantly refused to grow up had really struck a nerve with the public, agreed to have his chapters from *The Little White Bird* published separately, in 1906, under the title *Peter Pan in Kensington Gardens*.

With no published version of the play script made available until 1928, Barrie fashioned his play into a novel, calling it *Peter and Wendy* and publishing it in 1911. In time, Wendy's name was removed from subsequent printings, and the book would be firmly implanted in people's minds as *Peter Pan*, with many assuming that this marked the character's debut. In 1924 Paramount released the first official film adaptation of the play, once again sticking with the female casting tradition, putting Betty Bronson (who was, at least, a relatively young seventeen at the time) in the lead, with Ernest Torrence as Hook. Tinker Bell was now able to be seen as a person rather than a beam of light, with Virginia Browne Faire in the role.

The 1950s brought the character into the public consciousness in a major way. First the play was revived in 1950 on Broadway, but with a handful of Leonard Bernstein songs inserted into the story. Starring Jean Arthur (who would turn fifty during the run) and Boris Karloff, the show racked up 321 performances. Three years later Peter finally became the boy he should have been all along when Walt Disney released his animated take on the story, with sixteen-year-old Bobby Driscoll providing the voice. This had its own new set of songs, which were contributed by Sammy Fain, Sammy Cahn, Oliver Wallace, Ted Sears, and Winston Hibler.

The "King of Fun" Strikes!

Captain Hook (Dustin Hoffman) strikes a piratical pose for his shipmate, Smee (Bob Hoskins), and his captive, Jack Banning (Charlie Korsmo), in this trading card image from *Hook*.

With forty-year-old Mary Martin in the lead, *Peter Pan* then became a full-out Broadway musical in 1954 with yet another new batch of tunes, these by Carolyn Leigh, Mark Charlap, Jule Styne, Betty Comden, and Adolph Green. Although this would run shorter than the Arthur-Karloff version (152 performances), its transformation into a live 1955 television special (subsequently restaged in 1956 and then preserved on tape for a 1960 telecast) turned it into a treasured classic. Because of these versions, *Peter Pan* pretty much became firmly embedded in the mind of a generation as a musical.

Hook did not set out to top or repeat any of these; instead, it was intended to create a whole new spin on the legend, a sequel of sorts. Writer Jim V. Hart came up with the concept of a grown-up Peter Pan and a Captain Hook who had survived his run-in with the hungry crocodile, based on theories and speculation provided by his questioning son. Hart had originally worked with writer-director Nick Castle on developing this into a screen story with the idea of the latter directing. Once Spielberg's former agent, Mike Medavoy, ended up in charge of TriStar, he knew that this would be the angle on the Pan legend to get Spielberg interested in finally directing some version of the story that had been forever associated with him by both his fans and detractors. While Spielberg had alternately declared that he was not interested in directing a *Peter Pan* film and that he was destined to do so, the latter won out, turning *Hook* into a highly desirable and potentially very lucrative property. Although Dustin Hoffman managed to be lured into playing the flamboyant and despicable Captain Hook, he requested rewrites and revisions for his character (who despite having the title role was very much in a subordinate position to the actual protagonist, Peter Banning), with Malia Scotch Marmo hired to do so. Similarly, it was decided that Tinker Bell (who, in Barrie's original concept, had no human speaking voice but tinkled like a bell, per her name) needed to have her dialogue beefed up. Actress-turned-author Carrie Fisher was given this task but received no onscreen credit among the writers.

Hook made several direct references to the Barrie story: the elderly Wendy would still inhabit a London home with the address of Number 14 (there was never a specific street mentioned), and Peter's children would be taken from the same nursery where Wendy and her brothers John and Michael had been coaxed away by Peter Pan in the original tale. The premise of getting Peter Banning and his family over to England involved the elderly Wendy having a wing of the Great Ormond Street Hospital in London dedicated in her honor. This establishment owed its lasting existence to J. M. Barrie, as he signed over the copyright to *Peter Pan* to them in 1929, allowing them to benefit from its popularity. Although the copyright expired in 1987, the UK government granted the hospital the right to continue collecting royalties on productions and adaptations of the work in perpetuity.

A grown-up (and senile) version of one of the Lost Boys, Tootles, was now sharing the residence with Wendy and was given the final moment in the movie, being granted the ability to fly once again. The menacing crocodile had since been slaughtered and turned into a clock tower in the center of Piratetown, although not for a working timepiece, as Captain Hook—having never gotten over the fear of ticking that had come from within the ominous reptile—had ordered all clocks to be broken and therefore silenced. Perhaps fearing any accusations of racism, the tribe of Indians (ruled by Tiger Lily) on Neverland was missing from the updated story altogether; Barrie had not only referred to them frequently by the uncomfortable label of "redskins" but also called them Piccaninnies (!). Naming Peter Banning's son Jack could be looked on as an homage of sorts to Jack Llewellyn Davies, one of the five brothers who had captured Barrie's fancy in Kensington Park and inspired the Pan story in the first place. Insomuch as a major star, Julia Roberts, was signed to play Tinker Bell, it no longer made any sense for her to speak only in tinkling bell sounds, and she was instead given a human voice.

Although Barrie had very specifically indicated that Captain Hook had lost his *right* arm (as opposed to hand) because of Peter chopping it off, this version saw the wicked pirate sporting his eponymous hook as his *left* hand. The location of the horrific device had never been something set in stone throughout the years as far as its various adaptations and revisions were concerned. The Disney cartoon's Captain Hook and Cyril Ritchard in the Mary Martin musical wore it as per Barrie, but Boris Karloff in the 1950 production and Danny Kaye in a 1976 television musical adaptation both sported left-hand hooks.

Jurassic Park

So certain was Hollywood that Michael Crichton's story about a dinosaur theme park could be turned into cinematic gold that a bidding war erupted months before the novel's actual publication. Aside from them meeting his $1.5 million asking price, Crichton was most anxious to sign with Universal Pictures because Steven Spielberg's guaranteed participation in the project was part of the deal. Since Crichton had more than his share of screenwriting experience (including *Westworld* and *The Great Train Robbery*, both of which he also directed), Universal further sweetened his bank account by paying him another $500,000 to write the script. Crichton reshaped the structure of his tale into what he hoped would be something closer to a filmable script but made it clear that Spielberg should hire someone else to finish the job. In the meantime, the book was finally released in November of 1990, quickly working its way up to twelve on the *New York Times* Best Seller list on December 2, 1990. It would soon break into the Top 10 and stay there for the next several months, reaching its highest position, number six, on January 20, 1991.

Initially, Spielberg gave one of his *Hook* writers, Malia Scotch Marmo, a shot at the *Jurassic* script, but he wasn't happy with her efforts. Next, he turned to David Koepp on the strength of a bizarre black comedy—*Death Becomes Her*, which went into release in the summer of 1992—Koepp had written for former Spielberg protégé Robert Zemeckis. Koepp would turn out to be one of the most compatible collaborators for the director, who turned to him again for the *Jurassic Park* sequel, *The Lost World*; his remake of *War of the Worlds*; and the fourth *Indiana Jones* adventure, *Kingdom of the Crystal Skull*.

The beginning of *Jurassic Park* required a great deal of streamlining for the screen because there were many chapters and much mystery surrounding just what was happening off the coast of Costa Rica before the principals were introduced. At the start of Crichton's novel, a bleeding worker is brought by helicopter to a

Costa Rican fishing village where his escort, publicist Ed Regis, falsifies the events that caused his gashes, claiming they were a construction accident. When the injured teen dies with the word "raptor" as his last, the hints begin to drop as to something being amiss on that private island. This is followed by a little girl being bitten by a curious creature after her parents have taken the family to an isolated beach. Rather than retain this sideline incident for the new film, it was put aside and used as the opening scene for the eventual follow-up movie, *Jurassic Park: The Lost World*. The attack on the girl is, in turn, investigated by Dr. Marty Gutierrez, who encounters a howler monkey chewing on the remains of some sort of mysterious lizard, the pieces of which are shipped to the Tropical Diseases Laboratory in New York. It is here that technician Alice Levin is able to identify the curious creature as a dinosaur through a drawing the attacked girl has made. In the meantime, back in Costa Rica, a most unfortunate baby in its bassinet becomes a meal for some hungry lizards (who turn out to be Procompsognathus, or "Compys"), the sort of gruesome occurrence that was unlikely to end up being depicted onscreen. Koepp's screenplay tossed away all of this in favor of starting off with a more direct "bang"—depicting a raptor attack on a worker at the Jurassic Park compound.

The introduction of Grant and Ellie at the excavation site was retained in the script; however, in the novel they are visited by Bob Morris from the EPA, but onscreen the site becomes the location of their first encounter with John Hammond, who invites them to visit Jurassic Park. (He'd done it a less

Ian Malcolm (Jeff Goldblum), John Hammond (Richard Attenborough), Ellie Sattler (Laura Dern), and Allan Grant (Sam Neill) show signs of raptor rapture as a new egg hatches in *Jurassic Park*.

cinematically interesting way, by phone, in the book.) Crichton's version of Hammond was that of an egotistical and irresponsible jerk run amok, someone readers were hoping would meet a grisly fate (as indeed he does, being feasted on by Compys after falling down a hill). Here, as embodied by a grandfatherly Richard Attenborough, with a beard that made him the perfect Santa Claus for the following year's remake of *Miracle on 34th Street*, Hammond is more of a misguided dreamer, genuinely dismayed when his theme park of enchantment turns out to be a nightmare. Similarly, the film wisely made Hammond's granddaughter, Lex, less obnoxious than she is on the written page, as she is the sort of whiny, self-involved character who'd certainly be given a gruesome demise had she not been a child. In the film, she is not only likable, as acted by Ariana Richards, but near the climax she plays a key role in helping out, getting the park's system back up and running through her computer knowledge.

There continued to be several smart choices in improving Crichton's expansive and often pulpy work. Rather than have the visitors spot their first dinosaur from the helicopter above, Spielberg staged a far more memorable introduction on land, from a jeep, as Ellie reacts with disbelief at what she is seeing and turns Grant's head to share the wonder, as a herd of brachiosaurs chomp on vegetation. (Hammond gives no tour of the park to his visitors in the book.) Crichton had made publicist Ed Regis a member of the besieged party that experiences the terrifying T-Rex attack, having him share one of the Land Rovers with the two children, Lex and Tim, while Grant and Ellie, along with mathematician Ian Malcolm and lawyer Gennaro, ride together in the other vehicle. Regis is the designated victim in the book, being eaten by a baby T-Rex trying to get to Grant and the kids. As there are precious few audience members who would not get a vicarious delight seeing a lawyer getting munched by a prehistoric predator, Gennaro becomes the casualty onscreen, being unforgettably snapped up by the T-Rex while hiding in a toilet. Regis was left out of the movie altogether.

Although the film kept the plotline of Grant having to get the two youngsters back to safety following the T-Rex attack, there was depth added to his character in Koepp's script, in which he initially announces his extreme dislike of children. This adventure ends up, therefore, serving as a bonding experience and a lesson in humanity for the paleontologist—a great touch. Crichton had provided more happenings during this trio's extended absence from the visitors center, having them take refuge in a shed where they find a raft, hoping to use the river to get back to home base, only to be terrorized once again by a hungry T-Rex. In the novel there is also an encounter at an aviary, where a Pterodactyl attempts to hoist Lex away until Grant saves her life.

The climax as featured in the novel has geneticist Dr. Wu killed in an effort to help Ellie (in the film it is presumed that he was one of the employees to evacuate the island during the storm); Malcolm seems to have succumbed to his injuries from the T-Rex attack, although we would find out this wasn't so when *The Lost World* was published; Grant injects eggs with poison, knowing the raptors will eat them; and Tim gets the power back on, thereby allowing him to kill off some raptors with the electricity from the wire fence covering the dome of the visitors center. Spielberg's film instead stages an unbearably tense scene of Lex and Tim hiding out in a kitchen from the raptors and then joining Ellie and Grant as they hope to escape from the voracious beasts by climbing atop a dinosaur skeleton exhibited in the rotunda of the center. Crichton had provided his degree of thrills, but Koepp and Spielberg had trimmed off some of the fat, bringing more focus to the excitement and making the plight of these characters far more engaging.

Crichton had made it clear that Jurassic Park was bombed by the National Guard after its survivors had fled the island, which meant that a sister island was concocted for the sequel, *The Lost World*, in order to keep the cash flowing in. The film kept its fate up in the air.

Perhaps the most surprising aspect of the film to come from the book was the use of actor Richard Kiley ("We spared no expense," Hammond boasts) as the unseen voice of the narrator during the park tour. Kiley was indeed mentioned as being the voice in Crichton's story, making it all too tempting to ask him to repeat the "role" for the movie version. His crisp diction was all too perfect, and he was also asked to provide the narration for the Jurassic Park River Adventure, which commenced in 1996, at the Universal Studios parks.

Schindler's List

When Australian author Thomas Keneally agreed to write an account of how Czech industrialist Oskar Schindler ended up saving the lives of more than a thousand Jews from certain death in Nazi concentration camps, he decided to approach it as a "novel" rather than declare it a straightforward, nonfiction piece of work. Published in the fall of 1982—here in the United States by Simon & Schuster and simultaneously in Great Britain under the title *Schindler's Ark* (Hodder & Stroughton)—the book was promptly purchased by Universal Pictures for a half million dollars and as a possible project for Steven Spielberg. In the meantime it went on to win the Australian Booker Prize for Fiction and the *Los Angeles Times* Book Prize as well. Spielberg knew that a film adaptation of such a shattering subject was a difficult sell and something he himself wasn't sure he was ready to tackle just yet. He kept it on his "to do" list for over ten years as a result.

Initially, Keneally himself was invited to do the adaptation, but like so many book writers not used to the idea of condensing novels into workable screenplays, what he handed in was too detailed, too long, or something akin to a miniseries. Next, Kurt Luedtke, who had won an Academy Award for adapting Karen Blixen's writings into *Out of Africa*, was selected but had no better luck in coming up with something filmable. Finally, Steven Zaillian got the job on the basis of having turned Oliver Sacks's account of a man brought out of a state of catatonia, *Awakenings*, into an awarded and surprisingly popular movie. Zaillian's ability to choose select events from Keneally's book and shape them into a powerful narrative was just one of the many remarkable things about the movie. A fascinating, richly detailed book that presented so much information as to defeat many a writer was given its due, while Zaillian also managed to bring the story to even greater life with dialogue and sequences not mentioned in Keneally's account.

In order to make sure that Oskar Schindler got all the glory he deserved, another humane German brought up in the book, Julius Madritsch, who operated a uniform factory from inside the Płaszów labor camp, had his contributions mini-malized to the point where it appeared unclear onscreen whether or not he was willing to cooperate with Schindler's plan to keep as many of their Jewish workers out of the camps as they could by purchasing them. Missing altogether, however, was Raimund Titsch, who was instrumental in smuggling food into the camp for the prisoners. It was actually Titsch with whom Schindler worked on compiling the lifesaving list of the title, but this task was given to his business manager, Itzhak Stern, in the movie. (There was a third party, Marcel Goldberg, involved in the further approval of the names. While this unscrupulous profiteer, who asked for bribes in order to placate him and would randomly remove names out of spite, was kept in the movie, he was not included in any sequences involving the compiling of the names.) Although Stern was very much a pivotal part of Keneally's story, his role was enhanced onscreen to make him a more constant presence, encouraging Schindler's beneficent efforts to be even greater. In Keneally's telling of the story, it was Schindler's office manager, Abraham Bankier, along with some other mem-bers of the Schindler work staff, who had to be rescued from one of the transport trains after failing to produce the mandatory blue-stickered identification papers. This moment was also rewritten so that Stern could be the hapless victim saved in the nick of time.

Reduced in importance in the script (due to time considerations) were Mietek Pemper—who was hired to be a typist for Commandant Amon Goeth and, because of his astonishing photographic memory, was later able to relate so many of his boss's crimes and atrocities, thereby providing sufficient evidence for Goeth's hanging—and Dr. Sedalek, a Zionist from a rescue organization in Budapest who came to Kraków to enlist Schindler to distribute money to contacts in the Jewish community and for the industrialist to give full reports on the atrocities witnessed, which, in turn, were to be passed along to the proper Allied authorities. Once Schindler moves his Jews to a safer factory in Brinnlitz, the movie gives the impres-sion that there was less threat or trouble with the S.S. regarding the treatment of the prisoners. Although the character of Josef Leipold, the camp commandant, is present, he is not depicted as being as dangerous as Schindler and his Jews felt him to be. Schindler had, in fact, made sure Leipold was transferred out of the factory before he caused any destruction. Similarly, the movie does not depict Amon Goeth—now less powerful due to having been arrested for black market dealings (another incident not dramatized in the movie) but no less intimidating—showing up at the Brinnlitz factory.

Despite the many examples of humanity shown by Schindler throughout the film, a crucial detail was omitted: after Schindler moved into an apartment in Kraków from which a Jewish family was forcibly evicted, he supposedly tracked them down and gave them some 50,000 złoty (Polish currency) in compensation.

Just as Goeth's eventual arrest and subsequent decline in authority was not explored onscreen, the movie also streamlined Schindler's amount of time spent under lock and key. The movie retained the most absurd and insulting of the indictments, Schindler admonished for kissing a Jewish girl at his party, but did not see any reason to include the others, one which took place early on during his work at the Kraków factory and the other later when he had transferred to

Brinnlitz; in each case, he was questioned over his finances and possible black market dealings.

One of the most memorable and frightening episodes in the movie is the accidental rerouting of Schindler's female workers to the death camp at Auschwitz until Oskar arrives to bargain for their lives and escort them safely back to his factory. This episode is understandably condensed for time and suspense. The women had, in fact, spent several *weeks* at the camp, and Oskar had first sent a woman as his emissary, basically finding someone who would be willing to offer herself up to the proper authorities at the camp in exchange for the release. This event was shortened to appear as if it all occurred within a few hours of time, with Schindler and only Schindler showing up to save the day.

Zaillian's script gave attention to hapless Helen Hirsch, condemned to serve Amon Goeth between beatings and assaults upon her, but figured she suffered enough without including a terrifying moment when Goeth orders her dragged into the yard for execution and only changes his mind at the last minute. Other incidents described in the book were handed off to different characters for greater impact. For example, it is the young pharmacy worker, Brackner, who in Keneally's version recounts his experience in escaping from the camp at Belzec by hiding inside the latrine, a scene given onscreen to tiny Olek, thereby creating a greater feeling of disbelief and shock in children being subjected to such an indignity.

Although there were exchanges between characters that were taken directly from the book, it was up to Zaillian to create certain scenes from scratch, and perhaps the most effective of these is Schindler's farewell scene before his factory workers. Whereas in the book Keneally recounted Schindler telling workers how

Itzak Stern (Ben Kingsley) sees a ray of hope for his fellow Jews when he's ordered to type up *Schindler's List*.

they must resist the urge at revenge and how the S.S. workers would be wise to return home peacefully without committing further acts of violence, the movie includes Schlinder breaking down as he comes to terms with the scope of what he did and what could have been done. Receiving an engraved ring from Stern and the workers, he then wonders aloud why he didn't sell additional items and raise money to save more Jews from extinction. The scene was a powerhouse for actor Liam Neeson and added a tremendous layer of further humanity upon the character, one who has risen above and beyond expectations and yet feels that his efforts have not been sufficient. It was this sequence alone that proved that Spielberg and Zaillian had created a masterwork that not only paid full tribute to its source but managed to enrich it further.

The Lost World: Jurassic Park

Fans of *The Lost World: Jurassic Park*, eager to check out the Michael Crichton novel credited as the source material, might have thought they had stumbled upon the wrong book, so marginally did it resemble what showed up onscreen. Universal Pictures knew they wanted a sequel to the global phenomenon *Jurassic Park* (1993) and were delighted that Crichton went and published his own follow-up two years afterward. This meant that there was further anticipation being generated in the literary world for more modern-day dinosaur adventures. Universal had already secured the rights to the property by the time of its September 20, 1995, publication. By October 8, 1995, the book had zoomed right to the very top of the *New York Times* Best Seller list, where it would remain for eight weeks straight. Once again proving that the public is most eager to experience what it already knows, this sequel to *Jurassic Park* outpaced its predecessor in popularity, staying in the top five for sixteen straight weeks. *Jurassic* had only gone as high as number six. Clearly a movie adaptation was more than a sure thing now. Spielberg called on David Koepp to once again provide a script, and he kept only a few characters and suggestions of key set pieces from the book. Otherwise, *The Lost World: Jurassic Park* was pretty much its own movie.

Crichton gave mathematician Ian Malcolm the central position in the book, as Malcolm was the one principal from *Jurassic Park* to return (his fate having been left somewhat vague). Although this was retained for the film, the screenplay saw fit to bring back John Hammond for plot exposition purposes (he had died in the first novel) and throw in some fleeing, superfluous appearances by his grandchildren, Tim and Lex, who had endured the first dinosaur rampage. The imperiled child this time around is twelve-year-old Kelly, who in the film is Malcolm's neglected daughter, whereas in Crichton's book she is merely an advanced student who knew him as a guest lecturer at her school. Her promotion to offspring gave the film a welcome bit of progress where Hollywood was concerned since the actress cast was black. No mention or issue was made of the fact that Caucasian Malcolm had an African American daughter. This also compensated for the fact that her cohort in adventures, eleven-year-old Arby—who in the book had joined her in stowing away in order to travel to Isla Sorna—was eliminated from the screen version. The boy had been Crichton's one African American principal. The movie also saw fit to keep Sarah Harding as the principal female, but she was upgraded to be Ian's current girlfriend, whereas she had only a passing relationship with him in the book.

In the novel, Malcolm teams up with Dr. Thorne to venture forth to another island near Costa Rica that appears to have been the production center for Jurassic Park, but their other purpose is to rescue a know-it-all scientist, Richard Levine, who has foolishly ventured there to see if the rumors about living dinosaurs are true. Koepp's script gave Malcolm a more plausible motivation for joining the expedition: he found out that Sarah has gone there. Worrying about his significant other rather than the fate of a self-centered, arrogant scientist made it a tad more feasible that Malcolm would dare risk tossing himself into the path of rampaging carnivores a second time. In the book, Crichton had dispatched a second team to the island for villainous effect: representatives from a genetics company called Biosyn, led by a particularly brutish and unpleasant fellow whose name, Lewis Dodgson, seemed to be a cryptic nod to the author of *Alice's Adventures in Wonderland*. Dodgson sails to the island with Sarah aboard only to ensure that she falls off the ship; he is unaware that she ends up surviving the plunge. Dodgson's efforts to steal the eggs of all of the species on the island result in some graphic deaths for his colleagues, Baselton and King. However, the most vicious demise is saved for Dodgson himself, as a T-Rex brings him to its nest, where he realizes he is dinner for her hungry children.

Koepp replaced Dodgson and his team with the more benign Roland Tembo and his hunters, who are on the island to trap dinosaurs to exhibit back in America. Needing a self-satisfied, unreasonable, and exasperating character to

Animal behaviorist Sarah Harding (Julianne Moore) is delighted to encounter a young Stegosaurus in *The Lost World: Jurassic Park*.

generate the plot and ensure that audiences loathed him in all his disregard for logic, safety, and consideration of others, Koepp replaced Levine with Hammond's snooty nephew, Peter Ludlow, who was given control of InGen and did his best to trash it up further. At least the film provided audiences with a somewhat satisfying punishment for this pompous fool, something Crichton had deprived readers of when it came to giving Levine his just desserts.

For the film, Dr. Thorne was dispensed with in favor of a younger video photographer, Nick Van Owen, while mechanics expert Eddie Carr *did* make the transition from page to screen, basically to be the one sympathetic character to be munched on by dinosaurs—in Crichton's book he is devourerd by raptors after falling from the high hide observation platform, and in Koepp's script he is torn apart by tyrannosaurs after heroically saving some lives; a cruel touch to have so graphic a demise for so undeserving a character. The principal sequence dramatized from the book was the expedition trailer being pushed by the angry tyrannosaurs in retaliation for the scientists daring to take their baby in order to help fix its broken leg. Whereas Crichton's version put only Malcolm and Sarah in this terrifying situation, stuck in the trailer as it dangled over the edge of a cliff, Nick was added to the mix in the film, and added tension was provided by having Sarah fall onto the slowly cracking windshield. An attack by vicious, chicken-sized dinosaurs nicknamed "Compys" was inspired by a sequence in the book, but whereas Dodgson had survived being besieged by the critters, the film's Dieter Stark was not merely nipped at but was pretty much devoured, per a later description of the aftermath by Tembo.

Amistad

Although it made no big deal of the fact, *Amistad* used William A. Owens's 1987 book *Black Mutiny: The Revolt on the Schooner Amistad* as its principal point of reference. David Franzoni's screenplay, however, was not credited as being a direct adaptation, and mention of Owens was not a part of the posters or advertising, as many of the print ads instead encouraged readers to look for the novelizations from Signet and Puffin Books. The movie's chief producer and the one who championed getting the project made for years, actress-choreographer-director Debbie Allen, had first come across the story of the rebellion aboard *La Amistad* three years earlier than the publication of Owens's book, having read volumes of essays by African-American writers published under the names *Amistad I* and *Amistad II*. Owens's depiction of the *Amistad* mutiny was ideal for adaptation, however, because rather than chronicle the events in straightforward manner, the author chose to tell the story dramatically, with dialogue that the participants in the events might have said. The facts surrounding these fabricated exchanges were otherwise as accurate as possible. As a result, Spielberg and his team stuck as closely as possible to what appeared to be the truth, with certain people left out mainly for brevity and an occasional unpleasant incident skipped over in order to maintain sympathy for the plight of the captured Africans.

While the movie informs us at the outset that the mutiny took place in 1839, it does not bother to keep us abreast of the timeframe otherwise. The original slave ship, the *Tecora*, that had taken Cinqué and his fellow Mendis from Lomboko on the west coast of Africa, departed there in early April of that year. *La Amistad* began its voyage out of Havana in late June, while the actual mutiny occurred on July 1. It was six weeks later, in August, when Lieutenants Gedney and Meade captured the schooner off Long Island, launching the trial that would be dragged out far longer than most viewers probably realized. By the time John Quincy Adams stepped forward to speak to the Supreme Court, it was late February of 1841. His plea for the rights of the captives would take far longer than the compact version onscreen, as his first speech lasted some four and a half hours, with more to come at a later date.

In order to dramatize the horror of the slave ships, a flashback depicted several hapless black captives being dumped over the side of the *Tecora* while chained together, a story related by a shaken Cinqué during the Middle Passage voyage, although there is no record of this actually happening on this particular ship at this particular crossing. The sequence was, however, enormously effective in summing up the debased inhumanity of the entire slavery system. The crew of the *Amistad* had also consisted of a black cabin boy, Antonio, who, being a slave himself and capable of communicating with the Cuban slavers, Ruiz and Montes, was spared by the mutineers as they killed the captain and the cook. Despite this being a chance to escape, his allegiance remained with the Spaniards. Antonio was not

In the prison yard, observing the behavior of Cinqué and the other captives, are a guard (Michael Massee), Theodore Joadson (Morgan Freeman), James Covey (Chiwetel Ejiofor), Roger Baldwin (Matthew McConaughey), and Warden Pendleton (Daniel von Bargen).

charged but was called on to testify at the Connecticut trial against Cinqué and the Mendis. This contrast between the Africans determined against all odds to attain freedom and one complacent in his servitude might have made for an intriguing subplot, but the character was dispensed with altogether in the screenplay.

The script also saw fit to eliminate the other two lawyers hired by the abolitionists to defend the Africans, Seth Staples and Theodore Sedgwick, and instead put the focus entirely upon the chief counsel, Roger Baldwin. A fictitious black abolitionist, Theodore Joadson, was worked into the storyline in order to establish that there were free men of color in New England and to give the captive Africans someone fighting for their cause who was not Caucasian. White filmmakers often faced criticism in depicting, no matter how accurate, stories in which black characters were obliged to be helped, saved, or advanced strictly through the intervention of Caucasians only. While it was accurate that an ensign on a British warship, James Covey, was eventually enlisted to translate for the Africans, one of the captives, Burnah, actually had some experience speaking English, and a previous interpreter, John Ferry, who was discovered by Yale linguistics Professor Josiah Gibbs, had made a futile effort to communicate with the prisoners as well. Again, the script wisely saw fit to streamline the story and remove these two less successful translators altogether, although Gibbs remained.

The captives were eventually moved to a different prison facility in Westville, Connecticut, and it was here that John Quincy Adams would meet Cinqué, not at his own home as dramatized in the film. There was also post-trial housing for the Africans before they would depart for home, at a farm in Farmington, where the abolitionists insisted on instructing them in English and Christianity, hoping to change them from their Mendi traditions, which the New Englanders looked upon as pagan and backward. This further obstruction in returning the men to their homeland would result in adding nearly another year onto their stay in America. By the time the ship *Gentleman* docked in Sierra Leone, it was January 15, 1842, which meant that Cinqué and the others had been forcibly absent from their village for nearly three years. While the movie accurately mentioned in its epilogue that Cinqué returned home to face a Civil War and the capture of his family into slavery, the darker aspects of his own behavior were not addressed. In absence of his previous wife, Cinqué took another, which put him in bad standing with the missionaries, who had established a base in Bonthe. Choosing to turn his back on them, he ended up in league with an unscrupulous trader, even going so far as to dabble in the slave trade, a terribly ironic turn of events that was enough to erase all the sympathy he had engendered during the course of the film. Not surprisingly, the necessary statement against the mistreatment of Cinqué and his fellow Mende tribesmen had been effectively made and this sad coda was deemed unnecessary to include onscreen.

A.I. Artificial Intelligence

Brian Aldiss's sci-fi short story "Super-Toys Last All Summer Long" was first published in the December 1969 issue of *Harper's Bazaar* and then the following year in an anthology collection of Aldiss's works under the title *The Moment of Eclipse*.

It was here that Stanley Kubrick read the piece and soon became obsessed with making a movie out of it. That Aldiss was initially surprised that someone saw the potential for a feature film in his decidedly brief tale is understandable. The motion picture basically took the germ of his idea and then expanded the seven-page piece in various directions.

The story has a frustrated Monica Swinton trying to cope with young David, who has taken away the rose she has plucked and has run off to float the flower in a wading pool, where he himself stands, getting his shoes wet. This incident is followed by the key line "She had tried to love him." Meanwhile, her husband, Henry, the Managing Director of Synthank, introduces the company's newest synthetic creation, a Serving-Man, a robot that will hopefully prove an invaluable addition to each household as well as fill a void in the lives of the lonely. Synthank has already proved successful with their synthetic tapeworm, which, when implanted in the small intestine, allows its host to eat up to 50 percent more without gaining pounds.

Although David has given reaching Monica his best shot, he fears he has failed and confides in his talking, mechanical bear, Teddy, that he is considering running away. As Henry arrives home with the Serving-Man to give it a test run, he is greeted by an elated Monica, who tells him they have won this week's parenthood lottery, which, since childbirth requires government permission, allows them to conceive a child. Despite the fact that Monica has come across sheets of paper in David's room on which the boy has written declarations of love for his mother, she and Henry contemplate sending him back to the factory; the boy, it turns out, is a synthetic creation as well.

For the motion picture adaptation, retained were the ideas of Monica and Henry adopting a robot boy and giving him a teddy bear as a loyal companion, along with the scene in which Monica sees David's touching efforts at expressing his feelings for her on sheets of paper. Otherwise, the screen story turned Aldiss's concept into a Pinocchio parallel that Stanley Kubrick had envisioned, about a boy's search to be real and to be loved by his human mother. Henry would no longer be in charge of the company that created David, there was no mention of the synthetic tapeworms, and a futuristic touch, which allowed the Swintons to readjust their windows to replicate various views in order to keep them from seeing the real, overpopulated world was no longer in evidence. The script now had Monica literally abandon David in the woods, thinking she is saving him from destruction by the lab that had manufactured him. It also added the entire journey to the Flesh Fair and the disturbing image of humans enjoying the brutal demise of their cyber "inferiors"; the surrogate father figure of fellow robot Gigolo Joe; the visit to the Vegas-like Rouge City; the flooded city of New York and David's descent into the waters to seek the Blue Fairy at the submerged Coney Island; and the jump forward in time to a world dominated by super cyber beings, which brings David together once again with Monica, although this time she is a genetically cloned version of herself.

Having worked directly with Kubrick on ideas for expanding his story for the screen, Brian Aldiss did publish two "sequels" featuring David. In "Supertoys When Winter Comes," David and Teddy end up innocently destroying Monica's

Teddy, David (Haley Joel Osment), and Gigolo Joe (Jude Law) find themselves among the decadent wonders of Rouge City in *A.I. Artificial Intelligence*.

now-cherished Super-Server, prompting the angry mother to dismissively tell David that he and Teddy are merely mechanical as well. This leads to David investigating her claim, thereby accidentally dismantling and "killing" Teddy. Realizing he is indeed a cyborg (smashing the plastic off his face), a distressed David "shuts down" the mechanisms running the futuristic house, and Monica is killed in the confusion. In "Supertoys in Other Seasons," David comes across the dumping ground for android parts, similar to the scene at the junkyard in "Shantytown" that appears onscreen. At this point Henry has come down in the world, his company having now been superseded by more up-to-date technology. He updates and then reactivates his son and his bear companion. Written in 1999 (the year Kubrick passed away), these follow-ups first appeared in the anthology *Supertoys Last All Summer Long and Other Stories of Future Time*, published in 2001 to coincide with the release of *A.I. Artificial Intelligence*.

Minority Report

Author Philip K. Dick didn't stick around long enough to realize what a frequent source of inspiration he'd become for filmmakers, passing away in March of 1982, only months before the first major adaptation of one of his works, *Blade Runner* (based on the novel *Do Androids Dream of Electric Sheep?*) debuted. Since that time such films as *Total Recall* (1990), *Paycheck* (2003), *A Scanner Darkly* (2006), and *The Adjustment Bureau* (2011) have been spun from his works, with varying degrees of success.

Minority Report was derived from his 1956 short story "The Minority Report," which first appeared in the anthology magazine *Fantastic Universe*. Being brief, screenwriters Scott Frank and Jon Cohen were obliged to expand upon it to bring it to feature length, taking some of the ideas and then coming up with a more substantial structure. Fantasy novelist Cohen (whose only screen credit this is to date) had written the first draft at the request of director Jan de Bont. This ended up in the hands of Tom Cruise, who thought this property would be the ideal one to finally allow him to work with Steven Spielberg. Spielberg then hired a more experienced screenwriter, Scott Frank, to embellish and revamp Cohen's script and flesh out the characters.

Although the character of John Anderton is Dick's central figure, he is referred to as an older man than the one played onscreen by Cruise. Anderton knows that the new associate assigned to him, Witwer, will inevitably replace him as the Commissioner at Pre-Crime and becomes increasingly paranoid that Witwer has set him up in order to take over his job sooner than anticipated. For the movie, Witwer became an outsider, an FBI agent (the screenplay relocated the action from New York City to Washington D.C.) sent to assess the operations and find a flaw in the system. Dick had the crimes foreseen by three Precogs, as in the film, but showed next to no compassion or concern for their hapless plight, which became a pivotal theme in the adaptation. Deformed and referred to callously as "idiots" because of their inability to interact with humanity, they are passive figures (as are the "twins" in the movie), and none of them become a crucial participant in the plotline as Agatha does in the screenplay.

Agnes (Samantha Morton) is foreseeing the future from within "The Temple" in this scene from *Minority Report.*

The movie retained the central premise of the protagonist surprised to discover that he is destined to kill someone he doesn't even know, but on the page that intended victim was a forcibly retired Army general, Leopold Kaplan. In the story, Anderton goes on the run in hopes of clearing his name but is abducted and taken to see his intended victim, Kaplan, who feels it is best to return the fugitive to the police. On his way back to Pre-Crime, the van he's being transported in collides with a truck and Anderton is rescued by a man named Fleming who explains the minority report concept, indicating that the Precogs are not all in agreement, as only two out of the three foresee Anderton killing Kaplan. Although Fleming insists that Anderton's wife, Lisa, who is also a member of Pre-Crime, has set the whole thing up to frame her husband, it turns out that Fleming is in league with Kaplan, who is hoping to expose the cracks in the Pre-Crime system and thereby allow the military to return to power and take charge of policing crime. Realizing the only way to prove that Pre-Crime *is* accurate is to kill Kaplan as had been predicted, Anderton does just that during a rally, knowing that he will be exiled to a distant planet as his punishment but saving his law enforcement organization in the long run.

Keeping the "man on the run" thread of the story, the script dispensed with the military takeover plotline, instead choosing to make a potent statement condemning Pre-Crime as a fallible system that infringes on Constitutional rights and incarcerates innocent people who haven't actually carried out their intended killings. To further humanize the tale for the movie, Anderton was given a backstory explaining his devotion to the Pre-Crime cause: having his young son kidnapped during a swim at a community pool, an event which shattered his life and brought an end to his marriage. In Frank's revamp, Anderton's wife no longer works for Pre-Crime but is divorced from him; however, she ends up drawn back into her ex's life and proves to be an essential participant in the finale when she rescues him from being unjustifiably sentenced to the containment prison facility. Cohen added the entire concept of the "eye scan," thereby introducing the marvelously unnerving subplot of Anderton having to change his eyes (by way of a scuzzy doctor played by an ideally cast Peter Stormare) and fake out the security "spyders" (another inspired touch) who come searching for him. It was just one of several embellishments that gave the story a more striking futuristic aura than Dick's tale, which was not heavy on descriptions.

Not a direct interpretation of Dick's intended tale by a long shot so much as an extended "take" on its core concept, *Minority Report* gave greater clarity to the enticing central theme than the maddeningly convoluted explanation of how each of the Precogs invalidated one another's visions, as summed up at the end of Dick's story.

Catch Me If You Can

Because the very reason Frank Abagnale Jr. had his life story turned into a big budget Hollywood movie depended on him being one of America's great con artists, imposters, and tall-tale spinners, one is left to contemplate just how much of his 1980 autobiography (written in collaboration with Stan Redding) consists of real facts, and how much was embellished for the sake of entertaining the reader. Therefore, Steven Spielberg and his screenwriter Jeff Nathanson can be forgiven for whatever liberties they took with the book's details in order to make for a snappier bit of filmic fun.

Young Frank's first scam, conning a Mobil gas station attendant out of $100, was not dramatized for the movie, perhaps because Frank Sr. ended up the victim, eventually owing $3,400 that his son had run up on his charge card. The film wanted to stress Jr.'s devotion to his forlorn dad, after all, and this might have seemed a callous treatment of the old man. There had also been a stopover at a Catholic Charities school for problem boys for young Frank, an episode not mentioned in the screenplay. Although Leonardo DiCaprio was able to pass himself off as a younger version of Frank Jr. for the early part of the storyline, the real Abagnale had been only fourteen at the time of his parent's divorce. Therefore, his exact age at the time was not mentioned in the dialogue to keep things more plausible.

In actuality, Frank Jr. did *not* get his Pan Am ID badge from the airline executive he interviewed, as depicted in the movie, but scored a card from a company that specialized in creating ID's, convincing them to make a sample with his fake name. His pilot's license, according to the book, came from a plaque-making firm in Milwaukee, after which Frank Jr. asked a print shop in Brooklyn to replicate the license, for a mere $5 fee. At one point, a Federal Aviation Agency complaint from

New Orleans resulted in the proper authorities meeting Frank's plane in Miami to question whether or not he actually worked for Pan Am, a tense situation dropped from the screenplay altogether.

Some of Frank Jr's stewardess hookups were deemed unnecessary for the film. One, named Diane, had connected him with a lawyer who, in turn, had suggested the charlatan pilot take the bar exam to practice law between flying assignments; another, called Rosalie, had tried to turn her duplicitous lover over to the cops after he had fessed up to some of his unsavory con man deeds— until he got wind of the betrayal and fled the scene. Versions of these incidents were instead threaded into the film's plotline that had him romancing hospital receptionist Brenda Strong (Amy Adams). A third stewardess in Abagnale's story, Monique Lavalier, had been the link to the French print shop—owned by her father—where Frank had ended up churning out fake Pan Am checks. Yet another lady in his life, an older woman identified as Kitty Corbett, had been instrumental in helping Frank to score a temporary passport while he was in Mexico, thereby allowing him to get to Europe. As with the flight attendants, this woman, as well as a trip south of the border, was nowhere in evidence on screen.

The book also found Frank slipping into the role of a sociology teacher at a Utah university, and even posing as an FBI agent in order to get back a forged check on which he had inadvertently scribbled his real name. The movie gave him enough faux professions to take up in order to get across the point that Frank was unstoppable when it came to posing as something he was not.

While most of this was going on, Abagnale was being pursued by an authentic FBI agent, one by the name of Sean O'Reilly, not Carl Hanratty, the name of his

Frank Sr. (Christopher Walken) pulls his "lost pendant" trick on an unsuspecting clothing store worker in order to get his son Frank Jr. (Leonardo DiCaprio) a suit in *Catch Me If You Can*.

fictional counterpart in the movie. Because the book had been told in the first person there was no depiction of events involving O'Reilly tracking Frank from the agent's point of view, which had to be dramatized for the screenplay.

The Terminal

Like *The Sugarland Express*, Spielberg's gentle comedy-drama *The Terminal* originated from the news headlines, but it deliberately set out to be "inspired by" the real events as opposed to being a direct dramatization of what happened. No real names were used, and none of the interactions or dialogue derived from true experiences, but as bizarre as the premise of *The Terminal* was, it was not made up.

Tom Hanks's character of Viktor Nazorski—a displaced foreigner (from the fictional country of Krakozhia) forced to take up residence in an airline terminal lounge in America when his country is closed off because of a civil war and, because of inadequate papers, denied access into the United States—was based on Mehran Karimi Nasseri. Nasseri was born in 1945 in an Anglo-Persian oil settlement in Iran to an Iranian father and a Scottish woman with whom Nasseri's father was having an extramarital affair. Because of his illegitimacy, Mehran was ultimately banished from the family following his father's death, which played a part in his dilemma. Although Hanks's character goes through a rough patch, his past life is never described as being anywhere near as unlucky as Nasseri's. Initially, his father's real wife sent him money in order to study in London, but once that ran out, Nasseri returned to Iran only to be arrested for allegedly protesting the Shah, an act which branded him a traitor and landed him in prison. He was eventually released and given an immigration passport on the condition that he not return to that country. Needing to find a country that would grant him refuge status, Nasseri ended up in Belgium in 1981. Wanting to visit Scotland with his papers, he was told there would be no problem. While onboard a boat for England, he sent his papers back to the Brussels office for the UN High Commission of Refugees, which meant he had no papers in England when he arrived. As a result, he was immediately sent back to Belgium, which then returned him to England. England then sent him by boat to Boulogne, France, where he was arrested and imprisoned for trying to enter the country illegally. Released, he was given forty-eight hours to leave France and attempted to fly to England. Again, he was returned to France, where in frustration he settled into the Zone d'attente, a holding area for passengers without papers in Terminal One at the Charles de Gaulle Airport, beginning on August 26, 1988.

Renouncing Iran and refusing to speak Farsi, Nasseri settled into his new "residence" and renamed himself Sir Alfred Mehran. There he remained with his luggage by his side, studying economics and writing in his diary. Sympathetic airport employees ended up giving him newspapers and food, although his main diet consisted of meals from McDonald's.

Eventually a lawyer named Christian Bourguet tracked down his papers and explained to Mehran that he now could travel to England. Because these papers were issued for an Iranian national under Sir Alfred's real name, he refused to sign them, choosing instead to remain in the airport. His strange appearance at the terminal brought him widespread media attention. Jean Rochefort played a thinly disguised version of Nasseri in director Philippe Lioret's 1994 French comedy film *Tombes du ciel*, the title of which roughly translates to *Fell from the Sky*, although its English title was given as the more suitable *Lost in Transit*. The movie received no US release. British composer Jonathan Dove made Nasseri's plight the subject of his 1998 opera *Flight*, commissioned by the Glyndebourne Opera; Alexis Kouros filmed a documentary about him, *Waiting for Godot at de Gaulle*, for airing on Finnish television in 2000. That same year Melissa Hibbard and Hamid Rahmanian shot a half-hour piece about the Kafkaesque situation, calling it *Sir Alfred of Charles De Gaulle Airport*. Michael Paterniti published an essay, "The 15 Year Layover," in the September 11, 2003, issue of *GQ*, right around the time Steven Spielberg's film went into production.

Nasseri, or Sir Alfred, was indeed still at de Gaulle at the time the movie was being shot and when it opened in June of 2004. In collaboration with British author Andrew Donkin, he related his story in a book, *The Terminal Man*, published that same year in the United Kingdom. By this point many had stated that Sir Alfred's state of mind was no longer clear and lucid, that his dilemma had taken its toll on both his memory and his credibility, thereby making certain aspects of his tale questionable in the extreme. Certainly, it was never the intention of the screenwriters or Steven Spielberg to make a tale as bleak as the real one ended up—the disintegration of a man's mind and spirit, a victim of an unreasonable level of government bureaucracy, a Catch-22 situation gone amok. Theirs was supposed to be a love story, an affirmation of the human spirit triumphing over impossible odds. What the filmmaker and his team had trouble overcoming was the cruelty inherent in placing a person in such a situation, something that couldn't help but come off as somewhat absurd and exasperating rather than richly comical or dramatically compelling no matter how light a tone Spielberg aimed for.

Although there was absolutely no reference made in the credits to Sir Alfred, nor in any of the production notes released by DreamWorks, it was reported that the company did pay the real-life "terminal man" a quarter

A simple ad for *The Terminal* with a clever double meaning.

of a million dollars in order to placate him and ensure that no lawsuits would be pending. Supposedly, when told that his alter ego would be played in the film by Tom Hanks, Nasseri was said to have asked, without intending humor, "Is he Japanese?"

Two years after the release of Spielberg's movie, Sir Alfred's failing health caused him to be hospitalized. His "residence" was dismantled although his red bench on which he sat and slept was kept. Following his hospital stay, he was put in a foster home in France and his condition left vague. Unbelievably, he was not the only person to suffer such a situation, as Hiroshi Nohara spent four months in Benito Juarez Airport in 2008; Zurach Malfa was stuck for ten months at Shariff Emma Taigo Airport waiting for refugee status in Canada; and Sanjay Sha staged a thirteen-month sit-in at Jo Mo Kenyata Airport. Nasseri's airport time topped them all, of course, at eighteen years.

War of the Worlds

The third of three seminal novels written by H. G. Wells that became among the most influential and pioneering works in the science fiction genre, *The War of the Worlds* was first serialized in *Pearson's* magazine in 1897, a few months after *The Invisible Man* had shown up in the same publication. Two years earlier he had given the world *The Time Machine*. The year following its serialization, *War* was published in book form in London by William Heinemann. The popularity of the work became even more pronounced following the *Mercury Theater on the Air*'s radio adaptation, which aired on CBS on October 30, 1938. Masterminded by Orson Welles, the story—instead of being presented as a straightforward adaptation—unfolded as if a real Martian invasion was taking place in present time, principally in a tiny town in New Jersey called Grover's Mill. So gullible were certain listeners that some bought whole hog that Earth was under attack, causing the broadcast to make headlines and remain, arguably, the most famous fictional program to ever go out over the airwaves. When next audiences were treated to an adaptation of the book, it came via Hollywood producer George Pal, who specialized in fanciful tales with some of the more elaborate special effects of their day. Released by Paramount in 1953 (seven years after Wells's death) and directed by Byron Haskin, *The War of the Worlds* was one of Pal's most entertaining offerings, although, like Orson Welles, he saw no reason to keep the story in H. G.'s original 1897 timeframe, instead setting it in the present in the vicinity of Los Angeles. In an era when science fiction did not dominate the box office, *War* did good business and ended up with the Academy Award for Best Visual Effects.

Steven Spielberg saw the work as a way of commenting on the frightening reality of terrorism by way of an impressive special effects show that utilized all the motion picture craft and technology not available to Pal and Haskin fifty-two years earlier. As with its predecessors, this adaptation was to be set in the present day, thereby making the alien invasion that much more urgent. Wells's story was told by a nameless narrator who, along with a scientist friend, observe, through a telescope, gas jetting out of Mars and unidentified objects seemingly being spit from the planet's surface. A cylinder lands in a field in Woking, a small town southwest of London, and unleashes destruction on the startled locals. Our narrator hurries his wife off to the safety of another town, returns to Woking, but then figures he'd best hightail it out of there as well, when even the military admits defeat in the face of the unstoppable enemy. Meanwhile, in London, the narrator's brother reports of refugees from nearby towns streaming into the city until the Martians reach this destination as well, causing him and others to flee. Our narrator finds himself obliged to hide out for an extended period of time with a curate whose doomsday rants threaten to expose them to the aliens, causing our hero to bring down the bellyaching clergyman with an axe handle. Just as all seems lost, the Martians are simply brought to a standstill because of their exposure to the Earth's bacteria.

In a nod of sorts to Orson Welles, Spielberg chose New Jersey as the setting for his version and gave his central hero a name, Ray Ferrier, an embittered ex-wife, and two children whose safety becomes his goal. The film closely followed Wells's description of the Martian fighting machines: they appear as enormous tripods from which they would scoop up hapless Earthlings and toss them into metallic carriers resembling a "workman's basket." (Pal's film had turned them into float-ing, saucer-like ships fronted by an extended arm with an iris emanating death

Tom Cruise and Steven Spielberg on the set of their second sci-fi collaboration, *War of the Worlds*.

rays, giving them the appearance of menacing desk lamps.) A sequence in Wells's book in which panicked citizens attempt to cross the Thames in a ferry was turned into one of the great set-pieces of Spielberg's career, only in his version the Earthlings were dumped off the boat by a rising Martian machine, whereas they had jumped for their lives in the book. Rather than have Ray endure a curate, David Koepp and Joshua Freeman's script combined this character with that of an artillery man encountered by Wells's narrator and turned him into a crazed farmer who offers shelter to Ray and his daughter until he needs to be dispatched, like his literary counterpart. In another Wells parallel, this character was named Ogilvy, which had been the name of the astronomer destroyed by the Martians early on in the story, at their initial landing site in Woking. The extended Ogilvy sequence, a terrific example of Spielberg creating tension and holding complete audience interest while working in a confined and limited space, did recreate Wells's description of an alien tentacle entering the hiding space.

There was also a visual realization of the novel's mention of red-colored growths sprouting throughout the English landscape because of seeds brought by the extra-terrestrials. Finally, Spielberg gave his hero a version of Wells's happy ending, reuniting him with both his children, just as the nameless narrator in the story had found his way back to his wife.

Munich

The shocking massacre of eleven Israeli athletes by Arab terrorists during the 1972 Munich Olympics was a horror played out before a stunned audience and therefore sufficiently documented to be later written about and dramatized. (Television weighed in with *21 Hours at Munich*, which starred William Holden as the Munich chief of police, and aired in November of 1976.) In contrast, the aftermath and the vengeance wreaked by a covert team of Israeli assassins on the terrorists was something kept secret from the world and therefore a story clouded in a great deal of speculation, missing details, and information that simply could not be shared. Journalist George Jonas made contact with one of the surviving members of the team and got the story from *his* point of view, verified it to the point that he was satisfied that his source (identified only by the pseudonym "Avner" but revealed later to be Juval Aviv) had told it like it was, and published his account of the mission, *Vengeance* (subtitled *The True Story of the Israeli Counter-Terrorist Team*), in June of 1984. Jonas's book was quickly taken to task by various skeptical journalists and denounced by some respected Israelis, including Army Commander (and future Prime Minister) Ariel Sharon and Mossad (the country's intelligence agency) Director Zvi Zamir, who doubted the validity of the information. Helped by the debate, Jonas's book (written like a novel rather than a dry listing of facts for more readable impact) sold well enough for the CTV Network in Canada to buy it and turn it into a television movie, *Sword of Gideon*, two years later.

Gideon (adapted by Chris Bryant and directed by Michael Anderson) told only so much of the story, giving over its nearly three-hour running time to just three of the successful assassination attempts (Wael Zwaiter's shooting in Rome, and the Paris explosions that killed Mahmoud Hamshari—via his telephone—and

Mohammed Boudia in his car). The aborted siege on a church where two of the terrorist leaders were thought to be meeting was covered, as was the vengeful killing of a female assassin who had tricked a member of Avner's team into bed and murdered him. Avner's helpful French source, referred to as "Papa," became someone who was recommended by Avner's father, himself a former agent. There was no such connection made in the book. The first American showing of this film took place on HBO on November 29, 1986.

Munich went back to the source and with more fidelity, although the author would later express displeasure with what he felt was too sympathetic a portrayal of the terrorists, arguing that Steven Spielberg and his writers seemed to equate terrorism with counterterrorism. *Munich* took the time to dramatize five of the successful "hits" that involved Avner and his team: Wael Zwaiter's shooting in his hotel lobby; Mahmoud Hamshari being killed off by a bomb planted in his phone; the hotel explosion that eliminated Abad al-Chir; the trifecta of assassinations that involved outside assistance in Beirut; and Zaid Muchassi nearly avoiding a fatal bombing until Hans takes it upon himself to lob a grenade into his hotel room to get the job done. Those missing were two other Paris jobs: Basil al-Kubaisi being shot dead on the street and the car bomb that killed Mohammed Boudia. Also included were the unsanctioned retaliation killing of Carl's female assassin and the bungled attempt to kill the most desirable target, Ali Hassan Salameh, which

Israeli Prime Minister Golda Meir (Lynn Cohen) and her team, including General Nadav (Sharon Cohen Alexander) and General Zamir (Ami Weinberg), discuss how to retaliate for the Olympic slayings in this scene from *Munich*.

resulted in the shooting of an unidentified Arab guard (who is given a more cinematic moment of falling dead in a swimming pool).

The screenplay gave more suspense to some of these events in order to prolong the inevitable for maximum audience tension and also to emphasize the risk involved that put innocent lives in harm's way. In the film, Hamshari's daughter returns early to the apartment, her arrival blocked by a truck that has pulled in front of Robert and his remote control for the bomb. Unaware of her reappearance on the scene, Robert nearly triggers the switch until delayed in the nick of time by Avner. This presented Spielberg with the perfect opportunity to pull off one of his nail-biting tour de force sequences, cutting between the participants for maximum impact, although no such moment was described in Jonas's retelling of the mission.

The script took liberties with the bombing of Abad al-Chir's hotel room, adding a sequence in which Avner and the terrorist leader actually talk to one another like civilized human beings on their respective balconies (Avner's room was not next to the other man's in the actual event), putting a more ironic spin on the predestined outcome. In addition, this was made more lethal by having Robert's makeshift bomb turn out to be more destructive than intended, harming the couple in the room next to al-Chir's and giving a further dose of humanity to the dangerous repercussions of vengeance. According to Jonas, this particular bomb did its job without further effect on the other hotel occupants.

While all exchanges between Avner and his father, himself a former Israeli agent, were deemed unnecessary for the story being told here, a few scenes were created expressly for the motion picture, chief among them an intriguing dialogue between Avner and one of the PLO agents he and his men have mistakenly been asked to share a safe house with during their mission to Athens. Because they are led to believe that Avner and his men are members of the ETA—a Basque nationalist organization—the Baader-Meinhof Group, and the African National Congress, one of the PLO agents feels free to express his negative feelings about the Israelis to Avner, making for a wry statement about the blindness of prejudice and the unreasonable motivations of the Palestinian cause. Also added was an aborted attempt to make contact with chief target Ali Hassan Salameh on a rainy London street at night, as Avner is interrupted by a pack of American drunks, one of whom mistakes him for someone else, a diversion that may or may not have been a set up by the CIA. An actual foiled attempt to assassinate Salameh—who was in Glarus, Switzerland, to meet at a church with fellow terrorist leader Abu Daoud—was not addressed in the movie.

Although Jonas had indicated in his book that Avner had one meeting with "Papa," the mysterious head of Le Group, the screenplay added a scene in which Avner meets up with Papa and Avner's face-to-face contact, Louis, in Paris. Here Papa gave him the needed information on the whereabouts of the female assassin responsible for Carl's death and advised Avner to put an end to the operation as he and his team were now being hunted themselves.

According to Jonas's account, following his decision to leave the Mossad behind, Avner is horrified to learn that his daughter was nearly kidnapped while leaving kindergarten. It is this final threat that causes him to storm into the Israeli consulate and demand the agency stop intimidating his family. Surprisingly,

Spielberg and his scripters opted not to use this highly dramatic turn of events as the prime motivating force for Avner's confrontation with the Deputy Consul, instead basing Avner's explosive anger on his overall fear of being stalked rather than a singular incident. A further underhanded move on the part of the Mossad, draining Avner's bank account after he has severed his ties with the agency, was also left out of the film script.

For a final meeting between Avner and his Mossad contact, Ephraim, the screenplay made it clear that two of the men killed as part of the mission, Zwaiter and Hamshari, were guilty of their involvement in *other* terrorist activities unrelated to the Munich massacre. This scene also emphasized Avner's guilt in choosing assassination over bringing the accused men to Israel to stand trial for their crimes and the realization that counter terrorism begets nothing more than further terrorism springing up in the place of those expunged—a point made clear by having the World Trade Center loom large in the background, an image made necessary at that point through CGI.

The Adventures of Tintin

According to Steven Spielberg, the first time he became aware of the name Tintin was when a reviewer compared the exploits of Indiana Jones in *Raiders of the Lost Ark* to the kind of cliff-hanging, somewhat tongue-in-cheek, globe-trotting adventures the youthful hero of Belgian cartoonist Hergé's (the pen name of Georges Remi) comic strip was known to excel at. It was understandable that Spielberg wasn't all that clear on just who this character was, Hergé's books never reaching the degree of tremendous popularity here that they had in Europe, despite having been translated into English and distributed in the United States since the 1950s. (There had also been two live-action French features based on the character, produced in the 1960s, but they had never been imported into the States.) By the time Spielberg took an interest in the series and actually spoke with Hergé about the possibility of turning them into a grand-scale motion picture epic, the cartoonist had already laid down his pen on his franchise, having published in 1976 his last Tintin adventure (*Tintin and Alph-Art*), the twenty-fourth in a series that had begun back in 1929 with *Tintin in the Land of the Soviets*. Shortly after Hergé's death in 1983, it was made known that Spielberg's Amblin entertainment had purchased the stories to develop into a movie, with *E.T.* writer Melissa Mathison given the job of adapting them. This project ended up way down the priority list on Spielberg's busy schedule, and in the interim HBO ran a Canadian-French-produced cartoon series made from the books, starting in November of 1991, the debut episode being "The Crab with the Golden Claws."

With the new millennium, Tintin was once again in Spielberg's sights, still with the idea of doing the movie as a live action adventure. Figuring he'd have to computer animate Tintin's faithful dog Snowy in order to get him to take direction and behave and respond in ways beyond that of a normal canine, Spielberg contacted *The Lord of the Rings* director Peter Jackson to see if his team of special effects experts in New Zealand could pull it off. With the development and perfecting of motion-capture technology, the two filmmakers decided this was the direction to go for the overall concept and to make this a collaboration of talents, Jackson being a Tintin fancier from way back. Rather than take a single Tintin story and adapt it (the books being more suited for a half-hour or one-hour format), they would combine elements from several. Although the full title during production was frequently reported as *The Adventures of Tintin: The Secret of the Unicorn*, that story (first published between 1942 and 1943) would be only one of several used as the source. In addition to *Unicorn*, they would fashion a screenplay out of pieces of *The Crab with the Golden Claws* (1941) and *Red Rackham's Treasure* (1943), which had initially been presented as the follow-up installment to *Unicorn*.

The film does resemble *Unicorn* at first. In both the book and onscreen, the inept detective duo the Thom(p)sons are on the lookout for a pickpocket, and Tintin comes across a model ship, which he buys at the Old Street Market in Brussels. Having lost out on buying the model, the villainous Sakharine comes to Tintin's apartment hoping to purchase the ship. Snowy ends up breaking the model (not while chasing a cat, as the script writers saw fit), but here the resemblance between the screen and page was thrown off by the appearance at Tintin's place by Captain Haddock. Spielberg wanted the movie to include the young reporter's first encounter with the liquor-loving, cantankerous seaman (as had taken place in *Golden Claws*) and therefore postponed any appearance by Haddock until later. Although Tintin confronts Sakharine about the sudden disappearance of the model (at his apartment, not at Marlinspike Hall, as in the movie), Sakharine does not continue throughout the original *Unicorn* story as the chief villain.

The film had Tintin kidnapped by Sakharine's thugs and placed in a crate that is transported aboard the *Karaboudjan*, where he meets up for the first time with

Captain Haddock, Tintin, and Snowy quickly recover after crash landing their plane in *The Adventures of Tintin*.

Haddock. Part of this turn of events came from *Crab*, wherein Tintin boards a ship of the same name because of a note found in a body at sea and then is subdued by shipboard thugs who had taken over the vessel from Haddock and who lock him in his cabin. Tintin using Snowy to gnaw at his ropes and then climbing out the porthole up to Haddock's cabin was retained in the movie, thereby recreating the first Tintin and Haddock meeting pretty faithfully. *Unicorn* had included Tintin getting chloroformed and put in a crate, but he had ended up imprisoned in Marlinspike Hall by criminals known as the Bird Brothers. The pickpocket had reentered the *Unicorn* story when it is revealed that he has Tintin's wallet, in which two needed parchments had been kept. In the film, the Thom(p)sons recover the wallet, which contains only one of the parchments, and they bring it to Tintin while he is having his adventures in Bagghar.

Tintin and Captain Haddock had escaped by lifeboat in *Golden Claws* in a series of events much like those depicted in the movie, with the Captain setting a fire in the boat, Tintin shooting down a seaplane and eventually disarming the pilots, the vehicle crashing in the desert, and Tintin and Haddock being rescued by Lieutenant Delacourt, who takes them to safety at a desert fortress. There were some revisions to these scenes. The film script added an example of Haddock's alcohol dependency causing further trouble, having him foolishly try to extinguish the fire with a splash of whisky, the resultant explosion causing himself and Tintin to end up seated on the capsized vessel. In Hergé's version they had ended up this way battling over a bucket of water and thereby tipping over. The plane ride also added some comical bit of liquor consumption, with Haddock helping to keep the seaplane running by belching his alcoholic breath into the tank. The curiously brutal moment of him smashing a bottle over poor Tintin's head and thereby causing the crash was wisely excised, but Tintin's compassionate saving of the thugs who had tried to kill them in the first place, pulling them from the plane wreckage, was no longer included onscreen either. Instead, the two men managed to parachute out of the diving plane before its landing.

Although the film had Tintin and Haddock end up in Bagghar, their adventures were now quite altered from the Hergé originals. In *Golden Claws* they had subdued Omar ben Salaad, the ringleader of the opium smugglers who'd been using the crab tins to move their product. The movie had a character of a sheik who held the third ship model in his possession. Although he somewhat resembled ben Salaad in appearance, he now became a benign victim of Sakharine's efforts to steal the ship and the parchment within. This sequence in the movie included the appearance of another character who had popped up in the *Tintin* stories, although not in *Golden Claws* or *Unicorn*. Dubbed the "Milanese Nightingale" the comical opera diva was first seen in *King Ottokar's Sceptre*, the eighth Tintin adventure. Although her signature aria had been "The Jewel Song," the film script chose another piece for her to sing, Gounod's "Ah, je veux vivre" from *Romeo et Juliette*.

As the wrap up for the movie, Spielberg chose the ending of *Red Rackham's Treasure*, wherein Tintin and Haddock had discovered a statue with a globe at the foot of it, in which lay the treasure. Prior to this, Hergé's story had Tintin descending into the ocean depths in a submarine fashioned to look like a shark in order to hunt for the submerged loot. No doubt Spielberg deliberately chose to bypass any shark imagery, having already covered that territory thirty-six years prior.

War Horse

For Spielberg, this film was an unusual example of an adaptation, having derived from both a novel and a play, making it the first instance in which he directed a work that had origins of any sort in live theater. Curiously, although the credit for both Michael Morpurgo's book and Nick Stafford's theatrical adaptation were evident at the close of the movie, the poster and print ads chose to emphasize only the connection to Morpurgo's work. It was perhaps a ploy to placate skeptics who wondered how the very theatrical piece could make the transition to film.

The book, intended for younger readers, made its debut in Morpurgo's native England in 1982, published by Kaye & Ward, and then appeared in America the following year, from Greenwillow Books. Told from the point of view of its equine protagonist, Joey, it hardly seemed like the sort of thing to bring to life onstage, and Morpurgo expressed disbelief when Nick Stafford proposed the idea. The stage approach, however, was to be highly stylized and steeped in the wonder of pure theater, with life-size horse puppets (three people operating each horse) created by Adrian Kohler and Basil Jones of the South African Handspring Puppet Company and choreographed by Toby Sedgwick. Opening at the Olivier Theater at London's Royal National Theater on October 17, 2007, under the direction of Marianne Elliott and starring Luke Treadaway in the central role of young Albert Narracott, *War Horse* became the sensation of the season. After its limited run ended in February of 2008, the play was brought back to the National in September of that year. When this run wrapped in March of 2009, the play already had a West End theater booked because of the high degree of public interest. (There was much news made about the fact that Queen Elizabeth not only attended a performance but invited the puppet company to bring their "horses" to Windsor Castle.) The transfer opened at the New London Theater on March 28, 2009, and would run another seven years. Prior to this the book was adapted for BBC Radio 2 in a one-hour format to commemorate the ninetieth anniversary of Armistice Day, which aired on November 8, 2008, with Timothy Spall narrating the voice of Joey. It was during its London run that Steven Spielberg's producing partners, Kathleen Kennedy and Frank Marshall, caught the show and recommended it highly to the director, with DreamWorks buying the rights even before Spielberg actually saw the play himself, this not happening until February 1, 2010.

Spielberg's film went into production and finished shooting some six months before *War Horse* had its Broadway debut, opening at the Vivian Beaumont Theater at Lincoln Center on April 14, 2011. All of this attention on the property was a publicity plus for the movie, which would play in movie theaters and then be available in home viewing formats while Stafford's adaptation ran in New York and then began its US tour, commencing in Los Angeles on June 14, 2012. If the 718-performance Broadway run was far outshone by the London production, the New York production fared better come awards season than it had in the United Kingdom, winning Outstanding Play accolades from the Drama League, the

Drama Desk, Outer Critics Circle, and, most significantly, the Tony Award committee, from which it won five total.

Television documentary producer Revel Guest had already expressed tremendous interest in making a movie version of Morpurgo's book years before the stage play came to fruition. To adapt the piece she turned to Lee Hall on the basis of his screenplay and subsequent musical stage adaptation of *Billy Elliot*. Bringing Morpurgo into the mix, the three collaborators even considered the possibility of making an animated movie as the one way of getting away with having the horses speak. Hall had finished his first version of the script prior to the play's London premiere; it therefore owed any later changes or revisions to Stafford's new take on the book. Although the original plan was to produce *War Horse* as an all-British production, DreamWorks' interest changed all that. There was also the need to flesh out characters, add humor, and strengthen certain aspects of Hall's screenplay, and therefore Richard Curtis—who had achieved great success as a screenwriter with *Four Weddings and a Funeral*, *Notting Hill*, and *Love, Actually*, among others—was hired to do the rewrite.

Because the story was no longer being told from Joey's point of view, the film followed the direction of the play by including scenes outside of the horse's direct involvement. Chief among these was an extended sequence in which Albert; his friend from back home, Andrew; and David, the son of the Narracott's cursed landlord, Lyons, find themselves in the trenches at the notorious Battle of the Somme, facing the horrors of war in close-up. (In a chilling moment, a sergeant

Lyons (David Thewlis), given shelter by his umbrella-toting cronie (Martin D. Dew), believes that Joey will never make a decent plow horse, but Mrs. Narracott (Emily Watson) is not so sure, in this scene from *War Horse*.

ominously reminds his men that "If anybody turns back . . . You take this rifle and you shoot them dead.") Also added to the screenplay were a pair of young German soldiers who, fed up with their lot, desert and end up at the farm of a Frenchman and his granddaughter. This led to one of the most haunting compositions of Spielberg's entire career, when the boys are taken to be shot by a firing squad, their actual killing momentarily blocked by a descending sail of the windmill where they have been hiding.

Morpurgo's book begins with a prologue that tells of a portrait of a horse that has hung for years on the wall of an English pub before it leads into this horse's tale. Although Captain Nicholls sketching Joey was retained for the film (in the book he had actually spoken to the horse while doing his artwork, but this wasn't shown on screen) and the portrait was sent to Albert following the commander's death, there was no modern-day lead-in for the film. Stafford had wisely given some tension to the auction at which Joey is purchased by an irresponsible Ted by adding a mocking competitive bidder, Arthur Warren, and his smug offspring, David. Versions of these characters appeared onscreen, although Arthur was now dubbed merely "Lyons" and his "villainy" was compounded by having him be the Narracott's taunting landlord, while his son later showed up in the movie as Albert's superior in the trenches.

Although Stafford's script had retained the little French girl named Emilie, onstage she now resided not with her grandfather but with a woman named Paulette, whose relationship to the girl was not made clear. Spielberg's movie retained Morpurgo's character of Emilie's grandfather, as well as his appearance near the finale at the auction, where he wins Joey but has a change of heart when he meets Albert. There had been no such interaction on the stage. Whereas in the book Joey and Topthorn continued to be used to haul artillery even after ending up at the French farm, the film wisely made this a respite of sorts for the two horses, a peaceful escape from the battle lines, with the two horses bonding with their new young owner and her grandfather until they are discovered and cruelly taken away by the Germans. As in the book and stageplay, Joey and Topthorn end up in the care of a compassionate German soldier named Friedrich (referred to derogatorily on the page as "Crazy Friedrich," despite him being the sensible one who simply wants to get away from the gunfire), but Spielberg chose not to have him be another war casualty, as Morpurgo and Stafford had, instead letting him be dragged away from Topthorn's corpse as he encourages Joey to run for his life, as he wishes he himself could do.

Following the staging of one of the most stunning and heart-pounding sequences in Spielberg's entire film output—in which the terrified Joey dashes through and over trenches during the persistent shattering of shells and gunfire in an effort to leave the insanity of war behind him, only to find himself unable to escape—a key sequence from the book and stage was retained but made even more harrowing and poignant. Morpurgo had Joey end up in No Man's Land, standing between rows of barbed wire and therefore in the center of enemy lines, observed by both the English and Germans. Spielberg staged the scene so that the hapless horse had caught himself up in so much barbed wire during his dash for safety that it had brought him down and pinned him to the ground helplessly, a disturbing image of innocence disabled by human barbarity.

Again, having missed an opportunity for some dramatic tension, Morpurgo merely had Joey, sick with tetanus, end up at a vet hospital where he is at last reunited with Albert after recognizing his voice. There had been an extended nursing of the horse by Albert and the other members of his company, who blocked out light and put Joey in an elaborate sling to help him heal. Stafford had come up with the brilliant idea of having poor Albert temporarily blinded by the deadly chemical gas that had been a vicious new addition to warfare during the First World War. This put Joey's owner in close proximity with his beloved horse, although he was not initially aware of it because of his lack of vision. This turn of events was wisely transferred over to the screen version for a maximum emotional impact.

In Morpurgo's book, during his stay in the vet hospital, Albert confides to Joey that during his pet's absence he had gotten himself a girlfriend back home. At the book's end Joey returns to England to stay with Albert and his love, Maisie, who became his wife, but the girl isn't able to work up any affection for this third party in her family. Although this offered some amusing opportunities for humor at the expense of a wife-horse rivalry, the film script felt it more effective to let Joey and Albert be the only couple at the wrap-up, it having been their love story all along.

Lincoln

The source credit for *Lincoln* reads "Based in part on the book *Team of Rivals: The Political Genius of Abraham Lincoln* by Doris Kearns Goodwin." The phrase "in part" might even be overstating the case. It was certainly good publicity to be aligned with Kearns Goodwin's magnificently detailed account of the sixteenth president's contributions to America, politics, and the world in general, but one could see the movie and read the book and not really make much of a direct connection between the two.

Ten years in the making, *Team of Rivals* was published in 2005 to great acclaim, the concept (and hence the title) being that rather than simply focusing on Lincoln, this historical tome also examined the lives of the three men who ran against him in the 1860 Republican primary: William Seward, Salmon Chase, and Edward Bates. What had impressed Kearns Goodwin was that rather than dismiss these men as having once been his rivals for the coveted office, Lincoln knew their strengths could be beneficial to him and to his goal of abolishing slavery in America and appointed each one to his cabinet. Seward became his irreplaceable secretary of state and eventually his foremost ally in Washington, Chase took on the job of secretary of the treasury, and Bates assumed the role of attorney general. Of course Lincoln remained the center of attention throughout the story, but Kearns Goodwin kept us up on each of the other politicians as the Civil War unfolded and the country faced an unprecedented crisis.

Tony Kushner's original script had tried to encompass much, much more of Lincoln's story until it became evident that this approach was more suitable to a miniseries than a theatrical feature film. When it was decided to narrow the focus to Lincoln's attempts to get the Thirteenth Amendment passed by Congress and therefore abolish slavery forever, this whittled the timeline down to the last four months of his life, January through April of 1865. This meant that Chase and Bates were now out of the picture altogether, both men having stepped down from their posts before the events taking place unfolded. Only Seward remained an important figure, meaning that that the screenplay was starting from about

Tony Kushner's script was made available for fans of *Lincoln*.

page 686 of the book. Kushner's script was obliged to create scenes that were not specifically referred to at all in Kearns Goodwin. The screenplay's depiction of Mr. and Mrs. Jolly coming to Lincoln for his assistance was based on the many office seekers and citizens to whom the president generously opened his door; none of the discussions between Lincoln and his eldest son Robert about the young man's desire to participate in the war were addressed in the book either. Pennsylvania representative Thaddeus Stevens now took on a far larger and more substantial role in the film, having rated a few passing mentions on the written page. He was not only included in a scene in which he was dryly berated by Mrs. Lincoln for questioning her spending money to upgrade the White House, but he was given the most progressively personal motivation for his crusade to have the amendment passed, as toward the end of the film he was seen returning to his home and crawling into bed alongside his African American housekeeper, giving her a kiss in triumph for this historical accomplishment.

Although Kushner's script carried forth several mentions in Kearns Goodwin's book of Lincoln's frequent desire to pardon deserting soldiers, the specific incident the president recounts onscreen to personal assistant John Hay of a young private deliberately maiming his horse was not taken directly from the book. A favorite Lincoln anecdote about the portrait of George Washington hung in a British bathroom was retained, although it was moved from his law circuit years to a later spot when the President and his cabinet, in the telegraph room, awaited word of the taking of Fort Monroe. Bits of dialogue quoted directly from Lincoln (his speech to his cabinet in which he declared himself "cloaked in great power;" his comparing obtaining votes for the amendment to whaling, etc.) were also used in the screenplay. Although the issue of black soldiers being given less pay than their white equivalents was featured in an early scene of Lincoln speaking with some enlisted men, this had actually first been brought up in Kearns Goodwin's book by the leading black abolitionist of his day, Frederick Douglass, during a White House meeting as early as 1863. Douglass had no place in the screen adaptation.

There was no mention of Lincoln's very curious assumption that, after the slaves were freed, most of them would be only too happy to leave the country and set up separate colonies elsewhere; the President never quite believed that it was possible for black and white to coexist peacefully, a fact that made him seem far less open-minded and optimistic. Another proposal, to give millions to the South if all resistance to national authority would cease by April 1, 1865, along with additional funds if the Thirteenth Amendment was ratified by July 1 of that year, was adamantly vetoed by Lincoln's cabinet and represented one of his greatest disagreements with them. This also played no part in the onscreen story.

While Kushner had done a superlative job of integrating the debate over the Thirteenth Amendment with the humanity of the President and those around him, just as Kearns Goodwin had done in her book, it hardly seemed necessary to single out her writing as the point of reference for *Lincoln*. If, however, seeing the film led audiences to pick up a copy of *Team of Rivals* because of its movie cover tie-in, then it was most beneficial to all.

Bridge of Spies

Although it did not credit a specific source, this account of the exchange of a Russian spy for an American U2 pilot had been well documented prior to Steven Spielberg's film on the subject.

On Saturday, February 10, 1962, Russian Colonel Rudolf Abel was handed over to the authorities representing his country on the Glienicke Bridge, a link between East and West Berlin over the Havel River. In turn, US Air Force pilot Francis Gary Powers, who had been enlisted by the CIA to join its U2 program of flying reconnaissance missions over Russia, was given to the US authorities, which included the attorney who had been instrumental in negotiating the deal, James B. Donovan. On March 23, 1964, Antheum Books published Donovan's firsthand account of the events from his point of view, *Strangers on a Bridge: The Case of Colonel Abel*, which principally focused on Rudolf Abel's capture by the FBI and Donovan's defense to keep his client from facing execution. Eight years later, Powers (collaborating with Curt Gentry) published *his* version of the events, *Operation Overflight: The U2 Spy Pilot Tells His Story for the First Time.* This was an account of how Powers had been shot down over Russia on May 1, 1960, and his interrogation and plight as a prisoner there, with the story eventually leading up to his exchange. It was this account that was used as the basis for the 1976 NBC television movie *Francis Gary Powers: The True Story of the U2 Spy Incident.* In it, Lee Majors appeared as Powers, James Gregory was a cantankerous James B. Donovan, and Charles Macaulay showed up as the Colonel.

BBC writer Matt Charman got the *Bridge of Spies* project generating after reading a footnote in a John F. Kennedy biography mentioning Donovan and an unrelated incident, in which the lawyer negotiated the release of 1,113 US prisoners from Cuba. This led Charman to research the man behind this act, thereby introducing him to the story of the Berlin exchange. Charman pitched the idea for a spy thriller to the Hollywood studios, a risky proposition insomuch as it was a period piece which gave more attention to logistics and human interaction than action. DreamWorks, however, was interested in Charman's proposal, which led to Spielberg choosing it as his next directorial project. Although the structure of Charman's screenplay was pretty much retained, Spielberg felt it needed stronger characterizations and brought aboard the esteemed Coen Brothers to do a polish.

The script would concentrate on the events leading up to the exchange that took place on February 10, which involved not only Abel and Powers but also an American student from Yale University, Frederic Pryor, who had been accused of espionage when his research on trade behind the Iron Curtain uncovered material regarded as confidential. There had been a third American arrested for espionage by the Russians, Marvin Makinen, who was caught taking illegal photographs of a military installation while touring the country. He was tried and sentenced to eight years in prison. Although Makinen's plight also became one of great concern to the US government and had occurred just around the time Donovan was trying to negotiate the Abel-Powers-Pryor deal, it was eventually decided that he could not be included in the swap and that his release would come at a later time. Because the outcome of Donovan's deal did not end up including Makinen (he was finally released in October of 1963), it was deemed unnecessary to clutter up the story with another character.

Some facts were altered in some instances simply to keep from having to create further locations or sets, which thereby kept down the budget. Donovan had been informed of his assignment to handle the Abel case while on vacation in the Adirondacks, but onscreen he was instead told in the confines of his law offices. Similarly, Abel's arrest did not occur in Brooklyn but in a Manhattan hotel room, where he was confronted by the FBI while naked on his bed. Putting him in underwear, minus his false teeth, was humiliating enough for the movie version, which wasn't looking for an R rating anyway. Also omitted was Abel's initial incarceration following his arrest, as he was taken to an illegal alien detainment camp all the way over in Texas. The screenplay gives the impression that he remained in the New York area from the time he was captured by the FBI. Insomuch as this version of the events would not focus specifically on Abel's trial, it only briefly touched upon Donovan's key defense, pointing out the illegality of how his client's possessions were confiscated for evidence. In the film, this defense is quickly dismissed by the biased judge. Two key witnesses for the prosecution were a fellow spy who had informed on Abel, Reino Hayhanen, and an American sergeant, Roy Rhodes, who had ended up providing the enemy with government information. Donovan discredited both as bringing forth no important evidence to condemn his client. Neither man was even mentioned in the film script. One intriguing bit of information was passed over as well: the fact that it was Francis Gary Powers's father who got the ball rolling on swapping his son for Abel, when he himself wrote to the latter in prison, pleading for his help in the matter. This being mainly Abel's story, the Powers family was not included in the film.

A few moments of unrest were put into the screenplay in order to add a bit more dramatic tension: Donovan's home being shot at by a passing car while his daughter innocently watches television, and the lawyer being made to give up his winter coat by a group of street hoods during his tense walk through the streets of East Berlin. Although Donovan had made mention in his book of the negative phone calls and letters he received berating him for defending a Russian spy, there was no account of any such shooting happening. Similarly, although he had recounted his confrontation with the German hoodlums, there was no indication in his writing of his coat being sacrificed in order to avoid any harm.

For maximum visual interest, the climax on the bridge was staged in the film to take place *before* dawn, allowing for Spielberg's cinematographer, Janusz Kaminski, to do a particularly evocative job of creating mood and atmosphere to spare—wintery, dark, and unfriendly in appearance. The actual exchange took place, in fact, a bit later than that, between 8:20 and 8:40 a.m., according to Donovan's account. There was also no painting given to the lawyer by Abel, although the latter would send him sixteenth-century editions of *Commentaries on the Justinian Code* (in Latin, no less) as a show of his appreciation, knowing Donovan was a collector of rare books. The portrait of Donovan turned out to be a better cinematic prop to use that could engender an emotional smile from its subject and get a more appreciative response from the audience as well.

The BFG

Roald Dahl's timing couldn't have been better for the publication of his children's novel *The BFG* in October of 1982. Three months earlier, the newspapers were abuzz with a bizarre incident in which a prowler managed to sneak into Queen Elizabeth's bedroom at Buckingham Palace and spent about ten minutes sitting on Her Majesty's bed, talking with her until the proper authorities could come and cart him away. Because Dahl's book has a sequence in which the title character (an abbreviation for Big Friendly Giant) deposits the regular-sized heroine, Sophie, on the windowsill of the Queen's bedroom to speak to her about the cannibalistic problem among the Big *Un*-Friendly Giants, it seemed hard to believe that the author had written this *before* the real events took place.

Despite the fact that there would later come a perfectly nice animated adaptation of the book—done for Thames television and originally broadcast on Christmas Day of 1989—the timing of the book's release was also prescient for another reason. The year 1982 was far and away the year of *E.T. the Extra-Terrestrial*; what Roald Dahl thought about it (if he thought about it at all) is anybody's guess, but he could hardly have imagined that its director would be adapting his story for the big screen, thirty-four years later, twenty-six years after Dahl's passing, and with *E.T.*'s screenwriter, Melissa Mathison, no less.

Having been a fan of the book for years and having read it to his children, Steven Spielberg wanted to do a very respectable adaptation of the work. Knowing that the present state of special effects could finally do it justice, he utilized motion capture to seamlessly put his actors into the storyline and to allow them to interact believably with one another regardless of their size differences. Perhaps its fidelity to the source was what kept it from being something very special. *The BFG* was pleasant enough as a book and pretty much stayed on that unremarkable level when blown up on the big screen.

The changes made in Mathison's screenplay were minor but worth noting. Unlike Dahl, Sophie's first sighting of the giant on the street outside her orphanage did not include the little girl seeing BFG use what she would refer to as his "dream-thing" to place dreams into the heads of the Goochey children down the street. For the film, she would not see this demonstrated by her oversized friend until later. All references to the various countries where the nine bad giants have eaten hapless citizens were eliminated, thereby dispensing with the jokes attached to each. Bonecrusher, for example, had a preference for Turks because he liked the taste of turkey, but he and his cohorts all avoided Greeks because they felt Greece was greasy, and so on. Perhaps because in the age of political correctness there was no way to make light of countries without it seeming like a thoughtless slight, giant consumption was made worldwide but generic. To avoid implying that the world of very huge beings (or "beans" per BFG's language) was sexist, the script also got rid of the explanation that BFG had no mother simply because there were no such things as female giants (this assessment having been written a few years before such a lady made a memorable appearance in the musical *Into the Woods*). Although no women of an unusual size were seen onscreen, there didn't seem to be any reason to stress this point and knock out all kinds of spin-off and sequel possibilities.

The Puffin movie tie-in edition of Roald Dahl's book.

To put Sophie in less potential peril, Mathison moved her from BFG's pocket to a derelict automobile during the scene in which her friend is cruelly tossed about by the larger members of his species. In Dahl's story, Sophie had also taken to riding on and in BFG's ear for their trip to and from London, but this was not dramatized in the movie, missing a potentially wondrous bit of imagery that might have drawn parallels (favorable or not) to Sabu's magical ride while holding genie Rex Ingram's ponytail in *Thief of Baghdad*. Also missing from Dahl-to-screen was a scene in which BFG blows a particularly nasty dream into Fleshlumpeater's mind, freaking him out and causing him to think that he is being attacked by the very same Jack the Giant Killer from the storybooks. Jack received no mention in the script, perhaps as a way of not drawing attention to the fact that a similar gathering of unpleasant giants had already taken place in Bryan Singer's 2013 fantasy *Jack the Giant Slayer.*

Gone too, unfortunately, was Roald Dahl's self-referential mention. When BFG explains that he learned to write the labels for his dream jars by reading a book he had "borrowed" from one of his jobs, the novel in question turns out to be *Nicholas Nickleby*, which he credits to "Dahl's Chickens" in his customary word-twisting way. The same book appeared onscreen, but as the one Sophie was reading while being stolen away.

Alas, some of Dahl's darker bits of whimsy were sacrificed. There was no mention of piles of bones being found under the windows of the children snatched away by giants; of the owner of Sophie's orphanage, Mrs. Clonkers, punishing the girls by locking them in a dark cellar without food or drink; nor of the need to wipe off the sword used at Buckingham Palace to feed BFG—it still having dried blood on it, being the very blade used to behead poor King Charles I. The movie did see fit to have the Queen and her staff subjected to some "whiz-popping" after sampling some of BFG's prized drink, Frobscottle (if the story already involved farting, why not make it regal?), and moved the location of the imprisonment for the giants from a huge hole in the ground to a distant island. Although the movie looked pretty much timeless in its depiction of both the real and the fantasy world of England, the script added a reference during the Queen's transatlantic phone call to "Ron and Nancy," thereby placing it in the 1980s, the era in which the novel was written.

3

Spielberg Directs for Television

His Fifteen Credits for the Small Screen

Television was where it all began for Steven Spielberg, but his talent was too vast for its confines. Nobody, after all, thought of it as a director's medium. That was what motion pictures were all about, but to achieve this aim so many ambitious directors were first obliged to ply their trade on the small screen.

Signed to a contract with Universal Television in the fall of 1968, Spielberg was pretty much handed his assignments and treated as just another name in the talent pool to choose from. But his work was assured and interesting right from the very start, despite his own frequent dismissal of so much of what he did there. Looking back on his five-year apprenticeship, there is nothing on his résumé to feel embarrassed about and plenty that was done with proficiency and more than a glimmer of creativity. When the breakthrough came in 1971 with *Duel*, the twenty-four-year-old had not only proven himself but was clearly displaying capabilities beyond his years. It was predestined that he end up in motion pictures, where he would have more time and autonomy to create works more to his liking and that reflected something of his own personality and soul.

He did not leave the medium behind completely, however, once his film career took off like a rocket in the mid-1970s. He returned amid much publicity in the 1980s to direct two episodes of a series he produced, *Amazing Stories*. There were also quieter contributions, as seen below.

1969–1970 Season

Night Gallery (Pilot movie: "Eyes" segment)

Shown on NBC, Saturday, November 8, 1969, 9:00 p.m. EST

A Universal Studios production. Starring Joan Crawford (Claudia Menlo), Barry Sullivan (Dr. Frank Heatherton). Costarring Tom Bosley (Sidney Resnick). With Byron Morrow (George J. Packer), Garry Goodrow (Lou), Shannon Farnon (1st Nurse). Hosted by Rod Serling. Produced by William Sackheim. Written by Rod Serling, based on his story. Directed by Steven Spielberg.

There is no overstating the importance of this credit in the Steven Spielberg canon; it was his first professional directing job and the work that gave him his first wide exposure in the entertainment industry. That Sid Sheinberg and the executives at Universal Studios had enough faith in him, on the basis of his short film, "Amblin," to let the twenty-two-year-old novice not only helm a segment of a pilot for a series created by one of the medium's iconic writers, Rod Serling, but one that starred one of the biggest names from Hollywood's so-called "golden" era, Joan Crawford, cannot be underestimated. Not surprisingly, as is often the case with any artist who becomes more accomplished and more assured with experience, Spielberg later had no qualms about dismissing his work here, calling it "terrible" and berating

Twenty-two-year-old Steven Spielberg tackling his very first professional directing job, *Night Gallery*, starring Joan Crawford.

himself for showing off, trying to add some artful touches to what was basically standard television fare. This is understandable, as it's never humble to declare your maiden effort an across-the-board triumph, but it's safe to say that Spielberg was being unnecessarily harsh in his self-assessment.

Because it introduced Spielberg to modern cinema aficionados, "Eyes," the middle section of the *Night Gallery* trilogy pilot, has come under a greater deal of scrutiny than just about any other segment of Rod Serling's anthology follow-up to his revered *The Twilight Zone.* It is certainly the standout of the three segments, the only one that doesn't make a painting a crucial element in the story, and the only one that doesn't require any supernatural elements to embellish it. Each story in the trio requires the main protagonist to be punished for his or her wicked behavior. The surrounding chapters were: Boris Sagal's opening segment, "The Cemetery," featuring Roddy McDowall as an abominably insensitive offspring desperate to claim an inheritance; and Barry Shear's closing chapter, "Escape Route," starring Richard Kiley as an ex-Nazi who thinks he has avoided detection while hiding out in South America.

In "Eyes," Crawford starred as Claudia Menlo, a monstrously bitter Manhattan multimillionaire who has been blind since birth and who believes that her money can purchase whatever and whomever she pleases. Eager to have at least a momentary look at the world that has been denied her, she comes up with an audacious plan. Having found an "inconsequential hoodlum," Sidney Resnick (Tom Bosley), willing to give up his own eyes to pay his bookie a $9,000 debt, she blackmails her doctor (Barry Sullivan) into performing an operation that will re-graft the optic nerves from her donor's eyes to her own, allowing her sight for a twelve-hour period. This being a morality play, Miss Menlo is in for a rude awakening when her moment arrives; her bandages are removed just as the city experiences a blackout, a cruel twist of fate for a woman who has unleashed her own degree of cruelty upon others.

If Spielberg indulges in some tricks ("It turned out to be the most visually blatant movie I've ever made," he would later declare), they only add to the atmosphere of unrest. A close-up of a bauble hanging from a chandelier, placing Dr. Heatherton upside in our view, suggests the events to come, which will turn the physician's life upside down. It is a distortion of the actual visual, the very theme of Serling's script. Quick cuts bringing us closer to Miss Menlo's angry face as she barks out the various items she demands she must see are dramatically effective in emphasizing her formidable presence. A transition between Menlo's apartment and a children's playground is done with a spinning camera, the point of which is made clear when we realize Sidney Resnick is confronting his bookie on a roundabout, the thug enjoying tormenting his hapless prey with the constant motion of the ride. The preparation for the operation is shot through a montage of images of both Menlo and Resnick being wheeled into the operating room as we hear their thoughts in voice-over, giving the sequence an ominous touch. An overhead shot melds donor and recipient's eyes until they are one, an effectively creepy visual keeping in the macabre tone of Serling's style. A surreal shot of smashing glass (obtained by literally dropping a pane of glass off a parking deck on the Universal lot) is a memorable substitute for the actual sight of Miss Menlo plunging to her demise from her penthouse apartment. It all works quite well.

Although Spielberg would later speak of having to work extra hard in order to win over the skeptical crew, who felt it was some sort of joke to have someone this green calling the shots, he had nothing but praise for his legendary star. While Crawford may have earned a reputation for being tough and difficult at times, she was surprisingly encouraging to the young neophyte, and he would later speak only in positive terms of his interaction with her. "Directing Joan Crawford was like pitching to Hank Aaron your first time in the game," Spielberg later said. "Once she knew I had done my homework . . . she treated me like I was The Director. Which, of course, I was, but at that time she knew a helluva lot more about directing than I did." He did coax a strong performance of out her, keeping her from lapsing into histrionics of the sort she was guilty of slipping into over the years. Her scenes with Barry Sullivan prove that Spielberg was proficient with guiding actors, his capabilities stretching beyond the technical side of directing. Sullivan would, in fact, end up in two more of Spielberg's television efforts (*The Name of the Game* and *Savage*), tying him with Richard Dreyfuss (and later Mark Rylance) as the star with which he collaborated the most until Harrison Ford, and then Tom Hanks, one-upped them both with four and five Spielberg credits, respectively.

While Spielberg filmed his segment as early as February of 1969, the program did not air until November of that year, in the coveted *Saturday Night at the Movies* timeslot. Although *TV Guide* ran a close-up to draw attention to the presentation, there was no mention in the copy of who had directed any of the segments. Rod Serling was the "name" to your average viewer, after all. The *Night Gallery* series premiered more than a year later, as the second offering of NBC's *Four in One* omnibus. During its first season, Spielberg would return to helm the segment entitled "Make Me Laugh."

Marcus Welby, M.D.: "The Daredevil Gesture"

Shown on ABC, Tuesday, March 17, 1970, 10:00 p.m. EST

Starring Robert Young (Marcus Welby M.D.), James Brolin (Steven Kiley, M.D.). Costarring Elena Verdugo (Consuela Lopez). Guest Stars: Marsha Hunt (Mrs. Bellows), Frank Webb (Larry Bellows), Susan Albert (Claudia Bellows). Executive Producer: David Victor. Produced by David J. O'Connell. Created by David Victor. Written by Jerome Ross. Directed by Steven Spielberg.

Following a long waiting period when he wasn't certain whether Universal was going to entrust him with another assignment or not and when he had had no luck shopping around possible ideas for feature film projects, Spielberg finally landed a second directing gig, his first on an established weekly series. As television shows go, he couldn't have scored higher, at least in terms of ratings, because *Marcus Welby, M.D.*, shortly after its debut in September of 1969, quickly became ABC's most watched program on its primetime lineup. (Being scheduled against the rather tepid competition of CBS's potpourri of news and specials, and NBC's latter hour of its Tuesday night movie, helped immeasurably in it being the go-to program of that hour when the new fall season arrived.) When it came to audience attention, this would be, by a wide margin, the most popular of the shows for which Spielberg would direct. (By the following year, *Welby* had grown so tremendously in popularity that it was ranked number one in the Nielsen ratings for the 1970–1971 season, making it the very first ABC series to ever reach the top spot.)

As with Joan Crawford in *Night Gallery*, Spielberg found himself giving direction to another industry veteran, Robert Young, who had, in fact, acted in films with Crawford on multiple occasions. As the very hands-on general practitioner who shared an office with a young, motorcycle-riding apprentice doctor, Steven Kiley (James Brolin), Young was many people's idea of the wise and caring physician, the sort that could hardly exist in the real world, although his knack for being seemingly everywhere and dispensing advice (sometimes outside his medical expertise) at the drop of a hat made him something of a self-righteous busybody to others. The formula had been set since the premiere: a guest star was challenged by an illness in the opening sequence and Dr. Welby or Kiley would be right on the case by the time credits arrived, sometimes because there was a personal connection. The illness for Spielberg's episode was hemophilia, and the episode dealt with a young high schooler (Frank Webb) frustrated by his overly cautious mother's (Marsha Hunt, Young's costar twenty-eight years earlier in the MGM wartime B, *Joe Smith, American*) insistence that he not participate in school activities, lest such extreme physicality lead to fatal bleeding. The episode raised the issue of allowing the afflicted to make his own decisions on his potential fate and of being willing to take risks to ensure something akin to a normal life, despite Dr. Kiley's warning, in a nod to the episode's title: "You might wind up paying a stiff price for a daredevil gesture."

Hardly adding anything innovative to the carefully calculated formula, Spielberg delivered what *Welby* fans had already come to expect. Perhaps the one aspect worth mentioning in his assignment was the especially dedicated performance he coaxed out of young Frank Webb as the tortured teen. Neither overly solicitous to his adult advisers nor a tenacious hellion, never self-pitying in his need to break out of his unfortunate state, Webb was the closest thing to a relatable teenager on view. (The actor had, by coincidence, attended the same Phoenix high school that Spielberg had done time at before his move to California.) He was a welcome contrast to the rather wholesome portrayals of his fellow students—representations that were reflective of the time, when television wasn't ready to rock the boat too harshly when it came to generational confrontations and examining the complex behavior of youth. Alas, Webb would leave acting shortly thereafter only to be killed in a car accident at the age of twenty-six.

At season's end, ABC had not only those enviable ratings to celebrate, due to their decision to put creator David Victor's medical drama on the air, but also favorable critical response for the show's efforts to bring various issues to the table and do so with a degree of restraint and lack of melodrama. There was support from various medical groups and Emmy Awards for Young, Brolin, and the show itself, which won Outstanding Dramatic Series. Insomuch as this was a reward for a season's worth of quality programming, one can include Spielberg's contribution in the mix, as it gave him, in a roundabout way, his first mention from the Television Academy.

By the time *Marcus Welby, M.D.* finished its seven-season run in May of 1976, Steven Spielberg had long ago left the medium of television behind and become the hottest director in film.

1970–1971 Season

Night Gallery: "Make Me Laugh"

Shown on NBC, Wednesday, January 6, 1971, 10:00 p.m. EST

Starring Godfrey Cambridge (Jackie Slater), Tom Bosley (Jules Kettleman). Special Guest Star: Jackie Vernon (Chatterje). Written by Rod Serling. Directed by Steven Spielberg.

Nobody came away particularly happy over Spielberg's second stab at a *Night Gallery* segment. The pilot he'd contributed to for Rod Serling's new omnibus series had proven successful, and NBC agreed to add the show to the 1970–1971 schedule, albeit not for the entire season. The idea was to make it part of an "umbrella series," which would go under the name *Four in One*, a quartet of dramas, each one presented consecutively for six weeks, broken up by specials filling the time slot. Once the season ended, the episodes would then be shown in rotation. *McCloud*, headlining Spielberg's future *Duel* star, Dennis Weaver, as a cowboy lawman in Manhattan would come first, followed by Lloyd Bridges in *San Francisco International Airport*, then *Night Gallery*, and, finally, *The Psychiatrist*, with Roy Thinnes in the lead. *Night Gallery* ran its season from December 16, 1970 through January 20, 1971, with Spielberg's episode, "Make Me Laugh," shown as part of the fourth week's installment, sharing the hour-long slot with "Clean Kills and Other Trophies," directed by Walter Doniger and starring Raymond Massey.

Godfrey Cambridge gained notoriety as a stand-up comic during the 1960s commenting deftly on race and the black experience, and he had only just the previous year made a successful transition to starring roles in feature films, with both *Watermelon Man* and *Cotton Comes to Harlem*. Here he portrayed Jackie Slater, a second-rate comedian desiring nothing more than the knack to make people laugh, seemingly unaware of his terrible choice of material and lackluster delivery. First seen bombing during an engagement in Perth Amboy, New Jersey, a despondent Slater meets up with a mysterious guru (Jackie Vernon) who agrees to grant him the gift he desires, since he himself is under pressure to perform one more miracle before midnight. Warned that there are risks to such a wish, the audience is instantly made aware of Slater's fate when a bartender goes into convulsions merely hearing the comic speak. Great success follows, only Slater remains discontented, being one more comedian eager to prove his serious side as well. Blowing an audition for a play with the intriguing title "How to Stuff Bread-Dressing," the preoccupied comedian wanders into traffic and is killed. (Spielberg ending the episode on the crying face of the flower lady Slater was crossing the street to confront was a nice touch.)

The curious casting of ultradeadpan stand-up Jackie Vernon, sporting dark makeup in order to pass as an Indian, led audiences to wonder if this was one of the less serious outings that Serling would toss off now and then, undercutting what was already something of a predictable Faustian plotline. Perhaps disengaged by the material, Spielberg once again rankled the front office by some of his choices, and the studio went so far as to replace the original actor cast as Cambridge's manager, Eddie Mayehoff, with Tom Bosley, although this was not a reunion for actor and director, since Jeannot Szwarcz (future director of *Jaws 2*) was called upon to do the reshooting. Spielberg felt further undermined when his original casting choice to play the theater director holding the audition was replaced, without his consent, by Tony Russel. An unimpressed Serling would comment harshly on what had been done to his script, declaring the finished product "a piece of crap."

There would be no more *Night Gallery* jobs for Spielberg, although the show (along with *McCloud*) was renewed for the following season (the two other pieces of the *Four in One* experiment were declared too weak in the ratings to make the cut), this time as its own stand-alone series shown on a weekly basis.

This marked the first time Spielberg would collaborate with art director Joseph Alves, Jr., who would work for him in this capacity on his first three theatrical features.

The Name of the Game: "LA 2017"

Shown on Friday, NBC, January 15, 1971; 8:30 p.m. EST

Universal Studios presents Gene Barry (Glenn Howard). Starring Barry Sullivan (Vice President Dane Bigelow), Edmond O'Brien (John Bergman), Severn Darden (Cameron), Paul Stewart (Dr. Rubas), Louise Latham (Helen). Special Guest Star: Sharon Farrell (Sandrelle). Executive Producer: Richard Irving. Produced by Dean Hargrove. Written by Philip Wylie. Directed by Steven Spielberg.

Although this was officially another series episode, *The Name of the Game* was not a typical series. Given a ninety-minute slot, it was something more akin to a television movie in length, thereby making this the most extensive professional Steven Spielberg credit to date. Rather than following the exploits of the same protagonist week after week, *Game* was a triple series. Stars Gene Barry, Tony Franciosa, and Robert Stack each carried their own self-contained episodes, and therefore which of the men would be the central focus varied from week to week. They did, however, work for the same company, Howard Publications, and the one recurring character from episode to episode was their shared editorial assistant, Peggy Maxwell, played by Susan Saint James, who had made her television debut in the 1966 pilot from which all this derived, *Fame Is the Name of the Game*. Gene Barry portrayed Glenn Howard, the owner of the publishing empire.

Spielberg's episode, however, did not stick to the basics (Saint James was nowhere on hand), being a fantasy which placed Glenn Howard in a future Los Angeles. Driving to a conference where he hopes to speak with the President about the dire state of the environment, Howard passes out at the wheel, only to awaken in an unfamiliar, desolate future. Driven to an underground facility, the confused publisher is told that he is now in the year 2017 and that the city has relocated beneath the Earth because of dangerous toxins that have destroyed the atmosphere. Howard becomes increasingly skeptical as the new way of living, which includes selective sterilization of the remaining citizens in order to control the outcome of all future children, is explained to him. It is clear that Howard has found himself in a totalitarian state where those in power are reinventing the world to their satisfaction, and his only hope of escape is the so-called "underground" movement of rebels who are eager to prevent further destruction of the surface.

This was a stand-out assignment for Spielberg to receive, and he gave the episode the proper nightmarish quality required without overstating the case. Using an orange filter on the camera to indicate a polluted atmosphere, his opening sequence of Howard being discovered and saved by a duo of minions and driven to the underground bunker is punctuated by foreground shots of junked cars and skeletons, creating a vivid sense of unrest and dread. The subterranean world is one of soulless corridors, ever-present impersonal announcements coming over the intercom, and menacing bureaucrats, sometimes filmed in silhouette; the other denizens of this world are a collective impersonal lot, seemingly anesthetized in their behavior. The creepy atmosphere reaches its peak when Howard is given a chance to meet one of the few survivors from the Earth he once knew. Tracking the camera in slowly toward actor Edmond O'Brien—as once eminent bio chemist John Bergman, who sits zombie-like and sweating in the center of an operating theater, bound in a straitjacket—Spielberg further creates an unsettling tone by sometimes filming Bergman from below and at other moments in extreme close-up. In a single scene, the character transitions from seemingly mad to pitiable. Between Bergman's recitations of the failings that led to this ecological disaster, we hear comments from Howard and the distrustful psychiatrist Cameron (Severn Darden), given an otherworldly echo by the sound department. It is a highly distinctive sequence that raises the episode miles above the typical weekly television fare.

Cecil Smith in *LA Times* called the episode "a bone-chilling experience . . . Young (23) Steven Spielberg directed the film with a remarkable sense that he was opening the door to an inferno and a clammy atmosphere of stark reality—no moonglow."

With respected science fiction author Philip Wylie (the novels *The Gladiator* and *When Worlds Collide*, among others) responsible for the chillingly apocalyptic script, this episode was deemed enough of a special accomplishment that it rated a showing at the Ninth Annual Festival of Science-Fiction Films in Trieste in July of 1971, being treated as a feature, given it's seventy-five-minute length. It was a giant leap forward for Spielberg because the job he did here earned the admiration of the top brass at Universal, more and more of whom were coming to the realization that they had something better than just a journeyman television director on their hands.

Louise Latham, playing Barry Sullivan's ever so delicate but clearly unhinged wife, was the one principal performer from Spielberg's television years that he would carry over with him into his first feature film, giving her the role of the baby's foster mother in *The Sugarland Express*. He would call on *Game* star Gene Barry much further down the line, when he asked him to do a cameo at the finale of Spielberg's new version of one of Barry's most notable films, *(The) War of the Worlds*. Author Wylie was one Spielberg collaborator who would never be made aware of the staggering later success and increasing prominence of the man who had helmed his story; he died of a heart attack by the end of the year that this episode aired.

The Psychiatrist: "The Private World of Martin Dalton"

Shown on NBC, Wednesday, February 10, 1971, 10:00 p.m. EST

Starring Roy Thinnes (Dr. James Whitman). Also Starring Luther Adler (Dr. Bernard Altman). Guest Stars: Jim Hutton (Robert Dalton), Kate Woodville (Janis Dalton). Costarring Stephen Hudis as Martin Dalton. Executive Producer: Norman Felton. Produced by Jerrold Freedman. Created by Richard Levinson and William Link. Written by Bo May. Directed by Steven Spielberg.

Discounting *Night Gallery* (since his first assignment was a pilot segment, followed later by an episode segment), *The Psychiatrist* marked the one time during his Universal contract that Steven Spielberg would be enlisted to direct *two* episodes of the same series. *The Psychiatrist* had a very short life span, the briefest run of any of the series he worked on, although he would later look on this as one of the better experiences apprenticing on the small screen. As the fourth in a quartet of series that made up the one-season omnibus *Four in One*, this well-intended drama about a Los Angeles therapist aired for a mere six episodes, this one being the second to be shown. The show was scheduled against one of the season's Top 10 Nielsen hits, *Hawaii Five-O*, on CBS, and of the four "mini" series in the quartet, *The Psychiatrist* fared poorest in the ratings. This and *San Francisco International Airport* were dropped by NBC after a single season.

This episode involved Martin Dalton, a rambunctious, difficult young boy whose excessive exaggerations, obsession with comic books and flights of fancy, as well as his bad habit of stealing, cause his mother to turn to psychiatrist James Whitman (Roy Thinnes) for help. It turns out that Martin's emotional outbursts of discontentment, calling his parents liars and snubbing his affectionate younger sister (Pamela Ferdin), are not quite as unfounded as they seem, as he had the misfortune of stumbling upon his adoption papers, a matter never disclosed within the family.

Spielberg's most impressive accomplishment here was his handling of the scenes between series star Roy Thinnes and thirteen-year-old Stephen Hudis, this marking the first time he proved adept at guiding a youngster through a difficult leading role. Young Martin's behavior, all but bouncing off the walls with discomfort and angst, are believably those of a child his age, and are well modulated to the degree that they draw the audience into his troubles rather than alienate them. Hudis (doing a very good job of disguising his UK origins) would make a career change later in life, becoming a stuntman and coordinator, though his many jobs never included any Spielberg projects.

An effective bit of direction takes place during a walk among the private planes at an airport, as Martin's dad (Jim Hutton) explains the adoption situation at last. Spielberg allows his high angle camera to pace itself with the two as they walk, brings it down to earth for what appears to be a heartfelt understanding between the boy and his dad, only to cut to a rapid tracking shot when Martin balks at hearing his sister referred to as his parents' "real" child (biologically), the boy racing off, the camera remaining below his waist as he runs towards it. This scene also marked the first time in his professional career that Spielberg would give attention to his lifelong interest in flying and airplanes.

This episode also contains some of the more fanciful sequences ever staged by Spielberg. These include the darkly hypnotic dream in which Martin relives finding his adoption papers, Dr. Whitman showing up in what appears to be a military uniform as the rest of the Dalton family, Martin's sister included, nestle comfortably together in bed, bathed in a blue light, the distressed boy repeatedly shouting "They're not my parents!" for maximum, annoying effect. Another dream sequence gets downright chaotic as a jumble of images flash with staccato cuts, as if to remind us that this is the early 1970s, the picture often turning into brightly colored negative images, jerkily edited family moments, and footage from the Japanese kiddie matinee favorite *King Kong vs. Godzilla* (!) More subdued, but no less odd is a sequence introduced by the disoriented visual image of a spinning book rack, leading to one of Martin's thieving endeavors. This curious scene is punctuated by the wailing screams brought forth by a toy store clerk (Peggy Mondo), who frantically chases young Martin from the premises, only to step on the very object she was hoping to stop him from stealing. "Martin Dalton" allowed Spielberg, if nothing else, to cut loose in unexpected ways within the confines of weekly Universal-produced mass-market entertainment.

The Psychiatrist: "Par for the Course"

Shown on NBC, Wednesday, March 10, 1971, 10:00 p.m. EST

Starring Roy Thinnes (Dr. James Whitman). Also starring Luther Adler (Dr. Bernard Altman). Guest Star: Clu Gulager (Frank Halloran). Costarring Joan Darling (Mary Halloran), Carl Reindel (Larry Wilson), Michael C. Gwynne (Blaine), David Astor (Dr. John Abarth), Bruce Glover (Stan Brewster), Gene Kearney (Stewart). Executive Producer: Norman Felton. Produced by Jerrold Freedman. Teleplay by Thomas Y. Drake and Herb Bermann, and Jerrold Freedman and Bo May. Story by Thomas Y. Drake. Directed by Steven Spielberg.

Spielberg's second episode for *The Psychiatrist* was, in fact, the last of the six aired. If the show itself made little impact on the television landscape, it did provide the director with one of his happier experiences in the medium. He would frequently speak of this particular episode as the one he was more satisfied with than any of the others series installments assigned him.

Clu Gulager was cast as Frank Halloran, a golfer eager to get back to the game following a cancer diagnosis but unaware of just how serious his disease is. Eventually, he comes to the realization that he must face his demise quicker than he imagined. What made an already well written episode something deeper was the inclusion of a scene of Dr. Whitman and his fellow staff members discussing how they must cope in a professional capacity with bestowing upon their patients the awful news that their numbers are up. Rather than this merely being a weepie trying to milk tears from a character's sad farewell, "Par for the Course" therefore offered up some food for thought.

Spielberg was again given free rein to direct the episode as he saw fit, and excelled in bringing off some emotional highlights, notably the image of Halloran watching a tape of the golf match (on an early reel-to-reel recorder) in which his initial collapse has been captured. Cutting between the silent footage, Gulager's saddened reaction, and the trophies and photos chronicling his triumphs that adorn the room, the director created a moving mini-portrait of a life that is slipping away, without a single line being spoken. Later, he delivers the goods in Halloran's death bed decline, at one point shooting the prone patient in close-up from below the chin, as, in his confusion, he asks the onlooking Dr. Whitman, "Tell me, Jim, tell me," before expiring. Having again coaxed an outstanding performance out of one of his actors, this was proof that Spielberg had the chops to go for a gut reaction, done with flair but never falling back on cheap manipulation. His own favorite moment of the episode finds Halloran's seemingly rock-steady wife (Joan Darling) calling her mother at a hospital pay phone to break the bad news, enduring pesky questions from the operator before turning from the camera and losing her cool, as the camera slowly pulls back from her.

Curiously, "Par for the Course" was interwoven with another *Psychiatrist* episode, "The Longer Trail" (directed Douglas Day Stewart), and released on home video in 1990 by ACE under the name *The Visionary*. Spielberg's name featured prominently on the box cover, giving buyers the impression that they were uncovering a lost, unknown item from his past.

Joan Darling (who was also featured in Spielberg's *Owen Marshall* episode) would later turn to directing, her credits behind the camera including two episodes of *Amazing Stories*, "The Sitter" and "What If . . . ," the latter written by Steven Spielberg's oldest sister, Anne.

1971–1972 Season

Columbo: "Murder by the Book"

Shown on NBC, Wednesday, September 15, 1971, 8:30 p.m. EST

Starring Peter Falk (Columbo). Guest Stars: Jack Cassidy (Ken Franklin), Rosemary Forsyth (Joanna). Special Guest Star: Martin Milner (Jim). Created and Produced by Richard Levinson and William Link. Written by Steven Bochco. Directed by Steven Spielberg.

Spielberg had clearly made an impression on the suits running Universal Television because his episode of *Columbo* was chosen to launch the new series despite the fact that it had been the fourth one filmed. If creators Richard Levinson and

William Link were hoping to get things off with a bang, the young director served them well.

This was not, however, the first time television audiences were exposed to Peter Falk's now-classic creation of the rumpled private detective with no first name, whose seemingly scatterbrained style of interrogation belied a brilliant mind that took great delight in seeing the guilty sweat it out while he tightened the noose. A full three years earlier, Columbo had shown up as the star of an *NBC World Premiere* movie, *Prescription Murder*, a proposed pilot that failed to make the grade, and then again, early in 1971, with *Ransom for a Dead Man*, the pilot which did the trick. *Columbo* was added to the lineup of another of NBC's multiple series, *NBC Mystery Movie*, this one also consisting of *MacMillan and Wife* (Rock Hudson and Susan St. James), as well as a returning favorite, *McCloud* (Dennis Weaver), which had, the prior season, swapped off with *Night Gallery*.

Given a tight script by Steven Bochco (Spielberg would call it the best of those he was given while directing episodic television), Spielberg handed in one of his finest jobs, bringing out the best in the show's villain, Jack Cassidy, who was always so good at smarmy duplicity and who in this episode brilliantly matched wits with the unflappable Falk. Starting the episode off with the ominous approach of Cassidy's car as seen from the window of his writing partner's (and ultimate victim's) office, as the sound of typewriter keys fills the soundtrack, "Murder by the Book" bounced along at a good clip and did the job of establishing a show that would soon become a six-season favorite for detective fans. The story centered around Ken Franklin (Cassidy), a no-talent coauthor who has, in fact, never actually contributed to the writing of a series of mystery novels (one of which he inscribes, in a key plot point in the show, is wittily titled, for those in the know, *Prescription Murder*) penned by his collaborator (Martin Milner). Franklin cleverly sets up an alibi in order to bump off his partner, who has decided to move on and work solo, leaving his faux collaborator in the lurch.

Filled with low-angle shots and menacing close-ups (notably an exchange of shadowy faces in the lobby of a theater between Franklin and his blackmailer, Lily La Sanka), the episode brought comparisons to the master of the genre from the *Washington Post* review, which noted Spielberg's "felicitous Hitchcockian touches here and there." The program also made stunning use of the scenery around Big Bear Lake, site of Franklin's cabin and the scene of both crimes, as the slithery killer makes sure to dispose of La Sanka (Barbara Colby) in the famed body of water after he has conked her on the head with an empty champagne bottle. (In a tragic irony, Colby was actually murdered four years later, shot to death in a parking garage, shortly after joining the cast of the sitcom *Phyllis*.)

The producer behind the project who hired Spielberg was Richard Irving, who was the uncle of actress Amy Irving, who would end up, fourteen years down the line, as Steven Spielberg's first wife. *Columbo* was followed in its Wednesday night lineup by the second season of *Night Gallery*, the property that had given Spielberg his first professional directing job, and one which he had since left behind, never to return.

Owen Marshall, Counselor at Law: "Eulogy for a Wide Receiver"

Shown on ABC, Thursday, September 30, 1971, 10:00 p.m. EST

Starring Arthur Hill (Owen Marshall), Lee Majors (Jess Brandon). Also starring Joan Darling (Frieda Krause). Guest Stars: Stephen Young (Coach Dave Buckner), John David Carson (Marty Cardwell), Brad David (Cliff Holmes). Executive Producer: David Victor. Produced by Jon Epstein. Created by David Victor and Jerry McNeely. Written by Richard Bluel. Directed by Steven Spielberg.

As a result of the success of *Marcus Welby, M.D.*, that series' creator, David Victor, teamed with Jerry McNeely (who'd written several *Welby* installments) to transplant the wizened veteran-young apprentice format from the hospital to the courtroom and came up with *Owen Marshall, Counselor at Law*. Arthur Hill (who had won the Tony Award for creating the part of "George" in the original Broadway production of *Who's Afraid of Virginia Woolf?*) assumed the role of the titular dignified lawyer, full of experience, sage advice, and comfort, while Lee Majors (with *The Big Valley* in his past and *The Six Million Dollar Man* about to arrive in his future) was his youthful partner, former pro-footballer Jess Brandon. Both characters even made crossover appearances on *Welby*, putting them in the same fictitious universe. In light of Spielberg's *Welby* credit, it came as no surprise that Universal assigned him to this show as well, although he balked at the original episode offered him, which involved an opera singer, and instead opted to do this football-based story. It was aired as the fourth episode of the premiere season.

Richard Bluel's script made a potent statement about the obsessive, kill-or-be-killed nature of not only those playing and coaching the game, but the fans. This criticism appealed to the director, who had experienced this sort of worship of sports in his high school days, being a decidedly non-athletic outsider to this world, although he honed his moviemaking skills by filming some of the games. This experience played right into several sequences in the program, notably the scrimmage seen in the opening credits, shot in slow motion minus any audio.

After a young player (a pre-*Happy Days* Anson Williams) collapses in the locker room and dies, the high school coach, Dave Buckner (Stephen Young), is brought up on murder charges, and the team's student manager, Marty Cardwell (John David Carson), claims that the amphetamines given to the late athlete were a direct result of the coach's orders. Rather than Marshall, it is Brandon who takes center stage in the courtroom, coming to the aid of his fellow former footballer. He eventually proves that Cardwell and his teammates were the ones providing the uppers and that Buckner was oblivious to this fact.

Spielberg's direction subtly signaled the diminished nature of the doomed athlete as he is being given his pep pills by his team manager, having the footballer's image dominating the foreground and then reversing the shot so that the pill provider now loomed large. Later, he dared to shoot the most guilt-ridden of the teammates through the spokes of a film projector as a documentary of the game unspooled in court, a fancy shot that actually worked.

While *Owen Marshall* never achieved the ratings high or Emmy acknowledgement of its predecessor (in its three-year run it would receive not a single mention from the Television Academy), it was another worthy credit for the director to add to his growing résumé.

Duel

Shown on *ABC Movie of the Weekend*, ABC, Saturday, November 13, 1971, 8:30–10:00 p.m. EST

Starring Dennis Weaver. Produced by George Eckstein. Teleplay by Richard Matheson, based on his published story of the same name. Directed by Steven Spielberg.

Duel is, beyond a doubt, the single most significant television credit on Steven Spielberg's résumé, the project that stands so far apart from the rest that historians and fans have happily grouped it in with the filmmaker's theatrical work. It was, after all, deemed good enough to release in movie theaters in Europe and important enough in the trajectory of his career that it even received a delayed run in American cinemas, more than a decade after its small-screen debut. It has been studied as frequently and as closely as any of his actual motion picture features, and it stands out not only among his work but in the television movie genre overall.

ABC's *Movie of the Week* set the tone for what became a small-screen tradition for years. Although there had been standalone projects starting in 1964 that were considered television movies (some of which served as pilots for possible series), these had aired in the timeslots held aside for theatrical features. When it debuted in September of 1969, *Movie of the Week* marked the first time a weekly series was dedicated to premiering movies made expressly for the medium, filling a ninety-minute space, thereby allowing for approximately seventy-four minutes of story, and the rest for commercials and bumpers. Made fast and efficiently, many compared these to the "B" features that had filled cinemas for years, and not always favorably. The series did deliver a watchable batch of movies of various genres and became popular enough to end up in the Nielsen Top 10 for its second season, thereby prompting ABC to expand the field by adding a second night of such programming, airing on Saturdays between 8:30–10:00 p.m. EST. Launched in September of 1971, this new lineup of films was officially called *ABC Movie of the Weekend*, and it was here that *Duel* was first seen.

Amidst the traditional television movie fodder of the day, *Duel* couldn't help but stand out. It had been preceded the week earlier on *Movie of the Weekend* by the thriller *Revenge!*, which cast Shelley Winters as a nutcase out to torture the man she thinks killed her daughter, while the Tuesday *Movie of the Week* put Helen Hayes and other elderly stars in a mild comedic mystery, *Do Not Fold, Spindle or Mutilate*. By the time the first commercial break arrived in the original telecast of *Duel*, audiences were spellbound by the very bare-bones premise unfolding before them: hapless motorist David Mann (Dennis Weaver) being relentlessly pursued by an unseen truck driver on desolate California roadways. As the tale continues to build suspense, there are only minor interactions with other characters along the way, the driver of the taunting truck is never seen, and there appears to be no rational motive for why he is doing what he is doing. That this unfathomable event seemed to have no letup and hooked viewers no matter how implausible it became was a testament not only to Richard Matheson's taut writing but, because it was unlike any other television movie out there, to the execution to the director. *Duel* became one of those unusual small-screen dramas that had people talking about it and remembering it long after most of the output on *Movie of the Week*(*end*) had faded away.

What was remarkable about *Duel* was that the whole project came to fruition, and so impressively, all within the course of the same year. Matheson's original story was published in *Playboy* in April of 1971, was soon purchased by Universal Television for producer George Eckstein, and found its way to Spielberg via his personal assistant. Matheson adapted his story and had the shooting script ready by mid-August. Pulling off something that could be so cinematically visual on television was a challenge Spielberg welcomed, and he rallied enthusiastically for the job.

Spielberg and his team were given a $750,000 budget, seventeen days of pre-production, fourteen days of location shooting (mostly in the canyons around Angels Crest and Soledad in Southern California) to commence on September 13, and six weeks of post-production, with the understanding that the completed movie be edited, scored, and ready for the scheduled airdate of November 13, 1971. Using a giant wall map on which he charted the hapless motorist's journey and index cards storyboarded with each shot he envisioned, Spielberg created an astoundingly varied visual look to a story that could have become repetitive. Because so much of the picture would involve a treacherous game of cat and mouse between two moving vehicles, two of Hollywood's best-known stunt drivers were enlisted for the project: Dale Van Sickel to fill in for Weaver during the more reckless bits, piloting the 1971 red Valiant chosen for the role, and Cary Loftin, who would be the truck driver the entire time since his face would never appear on camera. He would be at the wheel of a 1955 Peterbilt oil tanker that was deliberately uglified by the prop

A man... a car... and
10 tons of rolling death
right behind them

DUEL

Starring Dennis Weaver
A World Premiere
Movie of the Weekend
8:30

A-18 TV GUIDE

The original *TV Guide* ad for the first telecast of *Duel*.

department, who adorned it with mud and dead bugs for maximum demonic impact. Camera mounts were attached to Weaver's car for select shots, while others involved using a handheld camera so that the actor could be shot in extreme close-up within the car in order to capture the mounting terror on his face. Getting rid of as much of the dialogue and voiceover thoughts of his protagonist that he felt would be acceptable to the executives at Universal Television, Spielberg created something even more nightmarish and exciting than Matheson's original tale.

Duel was publicized in TV Guide with an ad picturing a screaming Dennis Weaver in the foreground and the demonic truck behind him, with the copy proclaiming, "A man . . . a car . . . and 10 tons of rolling death right behind them." Although it did not warrant the magazine's prestigious designation of a "close-up," allowing its entry to jump out from the other offerings that evening, the capsule summary did, in fact, end with the line: "Directed by Steven Spielberg."

According to Variety, thanks to Duel, Movie of the Weekend posted its highest ratings to date, ending up for a tie in twenty-seventh place among that week's programs, which was fitting, as Hollywood Reporter declared it the "finest so far of the ABC Movies of the Weekend." There were further raves, including one by Cecil Smith of the LA Times, who declared it the "Best TV Movie of 1971," adding that it was a "classic of pure cinema." It was comments like that that encouraged Universal to do something more with the film. In an unusual move, they actually requested that Spielberg and Matheson expand on the story and shoot some additional footage in order to pad the film out to a ninety-minute length. These new scenes included Weaver pulling his car out of his garage at the start; stopping at a gas station in order to call his wife, indicating that they had some harsh words the previous evening; pausing to help a stranded school bus until he is forced to take off because of his menacing nemesis; and having his car pushed onto a railroad track by the truck. None of them added much value to what had already been a compact thriller, one that had careened along quite nicely without this excess fat. Both Spielberg and Matheson would later speak regrettably of being obliged to put in the extra footage, although this version continued to circulate for years.

With these additional sixteen minutes, Duel was released regionally in England in October of 1972 and then, finally, in November, in London, where it was treated with the sort of respect and acclaim seldom accorded television movies. Universal was even more excited when the movie posted grosses of $12,000 in just the first week at its exclusive booking at the Universal Cinema in Piccadilly Circus. (In the interim, ABC chose not to rerun the film on the Movies of the Week(end) series during the remainder of the 1971–1972 season.) There were further theatrical openings throughout Europe and Asia into 1973.

The first prize for Duel came at the twelfth International TV Festival of Monte Carlo, where Spielberg received a special mention as Best Director. (Patrick Garland won the festival's Silver Nymph Award for Best Direction for The Snow Goose; neither men ended up with a nomination from the Directors Guild of America.) At the close of the 1971–1972 television season, Jack A. Marta received an Emmy nomination for his cinematography, while the film's sound editing team (consisting of Jerry Christian, James Troutman, Ronald LaVine, Sid Lubow, Richard Raderman, Dale Johnston, Sam Caylor, John Stacy, and Jack Kirschner) brought the movie its sole Emmy win. The Golden Globe Awards were more generous, actually nominating *Duel* as Best Movie Made for TV, although it ended up losing to NBC's *The Snow Goose.*

Once *Jaws* made Spielberg the most famous director in Hollywood, the appreciation for *Duel* really began to increase, and it became the early effort most credited with displaying his directorial finesse and creativity. After the double punch of *Raiders of the Lost Ark* (1981) and *E.T. the Extra-Terrestrial* (1982) made him nothing less than a household name, Universal assumed they could squeeze some further coin out of *Duel* by distributing it to theaters in its extended form. This was a unique treatment for a television movie. Although certain notable dramas like *My Sweet Charlie* and *Brian's Song* had been given brief theatrical runs not long after they had made their debuts on television, it was unprecedented to do this more than a decade later. Oddly, the announcement that *Duel* was going to end up in theaters did not keep the film out of syndicated circulation, and it could be seen playing on the small screen that very same year. It was released in New York at the Manhattan Twin on April 14, 1983, with a special boxed credit in the ad stating, "The first film directed by Steven Spielberg." Because it now had some naughty words and, perhaps, because of the intensity of the situation, it was rated PG and referred to as a Universal "re-release." Although there were those curious to see on the big screen the fabled thriller that launched the career of one of the great contemporary filmmakers, business overall was mild.

Something Evil

Shown on *The New CBS Friday Night Movies*, CBS, Friday, January 21, 1972, 9:00–10:30 p.m. EST

Sandy Dennis (Marjorie Worden), Darren McGavin (Paul Worden) Also starring Jeff Corey (Gehrmann), Johnny Whitaker (Stevie Worden), John Rubinstein (Ernest). Special Guest Star: Ralph Bellamy (Harry Lincoln). Produced by Alan Jay Factor. Written by Robert Clouse. Directed by Steven Spielberg.

No sooner had Steven Spielberg finished his bravura job on *Duel* than he accepted another TV movie directorial assignment, the first and only dramatic one he would do in the medium that was *not* a production of Universal Studios. The first of his "ghost" stories (*Amazing Stories* would feature the other one) was a CBS production and presentation (all of his other early small-screen directing efforts were shown on either NBC or ABC).

During a day trip, amateur artist Marjorie Worden (Sandy Dennis) asks her husband, television director Paul (Darren McGavin), if they might be able to buy the ramshackle old house in the Pennsylvania countryside that she is capturing on canvas. Despite Paul's reluctance to adapt to a two-hour commute into New York, the Wordens make the move, which they will soon regret. In no time, Marjorie begins hearing strange sounds, witnessing weird behavior in her neighbors (one of them has a habit of spreading chicken blood, which might be a fairly dependable tip-off that something's amok), and turning to a believer in the occult (Ralph Bellamy), who tells her in no uncertain terms that he's already had a scrap with the Devil himself.

While in no way a major credit on the Spielberg resume, and certainly a bit of a slip backwards following the highly distinctive *Duel*, this thriller was nevertheless effectively done and performed with a commendable degree of restraint by Sandy Dennis, an actress known to fall back on fidgety ticks and mannerisms on occasion. Here, she portrayed a troubled and increasingly desperate mother facing an escalating terror and drew you into her plight rather than keeping the audience at arm's length. Spielberg built the suspense in a measured, believable manner (a scene in which Dennis, in the dead of night, investigates the eerie sounds of a whimpering little girl was staged and pulled off with just the right degree of atmosphere and tension), doing his best to keep the behavior of the oddballs Dennis and her family encounter around their new country digs menacing rather than silly. There was certainly more restraint in evidence here than in Spielberg's far better known "ghost" feature (for which he provided the screenplay and supervised the production of), *Poltergeist*, which took the idea of a suburban family shaken by supernatural events and buried it with special effects that went for cheap shocks rather than honest chills. It is only toward the end of *Something Evil* that the whole thing begins to lose its grip in a similar manner, when the Worden son (played by onetime *Family Affair* cast regular Johnny Whitaker) becomes more blatantly devil-possessed, causing the sort of ludicrously effects-laden battle between the forces of good and evil that has defeated countless directors.

This production marked the first time Steven Spielberg allowed himself to be seen "acting" on camera, in this case playing a techie in a scene in a recording studio where Darren McGavin is directing an actress through a dubbing session. That actress, Margaret Avery, would benefit from her participation in this telefeature when, thirteen years later, she scored the role of Shug Avery in Spielberg's film *The Color Purple*. In an earlier scene, a party was captured with one fluid take as the camera picked up sound bites and glimpses of the guests and as a flaky actress places medallions around the attendants' necks to ward off demons. Among the revelers was future *Jaws* writer Carl Gottlieb, seen chatting up another guest. ("And that was the time that Hal Clement caught black water fever.") The writer of the teleplay, Robert Clouse, would find himself cherished by fans of the martial arts genre the following year, when he directed one of the most highly regarded of them all, *Enter the Dragon* with Bruce Lee. Director of photography Bill Butler would not only work on Spielberg's follow-up project, *Savage*, but would also serve as his cinematographer on *Jaws*.

With a rating of twenty-three, *Something Evil* bested its network competition: ABC's lineup of *Room 222*, *The Odd Couple*, and *Love American Style*, and NBC's rerun of the Yul Brynner western *Return of the Seven*.

An anonymous reviewer for *the Atlanta Constitution* hailed the telemovie as "by far the best of the recent shows about an evil presence," which presumably can be looked on as *some* sort of praise.

1972–1973 Season

Savage

Shown on the *NBC Saturday Night World Premiere Movie*, NBC, Saturday, March 31, 1973, 9:30–11:00 p.m. EST

Starring Martin Landau (Paul Savage), Barbara Bain (Gail Abbott). Guest Stars: Will Geer (Joel Ryker), Paul Richards (Peter Brooks), Michele Carey (Allison Baker). Special Guest Star: Barry Sullivan (Judge Daniel Stern). Costarring Louise Latham (Marian Stern), Susan Howard (Lee Reynolds), Dabney Coleman (Ted Seligson), Pat Harrington (Russell). Produced by Paul Mason. Executive Producers: William Link and Richard Levinson. Teleplay by Mark Rodgers and William Link and Richard Levinson. Story by Mark Rodgers. Directed by Steven Spielberg.

Just when Steven Spielberg assumed that the attention brought upon him by *Duel* meant he could now move out of television and on to features, Sid Sheinberg and Universal sprang another small-screen assignment upon him, much to his displeasure. Spielberg wanted to get *The Sugarland Express* up and running at this point, but Sheinberg had a script by Mark Rodgers (originally called *The Savage Report*) that looked like it could work as a potential pilot for a series, and his protégé was under contract, after all. The studio's much lauded team of William Link and Richard Levinson looked at the same script, knew it needed much improvement, and did a rewrite on it, whipping it in to presentable shape and hoping they could add Spielberg to the mix to make it look even better. According to Link, he pressured Sheinberg behind Spielberg's back to make him take on the job.

All this said and done, the resulting seventy-five-minute pilot, retitled *Savage*—the second half of a double feature of unsold pilots, with *Hitched*—was another solid directing job and hardly the endurance test this initial resistance might indicate. Real-life couple Martin Landau and Barbara Bain were cast as TV news anchorman Paul Savage (star of station NYES's *The Savage Report*) and his producer, Gail Abbott, but their determination to get to the bottom of a story made the drama play more like a police procedural. Indeed, Network News President Ted Seligson was heard to remark, "We ought to get out of television and start a detective agency."

When a frightened young woman (Susan Howard) comes to Paul with an incriminating photograph of herself and recently appointed Supreme Court Judge Daniel Stern, she asks for $5,000 for *The Savage Report* to have exclusive rights to the picture and the facts. No sooner has the deal been proposed when the woman ends up plunging from her fifteenth-floor terrace. Savage wants to know the truth behind what he's certain was murder, leading him to a model (Michele Carey) who turns out to have been yet another attractive mistress in the secret life of the randy judge.

Spielberg delivered the goods in an early sequence in which Gail and her team frantically ready the stage for Paul's show while anxiously awaiting his delayed arrival by helicopter. Cutting back and forth between Gail, the control booth, the ticking clock, and glimpses of the technical equipment adorning the studio, the director created a thrilling opening that promised good things to come. This unheralded three minutes of screen time was one of the best things he had done during his apprenticeship in the medium. There were also evocative touches, such as a low angle long shot of a cat slinking across the railing of the terrace from which our hapless victim has just been thrown; the Judge's unhappy wife (Louise Latham) sitting in darkness, framed only by the glow of a birthday candle as her philandering husband and his friends try to cheer her up with a chorus of "Happy Birthday"; and a spot-on recreation of the sort of perfume ads that were prevalent at the time. There were fine performances from Landau and Latham, and especially from Will Geer, as the seemingly folksy but menacing millionaire whose desire to influence the power players in Washington sets the diabolical plot in motion.

Latham was rewarded for her good work here with the key role as Baby Langston's foster mother in *The Sugarland Express*. Similarly, Bill Quinn, shown in a brief one-scene role as a senator calling Savage on the phone, no doubt stayed in Spielberg's mind when he was looking for elderly thespians for his *Twilight Zone: The Movie* segment, giving him the principal role of the senior citizen who wishes to return to his youthful state. Barry Sullivan was back for his third and final role in a Spielberg-directed project, and Spielberg's friend and future *Jaws* scribe Carl Gottlieb showed up as a stagehand during the tour de force TV studio sequence.

Pretty much tossed away as the second half of a "two-for-one" double bill on NBC's *World Premiere* of unsold pilots (*Hitched*, starring Spielberg's future *Lincoln* costar, Sally Field, was the other), *Savage* didn't excite anyone enough to warrant being turned into a weekly series. On the night of its original airing, March 31, 1973, Steven Spielberg was attending the very first American Film Institute Tribute, to John Ford, having just returned from Texas after completing *The Sugarland Express*.

1983–1984 Season

Strokes of Genius

Shown as a four-part documentary series on PBS, Tuesday nights in the New York market, 10:00 p.m. EST

Each week this documentary series looked at the life and work of some of the giants of Abstract Expressionism, with each segment being directed by a different filmmaker. For the wraparound segments, Dustin Hoffman appeared on camera and gave some background on the artist and information on what viewers were about to see. Courtney Sale (Ross), who conceived and produced the series, was the wife of one of Steven Spielberg's closest friends in Hollywood, Warner Bros. executive Steve Ross. As a result, she managed to persuade the filmmaker to very unobtrusively direct Hoffman in these brief introductions, and Spielberg pretty much placed the camera in the expected spot and let the sequence roll in a straightforward fashion. He took no onscreen credit for his contributions. Apart from doing a favor for a friend, it did give him the opportunity, years before their official motion picture collaboration on *Hook*, to direct an actor he had always admired.

The four episodes were:

Jackson Pollock: Portrait (Episode 1: May 8, 1984), written and directed by Amanda C. Pope.

Arshile Gorky (Episode 2: May 15, 1984), written and directed by Charlotte Zwerin, and *Franz Kline Remembered*, directed by Carl Colby.

De Kooning on de Kooning (Episode 3: May 22, 1984), written and directed by Charlotte Zwerin.

David Smith: Steel into Sculpture (Episode 4: May 29, 1984), written by Jay Freund and Karen Lindsay and directed by Jay Freund.

1985–1986 Season

Amazing Stories: "Ghost Train"

Shown on NBC, Sunday, September 29, 1985, 8:00 p.m. EST

Starring Roberts Blossom (Ole Pa Globe), Scott Paulin (Fenton Globe), Gail Edwards (Joleen Globe), Lukas Haas (Brian Globe). Supervising Producers: Joshua Brand, John Falsey. Production Executives: Kathleen Kennedy, Frank Marshall. Produced by David E. Vogel. Developed by Steven Spielberg, Joshua Brand and John Falsey. Teleplay by Frank Deese. Story by Steven Spielberg. Directed by Steven Spielberg

Because he did the wraparound segments of *Strokes of Genius* with no credit, this premiere episode of Steven Spielberg's much-publicized anthology series was considered by most of his admirers to be his return to directing on the small screen, after more than a decade away, during which time he had become the most successful filmmaker in Hollywood. It was good publicity for the show to launch it with Spielberg in the director's chair, but that also raised expectations quite high for the finished product to be something outstanding and spectacular (not to mention "amazing") and the fate of the series ended up being hung upon this maiden effort. If "Ghost Train" came off as slight to many viewers, they would come to realize in the passing weeks that this was, in fact, one of the better episodes, played with a pleasing simplicity, evoking a certain degree of mystery and wonder, and directed with the right balance of whimsy and dramatic feeling.

Roberts Blossom (who had played the farmer claiming to have encountered Bigfoot in *Close Encounters of the Third Kind*) was given the starring role of an imaginative grandpa come to live out his final years with his son and his family. Dismayed to see that they have built their new house directly in the path of the former train line that once went through the land, "Ole Pa" grows increasingly worried when he gets wind that the train he missed years ago as a boy will be returning that very night to take him on the journey he never finished. It turns out that he had fallen asleep on the tracks, causing the locomotive to have an accident. Only young Brian, the grandson who idolizes him and his tales of the past, believes the old man's warnings to evacuate the premise, but the two dreamers are challenged by Brian's more pragmatic parents.

The episode benefited tremendously from the casting of Blossom, the sort of crusty old character player who was adept at erasing any trace of false sentiment in the codgers he usually played, never falling back on cute tricks, making Ole Pa's fanciful musings appear not only rational but preferable to his bland surroundings. He was matched beautifully by nine-year-old Lukas Haas, who earlier that year had made a deep impression as the terrorized Amish boy in *Witness*, opposite Harrison Ford. Their rapport comes across as heartfelt and utterly convincing, an outstanding example of Spielberg's easy handling of child actors, raising them up to an equal level with their more experienced adult costars.

Spielberg created a fine sense of encroaching danger during the big climax, starting with the distant sound of the real train filling the soundtrack as the camera tracked slowly towards Haas as he rests his ear on the tracks of his toy train set. Allen Daviau's camerawork filled the darkened house with eerie shafts of light, while the special effects team gently shook and rumbled the set with the right degree of tension before delivering the big bang as the period train engine smashed its way through the suburban dwelling. There was often a feeling of crossing the wonderment of *Close Encounters* with the suburban terror of *Poltergeist*, although this twenty-five-minute piece was far more successful in keeping the supernatural in control than the latter.

Placing his offscreen partner Amy Irving in period clothing aboard the train for a silent cameo as one of the ghostly passengers meant that this was the only instance in which Spielberg directed his first wife in any of his projects. She was joined in the scene by her mother, actress Priscilla Pointer, as well as one of Spielberg's *E.T.* cast members, Drew Barrymore. There was some sprightly humor in that sequence, provided by a pair of train engineers reacting with puzzlement to the modern surroundings of the kitchen they have just trashed—refrigerators, six packs of beer, and Mr. Coffee machines.

The whole thing worked quite nicely and got what turned out to be a highly uneven series off to an acceptable start, although many reviewers and audiences weren't in the mood to give Steven Spielberg a break. Somebody this popular in the world of cinema wasn't eligible for kudos in this medium as well, and to many "Ghost Train" was all too precious and unexceptional to warrant the hallowed treatment Spielberg and his new show were being given by NBC.

Amazing Stories: "The Mission"

Shown on NBC, Sunday, November 3, 1985, 8:00 p.m. EST

Starring Kevin Costner (Captain), Casey Siemaszko (Jonathan), Kiefer Sutherland (Static). Supervising Producers: Joshua Brand, John Falsey. Production Executives: Kathleen Kennedy, Frank Marshall. Produced by David E. Vogel. Developed by Steven Spielberg, Joshua Brand and John Falsey. Teleplay by Menno Meyjes. Story by Steven Spielberg. Directed by Steven Spielberg.

Steven Spielberg's second directorial credit on *Amazing Stories* turned out to be the longest presentation of the series, the only episode shown in an hour time slot. He was the boss, after all, the whole reason the show was on the air in the first place, and NBC was still happy to accommodate his needs despite the less than stellar ratings the anthology had posted since its September debut. The elongated running time knocked *Alfred Hitchcock Presents* off the Sunday schedule, but as a compensation that series was allowed to follow a completely different episode of *Amazing Stories*, being shown later that same week in a special time period, on Tuesday, November 5. To script his own story, Spielberg engaged the services of the man to whom he had entrusted the screenplay of *The Color Purple*, Menno Meyjes.

Continuing Spielberg's fascination with flying and paying tribute to his father's experiences as a World War II pilot, "The Mission" was a male-dominated piece set almost entirely aboard a bomber plane flying its twenty-fourth mission. The Captain (Kevin Costner, who had starred earlier that year in the Amblin Entertainment film *Fandango*) isn't keen on having his squadron's lucky turret gunner, Jonathan (a highly appealing Casey Siemaszko in a standout performance), onboard this time out, but at the insistence of his men, he changes his mind. When a propeller from an enemy plane is sent hurtling into the craft, the

A lobby card for the European theatrical release of a compilation of four *Amazing Stories* episodes, including one directed by Spielberg, "The Mission." Casey Siemaszko and Kevin Costner are seen in the foreground.

wreckage trapping the hapless gunner in his compartment, Jonathan uses his artistic talents to save himself and his fellow fliers.

The opening sequence was a promising one, with Spielberg staging a variety of actions in one continuous shot: the camera starting on a close-up of a sketch pasted on the window of Jonathan's turret and then pulling back under the plane to introduce the Captain as he greets his men; concentrating on a foreground argument between the Captain and his radio man, Static (Kiefer Sutherland); a pan upward to include the conversation of the technicians working on the plane's propeller; the arrival of a replacement gunner, staged in the distance, which includes a bit of throwaway slapstick when the eager recruit bumps his head on the nose of the plane; the appearance of Jonathan himself; and the boarding of the plane as the camera tracks up to the painted emblem of a voluptuous lady posed atop a bomb with the words "Hello Adolph!" The indoor set, bathed in vaporous smoke, gave the whole thing the deliberately old-fashioned feel of a World War II fantasy set in heaven, four years before Spielberg would direct his updated remake of just such a movie, *A Guy Named Joe*. The episode kept up this exciting level of cinematic energy as the camera tracked and glided throughout the bomber as each of the crew members was introduced and their fondness for their "lucky" gunner made evident. As Jonathan's plight becomes seemingly hopeless, Spielberg pulled off one of his most emotionally satisfying scenes, as each of the shaken crew members, believing this to be their last such time, reach into their doomed comrade's accidental entombment and touch his head for good luck, as the poor man tries in vain to fight back tears.

So good was the bulk of "The Mission" that it only made the fantasy twist, insisted upon by the very theme of the series, that much more ridiculous and, frankly, irritating when it arrived, as it pretty much pulled the rug out from under viewers who had been totally engaged by the human nature of the piece thus far. Having Jonathan quickly sketch up a pair of wheels that, in turn, materialize on the damaged plane in cartoon form, thereby allowing the Captain to land the aircraft and save the day, was almost too goofy to comprehend. It was a cop-out to an otherwise sharply fashioned episode and executed in such a way that it played as borderline embarrassing in light of all that good work that came before it.

Regardless of its silly denouement, there was no denying that Spielberg's direction was masterful, and the Television Academy did not want to pass up a chance to at least once put him in the running for a directorial Emmy Award. He was nominated for this episode for Outstanding Directing in a Drama Series, competing with four directors helming episodes for weekly series that had continuing characters. Georg Stanford Brown would beat Spielberg out, however, for his work on the "Parting Shots" episode of *Cagney & Lacey*. (The cop show also won the Emmy for Best Dramatic Series that same year.)

For the remainder of *Amazing Stories*'s two seasons on the air, Spielberg would stick to his job as executive producer while occasionally providing storylines. "The Mission" marked his last direction of a dramatic piece in the television medium to date.

1999–2000 Season

The Unfinished Journey

Shown as part of the special *America's Millennium*, CBS, December 31, 1999, 10:00 p.m. EST

While not specifically created for television, this eighteen-minute short debuted at the Lincoln Memorial during the New Year's Eve celebration of the new millennium, which was broadcast live on CBS. As part of a three-day, $12.5 million party to ring in 2000, Washington D.C. included as its centerpiece a brand new work from Steven Spielberg, "The Unfinished Journey," which was basically a collage of photographs and historical footage combined to show the accomplishments, triumphs over adversity, and milestones of the twentieth century. Seen were glimpses of immigrants landing on Ellis Island; the stock market crash; the construction of various buildings and bridges; the coming of motion pictures, television, and computers; assembly plants in operation; marches for the rights of blacks, women, and gays. It was reasonably uplifting and worthy of the event without looking much different than so many other montages depicting American history. Accompanying the visuals was a new piece of music written and conducted by Spielberg's favorite composer, John Williams, while inspirational speeches from the likes of Abraham Lincoln (it was staged in front of his memorial, after all) and Martin Luther King, Jr. were read by President Bill Clinton, Edward James Olmos, and Sam Waterston.

The CBS special went under the banner heading of *America's Millennium* and was aired over a three-hour time slot, beginning at 10:00 p.m. EST. Will Smith was the host; George Stevens Jr. and Quincy Jones produced it. Spielberg's movie was shown at the 11:30 point, with giant screens placed in front of the memorial itself and around the reflecting pool. This addition to the festivities was considered important enough to be a crucial part of the advertising, Spielberg's name still being an obvious selling point to get folks to pick this one over the many other Millennium specials airing that night. Starting in 2000, Williams would conduct his piece and show the film throughout the country, with different narrators.

4

Spielberg on Location

Where Steven Spielberg Shot Each of His Films

S teven Spielberg entered the world of filming when location shooting had become the norm, as directors of the post-studio era were eager to bring more realism to their projects by shooting at actual locations rather than seeing them simulated on a backlot or soundstage. As a result, Spielberg has taken us all over the world to experience his stories, sometimes finding the precise spot to recreate a moment in history, in other instances having one place stand in for another through movie trickery. The adventures of Indiana Jones would not be as exciting without their exotic foreign locales, *Schindler's List* would not be as urgent or authentic if it did not unfold in some of the actual Polish locations where the real story took place, and *War of the Worlds* would not have been as frightening without the thought of New Jersey being destroyed by an alien attack.

Duel

One of the remarkable accomplishments of *Duel* was just how quickly the whole thing was filmed, with Spielberg and his team working against the clock to meet a preset airdate of November 13, 1971. Insomuch as the original story was set in California and because it was easier for the tightly budgeted program to shoot close to home, the highways required were found northeast of San Fernando in the Soledad Canyon and Angeles Forest region. Filming began on September 17, 1971 and, with a three-day overrun, ended on October 3, 1971.

In addition to several highway vistas repeated through the use of clever editing and varying angles, the production utilized a service station in Acton for the scene in which Mann (Dennis Weaver) notices the boots of his tormentor while they are both waiting for gas; the Angeles Forest Highway for the tense moment when Mann nearly collides head-on with another car when he is waved on by the trucker; the Sierra Highway, which, in Santa Clarita, provided two different stops: Chuck's Café—the interior being used as well for Spielberg's masterful and uninterrupted handheld shot that following Mann into the building, to the restroom, and out into the main area—and another filling station, this one in Aqua Verde, redecorated with caged reptiles and arachnids to become Sally's Snakerama. In Soledad

Canyon, Spielberg staged Mann sleeping at the railroad crossing, his efforts to enlist the aid of an elderly couple, and the truck's final drop from the cliff.

The Sugarland Express

Because so much of *The Sugarland Express* took place on highways and in cars, it made perfect sense to shoot the entire film on location in Texas for maximum authenticity. There would be no passing off Southern California as the flat vistas of the Lone Star State, nor would there be rear projection shots used behind the fugitives and their captive as they found themselves pursued by half the Texas State Department of Corrections. While the actual event upon which the screenplay was based had taken place between Port Arthur and Wheelock, the fictionalization of the story meant that none of these particular towns needed to be mentioned nor utilized for filming. Now the destination became Sugarland, a town supposedly located just over the border from Mexico, although there was, in fact, a real Sugar Land (two words), located closer to Houston. This caused a bit of confusion for locals who wondered why the chase, said to be leading the fugitives in a south-bound direction, made it sound by the mention of Sugarland/Sugar Land as if they were circling back northeast.

Obtaining the cooperation of the Texas Film Commission was not an easy thing. Although the police had managed to subdue the criminals in the real case, there was fear that a Hollywoodized version of the story might make law enforcement officials look bad. Spielberg and company assured them up front that no such thing would happen, although in the end there was indeed plenty of criticism of all parties involved, with a special degree of rancor held for the local populace who foolishly turn these petty lawbreakers into some sort of "fifteen minutes of fame" heroes, so in need are they of momentarily brightening their own drab lives. If the citizens of Texas were coming in for some unkind scrutiny, at least they would be placated by acting out their own shortcomings. Hoping for a genuine feel of the state, Spielberg cast some fourteen parts using people from the Houston area and forty-eight roles in San Antonio. Among those chosen were Merrill L. Connally, brother of the former governor, John B. Connally, who entered the history books in notoriety for being wounded while riding with President Kennedy during his fatal shooting in Dallas. Merrill would play the foster father of the baby Lou Jean and her husband want back, at one point offering his own weapon to help the snipers bring down the offenders. The actual kidnapped patrolman from the real-life case, Kenneth Crone, was asked to take the role of a Texas deputy helping to identify the stolen car's proper owner.

While several local cars volunteered their services for the many scenes of the seemingly endless line of vehicles following Lou Jean and Clovis, the film company purchased some twenty-three used cop cars from the Texas Department of Public Safety to ensure that they could do with them what they pleased.

Filming began on January 15, 1973, in the Houston area, with the filmmakers using the Beauford H. Jester pre-release center on Jester Road in Richmond for the opening scene in which Lou Jean casually springs her husband from the facility only four weeks before his scheduled release. The scene of Lou Jean (Goldie Hawn) and Clovis (William Atherton) disarming Office Slide (Michael Sacks) in order to take command over his patrol car was filmed in the bottomland near Sugar Land. The car crack-up that allows the Poplins to escape temporarily was shot at an intersection in the town of Converse.

Moving on to the San Antonio area, Autry's Chicken in Pleasanton stood in for the renamed Dybala's fast food stop, where Lou Jean orders some chicken while hanging out of the patrol car; this scene was followed by Officer Tanner (Ben Johnson) discussing the possibility of picking off the criminals by using a pair of snipers. A used car lot at SW Military Drive and Ascot Avenue became a key location as the overnight hiding place for Lou Jean and Clovis, as they manage to camouflage Slide's car among the other vehicles while watching a Universal release from 1973, *Sssssss*, and a Road Runner cartoon playing next door at the South Loop Drive-In. A shoot-out was staged here after the Poplins are spotted by a team of gun-happy hunters. The hunters responsible had been filmed leaving on their trip from Forsen Drive on the other side of the South PanAm Freeway. Lou Jean's daddy (George Hagy) was seen arriving by helicopter to speak on the police radio with his delinquent daughter at the Harlandale Stadium.

To sub for the fictional Sugarland, the town of Floresville, about thirty miles southeast of San Antonio, was chosen. The parade scene was staged on C Street, while the final destination of the Poplins, the foster home where the Loobys have been given custody of Baby Langston, was located at G and 3rd Streets. Insomuch as Sugarland is supposed to be located near the Mexican border, the finale was staged near the real thing, in Del Rio, with the police car coming to a stop in a riverbed near the prophetically named Amistad Dam.

Although scheduled for fifty-five days, the filming was delayed by weather conditions (including snow in the San Antonio area in February) and Hawn's temporary illness; it stretched out for sixty days, thereby bringing principal photography to an end in late March. The cost was approximately $2.5 million, certainly the smallest budget the director would *ever* work under on a theatrical motion picture. Because Universal decided not to release the picture in late 1973 as originally planned, the opening was delayed until the very end of March of 1974. This meant that one entire year had gone by between the end of principal photography and when the general public got to see the end result.

Jaws

The filming of Steven Spielberg's second feature was so elongated and hellishly over budget that it became the stuff of legend. Fortunately, the final product was so good that few people, outside of those involved in the shooting, gave much thought to how arduous the journey had been in getting it to come out right. More importantly, for Universal, the box office was so gigantic and the audience response so utterly phenomenal that cost overruns suddenly seemed trivial, and the studio was now ready to pat itself on the back for giving the director all the time he needed to achieve greatness.

Among other things, *Jaws* brought immeasurable attention to its principal location, Martha's Vineyard, an already desirable and isolated spot for both vacationers and residents that is some eighty-seven square miles in size and about seven miles from the mainland of the southeastern point of Cape Cod in Massachusetts. There had been very little filming activity there prior to Spielberg's shark epic, with the most recent production to use the island being a 1973 sex comedy with the unwieldy title *I Could Never Have Sex with Any Man Who Has So Little Regard for My Husband*. Because *Jaws* made such extensive use of the place to stand in for the book's fictitious Amity, and because of the movie's tremendous impact on pop culture, the two have been bound together for eternity.

Filming began under highly chilly temperatures on May 2, 1974. For the next two months or so, Spielberg and his team shot mainly on dry land where things went smoothly for the most part. Areas used on Martha's Vineyard included South Beach, for the discovery of the remains of the shark's first victim, Chrissie Watkins (Susan Backlinie); Edgartown, where scenes included a Fourth of July parade on Main Street as Chief Brody (Roy Scheider) makes his way into a hardware store, and the Norton and Easterbrook dock for the armada of fishing boats heading out to sea in hopes of trapping the beast; interiors in Edgartown included the police station, the medical examiner's lab and the town hall, for the meeting where Quint (Robert Shaw) scratches his fingernails on the blackboard to get everyone's attention. Cape Pogue, off Chappaquiddick, was the off-land site for the armada out at sea; on Gay Head a billboard welcoming visitors to Amity and its subsequent vandalized version—Help! A Shark!—were erected with the understanding, in deference to concerned locals, that it would be promptly taken down; a residence on East Chop Drive in East Chop on the northern side of the island became the

Steven Spielberg's troublesome shark, "Bruce," gets ready for his close-up on the Martha's Vineyard set of *Jaws*.

home of Brody and his family; a private beach in the Hartheaven section of Oak Bluffs was where a breakaway dock was built for the tense moment of two naïve locals trying to coax the deadly fish with a chunk of meat. At Menemsha, on the southwest side of the triangular island, Quint's boat shed was erected from scratch by the art direction team.

Getting increasingly watery, State Beach in Oak Bluffs was used for the terrifying attack on young Alex Kitner (Jeffrey Voorhees), which occurred while he was floating on his raft and was followed by a chaotic mass exodus of frightened swimmers; the same site hosted the Fourth of July sequence, which included a cameo by the book's author, Peter Benchley, and a prankster with a fake fin; Katama Beach on the south side of the Vineyeard was seen in the opening as the nighttime campfire frolic, although Chrissie's subsequent attack was shot further north in Cow Bay. Sengekontacket Pond, a saltwater estuary directly behind State Beach, was used for the scene in which a boater ends up having his leg chomped off while one of Brody's children freezes in fear and manages to escape harm. The American Legion Memorial Bridge, connecting State Beach and the Wildlife Sanctuary, where Brody and others were seen running in hopes of coaxing the imperiled children out of the water, ended up being nicknamed "Jaws Bridge" with the passing years.

Starting in mid-July, the company ventured into Cow Bay to shoot the film's tension-filled third act, only to discover that getting the mechanical shark they'd constructed to work was far less dependable than anyone anticipated. So much time was wasted setting up shots that proved useable that Spielberg ended up very cleverly creating far more dread and terror by *suggesting* the shark rather than actually seeing it as much as originally intended. The studio spent $3,500 to convert a working fishing boat called *Warlock* into Quint's *Orca*, while a second vessel, depicting the *Orca* during various stages of sinking, was built as well. The sinking scenes were shot in Katama Bay. By the time Spielberg was able to wrap things up in the Vineyard, it was September 16, and the original $4.5 million budget had more than doubled.

There was still more to do, however, with additional scenes shot back in California. Brody and Hooper (Richard Dreyfuss) locating in the nighttime fog what appears to be Ben Gardner's abandoned boat was done on a lake on the Universal Studios lot. Over at the MGM studio tank, the underwater cage scenes— in which the shark smashes the contraption to bits before Hooper manages to escape in time (with stuntman Dick Warlock standing in for Dreyfuss)—were staged. The waters off Santa Monica Bay provided the underwater shots for the opening credits scene and for Hooper managing to swim to safety in the reef below after the shark has destroyed his cage. Using money from his own pocket, Spielberg shot the sensational "jump-scare" moment of Ben Gardner's head bobbing into view in editor Verna Fields's swimming pool, while the image of the *Orca* planks snapping because the shark is ramming them on the other side was set up and filmed in the driveway of the movie's production designer Joseph Alves Jr. (whose only credit as director would be the 1983 sequel *Jaws 3-D*).

Close Encounters of the Third Kind

Because the success of *Jaws* had rocked the very foundations of the movie industry, Steven Spielberg was in the enviable position to film his next movie pretty much on his own terms. Unlike the efficient manner in which he would later shoot pretty much all of his pictures, his long-gestating dream project, *Close Encounters of the Third Kind*, was filmed over an elongated period of time, with pieces here and pieces there shot and stuck in as new ideas and concepts emerged along the way.

Figuring they needed to get their foot in the door and then worry later on at the certainty of the budget escalating, Spielberg and his producers, Michael and Julia Phillips, managed to convince Columbia Pictures that they could get the science fiction epic about man's contact with extraterrestrials made for an acceptable $2.8 million, all the while knowing this price tag was unfeasible. By the time the whole thing wrapped the cost had skyrocketed to $19,400,000, meaning Columbia had a lot riding on what had become the most expensive motion picture they had yet distributed. Fortunately, *Close Encounters* turned out to be another Spielberg smash, giving everyone a happy ending, which, like *Jaws*, made the industry suits forget about how nervous they had been while the production was getting out of hand.

That *Close Encounters* was not going to be your average production was evident from the start, when Spielberg declared that even adjoining the two largest soundstages at the Burbank (Warner Bros.) Studios could not accommodate the scope of what he envisioned for the landing field set needed for the climax. Instead, he went scouting around the country for an enclosed space that could serve as a makeshift soundstage, settling on an abandoned airplane hangar at Brookley Airforce Base in Mobile, Alabama. Even this required some alteration, the 300-foot length expanded another 150 feet by building a tubular steel frame to be surrounded by a black, wraparound tarp. The "box canyon" set, as it was called, consisting of a landing field and technical apparatus, supposedly situated near the base of Devils Tower, took some three months to construct at a cost of $700,000. Because a second hangar, situated next door could be filled with some additional sets, Mobile pretty much became the key base of operations. Hangar II would house the "Crescendo Summit," the bend of the road where Roy Neary (Richard Dreyfuss) and others spot a series of small spacecraft sweeping by, and "the Notch," where Neary and Jillian Guiler (Melinda Dillon) find themselves hidden among the rocks at the base of Devils Tower, observing the events happening in the box canyon.

Alabama became the state of choice for a few exteriors as well. A house at 1613 Carlisle Drive East in Mobile was purchased by Columbia so that it could stand in for the Neary home, the most memorable use of it showing Neary in his bathrobe pulling up bushes and shoveling dirt in manic fashion to build his visionary "mountain" in his rec room. The neighborhood was fairly new at the time, which meant there were several other houses on the block not yet occupied. An office building in downtown Mobile was used for the Air Force debriefing scene in which the military attempts to quickly debunk the claims of Neary and other witnesses. Over on the other side of Mobile Bay, east of Highway 181, in the town of Fairhope, was the farmhouse from which Jillian's young son, Barry (Cary Guffey), is abducted by aliens. The evacuation scene, with several frantic locals being ushered onto a train in order to get them away from the faux gas attack near Devils Tower, was filmed in another Alabama location, Bay Minette. The railroad crossing where Roy has his initial UFO encounter, with all the metal within his truck losing gravity, was also shot in Mobile. All of this shooting was happening between May 31 and Labor Day of 1976.

Prior to this, the production had unofficially begun at the tail end of 1975 simply for the sake of allowing the participants who were putting up some of the money (Time Inc. and EMI, Ltd. would end up providing some $7 million of the budget) to write their investments off on their taxes. The scene at what is supposed to be the Indianapolis Air Traffic Control Center—where controllers listen to reports from a pilot of possible UFO sightings—was shot in an actual air traffic facility in Palmdale, California, on December 29 and 30.

The official start of filming began on May 17, 1976, around Devils Tower National Monument in the northeast corner of Wyoming. Needing an imposing and unforgettable natural formation that would ingrain itself in the subconscious of Roy Neary and the other witnesses, Spielberg ended up choosing one of the most distinctive sites in the American West, a 1,267-foot-tall laccolith butte whose flat top looked as if the upper portion of the rock edifice had been sculpted off in a clean slice. It was, in fact, the very first US site to be officially declared a National

Lineman Roy Neary (Richard Dreyfuss) is dazzled by the extraterrestrial light in *Close Encounters of the Third Kind*, filmed in Mobile, Alabama.

Monument, seventy years before *Close Encounters* would set up camp there. The already striking formation became that much more famous with the release of the movie and would forever be unequivocally identified with it. Neary's approach to the site and the efforts by the military to stop him were shot on and around Highway 24, while a base camp where the army attempts to remove Neary and the others from the premises by helicopter was built near the monument. There were also scenes shot on a rocky incline around the tower when Roy, Jillian, and another witness, Larry Butler (Josef Sommer), are being chased by the authorities.

Following the shoot in Alabama there were still key sequences to be filmed, including Lacombe (Francois Truffaut) and his team encountering a huge crowd of people chanting the five-note *Close Encounters* signal repeatedly. After multiple postponements, this scene, which climaxed with the crowd pointing upward to the sky in unison, was captured in late February of 1977 on a hill outside the village of Hal, in India, about thirty-five miles from Bombay. Portions of the police car chase, which ended with a dangerous stunt involving one of the vehicles breaking through a guard rail and landing with a crash below, was done in San Pedro, California. (The Vincent Thomas Bridge toll booths there were used for the gag of the UFOs zipping through.) While massive amounts of special effects work, overseen by Douglas Trumbull, were being created and perfected at his Future General company in Marina del Rey, Spielberg had come up with a new opening for the picture which required yet another location, El Mirage Dry Lake in the Mojave Desert, where Lacombe and his team are brought to see a collection of World War II bombers that have miraculously reappeared, decades later, looking brand new.

The radio telescope lab, where amateur interpreter David Laughlin (Bob Balaban) figures out that the numbers being transmitted from the aliens are in fact map coordinates was created at the Burbank Studios ranch, while the actual Burbank Studios was finally utilized after all: its woodworking mill on the lot became the building where Major Walsh (Warren Kemmerling) plots the poison gas hoax and a team of pilgrims in red jump suits board a bus that takes them to the Wyoming rendezvous. Insomuch as special effects, as well as various last minute efforts to shape and tweak the whole thing, were still going on right up to the November 1977 opening, and because Spielberg ended up filming yet more footage for the revised, 1980 reissue of the picture, *Close Encounters* certainly ranked as the longest shoot of his career.

1941

Considering the deliberately over-the-top, artificial nature of *1941*, it's strange to think that Steven Spielberg originally contemplated doing some location work at the actual intersection of Hollywood and Vine. Hoping to redress the standing buildings to look as they did at the outbreak of World War II, he then planned on staging the crash of a fighter plane on the spot. This, along with the fact that the planned schedule would shut the busy area down for a ten-day stretch and end up costing the production some $1.5 million, caused everyone to reconsider. *1941* was a period piece, a live-action cartoon, a potential art director's dream; so why not just use as many backlots, special effects, and studio soundstages, and as much matte work, as possible?

While Spielberg had the backing of both studios for which he'd recently directed their biggest box office hits, Universal (*Jaws*) and Columbia (*Close Encounters*), it was at the latter's studio where the bulk of the filming would be done. (The production base of operations, however, where much of the building of the sets and props took place, was in an empty airplane hangar at Lockheed in

For those anxious to know how they broke all those props, there was a Ballantine book about the making of *1941*.

Burbank.) At that time Columbia was no longer headquartered in the Sunset and Gower facility that it would have occupied in 1941, but instead it had combined forces with Warner Bros. in order to alleviate their financial problems, moving into the Warner Bros. lot in Burbank in 1971. The lot was officially renamed the Burbank Studios.

Shooting did not, however, officially begin here, but at MGM in Culver City. Needing a massive water tank, the production took over the largest of these at any of the studios, on Stage 30, most famous for being used in various Esther Williams water ballets over the years. Here a miniature (measuring 90 × 110 feet) of Ocean Park Amusement Pier was constructed over the tank, with detailed reproductions of buildings measuring to scale—a half inch for every foot. A twenty-seven-foot model of a Japanese submarine was built in the tank for the sequence near the close of the film, when an eager Commander Mitamura (Toshiro Mifune) and his crew start firing shells at the mostly empty park and at the hapless air-raid wardens (played by Murray Hamilton and Eddie Deezen in roles originally envisioned for Jackie Gleason and Art Carney) trapped in a stationary Ferris wheel. The wheel, designed to be the centerpiece of the scene, was eleven feet tall, and was required to be shot from its hinges by the enemy and then roll, much like a tire, down the pier and into the water. Filming began on October 28, 1978, with this entire set and the special effects required to pull off the scene costing the production $1 million.

Photography involving actual cast members began on November 16 at Indian Dunes, located north of Santa Clarita and Magic Mountain amusement park, where the base camp for gung-ho Colonel "Madman" Maddox (Warren Oates) was set up. Because this area contained its own landing strip, Spielberg was able to stage loco Wild Bill Kelso's (John Belushi) arrival and his clumsy exit, which not only included an unscripted pratfall by the actor off the plane's wing (kept in the finished print) but his aircraft hitting a tower as it exited. This 200-acre location—one frequently used by filmmakers needing foliage, a running stream, or wide vistas without nearby buildings or lights to interfere—would enter notoriety as the site where the fatal helicopter crash occurred in the summer of 1982 during the filming of the John Landis segment of *Twilight Zone the Movie*. (The site closed in 1990.)

As an in-joke for those in the know, Spielberg returned to his roots to film the scene in which Kelso lands his plane on a desert highway in search of gas, utilizing the very same service station and café in Aqua Dulce, California, at which Dennis Weaver had encountered cages of snakes and tarantulas in *Duel*. To further emphasize the connection, the actress who had run the stop in that 1971 TV movie, Lucille Benson, was reprising her duties here.

Having dismantled the Ocean Park miniature, MGM's Stage 30 now made room for a full-size submarine hull, which allowed for another in-joke, the best in the film (and for many the funniest part of the picture). The same stuntwoman, Susan Backlinie, who had taken the fatal swim in the opening scene of *Jaws*, was summoned to reenact a similar moment, a gag thought up not by the screenwriters, Robert Zemeckis and Bob Gale, but Spielberg himself. This time the threatening underwater menace was not a shark but the periscope of the Japanese vessel, around which Backlinie was required to wrap herself, her body parts strategically arranged to hide her nudity, and be raised high above the soundstage pool. While all scenes set on the surfaced deck of the vessel were done here, the submarine's interior was built on a soundstage at the Burbank Studios.

Realizing the inconvenience of their original plan, Hollywood Boulevard would now rise on the backlot at the Burbank Studios, with the standing New York Street set redressed to look like 1940s Los Angeles, adorned with Christmas decorations including multiple Santas hoisted over the street, one of which was needed to collapse on Sgt. Tree (Dan Aykroyd) during the big fight scene, which required some 650 extras.

In addition to the outside of the U.S.O. club, this set would have, as its centerpiece, the facade of an old movie palace, the Hollywood State Theatre, the marquee of which would announce the showing of Disney's *Dumbo*. The interior of the theater, in which General Stilwell (Robert Stack) takes time out from military obligations to tearfully watch the flying elephant cavort on screen, was shot in the actual Los Angeles Theatre in the downtown area. While the real Stilwell had made reference to seeing this movie during the events fictionalized for *1941*, the filmmakers took artistic liberties with the facts. There was no Hollywood State Theater on Hollywood Boulevard, nor could *Dumbo* actually be seen in downtown Hollywood on the date the story was taking place. The animated feature did not have its Los Angeles premiere until the following week, on December 19, and was shown in two venues elsewhere in the vicinity, the Carthay Circle and the United Artists Theater.

The Hollywood Boulevard set was the location for a daring stunt in which a replica of Wild Bell's P-40 Warhawk airplane was supposed to crash following a dogfight. This required a 150-foot wooden ramp—which would launch the vehicle and allow it to skid onto the street and stop short of actually destroying portions of the facades—to be built across from one of the studio parking lots. When Spielberg found himself disappointed by the stunt, he ordered the ramp extended another hundred feet and the whole scene restaged for greater impact at a cost of a half-million dollars, one of too many examples of how freely money was tossed around on the production in hopes of giving the audiences more bang for their buck.

Rather than erect a set on a soundstage, the company chose instead to redress to period perfection an actual former nightclub in a residential section of Los Angeles to stand in for the U.S.O. club. Here were staged various snappy dance numbers and a fight between opposing military members, which included a Rube Goldberg sight gag with various objects falling into one another in a chain of mayhem and an unbilled guest bit by James Caan, clad in sailor blues, to help start the altercation. Similarly, a U.S.O. hostess was played by *Laverne & Shirley* star Penny Marshall, who also received no mention in the closing credits.

Long Beach Airport provided the airfield for the scene in which General Stilwell is startled by a bomb during his speech. Six T6 Trainers were rented from a skywriting team, and three B-25 Mitchell Bombers (one of which had been one of Eisenhower's planes) dressed the set, as well as a B-17 bomber plane, lent from an air force museum, in which Captain Birkhead (Tim Matheson) and Stilwell's secretary, Donna Stratton (Nancy Allen), have one of their rendezvous, their fumbling causing that bomb to roll out of the hatch.

Back at the Burbank Studios, additional soundstages were occupied by sets recreating the rooftops over Hollywood Boulevard, including one on which were positioned, surrounded by sandbags, characters named after Bill Mauldin's famous WWII cartoon soldiers, Willie and Joe. These were played by two more cast members from *Laverne & Shirley*, Michael McKean and David Lander, in blink-and-you-miss-'em cameos. A twelve-foot high section of the Ferris wheel was built indoors in order to shoot close-ups of Hamilton and Deezen (with his ventriloquist dummy, operated from out of sight by Jerry Layne), as well as a full-size operational one. Also done on the lot was the Inceptor Command center, which featured a quick appearance by famed filmmaker Samuel Fuller. For scenes taking place inside of the tank containing Aykroyd's motley crew (consisting of John Candy, J. Patrick McNamara, and a pre-stardom Mickey Rourke in his motion picture debut), a soundstage over at CBS Studio City studios was used. For the scene in which Birkhead and Donna crash their plane into the La Brea Tar Pits, a pond that made up part of the standing set for the ongoing television series *The Waltons* was utilized, with the water replaced by bentonite in order to give it a muckier, mud-like appearance.

The main non-studio location was that of the Douglas House—built at a cost of $260,000 in a section of Malibu called Nicolas Canyon County Beach and situated on a cliff overlooking the ocean. After misdirected chaos, which required Ward Douglas (Ned Beatty) to pilot a 40 mm antiaircraft gun and thereby lay havoc to his own home, the entire structure was dropped off the cliff to provide the movie with its all too fitting apocalyptic climax. Most of the cast principals were assembled on the cliffside in order to be seen in the swooping helicopter shot that capped the picture, but rethinking the storyline meant that both Slim Pickens (as a civilian taken prisoner) and Christopher Lee (as the German officer in league with the Japanese) could be spotted, despite the fact that the continuity gave no reason for how they got there, the latter having been dropped over the side of the submarine by his Japanese "allies," presumably to perish.

All of this filming was still going on as of late spring of 1979, with further shots done at a vacant building so that Spielberg could stage a gag of Sgt. Tree's tank crashing through a paint factory, getting covered with a rainbow of colors, only to take another detour into a turpentine factory, thereby emerging onto the street spotless. Another highly detailed miniature was built on the Burbank Studios' Soundstage 15 of Hollywood Boulevard, so that one of the most impressive special effects scenes in the movie could be carried off, as the planes piloted by Wild Bill and Birkhead engage in an impromptu dogfight over the famed strip. Mini versions of the aircraft were strung along wires in order to make them spin and flip like actual working planes. Also constructed in miniature was a model of the landscape of the Los Angeles basin. The shoot would cease after some 247 days at a cost of $27 million. It had been a goal of Steven Spielberg's to make a movie in which he could basically "break a lot of stuff." At this, he had succeeded.

Raiders of the Lost Ark

The adventures of a globetrotting hero were, of course, going to require some globetrotting, so the world's first Indiana Jones epic found him cavorting on all kinds of sets and locations passing themselves off as someplace else altogether.

Needing a submarine for the sequence in which the Nazis catch up with Indy (Harrison Ford) and Marion (Karen Allen) aboard a pirated cargo boat, the production realized the title vessel of the not-yet-released German film *Das Boot* (which would not have its US theatrical premiere until February of 1982, several months after the opening of *Raiders*) was available for use in La Rochelle on the western coast of France. Although it had not intended to add this country to the original schedule, the production commenced shooting here on June 23, 1980, with not only scenes of the Nazis overtaking the *Bantu Wind* and stealing back the ark but also with Indy swimming to the sub and boarding it, to the cheers of the *Bantu* crew; the ark being unloaded in the sub-pen after it reaches the Nazi island hideout (where Indy overpowers two different guards in order to secure a uniform); and Indy and Marion bidding goodbye to Sallah (John Rhys-Davies) on the docks prior to boarding the ship. France therefore was pretending to be Egypt, and the Passage of Antioch was passing itself off as the Mediterranean.

Following this stopover, the production took up eight of the nine soundstages at EMI Elstree Studios in Borehamwood, England, starting on June 30. It was here that producer George Lucas had shot much of *Star Wars* and had been very pleased with the British crews and facilities. Among the many interiors created by production designer Norman Reynolds was the Peruvian Temple (shot on Stage 4) that Jones and his greedy accomplice, Satipo (Alfred Molina), dare to enter in the opening sequence, packed for maximum atmospheric dread with tarantulas, maggots, blow dart walls, cobwebs, hidden spikes, a rolling boulder, a bottomless chasm, and a booby-trapped pedestal for the target of Indy's hunt, the golden Chachapoyan fertility idol. On Stage 3 was built another of Reynolds's memorable sets, the Well of Souls—the subterranean location of the ark, guarded by a pair of towering Egyptian statues and, more ominously, a "moving" floor consisting of snakes of all shapes and varieties, numbering somewhere between 6,500 to 10,000, depending on the source. Although Harrison Ford and Karen Allen were required to wade among them, their face-to-face confrontation with a hooded cobra was filmed with a protective sheet of glass between them.

Elsewhere at the studio, among the various stages, were the sets for: Imam's (Tutte Lemkow) house, where Sallah stops Indy from swallowing a poisoned date in the nick of time, while an evil Nazi monkey ends up less fortunate; the Map Room, where Indy is able to pinpoint the precise location of the ark on a miniature of the city of Tanis using the Staff of Ra; a portion of the warehouse where the ark ends up among hundreds of other questionable crates (the bulk of the final shot was done with a matte painting accomplished later on, fashioned around the image of actor Fred Gambia as the porter pushing the cart); the catacombs where Marion has a hellish encounter with some aged cadavers; Marion's Nepalese tavern, which goes up in flames after the creepy Toht (Ronald Lacey) and his goons try to get hold of the valuable medallion/headpiece needed to locate the ark; the cabin of the *Bantu Wind*, with Indy playfully coaxing a kiss on the lips from Marion while directing her to other parts on his body that are *not* hurting; the tent at the digging site where Marion is being held prisoner by Belloq (Paul Freeman); Indy's house, for a brief meeting with his colleague, Marcus Brody (Denholm Elliott); the nighttime sequence with Indy, Sallah, and their aides unearthing the entrance to the Wells of Souls (because a mystical, stormy sky was envisioned for the background, this meant the shot could be done indoors, with a blue screen behind the actors with the effects added later); and the altar where Belloq and the Nazis foolishly open the ark as Indy and Marion are tied, back to back, to a pillar. This

Indiana Jones (Harrison Ford) must contend with his greatest fear, snakes, as he and his accomplice, Sallah (John Rhys-Davies), find themselves in the Well of Souls, filmed on Stage 3 at EMI Elstree Studios in England.

last set required only the base portion to be built. The sky and surrounding area beyond the rocks was later matted in, as were, of course, the visual effects for the unexpected and apocalyptic destruction that erupts for one of the many scenes that made the movie so thoroughly satisfying for audiences.

During the stay in England, the production spent some time at the Royal Masonic School for Girls in Rickmansworth, Hertsfordshire, located about a half hour to the west of Elstree Studios. This provided the classroom for Professor Jones, where he is amusingly flirted with by a female student with "love you" written on her eyelids, and he is also given an apple by a shy male student, who may or may not have similar feelings for the teacher, depending on your interpretation of the moment; the assembly hall, where Indy and Marcus meet with the government officials who want the former to find the ark before the Nazis do; and the (D.C.) war office, where Indy finds himself deeply dissatisfied with the same officials when they will not provide him with direct answers to what is going to happen to the ark. Shooting in England finished up on August 29.

Starting on September 1, the company relocated to Tunisia, which was filling in for Egypt. The main set, covering some one hundred acres was the Tanis dig, in Sedada, near Tozeur. Tozuer was where the airstrip was built for the Flying Wing Nazi airplane to be positioned during a battle between Indy and a hulking, bald mechanic (Pat Roach), as Marion tries to free herself from the gunner turret on the wing. (The pilot Karen Allen was seen knocking out at the start of the sequence was the movie's producer, Frank Marshall.) There were also further scenes staged here inside of the tent where Marion is held captive, including an amusing gag with Toht involving a seemingly threatening torture apparatus that turns out to be nothing more than a coat hanger (a joke once intended for *1941*).

Before the principals and key crew arrived in Tunisia, second unit director Michael Moore had already begun shooting what would turn out to be perhaps the most stunning, tour de force sequence in the movie, Indiana's determined attempt to board the truck containing the ark and capture it back from Belloq and his Nazi cohorts. Closely following the storyboards Steven Spielberg had designed, shooting began on August 21 with a specially built truck made to resemble an American GMC from the past, although it wasn't exactly an accurate one to the time frame of the film, as it looked more like a 1943 model. Stunt men filled in for Harrison Ford, including, most unforgettably, Terry Leonard, who wowed the company as well as film fans for decades to come when he risked inching his way under the moving truck before being dragged behind it while holding on to a whip. It was moments like this that so captured the fancy of the millions who kept turning out for *Raiders* that following summer.

Ford would join this unit in mid-September to enact his close-ups during the chase, gladly jumping into many daredevil shots that might have scared off many other stars. All of the truck sequences were shot near Metlaoui, mostly on Paradise Road. In Kairouan, television aerials were removed by the film unit so that they could pass the city off as Cairo, circa 1936, as seen from the terrace of Sallah's home. This town also provided the settings for Indy's encounter with Belloq at a bar; the bazaar where Jones desperately knocks over some baskets in hopes of finding Marion in one; and Omar's Garage, where Indy manages to hide the truck from the flummoxed Nazis with the help of some locals. As fitting as the country was for the settings needed, the shoot became a difficult one, simply because the average temperature would surpass one hundred degrees on a typical day, causing fatigue and illness among an exorbitant number of cast and crew members. This also caused Spielberg to streamline some scenes that would have required more time in the sun and more complicated shots. As a result, one of the best remembered and funniest moments in the entire movie came out of this eagerness to move on from the location, when a fight with a towering Arab in the marketplace was dispensed with, Indy instead wearily shooting him with his gun after the imposing fellow has shown off a flashy display of swordplay.

From September 30 through October 9, 1980, the production filmed at Halemano Falls at Puhi on the island of Kuai in Hawaii for the opening sequence supposedly taking place in the jungles of Peru. The wonderfully old-fashioned "starry" introduction of Indiana Jones (coming forth from the shadows) was filmed in front of the waterfalls here, while this was also the location of the entrance to the booby-trapped temple and of the chase by the Hovitos warriors leading to Indy's getaway plane. The biplane was situated on the Huleia River, pretending to be the Urubamba River. Principal photography was wrapped fifteen days early, but there were additional shots added down the line.

While the special effects were being dealt with at George Lucas's Industrial Light & Magic studio, Harrison Ford reported to the Richmond Marina (north of Berkeley, California) in November of 1980 to film Indy leaving for his trip aboard a China Clipper (actually the *Solent IV* built by Howard Hughes), unaware that he is being followed. In January of 1981, Ford and Allen filmed the penultimate scene in the movie, where Indiana and Marion leave what is supposed to be a Washington, D.C., government building, utilizing San Francisco's City Hall instead.

E.T. the Extra-Terrestrial

While *Raiders of the Lost Ark* kept bringing in the customers in such record-breaking numbers that it redeemed Steven Spielberg from the bungle of *1941* and turned him, yet again, into Hollywood's golden boy, the filmmaker quietly began production on his follow-up feature. Envisioning something on a smaller scale than his last three projects, Spielberg hoped to shoot his new science fiction tale swiftly and efficiently, without too much information being leaked in advance. Indeed, the title was initially released to the press as the generic *A Boy's Life*, which sounded more like a cub scouts adventure, and those involved in the production were sworn to secrecy, although one source at the time had this to say: "It's about a group of kids who find an alien and hide it from their parents by keeping it in a closet." This blunt summation wasn't accurate to a fault, insomuch as the kids in question no longer had a father in their lives, but otherwise put the matter in a nutshell, for those who like things that way. It was, of course, how Spielberg told the story that made it all matter.

The production did not even utilize the studio facilities of the company that was releasing it, Universal; Spielberg instead chose to head south and set up shop at what had started life back in 1918 as the Culver Studios, built by silent film pioneer

Thomas Ince. In the intervening years the facility had gone through a plethora of different names dependent on who was in residence, most famously Selznick International (*Gone with the Wind* was shot there) and Desilu-Culver (purchased by Lucille Ball and Desi Arnaz). At the time *E.T.* filmed there, it went under the name Laird International Studios. (It is presently, once again, called Culver Studios.) Three sound stages on the lot were used. One was filled entirely by a faux forest that served as the landing site of E.T.'s spaceship as it appeared at the start and finish of the picture, with the spaceman and his fellow travelers searching for plant specimens before having to hightail it off the planet when the authorities arrive. Another stage held the downstairs and backyard of Elliott's home, the latter location being where the boy and his unearthly friend first meet, when the latter tosses back a baseball from a shed and then is coaxed into following Elliott (Henry Thomas) by a trail of Reece's Pieces. (It has been extensively reported that M&M seriously messed up by not cashing in on this phenomenal bit of product placement when they turned down the offer to participate on the basis of E.T. being too "ugly" to be associated with.) The third stage housed the upstairs bedrooms, most importantly Elliott's, which contained that aforementioned closet in which E.T. hid among a profusion of stuffed animals in one of the movie's funniest scenes.

Shooting began on September 8, 1981, with the Culver City High School on Elenda Street, less than two miles west of the studio, filling in for Elliott's grammar

White Oak Avenue in Granada Hills, California, was "elevated" to cinematic immortality when Steven Spielberg chose it for a key moment during the big chase scene in *E.T. the Extra-Terrestrial*. Left to right: Michael (Robert McNaughton), Tyler (Tom Howell), Greg (K. C. Martel), Elliott (Henry Thomas), and E.T.

school, where he manages to get drunk through his symbiotic connection with his boarding space alien; unleashes a science class full of frogs; and kisses a pretty girl (Erika Eleniak) because E.T. is home watching a key scene from John Ford's *The Quiet Man* on television. A sequence with Harrison Ford playing the principal of the school was planned but dropped, as was screenwriter Melissa Mathison's appearance as a school nurse.

For the exteriors of Elliott's neighborhood, Spielberg took his production up to the San Fernando Valley to the town of Porter Ranch, about a half-hour drive northwest of Universal City. The streets of this town were home to the bus stop scene in which Elliott is taunted by his brother's friends; the famous Halloween sequence in which E.T. is hidden under a ghost sheet as he reacts favorably to a child dressed as Yoda from the *Star Wars* saga; and the climactic chase, first with the stolen van and then with the police authorities chasing Elliott, Michael (Robert McNaughton), and Michael's friends on their bicycles. This last sequence includes a trip through Porter Ridge Park, past a distinctive caterpillar playset which remains there to this day. For the most memorable scene in the chase, however, in which Elliott and his fellow cyclists are suddenly elevated by E.T. while being pursued by the determined authorities, White Oak Avenue in Granada Hills, a few miles south of Porter Ranch, was used. A then-undeveloped area overlooking Porter Ranch, where Gertie (Drew Barrymore) is seen waiting to change places with E.T., has since become Stewarton Drive. Another elevated area, Wilbur Tampa Park, was where "Keys" (Peter Coyote) and his team first see the town where the alien visitor is being sheltered. Wanting a house with a mountain looming behind it, Spielberg went further east to Tujunga, where he found the perfect dwelling to play Elliott's home, hidden back from the road at the top of a long driveway, at 7121 Lonzo Street. Scenes of vehicles leaving this site were edited together with the Porter Ranch locations.

Interspersed with soundstage recreations was Redwood National Park in Crescent City, California, for Elliott's memorable flight into the forest to help E.T. contact his home planet. At nearby Little Mill Creek, the sad moment when Michael encounters the hapless alien lying face down, hanging on to his last bit of life, was filmed.

The production wrapped in early December of 1981, four days ahead of schedule, followed by the necessary special effects work that included the image that came to define Steven Spielberg's entire career and became his Amblin Entertainment logo: Elliott flying his bicycle past a full moon with E.T. hidden in the basket on the handlebars. While this was going on in early 1982, the title was finally announced as *E.T. the Extra-Terrestrial*, although the picture became so famous, so thoroughly a part of pop culture and motion picture history, that only the first two initials needed be spoken for instant recognition.

Twilight Zone: The Movie

Steven Spielberg's twenty-one-minute contribution to the cursed multi-storied *Twilight Zone* feature was meant to look small and simple, with a good deal of the action taking place either inside a senior citizens' home or on its surrounding property. Rest home interiors and the nighttime game of "Kick the Can," in which the elderly residents suddenly find themselves transformed back into their younger selves, were done on the Burbank Studios (Warner Bros.) soundstages. For the daylight exteriors of the Sunnyvale Rest Home, which included the sequence of the hapless Leo Conroy (Bill Quinn) being rejected once again by his son, and the finale, in which the mysterious Mr. Bloom (Scatman Crothers) departs after bestowing his wisdom on most of the residents, the Colonial Revival-style Heritage Valley Inn (built in 1888) at 691 North Main Street in the town of Piru, California, about an hour northwest of the studio, was selected. Around the corner, a house on Church Street became Mr. Bloom's next destination, a convalescent home called Driftwood.

Indiana Jones and the Temple of Doom

For the eagerly anticipated second "chapter" in the intended Indiana Jones trilogy, Steven Spielberg and George Lucas chose to actually step *back* in time, setting the second installment one year before *Raiders of the Lost Ark*, in 1935. The original title was *Indiana Jones and the Temple of Death*, which should have tipped off those who suddenly decided to be all bent out of shape about the movie's darker tone, and the intended principal location was to be India. *Death* became *Doom*, and although the setting for the story remained India, that country had too many demands regarding Willard Huyck and Gloria Katz's screenplay, so the production went elsewhere for its backdrops. Before shooting proper commenced, the second unit journeyed to Macao to shoot exteriors for the rickshaw-Dusenberg chase that was supposed to be taking place in Shanghai, outside of the Obi Wan nightclub.

From April 18 to May 2, 1983, the *Doom* group filmed in Sri Lanka, which, in movie history, had most famously served as the location for David Lean's Academy Award-winning *The Bridge on the River Kwai* back in 1957, when the country was known as Ceylon. The Oodewella and Hantana tea plantations in Kandy stood in for the Mayapore Hills (which included the elephant-riding scenes) where two versions of the village (prosperous and decimated) from which the children have been stolen by the Thugee villains were constructed. The Kandy River was used for the end of Indy (Harrison Ford), Short Round (Ke Huy Quan) and Willie's (Kate Capshaw) river journey, where the Shayman (D. R. Nanayakkara) spots them from the riverbank. Near Victoria Dam, portions of the thrilling rope bridge climax were shot.

Returning to EMI Elstree Studios in Borehamwood, England, where *Raiders* had been shot, the production took up eight of the facility's nine soundstages for the many interior sets. Shooting began here on May 6 and continued through July 15. Sets included the campsite where Willie keeps encountering various jungle critters while an oblivious Indy and Short Round converse (this replaced an intended boa constrictor scene that was disposed of because leading lady Kate Capshaw found herself in a total state of discomfort trying to work with the reptile); the Pleasure Pavilion, which provided the movie with one of its funniest "gross-out" scenes, with Indy and company expected to dine on such delicacies as chilled monkey brains (the "brains" actually consisted of custard with raspberry sauce) with their Pankot Palace hosts; the terrifying temple altar (a fantastic creation by production designer Elliot Scott, built on Stage 2) used for sacrificing the hapless victims into the fire below; the Palace interiors that included Indy's and Willie's guest suites; Mola Ram's chamber; and the interior of the nightclub in which Willie and her chorus girls perform an unforgettable rendition of "Anything Goes" in Mandarin. Stage 6 housed the elaborate roller coaster-like mining tunnels and tracks, as well as the quarry cavern where the hapless youngsters are held under the lash by their captives (nasty images that prompted some of the more unforgiving complaints from those who found the movie too dark for their tastes).

During filming, leading man Harrison Ford was rendered unavailable because of back problems, requiring him to leave the production in order to have an operation done back in Los Angeles. Spielberg shot around him as much as possible, either concentrating on moments that did not require Ford on camera or by using a double, as was frequently in evidence in the fight between Indy and a muscular Thuggee in the quarry cavern. After a while it was simply too difficult to keep working around the movie's protagonist and the production actually shut down for a three-week period. Over in California, Spielberg's *E.T.* cinematographer, Allen Daviau, shot the raft's plunge from the faulty airplane and its run down a

A mine car becomes a treacherous rollercoaster as Short Round (Ke Huy Quan), Willie Scott (Kate Capshaw), and Indiana Jones (Harrison Ford) try to flee the pursuing Thuggees in *Indiana Jones and the Temple of Doom*. The coaster tracks were built on Stage 6 of EMI Elstree Studios.

snowy mountainside at Mammoth Mountain Crest's Ridge Run ski area. For the moment of the raft flying into the air before landing in the river, Lumsden Bridge at the Tuolomne River was chosen.

When Ford became available again, filming resumed at EMI Elstree, with the tunnel exit, the cliffside, and the rope bridge created on the backlot for the battle between Mola Ram and Indy over the crocodile-infested river. Also built there was the courtyard of the Pankot Palace for Indy, Willie, and Short Round's arrival, and the liberation of the captive children. For the scenes set inside the cargo plane, a stage at the Industrial Light and Magic studio back in California was utilized. The Hamilton Airforce Base in Novato, north of San Rafael, became the site of the departure of the cargo plane from Nang-Tao Airfield, which included a visible cameo by a British-accented Dan Aykroyd. ("Unfortunately, you will be riding on a cargo of *live* poultry.") That same scene featured Spielberg, Lucas, and producer Frank Marshall dressed in period costumes to play extras, although to the uninformed viewer they are hardly noticeable in the finished print.

Principal photography came to an end on August 26, 1983, although there were later inserts done in the California Sierras for the raft scene, alligator footage for the treacherous plunge from the rope bridge shot at the Gatorland Zoo and Alligator Farm in St. Augustine, Florida, and an abundance of special effects trickery done at ILM.

The Color Purple

This is an outstanding example of how efficient Steven Spielberg had become as a filmmaker. It is highly impressive to think that he shot this film over the summer of 1985—encompassing a little less than three months—and had the whole thing edited, scored, and ready to go for Christmastime, handing world audiences one of the best pictures of the year.

After scouting various southern locations, including the book's setting of Alabama, the filmmaker settled on North Carolina. But before the company moved east, he scheduled interior shots to be done at Universal Studios over a three-week period so that he could be present when his partner, Amy Irving, gave birth to their child. Filming began at the lot on June 5, 1985, with scenes set inside Harpo's (Willard Pugh) "jook" joint, upstairs rooms at Mr. ____ 's (Danny Glover) house, and the bedroom at Pa Harris's (Leonard Jackson) house for the birth of young Celie's (Desreta Jackson) child, coincidentally recorded the very day, June 13, the Spielberg-Irving offspring, Max, arrived.

During July and August the company was stationed in Anson County, North Carolina, the main location being a farmhouse built by one of the county's wealthiest citizens, James Bennett, on Diggs Road in Wadesboro in 1835. At the time of filming, it was owned by a family named Huntley but had been vacant for years. Having leased the property over a six-month period, six weeks were spent landscaping it so that fields of tobacco would grow along with pearl millet and sunflowers. This would serve as Mr. ____ 's farm, where Celie comes to live and basically endures years of abuse and indentured servitude from her bullying husband and his ungrateful children. Indeed, at first sight of the place, the hapless woman has

Whoopi Goldberg receives direction from Steven Spielberg on the Wadesboro, North Carolina, set of *The Color Purple*.

a rocked heaved at her head by one of the abominable brats. Needing another house not too far away to serve as Harpo and Sofia's (Oprah Winfrey) home, one was built from scratch and then converted into the "jook" joint at which Shug Avery (Margaret Avery) sings her song of devotion to now grown-up Celie (Whoopi Goldberg) in one of the movie's most memorable scenes. The church where Shug brings her fellow singers in order to finally confront her father (John Patton Jr.) was a building transported to the property.

All of the scenes taking place in town were shot in and around North White Street in Marshville, North Carolina, approximately a half hour west of the Wadesboro farm. These included the exterior of the general store where Celie first sees the baby she knows is the one she was forced to give away. The streets were covered with dirt to give the location a more antiquated feel, and it was here that Sofia had her unfortunate encounter with the Mayor (Phillip Strong) and where the deliriously self-involved Miss Millie (Dana Ivey) did her reckless driving.

A second unit was sent to Masai country in Kenya to film shots of Nettie's life in Africa, with Spielberg's trusted producer, Frank Marshall, directing these scenes.

Empire of the Sun

Steven Spielberg had the tremendous advantage of being able to film his adaptation of J. G. Ballard's Shanghai-based novel in the city itself, becoming the first major production from the West to do so. Because the city had changed so little in the forty-six years since the story took place, actual authentic backdrops could be photographed and still be passed off as 1941. Therefore, the former Hong Kong and Shanghai Banking Corporation (HSBC) building (and later offices of the Shanghai municipal government), the huge structure looming over the massive exodus through the streets of the city in the waterfront area known as the Bund, was true to the period, having been completed in 1923. Filming began in this area on March 2, 1987.

For a three-week period Spielberg and company shot in Shanghai. Additional locations there included the pyramid-topped Peace Hotel (once called the Cathay, as in the film) at Nanjing Road, where young Jim (Christian Bale) innocently signals to a ship in the harbor only to be stunned by a blast, signaling the beginning of the Japanese takeover; the Waibaidu Bridge, connecting the Huangpu and Hongkew districts, where Jim and his family, while clad in their masquerade costumes, are chauffeured through the crowd of destitute and desperate Chinese citizens; and Sgt. Ignatius Cathedral (Xujahui Catholic Church), where the chauffeurs of the wealthy, displaced Brits wait outside while Jim and his schoolmates finish singing the choral number "Guo San." The Capitol Theatre at Chapoo Road was shown hosting the 1939 remake of *The Hunchback of Notre Dame*, although Ballard's book had accurately described it as premiering in the city at the Cathay Theatre. Because the unit needed to indicate that bombs had gone off in the city, they created their own fake "smoke" by burning rubber tires in the area of Fen Yang Road. This incident resulted in such an overabundance of temporary air pollution that the movie wound up with some unwanted publicity when Warner Bros. was fined $13,500 by the city.

During the evacuation of Shanghai, Jim (Christian Bale) comes to the terrifying realization that he's been separated from his parents in this scene from *Empire of the Sun*, filmed in a section of the city known as The Bund.

It was then over to England, where, beyond shooting some interiors at Elstree Studios, Legh Road in Knutsford, Cheshire, passed itself off as the avenue on which the Graham family lived, this street having the same sort of architecture preferred by the expatriate Brits in the English settlement in Shanghai. The interiors of the Graham home were shot elsewhere, in the village of Sunningdale in Berkshire. For the scene in which Jim and hundreds of other captured English expats are placed in a factory-like detention center before being shipped to their prison camp, a building at the abandoned gasworks in Beckton in East London was utilized. Not long before this, Stanley Kubrick had used this same area to film a good deal of his Vietnam opus *Full Metal Jacket*.

Starting on April 22, the company moved the remainder of the shoot to Spain. There, nine miles southwest of Jereze de la Fontera, the Soochow prison camp facility was constructed, as was the nearby airfield where Jim enviously watches the kamikaze pilots taking off. Also constructed here was the stadium where the prisoners, following their release, come across a horde of stolen goods and valuables scattered carelessly on the field. The construction of these sites accounted for roughly a third of the $30 million budget.

Principal photography concluded on June 18, 1987, coming in five days ahead of schedule for a seventy-two-day shoot.

Indiana Jones and the Last Crusade

Steven Spielberg and George Lucas took a third trip to the Indiana Jones well to close out the decade and came up with yet another winner, allowing Indy (Harrison Ford) to globe-trot his way through some more striking locations, this time with his dad (Sean Connery). Originally conceived under the name *Indiana Jones and the Monkey King*, the finished product had nothing whatsoever to do with monkeys or kings. Several writers took a crack at developing George Lucas's ideas into a script: *The Color Purple*'s Menno Meyjes (who would end up with a story credit with Lucas), *Gremlins*' Chris Columbus, *Empire of the Sun*'s Tom Stoppard (under a pseudonym), and finally *Innerspace*'s Jeffrey Boam, who would deliver the goods and end up with sole screenwriter credit on the finished print.

Principal photography commenced on May 16, 1988, in Spain, which was able to sub for the city of Iskenderun (the former Alexandretta) in Turkey, as well as Germany. Through June 1, the company shot at Bellas Artes, which stood in for the Sultan of Hatay's (Alexei Sayle) palace; Almeira, for the street in Iskenderun, where Sallah (John Rhys-Davies) accidentally puts Marcus Brody (Denholm Elliott) into the truck of his kidnappers; Playa de Mónsul, southeast of Almeira, where one of the film's best sequences was staged, as Professor Jones improvises a clever ploy to bring down the Nazi airplane that is bent on killing him and his son, grabbing an umbrella and scaring a flock of seagulls (the actual birds used were doves) to fly upward into the path of the offending aircraft; Rodquilar, for the scene of the plane following Indiana and his dad into the tunnel, losing its wings in the process; an airfield in Mojacar, for the scene in which the Joneses crash their plane; and Guadix, for the Iskenderun railroad.

Between June 5 and August 5, the production returned to the same UK facilities used in the previous Indy films, Elstree Studios, on Shenley Road in Borehamwood. Here the interiors of Baron Brunwald's castle were created in order to catch fire during the memorable scene in which Indy and Dad are tied back-to-back. Also taking up various stages were the temple in which the climactic set piece takes place, with Indy carefully maneuvering the Jehovah stones and then encountering the ghost of the knight (Robert Eddison) in the grail room, and the abyss into which the duplicitous Elsa (Alison Doody) plunges, while Indy ends up rescued by his father. There were also the interior of the Biblioteca Nationale, where Indy figures out the clue of how to access the catacombs below; the catacombs themselves, which required dozen of rats to cause Indy and Elsa to squirm as they make their way to the knight's tomb; the deck of the Portuguese freighter *Coronado*, where Indy manages to retrieve the valuable cross that had been pinched from him as a teenager; Indy's school office; and Professor Jones's house, which ends up ransacked by his abductors. On the backlot were shot the motorcycle escape from the Baron's castle, and the tense moment when Indy slugs

Professor Jones (Sean Connery) and his son, Indiana (Harrison Ford), find themselves in another hair-raising dilemma, bound back-to-back in a burning Nazi castle in *Indiana Jones and the Last Crusade*, filmed at Elstree Studios in England.

it out with Kazim (Kevork Malikyan) aboard a motorboat as they get closer and closer to a giant propeller.

While in England, Spielberg and company dressed up the interior of the Royal Horticultural Halls and Conference Center at Vincent Square in Westminster to play the interior of Berlin's Tempelhof Airport. (The exterior was the headquarters of the US naval station on Treasure Island in San Francisco Bay.) As the backdrop of the Nazi's book-burning rally, at which Indy finds himself inadvertently receiving Adolf Hitler's autograph on his father's precious diary, the majestic and highly photogenic Blenheim Palace located in Woodstock, Oxfordshire, was chosen. This continued to become a highly desirable location over the years, appearing in everything from Kenneth Branagh's *Hamlet* (1996) to the Sean Connery romp *Entrapment* (1999), until Spielberg himself made a return visit for *The BFG*. The affluent UK suburb of Mill Hill in the London Borough of Barnet became the street outside of Professor Jones's home; the Tillbury Dock in Essex stood in for the Venice boat chase; and the Royal Masonic School in Rickmansworth once again played Dr. Jones's school, as it had in *Raiders*.

A single day of filming in Venice captured Indy and Brady meeting Dr. Snyder, who turns out to be the beautiful Elsa, and the exterior of the Bibiloteca, located on Campo San Barnaba, where Elsa and Indy make their way into the plaza through a manhole within the outdoor café. Moving on to Jordan, the journey to the hidden grail temple through the Siq, a narrow fissure in the surrounding cliffs, was shot in Patra in the Edom Mountains.

During the first part of September, the unit came to America to film the prologue, in which the audience is made privy to how their intrepid adventurer got his scar, his fedora, and his fear of snakes. The circus train chase and fight was filmed on a stretch of the Cumbres and Toltec Scenic Railroad in Colorado. The beginning of this sequence, with Young Indiana (River Phoenix) and his scout troop coming across the thieves in the cave, was done in Utah's Arches National Park. This allowed the filmmakers to photograph yet another peak for the famous Paramount logo to fade into, a clever bit of business that had started each Indy epic.

Although principal photography was considered finished by mid- to late September, Spielberg wanted more action for the picture and therefore came up with the idea of Indiana and his dad being pursued by the villains in a motorcycle and sidecar. Although this was supposed to be Germany, a more convenient wooded area was found in Fairfax, California, approximately twelve miles southwest of George Lucas's studio facilities at the Skywalker Ranch. At the start of 1989, one more pivotal moment was thought up, a spectacularly photographed ride into the sunset on horseback by Indiana, Professor Jones, Brady, and Sallah (or at least their stand-ins), which was shot near Amarillo, Texas.

The final cost of the two-hour-and-seven-minute movie (the longest of the Indy adventures) was $55,364,887, more than double the budget of *Raiders of the Lost Ark*, but it was well worth the investment. Perhaps even an Indiana Jones movie of inferior quality would still have brought in the crowds, but this one was better than anyone had any reason to expect, with the addition of Sean Connery as the older Jones, which not only added box office appeal but proved to be just the unique aspect that made this installment instantly standout and allow for deeper character development and a higher level of wit and humor.

Always

Filming commenced on Steven Spielberg's long cherished project, a remake of the 1943 MGM fantasy *A Guy Named Joe*, on May 15, 1989, a week and a half before *Indiana Jones and the Last Crusade* opened in theaters. Because he had become such an efficient filmmaker, this meant that he had every intention of shooting the picture and then shaping it in post-production to have it ready in time for the Christmas season. As a result, 1989 became the first year that his fans and followers would see *two* Steven Spielberg directorial credits released.

Taking the World War II-based story away from its military setting and revising it as a modern-day tale of aerial firefighters, Spielberg needed forest backdrops and therefore settled on the Pacific Northwest. An airfield seven miles south of the town of Libby, Montana, became the base of operations for the firefighting unit as seen in the opening scenes in which Pete (Richard Dreyfuss) and Al (John Goodman) fly their missions, and then Dorinda (Holly Hunter) takes up the plane to make Pete see just how nervous *his* recklessness makes *her*. The Kootenai National Forest north of the airfield became the setting for the firefighting scenes, with the film crew using a partially cleared area that had already been burned, as well as constructing forty-one nonflammable trees piped with propane, allowing them to set and reset fires to them according to the needed shots. These were also intercut with actual footage of real blazes recorded the previous year in Yellowstone National Park. The US Forestry Service worked closely with the company to ensure that nothing went up in flames for the sake of entertainment. Bull Lake, west of Libby, was used for the opening scene in which a pair of fishermen are startled by Pete nearly landing his plane on top of them, and for Dorinda's crash near the finale.

Spielberg's company went further west to the airfield at Ephrata, Washington, to portray the firefighters' training base in what is referred to in the script as Colorado. This was where the now dead Pete first returns to discover that his human friends cannot see or hear him but can "feel" his presence, thereby allowing him to coach aspiring pilot Ted Baker (Brad Johnson) and to talk Dorinda through the dangerous mission at the film's climax. Dorinda's home was a set built there by the production company. The Billingsley Ranch in nearby Pallisades, Washington, was where Al perched on his beach chair and watched the pilots train, only to have flame retardant dumped upon him due to Pete's mischief. Pete's chat in the hereafter with his spiritual guide Hap (Audrey Hepburn) included a walk through a wheat field in the town of Sprague, south of Spokane.

To ensure further safety, miniature planes were constructed at a one-fifth scale and then flown and filmed at 20–30 mph. There were two separate forest sets made for these effects. The outdoor one was constructed on an abandon airstrip near Tracy, Montana, with hundreds of Christmas trees set ablaze to look like the full-scale thing and shot from a speeding camera car. For nighttime shots, a similar set was built inside of the Bethlehem Steel Plant near San Francisco. Whereas the

Having arrived in the afterlife, Pete Sandich (Richard Dreyfuss) receives a haircut from his heavenly contact, Hap (Audrey Hepburn), in this scene from *Always*, filmed in the Kootenai National Forest in Montana.

outdoor miniature planes could be operated by radio control, the interior planes were suspended from a wire rig. A studio tank at Universal was used for the sequence of Dorinda being coaxed out of the water by Pete's spirit. Principal photography was finished by early August.

Hook

For the unreal world Steven Spielberg wanted to create for *Hook*, the idea was for the majority of the movie to be done indoors, with all scenes taking place in Neverland shot on soundstages or using matte paintings or bluescreen effects. The facility chosen was the Sony Pictures Studios in Culver City, California, during the period when it was going through its transformation from what had been the base of operations for Metro-Goldwyn-Mayer since 1924 to the headquarters of Columbia Pictures and its subsidiaries. Filming began on February 21, 1991.

Rather than save some of the bluescreen technical work to be done up north at the Industrial Light & Magic studios, Spielberg wanted it done concurrently with the production, mainly because all of Julia Roberts's scenes as Tinker Bell (save for the brief sequence where she grows to normal size and kisses Robin Williams) required this process and therefore needed the guiding hand of the director. Bringing her character to life would, in fact, turn out to be one of the more complicated aspects of the already complicated production, as her wings, fairy dust, and glow required separate effects ultimately combined into one. Reports from the set of dissension between Spielberg and Roberts (who was going through a personal meltdown, this being the time of her career when she was at the height of intense media scrutiny) flooded the news, and rumors began to circulate that she might be replaced by another big-name performer, although these rumors, of course, were unfounded. Whatever the reason, hers turned out to be the one miscalculated performance among the adult principals in the film.

John Napier, who had designed the Broadway sensations *Cats* and *Les Misérables*, was brought aboard as the visual consultant, working with production designer Norman Garwood (who had earned Oscar nominations for *Brazil* and *Glory*). The most impressive set built for the production (housed inside Stage 27) was the *Jolly Roger* pirate ship (this alone cost $1.5 million) and its surrounding dock area. The recreation of a seventeenth-century frigate (complete with a skeleton masthead figure) was 170 feet long, 35 feet wide, and 70 feet high at the mainmast. It became a go-to site during filming for various luminaries and industry colleagues. The Piratetown buildings by the dock were ship-shaped as well, the intention being for them to look as if they had been constructed from scuttled vessels. The remainder of the town was housed on a separate stage and included a clock tower made from the remnants of Captain Hook's (Dustin Hoffman) other nemesis, the crocodile that had pursued him relentlessly in J. M. Barrie's original work.

On Stage 30 (famous for containing Esther Williams's water ballet pool and previously used by Spielberg for scenes in *1941*) was constructed the "Never Tree" where the Lost Boys resided in their various individual huts high above the ground, safe from their pirate foe, who, according to the script, had destroyed their prior underground dwelling from the original story. This set included a track wrapped around the trunk for some very un-Barrie-like skateboarding by the lads. A striking matte painting was used for longshots that gave the impression that the tree was perched on a vertical rock. This was combined with actual footage shot in Hawaii, bringing the elements together for a visually seamless look. Another stage was surrounded in bluescreen so that Peter Banning (Robin Williams) could be simulated flying in a harness on cables (later digitally removed), sometimes as high as thirty feet in the air.

For the opening scene of Maggie Banning (Amber Scott) and her classmates performing in a grammar school production of *Peter Pan*, the production moved off the lot to an auditorium in the soon-to-be-demolished buildings at Our Lady of Loretto-Bishop Conaty Hill School in Los Angeles. The banquet hall where the normally distracted Peter gives a heartfelt speech about Granny Wendy (Maggie

Smith) being honored with a wing of the Great Ormond Street Hospital was supposed to be happening in London but was, in fact, filmed at a ballroom in Los Angeles' Park Plaza Hotel, located across from MacArthur Park. This Art Deco establishment (a one-time Elks lodge) was no longer operating as a hotel but was frequently used as a filming location. For the one principal outdoor setting in the movie—where Jack Banning (Charlie Korsmo) is crushed that his father has not bothered to attend his baseball game and has instead sent a flunky to videotape it—Pote Field in Griffith Park fit the requirement.

Although budgeted at $40 million, with the principal actors all forfeiting their normally high salaries and instead opting to take a share of the film's gross box office receipts, the production became one of those unfortunate slogs that got out of hand, reportedly ending up costing somewhere between $62 and $70 million and not wrapping until late August, delaying star Dustin Hoffman from reporting for reshoots on his previous assignment, *Billy Bathgate*. Following production, TriStar had dismantled rather than destroyed most of the sets with the idea of using them as part of a Peter Pan theme park in Orlando, Florida, but there turned out to be no great demand for this, and the idea was quietly scrapped.

Jurassic Park

While this was another impressive example of Steven Spielberg getting a seemingly difficult shoot done in a relatively tight amount of time, it should be noted that a great deal of pre- and post-production work went on surrounding the filming dates. Once Universal purchased Michael Crichton's book prior to publication in 1990, Spielberg set loose the special effects team at Stan Winston's studio (where the life-sized "puppets" would be built) and ILM (who would handle the computer-generated images) to do test runs on whether or not they could pull off making the dinosaurs appear as realistic as possible. Over a two-year period, both Winston and ILM rose dazzlingly to the challenge, foraging another breakthrough in visual effects movie magic. The seamless marriage of hydraulically activated (often done in pieces, depending on the shot) and computer-created creatures would turn out to be one of the most talked-about accomplishments of the finished movie. Gone were any of the herky-jerky movements or lifeless performances that had come from animatronic or miniaturized cinematic dinosaurs of the past.

Needing a tropical paradise that could pass itself off as an island off the coast of Costa Rica, Spielberg chose Kauai, the second to last most westward of the eight Hawaiian Islands. It would serve not only as Isla Nublar, John Hammond's (Richard Attenborough) private resort on which Jurassic Park is built, but would pass itself off as the Dominican Republic, where lawyer Donald Gennaro (Martin Ferrero) drops by the Mano de Dois Amber Mine to see where an entrapped insect has been discovered, and San Jose, Costa Rica, where slovenly employee Dennis Nedry (Wayne Knight)—in order to steal for a rival organization—receives a shaving can in which to place dinosaur embryos.

Starting on August 24, 1992, the company spent three weeks on the island, where several sets to be used exclusively for exteriors had been built at various locations over the summer. These included the Valley House Plantation Estate near Kapaa, where the visitor center was built; the Olokele Valley for the electrified fence, where Spielberg brilliantly intercut between Ellie (Laura Dern) trying to switch the power back on and Dr. Grant (Sam Neill) and the children, Tim and Lex (Joseph Mazzello and Ariana Richards), scaling the obstruction, unaware of how close they are to being fried to death; Allterton Garden, where Grant comes across the egg and realizes that the dinosaurs are indeed reproducing; Blue Hole canyon, for the daytime glimpses of the T-Rex pen, where a goat is brought to the surface in hopes of tempting the creature out of hiding; Jurassic Kahili Ranch was the setting for Grant and the other visitors getting their first look at the prehistoric beasts, as a computer-generated brachiosaurs nips at a tree branch; and Ranchand Limahuli Garden, for the opening scene in which a hapless park employee is pulled into the crate by a vicious, unseen dinosaur. For the visitors' arrival at Isla Nublar, a helicopter flew them over Na Pali Coast and through the Hanapepe Valley before landing at a helipad by the Manawaiopuna Falls. The most famous exterior set was the imposing gate through which the Land Rovers drove at the start of their unfortunate tour. It was erected near Mount Wai'ale'aale. Although the structure was taken down, as is the usual custom following filming, two of the poles that straddled the road remained behind.

On the last scheduled day of Kauai shooting, Hurricane Iniki hit the island, forcing the cast and crew to take refuge and postpone the next intended sequence: Grant and the children escaping from a rampaging herd of gallimimus. It was finally shot, two weeks later than intended, not on Kauai but at the Kualoa Ranch on the Island of Oahu. Apart from this and a side trip to Red Rock Canyon in the Mojave Desert (filling in for the Badlands of Montana) for the sequence in which Hammond thoughtlessly lands his helicopter at Grant and Ellie's archeological dig, the rest of the filming was done on soundstages back in California.

Five stage were taken over at Universal Studios: Stage 24 for the kitchen where Tim and Lex have their tense cat and mouse game with the raptors, enacted by a combination of puppets and performers in dinosaur suits; Stage 23 for the interior of the maintenance shed where Ellie winds up finding a piece of chief engineer Ray Arnold (Samuel L. Jackson) and another hungry raptor; Stage 27, where a giant tree was constructed, first with hydraulic rigs in order to slowly drop the Land Rover down it as Tim and Grant struggle to get free, and then redressed to play the more comforting plant in which Tim, Grant, and Lex are visited by a harmless brachiosaur. This stage was also dressed for the outdoor scenes in which Muldoon (Bob Peck) is killed trying to hunt down the raptors and where Nedry met his suitable demise by a persistent, spitting dilophosaurus. Stage 28, which housed the park control room (the computer technology seen in the movie costing more than $1 million) and the hatchery, where a baby raptor emerges harmlessly into the new world; and the largest stage at the studio, Stage 12, where the rotunda of the visitors center was adorned with the skeletons of a battling T-Rex and an alamosaurus, from which Grant, Ellie, and the kids hang on for dear life in a new sequence suggested by Spielberg for the computer wizards to enhance in post-production with a real-life confrontation between the raptors and the T-Rex.

Needing a larger soundstage than Universal could provide for the film's unforgettable nighttime scene of the tyrannosaurus attacking the Land Rovers, the company rented out Stage 16 at Warner Bros. Stan Winston's twenty-foot tall, 13,000-pound animatronic T-Rex was used to wreak havoc during a relentless downpour in one of the most tensely staged and supremely satisfying sequences in the director's career.

Following the end of principal photography on November 30, 1992, the next six months were put in the hands of the special effects experts at Industrial Light & Magic, where computer-generated images of the dinosaurs were used in the gallimimus stampede; the initial appearance of the brachiosaurus by Hammond's enthralled visitors (Sam Neill bending over to catch his breath was a nice touch in showing the wonder such a moment would give a paleontologist); the T-Rex chasing after the Land Rover in the storm; and the fight in the rotunda between the T-Rex and the raptors, which ended in one of Spielberg's slyest touches—the banner proclaiming "When Dinosaurs Ruled the Earth" floating down from its riggings in front of the raging tyrannosaurus. Universal, knowing it had a winner on its hands—albeit a winner that came at a cost of $63 million—had no qualms about spending approximately as much to market their thrilling adventure, which took the world by storm, surpassing even their wildest box office expectations. Clearly, Dinosaurs *were* ruling the Earth, at least in 1993.

Schindler's List

Having delivered Universal Studios their biggest financial success of the 1970s with *Jaws* and their greatest worldwide smash of the 1980s with *E.T.*—and about to enrich their coffers even further with *Jurassic Park*, which would prove their top moneymaker of the 1990s—Steven Spielberg still was faced with hesitancy and reluctance when he wanted to proceed with his riskiest project, *Schindler's List*. He wanted it shot in Poland on as many of the actual locations as possible, which was acceptable, but he also planned to shoot it in black and white, believing that the Holocaust represented the absence of color. While the front office caved into this seemingly non-commercial proposal, they insisted the budget be kept at a cautious level, and this the filmmaker managed to do, bringing in the epic production at a very reasonable $22 million. This was the last time a Spielberg movie would carry a price tag under the $30 million mark.

The principal location was Kraków, which had experienced so few architectural changes in the fifty years since the story took place that Spielberg could take advantage of the city looking so timeless. Starting on March 1, 1993, he commenced shooting there on Poselska Street, with the scene of the Schindler factory workers being ordered by the Nazis to shovel snow—tons of the real thing having been trucked in from the skiing resort in Zakopane on the Slovakian border. It was also on this street that a guard would abruptly shoot dead the one-armed worker (Henryk Bista) who had only just recently thanked Schindler for hiring him. On Ciemna Street was filmed the scene of Poldek Pfefferberg (Jonathan Sagalle) managing to escape certain execution by Amon Goeth (Ralph Fiennes) and his men by clearing suitcases off the road for the SS and then clicking his heels for maximum fawning effect. Inside a building on the corner of Skawińska and Krakówska Streets, the headquarters of the Judenrat (Jewish Senior Council), where Schindler (Liam Neeson) first meets the man who will become his business manager and his conscience of sorts, Itzak Stern (Ben Kingsley), was created. On Krzyza Street was filmed the scene of the Nazi soldiers humiliating the Orthodox Jews by cutting their payos (sidelocks) off. The stairs under which young Adam Levy (Adam Siemion) hid Mrs. Dresner (Miri Fabian), after she wasn't allowed inside the hidden compartment in her neighbor's apartment, were located in the courtyard entered through 12 Jozefa Street. The actual apartment the real Schindler had moved into and thereby forced the Nussbaums to vacate, located at 7 Straszewskiego Street, was used for the film. Here, Schindler is interrupted in the act of sex by Poldek Pfefferberg with the news that Stern is about to be transported off to the camps, and he later has an uncomfortable moment when both his wife and mistress end up in the same location; the industrialist was used to juggling his women so that they could remain willfully oblivious to the other's existence. The church where Schindler first meets up with Poldek and the other black marketers was the fourteenth-century St. Mary's Basilica at plac Mariacki (Marian Square).

For the hypnotically filmed introduction to Oskar Schindler—in which Spielberg's camera follows him into a restaurant, where he manages through charm, liquor, and money to persuade a group of SS officers to bring their party over to *him*—the ballroom of a former officers club, referred to as the Army Casino and later the Avangara Restaurant, at Mikolaja Zyblikiewicza 1, was chosen for the setting. The scene when Schindler and his mistress Ingrid (Beatrice Macola) go horseback riding and stop atop the hill where they watch with abject horror as the Nazis liquidate the Jewish ghetto was shot on the southern side of the Vistula River at Lasota Hill, the location of the actual incident having since been obscured by too many trees to provide the view necessary.

The actual Jewish ghetto in a section of the city called Podgórze had gone through too much alteration over the years and had lost a great deal of its period look, requiring the cameras to instead film around Szeroka Street in the Kazimierz district, where an entrance gate and pieces of the ghetto wall were constructed by the production team. This area paid host to the horrific seventeen-minute sequence in which Goeth and his SS troops liquidate the ghetto, callously shooting the uncooperative and elderly, as Schindler watches from the hilltop and while a girl in a red coat (Oliwia Dabrowska) wanders about aimlessly amid the carnage, in one of the most shattering scenes ever committed to film. For the moving sequence of hundreds of Jews forced out of their homes and herded together to cross into the ghetto, Spielberg shot on the Pilsudski Bridge (officially called Most Marszałka Józefa Piłsudskiego) over the Vistula River. In order to ease traffic flow and because there would be too many modern buildings in the shot, the actual direction of the exodus was reversed, so that the populace was, in fact, marching *away* from where the actual ghetto had been rather than toward it. Approximately 800 extras were hired for the scene.

Spielberg was fortunate that Oskar Schindler's enamelware factory, so crucial to the story, was still standing, at 4 Lipowa Street (Ullica Lipowa 4), in the section of Kraków called Zablocie, south of the Vistula River, allowing for shots of the exterior and of the long staircase going up to his office. Because it was still an operating factory (though not manufacturing enamelware, it was used instead by a telecommunications company), a different interior was required. An old enamelware building in Olkusz, about forty kilometers north of Kraków, provided the actual factory works and machinery as well as the upstairs offices of Oskar Schindler. It was here that his fateful birthday party was held in which he ended up arrested for daring to kiss a Jewish girl (Magdalena Dandourian) in appreciation for a cake made by his workers. Needing yet another factory once Oskar moved his works and purchased his workers to get them to the safer location of his hometown of Brnenec (or Brinnlitz in German), Czechoslovakia, Spielberg chose an old building belonging to the Active Society for Chemical Industry in the Bonarka section of the city. It was here that the Jewish workers were informed that

Commandant Amon Goeth (Ralph Fiennes) indulges in some horrifying "target practice" from the balcony of his villa, which overlooks the Płaszów labor camp, in *Schindler's List*. The camp and the villa were built in the Liban Quarry in Poland.

the war was over and that they were no longer prisoners. Outside the factory, Spielberg filmed the emotionally wrenching farewell scene in which Schindler breaks down, wishing he could have done more to save additional lives.

The Kraków Główny railway station was the setting for two different acts of Schindler's heroism. In one, he arrives angrily after hearing that Stern has been mistakenly arrested and placed in one of the cattle cars in order to be shipped to a concentration camp. Using his clout for humane reasons but making sure he never displays an iota of sentiment or emotional concern to his employee, he intimidates the guards on duty into complying with his bidding, stopping the trains and coming to the rescue in the nick of time, in just one of many satisfying scenes in the film. Later, the same location was used for the scene in which Schindler pretends to want to amuse himself and the Nazis by hosing down the cattle cars, making it appear as if the prisoners within are being humiliated, when in fact they are grateful for the drops of water as a temporary relief from the oppressive heat.

The actual Płaszów forced labor camp, where Schindler's workers had been imprisoned and where a great deal of the story would take place, had been dismantled by the Germans in an effort to cover their crimes once they realized the Soviets were approaching Kraków. Rather than reconstruct the camp on the actual site, Spielberg chose the Liban Quarry north of the actual area. There, production designer Allan Starski oversaw the building of thirty-four barracks as well as the hilltop villa of the commandant, Amon Goeth, and the construction of these structures was shown within the film itself for story purposes. The interior of Goeth's villa—where the officer's various orgiastic parties and staff meetings were held, as well as his card game for the fate of his abused servant girl Helen Hirsch (Embeth Davidtz)—was constructed at a television studio in a neighborhood of Kraków called Leg.

For the frightening sequence in which Schindler's female workers are accidentally rerouted to the Auschwitz-Birkenau camp, Spielberg was denied permission to film within the actual grounds, although it had initially been assumed that this would be possible. Not wanting to create a fuss over so sacred a place, he instead had his production crew build barracks *outside* the front gates, located in the town of Oswiecim.

Although the film had excelled in power beyond anyone's wildest expectations, Spielberg dreamed up a finale that was simply inspired in its simplicity and that much more beautiful in its emotional payoff. Rounding up as many of the surviving Schindler's Jews who had been portrayed in the film, he took his cast to the Mount Zion Catholic Cemetery in Jerusalem where Oskar Schindler was buried. The actors were asked to walk with their real-life counterparts past the grave and place a stone upon it, per the Jewish custom. This had been preceded by a marvelously uplifting scene, filmed on a nearby hill, in which the actors, in 1940s ragged attire, walked toward the camera singing "Yeroushalaim Shel Zahav (Jerusalem of Gold)" before the movie made its transitional return to color and the Schindler Jews, in modern garb, materialized in their place. With this, the production wrapped on May 23, 1993.

The Lost World: Jurassic Park

While it seemed a not unattractive idea to return to the tropical shores of Hawaii to film the sequel to the monster hit *Jurassic Park*, the bulk of the project ended up shooting closer to home. The principal setting was no longer Isla Nublar but a sister island called Sorna, which meant that exact locations need not be duplicated. Although there would be some establishing shots using Kauai, it was decided Sorna was going to have a more forestal look, so two coastal parks in Northern California, north of Eureka, were selected.

Shooting began on September 4, 1996, at Prairie Creek Redwoods State Park in an area called Fern Canyon. Here, the most repulsive member of Roland Tembo's hunting party, a slithery fellow by the name of Dieter Stark (Peter Stormare), was given the sort of demise appropriate for hissable villains: being devoured by a horde of "Compys" (*Compsognathus longipes* dinosaurs), described in the novel as the size of chickens but possessing a much more voracious appetite. Here the little critters were required to overwhelm and bite their victim, which meant that some wire controlled models were used for close-ups while their more physical movements would be created later in the ILM workshop using CGI. Prairie Creek would also be the location of Sarah Harding's (Julianne Moore) encounter with a baby stegosaurus (a model created by Stan Winston and his team) and the larger variety of the beast (CGI generated); the "high hide" cage being prepared for hoisting into the trees; and many scenes of Ian Malcolm (Jeff Goldblum) and his team trekking through the woods. To give the location a more Central American feel, much studio-manufactured foliage adorned the real stuff.

Moving south, Patrick's Point State Park provided further glimpses of activity on Isla Sorna: the hunters rounding up some dinosaurs—pachycephalosaurs—in a scene that was later inserted through computer trickery and was reminiscent of Howard Hawks's Africa-based *Hatari!*; Malcolm and his team watching the spectacle from the high rocks (using Ceremonial Rock); and the camp scenes involving the trailer. Following a three-week shoot here, the company settled in at Universal Studios, where the majority of filming would take place.

A pair of T-Rexes, male and female, were created on Stage 24 by Stan Winston for close-ups. Operated on hydraulic lifts and weighing some 18,000 pounds each, it was deemed easier to create sets around them rather than continually move them from stage to stage. Therefore, although the nighttime attack on the trailer by the T-Rexes (staged for maximum impact by Spielberg) was shot mostly on Stage 27, the scene with the dinosaurs peering menacingly into the vehicle where Sarah and Malcolm are nursing their offspring back to health was done at this location. Additional soundstages on the lot in Universal City held such sets as the hunters' camp (which is raided at night by a selection of dinosaurs), the T-Rex nest, and the ravine where the visitors find themselves running from the T-Rex. Outdoors, on the backlot, the production built the abandoned laboratory compound where Malcolm, Sarah, and Nick Van Owen (Vince Vaughn) fight off a pack of vicious velociraptors. Here, the cast was throttled and thrown about (or, in one of the sillier moments, displayed gymnastics prowess) while fending off the nasty creatures before helicopter rescue arrived.

The unleashing by Sarah and her friends of the dinosaurs captured and caged by Roland and his hunters was done at the Los Angeles County Arboretum, a nearby horticultural preserve. In a field in Newhall, California, elephant grass had been planted by the production months earlier so that they could stage the eerie raptor attack on the hunters, which was made more ominous by having the predators trample the tall grass in straight lines as they approach their unsuspecting prey.

Because the big finale was going to take place on bustling neighborhood streets, the Media Center in Downtown Burbank was chosen to pass itself off as San Diego. Here, screaming crowds fled in terror and a bus was rammed into a video store, all because of a rampaging T-Rex who would be placed in later through the miracle of special effects. The movie's screenwriter, David Koepp, was given a cameo (billed cheekily in the credits as "Unlucky Bastard") as a terrified pedestrian who ends up getting laid to rest by the T-Rex in front of Crown Books on San Fernando Boulevard. Further northwest, Granada Hills was the setting for the scene in which a Union '76 gas station ball rolls down the street (on Balboa Boulevard) and for the T-Rex's nighttime visit to a typical suburban home (17917 Mayerling Street in the Greyhawk Ranch development), where he takes a drink from a backyard pool, much to the surprise of a little boy (Colton James). The interior of the boy's bedroom was constructed back on Stage 24, because the Stan Winston T-Rex was needed for the shots.

The docks of San Pedro stood in for the waterfront of San Diego (the crashing of the ship into the dock, however, was done with miniatures at the ILM Studios after principal photography), and the Mayfair Catholic Girls' School in Pasadena provided the interiors of John Hammond's (Richard Attenborough) New York mansion, allowing for cameos by *Jurassic Park* cast members Joseph Mazzello and Ariana Richards.

The company finally did make it back to Hawaii, toward the end of the shoot, for the opening scene in the film when the little girl (Camilla Belle) strays from her family's picnic on the beach and encounters a seemingly friendly Compy (operated by wires) before a more aggressive pack of creatures surround her and the screaming starts. Principal photography ended on December 11, 1996, and the remaining material was done in the special effects shops at ILM.

Amistad

Considering the obvious amount of accurate detail and care that went into the filming of this historical account of the slave insurrection aboard *La Amistad* and its aftermath, this was yet another Steve Spielberg production that was shot in a relatively short amount of time. The director's days of endless shooting schedules of the 1970s were a thing of the past.

Filming began on February 18, 1997, with the interior hull of the *Amistad* recreated on Universal Studios's Stage 12, and depicted the opening sequence in which Cinqué (Djimon Hounsou) manages to unshackle himself using a screw. For the scenes above deck that required either stormy seas or the darkness of the nighttime, an 85 percent scale model of the schooner was constructed at a hangar in

Van Nuys, California. Built on a system of air bags, this allowed the crew to control the rocking movement of the ship. The takeover of the ship, which of course set the whole story in motion, was the key sequence filmed here.

Moving cross country, the production settled in Newport, Rhode Island, in early March, and transformed Washington Square, in the city's historical district, into New Haven, Connecticut, circa 1839–41, for street scenes (parking meters removed, street lamps replaced by gas lamps), including the transportation of the chained slaves to the courthouse. The 1739 Colony House in this square served as the location of the courtroom scenes in which lawyer Roger Baldwin (Matthew McConaughey) defends the prisoners. A room in this building would also serve as Baldwin's office, where he is seeing writing a letter to John Quincy Adams (Anthony Hopkins), pleading for his help in the case. The exterior of the jail was built in Queen Ann's Square in front of Trinity Church. Not having time or need to zip over to Spain for mere interiors, Marble House, one of Newport's famed Gilded Age mansions, became the Spanish Royal Palace for scenes involving eleven-year-old Queen Isabella (Anna Paquin). There were also quick glimpses of Rosecliff mansion and St. Mary's Church, where Judge Coglin (Jeremy Northam) was seen pondering his decision on the case. Spielberg and crew also filmed at Jamestown at Fort Wetherill Beach for the scene of the Africans rowing ashore to what they have been led to believe is Africa, while the moment of them filling their buckets with water was done at the Hope Farm in Bristole. The house on this property also stood in for the outside of John Quincy Adams's home. The production moved to Providence, Rhode Island's state capital, so that the State House could stand in for 1840s Washington, D.C.

Needing a seaport they could easily convert to the nineteenth century, the production chose Connecticut's Historic Mystic Seaport for scenes in which the slaves are transported from the *Amistad* and in which Baldwin and abolitionist Theodore Joadson (Morgan Freeman) go looking awkwardly for black men they hope can speak the dialect of the captured Africans. A fleeting shot of land was needed as a point of view from Cinqué's lifeboat and Point Bluff in Groton was chosen after assurance that no film crew trucks would spoil the natural beauty of the place.

Despite Spielberg's better efforts to shoot John Quincy Adams's final speech in the actual Old Supreme Court Chamber where it happened (going so far as offering a donation of $250,000 to the Capitol Preservation Commission), the Senate Rules Committee held firm on its ongoing policy of *never* allowing anything to film there. Instead, the room was built from scratch on a soundstage at the recently constructed Sonalysts Studio in Waterford, Connecticut. This scene featured a role for eighty-eight-year-old retired Supreme Court Justice (1970–1994) Harry Blackmun reading the court decision of Justice Joseph Story, who had held the same seat as Blackmun from 1812 to 1845.

For an amusing scene in which Adams appears to be sleeping during a meeting of the House of Representatives, the Massachusetts State House in the capital city of Boston was used. While in the New England area, footage of *La Amistad* at sea was shot with Maryland's state ship, *Pride of Baltimore II*, standing in for the real thing.

Back in California, off the coast of San Pedro, a filming platform was utilized for shooting some of the most wrenching scenes in the movie, including the voyage of the captured Sierra Leoneans from Africa to Cuba aboard *Tecora*. This time the state ship of California, the *Californian*, became the vintage vessel.

In late April, scenes were shot at Castillo San Felipe del Morro (a sixteenth-century structure that had been occupied by the US military from 1898 until 1961) in San Juan, Puerto Rico, standing in for the Lomboko Slave Fortress that had been located in Sierra Leone. This was used in the flashback of Cinqué relating his tale of how he was captured and brought to the fort prior to transport across the ocean. It was also the sight of the joyful liberation of the captives (accompanied by John Williams's rousing adaptation of "Dry Your Eyes, Afrika") once the facility is deemed unlawful. The decimation of the fort, obviously, required special effects, since del Morro had for years been a museum designated by the National Park Service.

Saving Private Ryan

Steven Spielberg started things off on a grand scale for his World War II epic, doing nothing less than recreating the D-Day landing that had taken place at Omaha Beach in Normandy, France, on June 6, 1944. There was no thought of using that actual location, however, because it had since been declared a histori-cal landmark and had been altered enough to make it difficult to fill in for itself anyway. England was the next option, but when the military refused to loan the filmmaker their troops as extras, Spielberg jumped across St. George's Channel to Ireland who promised not only some enticing tax breaks but the use of some 750 members of the Irish Army Reserve (a.k.a. *Fórsa Cosanta Áitiúil*, or the F.C.A.). The coastline was scattered with Teller mines, barbed wire, iron hedgehogs, and concrete pillboxes, with a dozen World War II landing craft (a.k.a. Higgins Boats) transported from Wexford Harbor to the beach to drop the hapless soldiers directly into the line of fire. Starting on June 27, 1997, Corricloe Beach in County Wexford in the Southeastern part of the country became Normandy for a three-week shoot that captured the hellish nature of battle unlike any film before it had done, with handheld cameras placing the audience directly into the path of oncoming artillery, with soldiers being picked off mercilessly, bloodily and grue-somely, in one of the most frightening, unnerving, and authentic sequences of the decade. This tour de force piece of filmmaking encompassed the first half hour of the lengthy story and would become one of the most talked about set pieces of Spielberg's career, one that no doubt was instrumental in him taking home the Academy Award for Best Director that year.

From there it was back to England, where three blocks of the war-shattered French village of Ramelle (a fictional name created for the film) were constructed at the former airfield and aircraft factory in Hatfield, located about eighteen miles north of London in the county of Hertfordshire. There, not only did Captain Miller (Tom Hanks) and his company finally encounter their goal, Private James Ryan (Matt Damon), but they engaged in a fierce battle to fortify a bridge in the

For the big climax of *Saving Private Ryan*, the fictional French village of Ramelle was created from scratch on a former airfield in Hatfield, England. Pictured: Pvt. Mellish (Adam Goldberg), Pvt. Parker (Demitri Gortsas), Cpt. Miller (Tom Hanks), Pvt. Ryan (Matt Damon), Cpl. Henderson (Maximilian Martini), and Sgt. Horvath (Tom Sizemore).

center of the ruined town, a conflagration that further wrecked the structures and tragically brought too many lives to an end in another incredible display of great filmmaking.

Also in England, Thame Park became the site of the machine-gun nest where the company's medic (Giovanni Ribisi) loses his life and Miller's men fight over whether or not to execute a German soldier (Joerg Stadler) insistent on his devotion to American pop culture. In that same location, a chapel became the church where Miller and his exhausted squad relax for the night, with the Captain conversing with their nervous interpreter (Jeremy Davies). In an amazing example of movie trickery, the Iowa farmhouse where poor Mrs. Ryan (Amanda Boxer) receives the devastating news that three of her boys have died in battle was shot not back in the Midwest but also in England—the Ryan home built by the production department on Gunsite Road near West Kennett in Wiltshire county, some two and a half hours west of London.

France did finally play a part in the movie, providing the location for the bracketing scenes set in the present day when the elderly Ryan (Harrison Young) and his family visit St. Laurent Cemetery at the Normandy American Cemetery and Memorial, in the town of Colleville-sure-Mer, located near the actual beach where the battle took place. Principal photography concluded on September 13, 1997.

A.I. Artificial Intelligence

By its very concept, *A.I.* was basically an indoor movie, one that required a great deal of technical and computer graphics to enhance the visual look. Several scenes would therefore be a combination of live actors and standing sets, blue-screen mattes, miniatures, and CGI-added enhancements. Because the late Stanley Kubrick had an exclusive pact with Warner Bros., that studio became the co-producer, along with Spielberg's DreamWorks company, and would supply the soundstages needed for the film. Filming began on August 17, 2000, and principal photography would wrap three months later in November.

The ultra-sleek interior of the Swinton home, where a good deal of the first chapter of the story would take place, was created on Soundstage 16 at Warner Bros., while the largest set—the crossroads of the sleazy, Vegas-like pleasure center, Rouge City—was constructed on Stage 20. Opulently vulgar buildings and flashing signs filling out the background, recreated by designer Rick Carter from the concept designs of Chris Baker, were computer generated and bluescreened behind the actors. Additional sets were built at the studio for the Cybertronic lecture room, Dr. Hobby's (William Hurt) study, and the hospital where the Swintons' comatose son Martin (Jake Thomas) is encased in an isolation tube. Because Steven Spielberg wanted a realistic look to the ice melting from the amphibicopter that "mecha" child David (Haley Joel Osment) has been encased in for 2,000 years, eighty tons of actual ice were shipped in each day and set up three hours before shooting. The underwater version of the decimated Coney Island was done principally with miniatures at the Industrial Light & Magic Studio. Shot "dry for wet," in industry parlance, the set was instead given an eerie, watery look via smoke and further made to look aquatic through CGI effects.

The most unusual interior space used for filming was the geodesic dome located at the harbor in Long Beach, California, next to the Queen Mary. Built at a cost of $4 million in order to house Howard Hughes's legendary wooden airplane, *Spruce Goose*, at 135,000 square feet it was larger than any soundstage in Hollywood. Once the *Goose* vacated the premise in 1992, after only nine years of exhibition, and relocated up to Oregon, the space became a desirable one for shooting movies, having served this purpose on such other Warner Bros. features as *Batman Forever* and *Batman and Robin*. Inside the dome, the arena-like Flesh Fair set was constructed, consisting of bleachers, a stage, and a sadistic series of props that were used to destroy the hapless robots on display for the "entertainment" of the vicious humans. The set was also used for the Moon Gondola scenes, in which Johnson-Johnson (Brendan Gleeson) and his crew hunt down unregistered mechas to bring to the fair. Dialogue in the film indicates that this action was taking place outside Haddonfield, New Jersey—no doubt an in-joke on Spielberg's part, as the director spent part of his youth living in this area.

The *A.I.* company traveled up to Oxbow Park in Oregon for the scenes of Henry Swinton (Sam Robards) and his wife Monica (Frances O'Connor) driving along the wooded roadway in their futuristic car and for the heart-wrenching scene in which Monica deposits the distraught David in the woods, believing she is doing him some good.

Minority Report

For a glimpse into the future that was both sleek and soulless in appearance, Steven Spielberg found locations in both California and Washington, D.C. (the story's setting), and then enhanced them a good deal with seamless special effects (supposedly 481 visual effects shots total, the most since *Close Encounters*). He then had his cinematographer, Janusz Kaminski, give the visuals a somewhat washed-out, disorienting sheen, which gave the whole movie the unsettling feel necessary for a dystopian look at a police state run amok.

Principal photography began on March 22, 2001 (the director was obliged to postpone the date by a few weeks so that his star, Tom Cruise, could finish shooting Cameron Crowe's *Vanilla Sky*), in Los Angeles on sets built at the 20th Century Fox Studios. Chief among these was the centerpiece of the story, "The Temple," a reference to the Pre-Cog chamber in which the three "mutant" beings capable of foreseeing criminal acts lay partially submerged in a pool, looking decidedly trapped and uncomfortable in their eerie enclosure as John Anderton (Cruise) and his team monitor their predictions from above. For a key part of the chase sequence, one that perfectly blended both suspense and humor in the trademark Spielberg tradition, Hennesy Street (built for the 1982 musical *Annie* and named after that movie's set designer, Dale Hennesy, who passed away during that picture's production) on the Warner Bros. backlot was used. Here, Gordon Fletcher (Neal McDonough) and his fellow Pre-Crime cops descended upon a fleeing Anderton in their hover packs, which required dangling the actors from wires above the set.

On Spring Street in downtown Los Angeles, the twelve-story El Dorado Hotel, built in 1914 and in a state of disrepair by the time Spielberg and company shot there, was used for the downtrodden flophouse in which Anderton takes refuge after having his eyes swapped. His discomfort is made that much more intense as Fletcher and his pursuing team toss creepy electronic "spyders"—much like four-legged miniature storm troopers—on the floor so that they can comb the building and put the residents in a state of fear. The structure was later rehabbed to turn into loft housing.

The film also utilized some of the less glamorous streets in this same area for the scene in which Anderton goes jogging at night in "the sprawl" in order to score some "clarity" from a dealer (David Stifel) with no eyes. Another site that had fallen on hard times but was redecorated to appear onscreen as if it was in perfectly functional futuristic working order was the Hawthorne Plaza Shopping Center in Hawthorne, located not far from the Los Angeles International Airport. Because of the economic decline in the area, the mall had shuttered by the time of filming, allowing the art department to create a shopping plaza circa 2054 in which annoying hologram ads hawk wares directly at each passing customer. One of the most suspenseful and cleverly staged scenes in the movie took place here: Anderton drags the hapless Pre-Cog Agatha (Samantha Morton) with him while fleeing from his fellow cops, and the clairvoyant helps him dodge detection by correctly anticipating what random objects can serve as his shield.

For Anderton's surprise visit to the secluded Maryland home of Pre-Crime creator Iris Hineman (Lois Smith), the Descanso Gardens in La Cañada Flintridge, California, east of Burbank, provided the dense foliage, which was made deadlier by the inclusion of some poisonous thorns and living plants that wrap themselves around the unsuspecting fugitive. Angelus Plaza, a senior housing complex located at 255 South Hill Street, next to the fabled Angels Flight funicular railway in the Bunker Hill district of downtown Los Angeles, was used for the building in which Agatha sees Anderton shooting Lee Crow (Mike Binder), a fellow he doesn't even know.

In the nation's capital, the opening "near-murder"—when Anderton and his team manage to pinpoint the correct neighborhood and stop Howard Marks (Arye Gross) from stabbing his philandering wife—was filmed in front of the 1700 block of a series of 1920s row houses on C Street SE in the Capitol Hill section of the district (across from a triangular park). The neighborhood is referred to in the script as being the Barnaby Woods area, which is actually in Georgetown. That northwestern section of D.C. *was* used for the scene when Anderton takes Agatha into a Gap store on Wisconsin Avenue NW in order to get her some less curious attire to wear in public. This was good news for fans of the venerable clothing establishment, leading costumers to believe it would still be around fifty years in the future.

The historic 1901 Beaux-Arts hotel, the Willard InterContinental, located at 1401 Pennsylvania Avenue NW, north of the White House, became the setting for the film's climax, when Pre-Crime director Lamar Burgess (Max von Sydow), thinking he is there to celebrate the triumphant passage of the National Pre-Crime bill, is instead startled to see information from Agatha's mind uploaded to a screen in the ballroom. Further south at 1300 Pennsylvania Avenue, the Ronald Reagan Trade Center (named after the President who requested a special screening of *E.T.* at the White House) was used to portray the exterior of the Office of Pre-Crime, where Anderton is seen injecting himself with a paralytic enzyme to deliberately distort his face, as a tour guide (Keith Flippen) cheerfully hosts an explanation of the workings of the law enforcement agency.

Outside D.C., Gloucester Courthouse, Virginia, provided the road on which Anderton was seen driving a Lexus (the newly made car he took off in after the battle with the FBI at the factory) in order to reach Dr. Hineman's house and the lovely waterfront home of his ex-wife Lara (Kathryn Morris), where she is visited first by FBI Agent Witwer (Colin Farrell) and later by Anderton himself, who brings along Agatha to shelter her from the pursuing police. This was shot at 6223 Ware Point Road on a peninsula between the Ware and North Rivers. The isolated log cabin where the Pre-Cogs find solitude away from their cruel exploitation was Butter Island, located in East Penobscot Bay, a part of Deer Isle in Maine.

The four-month shoot concluded on July 28, 2001. It would be nearly a year before the picture was actually released into theaters.

Catch Me If You Can

Despite the fact that *Catch Me If You Can* stretched over six years of time and required so much globetrotting on the part of its criminal protagonist, Frank Abagnale Jr. (Leonardo DiCaprio), Steven Spielberg prided himself in filming it fast and efficiently. Starting on February 11, 2002, the movie began shooting in the Southern California area, which would fill in for all kinds of places in various parts of the country. The lavish New Orleans home lived in by the parents of Frank's betrothed, Brenda (Amy Adams), was the Crank House, a two-story Victorian built in 1882, located at 2186 East Crary Street in Altadena (north of Pasadena), California. The exterior was captured most extensively during Frank and Brenda's aborted engagement party, while the interiors of the house included the bedroom from which Frank escaped through the window once he realized FBI Agent Carl Hanratty (Tom Hanks) had caught up with him once again. In Pasadena itself, a house at 3077 East California Boulevard became the Long Island residence of Frank's newly married mother Paula (Nathalie Baye), where Hanratty springs upon the surprised woman the fact that her felonious son owes $1.3 million, and where, later, Frank peers in enviously through the windows at Christmastime to see the family life he cannot have. The latter scene required the standard Hollywood magic of making fake snow to give the proper East Coast atmosphere.

The famous Union Station in downtown Los Angeles was redressed to pass itself off as the Miami bank where Frank flirts with an assistant manager (Elizabeth Banks) in order to learn about the check-coding machine. Although Frank is supposed to be attending high school in Eastchester when he is mistaken for a substitute and decides to run with the ruse, Bellarmine-Jefferson High School in Burbank was used for filming but had its name retained in the script when the real sub (Maggie Melin) arrives and declares she would never take a job from this particular school again. Frank's auditioning of the Miami college girls to be his stewardesses in order for him to escape was staged in the auditorium of the Ebell of Los Angeles Woman's Club at 4401 West Eighth Street at Lucerne Boulevard in Los Angeles. The Old Orange Courthouse in Santa Ana was where Frank enthusiastically gives his legal speech, copied from *Perry Mason* to a disbelieving judge. The Ambassador Hotel, for years a venerable site on Wilshire Boulevard, had by the time of filming closed its doors to guests but still hosted movie shoots. It was here that Frank is seen putting together his fake TWA checks, submerging plastic plane models in the bathtub to remove their airline decals, and where he has his "go fish" encounter with a costly prostitute (Jennifer Garner) who wants him to sign over one of his fake checks to her. The New Rochelle house from which the Abagnales are evicted because of Frank Sr.'s inability to pay his debts was located at 12075 Valleyheart Drive in Studio City.

Hollywood did play Hollywood itself for the scene in which Hanratty and his aides show up at the Tropicana Hotel to inquire about some forged checks, only to be told the man responsible is still in occupancy there. The back section of the Roosevelt Hotel on Hawthorn Avenue, which resembled a two-story motel rather than the high-rise apartment building that faced Hollywood Boulevard, provided the location, which included a built-in pool and was dressed in colorful early 1960s decor. After duping Hanratty into believing he's someone else, Frank is seen fleeing on Hawthorn Avenue. The Quality Café on West 7th Street, a frequently used Los Angeles location, was the coffee shop where a friendly waiter (Jeremy

Steven Spielberg and Leonardo DiCaprio (in his Italian knit shirt) watch the playback of a scene from *Catch Me If You Can*.

Howard) informs grumpy Carl that the "Barry Allen" on his report is the name of a comic book character, the Flash.

About fifty minutes east of Los Angeles, off Interstate 10, the Ontario Airport became Miami International Airport, where Frank realizes his rendezvous with Brenda will not work out because she's in league with the feds, and where one of the most delightful images of the movie was shot: Frank linking arms with a bevy of beautiful stewardesses as they parade into the terminal to the strains of Frank Sinatra singing "Come Fly with Me." Inside a former aerospace factory building in Downey, which had recently become part of the Downey Studios facility, the FBI offices were constructed for the scenes in which Hanratty answers the phone while working one of his lonely Christmas Eves. At the end of the film this becomes Frank's new place of business when he reluctantly agrees to leave crime behind and join the good guys.

Over on the East Coast, Spielberg filmed for the very first time in Manhattan, with Frank seen striding proudly up Park Avenue in his pilot's uniform. Earlier in the story he is seen making a call from a phone booth, the camera panning down from the top of what would have been the Pan Am building when the movie was taking place but what had since become MetLife. There is also a shot of Frank's newly purchased Aston-Martin (patterned after the one Sean Connery drove in *Goldfinger*) zipping around the corner and onto the avenue. Over in Brooklyn, the spectacular interior of the Williamsburgh Savings Bank, in the Bank Tower at 1 Hanson Place, became the inside of the Chase Manhattan Bank where Frank Sr. (Christopher Walken) tries to charm a loan out of one of the managers to no avail. Outside, he had dressed up the younger Frank in a suit in order for him to appear as if Frank Sr. had been driven there by a chauffeur, but that moment was not shot outside this location but behind Brooklyn's Borough Hall, in front of the Municipal Building.

Heading north, the town of Yonkers was where the Abagnales are shown coming down in the world, moving into an apartment building in what is supposed to be Eastchester. This was located at 108 Buena Vista Avenue. Frank is seen running down this same street after receiving the awful news that his parents are divorcing. Larkin Park in Yonkers stood in for a square in Washington, D.C., where Hanratty is seen placing a call from a phone booth when he comes to the conclusion that his suspect must be *very* young because of his interest in comic books. The Prestige Laundromat at 151 Lake Avenue in the same city became the site of Carl's hapless night spent seeing his clothes turned red, a scene hilariously contrasted with his suspect spending the night with a high-class hooker. There was some quick filming in New Jersey, at the Highland Avenue train station in Orange, for the moment when a distraught Frank tries to write a check in order to get a railway ticket to New York.

One of the most striking locations used in the film shows up in two separate scenes. The TWA Flight Center at John F. Kennedy Airport in Queens, New York—with its futuristic, sleek shell-roof design and curvy interior created by Eero Saarinen—was considered an architectural marvel when it opened in 1962. Frank is seen walking through the main terminal when he is asked by a TWA ticket agent (Jane Bodie) if he will be "deadheading." Toward the end of the film, Frank, while walking through one of the airport's spacey-looking ramp tunnels, is stopped by Hanratty, who tells him he's not being chased by anyone while hoping Frank will return to his FBI job on Monday.

Rather than fly to France, the town of Montrichard was portrayed by Place Royale in Quebec City in Montreal, where Carl leads Frank out into the square after arresting him in the print shop, as a choir sings outside of the church behind them. This was the Church Notre-Dame-des-Victoires. The production team also found an abandoned penal facility in Montreal to sub for the Perpignon Prison in France. Shooting ended in Canada on May 4, 2002.

The Terminal

For a movie that didn't exactly astound in theme or emotional payoff, *The Terminal* did have one aspect that *was* pretty amazing, although few people gave it much notice or credit. The movie looked so convincingly as if it was taking place in a genuine, functioning, modern-day, state-of-the-art airline terminal that it came as a surprise to many that it wasn't actually filmed in one. Realizing that it was not feasible to work freely and without interference in an operating terminal over a two-month period, Steven Spielberg asked production designer Alex McDowell to build one from the ground up and to do so in such a way that it would pretty much fool anyone into thinking it was authentic. For what McDowell had in mind, there simply wasn't a large enough soundstage in Hollywood to accommodate it,

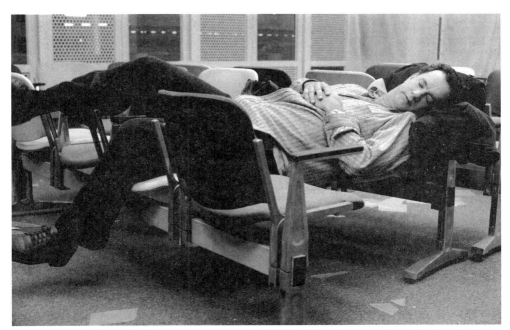

Viktor Navorski (Tom Hanks) at rest on his makeshift "bed" in this scene from *The Terminal*, shot on a set built inside an airplane hangar in Palmdale, California.

so, most fittingly, an airplane hangar would have to do. A suitable one was found at the Palmdale Regional Airport, about sixty miles northwest of Universal City. The hangar had once been used to house and service 747 planes and had room enough for six at a time.

McDowell's set would consist of three levels of shops, restaurants, and services, and real companies—knowing this was great publicity for them—participated in the decor. These included Sbarro, La Perla, Baja Fresh, Hudson News, Starbucks (of course), Nathan's Famous, Baskin-Robbins Ice Cream, Cambridge Soundworks, Borders, and more. McDowell and his team worked for twenty-one weeks constructing the self-supporting structure out of steel, with granite floors, four working escalators, and a glass circumference that gave it the feeling of an atrium. Since this structure was contained within another building, it required a very precise lighting design, allowing it to look like various times of the day, with a track of 100,000 lights placed along the ceiling of the hangar. Also required were a gigantic matte painting of the airfields that were supposed to be outside the structure and a blue screen upon which would be projected incoming and outgoing flights to ensure that the background seemed appropriately busy when it needed to. The finished set was 750 feet long, 300 feet wide, and 70 feet tall, leaving just enough room outside of it for the technical setup needed to bring it to life. It first appeared onscreen when Homeland Security officer Thurman (Barry Shabaka Henley) escorts trapped foreigner Victor Navorski (Tom Hanks) down a corridor and through a pair of doors, which was captured by Spielberg and cameraman Janusz Kaminski in a splendid, spinning shot that made it seem like a thriving, pulsating wonderland, before the mundane, impersonal nature of it all could be absorbed.

At a hangar directly next to the one housing this set were further sets necessary to bring the airport to life, including the Homeland Security Offices and the seemingly neglected Gate 67, where Viktor is obliged to create his temporary "home" among the uncomfortable airport lounge seats. This set was required to spring to life from its moribund state when Viktor joined Karl Iverson (Jude Ciccolella) and his construction crew in finishing the walls and, ultimately, creating his own fountain. Filming began in the Palmdale hangars on October 1, 2003.

A real airport, however, was still needed for the opening sequence of the immigration nightmare of getting through customs, the domain of unflappable Homeland Security Chief Frank Dixon (Stanley Tucci). Following the Palmdale shoot, the company flew to Mirabel, Quebec, Canada, in order to use the Montreal-Mirabel International Airport. This would stand in for what was supposed to be John F. Kennedy International Airport in Queens, New York, the locale mentioned only briefly in the dialogue. The scenes of Viktor finally leaving the terminal and of custodian Gupta Rajan (Kumar Pallana) approaching a landing plane with his mop in hopes of making sure Viktor would allow him to be arrested for his past crimes and detain himself no further for the cleaning man's benefit were shot outside the airport. The latter scene required the loan of a Boeing 747 from United Airlines. The concluding scene of Viktor traveling by cab was shot in Times Square, New York, and the movie wrapped on December 12, 2003.

War of the Worlds

Rather than set his take on H. G. Wells's classic novel in the author's native England, Steven Spielberg instead paid homage to the other Well(e)s forever associated with *The War of the Worlds*, Orson, whose 1938 radio adaptation had the Martians first being sighted in the tiny town of Grovers Mill, New Jersey. Spielberg made his protagonist, Ray Ferrier (Tom Cruise), a Jersey resident and therefore did some shooting in the Garden State. Filming began there on November 8, 2004, in the Ironbound district of Newark at an intersection known as Five Corners, where Ferry Street, Merchant Street, and Wilson Avenue come together. The dramatic introduction of the aliens—in which several citizens converge near a hole in the middle of the street only to be stunned when a gigantic tentacled object rises from the earth and begins zapping folks left and right—was shot here. The intersection's most prominent building, St. Stephan's Grace Community Church, gets a beating as the walls crumble and the glass breaks, although this was all done later, of course, through the miracle of computer-generated imagery.

Although the story made it appear that this spot wasn't far away from Ray's home, the actual site of the Ferrier house was about a half hour's drive away, at 11 John F. Kennedy Boulevard at the southern point of the city of Bayonne. The row houses here had the dramatic backdrop of the Bayonne Bridge (connecting them to Staten Island), which was blown up in chaotic CGI fashion as Ray and his two children (Dakota Fanning, Justin Chatwin) race from their block in the only useable car in the neighborhood. That car had been "borrowed" by a frantic Ray from the gas station down the end of his street, but there was no such service center there, requiring production designer Rick Carter's team to build one on a little league field under the bridge arches.

The company then made a stopover in Howell Township at the Ardena Acres development, where a house on Canterbury Way became the home of Ray's ex-wife Mary Ann (Miranda Otto), a temporary shelter for the fleeing family until

Aliens over Newark! The first tripod rises over the Five Corners intersection of the city in this scene from *War of the Worlds*.

they wake up and find the place has been decimated by a crashed airplane. The trashed neighborhood, however, was done across the country on the backlot at Universal Studios, requiring the purchase of a 747 plane to cut into pieces. The opening scene of Ray working at his job hoisting containers was filmed in Red Hook, Brooklyn, which is located across Upper New York Bay from Bayonne. For the finale, when Ray and Rachel finally reach their destination in Boston, the film used Carroll Street between 7th and 8th Avenue in the Park Slope section of Brooklyn to stand in for Beantown. This moment was of special note because the stars of the original 1953 film of Wells's story, Gene Barry and Ann Robinson, put in silent cameos as Mary Ann's parents.

The small village of Athens, New York, appeared as itself for one of the most exciting sequences of Spielberg's career, when the Ferriers and other escaping earthlings try to board a ferry only to panic when the alien tripods arise on the hill above them. Some 1,000 extras were asked to march down Second Street toward the Hudson River, although the town had no actual ferry. The ferry dock was constructed expressly for the movie, as were the crossing gate and railroad tracks (across Water Street) where Ray and the crowd are startled to see a fiery train zip past them. For the capsizing ferry, foam duplicates of automobiles with battery powered headlights were toppled into the water. Although the terrifying scene of the Ferriers having their car taken from them at gunpoint appears to be in the same location, it was actually shot all the way over in Piru, California, a town that Spielberg had already used for his segment of *Twilight Zone: The Movie*.

The city of Naugatuck, Connecticut, stood in for another part of Boston, where an alien tripod is finally defeated and collapses upon a factory building. A former Uniroyal chemical plant on Elm Street became the scene of the altercation. Further north, in Windsor, Connecticut, the eerie moment of Rachel getting shaken by the sight of dead bodies floating in the water was shot at the Farmington River.

The exodus of the wearied citizens walking through the peaceful farm country was done in Raphine, Virginia, where a farmhouse on Pisgah Road is visible as the backdrop. The line of National Guard trucks and tanks that so intrigues Ray's son Robbie was filmed on Decataur Road in nearby Brownsburg.

Universal Studios would also provide a street set on the backlot for the moment when a car crashes through a store window as Ray attempts to flee the Martian rays in Newark, while the tank on Stage 27 became the Hudson River, where the Ferriers and other ferry passengers are dropped into the water and nearly crushed by the cars falling from the vessel. The basement dwelling of nutcase Harlan Ogilvy (Tim Robbins), where Rachel and Ray must try to remain silent when an alien tentacle comes searching through the hiding place, was a set on a soundstage at 20th Century Fox, as was the outside of the farm house, where Ray sees the endless mess of red weeds that has started engulfing the landscape and where he and Rachel are snatched up by the tripod. They end up among other frightened humans inside giant metal baskets, but these scenes were done at yet another studio, Sony, in Culver City. A section of the Agua Dulce Movie Ranch known as Mystery Mesa was the setting for the nighttime hill battle between the military and the Martians, when Robbie decides he wants to join the fight and Ray must choose between which of his children to protect.

Principal photography on the costly production came to a close on March 8, 2005, after which there were some three months of post-production to perfect the special effects, which included a stunning image of one of the menacing tripods slowly hulking its way through Newark—certainly one of that city's most memorable appearances on film.

Munich

The original idea was to dramatize the 1972 Munich Olympic massacre and its aftermath by shooting in as many of the actual locations where the events took place. This, however, was not feasible, financially speaking. The project was a risky enough one where the box office was concerned, so costs needed to be kept as low as possible. To this end, the *Munich* team—figuring most audiences would be none the wiser—wound up filming principally in two countries where *none* of the action takes place in the script, Malta and Hungary, which also filled in for various other locales.

Shooting began in Malta on June 29, 2005, which was coincidentally the very same day that Spielberg's previous movie, *War of the Worlds*, was opening around the United States. Over a six-week period the production would film at various spots around the Mediterranean island, located south of Sicily. The Primera Hotel on Triq Halel in Bugibba, on the northern coast, became the Cyprus Hotel, where the bomb is planted under the bed, causing a far greater explosion than the team of assassins was anticipating. A café in the same city stood in for the scene of several Israelis gathered around the television and reacting to the news of the killings in Munich. In Sliema, the walkway by Triq it-Torri (Tower Road) was used to represent a promenade in Tel Aviv where Avner (Eric Bana) and his Mossad contact, Ephraim (Geoffrey Rush), discuss—while eating baklava—the assignment and how the team of assassins will be paid. At Republic Square in the capital city of Valletta was staged a scene supposedly taking place in Rome: Avner being introduced by his friend Andreas (Moritz Bleibtreu) to an Italian contact (Yvan Attal), who gives him the whereabouts of his first target, Wael Zwaiter (Makram Khoury). In this same locale, the British Hotel on Triq il-Batterija (Battery Street) became the Aristedes Hotel in Athens, where an uncooperative bomb causes Hans (Hanns Zischler) to skip protocol and toss a grenade into the target room. After this ruckus, there is a shootout in front of the establishment, during which Ali (Omar Metwally), the PLO leader who had argued earlier over politics with Avner, is gunned down by Carl (Ciarán Hinds). Across the Grand Harbor in Cospicua, the bizarre scene of the Israeli assassins arriving by boat and some of them changing into drag in order to carry out their job in Beirut was filmed.

Moving over to the southern side of the island, the outdoor café scene (happening onscreen in Rome) in which Avner and his team meet following their first successful hit was shot in the central square in front of Collegiate Church of St. Paul. A derelict house in the same town became the Athens safe house where Avner's team ends up accidentally having to share the place with members of the PLO. Elsewhere throughout the island, private residences stood in for Avner and his wife Daphna's (Ayelet Zurer) home in Tel Aviv, various safe houses, and

Golda Meir's (Lynn Cohen) apartment, where Avner is taken and offered his dangerous and lengthy retaliation mission. The hospital where Daphna gives birth to her daughter was St. Dorothy's Senior School in Haz-Zebbug, and the Malta International Airport stood in for the Lod Airport in Israel.

Another six weeks found the company shooting in Hungary. The grounds of Budapest's Puskas Ferenc Stadium stood in for the Olympic compound where the Arab assassins scaled the fences and began their assault on the Israeli athletes at Connollystrasse 31. The quarters where the athletes try to fight off the invading killers was recreated on a set built at an abandoned ice rink in Budapest due to the fact that there were no actual soundstages available at the time. The Frankfurt safe house where Avner is first introduced to his team members was constructed there as well. The horrific killings of the athletes and their coaches, which had taken place at the Furstenedlbruck Air Base outside of Munich, was recreated at Tököl, a World War II military airfield at Halásztelek, south of Budapest near the Danube River.

Wael Zwaiter, the first target, is seen giving his recitation on *Arabian Nights* in what is meant to be Rome, but this was filmed near the Budapest intersection of Dalszinhaz and Andrassy Streets, with the columns from the Opera House visible in the background. Avner and Robert (Mathieu Kassovitz) are then seen passing under those same columns and walking directly across Dalszinhaz to Zwaiter's building, where they shoot him through his grocery bag.

The tense moment when the Mossad nearly blow up the daughter of one of their targets with a bomb that has been planted inside a telephone was filmed on Aulich Street and Bathory Street, passing itself off as Paris. A mere ten minutes away, Budapest around Anker Koz and Asboth Streets then became London during a heavy rainfall, when Avner attempts to kill Salameh (Mehdi Nebbou)

Making a bigger bang than they had anticipated, Carl (Ciarán Hinds) and his fellow assassins (Hanns Zischler and Mathieu Kassovitz) quickly hightail it away from their target in this scene from *Munich*. The Primera Hotel in Malta stood in for the Cyprus Hotel.

only to have some drunken Americans (and possible CIA agents) interfere and thwart his efforts. For the London hotel where Avner wisely rejects the advances of a beautiful woman (Marie-Josée Croze) but Carl falls prey to her lethal charms, the Marriott Budapest on János utca (Janos Street) provided the interior. For one of the most hauntingly filmed scenes, in which Avner and Steve come across a slain Hans propped up on a park bench, Margaret Island was used, with the Margit híd (or Margaret Bridge) dominating the frame, and, in an effective touch, several lights in the city are extinguished simultaneously in the background. Avner and the surviving members of his team were seen leaving Paris by train, but the station used was the Budapest-Nyguati Railway Terminal.

Finally deciding to use a country to play itself, Spielberg took his crew to Paris, where Avner meets Louis (Mathieu Amalric) at a market on the Pont de Bir Hakeim, a double-decker bridge over the Seine, with the Eiffel Tower featured prominently in the background to make it clear that this most certainly is *not* Budapest. Another location in the city found Avner, Louis, Robert, and the mysterious information provider known as "Papa" (Michael Lonsdale) at the outdoor café La Cave Bourgogne at Place Saint Medard, where Avner is told he himself is now being hunted and is advised at this point to quit his assignment. Having no luck finding a suitable location while in Hungary, a farmhouse outside of Paris was used for Papa's secret compound.

Hoping to hide away in America and live a peaceful existence, Avner, Daphna, and their daughter take up residence at 259 Clermont Avenue, near DeKalb Avenue in the Fort Greene section of Brooklyn, only to have the former assassin worry that every passing car is trailing him. For the final exchange between Avner and Ephraim, Gantry Plaza State Park in Long Island City was used, with the famous Pepsi Cola sign (which was later granted landmark status) visible during their discussion. More importantly, the location allowed for a view of downtown Manhattan across the East River, where the special effects artists recreated a digital version of the World Trade Center to remind audiences that there was indeed no end to terrorism in our lives. Filming ended on September 29, 2005, with *Munich* opening in theaters less than three months later.

Indiana Jones and the Kingdom of the Crystal Skull

For the long-anticipated return of one of the iconic creations of eighties cinema, Steven Spielberg and George Lucas went a different route when it came to locations, choosing to keep their actors in the United States, while the second unit staff did the necessary background plates and establishing shots outside the country.

Using the code name *Genre*, the fourth Indiana Jones adventure began principal photography on June 18, 2007, in New Mexico, with Deming Municipal Airport serving as the exterior of the Area 51 military hangar where Indy (Harrison Ford) and his cohort Mac (Ray Winstone) have been brought (by way of a car trunk) by villainous Irina Spalko (Cate Blanchett) and her Russian henchmen. On the grounds of the airport, the production built a fake "Doom Town" village to be deliberately bombed in a nuclear test, with Indy stuck there right in the middle of the prefabricated town, which consisted of cheery mannequins in candy-colored wholesome settings. The quick-thinking Indy, placing himself inside a refrigerator as a safety precaution, ends up landing—in a Wile E. Coyote-style gag—in a gravel pit that was filmed on Corralitos Road in Las Cruces and was also the sight of where the rocket sled comes to a halt. The opening scene of the fake military convoy racing with the reckless teens was shot on Route 84 in Abiquiu in the desert area north of Albuquerque.

Indy's fictitious university, Marshall College, this time utilized Yale in New Haven, with Room 113 in Harkness Hall standing in for Professor Jones's classroom. Several streets in town were closed off to stage the motorcycle chase, with Indy perched on the back of Mutt Williams's (Shia LaBeouf) bike as the Russians pursue them. The stunt gag of them skidding to a halt in the study hall so a student (played by Chet Hanks, son of frequent Spielberg leading man Tom Hanks) could ask the Professor a question was done at the University Commons in Woolsey Hall, while a statue of Indy's late colleague and mentor Marcus Brody (Denholm Elliott, who played him in *Raiders* and *Last Crusade* and who had passed away in 1992) was placed in the university quad so it could be beheaded as a sight gag. Needing a period locomotive, Spielberg filmed Mutt speaking to Indy from the train at the Essex Steam Train and Riverboat exhibit in Essex, Connecticut. Indy and Mutt discussing the disappearance of Professor Oxley in the campus diner (named Arnie's, in tribute to Spielberg's dad) before starting a fight as a diversion, thereby leading to the motorcycle chase, was shot on the backlot at Paramount Studios.

This being modern Hollywood, however, this Paramount release was not confined to using only that studio's space. *Crystal Skull* would end up using four other studios for its elaborate sets. The newest (and shortest lasting) was the Downey Studios, a facility that had opened its doors in the late 1990s for filming, having been the Rockwell International plant for the building of various vehicles for the space program. The interior of Area 51 was constructed there and consisted of dozens of crates of highly classified artifacts, with the titular prop from *Raiders of the Lost Ark* making a cameo appearance before the eruption of the big battle and chase. The launching spot of the rocket sled, where Indy slugs it out with Spalko's main flunky, Dovchenko (Igor Jijikine), was filmed here as well, as were the caves of the Akator Cliffs, full of cryptic ancient paintings adorning the walls, and the Akator rotunda, where a tribe of threatening warriors emerge from the walls to pursue Indy and his group. Within five years after filming, Downey Studios was closed and demolished to make way for a shopping center.

Back at the more durable studio spaces in Southern California, *Crystal Skull* settled in at Universal, where a number of locations were created on soundstages: the interior of Indy's home, where he converses with Dean Stanforth (Jim Broadbent); the sanitarium interior, where Mutt and Indy notice the cryptic scribblings on Oxley's former cell; and the desolate cemetery, where Mutt and Indy are attacked by some blowpipe-wielding killers specializing in martial arts moves. A Peruvian village was constructed on the backlot, as was the top of the Great Stone Temple and the steps from which Indy and his party are seen racing away from the warriors. After sand pours out of the temple's base, four towers converge at the top of this structure to form an obelisk—just the sort of outrageous and spectacular

Irina Spalko (Cate Blanchett) tries her psychic powers on Indiana Jones (Harrison Ford) while her henchman, Dovchenko (Igor Jijikine, left), looks on in *Indiana Jones and the Kingdom of the Crystal Skull.* The Deming Municipal Airport in New Mexico provided the location for this sequence.

mechanism this movie franchise specialized in. Also on the lot was the plot of land where Oxley wards off the giant ants with the mystical crystal skull of the title, while Dovchenko doesn't fare so well, not only getting overwhelmed by the hungry insects but being carried off into their lair for additional feasting. There was also a funny sight gag of Indiana's trademark fedora being abducted by the ants, before being snatched up by its owner. The ants were, of course, later added through computer effects.

Down at Sony Studios (formerly MGM) in Culver City, the production constructed the Soviet base camp in the Amazon jungle where both Professor Oxley and the returning costar of *Raiders*, Karen Allen, first make their appearances; the tent interior where Indy is held hostage; and the most entertaining of the sets—the stone staircase with the retractable steps. This last set was constructed in two separate pieces and required the actors to be attached to safety wires as they scampered down the steps and as stagehands pulled the stone pieces back into the walls for maximum thrills. At the base of the stairs was a pool of water with the spiked corpses of less fortunate conquistadors who weren't able to outrun the tricky contraption.

It was at Warner Bros. that the elaborate door that required the crystal skull to open it and the circular throne room, seating a collection of thirteen skeletal aliens around the perimeter, were built for the big climax, although the sequence was so dependent on special effects that a great deal of it was acted against green screens on another set altogether. The escape route for Indy and his party, with a series of stone wheels and steps leading into the circular chamber that ends up flooded and thereby sends our heroes rising upward to rousingly cap off their ordeal, was also shot on the Warner Bros. stages.

During these soundstage excursions there had also been a trip to Hawaii, to the Shipman Estate on the eastern coast of the "Big Island" of Hawaii, in Hilo, where the chase scene between Spalko and Indy was staged, the highlight of which was a sword fight between the Russian villainess and Mutt. This sequence also required a great deal of additional soundstage filming. While in the fiftieth state, the company also shot what was supposed to be the base of the waterfalls after Marion drives over the three drops, with Kulaniapia Falls standing in for Peru. The second unit had captured spectacular images of Iguaçu Falls in Argentina, right on the Brazilian border, so that the principals would appear to be navigating these particular waters.

The wedding of Indy and Marion was staged at the First Christian Church of North Hollywood in Studio City, while the arrival in Peru, at what was supposed to be the rather forlorn looking Aeroporto de Nazca, was actually shot at Eagle Field in Firebaugh, northwest of Fresno, California. Principal photography finished a bit behind schedule on October 11, 2007. The post-production special effects included creating a miniature version of the "Doom Town" up at the Skywalker Ranch in order for it to be blown away by a nuclear blast.

The Adventures of Tintin

Although *The Adventures of Tintin*, being a motion-capture production, had no actual "locations" on which to shoot, it did require being created and put together at two different sites that were 6,700 miles apart. Producer Peter Jackson's Weta Workshop, located on the Miramar Peninsula in Wellington, New Zealand, was initially contacted by Steven Spielberg to do a CGI-version of Tintin's faithful dog, Snowy, for what was at that time intended to be a live-action adventure. Once the idea shifted to a full out motion-capture production, Weta became responsible for coming up with a look for the movie, creating preliminary art work of backdrops, buildings, props, character clothing, and so forth. By the fall of 2008, some $30 million had already been spent on scripts, character design, initial animation, and 3-D tests.

All of this went on prior to Spielberg's actual filming, which was done at the Giant Studios, located in West Lost Angeles, north of the Playa Vista campus. Starting on January 26, 2009, he guided the actors through their roles as they enacted the adventures on a bare set (referred to as the Mocap Volume) with a minimum of sets or props. (For example, because the scene aboard the *Karaboudjan* required the performers to react to being tossed about, a makeshift piece of the ship was constructed at the studio to allow them move about accurately.) Leading actors Jamie Bell, Daniel Craig, Andy Serkis, Nick Frost, Simon Pegg, and others were required to wear leotards with dots corresponding to certain parts of the body painted on them. Surrounding them on the stage were several cameras, which picked up each of these dots, communicating their movements to a central computer. This procedure was repeated with the actors' faces as well. In addition to being covered with the same special motion-capture paint, which was specifically placed on the twelve main muscle groups of the face, they wore a helmet upon which was strapped a small camera pointing directly at them so that its footage could be fed into a specially developed facial tracking software, which was, in turn, fed into a computer and matched onto the computer-generated character's face. Sometimes holding the camera himself, Spielberg was able to work fast, at times capturing as many as seventy to eighty shots a day. He completed all of the principal photography by mid-March, logging thirty-two days of actual shooting.

At this point, the filmed footage was handed over to Jackson's team, who were now at the Weta Digital facility in Wellington, where they were to spend another eighteen months computer designing the physical look of the characters, locations, surrounding structures, and so forth. They sometimes adhered to the original Hergé designs but in other instances opted for a different visual approach, according to Spielberg's request for how he wanted the finished film to look. Although Hergé's original artwork was used as the launching point for many of the designs, it was decided that his work was often too spare and required a more lavish, detailed look. This leg of the production dragged on long enough for a full two and a half years to pass between the end of actual shooting and the premiere in Belgium in October of 2011.

War Horse

For his filming of Michael Morpurgo's horse tale, Steve Spielberg used some of the most beautiful backdrops to ever appear in his films, as the chief setting of *War Horse* was the lush, picture-postcard green hills of Dartmoor National Park in Devon County, located in the England's South Western Peninsula. There, an abandoned building—the Ditsworthy Warren House, near Sheepstor—was redressed to become the Narracott farmhouse, with a barn, necessary for the storyline, built from scratch nearby. The location was ideal for shooting purposes, as there was not another building to be seen for miles around at any angle, giving it the peaceful feeling of isolation Spielberg was seeking. Shooting began here on August 6, 2010, with additional scenes utilizing Meavy, Comestone Tor, Haytor, and Ringmoor Down.

From mid- to late September, the company used another beautiful spot that seemed authentic to the movie's World War I-era setting: the village of Castle Combe, about twenty miles east of Bristol. Looking quaintly stuck in time, this town had frequently been cited as the prettiest in England and had already been used quite extensively in other period pictures, chief among them the 1967 musical *Doctor Dolittle*. There, Ted Narracott (Peter Mullan) is seen bidding for Joey on the Market Cross near the start of the film, and a heartbroken Albert (Jeremy Irvine) is forced to bid his beloved horse goodbye when his dad sells him to Captain Nicholls (Tom Hiddleston), as the military takes over the streets hoping to recruit some soldiers for the cause.

Stratfield Saye, the former home of the Duke of Wellington, acquired after his triumph at the Battle of Waterloo, was used to represent the cavalry headquarters

Steven Spielberg guides Jeremy Irvine through a scene on the Devon County set of *War Horse*.

where Joey is taken after becoming Nicholls's possession. On the grounds of this estate was filmed the exciting cavalry charge that memorably commences as the soldiers spring up from a waving wheat field and onto their mounts in unison before thundering into the fray, leading to the unfortunate but certain death of poor Captain Nicholls.

Although the action of the story moves over to France to subject poor Joey and the various soldiers he encounters along the way to the hell and muck of the battlefield, the film unit stayed in England to shoot all of these sequences, including those set on the French farm and at the windmill, where Spielberg staged one of the most effective shots of his career: the blades covering the sad execution of the deserting German soldiers. At Bourne Wood in Farmham, Surrey, the sloped incline was thoroughly muddied up for the scene in which Topthorn—trying to drag heavy artillery for the Germans—is savagely pushed to the limit of endurance, having been designated the on-the-spot replacement for the previous horse that was shot dead for his failure to perform.

The Wisley Airfield, also in Surrey, outside of Woking, was covered in barbed wire, mud, and corpses to become the grim location of the Battle of the Somme, where Albert and his friend Andrew Easton (Matt Milne) find themselves among the terrified soldiers asked to climb out of their ratty trenches and run directly into the line of fire. This also became the sight of the thrilling and unsettling sequence in which Joey makes a mad dash in hopes of escaping his plight only to end up wrapped in barbed wire and brought down smack in the middle of no-man's-land, where his misfortune brings together the opposing enemy for a brief moment of understanding. The emotional climax, when Joey is declared beyond help by the doctor (Liam Cunningham) and is ordered to be shot, was filmed in a section of the Luton Hoo Estate referred to as the Home Farm Buildings, in Luton, about an hour north of Central London. Shooting on the picture wrapped on October 27, 2010.

Lincoln

For his dramatization of the last four months in the life of the sixteenth president, Steven Spielberg took his cast and crew to Virginia, where all of the filming of *Lincoln* would take place. (Initially the dummy title of *Office Seekers* was used on the project.) Shooting there would last little more than two months, starting on October 11, 2011, and wrapping on December 19. Ironically, insomuch as it served as the capital of the Confederacy during the war between the states, Richmond now paid host to several scenes set in Washington, D.C. The Virginia State Capitol building in the middle of Capitol Square on Bank Street served a two-fold purpose. Production Designer Rick Carter (who would win an Oscar for his efforts) added a portico to the north side of the building so that it could pass itself off as the exterior of the White House, and chief among the scenes shot there was Lincoln's (Daniel Day-Lewis) discussion on the slavery amendment with his wife's companion Elizabeth Keckley (Gloria Reuben). The steps of the building would also fill in for the Capitol in D.C., in the flashback that concluded the movie, with Lincoln speaking his famous "with malice toward none" Second Inaugural Address.

Carter and Spielberg had hoped to use a House of Representatives set constructed for the last *Transformers* movie only to find out that it had already been dismantled. Therefore, the legislative chamber in the Virginia State Capitol, with alterations to keep it accurate to the 1865 time frame, now became the House and therefore the setting for many scenes in the movie, with fiery debates, as well as insults, swapped back and forth between radical Republican Thaddeus Stevens (Tommy Lee Jones) and grandstanding Democrat Fernando Wood (Lee Pace). The filmmakers had to make do with the fact that this particular area was about half the size of the actual House of Representatives, figuring if they were creating enough compelling drama and Spielberg was setting his camera up at enough interesting angles nobody but the most fervid historians would notice or care.

The Governor's Mansion, located on Governor Street near Capitol Square, became the exterior of the home of Preston Blair (Hal Holbrook), the Republican Party founder Lincoln enlists the aide of in order to help push the Thirteenth Amendment through. In the film, Blair is seen outside the building being lovingly put in his carriage by his daughter Elizabeth (Julie White) for his long ride (ironically) to Richmond. The interior of the house was used for the reception room of the White House, where Mrs. Lincoln (Sally Field) takes Stevens to task for checking up on the money she used to refurbish the decaying presidential residence. Staying in the neighborhood, another house on Governor Street, diagonally across from the Governor's Mansion, at 219–223, became Thaddeus Stevens's home, where he returns joyfully to show the amendment bill to his housekeeper, Lydia Smith (S. Epatha Merkerson), who happens to be his lover as well.

The telegraph room of the war department—where Lincoln tells his George Washington joke, much to the irritation of Edwin Stanton (Bruce McGill), and later speaks philosophically with two of the telegraph operators (Adam Driver, Drew Sease), asking them whether we choose to be born—was built at the Ninth Street Office Building, at 202 North Ninth in Richmond, also adjacent to the Capitol Plaza. West of the Capitol, on West Broad Street, the November Theater (which had original opened in 1911 as the Empire Theater) was used twice in the story. It is first seen as the opera house where the president and Mrs. Lincoln watch from their private box as Mary threateningly goads her husband to make sure the amendment is passed in order to keep their son Robert (Joseph Gordon-Levitt) out of the war. Later, it became D.C.'s Grover's Theater, where Lincoln's younger son Tad (Gulliver McGrath) is horrified to hear the news of his father's assassination.

Robert Lincoln (Joseph Gordon-Levitt) seems to be having second thoughts about enlisting in this scene from *Lincoln*. Petersburg, Virginia's Old Towne section provides the backdrop.

At Maymont, a Victorian estate located near the James River in Richmond, the brief scene following the Confederate Army's surrender at the McLean House at Appomattox Courthouse, when the Union Army shows an impromptu display of respect for the defeated Robert E. Lee (Christopher Boyer) by removing their hats, was filmed, as was Abraham and Mary's carriage ride, a moment of respite before the Ford's Theater tragedy.

Petersburg's Old Towne section was crucial for providing period buildings for several scenes. The City Market (actually built post-Civil War in 1879) on East Old Street was the setting for Lincoln's first appearance in the film, following the Battle of Jenkins' Ferry, when he listens to the grievances of a black soldier (David Oyelowo), who then joins two white soldiers (Dane DeHaan and Lukas Haas) in reciting the Gettysburg Address. The interior of this same octagonal building was also used as Grant's headquarters, where Grant (Jared Harris) and his men listen to the news over the telegraph of the decision on the Amendment. Around the corner on River Street, the Union Station stood in for the Naval Department, where Lincoln awkwardly gives his brief flag-raising speech. On that same street, the upper floor of the South Side Depot became the tavern where Secretary of State William Seward (David Strathairn) meets with the three political operatives (James Spader, John Hawkes, and Tim Blake Nelson) he hopes will sway voters to back the Thirteenth Amendment. This same building was the exterior of the army hospital where Lincoln takes his son Robert in hopes of persuading him not to enlist after witnessing the blood and brutality of war. Over on Cockade Alley, the Brickhouse Run restaurant was the backdrop for the scene in which an impatient democrat (Michael Ruff), who has no intention of listening to W. N. Bilbo's (Spader) sales pitch for the amendment, pulls a gun on him to scare the pest away. On that same street was the home of Senator William Hutton (David Warshofsky), where Hutton slams the door in the face of Richard Schell (Nelson), knocking off the wreath hanging there in memory of his brother. Later, Lincoln himself comes here to speak with Hutton, who admits to being a prejudiced man. Old Street also passed itself off as Pennsylvania Avenue in D.C. for the scene in which Lincoln and Seward discuss the chances of obtaining votes during a carriage ride.

Heading northwest up the James River, the production used a private estate in Goochland for the scenes of the *River Queen* side-wheel steamer docked at City Point, where General Grant welcomes the peace commissioners from Richmond (Jackie Earle Haley, Michael Shifflett, and Gregory Itzin). The interior of the boat was built at the AMF warehouse up in Mechanicsville, located about nine miles northeast of Capitol Square in Richmond. At this facility, Carter and his design team also recreated the entire second floor of the White House, where Lincoln had his private quarters and where, just down the corridor, he held his cabinet meeting, there being no West Wing at the time of the story. The bedroom in the Peterson House in D.C.—where Lincoln was carried after being shot at Ford's Theater across the street—was also built here to stage the death of the beloved chief executive, with all of the actors documenting the sad moment by being positioned according to famous illustrations of the time.

Bridge of Spies

After brief visits to New York for *Catch Me If You Can* and *The Terminal*, Steven Spielberg did more extensive shooting in the area for his Cold War drama. Starting on September 8, 2014, using the placeholder title of *St. James Place*, he took his cameras to Manhattan, beginning with a shot of James B. Donovan (Tom Hanks) walking up the steps of the Federal Courthouse at Foley Square, the building filling in for the US Supreme Court, per an onscreen chyron. The interiors were also used for Abel's trial. There was further Manhattan filming at the Broad Street subway station, dressed in 1957 style, for the scene at the start of the movie when Rudolf Abel (Mark Rylance) is pursued by a pair of FBI agents; a vintage train car from the New York City Transit Museum in Brooklyn Heights was used. The New York Bar Association at 42 West 44th Street welcomed the production into its offices so that they could stand in for Donovan's place of business, the firm of Watters, Cowan & Donovan. Here, Donovan receives the startling news that he has been chosen to represent Abel, who is accused of spying for Russia.

Over in Brooklyn, where the first portion of the movie was set, Abel is seen leaving his studio in the neighborhood affectionately referred to as DUMBO (Down Under the Manhattan Bridge Overpass). Further north, Abel is seen painting a picture in Astoria Park, although his mission there is two-fold, as we see him reach under the bench on which he is sitting and retrieve a coin, which we will soon find out has a message from his Russia contact in it. When the FBI finally decides to rush in and arrest Abel, it is at a building in the Astoria section of Queens near the intersection of 18th Street and 26th Avenue. Under heavy artificial rain, the night scene in which Donovan can't get a cab was filmed before the Appellate Division building on Monroe Place. Realizing he's being followed, Donovan then ends up crouching behind a car where he is finally confronted by Agent Hoffman (Scott Shepherd). This was filmed near the intersection of Hicks and Pineapple Streets. The prison courtyard where Abel reads a letter from his "pretend wife" sent from East Germany was shot at the Queens Detention Center.

In Brooklyn's Flatbush-Ditmas Park neighborhood, an attractive 1902 Victorian house located on 17th Street between Dorchester Road and Ditmas Avenue was chosen to portray the Donovan house, although at the time the events were taking place the lawyer and his family had moved into a bi-level apartment overlooking Prospect Park. The exterior of the house was used as well, although only its bottom floor. Among the scenes set here was the family discussion at the dinner table about Donovan taking the case. Trick windows made of sugar were put in for the unexpected moment in which Donovan's older daughter (Eve Hewson) is scared out of her wits when bullets are sprayed at the house while she's watching television. The upstairs of the house, for the scene of Donovan's son (Noah Schnapp) filling his bathtub as a "Red Scare" precaution, along with the scene of the exhausted counsellor coming home at the end of his ordeal and finally flopping on his bed for some rest, was a set created at the Steiner Studios. The cell in which Donovan first meets Abel and in which they later listen to Shostakovich together was also built there.

Flying overseas to Berlin in October, the film utilized Palais am Festungsgraben ("Palace on the Moat") to play the Russian Embassy where Donovan meets up with Abel's very dramatic "wife" (Petra Maria Cammin) and later his desired contact, Vogel (Sebastian Koch). The Berlin Messe, an exhibition hall built during the Nazi regime, became the massive Moscow courtroom at which Lieutenant Powers (Austin Stowell) is tried and sentenced to great applause. The no-longer-operating Flughafen-Berlin Tempelhof Airport, scene of the post-war airlifts, was used for Donovan's arrival in Berlin and later when Donovan and Powers leave the country on the cargo transport plane. The cockpit of Powers's U2 plane was built here to recreate its actual crash. A former political prison, Honhenschönhaussen, provided the cell and corridors for the scene in which Powers is dragged indelicately

Tom Hanks and Steven Spielberg discuss a scene next to a recreation of the Berlin Wall on the Wroclaw, Poland, set of *Bridge of Spies*.

to his various interrogations and receives buckets of water in his face from the KGB agents, who are not kidding around. The same building was used for the East Berlin detainment cell in which Donovan is placed after passport trouble. The Friedrichstrasse checkpoint, where Donovan jumps the line and is given priority to enter because he is an American, was created under the Gleisdeieck viaduct of the U-Bahn station. The motel where Powers and the other fliers meet for their lie detector tests was a set built in a Berlin parking lot. The Schloss Marquardt in Potsdam was the setting for the tense scene in which Vogel—believing Donovan is playing the Germans and the Russians against one another—suddenly turns on him.

The key location that gave the film its title was the real thing, the Glienicke Bridge (or Glienicker Brücke), where the actual exchange of Rudolf Abel and Francis Gary Powers had taken place on the morning of February 10, 1962. Connecting Berlin and Brandburg over the Havel River, this particular structure had been built in 1907. Because it was still a very busy road and simply could not keep operating while filming stopped and started, the production took complete control of it over a weekend with the city's permission.

Needing a city that still had the shabby and forlorn look that East Berlin possessed at the time of the story, the filmmakers ended up in Wroclaw, in western Poland, not far from the German border. Three hundred feet of the Berlin Wall under construction was set up on Miernicza Street for the scene in which US student Frederic Pryor (Will Rogers) initially crosses into East Berlin and then is arrested on his return visit. He is later seen being delivered to Checkpoint Charlie, which was also recreated in Wroclaw, at Kurkowa and Ptasia Streets. European shooting wrapped in early December. Additional sequences involving actual U2 planes were shot later down the line at Beale Airforce Base in Yuba County, California.

The BFG

Because Steven Spielberg's adaptation of Roald Dahl's children's book would require a combination of live actors and motion-capture performances, he couldn't rely on the means of filming he'd helped perfect on *The Adventures of Tintin*, merely shooting his actors on a blank stage while they wore motion-capture suits. Instead, he wanted his cast to be acting opposite one another as much as physically possible, no matter if they were great big fifty-foot-tall giants, smaller giants of a mere twenty-four feet in height, or just plain people. To this end he sometimes had multiple versions of the same set built to accommodate which characters were inhabiting it. Needing a great deal of space, he chose a former warehouse in Burnaby, outside of Vancouver, British Columbia, that had been converted into studio space in the early 2000s and renamed Mammoth Studios. Located on Underhill Avenue, it offered three impressive soundstages for use. Shooting began there on March 23, 2015.

Prior to the actual start of production, Spielberg staged a test run and invited members of his creative team to don motion-capture suits and act out the entirety of *The BFG* in the garage of his summer home in the Hamptons, blocking each scene and then recording it on a handheld camera.

The stages at Mammoth were filled with Sophie's (Ruby Barnhill) orphanage and the cobblestone London streets outside the building; a home in Amsterdam where BFG (Mark Rylance) and Sophie deliver a boy's dreams; the ballroom of Buckingham Palace, where BFG shares the "pleasures" of drinking Frobscottle with her majesty Queen Elizabeth II (Penelope Wilton); the queen's bedroom, where she is first startled to see Sophie plunked down at her window; and BFG's cavern hideaway. The last was an example of a setting that required the set to be produced in triplicate, scaled in correct perspective for Rylance, as BFG, to roam around comfortably; reduced somewhat in scale so that Fleshlumpeater (Jemaine Clement) and the other intruding giants could appear confined and hindered by the space; and, finally, filled with suggestions of various oversized props within the dwelling, so that Barnhill, as Sophie, would be properly dwarfed by her surroundings. In scenes involving both BFG and Sophie, a two-story platform was erected for Rylance to stand on so that the two actors could feel the necessary emotional interaction, rather than having the pair of them act against green screens or a prop suggesting the missing actor. Shooting would go on at the studio until June 16.

After this, additional locations were shot in Scotland to be used as "plate shots" for the backdrops for Giants Land, with several striking vistas on the Isle of Skye, Shiant Islands; the Orkneys, in the northernmost part of the country; Bamburgh Beach; and the Highlands. There were also establishing shots outside the actual Buckingham Palace in London, while Blenheim Palace in Woodstock, Oxfordshire, provided its gardens for the scene in which BFG is confronted by the Queen's guards.

5

Scripted by Spielberg

When the Director Received an Onscreen Writing Credit

T he best filmmakers are great storytellers, and it is often the director whom your average moviegoer equates with the "creation" of what they are seeing on screen. While any director of value has been known to work in close collaboration with their screenwriters, this does not always mean they are willing or justified in taking an onscreen credit in the writing department. Certainly Steven Spielberg worked with Carl Gottlieb while on location to get the *Jaws* screenplay into shape, and Melissa Matheson took the director's concept and ideas to construct her Oscar-nominated script for *E.T. the Extra-Terrestrial*, but in neither case did he receive any official mention as a writer.

Because he is said to be overflowing with story ideas, occasionally these have been committed to paper and then to film, with Steven Spielberg actually being credited for the writing. To date, only two of his own directorial efforts contain a "Screenplay by" mention, while the bulk of his "story" contributions came on television, by way of his two-season omnibus series *Amazing Stories*.

Here are the instances where Steven Spielberg received an onscreen writing credit of some sort.

Ace Eli and Rodger of the Skies

(20th Century Fox; April 11, 1973)

Starring Cliff Robertson (Ace Eli Walford), Pamela Franklin (Shelby), Eric Shea (Rodger Walford). Costarring Rosemary Murphy (Hannah), Bernadette Peters (Allison), Alice Ghostley (Sister Lite), Kelly Jean Peters (Rachel), Don Keefer (Mr. Parsons), Patricia Smith (Mrs. Wilma Walford), Royal Dano (Jake), Robert Hamm (Dumb Dickie), Herb Gatlin (Frank Savage), Arthur Malet (Brother Watson), Ariane Munker (Ariana Chase), Hope Summers (Laura), Jim Boles (Abraham), Lew Brown (Harrison). Music by Jerry Goldsmith. Screenplay by Chips Rosen (Claudia Salter). Story by Steven Spielberg. Produced by Boris Wilson (Robert Fryer and James Cresson). Directed by Bill Sampson (John Erman). 89 minutes. (PG)

A milestone insomuch as it marked the very first time Steven Spielberg's name was seen in the credits of a theatrical motion picture, *Ace Eli and Rodger of the Skies* was otherwise a project nobody connected with it had anything good to say about.

Hoping to entice one of the studios with a project he himself could direct, Spielberg came up with the storyline for a period piece about a barnstorming pilot and his difficult relationship with his hero-worshipping son, who follows the old man around the country as a participant in his traveling air show. At the time, Spielberg was under the guidance of agent Mike Medavoy, and he persuaded another of Medavoy's clients, Claudia Salter, to collaborate with him on coming up with a screenplay. Steven took Claudia's script to Fox in 1969, managing to interest production head Richard D. Zanuck, who would play an important part in Spielberg's career down the line. Initially, it appeared that Spielberg would get his wish to direct, when the project was announced in early January of 1970, with Joe Wizan as producer. Once Robert Fryer and James Cresson took over the property, they were adamant about getting someone with more experience behind the camera. The job, instead, went to John Erman, who, like Spielberg, had worked on *Marcus Welby M.D.*, among many television assignments, as well as having just done a feature for Fox, *Making It* (1971).

Filming on the $2.5 million production began in July of 1971 in Kansas, but a year later something had clearly gone wrong when 20th Century Fox kept dropping *Ace Eli* off the upcoming release schedule. By the time it finally arrived in select engagements (including D.C.) on April 11, 1973, industry insiders were well aware that the opening titles were full of pseudonyms, a sure sign of disenchantment. Erman was now "Bill Sampson," Salter was "Chips Rosen," and Fryer and Cresson together became "Boris Wilson." Perhaps figuring it was better to have your name up on the big screen than not at all, only Spielberg kept his proper credit, although he was as disgusted by what had been done to his original premise as the others. He would later refer to it as a "sick film."

The eighty-nine-minute film was certainly made with professionalism, although there was a distinctively sour tone to so much of it, as the relationship between the selfish, womanizing dad (Cliff Robertson) and his loyal but hapless boy (Eric Shea) was decidedly unsentimental, bordering on the unpleasant. Their itinerant lifestyle with the backdrop of the Depression era Midwest ended up giving it an unintended (and unfortunate) similarity to a superior concurrent release, Peter Bogdanovich's *Paper Moon*, which the public went for in a far bigger way than they did *Ace Eli*.

One bright spot was the introduction of stage performer Bernadette Peters in her very first motion picture, playing a prostitute who offers her services to Robertson in exchange for air rides. Also seen in the cast, partnered with Alice Ghostley as charlatan evangelists, was Arthur Malet, who did get his chance to be directed by Spielberg, twenty years later, as the grown up Tootles in *Hook*.

The Sugarland Express

Seeing Steven Spielberg's name among the writing credits on his very first theatrical release might have led people to believe that this was the norm and that he might become one of those multi-hyphen filmmakers who often put pen to paper before stepping behind the camera. His credited contributions as such would turn out to be very sporadic.

He was the one who first encountered the real life story of the Texas couple, Bobby and Ilae Faye Dent, who, in their foolish efforts to reclaim their offspring, had caused a surreal police caravan to trail them to their destination. Not wanting to present this as a "biographical" reenactment of the life and crimes of these two, Spielberg revamped the incident so that he would not be beholden to accuracy or to motivations that came from anywhere but the screenplay and the new characters he helped to create. He would work on the storyline with his hired screenwriters, Hal Barwood and Matthew Robbins, taking first billing in the "Story by" credit, followed by the requisite spelled out "and" before their ampersand teaming, indicating that their writing was recognized by the Writers Guild as a collaboration, with their director a separate entity.

Close Encounters of the Third Kind

A unique credit in Steve Spielberg's career, this marked the first time his name appeared as the screenwriter of one of his own directorial efforts. It would not happen again until twenty-four years later, when he also received a solo screenplay credit on *A.I. Artificial Intelligence.*

The origins of his grandiose epic about a peaceful meeting between Earthlings and extraterrestrials was inspired by a memorable moment in Spielberg's childhood when his father woke him in the middle of the night with the idea of the two of them sharing the spectacle of seeing a comet. What they witnessed instead was a spectacular meteor shower that left the ten-year-old future filmmaker pondering the mysteries of what exactly lay out there beyond the stars. Once he had made the leap into professional show business, he became increasingly fascinated by the continuing obsession with the topic of UFOs so many people had had since the late 1940s, this phenomenon having prompted the military to establish a committee to investigate claims of UFO sightings and thereafter basically discredit them. Dr. J. Allen Hynek had been in charge of this committee, which eventually went under the heading Project Blue Book, and the esteemed astronomer made the leap from skeptic to a man convinced that the government's handling of these reports were biased and uncharitable in their findings. He published a book, *The UFO Experience: A Scientific Inquiry*, in 1972, which told of his findings and theories, and ended up giving Spielberg his eventual title. According to Hynek there were three stages of UFO encounters: the First Kind was a sighting, the Second Kind proof of existence, and the Third Kind actual contact with alien life-form. At first Spielberg did not set out to make a direct reference in his intended story; he instead harkened back to the final speech at the end of the classic 1951 sci-fi thriller *The Thing from Another World* and called his treatment *Watch the Skies.*

The initial approach was to make a direct connection to Project Blue Book, with the protagonist of Spielberg's fictional tale being a committee member of this organization, an investigator who comes to the realization that there is a government cover-up regarding the whole UFO issue. His own skepticism on the subject would do a complete turnaround, leading up to an eventual alien encounter.

Because this was his dream project, it is not surprising that Spielberg was very adamant about what he felt was right for the film and what was not. Not considering himself a screenwriter, however, he felt obliged to find someone with more experience in this area to take a crack at fleshing out his ideas. Once Julia and Michael Phillips got involved as the producers, they suggested Spielberg use Paul Schrader, who had just written a very intense and dark drama about a disturbed New York cabbie who hopes to make his mark by assassinating a political candidate and rescuing an underage prostitute from her life on the streets. *Taxi Driver* was to become the next Phillips production, following up their Oscar-winning triumph of *The Sting.*

The Phillipses and Spielberg cultivated the interest of 20th Century Fox head Alan Ladd Jr. in their UFO concept, but the executive was confounded by their choice of Schrader to write the script, figuring he was the absolute wrong person for the job. As a result, the project was dropped by Fox and suddenly up for grabs

One of the many merchandising items related to *Close Encounters of the Third Kind*, the first film for which Spielberg received solo screenwriting credit.

until Columbia Studios executive David Begelman was sold on the idea. With Spielberg placating Columbia that they could make the whole film for less than the $3 million cap the studio had imposed on all upcoming projects, *Watch the Skies* was finally ready to move into becoming a reality, and the announcement was made in the fall of 1973 that it would be a new Columbia feature. Alan Ladd Jr's reservations, however, were well founded when Schrader handed in a grim and far too religiously themed screenplay, which he entitled *Kingdom Come*, about a man's struggle to convince the world that he is correct about his UFO theories. Insomuch as Schrader became known for his very angry, often heavy-handed and sour scripts, it is odd than anyone thought he was a good match for the kind of optimistic film Spielberg had in mind. Spielberg minced no words in describing how awful he thought the script was, and Schrader was off the project.

The next one to take a swing at it was someone with relatively little screenwriting experience, John Hill, who had impressed the Phillipses with a screenplay he written, *Far as the Eye Can See,* which never ended up getting made. Utilizing Spielberg's ideas, he came out ahead of Schrader, his draft called *Meeting of the Minds,* but it was clear that nobody was going to be able to get inside the director's head and fulfill his needs. The logical step seemed to be for Spielberg himself to take charge of the screenplay, a proposal that Columbia was happy to accept.

He did not, however, remain the sole writer on the project, turning at one point to Jerry Belson, best known for writing for such sitcoms as *The Dick Van Dyke Show* and *The Odd Couple,* in hopes that he could bring more humor to the property and perhaps revise some of the scenes between the tormented protagonist, Roy Neary, and his family. Along the way, Spielberg would also seek out contributions from Hal Barwood and Matthew Robbins, the two men who had written his very first feature, *The Sugarland Express.* They helped to shape scenes already written, were called back late in the game when Spielberg realized he needed some entirely new scenes in order to bring clarity and drama, and wrote the new introductory sequence of Lacombe and his team showing up in a desert windstorm after a fleet of missing World War II fliers have materialized.

In the end, however, the Writers Guild deemed Spielberg the chief creator of the screenplay, and he alone would receive on-screen mention. In addition to his screenplay credit, it was Steven Spielberg's name that appeared on the cover of the novelization published to coincide with the release of the movie, making one wonder how so busy a director managed to work book writing into his schedule. The *Close Encounters* novel, however, was not actually his, but the work of novelist Leslie Waller. Dell Books was well aware that putting the increasingly famous director's name on the cover was likely to engender more sales than Waller's would.

Poltergeist

(MGM, June 4, 1982)

Starring JoBeth Williams (Diana Freeling), Craig T. Nelson (Steve Freeling), Beatrice Straight (Dr. Lesh), Dominique Dunne (Dana Freeling), Oliver Robins (Robbie Freeling), Heather O'Rourke (Carol Anne Freeling). Screenplay by Steven Spielberg,

Michael Grais and Mark Victor. Story by Steven Spielberg. Produced by Steven Spielberg and Frank Marshall. Directed by Tobe Hooper. 114 minutes. (PG)

Steven Spielberg's name appears four times in the opening credits of *Poltergeist*; first, heralding the film as "a Steven Spielberg production;" then, as the top-billed screenplay writer (along with Michael Grais and Mark Victor); third, for providing the story; and, finally, as producer (sharing this task with Frank Marshall). But, as far as many people are concerned, he was also the director of the film, despite Tobe Hooper being listed as such.

Of all the motion pictures on which Spielberg's name appears outside of the final credit for director, this is the one people most readily associate with him and assume is actually his creation, through and through. And there is much to support the claim. Although Hooper was the man behind the camera, Spielberg was very much an overwhelming presence on set, making sure his vision was achieved, with many involved in the making of *Poltergeist* admitting that Hooper would defer to the better known filmmaker on many occasions to insure he was satisfied with

Time to clean the pool! Diana Freeling (JoBeth Williams) finds herself swimming with skeletons in *Poltergeist*.

what was being filmed. Producer Frank Marshall would later state, "Tobe was the director and was on the set every day. But Steven did the design for every story board . . . and he was on the set every day except for three days when he was in Hawaii." Steven also fessed up to designing the movie and being involved in all of the camera setups of specific shots. He and Marshall were also the supervisors of the entire post-production of the movie, overseeing the editing, special effects, sound recording, and soundtrack.

The origins of the story were very much Spielberg's, whose idea it was to make a horror film, not in a familiar "haunted house" or gloomy urban setting but in the blandest of prefab suburban developments patterned after the one he grew up in while living in Arizona. His own childhood fear of an ominous tree that stood outside of his bedroom window was worked into the script. He also claimed that *Poltergeist* was his criticism of the dominance of television in most family's lives since the whole plotline spun around the supernatural spirits entering the Freeling household by way of their TV set. The image of little Heather O'Rourke transfixed by the tube, her hands placed against its screen, was chosen for the poster that sold the movie and became perhaps the moment ("They're here . . . !!!") best remembered by viewers. Because Spielberg had frequently spoken of his obsession with the small screen, for which he would later produce a great deal of product, this "critique" of the ominous power of television over us all was as "safe" and toothless as the rest of the finished product.

The two men originally hired to bring Spielberg's story to life, Michael Grais and Mark Victor, had previously collaborated on an unusual episode of *Starsky & Hutch*, "The Vampire," in which John Saxon portrayed a psychopath who affixed fangs to his mouth in order to puncture the necks of his victims. According to Marshall, Spielberg then did a complete rewrite of their work but allowed them to retain a credit.

Wanting to hand the project over to someone else with more experience in creating a world of horror than he felt he was capable of, Spielberg sought out Tobe Hooper to helm the picture on the basis of his seminal 1974 thriller *The Texas Chain Saw Massacre*. That deeply unsettling and uncompromisingly terrifying account of some hapless travelers besieged by a family of unhinged murderers with a knack for dismembering their victims had struck many as a fresh, gut-wrenching way of creating nightmares. The very raw, visceral nature of *Massacre* was, in truth, at odds with the PG-rated vision of wholesome scares Spielberg had in mind, which proved to be the movie's undoing. In the end, *Poltergeist* played more like a candy-coated rollercoaster ride, letting the special effects and cheap shocks override genuine emotion and scares, with no sense whatsoever of any real impending threat to the blandly cookie-cutter family portrayed onscreen by a less than exciting cast.

Costing $10.5 million, *Poltergeist* opened just a week before *E.T.* This caused some to speculate that Spielberg might *not* have been able to direct both pictures, when in fact principal photography on the former took place between May and August of 1981, finishing up the month before the latter began filming. *Poltergeist* was originally saddled with an R rating by the MPAA, until MGM disputed the decision and won a more saleable PG. The picture struck a nerve with undemanding summer audiences, taking in $76,606,280 at the box office, thereby allowing Spielberg's name to leap that much further up the ladder of fame and recognition. It was also a rare hit for the once mighty studio during this era and the first Spielberg-produced entity that actually made money.

Considering the second-rate nature of the finished product, it was probably a wise decision on Spielberg's part to let someone else shoulder the blame. Hooper would diplomatically claim at the time that he was very happy with the collaboration and the amount of input from his producer-writer, but he balked at some of the initial advertising, which gave Spielberg a larger typeface on his credit than Hooper's. Legal action caused MGM to alter this accordingly. This did not mean that there was any animosity between the two, as Hooper and Spielberg would collaborate again—the former directing an episode of *Amazing Stories* five years later, and, many more years down the line, an episode of the alien abduction miniseries *Taken*.

Spielberg admitted to the press: "I felt a proprietary interest in this project that was stronger than if I was just an executive producer. I thought I'd be able to turn *Poltergeist* over to a director and walk away. I was wrong."

The Goonies

(Warner Bros.; June 7, 1985)

Steven Spielberg presents. Starring (in alphabetical order) Sean Astin (Mikey), Josh Brolin (Brand), Jeff Cohen (Chunk), Corey Feldman (Mouth), Kerri Green (Andy), Martha Plimpton (Stef), Ke Huy Quan (Data). Executive Producers: Steven Spielberg, Frank Marshall, Kathleen Kennedy. Produced by Richard Donner and Harvey Bernhard. Screenplay by Chris Columbus. Story by Steven Spielberg. Directed by Richard Donner. 114 minutes. (PG)

Skeletons! Bats! Mutants! Pirates! Liberace references! All of these and more were crammed into the very busy, very noisy storyline of *The Goonies*, Steven Spielberg's attempt to fulfill every (or almost every) young boy's fantasy of experiencing the sort of high adventure right there in your own backyard that seemed possible only in storybooks. Unlike *Poltergeist*, this time, after coming up with the concept, he left the screenwriting to someone else, Chris Columbus, the only name that appears in this capacity onscreen. (His script includes a self-referential mention of his own *Gremlins*.) Perhaps because he found an ideal outlet to bring his bottomless bag of ideas to life by producing them in a short-story format on television with *Amazing Stories*, this marked Spielberg's last story credit to date on a feature film.

In the picture-postcard town of Astoria, Oregon, young Mike (Sean Astin)—having discovered the map of legendary pirate One-Eyed Willie in his attic—persuades his motley group of friends to join him on the treasure hunt, leading them to hidden tunnels beneath an abandoned restaurant, where they run afoul of a family of cutthroat counterfeiters. Rapidly paced but staged and enacted with all the subtlety of someone slamming their hand repeatedly in a car door, *The Goonies* won no new converts to Spielberg's expanding world of summertime fantasy

Good enough for some: Mouth (Corey Feldman), Mikey (Sean Astin), Data (Ke Huy Quan), and Chunk (Jeff Cohen) go hunting for treasure in *The Goonies*.

entertainment, some of which, like this one, were clearly targeted at undemanding 1980s youngsters (who enjoyed a penis joke or two).

The movie deserved applause, however, for J. Michael Riva's splendidly detailed production design, the highlight of which was a full-scale pirate ship situated in a lake inside a cave (built at the Burbank Studios), and for Astin (in his screen debut), for being the only child actor on hand who didn't grate on one's nerves.

Included in the cast, as Astin's mom, was Mary Ellen Trainor, who had worked as an assistant on *1941*, ended up coauthoring a book on its making, and married its writer, Robert Zemeckis. Also on hand, as one of "the Goonies," was Spielberg's young discovery from *Indiana Jones and the Temple of Doom*, Ke Huy Quan.

Amazing Stories

Season 1

"Ghost Train" (See Chapter 3, page 100)

"The Main Attraction" (Season 1, Episode 2; October 6, 1985)
Starring John Scott Clough (Brad Bender), Lisa Jane Persky (Shirley). Teleplay by Brad Bird and Mick Garris. Story by Steven Spielberg. Directed by Matthew Robbins.

"He could not resist the incredible force," said the copy in the *TV Guide* ad, giving the impression that this episode was going to be more serious than it actually was. Unsubtly directed by Spielberg's cowriter on *The Sugarland Express*, Matthew Robbins, this was a decidedly goofy story of an arrogant high schooler (Clough), whose goal to be named prom king is sidelined when a meteor hits his bedroom and makes him magnetic.

This was the first professional writing credit for Brad Bird, who would go on to direct such top-notch animated films as *The Iron Giant* (1999) and *Ratatouille* (2007). He also showed up onscreen as one of the scientists investigating the meteor damage.

"Alamo Jobe" (Season 1, Episode 3; October 20, 1985)

Starring Kelly Reno (Jobe). Costarring William Boyett (Col. Travis), Lurene Tuttle (Harriet Wendse), Richard Young (Davy Crockett). Teleplay by Joshua Brand and John Falsey. Story by Steven Spielberg. Directed by Michael Moore.

The Black Stallion star Kelly Reno (whose final acting appearance this turned out to be) was cast as a fifteen-year-old Texas patriot participating in the doomed battle at the Alamo only to find himself thrown into modern-day San Antonio. The befuddled but determined teen gallops about the city in an effort to deliver an important missive from Colonel Travis to General Lefferts. The intriguing premise ended up being seriously shortchanged when the whole thing ended rather abruptly, as if the plug was pulled because the allotted time had run out.

Spielberg's cherished second unit director on *Raiders of the Lost Ark* and *Indiana Jones and the Temple of Doom*, Michael Moore (*not* the future documentary filmmaker), got a chance to call the shots here. This caused a bit of confusion, as there was yet another Michael Moore who showed up in the end credits, as the series' sound mixer.

"Mummy Daddy" (Season 1, Episode 4; October 27, 1985)

Starring Tom Harrison (Harold), Bronson Pinchot (Director), Brion James (Willie Joe), Tracey Walter (Ezra), Larry Hakin (Jubal). Teleplay by Earl Pomerantz. Story by Steven Spielberg. Directed by William Dear.

More Abbott and Costello than *The Twilight Zone*, this episode once again went for the silly rather than the eerie in this tale of an actor (Tom Harrison) whose confinement in his mummy costume during a film shoot gets him into trouble with some unsuspecting locals. When Harold is told his wife is about to give birth, he races to the hospital still garbed in his gauze only to be mistaken by some yokels for the legendary Ra Amin Ka, a rampaging mummy who, according to lore, was left behind by a gypsy carnival. Greg Cannom's detailed mummy makeup was the real attraction here.

This episode was paired with Spielberg's "The Mission" and Robert Zemeckis's "Go to the Head of the Class" to make up an *Amazing Stories* feature film for theatrical release in Europe in 1987.

"The Mission" (See Chapter 3, page 101)

"The Amazing Falsworth" (Season 1, Episode 6; November 5, 1985)

Special Guest Star: Gregory Hines (Falsworth). Guest Star: Richard Masur (Trent Tinker). Teleplay by Mick Garris. Story by Steven Spielberg. Directed by Peter Hyams.

This installment was considered "intense" enough for it to be scheduled at a later time on a "special night"; therefore it aired on a Tuesday at 9:00 p.m. EST, only two days after "The Mission" had been shown in an expanded timeslot that Sunday. Directed with a creepy sense of menace by Peter Hyams, this thriller was reasonably engaging up to the point when the "surprise" twist became a bit too obvious.

Gregory Hines played a psychic whose stage show consists of going through his audience blindfolded and touching select patrons, the physical contact allowing him to know hidden secrets about them. He is greatly disturbed when he realizes one of the men he has touched is the "Keyboard Killer," fresh from two murders.

"Fine Tuning" (Season 1, Episode 7; November 10, 1985)

Starring Matthew Laborteaux (Andy), Gary Riley (Jimmy), Jimmy Gatherum (George). Special Guest appearance by Milton Berle (himself). Teleplay by Earl Pomerantz. Story by Steven Spielberg. Directed by Bob Balaban.

This time Spielberg gives one of his *Close Encounters of the Third Kind* cast members, Bob Balaban, a chance to sit in the director's chair for another off-kilter episode. Three teens are thrilled to discover that their science project to build a television antenna to reach far-off parts of the United States has taken them *way* beyond that when they pick up signals from another planet. Turns out the aliens are not only big fans of old television shows; they've even produced copycat versions of some of our classics from the past, including *The George Burns and Gracie Allen Show* and *I Love Lucy* ("We never should've told them Lucy and Desi split up," one of the boys theorizes later, when the aliens become depressed). Coming to Earth in hopes of making contact with one of their small-screen favorites, they encounter Milton Berle taking a walk through Beverly Hills and try to entice him to leave Southern California behind for another galaxy.

Elements of the plotline bore an uncomfortable similarity to a film released earlier that summer, *Explorers*—directed by another Spielberg protégé, Joe Dante—in which three boys encounter aliens with a penchant for Earthling television.

In a cute nod to *Close Encounters*, the "Fine Tuning" teens and the aliens first communicate through music (on a clarinet, the instrument, coincidentally, that Spielberg himself knew how to play), only it's not the unmistakable five tones from the classic space movie that bond them but the three-note NBC chimes.

"Mr. Remote Control" (Season 1, Episode 10; December 8, 1985)

Starring Sydney Lassick (Walter Poindexter), Nancy Parsons (Grendel Poindexter). Costarring Philip Bruns (Mr. Beasley), Jeff B. Cohen (Ralph), David Stone (Maheshwara), Shawn Weatherly (Beauty Pageant Contestant). Teleplay by Douglas Lloyd McIntosh. Story by Steven Spielberg. Directed by Bob Clark.

Perhaps to make amends for chopping him out of the theatrical print of *1941*, Spielberg bumped frumpy character actor Sydney Lassick up to the star spot for yet another exercise in overkill. Henpecked Walter Poindexter is given a temporary respite from his miserable life when he purchases a television set with a remote control that can turn his tormentors into famous TV characters. His shrewish spouse now becomes June Cleaver (Barbara Billingsley) from *Leave it to Beaver*; his Hare Krishna older son is turned into Faceman (Dirk Benedict) from *The A-Team*; and his demonic younger son transforms into Arnold (Gary Coleman) from *Diff'rent Strokes*.

There are additional cameos from *Tonight Show* sidekick Ed McMahon, *Sanford and Son*'s LaWanda Page, *The Dating Game* host Jim Lange, and KITT, the talking car from *Knight Rider*. Bob Clark directs his actors—including Nancy Parsons, with whom he had worked in the *Porky's* comedies—to "go large."

If nothing else, the episode gives viewers a chance to see someone threaten overbearing exercise guru Richard Simmons with a gun.

"Santa '85" (Season 1, Episode 11; December 15, 1985)

Starring Douglas Seale (Santa Claus), Pat Hingle (Sheriff Horace Smyvie), Gabriel Damon (Bobby Mynes), Marvin J. McIntyre (Deputy Weatherby). Teleplay by Joshua Brand and John Falsey. Story by Steven Spielberg. Directed by Phil Joanou.

On his appointed rounds, poor Santa finds himself arrested for breaking and entering and confronts a disbelieving sheriff (Hingle) and a little boy (Damon), who uses St. Nick's reindeer to help the Jolly Old Elf break out of the slammer. A well-intended but featherweight entry, this served as a warm-up of sorts for Seale, who would later play Kris Kringle on the big screen, in the Disney comedy *Ernest Saves Christmas* (1988).

"Vanessa in the Garden" (Season 1, Episode 12; December 29, 1985)

Starring Harvey Keitel (Byron Sullivan), Sondra Locke (Vanessa Sullivan), Beau Bridges (Teddy Shearing). Written by Steven Spielberg. Directed by Clint Eastwood.

Significant for being the sole episode of the series to give credit entirely to Steven Spielberg for the writing, "Vanessa in the Garden" also had the added attraction of being the very first project for television to be directed by Clint Eastwood. (His only other effort in the medium was not a dramatic story but an episode of his own production, the documentary series *The Blues*.) With this stellar combination of names, it is odd that the segment ended up debuting in the week between Christmas and New Year's Day, normally a TV graveyard of reruns.

While being yet another one of the series' offerings to fall short of its goals, this ghost tale was one of the better first season efforts up to that point. Artist Byron Sullivan (a not quite ideally cast Harvey Keitel) finds his inspiration in his beloved wife, Vanessa (Eastwood's then-girlfriend and occasional costar Sondra Locke). After being told by his agent (Beau Bridges) that his work has landed him a show at an exclusive New York gallery, Byron is elated but then has his future shattered when Vanessa is killed in a freak carriage accident. Convinced he can never paint again, a despondent Byron is haunted by visions of his late wife, which proves a turning point in his uncertain future.

Although Spielberg's dialogue sounded a tad stilted coming from the mouths of Keitel and Bridges, there was a worthy message in his tale: a loved one's passing needn't mark the end of an artist's creativity but can instead inspire them to carry on.

This episode connected Spielberg back to his beginnings, as Keitel's paintings were created by the same man who did the portraits for *Night Gallery*, Jaroslav Gebr.

"No Day at the Beach" (Season 1, Episode 14; January 12, 1986)

Starring Charlie Sheen (Casey), Larry Spinak (Arnold), Ralph Seymour (Ira), Philip McKeon (Stick), Leo Geter (Evergreen), Tom Hodges (Tiny). Teleplay by Mick Garris. Story by Steven Spielberg. Directed by Lesli Linka Glatter.

Like the Spielberg-directed "The Mission," this episode captured the camaraderie of young soldiers as they embark on a dangerous confrontation with the enemy, but it also got tripped up by the series' insistence on adding a fantasy twist, one that merely came off as head scratching.

During World War II, a troop of soldiers pass the time on their transport ship by teasing the outsider of the group, naïve and clumsy Arnold. When they are pinned down during battle by artillery fire from a German pillbox, Arnold unexpectedly proves to be a hero . . . or does he?

This one was of interest because director Lesli Linka Glatter managed to shoot the episode in black and white (to help match the actual stock footage used throughout) and because of the similarities it now draws to *Saving Private Ryan*. In both, the soldiers must disembark from a landing craft onto a beach under heavy siege by the enemy, but mid-1980s network television dared not be as shockingly explicit in its depiction of wartime violence as Spielberg's later masterpiece.

Although Charlie Sheen rated top billing, the piece was definitely an ensemble. He would not have his breakthrough role, in Oliver Stone's *Platoon*, until the end of that same year.

"Gather Ye Acorns" (Season 1, Episode 16; February 2, 1986)

Starring Mark Hamill (Jonathan Quick), David Rappaport (Troll), Lois de Banzie (Alma), Mary Jo Deschanel (Francine). Special Guest Appearance by Royal Dano (Elmer). Teleplay by Stu Krieger. Story by Steven Spielberg. Directed by Norman Reynolds.

It's not hard to connect this tale to Steven Spielberg, as it has things turn out quite nicely for a boy (David Friedman) who listens to a troll's advice to "cling to the child in you for as long as you possibly can." Heeding the mysterious little man's words, Jonathan Quick forsakes his parents' wishes for him to study medicine and instead grows up to be a disillusioned vagrant, toting around his collectibles, until fate steps in.

One of the more engaging of Spielberg's storylines from Season 1, it also allowed its star, Mark Hamill, to have fun disguising himself under mounds of Rip Van Winkle-like hair to play a grizzled old drifter. The supporting cast includes future Oscar-winner Forest Whitaker as one of the men excited over Jonathan's rarities, which include the first comic book to feature Superman.

"Ben and Dorothy" (Season 1, Episode 18; March 2, 1986)

Starring Joe Seneca (Ben Dumfy), Lane Smith (Dr. Caruso), Louis Giambalvo (Dr. Templeton), Kathleen Lloyd (Samantha), Joe Regalbuto (Merle), Natalie Gregory (Dorothy). Teleplay by Michael de Guzman. Story by Steven Spielberg. Directed by Thomas Carter.

Aiming for the heartstrings, this is a sweet and simple story of Ben Dumfy, an elderly man who wakes up in the hospital after being in a coma for forty years. Having spent so much time in an unconscious state, Ben finds he is able to communicate with a little girl (Natalie Gregory) who is also in a coma, much to the surprise of her grieving but hopeful parents.

This segment benefited tremendously from the fine central performance of Joe Seneca, a late bloomer who received the bulk of his acting jobs past the age of sixty, following a career singing as a member of a group called the Three Riffs. The episode's writer, Michael de Guzman, had the dubious distinction of later scripting *Jaws, the Revenge* (1987).

"Mirror, Mirror" (Season 1, Episode 19; March 9, 1986)

Starring Sam Waterston (Jordan Manmouth), Helen Shaver (Karen). Special Appearance by Dick Cavett (himself). Costarring Tim Robbins (Jordan's phantom). Teleplay by Joseph Minion. Story by Steven Spielberg. Directed by Martin Scorsese.

For his final story contribution to the first season, Spielberg went for supernatural chills rather than silly thrills. Just to make things that much sweeter, he managed to persuade one of the cinema's red-hot filmmakers, Martin Scorsese, to helm the episode, which was the very first time he directed something for the small screen.

Sam Waterston gives it his all playing Jordan Manmouth, a self-satisfied horror author who is convinced that nothing *really* frightens him and who argues with talk show host Dick Cavett that the violence one sees in scary movies is there to disturb and delight people. When Manmouth returns home that night, he is startled to see the image of a disfigured man repeatedly appearing in every mirror in which he looks. His mounting fear takes him to the brink of madness and beyond. While Scorsese brings a good degree of unease and anxiety to the piece, the episode could really have used a better twist as its denouement.

The writer of this installment, Joseph Minion, had the year prior scripted Scorsese's dark screwball comedy *After Hours*. Obscured by makeup, Tim Robbins appeared as Manmouth's phantom twenty years before Spielberg directed him in *War of the Worlds*. Opening the episode are scenes from the Hammer horror film *The Plague of the Zombies* (1966).

Season 2

"The Wedding Ring" (Season 2, Episode 1; September 22, 1986)

Starring Rhea Perlman (Lois), Danny DeVito (Herbert), Louis Giambalvo (Haggerty), Bernadette Birkett (Tina), David Byrd (Mr. Rhine), Tracey Walter (Blaze). Teleplay by Stu Krieger. Story by Steven Spielberg. Directed by Danny DeVito.

For the second season opener, the series went for broad and dopey. Danny DeVito directed himself and his wife, Rhea Perlman, in this tale of a cursed wedding ring that turns a timid Atlantic City waitress into a sexual dynamo and would-be murderess. Overplayed (especially by Perlman) for minimum laughs, it was probably more fun on the set than the finished product was to watch.

"You Gotta Believe Me" (Season 2, Episode 5; October 20, 1986)

Starring Charles Durning (Earl), Mary Betten (Nancy), Ebbe Roe Smith (Theresa), Wil Shriner (James), John Roselius (Todd Johnson). Teleplay by Stu Krieger. Story by Steven Spielberg. Directed by Kevin Reynolds.

This is the best of the second season entries to have a story devised by Steven Spielberg. Earl has a vivid dream of the debris of a plane crash smoldering in his living room and the ghosts of its victims walking among it. Certain that this is not just an illusion but a premonition of something awful about to happen, Earl heads to the airport in an effort to stop the next scheduled flight from taking off.

Atmospherically directed by Kevin Reynolds (who had already scripted and directed *Fandango* for Amblin) and acted with just the right degree of paranoia by Charles Durning, this episode came pretty close to capturing the spirit of *The Twilight Zone*. The sight of a distraught Durning wandering the nearly vacant airport in his pajamas and bathrobe was a memorable one.

"The Greibble" (Season 2, Episode 6; November 3, 1986)

Starring Hayley Mills (Joan Simmons). Teleplay by Mick Garris. Story by Steven Spielberg. Directed by Joe Dante.

Feeling it necessary to clean out her young son's bedroom in order to rid him of some of his childhood keepsakes, housewife Joan Simmons is shocked when the incarnation of the monster in a storybook she's just heaved into the trash shows up and proceeds to eat every inanimate object in sight. Too foolish to be enjoyed by anyone but impressionable tots, it bares the unmistakable stamp of director Joe Dante. It is always nice to see Hayley Mills, however.

"Blue Man Down" (Season 2, Episode 14; January 19, 1987)

Starring Max Gail (Duncan Moore), Kate McNeil (Patty O'Neil), Chris Nash (DeSoto). Teleplay by Jacob Epstein and Daniel Lindley. Story by Steven Spielberg. Directed by Paul Michael Glaser.

Wracked by guilt when his partner is killed by a masked psycho, a police officer is given a new partner who helps him overcome his anxiety and track down the man responsible for the crime. Nicely played by Max Gail as the cop and Kate McNeil as the lady who inspires him, this episode played for the most part like a straight-forward police-procedural episode of a weekly cop series. Since every episode has *something* supernatural to it, it was pretty easy to guess the surprise twist.

High Incident: **Pilot**

(ABC, March 4, 1996; 9:00 p.m. EST)

Starring Matthew Beck (Terry Hagar), Dylan A. Bruno (Andy Lightner), Matt Craven (Lenny Gayer), Aunjanue Ellis (Leslie Joyner), Cole Hauser (Randy Willitz), David Keith (Jim Marsh), Catherine Kellner (Gayle Van Camp), Julio Oscar Mechoso (Richie Fernandez), Louis Mustillo (Russell Topps). Guest Starring Lucinda Jenney (Anne Bonner), Titus Welliver (Sgt. Crisco), Rocky Carroll (Jerry White). Created by Eric Bogosian and Michael Pavone and Dave Alan Johnson and Steven Spielberg. Executive producers: Steven Spielberg, Michael Pavone and Dave Alan Johnson, Eric Bogosian. Teleplay by Eric Bogosian and Michael Pavone and Dave Alan Johnson. Story by Steven Spielberg and Eric Bogosian and Michael Pavone and Dave Alan Johnson. Directed by Charles Haid.

So determined was Steve Spielberg to make his one-hour, mid-season police series work that he got involved beyond the creation and executive producer stage and actually contributed to the story of the pilot, the first time he received a writing mention on one of his television projects since *Amazing Stories*. This was the second series from DreamWorks SKG, following the quick demise of *Champs*, also on ABC, earlier that year.

Set in the fictional Southern Los Angeles city of El Camino (actually filmed in Chatsworth), *High Incident* was described by its creative team as a mix of *Hill Street Blues* (the director of this episode and the show's co-executive producer, Charles Haid, was one of that program's stars) and *Adam-12*, as it followed various members of the police force as they dealt with criminal matters both minor and major. The pilot episode had no single plot but episodically consisted of various police duos paired off in their squad cars swapping philosophies, inanities, and trivia while trying to break up a fight at a children's birthday party; chasing a fourteen-year-old suspect; carting away a nutcase street performer; and experiencing a shocking fatality when pulling someone over because of a faulty tail pipe. One officer, Jim Marsh (David Keith), is charged with harassment by a fellow cop (Lucinda Jenney) he slept with, a lawnmower becomes a bizarre symbol of closure, and audiences probably weren't too sure what to make of a scene that had Marsh pulling over a driver (Reed Rudy) because he was picking his nose.

So deeply involved in the series that he actually served at one point as a camera operator on the set, Spielberg no doubt added some personal touches to the first episode in a plotline involving a sensitive boy (Jameson Baltes) who is the only one in his apartment complex to speak up against an intimidating neighbor (Mike Starr). There were also references to *The Magnificent Seven, Shane, The Shootist*, and *High Noon* ("Who's Gary Cooper?") from an officer (Louis Mustillo) well versed in western-movie history.

Despite its best efforts to blend the personal lives of its protagonists and the unpredictable danger and lunacy of their day-to-day workloads, the series was devoid of fresh ideas and didn't have enough compelling characters or incidents (high or otherwise) onscreen week after week to make any sort of impact on television audiences. ABC gave it their best shot, however, to cultivate interest. The pilot was shown *twice* in its premiere week in March, as was, in a last-minute decision, episode number 2. After the first six episodes aired, *High Incident* stayed firmly under the top fifty in the Nielsen ratings for the 1995–1996 season but was given a second chance by the network at the urging of DreamWorks. Returning in August, the remaining four episodes were shown, running directly into the second-season premiere week in September, when audiences were offered both a Tuesday preview and the official debut in the new time slot, Thursday at 8:00 p.m. EST. ABC allowed the show to run the full season, but the ratings never improved, and it aired its last new episode on May 8, 1997.

So famous was the filmmaker by this point that Spielberg claimed that, while he participated in a ride-along to observe real police officers at work, "the guys being put in handcuffs were asking for my autograph."

A.I. Artificial Intelligence

A.I. marked the first time in twenty-four years that Steven Spielberg's name was credited on the screenplay for one of his own films (*Close Encounters of the Third Kind* being the only previous such instance). His "Screenplay by" credit was followed by the acknowledgement "Based on a Screen Story by Ian Watson," which preceded the mention of the source material, Brian Aldiss's short story "Supertoys Last All Summer Long."

Watson was a British science fiction writer whose works included novels like *The Embedding* and the "Black Current" series of books. After filmmaker Stanley Kubrick had purchased the rights to Aldiss's tale, he enlisted Watson to work with him in formulating ideas of how to expand on the seven-page story, seeing parallels to Carlo Collodi's classic children's novel *The Adventures of Pinocchio*, a comparison Aldiss was not keen on making. The Watson-Kubrick collaboration went on between May of 1990 and January of 1991. The director would also approach Arthur C. Clarke—the man whose story "The Sentinel" had inspired Kubrick's sci-fi masterpiece, *2001: A Space Odyssey*—and novelist Sara Maitland (*Daughter of Jerusalem*), but it was Watson's ideas and story outline that brought the concept closest to what Kubrick wanted. To further bring this world to life, Kubrick hired illustrator Chris Baker (who went under the professional name of "Fangorn") to provide a series of sketches for the visual look of the backdrops, sets, costumes, and characters.

During this long process, Kubrick kept Spielberg abreast of his intentions, marking a rare time he invited another filmmaker into his customarily secretive process of developing movies. Part of the reason Kubrick kept in touch with Spielberg was that he wasn't sure if he himself was the right person to bring the story to life onscreen; he proposed the possibility of producing the picture with Spielberg in the director's chair, believing the property to be "closer to your sensibility than mine." There was also hesitancy on Kubrick's part because he didn't feel that, as of the early 1990s, special effects technology had caught up with his vision, and he worried that bringing to life a robotic boy and placing him in the fantastical future world he had in mind couldn't be pulled off with conviction. Once he saw the technical marvels Spielberg's special effects team whipped up for *Jurassic Park*, Kubrick was now convinced the property had a future. Notorious for the amount of time spent between and *during* his films, Kubrick put *A.I.* on the backburner while he concentrated on *Eyes Wide Shut* instead. Only months before that drama made its debut in the summer of 1999, Kubrick passed away. This seemingly put an end to *A.I.* until Kubrick's widow contacted Spielberg, urging him to carry out her husband's vision. It was a mighty challenge, as Kubrick had a very distinctive style and a very devout following. Although there were millions excited at the prospect of a property that came from the minds of both Stanley Kubrick and Steven Spielberg, there were just as many detractors who placed them in opposing camps, the former often thought of as cerebral and distant, the latter a crowd-pleasing sentimentalist.

Because he had the family's blessing (an end credit would thank "Christiane Kubrick & the Kubrick Family"), Spielberg was now firmly committed to bring the property to fruition. Due to Kubrick's longstanding relationship with Warner Bros., that studio would serve as distributor in the United States, while Spielberg's company, DreamWorks, would handle exhibition elsewhere. Because Kubrick

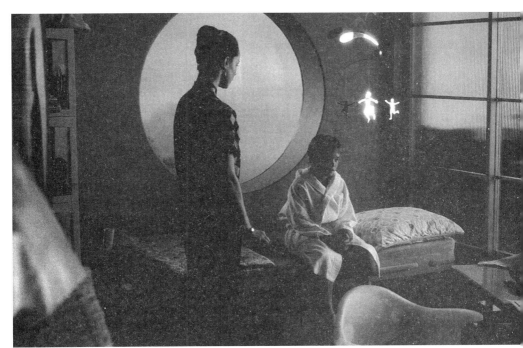

Monica Swinton (Frances O'Connor) tries to connect with her adopted "mecha" child, David (Haley Joel Osment), in *A.I. Artificial Intelligence*.

had taken Spielberg into his confidence and intimately shared his intentions as the project went through various stages for nearly twenty years, Spielberg was hesitant to give anyone else the job of writing it. "Steven understood, on so many levels, what this movie meant to an audience, what it meant to him personally, and what it had meant to Stanley," Spielberg's frequent producer Kathleen Kennedy was quoted as stating, in the Warner Bros. press notes on the film. "I don't think he could have sat down with any other writer and expect them to interpret what was in his head." To this end, Jan Harlan, Kubrick's brother-in-law and executive producer on his last four movies, made sure that Spielberg was handed all kinds of material Kubrick had pulled together over the years, including Baker's drawings, to ensure that what ended up onscreen would have as much of Stanley Kubrick in it as possible. In addition to the shared credit "an Amblin/Stanley Kubrick production," the one direct mention of the late filmmaker would come at the very end of the movie, with the title card "For Stanley Kubrick" placed before the Amblin Entertainment logo.

Spielberg would make frequent claims that the opening section of the picture, encompassing David's arrival at the Swinton household and his eventual abandonment by his adopted "parents," came mainly from Kubrick's vision, as did the controversial final twenty minutes, which took David thousands of years into the future and allowed him to fulfill his cherished dream of having a devoted mother. There was much speculation that the populist Spielberg had decided to add this coda so that the movie wouldn't end with the sad sight of David and his devoted Teddy sitting in the bottom of the sea, wishing to be a real boy. While many misinterpreted the final act as upbeat, it was, in truth, an even more chilling way to sum up the story, with only the "mechas" surviving mankind's annihilation, and the only way for the hapless robot boy to find happiness with the human world he so longed to be a part of—requesting that his long deceased human "mother" be brought back to life—being brought about through artificial means.

The mix of technological wonderment and dystopian dread—the heartfelt emotion that Spielberg brought forth from a potentially alienating, antiseptic otherworldly setting—and the disturbing depictions of cruelty toward the unjustly maligned cyborg race made for an incredibly rich and complex piece of writing. Steven Spielberg had not only brought his friend's cherished project fully to life with his consummate directorial skills but had fashioned a screenplay as intelligent and thought provoking as any professional writer skilled and versed in the field of science fiction.

6

Produced by Spielberg

From Amblin to DreamWorks and Beyond

n 1978, as a way of helping his protégé, Robert Zemeckis, get his directorial career launched, Steven Spielberg took on his first credit as executive
producer. Even though that film, *I Wanna Hold Your Hand*, had no box office
success to speak of, it put the director in the producer's chair for the first time
(none of his own directorial credits had yet to be produced by him up to that
point), opening up a whole new side to his growing status in the movie industry. In
1981, he formed Amblin Entertainment with fellow producers Kathleen Kennedy
and Frank Marshall. In time, the eventual company logo, taken directly from the
indelible moment in *E.T. the Extra-Terrestrial* when Elliott (Henry Thomas) rides
his bicycle past the moon, became as familiar to moviegoers as those of the major
studios. In 1997, Spielberg extended his reach further when he, along with David
Geffen and Jeffrey Katzenberg, created DreamWorks SKG to distribute not only
Spielberg's films but those of other moviemakers.

Listed in this chapter are all the movies outside of those directed (or written)
by Spielberg that bear his name in the credits as either a producer or executive
producer. There are several Amblin Entertainment and DreamWorks productions
not covered here because he either chose not to have his name listed or did not
involve himself directly in the producing end. Although many of these movies are
frequently listed as being Steven Spielberg offerings, this chapter is only concerned
with those for which he received onscreen credit.

Therefore, those movies *not* covered are as follows: *Fandango* (WB, 1985);
Harry and the Hendersons (Universal, 1987); *Akira Kurosawa's Dreams* (WB, 1990);
Cape Fear (Universal, 1991); *Noises Off* (Touchstone, 1992); *A Far Off Place* (Disney,
1993); *A Dangerous Woman* (Gramercy, 1993); *The Little Rascals* (Universal, 1994);
Little Giants (WB, 1994); *The Bridges of Madison County* (WB, 1995); *To Wong Foo,
Thanks for Everything! Julie Newmar* (Universal, 1995); *How to Make an American Quilt*
(Universal, 1995); *The Trigger Effect* (Gramercy, 1996); *Small Soldiers* (DreamWorks,
1998); *In Dreams* (DreamWorks, 1999); *The Flintstones in Viva Rock Vegas* (Universal,
2000); *Shrek* (DreamWorks, 2001); and *A Dog's Purpose* (Universal, 2017).

I Wanna Hold Your Hand

Universal, April 21, 1978

A Rose & Asseyev production. Starring Nancy Allen (Pam Mitchell), Bobby Di Cicco (Tony Smerko), Marc McClure (Larry Dubois), Susan Kendall Newman (Janis Goldman), Theresa Saldana (Grace Corrigan), Wendie Jo Sperber (Rosie Petrofsky). Produced by Tamara Asseyev and Alex Rose. Executive Producer: Steven Spielberg. Written by Robert Zemeckis and Bob Gale. Directed by Robert Zemeckis. Technicolor. 104 minutes. (PG)

Wanting to nurture new talent, Steven Spielberg helped guide this frenetic farce to the screen, allowing the two men who had caught his attention with their screenplay for *1941*, Robert Zemeckis and Bob Gale, to debut another of their scripts before the grandiose World War II comedy would even commence filming. To further sweeten the deal, Spielberg gave Zemeckis the opportunity to make his feature film debut behind the camera, thereby launching the career in this capacity of the future Oscar-winner (*Forrest Gump*).

As broad at times as *1941,* but full of a much more good-natured spirit and well-earned laughs, *I Wanna Hold Your Hand* captured a moment in pop culture history with an often infectious enthusiasm, as six teens from Maplewood, New Jersey, journey into New York in hopes of sneaking into the Plaza Hotel for a glimpse of the Beatles and perhaps even securing tickets to the Fab Four's now-legendary February 9, 1964, American television debut on *The Ed Sullivan Show.*

Although ads would very prominently place "Steven Spielberg Presents" above the credit for "a Rose & Asseyev production," the onscreen credits left it at "Executive Producer: Steven Spielberg," marking the very first time he received a producer credit of any kind on a motion picture.

Cast members Nancy Allen, Bobby Di Cicco, Eddie Deezen (playing the ultimate obnoxious Beatles know-it-all "Ringo" Klaus), Wendie Jo Sperber, and Dick Miller all ended up in *1941* the following year. The movie also featured Marc McClure (who later that same year would play Jimmy Olsen in *Superman*), Susan Kendall Newman (daughter of Paul), and Will Jordan, doing his patented Ed Sullivan impersonation. Despite the tepid response at theater box offices, the film found its share of admirers in subsequent years as a pay-cable favorite.

Used Cars

Columbia, July 11, 1980

Starring Kurt Russell (Rudy Russo), Gerrit Graham (Jeff), Frank McRae (Jim), Deborah Harmon (Barbara Fuchs), Jack Warden (the Fuchs Brothers). Executive Producers: Steven Spielberg and John Milius. Written by Robert Zemeckis and Bob Gale. Produced by Bob Gale. Directed by Robert Zemeckis. Metrocolor. 113 minutes. (R)

Despite the blemish of *1941* on their resumes, Steven Spielberg continued to have tremendous faith in the talents of Robert Zemeckis and Bob Gale, joining forces with their other mentor, John Milius, to executive produce their latest farce, the first movie to bear Spielberg's name that went out with an R rating.

Jack Warden went *very* broad as twin brothers who run rival used-car lots across the street from one another, the gentler sibling depending on blustery salesman Rudy Russo to bring in the customers by whatever means necessary. This leads to a promotion war with everything from strippers to camels employed with no consideration for taste or tact. The same could be said of the screenplay, which strained much too hard to be outrageous and only clicked in during the grand finale, when Russell and company race a caravan of ragtag autos (echoing *The Sugarland Express*) across the Arizona landscape to beat the clock and prove that they do indeed offer one mile of cars for sale. Terry J. Leonard's stunt crew excelled here, as did a charismatic pooch named "Peanuts," who pretty much stole the show from the humans on hand.

The box office response for this was just as meager as it was for *I Wanna Hold Your Hand*, which should not have come as much of a surprise. After all, how many people were expected to work up any enthusiasm to see a movie called *Used Cars*?

Continental Divide

Universal, September 18, 1981

An Amblin Production. Starring John Belushi (Ernie Souchak), Blair Brown (Nell Porter), Allen Goorwitz (Howard McDermott), Carlin Glynn (Sylvia). Produced by Bob Larson. Executive Producers: Steven Spielberg and Bernie Brillstein. Written by Lawrence Kasdan. Directed by Michael Apted. Technicolor. 103 minutes. (PG)

Notable as the first motion picture to have an "Amblin" production credit, this film was based on the screenplay that helped secure Lawrence Kasdan the job of writing *Raiders of the Lost Ark*. Although Spielberg briefly toyed with the idea of directing it, the movie ended up with *Coal Miner's Daughter*'s Michael Apted at the helm, and what showed up on the screen never for a moment hinted that there had *ever* been much in the script to get excited about. (Supposedly, Hal Barwood and Matthew Robbins worked on the writing as well.)

Toning down his buffoonish slob act considerably, comedian John Belushi was cast as muckraking *Chicago Sun-Tribune* columnist Ernie Souchak, whose explosive revelations about a corrupt city alderman prompt his editor (Goorwitz) to send him away on assignment. Against his better judgment, Souchak ends up in the Rocky Mountains spending time with a dedicated ornithologist (Brown) who is trying to preserve America's bald eagles. Needless to say, these disparate personalities fall in love. Too mild for Belushi fans expecting his usual shtick, this one wasn't even particularly fresh or satisfying fare for devotees of romantic comedy and went nowhere at the box office. (The picture opened on the same day that Kasdan's directorial debut, the modern noir *Body Heat*, expanded its run in cinemas. That one ended up faring better with the paying public.)

Regardless of the response at the turnstiles, it was probably a good idea for Belushi to stretch in hopes of making himself eligible for more varied roles after

Nell Porter (Blair Brown) and Ernie Souchak (John Belushi) become unlikely lovers in true Hollywood fashion in *Continental Divide*.

his industry "heat" had cooled and people tired of his coarse persona. But, less than six months after this picture premiered, he was dead of a drug overdose.

Poltergeist

MGM, June 4, 1982

(See Chapter 5, page 174)

Gremlins

WB, June 8, 1984

(See Chapter 8, page 275)

The Goonies

WB, June 7, 1985

(See Chapter 5, page 177)

Back to the Future

Universal, July 3, 1985

Steven Spielberg presents. Starring Michael J. Fox (Marty McFly), Christopher Lloyd (Doc Emmett Brown), Lea Thompson (Lorraine Baines McFly), Crispin Glover (George McFly), Thomas F. Wilson (Biff Tannen). Produced by Bob Gale and Neil Canton. Executive Producers: Steven Spielberg, Frank Marshall, Kathleen Kennedy. Screenplay by Robert Zemeckis and Bob Gale. Directed by Robert Zemeckis. Technicolor. 116 minutes. (PG)

During the 1980s, when Steven Spielberg's name kept popping up on all kinds of films and less observant audiences began to assume he was the director of each of them, this was one title of which he could have been proud to be wrongly thought to have helmed. After three uneven tries at presenting his protégés, Robert Zemeckis and Bob Gale, to the world with *1941*, *I Wanna Hold Your Hand*, and *Used Cars*, their fourth effort under Spielberg's aegis justified the faith he had in them all along. *Back to the Future* hit the bull's-eye in all departments: it earned critical praise, soared to the very top of the box office charts to become the highest-grossing 1985 release, took its place as one of the most fondly remembered of all movies of its era, and became looked upon as a bona fide classic in the realm of comedy and science fiction.

Using the always intriguing premise of time travel, Zemeckis and Gale's script took us to the unremarkable small town of Hill Valley, where teenager Marty McFly, after being shuttled back in a scientifically souped-up DeLorean DMC-12 sports car to 1955, encounters his own parents in their high school years. Because he has inadvertently interfered with the meeting that would set them on their destiny of getting married and therefore producing Marty as their offspring, Marty must do what he can to set things right before he erases his own existence. Assisting him is Doc Brown—the eccentric inventor of the time-traveling car that put him back in the wrong decade in the first place—who must also return Marty to the era in which he belongs, hoping to send him "back to the future" with the assist of a punctual lightning bolt.

What turned out to be one of the most lightheartedly enjoyable movies of the decade began in serious trouble when, a month after shooting had commenced in late November of 1984, it was decided that the original leading man, Eric Stoltz, wasn't registering with the necessary comedic sense, which required him to be replaced and a good deal of footage to be scrapped. (Fortunately, Stoltz would have his own star-making vehicle in 1985 to compensate, playing Cher's facially disfigured son in *Mask*.) Spielberg and Zemeckis turned to the actor they had strongly considered in the first place, Michael J. Fox, who was at the time committed to filming *Family Ties,* the television series that had turned him into a teen fan favorite. Fox made the risky choice of accepting the offer with the understanding that he would have to shoot his show during the day and the motion picture at night. The reshoots brought the budget up to $22 million, but the results were worth the expense.

The original poster for the top box office attraction of 1985.

On the Universal Studios backlot, the frequently used "Courthouse Square" set became the town center of Hill Valley, the centerpiece being the courthouse atop which sat a clock that became the key focus of the grand finale. This square required set dressing for both eras, thereby providing a good deal of humor from the thirty-year dissimilarity between then and now. The cleaner, more wholesome 1955 Hill Valley was complete with a Texaco service station with eager-to-please attendants; one of the local cinemas was playing *Cattle Queen of Montana*, which featured Ronald Reagan, the president at the time of *Back to the Future*'s release; gas cost nineteen and a half cents a gallon; and Studebakers were in fashion. In contrast, the 1985 local theaters had become an Assembly of Christ church and a porn theater, respectively; the Japanese Toyota company had replaced the US car manufacturer; Lou's malt shop became an aerobics center; the downtown businesses were diminished in desirability by a shopping mall outside of town; and the former green lawn in front of the courthouse was replaced by a parking lot. Few movies ever made so deft a statement about the decline of grace in America without making it the main focus.

Filming between January and April of 1985 with the new lead, the movie was rushed through post-production to ensure that it could make its early July release date. Helped no doubt by the recasting, since Fox was at the peak of his television popularity at the time, *Back to the Future* took off like a rocket and dominated the summer box offices, thanks to sensational word of mouth. Zemeckis had balanced the wonder and the laughs expertly, coaxing an especially inspired performance out of Christopher Lloyd, whose hyper weird facial tics and vocal reactions added immeasurably to the fun. The movie was soon one of the most quoted and referred to of its day, and it ended up with four Oscar nominations, for original screenplay, sound, original song ("The Power of Love"), and sound effects editing, winning the last. It was also a Writers Guild Award nominee and was in the running for Best Film at the Golden Globes and BAFTAs. "The Power of Love"—by Huey Lewis (who appeared in the movie, unbilled, as one of the teachers criticizing Fox's audition) & the News—reached number one on the *Billboard* charts.

Alas, all this success meant the inevitable heavy-handed sequels and cartoon series spinoff. Visitors to Universal Studios could see not only Courthouse Square as part of the tour but could experience a *Back to the Future* simulator ride, which was an attraction that opened in Florida in 1991, in Hollywood in 1993, and closed (at both) in 2007. That same year, *Back to the Future* had the honor of being added to the National Film Registry of motion pictures worthy of being cited as a way of bringing attention to the importance of preservation. It was the first of Steven Spielberg's non-directed producer credits to make the list.

Young Sherlock Holmes

Paramount, December 4, 1985

Steven Spielberg presents. Starring Nicholas Rowe (Sherlock Holmes), Alan Cox (John Watson), Sophie Ward (Elizabeth Hardy), Anthony Higgins (Professor Rathe).

Executive Producers: Steven Spielberg, Frank Marshall, Kathleen Kennedy. Written by Chris Columbus. Produced by Mark Johnson. Directed by Barry Levinson. Technicolor. 109 minutes. (PG-13)

A cute concept nicely executed, *Young Sherlock Holmes* posited the idea of the world's greatest fictional detective having met his companion in sleuthing, Dr. Watson, years earlier than Arthur Conan Doyle depicted it. In this stylish adventure, the two hook up as teenagers at London's Brompton Academy, where Holmes is already showing off his skills as a master of detection. A mysterious assassin causes the deaths of three elderly gentlemen after stinging them with a hallucinogenic dart, leading Holmes and Watson to a deadly cult of religious fanatics who are sacrificing young women at an underground temple.

A distinct improvement on Chris Columbus's previous Amblin screenplays for *Gremlins* and *The Goonies*, the film stayed true to the spirit of the Conan Doyle characters while adding the requisite 1980s dash of high energy and special effects (with some set pieces that resembled *Indiana Jones and the Temple of Doom* a bit too closely, perhaps). Rowe (playing a Sherlock capable of tears and a smile) and Cox (as a skeptical and uptight Watson) were ideally paired off, and there were some amusing nods to the Holmes legend, with Lestrade achieving his promotion to Inspector by riding on Sherlock's coattails for the first time; the famous deerstalker cap being inherited from Holmes's professorial mentor after the old fellow's demise; and Watson stopping his new schoolmate from smashing his violin because he feels inadequate at the instrument, after a mere three days of practice. Dennis Muren and his special effects team earned a well-warranted Oscar nomination, as the film contained one of the pioneering sequences in CGI technology, as a knight in a stained-glass window came to three-dimensional life to terrify a hallucinating clergyman.

Just as previous playful speculations and tributes to Conan Doyle's immortal creation—including Billy Wilder's *The Private Life of Sherlock Holmes* (1970), Anthony Harvey's *They Might Be Giants* (1971), and Herbert Ross's *The Seven Percent Solution* (1976)—had come up short at the box office, this pleasant romp fared no better with the paying public.

The Money Pit

Universal, March 26, 1986

Steven Spielberg presents. Starring Tom Hanks (Walter), Shelley Long (Anna), Alexander Gudonov (Max Beissart), Maureen Stapleton (Estelle). Executive Producers: Steven Spielberg, David Giler. Producers: Frank Marshall, Kathleen Kennedy, Art Levinson. Written by David Giler. Directed by Richard Benjamin. DeLuxe color. 91 minutes. (PG)

An uncooperative house could provide a few good laughs, as evident in the 1920 Buster Keaton short *One Week* and the snappy 1948 Cary Grant comedy *Mr. Blandings Builds His Dream House*, so Tom Hanks and Shelley Long took a shot at it, 1980s style, but, alas, the script was as shaky as their crumbling residence. As an entertainment lawyer watching his bank balance dwindle as he throws considerable cash into renovating a deceptively attractive fixer-upper (the filmmakers used a real eight-bedroom, three-story, white clapboard home in Lattingtown on Long Island—clearly more space than two people needed), Hanks proved yet again that he could work miracles with limp material. If nothing else, this film was his first opportunity to work on a Spielberg-related project. They would have more fruitful collaborations further down the line.

An American Tail

Universal, November 21, 1986

Steven Spielberg presents. With the voices of Cathianne Blore (Bridget), Dom DeLuise (Tiger), John Finnegan (Warren T. Rat), Phillip Glasser (Fievel Mousekewitz), Amy Green (Tanya Mousekewitz), Madeline Kahn (Gussie Mausheimer), Pat Musick (Tony Toponi), Nehemiah Persoff (Papa Mousekewitz), Christopher Plummer (Henri), Neil Ross (Honest John), Will Ryan (Digit), Hal Smith (Moe), Erica Yohn (Mama Mousekewitz). Executive Producers: Steven Spielberg, David Kirschner, Kathleen Kennedy, Frank Marshall. Created by David Kirschner. Story by David Kirschner and Judy Freudberg and Tony Geiss. Screenplay by Judy Freudberg and Tony Geiss. Produced by Don Bluth, Gary Goldman, John Pomeroy, Gary Goldman. Directed by Don Bluth. DeLuxe color. 80 minutes. (G)

Meet Fievel. In his search to find his family, he discovered America.

Steven Spielberg's first venture into animation and his first credit on a G-rated motion picture had an interesting premise. Following the plight of a family of mice, who leave Shostka, Russia, and sail to America in hopes of escaping the terror of their feline enemies, it also served as a metaphor for the Jews forced out of the same country because of anti-Semitic oppression. Well-intended and nicely animated by former Disney artist Don Bluth

The poster for Spielberg's first animated production, *An American Tail*.

and his team (who depict New York City, circa 1885), *An American Tail* was a bit too cute, too juvenile in approach, too insubstantial in its storytelling skills.

It did have the advantage of having a hit song in its score. Although the rendition of "Somewhere Out There" as performed in the story by the young Mousekewitz children, Fievel and Tanya, wasn't too comfortable on the ears, the reprise during the end credits, sung with far greater clarity and flair by Linda Ronstadt and James Ingram, really clicked. The single, on MCA records, became a staple on the radio airwaves throughout that winter and rose to number two on the *Billboard* charts on January 24, 1987. The songwriters (James Horner, Barry Mann, and Cynthia Weil) received an Oscar nomination.

An American Tail did surprisingly good box office business in an era when most animated features came from the Disney Studio, and so it warranted a sequel, *An American Tail: Fievel Goes West*, five years later. It also spun off a Saturday morning television series, *Fievel's American Tails* (1992); some direct-to-video titles, *An American Tail: The Treasure of Manhattan Island* (1998) and *An American Tail: The Mystery of the Night Monster* (1999); and Fievel's Playland, a Universal Studios theme park attraction aimed at the young. This attraction opened at both the Universal City and Orlando locations, in 1990 and 1992 respectively, closing in California in 1997 but remaining a part of the Florida park.

Innerspace

Warner Bros., July 1, 1987

Steven Spielberg presents. A Guber-Peters production. Starring Dennis Quaid (Lt. Tuck Pendleton), Martin Short (Jack Putter), Meg Ryan (Lydia Maxwell). Costarring Kevin McCarthy (Victor Scrimshaw), Fiona Lewis (Dr. Margaret Canker). Co-Executive Producers: Frank Marshall, Kathleen Kennedy. Co-Producer: Chip Proser. Executive Producers: Steven Spielberg, Peter Guber, Jon Peters. Screenplay by Jeffrey Boam, Chip Proser. Story by Chip Proser. Produced by Michael Finnell. Directed by Joe Dante. Technicolor. 120 minutes. (PG)

Inspired no doubt by one of the seminal science fiction movies of all time, Richard Fleischer's *Fantastic Voyage* (1966), this comedy from Amblin borrowed the premise of someone being miniaturized in order to enter another person's body and found every opportunity to dumb it down. Pilot Tuck Pendleton agrees to be shrunken to the size of a microbe in order to be injected into a lab bunny, but because of meddling outside forces, he instead ends up inside hypochondriac supermarket clerk Jack Putter. Director Joe Dante's curious talent for combining inertia and overkill managed to bring out the least in his cast (Robert Picardo as a foreign fence in technical equipment was especially unfunny), and the whole thing dragged on far too long for anyone to feel very good about it by the time it finally called it quits.

Dennis Muren and his team were the year's Oscar winners for Special Visual Effects.

*batteries not included

Universal, December 18, 1987

Steven Spielberg presents. Starring Hume Cronyn (Frank Riley), Jessica Tandy (Faye Riley), Frank McRae (Harry Noble), Elizabeth Peña (Marisa Esteval), Michael Carmine (Carlos), Dennis Boutsikaris (Mason Baylor). Associate Producer: Gerald R. Molen. Executive Producers: Steven Spielberg, Kathleen Kennedy, Frank Marshall. Screenplay by Brad Bird and Matthew Robbins and Brent Maddock and S.S. Wilson. Story by Mick Garris. Produced by Ronald L. Schwary. Directed by Matthew Robbins. Color. 106 minutes. (PG)

Aliens were back among us and smaller than ever. Spielberg's collaborator on the screenplay of *The Sugarland Express*, Matthew Robbins, received his one feature film directorial gig at Amblin and went for quirky but came up too cutesy to appeal to a vast audience, who may have felt they'd seen this sort of thing (from Amblin or elsewhere) one time too many. The original story was by Mick Garris, who had contributed to the writing on several installments of *Amazing Stories*. Could it be that this was one idea that was deemed too hard to cram into a twenty-five-minute teleplay and got the extended-feature treatment instead?

When the misfit residents of a crumbling Lower East Side brownstone are threatened with eviction by an evil land developer (are there any other kinds in

Brownstone residents Faye Riley (Jessica Tandy) and Marisa Estevel (Elizabeth Peña) are in awe of some teeny alien visitors in *batteries not included.*

the movies?), they are unexpectedly rescued by a miniscule family of flying saucers who feed on metal and can work miracles, like putting broken items back together again. It was nice to see real-life acting couple Hume Cronyn and Jessica Tandy (both in their seventies) receive star billing in a big-budget movie at this stage in their careers, and the special effects were worthy of an Oscar nomination they failed to receive, but this kind of good-natured, trivial contrivance added little luster to the Amblin reputation.

Who Framed Roger Rabbit

Disney, June 22, 1988

A Touchstone Pictures and Amblin Entertainment in association with Silver Screen Partners III presentation. Starring Bob Hoskins (Eddie Valiant), Christopher Lloyd (Judge Doom). Starring Charles Fleischer (the voice of Roger Rabbit), Stubby Kaye (Marvin Acme), Joanna Cassidy (Dolores). Directed by Robert Zemeckis. Screenplay by Jeffrey Price and Peter S. Seaman. Based on the book *Who Censored Roger Rabbit?* by Gary K. Wolf. Director of Animation: Richard Williams. Produced by Robert Watts, Frank Marshall. Executive Producers: Steven Spielberg, Kathleen Kennedy. DeLuxe color. 104 minutes. (PG)

This time an Amblin Entertainment presentation had a valid reason for playing at the high decibel level of a cartoon: a good deal of it was animated after all. *Roger Rabbit* brought live action and animation together with all the technical finesse the 1980s had to offer and was considered such a special effects marvel at the time that it rated a cover story on *Newsweek*. Although this sort of match-up had been executed with tremendous dexterity and charm in such earlier films as *Anchors Aweigh* (1945) and *Mary Poppins* (1964), these were done for select sequences. Director Robert Zemeckis set out to see if he and his team could pull it off for an entire feature, playing real people off cartoons seamlessly. In this respect, it worked. The strikingly colorful production made it seem like there once was a Los Angeles where human beings shared the world with drawn characters.

Starting out with a nearly full-length animated short subject, "Somethin' Cookin'," the film posited that its stars, Baby Herman (in truth a cigar-chomping squirt with the voice and libido of an adult) and hyperactive Roger Rabbit, were able to step off the set and exist in 1947 Hollywood. When the owner of the cartoon suburb of Toontown, Marvin Acme, is found dead after playing patty-cake with Roger's curvaceous wife, Jessica, the hapless bunny finds himself the chief suspect. Roger turns for help to the down-on-his-luck detective Eddie Valiant, who exposed Jessica and Marvin's dalliance, and soon the mismatched duo find themselves journeying through underworlds and fantasylands in an effort to crack the case.

Beyond its exuberant spirits (which eventually crossed over into a stridently undisciplined loss of control for the finale), the film benefited tremendously from the anchoring presence of Bob Hoskins in the leading role, the gruffly charismatic actor proving a great relief from the often exhausting eponymous leading hare. Another plus was the cascade of "guest appearances" by famous animated characters that filled the storyline, including Dumbo, the living brooms from *Fantasia*, Betty Boop, the penguin waiters from *Mary Poppins*, Mickey Mouse, Daffy Duck, Bugs Bunny, Yosemite Sam, the Three Little Pigs, Woody Woodpecker, Tweety Bird, Snow White, a singing sword resembling Frank Sinatra, and the inimitable Donald Duck. Jessica's sultry speaking voice was provided by Kathleen Turner, but her singing of "Why Don't You Do Right?" (previously a hit single for Peggy Lee) was done by Steven Spielberg's wife at the time, Amy Irving.

Who Framed Roger Rabbit was another box office smash for Amblin, earning $156 million in the United States, becoming the second highest-grossing 1988 release (after the year's Oscar-winner, *Rain Man*, a property Steven Spielberg once considered doing), and taking home Academy Awards for Film Editing, Visual Effects, Sound Effects Editing, and a special trophy to Richard Williams "for the animation direction and creation of the cartoon characters." There were additional Oscar nominations for Cinematography, Art Direction, and Sound.

Spielberg would also serve as executive producer on the three subsequent Amblin short subjects starring Roger and Baby Herman, each of them released theatrically to precede a Disney Studios release: *Tummy Trouble* (1989; positioned before *Honey, I Shrunk the Kids*); *Roller Coaster Rabbit* (1990; shown with *Dick Tracy*); and *Trail Mix-Up* (1993; with *A Far Off Place*).

The Land Before Time

Universal, November 18, 1988

A Lucas/Spielberg presentation. Produced by Sullivan Bluth Studios Ireland Ltd. With the voice talents of: Judith Barsi (Ducky), Burke Byrnes (Daddy Topps), Gabriel Damon (Littlefoot), Bill Erwin (Grandfather), Pat Hingle (Narrator/Rooter), Candy Hutson (Cera), Will Ryan (Petrie), Helen Shaver (Littlefoot's Mother). Executive Producers: Steven Spielberg, George Lucas. Co-Executive Producers: Frank Marshall, Kathleen Kennedy. Producers: Don Bluth, Gary Goldman, John Pomeroy. Screenplay by Stu Krieger. Story by Judy Freudberg, Tony Geiss. Directed by Don Bluth. Technicolor. 69 minutes. (G)

After losing his mother, a young "longneck" (that's brontosaurus, to us) journeys to the fabled "Great Valley" in search of food and vegetation and is joined by a "three-horn" (triceratops), a "flier" (pterodactyl), a "big mouth" (hadrosaurid), and a "spike tail" (stegosaurus). While it's commendable that this animated tale taught the importance of all species (races) overlooking their differences and bonding together, it was really done in by a fatal abundance of the cutes, with some overly precious horseplay between the prehistoric offspring and mawkish voice work (Judith Barsi being the chief offender) that made older audience members wish the adult dinosaurs, worried about where their next meal was coming from, had simply eaten their young.

Over the end credits, Diana Ross sang "If We Hold On Together," a James Horner/Will Jennings composition that proved a bigger hit in Japan than here. This very minor movie later brought forth a slew of direct-to-video sequels and a TV series (2007–2008), having done surprisingly well at the box office, taking in some $45 million in the United States. This only proved that one could probably make a small fortune if you were to create a genuinely *thrilling* dinosaur adventure, and one of its executive producers, Steven Spielberg, would, of course, do just that, five years later, with *Jurassic Park*.

Dad

Universal, November 10, 1989

Amblin Entertainment presents. Starring Jack Lemmon (Jake Tremont), Ted Danson (John Tremont), Olympia Dukakis (Bette Tremont), Kathy Baker (Annie), Kevin Spacey (Mario), Ethan Hawke (Billy Tremont). Executive Producers: Steven Spielberg, Frank Marshall, Kathleen Kennedy. Produced by Joseph Stern, Gary David Goldberg. Based on the novel by William Wharton. Written for the screen and directed by Gary David Goldberg. Color. 117 minutes. (PG)

Significant as the first Spielberg-produced film to not involve fantasy or comedy, *Dad* was, instead, an intimate family drama—a tearjerker to be sure—about one man's efforts to reconnect with his father before it's too late. Ted Danson (a last-minute replacement for James Caan) was outstanding as the high-powered executive who rushes home at the news of his mother's debilitating heart attack only to find that, just as his mother is beginning to recover, his father has developed cancer and may not have long to live. Jack Lemmon (adorned in Oscar-nominated

Jake (Jack Lemmon) and John Tremont (Ted Danson) coming to grips with mortality in *Dad*.

old man makeup by Dick Smith), Olympia Dukakis (as his pragmatic and often cantankerous wife), and Ethan Hawke (as Danson's distant son) all added immeasurably to material that now and then threatened to teeter into slushy sentimentality but earned its fair share of affecting moments.

Back to the Future Part II

Universal, November 22, 1989

Steven Spielberg presents. Starring Michael J. Fox (Marty McFly/Marty McFly Jr./ Marlene McFly), Christopher Lloyd (Dr. Emmett Brown), Lea Thompson (Lorraine McFly), Thomas F. Wilson (Biff Tannen/Griff Tannen). Executive Producers: Steven Spielberg, Frank Marshall, Kathleen Kennedy. Screenplay by Bob Gale. Story by Robert Zemeckis and Bob Gale. Produced by Bob Gale, Neil Canton. Directed by Robert Zemeckis. DeLuxe color. 108 minutes. (PG)

Back to the Future ended with a perfectly cryptic wrap-up that encouraged audiences to use their imaginations; there were no further explanations or continuations needed. But it also made a ton of money, so there was not just one but two sequels ordered, made back to back, with *Part II* coming to typify the very terribleness that too often comes from the misguided need to cash in on success. In the most convoluted fashion, Marty McFly is sent thirty years ahead to 2015, then back to 1985, and then back again to 1955, all in an effort to rectify what had gone wrong in his life and his hometown, mainly because of a sports almanac stolen by nemesis Biff Tannen. Despite being frenetic and sour, with mugging encouraged in place of comic finesse, ticket buyers showed up in big numbers, but clearly enough customers felt so thoroughly "had" that many passed on attending *Part III*.

In a self-referential dig at Hollywood's sequelitis, the HoloMax movie theater of the future advertised *Jaws 19*, directed by Spielberg's first offspring, Max. A hologram of a shark popped out of the marquee pretending to chomp passing pedestrians, prompting Marty to quip "Shark *still* looks fake." Fortunately, the real 2015 brought us the correct Spielberg directing something a bit more ambitious: *Bridge of Spies*.

If nothing else, Alan Silvestri's main theme, reprised from the first film, was still terrific.

Joe Versus the Volcano

Warner Bros., March 9, 1990

An Amblin Entertainment production. Tom Hanks (Joe Banks), Meg Ryan (DeDe/ Angelica Graynamore/Patricia Graynamore), Lloyd Bridges (Graynamore), Robert Stack (Dr. Ellison), Abe Vigoda (Chief of the Waponis), Dan Hedaya (Frank Waturi), Barry McGovern (Luggage Salesman), Amanda Plummer (Dagmar), Ossie Davis (Marshall). Executive Producers: Steven Spielberg, Kathleen Kennedy, Frank Marshall. Produced by Teri Schwartz. Written and directed by John Patrick Shanley. Technicolor. Panavision. 102 minutes. (PG)

While writer John Patrick Shanley deserved points for dispensing with typical romantic comedy formulas and going a bit "out there" for his directorial debut, *Joe Versus the Volcano* actually worked better when it went for the gentle rather than the quirky. The always watchable Tom Hanks played a hypochondriac who is stuck in a miserable job at American Panascope (Home of the Rectal Probe) and who is told he has a "brain cloud" and therefore only six months to live. Figuring he has nothing to lose, he accepts an offer from an eccentric millionaire (Lloyd Bridges) to travel all expenses paid to an island in the South Pacific and jump into a volcano to appease the gods, thereby, hopefully, allowing his "sponsor" to nab the rights to a rare mineral found on the island. Meg Ryan had fun playing three distinctively different women in Hanks's life, and the two performers displayed a nice chemistry that they would use to better effect down the line in *Sleepless in Seattle* (1993) and *You've Got Mail* (1998). Shanley also fared better the next time he stepped behind the camera, eighteen years later, to direct the movie version of his prize-winning play *Doubt*.

Joe Banks (Tom Hanks) and Patricia Graynamore (Meg Ryan) face their destiny among the Waponi Islanders in *Joe Versus the Volcano*.

Back to the Future Part III

Universal, May 25, 1990

Steven Spielberg presents. Michael J. Fox (Marty McFly/Seamus McFly), Christopher Lloyd (Doc Emmet Brown), Mary Steenburgen (Clara Clayton), Thomas F. Wilson (Buford "Mad Dog" Tannen/Biff Tannen), and Lea Thompson (Maggie McFly/Lorraine McFly). Produced by Bob Gale, Neil Canton. Executive Producers: Steven Spielberg, Frank Marshall, Kathleen Kennedy. Screenplay by Bob Gale. Story by Robert Zemeckis and Bob Gale. Directed by Robert Zemeckis. DeLuxe color. 118 minutes. (PG)

Easier to take than *Part II* but still inflicted with that tiresome, mechanical lack of inspiration that is the curse of sequels, this final, magic-free chapter did about $30 million less than its predecessor at the box office. When Doc Brown finds himself living in Hill Valley in the year 1885, he and Marty realize they must change destiny when they discover a tombstone indicating that the hapless Doc died after being shot in the back by villain Buford Tannen. Mary Steenburgen was added to the mix as Doc's nineteenth-century love interest, but she had fared better in the time-travel genre with the superior *Time After Time* back in 1979.

   Although this was its last theatrical entry, the *Back to the Future* "franchise" continued with a Saturday morning cartoon series (1991–1992), for which Christopher Lloyd provided live action intros and Steenburgen reprised the voice of her character; a simulator ride starring Lloyd and Thomas F. Wilson at the Universal Studios theme parks (1991–2007 in Orlando, 1993–2007 in Universal City); and a video game in 2010, with Lloyd supplying the voice of Doc Brown.

Gremlins 2: The New Batch

Warner Bros., June 15, 1990

An Amblin Entertainment picture. A Michael Finnell production. Starring Zach Galligan (Billy Peltzer), Phoebe Cates (Kate Beringer), John Glover (Daniel Clamp), Robert Prosky (Grandpa Fred), Robert Picardo (Forster), Christopher Lee (Dr. Catheter), Havilland Morris (Marla Bloodstone). Co-Producer: Rick Baker. Executive Producers: Steven Spielberg, Kathleen Kennedy, Frank Marshall. Written by Charlie Haas. Produced by Mike Finnell. Directed by Joe Dante. Technicolor. 106 minutes. (PG-13)

One would never have gotten the impression during the 1980s that the world was clamoring for a sequel to *Gremlins* (1984), but when the new decade arrived, Warner Bros. and Amblin gave them one anyway, with a budget nearly five times that of the original. The good news was that the screenplay by Charlie Haas (replacing Chris Columbus) took some genuinely witty satirical swipes at corporate megalomania run amok, with the model for John Glover's crassly insensitive billionaire Daniel Clamp being the chief megalomaniacal vulgarian of them all, Donald Trump. Resetting the chaos in Manhattan, the Gremlins now caused destruction at the Clamp office tower, the first totally automated structure of its kind.

The self-referential humor that resulted in some bizarre laughs included an introductory exchange between Daffy Duck and Bugs Bunny; the film itself supposedly breaking down in the middle so that the mischievous creatures can swap it with a nudist camp documentary; Tony Randall providing the voice of a brainy gremlin, singing "New York, New York"; and jars of laboratory acid marked "Do Not Throw in Face." A movie patron was heard to exclaim, "This is worse that the first one." It wasn't, but you still couldn't help but feel that your head was being forced into a blender for the sake of entertainment. There was far less public interest this time around, however, although those who attended no doubt got a kick out of seeing critic Leonard Maltin killed by the giggly monsters for giving their movie a bad review.

Arachnophobia

Hollywood Pictures, July 18, 1990

A Hollywood Pictures and Amblin Entertainment presentation. Starring Jeff Daniels (Dr. Ross Jennings), Julian Sands (Dr. James Atherton), Harley Jane Kozak (Molly Jennings), Brian McNamara (Chris Collins), John Goodman (Delbert). Co-Executive Producers: Ted Field, Robert W. Cort. Executive Producers: Steven Spielberg, Frank Marshall. Story by Don Jakoby and Al Williams. Screenplay by Don Jakoby, Wesley Strick. Produced by Kathleen Kennedy, Richard Vane. Directed by Frank Marshall. DeLuxe color. 110 minutes. (PG-13)

Apparently, Steven Spielberg's producing partner, Frank Marshall, had not gotten his fill of crawly things working on the Indiana Jones trilogy and decided that, for his debut behind the camera as a director, he would make spiders the focus of this relaxed thriller with droll undertones.

After a photographer (Mark L. Taylor) on assignment in Venezuela is bitten by a vengeful spider, the arachnid stows away in his transport casket, ending up in the peaceful suburban town of Canaima, California (actually filmed in Cambria, California). There he mates in the barn of spider-phobic Dr. Jennings and unleashes a clutter of poisonous arachnids for a reasonable amount of PG-13 chills. Jeff Daniels was well cast as the reluctantly uprooted urbanite who not only has to confront rampaging insects but also traditional small-town thinking, although the whole show was stolen by John Goodman, in a wittily underplayed turn as a no-nonsense exterminator.

Marshall proved himself adept at building tension, often shooting from the spiders' level of the action as they crawled onto the scene out of sight of their prospective prey, and he really came through staging the climax, as Dr. Jennings goes it alone and battles the killer bugs in his crumbling wine cellar. Probably too low-key and tasteful for the kills-and-thrills crowd, this was still a worthy entry to launch the Disney Studios' new subsidiary, Hollywood Pictures, although it would turn out to be the one and only Amblin Entertainment production released by them.

It's exterminator Delbert McClintock (John Goodman) to the rescue of Molly Jennings (Harley Jane Kozak) and the spider-infested town of Canaima, California, in *Arachnophobia*.

An American Tail: Fievel Goes West

Universal, November 22, 1991

Steven Spielberg presents. With the voice talents of John Cleese (Cat R. Waul), Dom DeLuise (Tiger), Phillip Glasser (Fievel), Amy Irving (Miss Kitty), Jon Lovitz (Chula), Cathy Cavadini (Tanya), Nehemiah Persoff (Papa), Erica Yohn (Mama), James Stewart (Wiley Burp). Created by David Kirschner. Story by Charles Swenson. Screenplay by Flint Dille. Executive Producers: Frank Marshall, Kathleen Kennedy, David Kirschner. Producers: Steven Spielberg, Robert Watts. Directed by Phil Nibbelink, Simon Wells. Color. 75 minutes. (G)

The surprising success of *An American Tail* brought forth the inevitable sequel but not the participation of animator Don Bluth. This time Fievel and his mouse family are conned into heading West by an opportunistic cat who wants to exploit them for their labor before devouring them. Labored and gooey, its only distinction was being the last credit of cinema legend James Stewart (who provided the voice of crusty old sheriff Wiley Burp). The hit song from the original, "Somewhere Out There," was reprised briefly in order to make a self-referential joke about its ubiquity, and John Cleese added a welcome sting to his line readings as the villainous Cat R. Waul. It was produced at Amblimation Studios in London.

We're Back! A Dinosaur's Story

Universal, November 24, 1993

Steven Spielberg presents. Voice Talents: John Goodman (Rex), Blaze Berdahl (Buster), Rhea Perlman (Mother Bird), Jay Leno (Vorb), René Le Vant (Woog), Felicity Kendal (Elsa), Charles Fleischer (Dweeb), Walter Cronkite (Captain Neweyes), Joey Shea (Louie), Julia Child (Dr. Julia Bleeb), Kenneth Mars (Prof. Screweyes), Yeardley Smith (Cecilia), Martin Short (Stubbs the Clown). Executive Producers: Steven Spielberg, Frank Marshall, Kathleen Kennedy. Produced by Stephen Hickner. Screenplay by John Patrick Shanley. Based on the book by Hudson Talbott. Directed by Dick Zondag, Ralph Zondag, Phil Nibblelink, Simon Wells. DeLuxe color. 72 minutes. (G)

Perhaps figuring the PG-13 *Jurassic Park* was a bit too frightening for the tots, Spielberg's Amblimation animated arm produced this G-rated cartoon for the *very* young to be released the very same year.

Through his wish radio, Captain Neweyes discovers that Earth children of the future want nothing more than to see real-life dinosaurs and convinces four such creatures to parachute into New York with the idea that they will take up residence at the Museum of Natural History. Things don't go quite as planned, and it's up to runaway Louie and his friend Cecilia to rescue their prehistoric friends from the evil Professor Screweyes.

Although the film had some eccentric casting touches by including newscaster Walter Cronkite and French chef Julia Child among its vocal talents, this mawkish cartoon offered little in the way of inspiration and quickly wore out even its mercifully brief running time. Captain Neweyes' spacecraft hovering over a circus tent at the finale brought the mothership of *Close Encounters* to mind, while another Spielberg homage during a romp in Times Square was far more direct and to the point: a theater marquee advertised *Jurassic Park*.

The Flintstones

Universal, May 27, 1994

Steven Spielrock presents a Hanna-Barbera/Amblin Entertainment production. Starring John Goodman (Fred Flintstone), Rick Moranis (Barney Rubble), Elizabeth Perkins (Wilma Flintstone), Rosie O'Donnell (Betty Rubble), Kyle MacLachlan (Cliff Vandercave), Halle Berry (Sharon Stone), Richard Moll (Hoagie), Elizabeth Taylor (Pearl Slaghoople). Executive Producers: William Hanna, Joseph Barbera, Kathleen Kennedy, David Kirschner, Gerald R. Molen. Co-Producer: Colin Wilson. Produced by Bruce Cohen. Written by Tom S. Parker and Jim Jennewein and Steven E. de Souza. Based on the animated series by Hanna-Barbera Productions, Inc. Directed by Brian Lavant. Color. 91 minutes. (PG)

Again with the dinosaurs! Amblin Entertainment collaborated with Hanna-Barbera on a live-action version of the latter's long-running, much-loved primetime animated series, a domestic sitcom set in the Stone Age, which ran on ABC from 1960 to 1966 and endured mightily in reruns. Audiences turned out in droves to see real actors recreate familiar actions and set pieces from the show, but there wasn't much more to it beyond that. The plot involved quarry worker Fred Flintstone being promoted to an executive position at Slate & Company, unaware that he is the pawn in a devious plan by Cliff Vandercave to embezzle money and blame it on the hapless new vice president.

Patriarch of a "modern Stone Age family": John Goodman as Fred Flintstone in *The Flintstones*.

As in the TV series, the fun came in the cheeky prehistoric parallels to modern times, with someone named Firestone inventing the wheel; a department store called "Marshy Fields" selling clothing by Halstone; the villains hoping to hightail it to Rocapulco; a swank eatery called Cavern on the Green; the drive-in movie theater playing *Tar Wars* by Gorge Lucas; and a children's playground called—what else?—Jurassic Park. Keeping in this spirit, the production was presented by Steven Spiel*rock*.

Casper

Universal, May 26, 1995

An Amblin Entertainment production in association with the Harvey Entertainment Company. Starring Christina Ricci (Kat Harvey), Bill Pullman (Dr. James Harvey), Cathy Moriarty (Carrigan Crittenden), Eric Idle (Paul Plutzker), and introducing Malachi Pearson (the voice of Casper). Co-Producers: Jeffrey Franklin, Steve Waterman. Executive Producers: Steven Spielberg, Gerald R. Molen, Jeffrey A. Montgomery. Written by Sherri Stoner and Deanna Oliver. Produced by Colin Wilson. Directed by Brad Silberling. Color. 100 minutes. (PG)

Dating back to 1939, Casper the Friendly Ghost first appeared in a book of that name written by Seymour Reit with illustrations by Joe Oriolo. This, in turn, led to a 1945 short subject from Paramount and then a whole slew of animated shorts throughout the 1950s, while at the same time the spirited fellow began popping up in comic books. Finally, a batch of further Casper adventures was created for Saturday morning children's television, airing from 1962 to 1969. Some found him adorable, but others were creeped out by the assumption that their kids were watching a program about a dead boy. In any event, gambling on the belief that the world apparently hadn't had their fill of the affable apparition, Amblin Entertainment brought him back to life (so to speak) as an animated figure acting opposite real actors asked to look spooked and dumbfounded.

James Harvey (so named as a nod to the founder of the comic books that showcased Casper, Alfred Harvey) was a therapist bent on connecting with what he called "the living impaired," figuring to make contact with his deceased wife. Hoping to get Casper and the Ghostly Trio out of her newly inherited haunted house so that she can get her hands on a hidden treasure, greedy Carrigan Crittenden hires Harvey to do the job only to have Harvey's daughter Kat bond with the lonely ghost child.

Dressed up with fanciful sets and state of the art animation, *Casper* was a vaporous concoction that quickly ran out of gas, settling into the sort of bombastic special effects show that was increasingly becoming the norm in "family" entertainment. Amblin had backed a winner, however, at least as far as finances were concerned, as the movie ended up as the eighth highest-grossing 1995 release, although it is doubtful most of those who saw it gave it all that much thought hours after seeing it. There were additional direct-to-video sequels and another TV series, *The Spooktacular New Adventures of Casper*, all from Amblin.

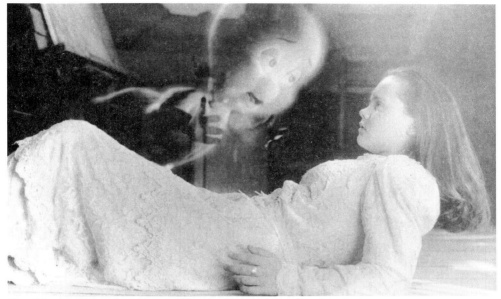

The Friendly Ghost himself greets Kat Harvey (Christina Ricci) in *Casper.*

Balto

Universal, December 22, 1995

An Amblin Entertainment presentation. Voice Talents: Kevin Bacon (Balto), Bridget Fonda (Jenna), Phil Collins (Muk and Luk), Bob Hoskins (Boris). Story by Cliff Ruby and Elana Lesser. Screenplay by Cliff Ruby and Elana Lesser and David Steven Cohen and Roger S. H. Schulman. Executive Producers: Steven Spielberg, Kathleen Kennedy, Bonne Radford. Produced by Steve Hickman. Directed by Simon Wells. Rankcolor. 78 minutes. (G)

What's with that dog statue that stands in New York's Central Park? This innocuous animated tale presented a fictionalized answer to that question, the story of a half-dog, half-wolf named Balto who overcomes his outcast status (shades of Rudolph the Red-Nosed Reindeer?) by leading a sled team through treacherous, snowbound Alaskan territory to bring antitoxins to Nome and stop a diphtheria outbreak. Bob Hoskins was clearly having fun broadly playing a Russian goose ("I was so scared I got people bumps!"), but the standout animated creations were a terrifying grizzly bear and a weird, telegraphic Bulldog named Morse.

While this was the best of the five traditionally animated Amblin features, it made little impact coming in the wake of Pixar and Disney's *Toy Story*, which brought computer animation into feature films and set the tone for the future in this genre, making this sort of artistry seem old fashioned and no longer of much interest to a wide audience.

Twister

Warner Bros., May 10, 1996

A Warner Bros. and Universal Pictures presentation of an Amblin Entertainment production. Starring Helen Hunt (Dr. Jo Harding), Bill Paxton (Bill Harding), Jami Gertz (Dr. Melissa Reeves), Cary Elwes (Dr. Jonas Miller). Executive Producers: Steven Spielberg, Walter Parkes, Laurie MacDonald, Gerald R. Molen. Produced by Kathleen Kennedy, Ian Bryce, Michael Crichton. Written by Michael Crichton and Anne-Marie Martin. Directed by Jan de Bont. Technicolor. Panavision. 113 minutes. (PG-13)

Storm chasers Bill (Bill Paxton) and Jo Harding (Helen Hunt) running in the opposite direction from a particularly nasty tornado in *Twister*.

This one was proof that there are large audiences out there who are looking strictly for special effects and big thrills, storytelling be damned. (The serviceable script was a collaboration between Michael Crichton and his then-wife, Anne-Marie, the "A-M" to whom the novel *Jurassic Park* was dedicated.)

While attempting to coax his estranged wife Jo into signing divorce papers, Bill Harding finds himself drawn back into his old job of "storm chasing," joining Jo's motley crew as they pursue one violent twister after another in an attempt to test a new device for studying tornadoes. That was the skeletal frame this project hung on, and at nearly two hours the thin concept wore out its welcome. The magicians at Industrial Light & Magic, however, really outdid themselves, creating an awesome spectacle of terrifying destruction that warranted well-deserved Oscar nominations for visual effects and sound. This was one movie that really benefited from being experienced in full Dolby Stereo sound.

Cary Elwes had little to do as a sneering rival; Jami Gertz was positively annoying as Bill Paxton's new girlfriend; Philip Seymour Hoffman went into goofy overkill as a gonzo storm enthusiast; and Jeremy Davies showed up to mumble a few lines two years before he joined Tom Hanks's company under Steven Spielberg's direction in *Saving Private Ryan*. An Oklahoma drive-in was wrecked dramatically during a showing of Stanley Kubrick's *The Shining*, and there were not only very definite references to *The Wizard of Oz* (Bill and Jo's tornado device was called "Dorothy" and stamped with a picture of Judy Garland on the side of its container) but further interest for Garland aficionados, when a twister hit Lois Smith's house right in the middle of a television showing of *A Star is Born*.

A costly endeavor that required the combined resources of two studios, *Twister* was a box office smash, earning an eye-opening $241,721,524 in the United States alone, becoming the second highest-grossing 1996 release.

Men in Black

Columbia, July 2, 1997

An Amblin Entertainment production in association with MacDonald/Parkes productions. Starring Tommy Lee Jones (Kay), Will Smith (Jay), Linda Fiorentino (Laurel Weaver), Vincent D'Onofrio (Edgar), Rip Torn (Zed), Tony Shalhoub (Jeebs). Co-Producer: Graham Place. Executive Producer: Steven Spielberg. Produced by Walter F. Parkes, Laurie MacDonald. Screen story and screenplay by Ed Solomon. Based on the Marvel comic by Lowell Cunningham. Directed by Barry Sonnenfeld. Technicolor. 98 minutes. (PG-13)

One of the bright spots on the Amblin Entertainment résumé, this adaptation of a little-known comic book series brought out the best in everyone involved. The film worked as an action-filled science fiction adventure while also having a sly sense of humor about its premise and therefore offering some genuine laughs as one of the summer's better comedies. Tommy Lee Jones, in prime deadpan form, was "Kay," a no-nonsense agent for MiB, a secret organization whose task it is to license, monitor, and police extraterrestrial activity on Earth. When his aging partner comes to the realization that he's no longer up to the task, Kay recruits a younger, smartass NYPD officer (Smith) to help him stop the more dangerous examples of alien infiltration. Chief among these is a bug that has taken over the body of an upstate farmer (D'Onofrio) and is on a rampage throughout New York in an effort to find a precious item that will allow world conquest for its species.

Ed Solomon's script had great fun with the dual "illegal alien" premise, at one point having Kay show his new partner the surveillance operations, including a map that keeps track of every registered alien on Earth at any given time. Visible on a picture screen are several examples of extraterrestrials comfortably hidden among us, including Sylvester Stallone, conservative Newt Gingrich, George Lucas, Dionne Warwick, Barry Sonnenfeld (the movie's director), Danny DeVito, and, of course, Steven Spielberg.

According to a *Newsweek* cover story, Spielberg's name was essential in getting the comedy off the ground, with Amblin coming aboard the production that Laurie MacDonald and Walter F. Parkes were already putting together. With a 3 percent profit participation deal, Amblin came away with ample rewards. *Men in Black* became the second highest-grossing US release of 1997, trailing (by a *wide* margin, as did everything else that year) *Titanic* but besting Spielberg's own *The Lost World: Jurassic Park* by some $20 million. Rick Baker and David LeRoy Anderson won Academy Awards for their makeup design (D'Onofrio received a particularly grueling workout with his face-sagging alien), and the picture earned additional Oscar mentions for art direction and Danny Elfman's music score. *MiB* even rated a Golden Globe nomination for Best Motion Picture – Comedy or Musical, but it lost out to *As Good as It Gets*.

An animated spinoff series premiered that same fall on Saturday mornings (Ed O'Ross and Keith Diamond provided the voices for Kay and Jay, respectively), with Amblin behind it but Spielberg's name not seen in the credits. There followed two theatrical sequels, and it doesn't take a genius to guess what they were called.

Deep Impact

Paramount/DreamWorks, May 9, 1998

A Zanuck/Brown production. Starring Robert Duvall (Spurgeon Tanner), Téa Leoni (Jenny Lerner), Elijah Wood (Leo Biederman), Vanessa Redgrave (Robin Lerner), Maximilian Schell (Jason Lerner), James Cromwell (Alan Rittenhouse), Ron Eldard (Oren Monash), Jon Favreau (Gus Partenza), Laura Innes (Beth Stanley), Mary McCormack (Andrea Baker), Richard Schiff (Don Biederman), Leelee Sobieski (Sarah Hotchner), Blair Underwood (Mark Simon), Morgan Freeman (President Tom Beck). Produced by Richard D. Zanuck, David Brown. Executive Producers: Steven Spielberg, Walter Parkes, Joan Bradshaw. Written by Bruce Joel Rubin and Michael Tolkin. Directed by Mimi Leder. Technicolor. Super 35 Widescreen. 120 minutes. (PG-13)

It was a race to see who could most loudly and profitably end the world in the summer movie season of 1998. While this $75 million production went for a gentler, more character-driven angle, Disney's *Armageddon* doubled the budget, added another half hour onto the story, and shook things up with more bang for your

Anchor Jenny Perner (Téa Leoni) has some bad news to bring the population about a massive comet in *Deep Impact*.

buck. If more ticket buyers turned out for the latter, *Deep Impact* had nothing to be ashamed about, bringing in some $140 million in the United States and, frankly, being the easier to take and more satisfying of the two spectacles.

An unidentified object in the skies turns out to be everyone's worst nightmare: a seven-mile long comet that is heading directly for Earth. As a solution, a gigantic spaceship is built in hopes that the combined efforts of an American and Russian crew can intercept and destroy the hurtling celestial object. But the best efforts don't always go as planned.

A lineup of such talented actors as Morgan Freeman (as the US President), Robert Duvall (as the veteran astronaut enlisted to help save the day), Elijah Wood (as the young astronomy club member who is the first to spot the offending comet), and Vanessa Redgrave (as the lonely divorcee resigned to the Earth's potential fate) added immeasurably to the proceedings, and, despite the smashing special effects, it was the human factor that delivered the goods in the end. Interestingly, a key sequence which had Manhattan hit by a tidal wave and therefore ending up under water looked almost like a warm-up to Spielberg's depiction of a submerged New York in *A.I. Artificial Intelligence*.

This film marked the first time Steven Spielberg had worked in collaboration with producers Richard D. Zanuck and David Brown since his 1975 breakthrough in *Jaws*.

The Mask of Zorro

TriStar, July 17, 1998

An Amblin Entertainment production in association with Zorro Prods. Starring Antonio Banderas (Alejandro Murrieta, "Zorro"), Anthony Hopkins (Don Diego de la Vega, "Zorro"), Catherine Zeta-Jones (Elena), Stuart Wilson (Don Raphael Montero), Matt Letscher (Captain Harrison Love). Executive Producers: Steven Spielberg, Walter F. Parkes, Laurie MacDonald. Produced by Doug Claybourne, David Foster. Co-Producer: John Gertz. Screenplay by John Eskow and Ted Elliott and Terry Rossio. Story by Ted Elliott and Terry Rossio and Randall Johnson. Directed by Martin Campbell. CFI Color. J-D-C Scope. 138 minutes. (PG-13)

Another high-water mark among the Amblin Entertainment output, this rousingly exciting adventure yarn brought back masked hero Zorro to the screen in all the opulent splendor and good spirits he deserved.

Originally created by Johnston McCulley for the pulp magazine *All-Story Weekly* back in 1919, the caped sword fighter, in the persona of Douglas Fairbanks, first showed up on movie screens the very next year in *The Mark of Zorro*, one of his best swashbucklers and a box office hit. Tyrone Power would don the mask successfully for a remake twenty years later, and there was further interest generated when Disney brought the character to television in 1957 and made a star out of Guy Williams. Things were less rosy when *The Mark of Zorro*, with Fank Langella in the lead, was remade for television in 1974 and when a cheapjack animated series, *The Tarzan/Lone Ranger/Zorro Adventure Hour*, included him among its lineup of heroes in 1981, the same year George Hamilton starred in a badly bungled spoof, *Zorro the Gay Blade*. It was therefore something of a risk to see if audiences still had much interest in the character.

Thanks to a well-plotted screenplay that was spiced with dollops of humor (but thankfully not enough to turn the film into a parody), a strong emotional backbone, and tremendous stunt work, *The Mask of Zorro* (borrowing the title of McCulley's final adventure) hit all the right marks. This time there were *two* Zorros on hand, with Anthony Hopkins as an aging swashbuckler who finds his life shattered when the wicked, soon-to-be deposed governor, Don Raphael, causes Zorro's beloved wife to be killed, tosses the masked hero behind bars, and steals away his baby daughter. Twenty years later, Zorro escapes from his prison and plots his revenge, enlisting to become the new Zorro, a petty thief who is himself hell bent on avenging the execution of his brother by a snarling army captain (Letscher). Old Zorro teaches Young Zorro not only to become a master swordsmen but to lend his services to the oppressed citizens of the territory of California.

Antonio Banderas, in one of his very best roles, was a witty and agile Zorro-in-training; Anthony Hopkins added tremendous gravitas and emotion as the aged swashbuckler, bent but far from broken; Catherine Zeta-Jones, as the devastatingly beautiful wronged daughter, was a terrific find for the part that helped launch her

The caped avenger returns to the screen, as seen in this ad for
The Mask of Zorro.

film career; and Stuart Wilson and Matt Letscher made for smoothly despicable bad guys. A combination swordfight and foreplay between Banderas and Zeta-Jones was a treat; a sequence in which Banderas (or rather his double) managed to remove a squadron of military riders from their horses was a stunt tour-de-force; and it was just the sort of grand entertainment (filmed entirely in Mexico) to please the masses in an old-fashioned sense. New Zealand director Martin Campbell's best effort behind the camera, *Zorro* grossed $93,830,000 in North America, earned Oscar nominations for sound and sound effects editing, was in the running for the Golden Globe (treated as a comedy) for Best Picture, and resulted in a sequel, *The Legend of Zorro*, seven years down the line.

The Last Days

October Films; October 23, 1998

Steven Spielberg and Survivors of the Shoah Visual History Foundation present a Ken Lipper/June Beallor production. Executive Producer: Steven Spielberg. Produced by June Beallor, Ken Lipper. Directed and Edited by James Moll. Color/Black and white. 87 minutes. (PG-13)

Surprisingly, it took this long for a theatrically released documentary to carry Steven Spielberg's name on it, but by any measure it was certainly an outstanding one. Five Hungarian Shoah survivors (all of whom speak English) are interviewed about their experiences leading up to their incarceration by the Nazis, the inhuman treatment they experienced, and their recovery after the liberation. Emphasized is the fact that despite their realization that they were not going to come out the victors, the Nazis still made it their goal to destroy as many Jews as possible in the waning months of World War II, a further vindication of their unspeakable depravity. Hearing the survivors' firsthand descriptions of the darkened box cars shipping them to the camps, the overcrowded barracks, and the ominous crematoriums bring the horror to life in ways even something as shattering as *Schindler's List* cannot replicate. Or, as one of the interviewees explains, "Unfortunately, it was much worse than what they show in the movies."

Those sharing their often emotionally crippling memories are Irene Zisblatt (from Polena), Renée Firestone (Ungvár), Alice Lok Cahana (Sárvár), Bill Basch (Szaszovo), and Tom Lantos (Budapest; who later became a California senator). Each is seen sharing their experiences with members of their families, in some cases taking them (and therefore us, the viewers) to the actual remains of the camps in search of some kind of catharsis or closure to their nightmares.

The movie received an Oscar-qualifying run in select theaters in October of 1998, which did the trick. It was named the Academy Award winner for Best Documentary Feature, with director James Moll and the first named producer, Ken Lipper, designated by the AMPAS as the winners, although they made sure that the other producer, June Beallor, came to the stage to share the moment with them. Moll extended a special thanks to a beaming and proud Steven Spielberg, who was sitting in the audience (later that night he would win his own Oscar for directing *Saving Private Ryan*), "for his strength of character and his vision in establishing the Shoah Foundation."

Jurassic Park III

Universal, July 18, 2001

An Amblin Entertainment production. Sam Neill (Dr. Alan Grant), William H. Macy (Paul Kirby), Téa Leoni (Amanda Kirby), Alessandro Nivola (Billy Brennan), Trevor Morgan (Eric Kirby), Michael Jeter (Udesky). Executive Producer: Steven Spielberg.

Produced by Kathleen Kennedy, Larry Franco. Written by Peter Buchman. Based on the characters created by Michael Crichton. Directed by Joe Johnston. DeLuxe color. 92 minutes. (PG-13)

Dr. Alan Grant agrees to return to Isla Sorna for a large amount of money. Sam Neill agrees to return to the *Jurassic* franchise, presumably for a large amount of money as well.

Turns out things aren't what they seem with this unwise trip to the second dinosaur island from *The Lost World*, a pair of concerned parents (Macy and Leoni) having conned Grant into being their guide in order to find their son, who had gone missing during a hang-gliding mishap. This was not a group that engendered much audience sympathy, making the swooping pterodactyls far more interesting to watch. By the time the travelers encountered a mixed group of dinosaurs grazing on a plain and John Williams's majestic score from the original movie soared to expected heights, even the most avid sequel fan must have sensed that everyone was merely going through the motions and that we'd dipped into this well one time too many. As these things went, at least it was relatively short.

Joe Johnston, who'd toiled for Steven Spielberg in various capacities on *Temple of Doom*, **batteries not included*, and *Always*, was in the director's chair, and Laura Dern briefly reprised her role of Ellie from *Jurassic Park*, letting audiences know that she and Dr. Grant did *not* end up together. The grosses were big, $180,190,000 in North America alone, but it took fourteen more years before Universal and Amblin resurrected the extinct ones again to further box office glory.

Men in Black II

Columbia, July 3, 2002

An Amblin Entertainment production in association with MacDonald/Parkes productions. Starring Tommy Lee Jones (Kay), Will Smith (Jay), Lara Flynn Boyle (Serleena), Johnny Knoxville (Scrad/Charlie), Rosario Dawson (Laura Vasquez), Tony Shalhoub (Jack Jeebs), Rip Torn (Zed). Executive Producer: Steven Spielberg. Produced by Walter F. Parkes, Laurie MacDonald. Story by Robert Gordon. Screenplay by Robert Gordon, Barry Fanaro. Based on the Malibu Comics series by Lowell Cunningham. Directed by Barry Sonnenfeld. DeLuxe color. 88 minutes. (PG-13)

Hollywood rule: Big box office begets big, unnecessary sequel. This time Jay must coax the now-retired Kay back into the Men in Black organization to help him stop a deadly alien (Boyle) from locating the Light of Zartha and bringing about Earth's annihilation. Straining very hard to duplicate the outrageous fun of the first adventure, *Black II* was full of bad ideas, from a double dose of Johnny Knoxville to giving Frank the Talking Pug a substantial role. No doubt it was the perfunctory screenplay that attracted Smith and Jones to return to their roles and not the $20 million salaries they were offered. It was the eighth highest-grossing movie of the year, so number *III* was ordered, although it took ten years to surface.

The Legend of Zorro

Columbia, October 28, 2005

A Spyglass Entertainment presentation of an Amblin Entertainment production. Antonio Banderas (Don Alejandro de la Vega, "Zorro"), Catherine Zeta-Jones (Elena de la Vega), Rufus Sewell (Count Armand), Nick Chinlund (Jacob McGivens), Julio Oscar Mechoso (Frey Felipe), Shuler Hensley (Pike), Michael Emerson (Harrigan), Adrian Alonso (Joaquin de la Vega). Executive Producers: Steven Spielberg, Gary Barber, Roger Birnbaum. Produced by Walter F. Parkes, Laurie MacDonald, Lloyd Phillips. Co-Producers: John Gertz, Amy Reid Lescoe, Marc Haimes. Screenplay by Roberto Orci and Alex Kurtzman. Story by Roberto Orci and Alex Kurtzman and Ted Elliott andTerry Rossio. Directed by Martin Campbell. DeLuxe color. Super 35 Widescreen. 131 minutes. (PG-13)

Another sequel nobody needed, seven years after the first, no less. Fumbling to create conflict, the new story finds Zorro and his beloved Elena breaking up over his failure to be a proper father to his son, Joaquin. Elena takes up instead with wealthy French count Armand who, anticipating the inevitable Civil War, is developing a secret weapon, extracting glycerin from soap. Antonio Banderas still made for a cheeky and dashing Zorro, but handing too much of the plotline over to his young offspring hardly compensated for the absence of a sorely missed Anthony Hopkins. The exciting climax involving a speeding train loaded with bottles of nitroglycerin was the highlight. This time, there was more interest in the international market than in the United States.

Memoirs of a Geisha

Columbia/DreamWorks, December 23, 2005

A Columbia Pictures, DreamWorks Pictures, and Spyglass Entertainment presentation of an Amblin Entertainment, Red Wagon production. Ziyi Zhang (Sayuri), Ken Watanabe (Chairman), Michelle Yeoh (Mameha), Koji Yakusho (Nobu), Yûki Kudô (Pumpkin), Kaori Momoi (Mother), Tsai Chin (Auntie), Cary-Hiroyuki Tagawa (The Baron), Gong Li (Hatsumomo). Introducing Suzuka Ohgo (Chiyo). Executive Producers: Roger Birnbaum, Gary Barber, Patricia Whitcher, Bobby Cohen. Produced by Lucy Fisher, Douglas Wick, Steven Spielberg. Screenplay by Robin Swicord. Based on the book by Arthur Golden. Directed by Rob Marshall. DeLuxe color. Panavision. 145 minutes. (PG-13).

Arthur Golden's novel *Memoirs of a Geisha* turned into the sort of surprise literary sensation that all authors dream of, becoming a staple on the *New York Times* Best Seller list for a two-year period. What's more, shortly after its debut, Hollywood came calling, the rights being purchased by Columbia Pictures for approximately $650,000, with none other than Steven Spielberg attached as director. In April of 1998, the filmmaker announced that he was very excited to make the book his next project, with shooting to begin by the end of the year or the beginning of the next. There were even specific casting choices announced to the press before Spielberg suddenly changed his mind and put the project on the shelf, opting to do *A.I. Artificial Intelligence* and *Minority Report* instead. By 2002, he had decided he would restrict his involvement to producing the movie with someone else taking over the direction. That job finally went to Rob Marshall, following his tremendous success in bringing the stage musical *Chicago* to the screen and to financial and Oscar glory. (One can't help but wonder: if Spielberg had stayed in the director's chair, would he have been subjected to the same kind of narrow-minded criticism he'd endured with *The Color Purple*, for "daring" to direct a story in which the majority of the characters were of a race different than his own?)

Golden's story followed the plight of Chiyo, a Japanese girl sold at the age of nine by her impoverished father to an okiya boarding house, where she is subjected to a strict and loveless upbringing in preparation for becoming a geisha (her name eventually changed to Sayuri), thereby robbing her of a life of her own choosing. An encounter with a kindly gentleman called "the Chairman" becomes her one hope to leave behind her oppressive existence, making it her goal to become a part of his life and win him over. As adapted for the screen by Robin Swicord, what had enthralled readers on the page came off as woefully devoid of stimulating drama, and Marshall's tasteful, stuffy direction made it even more of a slog to sit through. Gong Li sunk her teeth a bit too deeply into her showy role of the vengeful, failed geisha Hatsumomo, while Ken Watanabe, as the humane Chairman, and Michelle Yeoh, as Sayuri's mentor, fared best simply because they were so much less stilted than too many others in the cast.

Since it was the sort of movie that could be best described as "all dressed up with no place to go," it was fitting that the Academy found it a visual treat, bestowing Oscars upon it for costumes, art direction and cinematography. The public response was less lucrative than anticipated, hardly reflecting its red-hot literary history.

Monster House

Columbia, July 21, 2006

Columbia Pictures presents in association with Relativity Media an ImageMovers/Amblin production. Starring Steve Buscemi (Nebbercracker), Nick Cannon (Officer Lister), Maggie Gyllenhaal (Zee), Jon Heder (Skull), Kevin James (Officer Landers), Jason Lee (Bones), Catherine O'Hara (Mom), Kathleenh Turner (Constance), Fred Willard (Dad), Mitchel Musso (DJ), Sam Lerner (Chowder), Spencer Locke (Jenny). Screenplay by Dan Harman and Rob Schrab and Pamela Pettler. Story by Dan Harmon and Rob Schrab. Produced by Steve Starkey, Jack Rapke. Executive Producers: Robert Zemeckis, Steven Spielberg, Jason Clark. Directed by Gil Kenan. Technicolor. 3D. 91 minutes. (PG)

Figuring most kids grew up near a hostile neighbor who unleashed hell if they caught any intruders trampling on their property, *Monster House* took this premise even further and made a suburban house itself not only ominous in appearance but ready to eat unsuspecting children and their toys should they dare cross its boundaries. A combination of motion capture (five years before Steven Spielberg took the plunge into this area with *The Adventures of Tintin*) and animation gave the principals a somewhat dead look and there was no shortage of irritating characters on hand, making it all a bit of a chore to watch. The film did, however, end up as one of the nominees that year for Animated Feature, while its director, Gil Kenan, was later enlisted to helm another overstuffed thriller, the 2015 remake of *Poltergeist.*

Spell Your Name

Ukraine premiere: October 18, 2006

A USC Shoah Foundation Institute production. Executive Producers: Steven Spielberg, Victor Pinchuk. Producers: Mark Edwards, Douglas Greenberg. Director: Sergey Bukovsky. Film Plus in association with the Victor Pinchuk Foundation. Color. 89 minutes.

A collaboration between the USC Shoah Foundation Institute for Visual History and Education and the Ukraine-based Victor Pinchuk Foundation, this documentary examined the massacre of tens of thousands of Jews at the Babi Yar ravine in Ukraine through testimonies of several survivors. Following the movie's Kiev premiere (at which Spielberg was in attendance), the film played festivals but received no official US theatrical run. It debuted on DVD on July 18, 2012.

Flags of Our Fathers

Paramount, October 20, 2006

A DreamWorks Pictures/Warner Bros. Pictures presentation of a Malpaso/Amblin Entertainment production. Distributed by Paramount Pictures. Starring Ryan Phillippe (John "Doc" Bradley), Jesse Bradford (Rene Gagnon), Adam Beach (Ira Hayes). Produced by Clint Eastwood, Steven Spielberg, Robert Lorenz. Screenplay by William Broyles Jr., Paul Haggis. Based on the book by James Bradley, Ron Powers. Directed by Clint Eastwood. Technicolor. Panavision. 132 minutes. (R)

One of the glowing Amblin credits, this stirring and emotionally complex war drama marked the first cinematic collaboration between Steven Spielberg and Clint Eastwood. (Amblin Entertainment had co-produced Eastwood's 1995 drama *The Bridges of Madison County*, but Spielberg had no producer credit on it.) Twenty-one years earlier they had worked on an episode of *Amazing Stories* ("Vanessa in the Garden"), with Eastwood making his first venture in directing for the small screen, and Spielberg providing the script. This epic look at the real story behind what became perhaps the most famous photographic image of World War II, the raising of the flag on Iwo Jima, was, actually a dual project. While *Flags of Our Fathers* depicted the events from the American point of view, a companion movie, *Letters from Iwo Jima*, would show what happened on the Japanese side of the conflict. The two projects were filmed back-to-back.

With a $55 million budget, *Flags* was a large and impressive undertaking, but one which emphasized intimacy and personalized stories within the ambitious scope of its storytelling. Eastwood staged the US efforts to capture the sulfuric island of Iwo Jima (with Iceland subbing for it in most of the scenes) with a frightening sense of chaos and thrilling cinematic momentum. Tom Stern's stunning cinematography added to the bleak hellishness of the mission, almost entirely washing the color out of the picture during these sequences, which was, in turn, punctuated by flashes of explosions and blood in the full Technicolor process. Intercut between the ugliness of combat was the story of the three surviving soldiers (played by Ryan Phillippe, Jesse Bradford, and an especially good Adam Beach, as the most tragic member of the trio, Native American Ira Hayes) who planted the flag atop Mount Suribachi. Their less-than-glorious aftermath, having to play heroes for a public eager to find glory in war despite the fact that theirs was the second, posed shot of the actual flag planting, was made more pointless by the fact that the three other men who shared the moment with them would soon afterward die grisly deaths.

The screenplay by *China Beach* creator William Broyles Jr. and Paul Haggis—Eastwood's scripter for his previous Oscar-winner, *Million Dollar Baby*—gave full attention to its vast roster of players. Among them were Barry Pepper and Harve Presnell, both returning for another tour of duty, having been seen in *Saving Private Ryan*; Neal McDonough, who had appeared in military fatigues in *Band of Brothers*; Eastwood's real-life son, billed here as Scott Reeves; Spielberg's future *The Adventures of Tintin* star Jamie Bell; Tom McCarthy, who would go on to Oscar

Excitedly on their way to Iwo Jima, before the grim reality of war sets in, are Ignatowski (Jamie Bell), Bradley (Ryan Phillippe), Lundsford (Scott Reeves), Sousley (Joseph Cross), and Block (Benjamin Walker), in *Flags of Our Fathers*.

glory as the cowriter and director of the 2015 Best Picture winner, *Spotlight*; and Joseph Cross, who ended up a part of the White House staff in Spielberg's *Lincoln*.

Alas, the box office was soft, placing the movie below such disposable titles from that year as *Big Momma's House 2, Benchwarmers,* and *Date Movie*, proving that the audiences who would appreciate such projects were not motivated enough to patronize them in sufficient numbers. There were, however, a pair of Oscar nominations, for sound mixing and sound editing, and Eastwood was among those in the running at the Golden Globes for Best Director. Just to show his versatility, the director sang "I'll Walk Alone" over the opening credits, quite hauntingly.

Letters from Iwo Jima

Warner Bros., December 20, 2006

A DreamWorks Pictures/Warner Bros. Pictures presentation of a Malpaso/Amblin Entertainment production. Distributed by Warner Bros. Ken Watanabe (General Kuribayashi), Kazunari Ninomiya (Saigo), Tsuyoshi Ihara (Baron Nishi), Ryo Kase (Shimizu), Shidou Nakamura (Lieutenant Ito). Produced by Clint Eastwood, Steven Spielberg, Robert Lorenz. Executive Producer: Paul Haggis. Co-Producer: Tim Moore. Screenplay by Iris Yamashita. Based on the book *Picture Letters from Commander in Chief* by Tadmichi Kuribayashi. Directed by Clint Eastwood. Technicolor. Panavision. 141 minutes. (R)

This worthy companion piece to *Flags of Our Fathers* was a risky commercial prospect. The idea was to take most of the other movie's storyline and flip it so that viewers would now see the battle of Iwo Jima from the point of view of the Japanese. The first fifty minutes consisted of the build-up to the arrival of US troops on the island, as General Kuribayashi arrives with the increasingly hopeless task of fortifying Iwo Jima so that the Americans cannot use it as a base of operations for attacking the Japanese mainland. Kuribayashi tries to rally his troops with as much martinet fervor that he can muster but cannot help but display a humane streak, as he is well aware that to die the glorious deaths expected of them by the Imperial Commanders is not so easy to accomplish for some of the more terrified soldiers. Witnessing most of the carnage that unfolds is an affable private (Ninomiya)—a simple baker who wants nothing more than to return home to his wife and newborn child—whose confusion and inability to rise to heroic expectations make him all too human.

Like *Flags*, *Letters* was shot with a desaturated color scheme that emphasized the bleak setting. Having letters written to loved ones back home, read as part of the narration, was another masterstroke in making audiences understand that those who had been nothing more than faceless foes in the previous film had real lives of their own. It was quite unique to offer an American-financed motion picture in which nearly all of the dialogue was spoken in another language and only the lead, Ken Watanabe, was in any way recognizable to US moviegoers. Not surprisingly, despite the positive reviews, the box office was even weaker than it had been for *Flags*, even after the movie scored an Academy Award nomination for Best Picture. (This honor marked the first time Steven Spielberg ended up with a Best Picture Oscar nomination for producing a movie he himself did not direct.) *Letters* received additional mentions from the Academy for Clint Eastwood as Director and for Original Screenplay (despite being credited on screen as being based on a book) and Sound Editing, which it won.

Transformers

DreamWorks/Paramount, July 3, 2007

A di Bonaventura Pictures production, a Tim DeSanto/Don Murphy production. Starring Shia LaBeouf (Sam Witwicky), Tyrese Gibson (Sgt. Epps), Josh Duhamel (Capt. William Lennox), Anthony Anderson (Glen Whitmann), Rachel Taylor (Maggie Madsen), Megan Fox (Mikaela Banes), John Turturro (Simmons), Jon Voight (Defense Secretary John Keller). Produced by Don Murphy, Tom DeSanto, Lorenzo di Bonaventura, Ian Bryce. Executive Producers: Steven Spielberg, Michael Bay, Brian Goldner, Mark Vahradian. Screenplay by Roberto Orci and Alex Kurztman. Story by Roberto Orci and Alex Kurtzman and John Rogers. Based on Hasbro's Transformers action figures. Directed by Michael Bay. Deluxe color. Panavision. 145 minutes. (PG-13)

There are robots among us! Huge, clanking monsters—the benevolent ones calling themselves Autobots, the evil ones dubbed Decepticons—from the planet Cybertron come to Earth to seek a precious cube that has the power to make a major galactic mess of things. In order to camouflage themselves among the Earthlings, the hulking automatons can transform at will into mechanical devices, motor vehicles chief among them. When high schooler Sam Witwicky purchases a Camaro from a used car lot, he's stunned to realize his new set of wheels is one of those very robots. The Autobots are anxious to obtain a pair of glasses that belonged to Sam's great-grandfather and contain coordinates pinpointing the location of the cube.

Who would have thought that a series of toys unleashed on the world from Hasbro in 1984 would pave the way, more than twenty years in the future, for some astronomically expensive, incredibly noisy, unreasonably overlong action epics that large portions of the world couldn't get enough of? Knowing that the toys, not to mention their TV cartoon and comic book spinoffs, had a vast and enthusiastic following, Steven Spielberg formed an unfortunate alliance with the director who'd come to epitomize the sort of excessive effects-driven blockbuster that went for soulless overload over storytelling, Michael Bay. There was no denying that the special effects were seamlessly blended in with the real action to eye-popping effect, but it wasn't encouraging to think that this kind of hectic, ultra-loud and rather juvenile nonsense was exactly what select members of the moviegoing population were clamoring for, resulting in a US box office gross of more than $300 million. (The overseas figures were even bigger.)

Shia LaBeouf, as the reluctant hero, was a considerable asset to the overstuffed proceedings, throwing himself into the action with committed dedication when necessary and just as often giving a knowing wink to the absurdity of it all. Megan Fox was just the sort of outlandishly sexy pinup fans of this sort of thing expected a woman to look like; E.T. received a passing mention; and John Turturro went so far out of his way to chomp a piece of scenery or two that it was kind of fun having him around. There were Oscar nominations for those visual effects plus additional nods to the sound mixing and sound editing that kept those strident crunching noises coming at you at full volume. During the big climactic battle in downtown Los Angeles, the marquee on the Orpheum Theatre advertised a double bill of *A Place in the Sun* and *The Rose Tattoo*, perhaps as an ironic statement on the sort of adult-driven movie Hollywood *used to* concentrate on, a long time ago.

Eagle Eye

DreamWorks/Paramount, September 26, 2008

A K/O production. Starring Shia LaBeouf (Jerry Shaw/Ethan Shaw), Michelle Monaghan (Rachel Holloman), Rosario Dawson (Zoe Perez), Michael Chiklis (Defense Secretary Callister), Anthony Mackie (Major William Bowman), Ethan Embry (Agent Toby Grant), Billy Bob Thornton (Agent Thomas Morgan). Executive Producers: Steven Spielberg, Edward L. McDonnell. Produced by Alex Kurtzman, Roberto Orci, Patrick Crowley. Story by Dan McDermott. Screenplay by John Glenn and Travis Adam Wright and Hillary Seitz and Dan McDermott. Directed by D. J. Caruso. Deluxe color. Super 35 Widescreen. 118 minutes. (PG-13)

Following the funeral of his lookalike brother, Jerry Shaw is hounded by persistent phone calls from a mysterious voice ordering him to follow instructions to carry out acts of anarchy, his each move tracked by surveillance and helped along by technology unexpectedly working in his favor. He joins forces with a single mother (Monaghan) who has been subjected to the same torment under threat of killing her young son, and the two take off on the run from the FBI as it becomes apparent they are being roped into a terrorist plot.

This paranoia thriller was designed for maximum car-crashing impact and to be a modern, techno-savvy version of one of Alfred Hitchcock's favorite themes: the innocent man on the run. While it was always nice to warn audiences about the dangers of crossing the lines of privacy in the name of government security and of depending too much on machines to guide our future, bombastic thrills took the place of subtlety, and plausibility was pretty much tossed to the winds. Coming after the double box office bullseyes of *Transformers* (2007) and *Indiana Jones and the Kingdom of the Crystal Skull* (2008), audiences no doubt had developed a temporary interest in Shia LaBeouf, at least where action roles were concerned, and this ended up grossing more than $100 million in North America. An unbilled Julianne Moore provided the self-righteous voice of the pesky computer, ARIIA.

Transformers: Revenge of the Fallen

DreamWorks/Paramount, June 24, 2009

A Don Murphy/Tom DeSanto production, a di Bonaventura Pictures production, an Ian Bryce production. Starring Shia LaBeouf (Sam Witwicky), Megan Fox (Mikaela Banes), Josh Duhamel (Major Lennox), Tyrese Gibson (Master Sgt. Epps), Kevin Dunn

(Ron Witwicky), Julie White (Judy Witwicky), John Turturro (Seymour Simmons). Produced by Lorenzo di Bonaventura, Tom DeSantos and Don Murphy, Ian Bryce. Executive Producers: Steven Spielberg, Michael Bay, Brian Goldner, Mark Vahradian. Written by Ehren Kruger and Roberto Orci and Alex Kurtzman. Based on Hasbro's Transformers action figures. Directed by Michael Bay. DeLuxe Color. Panavision. 150 minutes. (PG-13)

You can't keep a good (or bad) robot down, not when there's money to be made. This time our reluctant hero, Sam Witwicky, starting anew in college, finds himself sucked back into the automaton war when he discovers a sliver from that coveted All Spark cube in his shirt. Because of it, strange symbols keep disrupting Sam's vision, and this makes him very desirable to the Decepticons, who propose their customary world-destruction threat unless they get what they want. This time it all ends with a crunchy, headache-inducing battle among the pyramids of Egypt, and along the way there is a brief sound bite of the *Jaws* theme on Bumblebee's car radio. At one point the battling bots wreck a library, which seemed all too depressingly symbolic of this enterprise. With all the grace of a truck filled with obsolete appliances dropping the unwanted machines into a deep landfill, this big, long, busy movie gave hungry audiences more of what they showed up for two years earlier, bringing in a scary $402,120,000 in the US alone!

The Lovely Bones

Paramount/DreamWorks, December 11, 2009

A DreamWorks Pictures in association with Film4 presentation of a Wingnut Films production. Starring Mark Wahlberg (Jack Salmon), Rachel Weisz (Abigail Salmon), Susan Sarandon (Grandma Lynn), Stanley Tucci (George Harvey), Michael Imperioli (Len Fenerman), Saoirse Ronan (Susie Salmon). Executive Producers: Tessa Ross, Steven Spielberg, Ken Kamins, James Wilson. Produced by Carolynne Cunningham, Fran Walsh, Peter Jackson, Aimee Peyronnet. Screenplay by Fran Walsh and Philippa Boyens and Peter Jackson. Based on the novel by Alice Sebold. Directed by Peter Jackson. Deluxe color. HD Widescreen. 136 minutes. (PG-13)

A departure for director Peter Jackson, made between Hobbits and gorillas, this sad drama still had its fair share of fantasy. The narrated line "I was fourteen years old when I was murdered on December 6, 1973" summed it up, as Susie Salmon relates her story from a kind of "in-between" afterlife, observing her family's shattered reaction to her disappearance and the eventual awareness of her death, as well as the progress of her killer, a creepy loner (Tucci) from down the block who suddenly has thoughts of disposing of Susie's inquisitive sister Lindsey (Rose McIver) as well.

This strange imbalance of depressing domestic unrest and weirdly kaleido-scopic special effects came to life in fits and starts, mainly because of the strong presence of Saoirse Ronan as the regretful and tragic heroine, and Stanley Tucci's subtly unnerving, Oscar-nominated turn as an unhinged predator who upends so many lives without remorse. Coming from a best-selling novel, this engendered some public interest at first but was too much of a miss to draw a large audience.

Hereafter

Warner Bros., October 15, 2010

A Kennedy/Marshall production, a Malpaso production. Starring Matt Damon (George Lonegan), Cécile de France (Marie Lelay), Jay Mohr (Billy Lonergan), Bryce Dallas Howard (Melanie), George McLaren (Marcus/Jason), Frankie McLaren (Marcus/Jason), Thierry Neuvic (Didier), Marthe Keller (Dr. Rousseau), Derek Jacobi (himself). Executive Producers: Steven Spielberg, Frank Marshall, Peter Morgan, Tim Moore. Produced by Kathleen Kennedy, Robert Lorenz. Written by Peter Morgan. Produced and Directed by Clint Eastwood. Technicolor. Panavision. 129 minutes. (PG-13)

A different choice of material for director Clint Eastwood, this slow, very muted, meditative drama about communication with the hereafter crisscrossed between three separate stories. After experiencing a devastating tsunami while on vacation, French journalist Marie Lelay is haunted by the glimpses into the afterlife she'd

Matt Damon as the tormented clairvoyant in *Hereafter*.

experienced when she nearly perished. In London, young Marcus yearns to contact his twin brother, who was hit by a car and killed after being chased by bullies. In San Francisco, George Lonergan tries to lead a normal life, tormented by the "gift" he has of making contact between the departed and their loved ones back on Earth. The three protagonists eventually converge at a book fair in London. (This leads to the movie's most effective scene, when George reluctantly agrees to make contact with Marcus's brother, bringing the surviving twin to tears of longing.)

Starting off with a frightening recreation of the 2004 Indian Ocean tsunami (earning an Oscar nomination for Michael Owens and his team), the movie approached the possibility of spiritual contact with seriousness, while also remembering to expose those charlatans hoping to make a buck off of people's suffering. A well-intended work that simply wasn't exciting enough to get anybody talking about its themes, this was a soft performer at the box office, although it did appeal to select critical factions.

True Grit

Paramount, December 22, 2010

Paramount Pictures and Skydance Productions present a Scott Rudin/Mike Zoss production. Starring Jeff Bridges (Marshal Reuben "Rooster" Cogburn), Matt Damon (LaBeouf), Josh Brolin (Tom Chaney), Barry Pepper (Lucky Ned Pepper), Hailee Steinfeld (Mattie Ross). Executive Producers: Steven Spielberg, Robert Graf, David Ellison, Paul Schwake, Megan Ellison. Produced by Scott Rudin, Ethan Coen, Joel Coen. Based on the novel by Charles Portis. Written for the screen and directed by Joel Coen and Ethan Coen. DeLuxe color. Super 35 Widescreen. 110 minutes. (PG-13)

There wasn't really any good reason to remake *True Grit*, which had been one of the highpoints of John Wayne's later career, winning him an Oscar and becoming one of the most popular and fondly remembered westerns of the Sixties. But, if you had to resurrect familiar material, at least the men behind it, the Coen Brothers, were talented filmmakers who did the job proficiently and with great reverence to the original source, the 1968 novel by Charles Portis. (They kept the sad epilogue which had been discarded in the first version.) The key to making it all work was getting the right actor to reprise the story's most unforgettable character, Marshal Rooster Cogburn, and here they hit a resounding bullseye in casting Jeff Bridges, whose eccentric, gravel-voiced rendering of the hard-drinking, ornery, disheveled but accomplished lawman was different enough in approach that it needn't be compared to Wayne's indelible performance.

After her father is senselessly killed by outlaw Tom Chaney, the fiercely determined, outspoken fourteen-year-old Mattie Ross hires Cogburn to track him down in hopes of bringing the criminal to justice. Joining them is Texas Ranger LaBeouf, and the trio forms a memorably disparate group, with the interplay among them being the real appeal of the film. Hailee Steinfeld, making her motion picture debut, was an inspired choice to play Mattie and carried the movie with the finesse of a veteran. A member of Tom Hanks's company from *Saving Private Ryan*, Barry Pepper, was especially good as the unctuous gang leader Lucky

Ned Pepper. The Coen brothers ended up with the biggest box office hit of their careers by a wide margin, with *True Grit* earning $171,100,000 at a time when there weren't all that many westerns being made. The film also received ten Oscar nominations, the most (to date) of any movie produced by Steven Spielberg outside of those he directed. In addition to Bridges and Steinfeld (curiously placed in the supporting category, despite having the most screen time), there were additional nominations for picture, the two directors, adapted screenplay, cinematography, art direction, costume design, sound mixing, and sound editing.

Super 8

Paramount, June 10, 2011

An Amblin Entertainment/Bad Robot production. Starring Kyle Chandler (Jackson Lamb), Elle Fanning (Alice Dainard), Joel Courtney (Joe Lamb), Gabriel Basso (Martin), Noah Emmerich (Nelec), Ron Eldard (Louis Dainard), Riley Griffiths (Charles), Ryan Lee (Cary), Zach Mills (Preston). Produced by Steven Spielberg, J. J. Abrams, Bryan Burk. Executive Producer: Guy Riedel. Written and directed by J. J. Abrams. DeLuxe Color. Panavision. 112 minutes. (PG-13)

J. J. Abrams's combination of suburban child's adventure and science fiction wanted to be an affectionate tribute to similar entertainments of the past (it was set in 1979), indirectly or not, created by the movie's producer, Steven Spielberg. To this end, there were echoes of *Close Encounters*, suggestions of *E.T.*, and maybe even a shout-out to *The Goonies*. Alas, rather than working as its own standalone fantasy, *Super 8* had a distinctly derivative feeling.

In the working class town of Lillian, Ohio (actually filmed in Weirton, in West Virginia's northern panhandle), teenage Joe Lamb and his friends are horrified when, during a night filming of their amateur zombie movie, they witness an epic train wreck. Having inadvertently captured the event on their super 8 camera, they realize this is no ordinary accident, as the crash unleashes from one of the boxcars a giant spider-like creature. The US Air Force descends upon the town in order to cover up the truth and stop the alien from what appears to be a destructive (and abductive) rampage. Falling back on "types," rather than fully dimensional characters, and bogus emotional highpoints, *Super 8* played strictly by rote. Despite the highly proficient filmmaking, there was little about it that seems fresh or inspired. It did, however, do a decent job of recreating the late 1970s, when Walkmans were new, monster model kits were still available, and bedroom walls featured "Keep on Truckin'" posters. There was also a nicely understated lead performance by newcomer Joel Courtney, the appealing hero of the piece.

Transformers: Dark of the Moon

Paramount, June 29, 2011

Presented in association with Hasbro. A di Bonaventura Pictures production, a Tom DeSanto and Don Murphy production, an Ian Bryce production. Starring Shia

LaBeouf (Sam Witwicky), Josh Duhamel (Will Lennox), John Turturro (Seymour Simmons), Tyrese Gibson (Master Sergeant Rob Epps), Rose Huntington-Whiteley (Carly Spencer), Patrick Dempsey (Dylan Gould), Kevin Dunn (Ron Witwicky), Julie White (Judy Witwicky), Ken Jeong (Jerry Wang). With John Malkovich (Bruce Bazos), Frances McDormand (Charlotte Mearing). Executive Producers: Steven Spielberg, Michael Bay, Brian Goldner, Mark Wheadan. Produced by Lorenzo di Bonaventura, Tom DeSanto and Don Murphy, Ian Bryce. Based on Hasbro's Transformers action figures. Written by Ehren Kruger. Directed by Michael Bay. DeLuxe color. Panavision. 3D. 154 minutes. (PG-13)

According to this chapter in the ongoing battling-robot orgy, the Apollo 11 Moon landing had a hidden purpose: to investigate a Cybertronian craft that had crashed there and that contained a device capable of putting an end to the war between the Autobots and the Decepticons. We know this is true because the real Buzz Aldrin shows up here to chat with chief automaton Optimus Prime about this cover-up. Worked into the plotline are the abandoned ruins of Chernobyl, three US Presidents (hero Sam Witwicky is given a medal by Barack Obama for enduring the previous chaotic adventures), a callous destruction of Daniel Chester French's iconic statue in the Lincoln Memorial (perhaps executive producer Steven Spielberg hoped to atone for this act by filming *Lincoln* later that year), and a deadly bird-like robot assassin called Laserbeak. This time Chicago was subjected to relentless annihilation via the Oscar-nominated special effects team, and this clanking noise went on even longer than usual, with the customary disregard for cohesion or subtlety. It clearly didn't matter an iota to the ticket buyers who made this celluloid clatter into the second highest-grossing movie of the year.

There were additional Oscar nominations for Sound Mixing and Sound Editing, and sci-fi geeks were no doubt in fanboy heaven because the voice of the duplicitous Sentinel Prime was provided by none other than *Star Trek* icon Leonard Nimoy (who had voiced an entirely different character in the 1986 animated feature *The Transformers*). Political commentator Bill O'Reilly showed up for a cameo, this being the sort of assignment worthy of him.

Cowboys & Aliens

Universal/DreamWorks, July 29, 2011

A DreamWorks Pictures, Universal Pictures, Reliance Entertainment presentation in association with Relativity Media, an Imagine Entertainment, K.D. Paper Products, Fairview Entertainment, Platinum Studios production. Starring Daniel Craig (Jake Lonergan), Harrison Ford (Woodrow Dolarhyde), Olivia Wilde (Ella Swenson), Sam Rockwell (Doc), Adam Beach (Nat Colorado), Paul Dano (Percy Dolarhyde), Noah Ringer (Emmett Taggart), Keith Carradine (Sheriff John Taggart), Clancy Brown (Meacham). Executive Producers: Steven Spielberg, Jon Favreau, Dennis L. Stewart, Bobby Cohen, Randy Greenberg, Ryan Kavanaugh. Produced by Brian Grazer, Ron Howard, Alex Kurtzman, Roberto Orci, Scott Mitchell Rosenberg. Screen story by Mark Fergus and Hawk Ostby and Steve Oedekerk. Screenplay by Roberto Orci and Alex Kurtzman and Damon Lindelof and Mark Fergus and Hawk Ostby. Based on

Platinum Studios' graphic novel by Scott Mitchell Rosenberg. Directed by Jon Favreau. DeLuxe color. Panavision. 118 minutes. (PG-13).

Consider this: since there are never going to be any alien landings on planet Earth except in the minds of fantasy writers, *why not* set a science fiction story in the old west? This not-so-outlandish concept originated from a 2006 graphic novel, and despite the instant amusement produced by the title, this was all meant to be taken quite seriously. Daniel Craig had the traditional role of the stranger who wanders into town and brings trouble with him, only in this case he isn't quite sure who he is or why there is an electronic bracelet strapped to his wrist—the curious contraption able to bring down alien spaceships when they suddenly swoop into town, terrifying the locals in the same way they would react if this were happening in modern times.

There was a strong degree of intriguing mystery throughout the opening scene as the motley citizens of Absolution, New Mexico, were introduced, and all of them were soon wondering just what in hell was going on. Why was beautiful Ella Swenson the only lady in town wearing a gun belt, and why did she seem to know more about the stranger than he did? How bad a man was bullying cattle rancher Woodrow Dolarhyde, or was he merely a misguided leftover product of Confederate bigotry with severe offspring issues? Was the man Jake Lonergan couldn't remember he was the villain depicted on those wanted posters? Were those tentacles that snapped up unsuspecting Earthlings a winking nod to the ones seen in Spielberg's version of *War of the Worlds* or a mere coincidence? And didn't that upside-down riverboat, stuck in the desert miles from water, bring to mind the ship found in the desert in the "Special Edition" of *Close Encounters of the Third Kind*? Director Jon Favreau kept the story moving briskly along, but after a spell those creepy CGI creatures (with extra arms appearing unexpectedly from their bellies) and their nefarious plans weren't as freshly offbeat as the initial concept. The result was an acceptable time-filler that wasn't really that much different (other than the fact that it had horses) than a dozen other big budget sci-fi adventures clogging cinemas in the new millennium.

This movie was the product of many collaborations helping to support the hefty $163 million budget, which included K.D. Paper Products—which was not just a cute name for someone's production company but really *was* a business, based in India, that produced paper products—and Ron Howard and Brian Grazer's company, Imagine Entertainment, marking the one time to date that Howard and Spielberg had any sort of film production interaction. Although the $100 million US gross meant that there were a substantial number of viewers *not* turned off by the title, the movie fell way short of its prospective goals.

Real Steel

Touchstone/DreamWorks; October 7, 2011

DreamWorks Pictures and Reliance Entertainment present a 21 Laps/Montford Murphy production. Starring Hugh Jackman (Charlie Kenton), Dakota Goyo (Max

Kenton), Evangeline Lilly (Bailey Tallet), Anthony Mackie (Finn), Kevin Durand (Ricky), Hope Davis (Aunt Debra). Executive Producers: Jack Rapke, Robert Zemeckis, Steve Starkey, Steven Spielberg, Josh McLaglen, Mary McLaglen. Producers: Don Murphy and Susan Montford and Shawn Levy. Screenplay by John Gatins. Story by Dan Gilroy, Jeremy Leven. Based in part upon the short story "Steel" by Richard Matheson. Directed by Shawn Levy. DeLuxe color. HD Widescreen. 127 minutes. (PG-13)

Just what the world needed—a live-action version of the 1960s super-toy Rock 'em Sock 'em Robots. Actually, this was an expanded (and *much* too long) adaptation of a short story by Richard Matheson, which had already received a brief and more direct dramatization by the author himself on a 1963 episode of *The Twilight Zone*.

A futuristic tale in which androids are now the participants in the sport of boxing, deadbeat robot operator Charlie Kenton suddenly has his hands full of both metal and flesh when he ends up taking care of the eleven-year-old son, Max, he'd given up years back. When the boy rescues a derelict "bot" from the junkyard, they turn the mechanical man (dubbed "Atom") into a champion on the fighting circuit. The real competition here was to see which of the humans came off as the least appealing character: selfish, formerly pugilist Charlie; his bratty, smug offspring Max; bellowing rodeo emcee Ricky; or cartoonish villains Farra Lemkova (Olga Fonda) and Take Mashido (Karl Yune). A somewhat lower level of robotic bombast for those who couldn't get enough of the *Transformers* movies, it earned an Oscar nomination for the seamless special effects by Erik Nash, John Rosengrant, Danny Gordon Taylor, and Swen Gillberg.

Men in Black 3

Columbia, May 25, 2012

Columbia Pictures presents in association with Hemisphere Media Capital, an Amblin Entertainment production in association with P+M Image Nation. Starring Will Smith (Agent J), Tommy Lee Jones (Agent K), Josh Brolin (Young Agent K), Jemaine Clement (Boris the Animal), Michael Stuhlbarg (Grffin), Alice Eve (Young Agent O), Bill Hader (Andy Warhol – Agent W), David Rasche (Agent X), Emma Thompson (O). Executive Producers: Steven Spielberg, G. Mac Brown. Produced by Walter F. Parkes, Laurie MacDonald. Written by Etan Cohen. Based on the Malibu Comics series by Lowell Cunningham. Directed by Barry Sonnenfeld. DeLuxe color. Super 35 Widescreen. 106 minutes. (PG-13)

The ten-year gap between sequels did not bode well for this third installment, but, in fact, this was a decided improvement over part II. This time Will Smith was upped to top billing, but that promotion was fully justified, not simply because of a commendable box office record but because Tommy Lee Jones gave over most of the running time to his younger self, as played by Josh Brolin, wittily aping the older actor's deadpan line readings.

This time a particularly nasty alien named Boris the Animal ("It's *just* Boris!!") is sprung from prison and travels back in time to kill the agent responsible for his missing arm. Since that agent just happens to be K, J finds it necessary to skip back to 1969 to save his partner's life and stop yet another potential destruction of mankind. Although the movie did not take full advantage of the time tripping, there was a scathing sequence subjecting J to the sort of racial profiling all too evident in that era. Because too many moviegoers are preset to plunk down their money on a familiar title, this one did good business, even if there was a clear drop off in interest from what had come before. Regardless, it was worth it if for no other reason than to hear Will Smith say the line, "You know, I don't have no problem pimp slappin' the shizit out of Andy Warhol."

Transformers: Age of Extinction

Paramount, June 27, 2014

A Paramount Pictures presentation in association with Hasbro, a Don Murphy/Tom DeSantos production, a di Bonaventura Pictures production, an Ian Bryce production. Starring Mark Wahlberg (Cade Yeager), Stanley Tucci (Joshua Joyce), Kelsey Grammer (Harold Attinger), Nicola Peltz (Tessa Yeager), Jack Reynor (Shane Dyson), Sophia Myles (Darcy Tirrel), Bingbing Li (Su Yueming), Titus Welliver (James Savoy), T. J. Miller (Lucas Flannery). Produced by Lorenzo di Bonaventura, Tom DeSantos and Don Murphy, Ian Bryce. Executive Producers: Steven Spielberg, Michael Bay, Brian Goldner, Mark Vahradian. Written by Ehren Kruger. Based on Hasbro's Transformers action figures. Directed by Michael Bay. Color. Panavision. 3D. 165 minutes. (PG-13)

Foolish Earthlings kept showing up at the box office, so a fourth installment of the world's loudest movie franchise was ordered. Unhappy that the skirmishing droids did the greatest amount of damage to Chicago since that city's famous fire, the military has ended their alliance with the friendly Autobots and all the robots, good or bad, are ordered to be hunted down. Turns out a CIA operative, Harold Attinger, isn't exactly looking out for national security and is, in fact, in league with a technology company called K.S.I. to create their own race of human-engineered transformers. Meanwhile, struggling inventor Cade Yeager and his teenage daughter are enlisted by Optimus Prime and his team of metal minions to put a stop to the enemy because, well, there's that world destruction thing motivating the bad guys again.

Cleaning house, all previous cast members were dropped in favor of a new lineup of humans, asked to look in awe at nothing, before the CGI specialists inserted the big metal guys into the shots. Since nobody was showing up for the people, it hardly mattered. Knowing these films drew big audiences in the Asian market, Hong Kong was chosen to be decimated during the climax, but the most interesting location was Chicago's shuttered Uptown movie palace, a sad reminder of a classier moviegoing era. Stanley Tucci, as the greedy corporate slime who changes his tune when he realizes the chaos he has wrought, added a welcome degree of self-aware cheek to the proceedings, but the whole thing was all too long, frenetic, and deafening for it to matter. Compared to the preceding films, there was something of a falling off at American box offices, but *Age of Extinction* was still very, very big in the world market, being the only 2014 release to top $1 billion internationally.

The Hundred-Foot Journey

Walt Disney Studios, August 8, 2014

A DreamWorks Pictures and Reliance Entertainment presentation in association with Participant Media and Image Nation, an Amblin Entertainment/Harpo Films production. Starring Helen Mirren (Madame Mallory), Om Puri (Papa Kadam), Manish Dayal (Hassan Kadam), Charlotte Le Bron (Marguerite), Michel Blanc (Mayor), Vincent Elbaz (Paul), Juhi Chawla (Mama Kadam). Executive Producers: Caroline Hewitt, Carla Gardini, Jeff Skoll, Jonathan King. Produced by Steven Spielberg, Oprah Winfrey, Juliet Blake. Screenplay by Steven Knight. Based on the novel by Richard C. Morais. Directed by Lasse Halstrom. Color. Hawk Scope. 123 minutes. (PG)

As a respite from all the special effects-driven spectacles he was producing, Steven Spielberg partnered up with one of his *The Color Purple* stars, Oprah Winfrey, for something far gentler and more dependent on human emotions. Leaving India behind and looking for a place in Europe to set up a new restaurant, widower Papa Kadam and his offspring settle on the quaint French village of Saint-Antonin-Noble-Val, operating their establishment, Maison Mumbai, in a building directly across the street from Madame Mallory's highly revered, upscale restaurant, Le Saule Pleureur. Having no tolerance for competition and used to getting her way, the imperious Madame declares war on her neighbors, well aware that the eldest Kadam son, Hassan, shows signs of being a chef of the highest caliber, the culinary artist who could help her to earn that second Michelin star she so greatly covets.

A clash of cultures and temperaments in which everything worked out very nicely, this was a pleasant addition to the summer movie lineup, with very winning work from Manish Dayal, as the talented young chef, and the formidable presence of the wonderful Helen Mirren, although her insufferable character asked for a great deal of patience from the audience before she could win them over. Overlong and rather meandering in the homestretch, this was nevertheless a quality piece that cast a spell on those seduced by cinematic depictions of cooking and turned into a profitable moneymaker.

Auschwitz

Allentown Productions, January 27, 2015

Produced by Steven Spielberg. Written by Lorna Graham. Directed by James Moll. Color. 15 minutes.

A collaboration between USC Shoah Foundation and the Auschwitz-Birkenau Museum, this short subject was first shown at the latter to celebrate the seventieth anniversary of the liberation of Auschwitz by the allies. The very direct narrative (as spoken by Meryl Streep) tells the full history of the camp, the name of which became synonymous with the atrocities of the Holocaust. It was made available the same month of its premiere on the USC Shoah Foundation channel, and then for Comcast Xfinity viewers as part of the annual *Days of Remembrance: PastForward* broadcast between April 15 and June 1, 2015. The following year it was screened at the Tribeca Film Festival as part of its "Past Imperfect" program, among other short documentaries addressing historical events.

Jurassic World

Universal, June 12, 2015

An Amblin Entertainment presentation in association with Legendary Pictures. Starring Chris Pratt (Owen Grady), Bryce Dallas Howard (Claire), Vincent D'Onofrio (Hoskins), Ty Simpkins (Gray), Nick Robinson (Zach), Jake Johnson (Lowery), Omar Sy (Barry), BD Wong (Dr. Henry Wu), Judy Greer (Karen), Irrfan Khan (Masrani). Executive Producers: Steven Spielberg, Thomas Tull. Produced by Frank Marshall, Patrick Crowley. Screenplay by Rick Jaffa and Amanda Silver and Derek Connolly and Colin Trevorrow. Story by Rick Jaffa and Amanda Silver. Based on characters created by Michael Crichton. Directed by Colin Trevorrow. FotoKem Color. Super 35 Widescreen. 124 minutes (PG-13).

Me and my raptor: Chris Pratt and a friend strike a pose in one of the biggest of all Amblin hits, *Jurassic World.*

"No one's impressed by a dinosaur anymore." So says uptight, officious park coordinator Claire, but the box office figures on this third sequel proved her very, very wrong. Taking in $652,270,625 in US theaters alone (from a staggering $208,806,270 opening weekend), *Jurassic World*, in terms of figures among 2015 releases, was topped only by the long-awaited *Star Wars* sequel.

Perhaps being a bit "meta," *Jurassic World* created the theme park John Hammond from *Jurassic Park* had envisioned, not only with gift shops and an IMAX theater but with chain eateries like Starbucks and Jimmy Buffett's Margaritaville on the premises. What had started as a thrilling adventure back in 1993 now became the franchise Universal Studios had longed for. Hoping the customers will keep booking passage to Isla Nublar, the greedy entrepreneurs behind the park start gene splicing to create fiercer beasts than the public has already seen. Needless to say, it is not too long before their latest creation, the Indominous Rex, a nasty cross between a T-Rex and a raptor, escapes from its pen and heads right towards the clueless tourists, creating the sort of havoc the ticket-buying movie customers are craving.

Chris Pratt made for a likable hero, and the special effects were incredible in their ability to dissolve the line between the real and the unreal, but movie audiences waited in vain for a bored teenager to be eaten in hopes that it will get him to stop looking at his iPhone. Such were the cinema's reflections of modern times.

There was a trip to the now-derelict original Hammond compound; the return of Dr. Wu (BD Wong) from the original 1993 cast; a glimpse of the famous *Jurassic Park* gates; and a *Jurassic Park* T-shirt worn by a staffer who pines longingly for the park that once was. Alas, with these grosses, can *Jurassic Universe* be far behind?

Five Came Back

Netflix, March 31, 2017

An Amblin Television, Scott Rudin, IACF production, in association with Passion Pictures and Rock Paper Scissors Entertainment. Executive Producers: Steven Spielberg, Justin Falvey, Darryl Frank, Scott Rudin, Eli Bush, Jason Sack, Barry Diller, Angus Wall, Linda Carlson, Jason Sterman, Ben Cotner, Adam Del Deo, Lisa Nishimura. Producers: John Battsek, Laurent Bouzereau. Written by Mark Harris. Directed by Laurent Bouzereau. Color/Black and white. 187 minutes.

Based on the book by Mark Harris, this is a stirring tribute to five great filmmakers who took time out from their busy Hollywood careers in order to put their skills to use for their country in a time of turmoil, documenting World War II in hopes of helping to sell the war, win the war, and build morale. Being up close to the conflict, however, would take a tremendous personal toll on each. "These filmmakers," says Steven Spielberg, "that came back with footage about the truth of that war were changed forever."

Rather than having historians give their thoughts on the importance of this mission, the film features five current directors, who reflect upon the contributions of their cinematic forebears and who have far more insight into what it takes to make a movie and what makes it work effectively than those outside the industry might have. Basically, each contemporary director aligns himself with a name from the past. Francis Ford Coppola speaks about John Huston; Guillermo del Toro reflects upon Frank Capra; Paul Greengrass on John Ford; Lawrence Kasdan on George Stevens; and Spielberg on William Wyler. Archival footage allows the five filmmakers from old Hollywood to speak their minds as well, and this is interspersed with highlights from their WWII contributions (including Huston's *Let There Be Light* and Wyler's *Memphis Belle*), their commercial Hollywood credits, newsreels documenting the era, home movies, audio interviews, and personal photos. Meryl Streep reads the connecting narrative.

The film received a theatrical run starting on the very same day that it was made available for viewing on Neftlix's streaming service as three separate installments: "The Mission Begins," "Combat Zones," and "The Price of Victory."

Naysayers need not accuse Spielberg of drawing attention to himself by appearing in as well as producing this project. Although a section is devoted to George Stevens and John Ford being assigned to film the D-Day invasion, there is no mention made of Spielberg's recreation of the event, *Saving Private Ryan*. Instead, the five modern directors make sure Capra, Ford, Huston, Stevens, and Wyler remain the focus and receive their due.

Finding Oscar

FilmRise, April 14, 2017

The Kennedy/Marshall Company presents, in association with USC Shoah Foundation and Friends of FAFG and Diamond Docs. Co-Produced by Scott Greathead, Stephen D. Smith, Nick Loud and Martin Singer. Executive Producer: Steven Spielberg. Producers: Frank Marshall, Ryan Suffern. Written by Ryan Suffern and Mark Monroe. Directed by Ryan Suffern. Color. 94 minutes.

Give the movies credit for sometimes bringing to our attention startling events that had slipped into obscurity with the passing years or had perhaps never been on our radar in the first place.

In 1982, Guatemala's despotic leader, General Efraín Ríos Montt, sent military troops to the village of Dos Erres, believing the citizens to be collaborating with rebel guerilla forces. Despite no evidence of this, the troops were ordered to eliminate everyone; the brutal massacre was symbolic of Ríos Montt's tyrannical rule, which went unpunished. Furthermore, President Ronald Reagan made no attempt to sever ties with the regime, instead declaring support for the general's efforts to put his opponents in their place. Through the efforts of the Famdegua organization, this and similar massacres were belatedly brought to light, leading to the discovery that two small boys had survived the Dos Erres carnage. One of those boys, Oscar Ramirez, becomes the focus of most of this well-intentioned but standard documentary, as efforts to contact him bring Famdegua members the hope that, as a firsthand witness, he can help bring those responsible for the killings to justice.

Transformers: The Last Knight

Paramount, June 21, 2017

A di Bonaventura Pictures, Hasbro Studios, Huahua Media, Ian Bryce production. Starring Mark Wahlberg (Cade Yeager), Josh Duhamel (Col. William Lennox), Anthony Hopkins (Sir Edmund Burton), Stanley Tucci (Merlin), Laura Haddock (Vivian Wembley), Jerrod Carmichael (Jimmy), Isabela Moner (Izabella), Santiago Cabrera (Santos), Glenn Morshower (Gen. Morshower), Tony Hale (JPL Engineer), John Turturro (Agent Simmons). Executive Producers: Steven Spielberg, Michael Bay, Brian Goldner, Mark Vahradian. Screenplay by Art Marcum and Matt Holloway and Ken Nolan. Story by Akiva Goldsman and Art Marcum and Matt Holloway and Ken Nolan. Directed by Michael Bay. Color. 3D. 149 minutes. (PG-13)

A fifth visit to the crunch bunch, with Mark Wahlberg returning from the previous installment as an Autobot supporter with a price on his head and teaming up with an English Lord (Anthony Hopkins) and an Oxford professor (Laura Haddock) to save the day. After skipping *Age of Extinction*, Josh Duhamel, John Turturro, and Glenn Morshower were back as well.

This one begins in the Dark Ages, allowing for an amusing cameo by Stanley Tucci as Merlin, and then jumps ahead to the present, giving audiences what they really want to see: state-of-the-art destruction, incoherent mayhem, and a lot of mumbo jumbo about the eminent demise of the planet. A powerful staff, given to Merlin by a Transformer of yore, is the key to saving the world, and somehow there is room among the chaos for Stonehenge, Nazis, and a C-3PO rip-off (as the dialogue states). The film's $400 million worldwide gross in less than two weeks only went to show that we were not quite out of modern cinema's Dark Ages just yet.

7

Small-Screen Spielberg Productions

Producing for Television

aving become the world's most successful filmmaker by the mid-1980s, Steven Spielberg made the surprise decision to take a detour from motion pictures in order to create a weekly series, *Amazing Stories*, figuring he now had an outlet to bring to life the many story ideas that had been building up in his head over the years. While this endeavor did not turn out as well as hoped, he returned to the medium, beginning in the 1990s, on a pretty consistent basis, first in the field of animation and later on nighttime television, eventually serving as producer or executive producer on series, miniseries, documentaries, and movies of varying degrees of quality and audience success. While his television work would hardly erase or even compare with his Olympian status in theatrical motion pictures, Spielberg has gotten behind some commendable projects and has brought home his share of awards as a result.

His credits in this capacity are as follows:

Amazing Stories

NBC, September 29, 1985–April 10, 1987; 8:00 p.m. EST

In late July of 1984 it was announced that Steven Spielberg would be returning to the place where it all started for him, television, at Universal and at NBC. He landed an unprecedented and quite enviable deal from the network to create and have total control over a half-hour, weekly anthology series in the vein of *The Twilight Zone*, with stories centering on the supernatural, science fictional, or otherworldly, as his name had become so readily connected by that point with the fanciful and the fantastic. The title, *Amazing Stories*, was inspired by a science fiction digest that had been published since 1926 and was a favorite of Spielberg's dad.

According to the deal, Steven would have a two-year commitment, providing forty-four episodes that would be aired regardless of whether the ratings were high or low. Each episode was given a pricey budget between $750,000 and $1 million in hopes of bringing motion picture technique and quality to weekly television, and Spielberg was given further control over all marketing and publicity. If

IT'S HERE!

AMAZING STORIES

Steven Spielberg
Executive Producer

This week's story directed by Steven Spielberg.
THE ADVENTURE BEGINS! 8PM 4₀

anything turned out to be "amazing" about the series, it was the fact that all twenty-four episodes for Season 1 were in the can and ready to go before the much-heralded premiere on Sunday night, September 29, 1985. Curiously, NBC decided to follow *Stories* on the schedule with a similar show—a revision of another anthology series, *Alfred Hitchcock Presents*. (Over at CBS, a new version of *Twilight Zone* was also premiering that September.)

Because Spielberg himself helmed the debut episode, "Ghost Train," there was enough audience interest to bring the premiere a 22.1 rating and a 34 share, designating the percentage of viewers actually watching television at that time, but not enough to match CBS's big winner, *Murder, She Wrote*, which was its fiercest competition in that time slot. This would remain the case as the season progressed, with each new offering losing out to Angela Lansbury's inimitable small-town sleuth, Jessica Fletcher. With Spielberg having declared in advance of the fall season that there were to be no advance previews for reviewers and press, the show was met with, not surprisingly, lukewarm to hostile critical reaction. Nobody was too thrilled or amazed by what they saw, and many within the industry began to resent the fact that no matter how pallid the response to it, *Amazing Stories* was around to stay for the contracted two-year duration.

There was one more episode directed by the boss, "The Mission' (November 3, 1985; it ran longer than the average episode and therefore was given an hour-long slot), but aside from that, he kept principally to providing the storylines for many installments, fourteen in all during Season 1. For "Vanessa in the Garden," he was also the one credited writer of the teleplay. At the end of the first season, the series ranked at number 40 with a 15.3 rating. The show ended up winning Emmy Awards in four categories: Hairstyling (for the episode "Gather Ye Acorns"), Cinematography and Sound Editing (both for "The Mission"), and, most impressively, Outstanding Guest Performer in a Drama Series (for John Lithgow and his performance in "The Doll," which Richard Matheson had originally written for *The Twilight Zone*). Spielberg was in the running for his direction of "The Mission," but lost to Georg Stanford Brown (for an episode of *Cagney & Lacey*).

When Season 2 rolled around, *Amazing Stories* still found itself in the same position, losing in the ratings to *Murder, She Wrote*. There were no more Spielberg-directed entries for this season, and the number of episodes for which he provided the stories was down to four. This time the show ended up tying for number 57 for the season, with a 13.7 rating. Its sole Emmy Award win this time out was for Outstanding Makeup, for the episode "Without Diana." *Amazing Stories* quietly faded into the sunset and was looked back upon as one of the decade's most ambitious but ultimately unrealized and unfulfilled projects.

Thanks to the clout of Spielberg, *Amazing Stories* did attract its share of interesting directors in its two-year, forty-five-episode (one more than expected from the initial announcement) lifespan. These included Clint Eastwood ("Vanessa in the Garden"), Bob Balaban ("Fine Tuning"), Burt Reynolds ("Guilt Trip"), Martin Scorsese ("Mirror, Mirror"), Timothy Hutton ("Grandpa's Ghost"), Irvin Kershner ("Hell Toupee"), Paul Bartel ("Secret Cinema" and "Gershwin's Trunk"), Peter Hyams ("The Amazing Falsworth"), Danny DeVito ("The Wedding Ring"), Robert Zemeckis ("Go to the Head of the Class"; this was the first television episode to ever be broadcast in Dolby Surround Sound), and Tobe Hooper (helming the very last episode of the series, "Miss Stardust").

The episode "What If . . . ?" was of note because it was written by Spielberg's sister, Anne. Menno Meyjes wrote the script for "The Mission" the same year he provided Spielberg the screenplay for *The Color Purple*. (For a complete list of episodes for which Steven Spielberg provided the stories, see chapter 5.)

Tiny Toon Adventures: The Looney Beginning

CBS, September 14, 1990; 8:30 p.m. EST

Although the series itself ended up on syndicated channels, this prime-time special to introduce it was shown on CBS, following a similar preview of *Teenage Mutant Ninja Turtles*. Bugs Bunny hosted the story of how the "Tiny Toon" adventures came to be when characters Buster and Babs developed the concept in lieu of their animator losing faith in the idea.

Steven Spielberg Presents Tiny Toon Adventures

Syndication, September 17, 1990–February 24, 1992; Fox, September 14, 1992–December 6, 1992; 4:00 p.m. EST

The spirit of the Looney Tunes was back in full force with Steven Spielberg's first venture into television animation. This was not just a tribute to the Warner Bros. cartoons that had become iconic, first through their exhibition in cinemas and then later as staples of the children's television market. The series actually included appearances by all the great WB animated characters who took supporting roles to the real stars, junior variations of themselves. Stars Buster (voice of Charlie Adler) and Babs Bunny (Tress MacNeille) were youthful rabbits in the tradition of sassy Bugs Bunny; Plucky Duck (Joe Alaskey) had the exasperated personality of Daffy Duck; Dizzy Devil (Maurice LaMarche) spun and sputtered with the energy of the Tasmanian Devil; Sweetie Pie (Candi Milo) was a chirpy little pink fowl akin to Tweetie Bird; Hamton J. Pig (Don Messick) was Porky Pig's counterpart; and so on. Elmyra Duff (Cree Summer), an overbearing little girl whose love for animals was more annoying than endearing, and Montana Max (Danny Cooksey), a bratty rich kid, were the stand-ins for Bugs's nemeses of the past, Elmer Fudd and Yosemite Sam.

Set in the world of Acme Acres, the youngsters attended Acme Looniversity ("institute of higher learning and lower comedy"), where they were taught by the real deals: Bugs, Daffy, Porky, Foghorn Leghorn, and others.

Frantic, colorful, and crammed full of puns, fourth-wall-breaking comments to the audience, unapologetic silliness, self-referential humor, animated versions of famous stars (including some who'd worked under Spielberg's direction, like Dustin Hoffman, Oprah Winfrey, and Julia Roberts), and pop culture parodies (i.e. the official debut episode, "A Quack in the Quark," was a send-up of Star Wars), Tiny Toon actually worked for what it was setting out to accomplish: appealing to both the kids and adult admirers who found a nostalgic tinge in the presentation. A pricy $25 million was spent on sixty-five half-hour episodes for the first season, and the show ran not as a weekly Saturday morning entry but as a five-days-a-week late afternoon offering, the idea being that it could be consumed as an afterschool attraction. It started airing in September of 1990 in syndication on 135 stations; Fox aired it for the third and final season.

A co-production of Amblin and Warner Bros. animation, Spielberg was credited not only as sole executive producer but had his name as part of the title. The episode "Cinemaniacs!" found Buster spoofing Indiana Jones (as "Pasadena Jones"), but other segments went better than that in their more direct references to the man in charge.

"Buster & Babs Go Hawaiian" featured Spielberg's actual speaking voice (see chapter 8, page 279). "KACME TV" (February 26, 1991) was a potpourri of television parodies, including a late, late show movie with a gigantic Elmyra terrorizing Tokyo. That movie was interrupted by a sales pitch for the

Acme Home Cartoon kit for those eager to make their own syndicated kiddie show. The box contained not only zany props but an executive staff, including "some guy who doesn't do anything but put his name on the picture." Out of the box fell a cartoon depiction of Steven Spielberg, who was then picked up, King Kong-style, by Elmyra, who thanks him for making her part bigger. He reminds her (in a voice provided by Joe Alaskey) that he made *her* bigger, not the part.

Although he is not mentioned by name, the director of Babs's appearance on the series *thirteensomething* (also the name of the episode, the first of Season 3, aired September 14, 1992) certainly looks like the Steven Spielberg cartoon that popped up on other episodes. The bearded fellow with the baseball cap reminds Bunny that her role of Alabaster is "a humorless character, given to fits of hopeless yet insightful teen angst." Frank Welker took up the task of imitating Steven for this one, as well as for a funny bit on the episode "Fox Trot" (September 16, 1992) entitled "Phone Call from the 405." During a chase scene, Buster and Babs receive a call from a displeased Steven. "Steven who?" Buster asks. "You know 'Steven who?' Our boss, the guy with the beard!" We are then treated to a glimpse of an animated Spielberg driving his car on the San Diego Freeway, giving a shout out to Michele Lee in the next vehicle. Figuring if you want something done right, you do it yourself, he proceeds to change the scene to his liking, watching his efforts on a monitor on his dashboard. Frustrated, Buster yanks him out of the car and into the scene, allowing *him* to be chased by the hungry Fox executives who have been pursuing the bunnies.

Tiny Toon Adventures won Emmy Awards for Outstanding Animated Program for its first and third seasons, thereby resulting in two trophies for Steven Spielberg, who shared the honors with Tom Ruegger, Ken Boyer, Art Leonardi, Art Vitello, Paul Dini, Sherri Stoner, Rich Arons, Byron Vaughns, Alfred Gimeno, and David West. The show begat the short-lived spinoff *The Plucky Duck Show*.

In addition to television specials, there was a theatrical short, *I'm Mad*, starring the Tiny Toon kids. It preceded the animated feature *Thumbelina*, a Warner Bros. release that debuted on March 30, 1994. Spielberg again had an executive producer credit.

Steven Spielberg Presents The Plucky Duck Show

Syndication, September 19–December 12, 1992; 9:00 a.m. EST

Billed as a "spinoff" of *Tiny Toon Adventures*, this series was something of a cheat when it came to declaring something "new" programming. The debut episode, "The Return of Batduck" (a send-up of that year's summer hit *Batman Returns*), was created specifically for this show, but the remaining twelve episodes consisted of shorts cribbed from *Tiny Toon*. The hyper, egotistical Plucky Duck, fashioned in the spirit of Looney Tunes' Daffy Duck, was the center of attention here, but audiences weren't buying this hybrid rip-off, and this duck was down by Christmas of that year.

It's a Wonderful Tiny Toons Christmas Special

Fox, December 6, 1992; 7:00 p.m. EST

A half-hour prime prime-time special spoofing Frank Capra's beloved 1946 film found Buster Bunny wishing he'd never been born after being fired as director of a Christmas pageant. Once again knowing who had the saleable name, the *TV Guide* ad let readers know that "Steven Spielberg presents a looney twist on a holiday classic."

Class of '61

ABC, April 12, 1993; 9:00 p.m. EST

Families and friends are torn apart when the War Between the States is declared in this two-hour offering on the *ABC Monday Night Movie*, the first time Amblin was behind a television movie, back when such things were still a regular occurrence in prime time. Among the young stars who would find success later on were Laura Linney, Joshua Lucas (playing George Armstrong Custer), and Clive Owen.

Family Dog

CBS, June 23–July 28, 1993; 8:00 p.m. EST

Spun from a 1987 episode of *Amazing Stories*, this prime-time series premiered (with back-to-back episodes) with a lot of advance negative buzz because it had been postponed for a two-year stretch after executive producers Steven Spielberg and Tim Burton expressed their displeasure with the finished product. Danny Mann was the voice of the neglected Binsford family pet, a role taken over from the original creator, Brad Bird. *TV Guide* wrongly credited Spielberg and Burton as "the creators."

seaQuest DSV / seaQuest 2032

NBC, September 12, 1993–September 13, 1995; 8:00 p.m. EST; *SeaQuest 2032*: September 20–December 27, 1995; 8:00 p.m. EST

Spielberg and Scheider—back in the water! This seemed like an ideal selling point, and the filmmaker, hot off the runaway success of *Jurassic Park*, managed to secure a twenty-two-episode, season-long commitment from NBC on this series, one of the most ambitious projects for the small screen up to that time. At $1.5 million an episode to produce, hopes were high. An undersea adventure set in the year 2018, the show followed Captain Nathan Bridger (Roy Scheider) as he commanded a state-of-the-art, thousand-foot-long submarine, the titular vessel (DSV stood for Deep Submergence Vehicle), created for exploring the oceans, which now paid host to underwater colonies and research centers. The supporting cast included

Stephanie Beacham as the ship's doctor and Jonathan Brandis as teenage techno wiz Lucas Wolenczak, but a dolphin named Darwin, which was able to communicate with the underwater team through a computer, stole most of the attention away. Aiming for something with a certain level of plausibility (scientific fact mixed in with the fiction), the series enlisted the technical advice of underwater scientist Dr. Robert Ballard, but this straightforward approached didn't help. Reviews were mostly negative, and although the two-hour premiere hit the bullseye by coming in second place for that week's ratings, the show did not maintain this strong level of viewer interest.

NBC and Amblin wanted their much-hyped series to work, however, and gave it a second chance, but with some major revisions. When the show returned for a second season in September of 1994, Beacham and several other "older" cast members were gone, replaced by more youthful characters, in hopes of appealing to this demographic. The tone became less serious and a bit more fantastical and therefore sillier, pretty much echoing what had happened to the show's prototype, *Voyage to the Bottom of the Sea*, back in the 1960s. Scheider did not mince words on how unhappy he had become with this turn of events, and the show remained a soft performer in the ratings.

Amazingly, this wasn't the end of the line for the show. NBC gave it chance number three, although Scheider asked not to be a regular participant anymore, instead agreeing to come back for select episodes. (He was seen in three.) The timeframe was jumped ahead, so the show was renamed *seaQuest 2032*, and Michael Ironside was brought in to play the new sub commander ("New Captain. New Mission. New Night!" the ads informed us, the show moving from Sundays to Wednesdays). All the retooling in the world could not overcome the fact that there wasn't great interest in the premise, and *seaQuest* was pulled from the lineup during Season 3 before the end of the calendar year. The remaining three episodes aired in West Coast markets only.

Steven Spielberg Presents Animaniacs

Fox Kids, September 13, 1993–November 12, 1994; 4:00 p.m. EST; The WB, September 9, 1995–November 14, 1998; 8:00 a.m. EST

"Zany" was the key word for this hectic offering of sketches, shorts, and blackout bits which starred three hyperactive Warners kids: brothers Wakko and Yakko, and their sister, Dot. After being unleashed on the world by the cartoonists of Warner Bros.' fabled "Termite Terrace," the three were locked away (as were their films, which "made no sense") in the studio's water tower, only to escape periodically and entertain us with their exploits.

As with the other Warner Bros. Animation/Amblin Entertainment collaborations, parody was in full, bombastic, often wickedly funny bloom. Given a jab in the ribs were *Jeopardy*, Gilbert and Sullivan operettas, *Les Misérables*, the Dalai Lama, *West Side Story*, Rasputin, Hitchcock's *The Birds*, *Apocalypse Now* (with Jerry Lewis in the director's chair), *A Midsummer Night's Dream*, *A Christmas Carol*, *The Karate Kid*,

Sherlock Holmes, Snow White, *The Sound of Music*, Ernest Hemingway, and *The Maltese Falcon*, to name but a few targets.

In the segment "Three Tenors and You're Out" (Season 3, Episode 3; September 16, 1995), a pair of crass squirrels (series regulars Slappy and Skippy) cause havoc at a Three Tenors concert by having a gigantic spaceship hover over the stadium and send out bass notes from "Take Me Out to the Ballgame" for a "sing-off" with the trio of opera legends—a spoof the famous climax of *Close Encounters of the Third Kind*. Inside the ship, Slappy informs us that she "decided to bring in the big guns," gesturing to her copilot, Steven Spielberg.

Joining the Warners in their own segments from time to time were Pinky and the Brain (who would receive their own spinoff down the line), Rita and Runt (the former a singing cat, voice provided by Bernadette Peters), Buttons and Mindy (a *Lassie* parody), Minerva Mink, and the six-foot-tall Chicken Boo, among others. The show began as a daily offering on the Fox Kids Channel for the first sixty-nine episodes and then moved over to the WB as part of the Saturday morning lineup for the remaining thirty. Tom Ruegger was the creator; the Warners voices were provided by Rob Paulsen (Yakko), Tress MacNeille (Dot), and Jess Harnell (Wakko); and there was a generous abundance of music and songs, most delightfully "Yakko's World" (Season 1, Episode 2; September 14, 1993), a rapid-fire listing of all the countries (written by Randy Rogel to the tune of the Mexican Hat Dance) that would have made Danny Kaye proud. (This song was included on the 1994 VHS compilation *Animaniacs Sing-Along: Yakko's World*, which gave Spielberg another executive producer credit.)

Richard Stone (composer) and Tom Ruegger (lyrics) won an Emmy for their exuberant title song (who could resist the lyric "there's baloney in our slacks"?). The series itself was twice (1996 and 1997) awarded the Daytime Emmy for Outstanding Animated Children's Program, Spielberg sharing the prize with a *long* list of contributors, including Ruegger, Rusty Mills, Liz Holzman, and Peter Hastings, also named in various capacities as producers.

Tiny Toons Spring Break

Fox, March 27, 1994; 7:00 p.m. EST

The animated gang from *Tiny Toon Adventures* rated their first prime-time special since the show joined the Saturday morning lineup, as Plucky, Babs, Buster, and other students from Acme Looniversity hopped on down to Fort Lauderdale. Since it was being shown during Easter season, the plot involved Elmyra mistaking Buster for the Easter Bunny, with a stopover at the annual White House egg roll.

While Babs and Buster are racing through an amusement park called *Fishyland World*, the sub from the Spielberg-produced series *seaQuest DSV* surfaces from a pool, with Captain Nathan Bridger popping out of its hatch only to be threatened by a shark. Since Roy Scheider played this role on the live-action show, it was inevitable that the cartoon version of him voice the line "We're going to need a bigger boat."

Tiny Toons' Night Ghoulery

Fox, May 28, 1995; 7:00 p.m. EST

It was only right that this prime-time special pay homage to Rod Serling's second anthology series, since it was on that show that this special's executive producer, Steven Spielberg, got his professional start as a director. Aside from parodying Serling's opening intros by having the host standing near paintings related to the upcoming tales, the omnibus featured a quick, cheeky spoof of *Duel*. The funniest bit, for those familiar with the original TV movie, had our beleaguered driver (played by Calamity Coyote) step into a roadside café after being pursued by the ominous truck only to find the vehicle itself sitting on a bar stool like the rest of the customers. Fittingly, the truck driver turns out to be the Coyote's nemesis, Little Beeper.

Although clearly made to air around Halloween of 1994, this special did not make it to the nighttime schedule until spring of the following year.

Steven Spielberg Presents Pinky and the Brain

The WB, September 9, 1995–November 14, 1998; 9:30 a.m. EST

The bouncy theme song (by Richard Stone) told it all, about two genetically altered lab mice set on world domination, or as the lyrics put it "to prove their mousey worth/they'll overthrow the earth." The ultraserious Brain (voice of Maurice LaMarche) came up with the outrageous plans, while the Cockney Pinky (Rob Paulsen, who received the 1999 Emmy as Outstanding Performer in an Animated Program) usually made idiotic remarks ("narf" was a key expression) as he misinterpreted his partner's every scheme. This Saturday morning animated series, created by Tom Ruegger, was derived from recurring segments on the previous WB cartoon show from Amblin, *Animaniacs*, and made its debut back-to-back with *Freakazoid!*

Although the animation was not much more inspired than most Saturday morning fare, the scripts had their share of amusingly nutty plotlines, witty deadpan remarks and off-the-cuff barbs at the expense of various pop culture figures to make it worth a look. The Lincoln Memorial statue was brought to life; game show host Wink Martindale received his own holiday; *Three's Company* star Joyce DeWitt ended up ruling the world; Brain disguised himself as Cher in order to infiltrate a celebrity golf tournament; cutesy comic strip *The Family Circus* was responsible for putting Pinky in the White House; Stooge Larry Fine showed up for an episode just to turn the comic duo into a trio; and there were spoofs of such movies as *A Clockwork Orange, The Third Man*, and *Around the World in Eighty Days*. Sometimes name actors were hired to provide guest voices, among them Roddy McDowall, Ernest Borgnine, Garry Marshall, Pam Grier, Michael McKean, Mark Hamill, Ed McMahon, Eric Idle, John Astin, Jeffrey Tambor, David Alan Grier, Olivia Hussey, and *Raiders of the Lost Ark* costar John Rhys-Davies.

Executive Producer Steven Spielberg himself came in for a poke in the ribs with the Season 3 episode "Schpiel-borg 2000" (November 22, 1997). Introduced with the reverence customarily bestowed upon the Commander in Chief (including a presidential seal), Spielberg (voiced by Frank K. Welker) thanks the audience for all the awards he . . . or rather, the show, has won (including the "Big Head of Pauly Shore Award for Most Unexpected and Unexplainable Success") and then shows a highlight reel of typical Pinky and the Brain mayhem (a "narf" montage, of course). But all is not what it seems, when it is revealed that the filmmaker is nothing more than a robot, controlled by Pinky. His functions include describing scenes from *Jaws, Jurassic Park*, and *E.T.*, but his real purpose is for Brain to carry out another attempt at world domination. "And if his box office numbers are any indication," the scheming mouse explains, "he has the potential to become ruler of the world." Another dream is crushed when the cybernetic clone self-destructs.

For its fourth and final season, the series was named Outstanding Special Class Animated Program, which gave Spielberg another Emmy for his mantle.

Steven Spielberg Presents Freakazoid!

The WB, September 9, 1995–June 1, 1997; 10:00 a.m. EST

It was only fitting that the title character had a habit of lapsing into Jerry Lewis-like stream of consciousness gibberish because this Saturday morning cartoon show was very much in the mode of the manic comedian, running the gamut from undisciplined chaos to very funny. The title character was a sixteen-year-old computer nerd named Dexter Douglas (a student at Harry Connick High School!?), who can will himself into becoming a volatile, somewhat idiotic superhero because of having been zapped into cyberspace. As per the title song, Freakazoid "runs around in underwear" while trying to solve crimes.

The tone was nutty and energetic and very meta, with fake commercials, fake important interruptions, and a slew of pop culture references which had become de rigueur for these shows. Sent up in loud fashion were the Clintons, socially inept fanboys, superhero sidekicks, Barbra Streisand, *The Godfather, The Poseidon Adventure*, and comedian Sinbad, among others. Appearing in their own segments were British superhero wannabe Lord Bravery (Jeff Bennett doing a John Cleese impersonation), a quartet of Lawn Gnomes, boy adventurer Toby Danger (spoofing the stilted animation and plotlines of the 1960s cartoon favorite *Jonny Quest*), a Robin Hood type in search of crime called the Huntsman, and two overweight crime fighters, Fatman and Boy Blubber. One of the show's writers, Paul Rugg, also provided the voice of Freakazoid, while there were guest voices galore, including Edward Asner as unfazed policeman Sgt. Cosgrove; Tim Curry as Dr. Mystico; David Warner as the brain-heavy villain the Lobe; and Bebe Neuwirth as the monotonously voiced Deadpan. Jonathan Harris voiced a character so clearly patterned after his signature role of Dr. Smith on *Lost in Space* that he was frequently asked if he was ever "on a TV show with a robot."

Behind-the-scenes shout-outs to the creative staff included glimpses of a cartoon version of Steven Spielberg. "Freakazoid is History" (November 11, 1995) had him showing up in a montage of famous movies, including *Jaws*; and in the episode "The Freakazoid," (September 14, 1996) he was part of a jokey bit in which the titular hero argued with Wakko from *Animaniacs* and Brain from *Pinky and the Brain* about which show "Steven" liked most. Journeying over to the Amblin offices, they were all taken aback when the famous filmmaker wasn't even sure who any of them were. "Next Time, Phone Ahead" (February 3, 1996) was a spoof of *E.T. the Extra-Terrestrial*, with recurring character Mo-Ron struggling to find a way to reach his alien cohorts.

Less of a hit than some of the other animated series, *Freakazoid!* ended up airing two seasons but running only twenty-four episodes total. Guaranteed to become a cult favorite, the series did endure for years on the Cartoon Network. For its second season it ended up with the Daytime Emmy Award for Outstanding Special Class Animated Program (somehow designated as such, and therefore not in competition with *Animaniacs*, which also won that year), having already taken home a trophy the previous year for Richard Stone and Tom Ruegger's screwy title song.

A Pinky and the Brain Christmas

The WB, December 13, 1995; 8:30 p.m. EST

The spliced mice received the own prime-time special, basically an episode of their series, with a Yule theme. The holidays, however, did not mean they would stop their nefarious behavior, as they journeyed to the North Pole to infiltrate Santa's workshop and mass produce a "Noodle-Noggin Doll" to hypnotize the populace and do Brain's bidding.

The time switch worked wonders because the show won the Primetime Emmy for Outstanding Animated Program, which included executive producer Steven Spielberg among its recipients.

Survivors of the Holocaust

TBS, January 8, 1996; 8:05 p.m. EST

One of the most worthwhile of all his television credits, Spielberg presented this one-hour documentary as part of the Survivors of the Shoah Visual History Foundation. The filmmaker's project to preserve on videotape the stories of those who survived the horror of the Holocaust came as a direct result of filming *Schindler's List*. At the end of the program, Spielberg appears on camera to explain the mission of the Foundation.

High Incident

ABC, 1996–1997

(See chapter 5, page 185)

The Lost Children of Berlin

A&E, May 31, 1997; 9:00 p.m. EST

This emotional documentary (hosted by Spielberg's *Amistad* cast member Anthony Hopkins) recounts the reunion of the survivors of Grosse Hamburgerstrasse, the last Jewish school in Berlin to be shuttered by the Nazis in April of 1942. The documentary was presented in association with Survivors of the Shoah Visual History Foundation and Fogwood Films (Sally Field's production company).

Toonsylvania

Fox, February 7, 1998–January 18, 1999; 9:30 a.m. EST

The first offering from Spielberg's DreamWorks Animation Studio was a horror spoof consisting of multiple segments, the principal characters being Dr. Frankenstein, Igor, and a monster called Phil. One of the doomed participants of *Jurassic Park*, Wayne Knight, provided the voice of Igor, so it was fitting that one segment involving a miniature golf course was entitled "Jurassic Putt."

Invasion America

The WB, June 8–July 7, 1998; 9:00 p.m. EST

Advertised as prime-time TV's first animated *dramatic* series (Hanna-Barbera's *Jonny Quest* had, in fact, beaten it to the dial, thirty-four years earlier), *Invasion America* premiered with two hour-long episodes (on consecutive evenings) before going to a half-hour format on Tuesday nights and then concluding with a ninety-minute installment.

Teen troublemaker David Carter (voice of Mikey Kelley) discovers that his absent father is the ruler of a distant planet and that David is destined to lead Earth in a fight against an alien rebellion. Chuck Barney in *The Austin American Statesman* called the show "a blend of *Jonny Quest, Star Wars,* and *Independence Day*," but that kind of endorsement did not bring in the high ratings or encourage the WB to pick it up for another season.

Among the voice talents on hand were *E.T.*'s Dee Wallace, James Sikking, Ronny Cox, *The Birds* star Tippi Hedren, Kristy McNichol, Lorenzo Lamas, *Star Trek*'s Leonard Nimoy, and Spielberg's fellow executive producer and the series' chief writer, Harve Bennett.

Steven Spielberg Presents Pinky, Elmyra & the Brain

The WB, September 19, 1998–December 12, 1998, 10:00 a.m. EST;
on *The Big Cartoonie Show*: January 16–April 10, 1999

Following three successful seasons on the air, Amblin decided to revamp the format of *Pinky and the Brain*, having the scheming mice end up in a pet store where they are taken home by a clueless little girl named Elmyra (voiced by Cree Summer). This made it a spinoff of a spinoff (the characters having started in *Animaniacs*), with an extra spinoff on the side (as Elmyra was also seen on *Tiny Toon Adventures*). Fans of the original expressed their displeasure with the new format, and only six episodes (consisting of two segments each) aired under this name. This revision also managed to drive writer and producer Peter Hastings to jump ship at Warner Bros. in favor of Disney. Starting in January, the remaining thirteen segments aired as part of a new compilation series, *The Big Cartoonie Show*, on the Saturday morning lineup.

Steven Spielberg was listed as the sole executive producer and once again got his name in the title. Maurice LaMarche and Rob Paulsen reprised their vocal roles as Brain and Pinky, respectively. This was the last Spielberg project in collaboration with Warner Bros. Television Animation.

Shooting War

ABC, December 7, 2000; 9:00 p.m. EST

It took the star wattage of Steven Spielberg and Tom Hanks to get one of the networks to air a two-hour documentary in prime time at this stage in television history. As an extension of their collaboration on *Saving Private Ryan*, Spielberg (as executive producer) and Hanks (as narrator, on and off camera) looked at the danger military combat cameramen faced while recording World War II battles for newsreels and as a way of preserving history. Taken from some 600 hours of archival footage, including, of course, the D-Day invasion depicted in *Private Ryan*, this special was directed and written by *Time* magazine film critic Richard Schickel.

Semper Fi

NBC, April 1, 2001; 9:00 p.m. EST

This was originally intended to serve as a pilot for a possible NBC series, but the network decided not to go ahead with it, despite reports that they had committed to thirteen episodes earlier that season. When no other network expressed interest, NBC showed the $5 million production as a standalone movie after knocking it off the schedule several times.

The premise was to look at the lives of a diverse group of raw recruits (played by, among others, Scott Bairstow, Vicellous Reon Shannon, Steve Burton, Michael

Peña, and Tammy Townsend) as they endured thirteen weeks of basic training at the Marine Corps Recruit Depot in Parris Island, South Carolina. Spielberg was executive producer along with the director, Michael Watkins, and the script writer, Jim Uhls.

Band of Brothers

HBO, September 9–November 4, 2001; 10:00 p.m. EST

This was "the big one," the most ambitious television project yet to bear Steven Spielberg's name, a record-breaking $125 million, ten-part miniseries adaptation of the acclaimed 1992 book by Stephen E. Ambrose documenting the missions of "Easy Company," the 506th Parachute Infantry Regiment, during World War II. The book had served as part of Tom Hanks's research for playing the role of Captain Miller in *Saving Private Ryan*, and he envisioned it as a follow-up to the previous miniseries he had produced to outstanding, Emmy-winning effect, *From the Earth to the Moon*. Although he and Spielberg would share the executive producer credit on *Band of Brothers* (the series was presented in association with DreamWorks and Hanks's company, Playtone), it was Hanks who was the real guiding force behind the project, and he not only received executive producer credit but also credit for co-scripting the first episode, "Currahee," and directing the fifth, "Crossroads."

Requiring 500 speaking roles and 10,000 extras, the production took some three years from planning to completion, much of it being filmed between April and November of 2000 in England, the principal base of operations being the Hatfield Aerodrome near London, which had already served as a location on *Private Ryan*. Actors Damian Lewis and Ron Livingston carried the largest amount of footage, although the whole intent was for the series to play as an ensemble, with certain characters given more emphasis in some episodes than others. Not surprisingly, the program occasionally suffered from the same problem often found in depictions of battle carnage, with the crosscutting, chaos, and confusion of it all, not to mention smudged faces under camouflaging helmets, often making it hard to determine what was happening to whom.

There were some highly effective sequences, chief among them the terrifying approach of planes toward the D-Day operation in France, as the aircraft are bombarded by the enemy, directed in Episode 2 by Richard Loncraine, and Hanks's stark and visceral staging of an assault on a battalion of German soldiers in Holland, in Episode 5. Episode 3 ("Carenton" directed by Spielberg's *Always* cinematographer, Mikael Salomon) was one of the standouts, basically following the story through the eyes of a shell-shocked Private Blithe (Marc Warren) as he overcomes his fears to fight heroically, only to die in a military hospital from his wounds long after the rest of his company have moved on. This episode, written by E. Max Frye, contained perhaps the most striking description of how to endure war, as Blithe was told by a superior officer: "The only hope you have is to accept the fact that you're already dead. And the sooner you accept that, the sooner you'll be able to function as a soldier is supposed to function—without mercy, without compassion, without remorse. All war depends upon it."

The enormous, mostly male cast included Simon Pegg, one of the future stars of Spielberg's *The Adventures of Tintin*; Neal McDonough, who would soon after appear for the director in *Minority Report*; pre-stardom Michael Fassbender and Tom Hardy; and Hanks's son, Colin.

Band of Brothers launched with the first two episodes (only two days before the terrorist attack on the World Trade Center) presented back-to-back and scored its

highest ratings, with approximately 10 million viewers. Although HBO remained pleased with the response to their investment, *Band* did not, surprisingly, maintain this level of audience interest, plunging to only half as many viewers by the time its last episode aired. The series, however, made a major splash in the Emmy nominations the following year, earning nineteen total. It ended up winning in six categories: Outstanding Casting, Single Camera Picture Editing, Sound Editing, Directing (encompassing all eight men who served in this capacity, those others, not mentioned above, being David Frankel, David Leland, David Nutter, Phil Alden Robinson, and Tony To), and Outstanding Miniseries, resulting in another statuette for Spielberg. It also won the Golden Globe Award in this last category as well.

We Stand Alone Together: The Men of Easy Company

HBO, November 11, 2001; 8:30 p.m. EST

This Veterans Day documentary aired a week after HBO showed the last episode of *Band of Brothers* and opposite ABC's unedited network debut of *Saving Private Ryan*. What it basically did was to tell the same story of *Band of Brothers* directly from the real participants, being a tribute to the men of Easy Company, the 506th Parachute Infantry Regiment of the 101st Airborne Division. Between newsreel footage, the modern-day interviews with members of the regiment included C. Carwood Lipton, Richard Winters, J. B. Stokes, Shifty Powers, Bill Wingett, Rod Strohl, among many others. Emphasized, as in the mini were the D-Day landing at Normandy, the liberation of Holland, the Battle of the Bulge, and the capture of Hitler's private mountaintop retreat, Eagle's Nest. Another collaboration between DreamWorks and Playtone, this program was Emmy nominated for Outstanding Non-Fiction Special, thereby bringing nominations to executive producers Steven Spielberg and Tom Hanks; co-executive producers Gary Goetzman and Tony To; the program's director, Mark Cowen; and its writer, William Richter.

Broken Silence

Cinemax, April 15–19, 2002; 7:00 p.m. EST

As part of Spielberg's ambitious project to record the testimonies of those who lived through Holocaust, he presented this series of five hour-long documentaries as part of Cinemax Reel Life under this banner title. The films in order of their showings were: "Eyes of the Holocaust" (by János Szász), "Some Who Lived" (by Luis Puenzo), "Children from the Abyss" (Pavel Chukhraj), "Hell on Earth" (Vojtech Jasny), and "I Remember" (Andrzej Wajda).

Price for Peace

NBC, May 27, 2002; 8:00 p.m. EST

This was another two-hour documentary that wouldn't likely have been shown on network television in prime time had not Steven Spielberg been involved. Aired on Memorial Day, this was another tribute to the heroes of World War II, specifically those who partook in the Pacific Theater. A co-presentation of the National World War II Museum in New Orleans, the special features interviews with various veterans. Spielberg's fellow executive producer, Stephen E. Ambrose—a military historian and the author of *Band of Brothers*—appeared as the onscreen narrator. (He would pass away later that same year.)

Taken

Sci-Fi Channel, December 2–6 and 9–15, 2002; 9:00 p.m. EST

This $40 million, ten-part, twenty-hour miniseries took some alien folklore and a few actual facts, combined them with a soap opera plotline of four generations of three different families affected by extraterrestrial contact, and spread the whole thing out over an epic fifty-year timeline, albeit with a decided emphasis on character over f/x. There were the Crawfords, who uncovered four alien bodies near Roswell, New Mexico, in 1947; the Keyses, who were subjected to various abductions; and the Clarkes, who bred a half-human/half-extraterrestrial (Anton Yelchin). The narrator was eight-year-old Allie Keys (Dakota Fanning, later to star under Spielberg's direction in *War of the Worlds*), who inherited her own alien powers; she was heard for the first six episodes and then played a pivotal part in the final four installments.

Among the myriad actors on hand were Matt Frewer (a future participant in *The BFG*), Emily Bergl, Joel Gretsch (who had just appeared in Spielberg's *Minority Report*), Eric Close, Ryan Hurst (who'd done a small role in *Saving Private Ryan*), Julie Benz, James McDaniel, Steve Burton, John Hawkes (who would work with Spielberg on *Lincoln*), Heather Donahue, Desmond Harrington, Catherine Dent, and Ryan Merriman. Because of the epic nature of the story, none of them appeared in *all* of the episodes. Sharing executive producer credit with Steven Spielberg was the series' writer, Leslie Boehm. Although sources state that the idea came from Spielberg, he was not credited as such onscreen. A co-production of the Sci-Fi Channel and DreamWorks Television, the show was very deliberately advertised as *Steven Spielberg Presents Taken*, as if his name was part of the title (a marketing decision on the part of the Earthlings at Sci-Fi). The director of the premiere episode ("Beyond the Sky") was Tobe Hooper, who had collaborated with Spielberg on *Poltergeist* twenty years prior.

The gamble paid off when the channel posted its biggest numbers up to that time, with 6.1 million viewers for the debut episode and an average of nearly

5 million each subsequent night. The show brought Spielberg another Emmy when it won Outstanding Miniseries (beating out *Napoleon* and *Hitler*—the minis, not the dictators).

Dan Finnerty & the Dan Band: I Am Woman

Bravo, June 2, 2005; 11:00 p.m. EST

There's no telling who might be drawn to your act, no matter how labored and one-note it might be. Dan Finnerty (a onetime member of another one-trick pony attraction, Stomp) became a cult favorite on the concert scene by performing obscenity-checkered versions of pop songs that had been hits for female singers. Steven Spielberg wanted more of the world to experience Dan, so he served as executive producer of this one hour-concert, his only such credit in this genre. McG (as in Joseph McGinty Nichol) served as director.

Into the West

TNT, June 10–July 22, 2005; 8:00 p.m. EST

This twelve-hour, six-week miniseries covering sixty-five years in the history of the American West was a dual multigenerational family saga, centering on both a white clan from Virginia and a Lakota family from the Great Plains. The two came together in marriage when Jacob Wheeler (Matthew Settle) wed Thunder Heart Woman (Tonantzin Carmelo). The epic went on to cover everything from the Gold Rush to Little Big Horn to the building of the railroads, with the idea of giving equal time to Native Americans and with careful attention given to presenting the culture with the utmost accuracy possible. William Mastrosimone was the principal writer, a different director was assigned to each episode, and the vast cast included Sean Astin, Beau Bridges, Tom Berenger, Josh Brolin, Jessica Capshaw (Steven Spielberg's stepdaughter), Keith Carradine, Rachael Leigh Cook, Joanna Going, Graham Greene, Lance Henriksen, Russell Means, Matthew Modine, David Paymer, Wes Studi, and a fellow by the name of Forest Fyre.

Costing some $50 million to make and therefore run frequently on the TNT schedule, the ambitious series was greeted with decidedly mixed reviews but scored good ratings and received sixteen Emmy nominations, including one for Outstanding Miniseries, putting Spielberg among the nominees. (He was the sole executive producer, while Larry Rapaport and David A. Rosemont were the producers and Kirk Ellis was the supervising producer.) *Into the West* brought home two Emmy Awards: for Outstanding Music Composition and Outstanding Single-Camera Sound Mixing.

On the Lot

Fox, May 22–August 18, 2007; 9:00 p.m. for premiere; 9:30 p.m. on Thursday for episode two; then 8:00 p.m. for subsequent episodes, EST

On the Lot was not a bad idea for a reality show for those who can stand reality shows, but the problem was that HBO's *Project Greenlight* had done it first and better. Spielberg (along with David Geffin) shared the executive producer credit with Mark Burnett, the king of the reality show concept who had given the world *Survivor* and *The Apprentice*, to name but two. The idea was to give a fighting chance to the many aspiring filmmakers out there by allowing them to compete for a development deal with Steven Spielberg's DreamWorks Pictures. The top fifty selected pitched their ideas to a panel of judges, which included actress Carrie Fisher and director Garry Marshall, among others. Then the thirty-six chosen from that batch were divided into twelve groups of three and asked to shoot a three-page scene in twenty-four hours. These folks, in turn, were whittled down to twenty-four contestants who were assigned to make a short film using five given sets. From the next chosen eighteen, an elimination process began and involved additional voting from home viewers based on their assessments of the short movies being screened. As the field narrowed, the contestants were given genres to work within—comedy, horror, action, and so forth—for their next projects. A drawback to the hour-long series was having to watch so much amateur work that wasn't particularly good or inspired. The reviews were dismissive, the ratings were poor, and there was no call for a second season.

On the finale, Episode 16, the winner was chosen—Will Bigham, who was awarded with $1 million, half of which was to be used for optioning scripts. To make the prize that much sweeter, Spielberg came walking through the gates of the DreamWorks complex on the Universal Studios lot to congratulate Mr. Bigham and present him with a key to his new office at the company. Alas, this did not lead to a career to equal his welcoming boss's. There would be no DreamWorks productions for the fledgling filmmaker. When he finally did get a feature made, five years later, it was a low-budget teen dramedy, *The A-List*, which sat in limbo for another few years before finally debuting on DVD and online streaming markets in 2015. It was distributed by Barnholtz Entertainment.

United States of Tara

Showtime, January 18, 2009–June 20, 2011; 10:00 p.m. EST

The origins of this series reportedly came from a conversation between Steven Spielberg and his wife about how each of us compartmentalizes our lives. From there it went to hiring hot, Oscar-winning screenwriter Diablo Cody (*Juno*) to fashion this concept into a series about a wife and mother of two who suffers from disassociative identity disorder, or, in layman's terms, multiple personalities.

Needing a talented lady to pull this off, the series lucked out in attracting the interest of Australian actress Toni Collette, who was required to play plain old Tara;

a sixteen-year-old party girl named T; an out-of-date 1950s housewife called Alice; and a redneck trucker named Buck. Making up the rest of the Gregson family were patient husband Max (John Corbett), troubled daughter Kate (future Oscar-winner Brie Larson), and homosexual son Marshall (Keir Gilchrist). Alternately comedic and dramatic in dealing with the difficult topic of a personality disorder of a most extreme kind, the series adhered to Showtime's customary approach, hoping to both shock and provoke with its often harsh, unpleasant tone.

Not unexpectedly, Collette nabbed an Emmy for her efforts for the first season and a nomination for the second season. As if the term "executive producer" was suffering from multiple personalities, Spielberg shared this credit not only with Cody but with Dave Finkel, Brett Baer, Craig Zisk, Darryl Frank, and Justin Falvey.

The Pacific

HBO, March 14–May 16, 2010; 9:00 p.m. EST

Having delivered so triumphant a collaboration with *Band of Brothers*, Tom Hanks and Steven Spielberg returned to HBO (under their respective Playtone and DreamWorks banners) nine years later to show the hell of war as it unfolded on the other side of the world. The project was, in fact, inspired by the number of favorable responses the original miniseries received from actual World War II veterans, who were now eager to see a similar depiction of the US offensive against the Japanese in the Pacific Theater of Operations. The result was perhaps an even more trenchant and unsettling portrait of warfare, a series whose firm mission it was to never forget the horror amid the heroism, delving deeply into the often abominable behavior on both sides of the battlefield, with an admirably steadfast refusal to present an upbeat, jingoistic version of war.

Like its predecessor, the series featured a vast ensemble, and it was peopled with so many characters that it was understandable if audiences got a bit lost at times trying to keep up with exactly who was who. For the most part the focus was on three real-life Marines: Private Robert Leckie (James Badge Dale), Gunnery Sgt. John Basilone (Jon Seda), and Cpl. Eugene Sledge (Joseph Mazzello, who, as a little boy, had dodged dinosaurs for Spielberg in *Jurassic Park* seventeen years earlier). Most episodes centered around specific battles, including those taking place on Guadalcanal, Pavuvu, and Okinawa, with a special emphasis given to the especially brutal experiences on Peleliu. Chapter 6 recreated a key moment of this bloody ordeal and was perhaps the standout episode, with the devastating assault on the Peleliu airfield strikingly directed by Tony To in all its chaotic, bloody confusion and terror. As Captain Haldane (Scott Gibson) tells an admittedly frightened Cpl. Sledge, "The man who isn't scared out here is either a liar or dead." Chapter 7 (directed by Tim Van Patten) was equally effective in detailing Sledge's continual disillusionment with the senseless bloodshed and perceived absence of compassion around him, as he battles the urge within himself to lose a grip on his own humanity.

Scripted mostly by Robert Schenkkan (who would later write another Spielberg-produced HBO project, *All the Way*) and Bruce C. McKenna (who had contributed to *Band of Brothers*), the mini was credited to personal reminiscences published by two of its principals: *With the Old Breed at Peleliu and Okinawa* by Sledge, and *Helmet for My Pillow* by Leckie, who, after serving, did, in fact, go on to become a journalist and professional author. There was also material gathered from interviews conducted with survivors and their relatives in order to get as much of the human story behind the history.

The budget was even bigger this time around, topping off at $200 million, the whole endeavor taking some seven years of planning and production, with filming taking place in Australia during 2008. The show launched with an acceptable 3.08 million viewers but fell off in the subsequent weeks, perhaps being a little

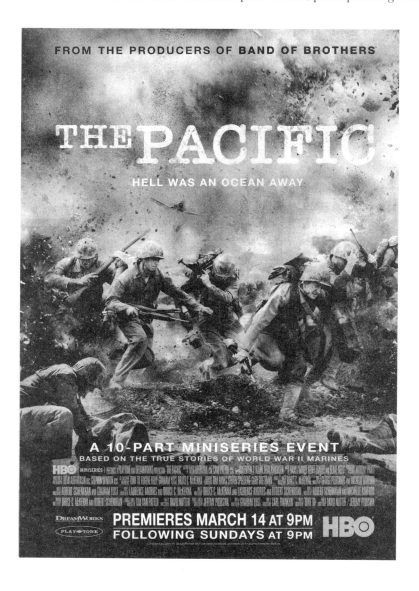

too rough to watch at times for those expecting whitewashed heroics. The reviews made it clear, however, that this was another exemplary credit for Hanks and Spielberg, ratings be damned.

With fifteen Emmy nominations, *The Pacific* was named Outstanding Miniseries, which included Spielberg among the designated winners. It earned additional trophies for its special effects, sound (editing and mixing), makeup (in two separate categories), casting, and art direction. In addition to Van Patten and To, the other directors were David Nutter, Jeremy Podeswa, Carl Franklin, and Graham Yost. It was also the Golden Globe winner for Best Miniseries or Motion Picture Made for Television, and it earned a Peabody Award, that particular honor shared by Van Patten, Podeswa, and Nutter.

Falling Skies

TNT, June 19, 2011–August 30, 2015; 10:00 p.m. EST

Continuing his negative take on alien beings depicted in *War of the Worlds*, this sci-fi series—which was executive produced by Steven Spielberg (along with Darryl Frank, Graham Yost, Remi Aubuchon, Justin Falvey, David Eick, and the series' creator, Robert Rodat, who had scripted *Saving Private Ryan*)—showed Earthlings at the mercy of a nasty race of six-legged, insect-like extraterrestrials called Skitters, themselves enslaved by a warring species known as the Espheni. In a nod to another Spielberg film, the bio-robots on hand here were called "Mechs," one letter off from the "Mechas" of *A.I. Artificial Intelligence*. Although 80 percent of the world's population has been wiped out, those remaining include resistance leader Tom Mason (Noah Wyle), a Boston history professor who has lost his wife to the alien conquest and had one of his three sons abducted by the invaders.

This time the show seemed to get on the good side of both reviewers and viewers and became TNT's big success for that first summer season. It returned for four more summers, although the ratings took a clear decline each year. Among the directors was Mikael Salomon, who had served as cinematographer on Spielberg's 1989 film *Always*.

Rising: Rebuilding Ground Zero

Discovery, August 25–September 1, 2011; 8:00 p.m. EST

This six-part documentary aired shortly before the tenth anniversary of the terrorist attacks on the World Trade Center. Hoping to find something positive to concentrate upon in light of the tragedy, this special documented the construction that has brought the sixteen-acre site in downtown Manhattan back to life. Episodes 1 and 2 ("Reclaiming the Skyline") were about the building of One World Trade Center; Episode 3 ("Stories from the Pile") was about the National 9/11 Museum, which houses remnants of the disaster; Episode 4 ("A New City") gave voice to 9/11 survivors who helped to repair the city; Episode 5 ("A Gateway to New York") took viewers into the transportation hub and its cathedral-like building;

and Episode 6 ("A Place to Mourn") explored the making of the 9/11 memorial. Three installments each were aired back to back on consecutive Thursday evenings.

Joining Steven Spielberg as executive producers were Justin Falvey, Jonathan Hock, William Hunt, Darryl Frank, Danny Forster, Kristy Sabat, Christo Doyle, Bernadette McDaid, Deborah Adler Myers, and Vincent Kralyevich. Ed Harris was the narrator.

Terra Nova

Fox, September 26–December 19, 2011; 8:00 p.m. EST

"At the dawn of the 22nd Century, the world is on the verge of environmental collapse. Mankind's only hope for survival lies 85 million years in the past." So read the intriguing titles that opened the premiere episode of this highly publicized and incredibly expensive series. Banking on dinosaurs being a sure thing, and a rarity on prime-time television, Fox went all out on this one, with reports of $14–16 million being spent on the pilot alone. When that two-hour effort didn't live up to expectations, it was pulled from the intended May 2011 preview for an overhaul and rescheduled for the fall.

The Shannon family of five (consisting of one child more than allotted by law) travels backward in time from the year 2149 in order to take their place in a jungle colony called Terra Nova (this set was built in Southern Queensland in Australia), where its inhabitants hope to correct the mistakes that caused mankind's shaky current environmental state. Outside the compound things aren't as promising, as there lives a separate colony of rebels calling themselves Sixers, who have split from Terra Nova, as well as those ever-present dinosaurs ready to stomp and chomp. Executive Producers Brannon Braga and Rene Echevarria summed it up as "*Little House on the Prairie* meets *Jurassic Park*." The Shannons were Jim (Jason O'Mara), an ex-cop; Elisabeth (Shelley Conn), a surgeon and Jim's wife; their teenage children Josh (Landon Liboiron) and Maddy (Naomi Scott); and five-year-old Zoe (Alana Mansour), their illegal offspring who they have smuggled into the past. The head of the Terra Nova colony is Commander Nathaniel Taylor (Stephen Lang).

Of course a production this big was going to have a lineup of producers to match, so Steven Spielberg was listed as executive producer along with the aforementioned Braga and Echevarria, as well as Jon Cassar, Peter Chernin, Justin Falvey, Darryl Frank, Aaron Kaplan, Kelly Marcel, Katherine Pope, and Craig Silverstein, not to mention David Fury and Alex Graves, on occasion.

Despite special effects (all of which were subjected to Spielberg's approval) that were every bit up to the standards of a big-budget theatrical feature, and that insistence that dinosaurs were a foolproof attraction, *Terra Nova* had unimpressive ratings from the start and never gained any real traction to become the season's hoped-for top-ten hit. It ended with a two-hour season finale in December, and after taking the high production cost into consideration, the network simply could not justify bringing it back the following season.

Smash

NBC, February 6, 2012–May 26, 2013; 10:00 p.m. EST

One of the more unusual endeavors on the DreamWorks television résumé, *Smash* (created by Theresa Rebeck) was not science fiction nor fantasy, although it didn't quite dwell in the real world. The idea of setting a weekly series in the sometimes ruthless realm of show business was intriguing, as was the concept of concentrating on the creation of a (fictitious) Broadway musical, *Bombshell*, about the life of the most famous cinema sex symbol of them all, Marilyn Monroe. The very dependable Marc Shaiman and Scott Wittman (*Hairspray*) were hired to write new songs and the cast was occasionally asked to break out of the storyline and sing, as if the series itself were a musical. Weak characters and an emphasis on ludicrous soap opera over hard-hitting drama did the show in, however, and it never developed

the excited and loyal fan base of Broadway musical aficionados it was hoping to cultivate.

Megan Hilty and Katharine McPhee were the ladies angling for the top spot on this show; Debra Messing and Christian Borle the songwriting team; Anjelica Huston the optimistic producer; Jack Davenport the martinet director. In the second season Jeremy Jordan and Andy Mientus were added to the mix as the writers of a supposedly less-conventional, Off-Broadway show, *Hit List*. Lots of talent from the New York theater scene showed up (Jennifer Hudson, Bernadette Peters, Lin-Manuel Miranda, Harvey Fierstein, Carolee Carmello, Christine Ebersole, Terrence Mann, Norbert Leo Butz, and more), which was the principal attraction. The ambitious series never rose out of the ratings doldrums, but against small competition, it got itself an Emmy Award for Outstanding Choreography (for Joshua Bergasse).

As executive producer, Steven Spielberg was listed along with Darryl Frank, Justin Falvey, Craig Zadan, Neil Meron, Shaiman and Wittman, David Marshall Grant, and Joshua Safran.

The River

ABC, February 7–March 20, 2012; 9:00 p.m. EST

Hot from his success creating the "found footage" sensation *Paranormal Activity* (2009) and too many sequels, Oren Peli took the concept of "documenting" supernatural events and applied it to this hour-long adventure series. When famous explorer and host of TV's *The Undiscovered Country*, Dr. Emmet Cole (Bruce Greenwood), goes missing during a trek to the Amazon (Hawaii and Puerto Rico subbed for the real locations), his wife (Leslie Hope) and son (Joe Anderson) set out with a documentary camera crew to find him, encountering creepy thrills along the way.

In addition to Peli and Steven Spielberg, the other executive producers were Michael Green, Darryl Frank, Justin Falvey, Zack Estrin, Jason Blum, and Steven Schneider.

Following the eighth episode, *The River*, like Dr. Cole, disappeared, only there was no longer a camera crew around to record what happened to it.

Don't Say No Until I Finish Talking: The Richard D. Zanuck Story

TCM, May 8, 2013; 8:00 p.m. EST

It was only fitting that Steven Spielberg served as one of the executive producers on this tribute to the late Richard D. Zanuck, insomuch as that man—being the producer of both *The Sugarland Express* and *Jaws*—had been instrumental in launching the director's movie career. Spielberg also appears onscreen, praising Zanuck as "a fantastic support system for me." Among the many others on hand to offer reminiscences are Clint Eastwood, Carl Gottlieb, Tim Burton, Michelle Pfeiffer, Sherry Lansing, Ron Howard, Johnny Depp, William Friedkin, Morgan

Freeman, Helena Bonham Carter, and Zanuck's son Harrison, who had acted for Spielberg thirty-nine years earlier, playing Baby Langston in *Sugarland*.

Laurent Bouzereau, responsible for creating so many of the extras on Spielberg's DVD releases, was the director, while Justin Falvey and Darryl Frank were the other executive producers. The documentary had first been shown the month before its cable television airing, at the TCM Film Festival.

Under the Dome

CBS, June 24, 2013–September 10, 2015; 10:00 p.m. EST

A mysterious transparent dome appears over the town of Chester's Mill (filming took place in North Carolina), trapping its residents inside and causing all kinds of paranoia and mayhem as the citizens, for three tension-filled seasons, face further obstacles, including caterpillar infestation, acid rain, dust storms, falling pink stars, fires, seizures, meningitis, and a meteor shower. This sci-fi summer series derived from Stephen King's 2009 novel *Dome*, which seemed to indicate that the best-selling horror master might have seen the uproarious 2007 theatrical feature *The Simpsons Movie*, in which the inhabitants of Springfield were confronted with the very same situation, albeit with funnier and less violent results.

Mike Vogel had a central role as a former US Special Forces operator named "Barbie," while others stuck inside the giant fish bowl included a disgraced journalist (Rachelle Lefevre) who ends up being declared protector of the Dome; a megalomaniacal councilman (Dean Norris) who sees this catastrophe as an opportunity to take charge of the town; the councilman's disturbed and dangerous offspring (Alexander Koch); and a radio engineer (Jolene Purdy) who manages to pick up strange signals from outside the sphere.

Ratings were huge for the first season, with an average 14.85 million viewers, making it the most watched series that summer. The second year's opener received its share of attention among genre fans because Stephen King himself wrote it. The audience declined over the remaining seasons, and there was just as much arguing over plot developments and storylines and the overall merit of *Under the Dome* as there was over *any* program in the sci-fi genre.

In addition to the ubiquitous Darryl Frank and Justin Falvey, Steven Spielberg's fellow executive producers on the show were Neal Baer, Stacey Snider, Jack Bender, Tim Schlattman, and Stephen King. CBS Television Studios produced in association with Amblin Television.

Lucky 7

ABC, September 24–October 1, 2013; 10:00 p.m. EST

Anything but lucky, this hour-long drama questioned how a windfall of cash could change one's life, and not always for the better, after seven employees of the Gold Star Auto Repair Shop in Queens win a shared $45 million lottery. The winning folks in question included an assistant manager (Matt Long), an ex-con (Stephen

Louis Grush), an overweight sales clerk (Lorraine Bruce, repeating her part from the British version), a woman dreading an arranged marriage (Summer Bashil), and a single mother (Anastassia Phillips).

Weak in execution and poorly reviewed, *Lucky 7* (adapted from a UK series, *The Syndicate*) fared so badly in the ratings that it became the first casualty of the 2013–2014 television season, being cancelled after only its second episode aired on October 1, 2013. The remaining six episodes were eventually made available on iTunes. Amblin produced the series in association with ABC Studios, and Spielberg was listed in the credits along with David Zabel, Jason Richman, Darryl Frank, Justin Falvey, and Kay Mellor.

Red Band Society

Fox, September 17, 2014–February 7, 2015; 9:00 p.m. EST

Another hospital show, but one where the patients show up as regularly as the staff. This Americanization of the Catalan series *Polseres Vermelles* was set in the pediatric ward of Los Angeles' Ocean Park Hospital (actually shot in Atlanta) and therefore centered on the lives and traumas of a group of long-term teenage patients, among them a monstrously mean cheerleader with an enlarged heart (Zoe Levin), an amputee undergoing rehabilitation (Charlie Rowe), and our narrator, Charlie Hutchison (Griffin Gluck), who comments on the action despite being in a coma. Oscar-winner Octavia Spencer was cast in the all-too-typical tough-but-caring head nurse role, and there was plenty of affected "attitude" in hopes of offsetting the manipulative stickiness. Following the first ten episodes, the series went on hiatus, as the network weighed the possibility of rallying

behind it and giving it a second chance, at a reduced licensing fee. Instead, it returned briefly to play its final three episodes and was gone from the schedule after airing back-to-back installments on February 7, 2015.

Red Band Society engendered a bit of controversy on the eve of premiering when some Los Angeles citizens took offense to bus ads that showed the cast lined up with graffiti scrawled next to them, giving blunt descriptions of each. Spencer's character was labeled "Scary Bitch," which was not appreciated by certain onlookers. NBC soon after removed the ads.

The series was produced by Filmax and Amblin Television in association with ABC Studios, and Spielberg's fellow executive producers were Sergio Augero, Darryl Frank, Justin Falvey, and Margaret Nagle.

Extant

CBS, July 9, 2014–September 9, 2015; 9:00 p.m. EST [season 1], 10:00 p.m. EST [season 2]

Astronaut Molly Woods (Halle Berry) returns from a thirteen-month solo mission in space to discover, much to her shock, that she has been impregnated, very possibly by an extraterrestrial. This would not be her first experience with unconventional parenting, as she already has to contend, back on Earth, with an android son (Pierce Gagnon), who was manufactured by her husband (Goran Visnjic) in an effort to compensate for them not being able to have children of their own.

Expecting great things from this series (created by Mickey Fisher), CBS actually ordered thirteen episodes to be produced without bothering with a pilot. As a financial safety net, however, they made a deal with Amazon to stream the program four days after airing. Clearly there were similarities here to *A.I. Artificial Intelligence*, such as having a mother find it difficult to show affection to a cyborg who is expecting to be treated like a beloved biological offspring. But just as too many audiences found *A.I.* too challenging, something didn't sit right with them here either. Nor was the critical response much help. Following encouraging debut numbers, it appeared that those who wished to watch *Extant* preferred to do so online, and the ratings continued to plummet. Much retooling was done for Season 2, such as dropping various subplots (and characters, including Molly's husband, as well as her friend, played by Camryn Manheim) and adding Jeffrey Dean Morgan to the storyline as a cop, but the show never rebounded.

Steven Spielberg executive produced with Fisher, Brooklyn Weaver, Darryl Frank and Justin Falvey, and Greg Walker. Amblin Television produced the series with CBS Television Studios.

The Whispers

ABC, June 1, 2015–August 31, 2015; 10:00 p.m. EST

The otherworldly being causing havoc in this summer series was an invisible but deadly "imaginary friend" called Drill who persuades young children to do his evil bidding, which includes a six-year-old girl luring her mother to a treehouse and then laying some guilt upon her, allowing the woman to fall to the patio below. Lily Rabe was an FBI investigator specializing in children; Milo Ventimiglia was her husband, a pilot who had been missing but then appears out of nowhere and may be a link to Drill; and Barry Sloane was a Defense Department official whose own daughter is one of the "possessed." Showing up from time to time as Rabe's mother and adding a bit of nostalgia to the series is Dee Wallace, the mom from *E.T. the Extra-Terrestrial.*

The series was a loose reworking of a Ray Bradbury story, "Zero Hour," from the 1951 compilation *The Illustrated Man.* Executive producing with Spielberg were Justin Falvey and Darryl Frank, Zack Estrin, Dawn Parouse, and Mark Romanek. The critics seemed to get behind this series more than audiences did. It lasted thirteen episodes.

A Clickety-Clark and Amblin Television in association with ABC Studios production.

Public Morals

TNT, August 25–October 20, 2015; 9:00 p.m. EST

One of the stars of Steven Spielberg's *Saving Private Ryan,* Edward Burns, was the whole show in this police procedural set during the 1960s. Burns, who had already done some multitasking in front of and behind the cameras with several independent features (including *The Brothers McMullen* and *Sidewalks of New York*), was *Public Morals'* leading man, creator, and an executive producer (sharing credit with Spielberg, Justin Falvey and Darryl Frank, and Aaron Lubin), as well as the sole writer and director of all ten of its episodes.

Burns starred as morally compromised Irish-American New York cop Terry Muldoon, who must walk a fine line between enforcing the laws through the New York Public Morals Division for which he works and keeping the city's gangland factions happy to maintain a shady but necessary balance of order. The Division was out to bring some semblance of control rather than eradicate crime.

With a solid thespian lineup that included Brian Dennehy as an aging mob boss; *Minority Report* cast member Neal McDonough as Dennehy's psychopathic offspring; Elizabeth Masucci as Muldoon's long-suffering wife; Michael Rapaport as Muldoon's partner; and Austin Stowell, who had just shot a role in Spielberg's *Bridge of Spies,* as a Muldoon cousin and fellow cop, the series had a gritty pull to it and received a good deal of critical support. Burns admitted there were deliberate nods throughout the show to various cinematic locations, props, and moments, going so far as to slip one in as a homage to Spielberg's 1960s-set drama *Catch Me If You Can,* with a shot on Park Avenue showing his character entering a phone booth much as Leonardo Di Caprio had done in Spielberg's 2002 movie.

Keeping up with the times, the day after the premiere, TNT made Episodes 1–4 of *Public Morals* available on demand. After a season of soft ratings, the show was not picked up for a second go-round.

Minority Report

Fox, September 21–November 30, 2015; 9:00 p.m. EST

For the first time, a television series produced by Steven Spielberg was derived from one of the theatrical films he directed. Whereas the twin Pre-Cogs from that movie were given short shrift in order to concentrate on the female, Agatha, this time one of the lookalike brothers, Dash (Stark Sands, who had been part of the ensemble of the Spielberg-produced *Flags of Our Fathers*), was promoted to the leading role. Set ten years after the finale of the movie, in which the Pre-Crime Unit was disbanded and the Pre-Cogs sent to live in seclusion from the rest of the world, the series had Dash return to civilization. There he hooks up with homicide detective Lara Vega (Meagan Good), who wants to use Dash's premonitory skills to solve crimes, putting him pretty much right back where he started.

Laura Regan appeared as Agatha, Dash's "twin" Arthur was played by Nick Zano, and there was actually a returning cast member from the movie, Daniel London, as the caretaker of the Pre-Cogs, Wally. William Mapother (cousin of the movie's star, Tom Cruise), who had played a creepy desk clerk in the film, showed up here as Agatha's neighbor, whom she blackmailed, knowing full well about his secret stash of cash. Max Borenstein, who'd done a commendable job of resurrecting *Godzilla* for a recent theatrical feature, was credited as the creator. He was also executive producer along with Spielberg, Justin Falvey, Darryl Frank, Kevin Falls, and Mark Mylod.

Another series that had no "thrill" factor to it to keep it from looking any different than the many weekly sci-fi adventures running rampant all over the tube, *Minority Report* received a collective shrug from reviewers and viewers, and posted weak ratings from the start. When the original thirteen-episode order was soon reduced to ten, the writing was on the wall, and the series became one more small-screen adaptation that would be thought of as a footnote to its superior cinematic source.

All the Way

HBO, May 21, 2016; 9:00 p.m. EST

Something refreshingly off the beaten track for Steven Spielberg, this was the first time a Broadway play served as the credited source of a television production he was involved with. A look at Lyndon Johnson's first year in the White House, this sharply written drama focuses principally on the often maddening political tactics the wily Texan used to get the Civil Rights Bill passed while still trying to court the favor of a bigoted Southern contingency for the upcoming 1964 election (echoing Spielberg's *Lincoln* and the sixteenth president's crusade to get the Thirteenth Amendment passed).

Robert Schenkkan's play had run 131 performances on Broadway, where Spielberg had seen it and instantly snatched up the rights. (Schenkkan had been a co-producer on Spielberg's *The Pacific* as well as writing four of its episodes.)

Alas, despite the fact that it ended up with Tony Awards for both Best Play and for Bryan Cranston's uncanny impersonation of the thirty-sixth president, it was not deemed worthy of being turned into a theatrical feature, as this sort of literate, thought-provoking drama was becoming an endangered species. Opening the play up from its theatrical roots and preserving Cranston's performance on film,

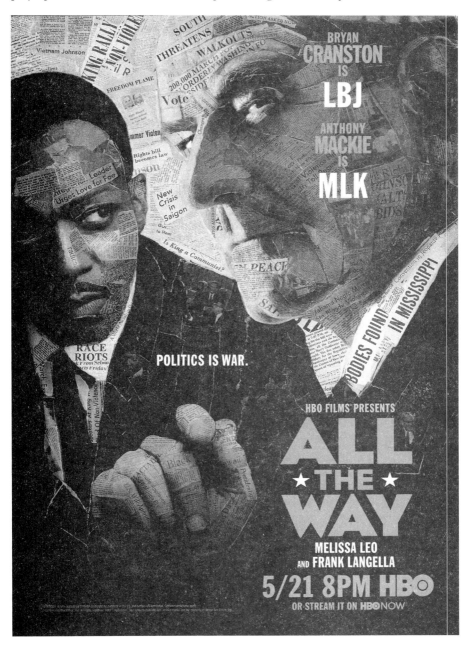

Schenkkan's adaptation also filled out many of its roles with a starrier supporting cast than had been seen onstage, including Frank Langella as Johnson's mentor-turned-opposition Sentator Richard Russell, Anthony Mackie as Martin Luther King, and Oscar-winner Melissa Leo as the ever-loyal Lady Bird Johnson.

Schenkkan, Cranston, and director Jay Roach all took producer credits alongside Spielberg, as did his Amblin partners, Justin Falvey and Darry Frank. Amblin shared the production duties with a Tale Told productions, Moon Shot Entertainment (Cranston's company), and Everyman Pictures (Roach's). The eight Emmy nominations it earned included those for Outstanding Television Movie (Spielberg among the nominees), Cranston for lead actor, and Leo in support.

Bull

CBS, Tuesday, September 20, 2016– ; 9:00 p.m. EST [Season 1]

"He'll get you off" was the attention-getting ad campaign for this legal drama, which was either an inducement or a deterrent to tuning in, depending on how one felt about the lead, Michael Weatherly (late of CBS's *NCIS*), and the show's premise. Weatherly plays another of television's brilliant minds, Dr. Jason Bull, an expert in human psychology, and the character is based on the early career of one of the show's creators, Dr. Phillip C. McGraw, known to the average viewer as "Dr. Phil." With his carefully chosen team, Dr. Bull profiles the behavior patterns of jurists, creating mirror juries and running mock trials, probing deeply and disturbingly into their personal lives through the use of high-technology. Although the series wants to make a case for the occasional need for undermining a corrupt and questionable legal system, this degree of meddling, and the Doctor's willingness to turn the tables in his client's favor for the right price, leaves one wondering just how much we are supposed to embrace this quipping know-it-all and his unethical techniques.

Despite a good deal of eye-rolling from the reviewers over the far-fetched premise, the series got off to a good start ratings wise, faring among the best of the fall's new offerings, getting itself quickly renewed for a full season, and for a second as well.

Spielberg was once again sharing executive producer credit with Justin Falvey and Darryl Frank, as well as Dr. Phil and his son Jay, *House, M.D.* creator Paul Attanasio, and Mark Goffman (*White Collar, Sleepy Hollow*).

8

Spielberg in Front of the Camera

W hen it comes to the general public being able to instantly identify a film director on sight, the list is small. Steven Spielberg is one of those few, mainly because his incredible degree of fame has pushed him into the spotlight, over and over again, on award shows, talk shows, commenting within documentaries, and showing up in extra features on DVDs. With this ubiquity comes the fun of putting him in front of the camera on occasion to do some "acting," so to speak. While hardly ready to compete with the professionals he's hired to perform in his own movies, Spielberg has proven to be an engaging presence on camera. His trademark appearance—bearded, bespectacled, customarily sporting a baseball cap—is memorable; his soft, slightly slurry, enthusiastic voice more interesting than many for whom acting is their principle means of income. Listed here are the highlights of Steven Spielberg either showing up before the lens to do something scripted, or those instances when only his voice was there for audiences to recognize.

Something Evil

CBS, January 21, 1972

A scene in Steven Spielberg's second official television movie finds commercial director Paul Worden (Darren McGavin) at work in a recording studio, listening to a singer (played by one of the future stars of *The Color Purple*, Margaret Avery) overdub the inadequate vocals of the ad's leading lady. Seen sitting at the control panel, sporting a bushy mustache, is Steven Spielberg in his first appearance *in front* of the cameras. The director *did* receive billing at the end of the program, along with several other bit players (including *Jaws* scribe Carl Gottlieb), although their roles were not specified.

Jaws

Universal, June 20, 1975

For the famously tense "third act" of *Jaws*, the three leads were left at sea with only a killer shark to share the screen with them. No other humans were seen for the last fifty-two minutes of the movie, but there was one other human *heard*. Coming through on the *Orca*'s radio is an Amity Point Life Station worker telling Quint, "We have Mrs. Brody on speaker," referring to the wife of the police chief. Although few would have been able to recognize it at the time of the movie's initial release, Steven Spielberg's subsequent fame and ubiquity on television interviews and award shows have made it quite clear to astute listeners that the voice is that of the director himself.

The Blues Brothers

Universal, June 20, 1980

Director: John Landis. Screenplay: Dan Aykroyd and John Landis.

If Steven Spielberg could direct a chaotic multi-million comedy (*1941*) featuring John Belushi and Dan Aykroyd, so could John Landis, handing in a $27 million extravaganza based on a pair of characters the two comedians had introduced in 1978 on the series that made them stars, *Saturday Night Live*. Musicians Jake and Elwood Blues were ultracool in their demeanor; wore black suits, black hats, and sunglasses; sang and danced their way through some blues numbers; and, frankly,

Steven Spielberg makes his onscreen motion picture acting debut as an office clerk during the climax of the John Landis comedy *The Blues Brothers*.

weren't really interesting enough to base a movie around. Nevertheless, when Belushi and Aykroyd's debut album as the Brothers, *Briefcase Full of Blues*, went to number one in 1979, it was inevitable that Hollywood would want to cash in on their heat with a vehicle.

The result was a hectic, messy mélange of weak comical set pieces; musical numbers from the likes of Aretha Franklin, James Brown, and Cab Calloway, among others; and a considerable amount of property damage, as the two petty thieves lay waste to most of Chicago as they are pursued by the police, a group of neo-Nazis, and Jake's spurned fiancée (Carrie Fisher) as they try to make the $5,000 needed to save Saint Helen of the Blessed Shroud Orphanage and deliver the cash to the Cook County Assessor's Office. The whole movie leads up to this latter destination and therefore to Steven Spielberg, who was invited by Landis (who had shown up for a cameo as a motorcycle messenger in *1941*) to make his official acting debut as "Cook County Clerk." Answering the door to the brothers, clad in plaid shirt and a sweater vest, and sporting a moustache, Spielberg delivered his first line—"Can I help you?"—with, if nothing else, more conviction than Franklin did with *her* dialogue. Accepting the payment and handing the boys their receipt, the trio is then surrounded by the law, rifles pointing in their faces, signaling the gig is up. At the time, it is doubtful most audience members would have realized who that guy was onscreen.

Indiana Jones and the Temple of Doom

Paramount, May 23, 1984

Sometimes cameos are done for the fun of those participating, not so much for the audience. Case in point: When Indiana Jones (Harrison Ford), Willie (Kate Capshaw), and Short Round (Ke Huy Quan) arrive at the Shanghai airport, they are greeted by an officious fellow named Weber, who informs them that he's managed to book them passage on a plane, with the drawback that they will be "riding on a cargo of live poultry." Viewers, no doubt, were acknowledging the fact that Weber was being played by comedian Dan Aykroyd, in an unannounced bit, thereby giving no attention whatsoever to the extras in the background. Among them, completely shielded from all but the most ocular wizards and wearing a pith helmet and missionary garb, is Steven Spielberg. Joining him are his producers, George Lucas and Frank Marshall, as well as costume designer Anthony Powell.

Gremlins

WB, June 8, 1984

Starring Zach Galligan (Billy Peltzer), Phoebe Cates (Kate Beringer), Hoyt Axton (Randall Peltzer), Polly Holliday (Ruby Deagle), Frances Lee McCain (Lynn Peltzer). Executive Producers: Steven Spielberg, Frank Marshall, Kathleen Kennedy. Produced by Michael Finnell. Director: Joe Dante. Screenplay: Chris Columbus. Technicolor. 106 minutes. (PG)

Steven Spielberg's unfortunate endorsement of Joe Dante resulted in another frenetic live-action cartoon from the undisciplined director, and it was a surprise box office hit, despite (or perhaps because of) its alternately nasty and moronic tone.

After inventor Randall Peltzer brings home a rare Mogwai for his son Billy's Christmas present, the teen inadvertently breaks the rules of *not* getting the creature wet or feeding it after midnight, resulting in a terrible horde of vicious gremlins that multiply and bring untold destruction to the small town of Kingston Falls.

When Randall has to leave town for an inventors' convention, we are given a quick glimpse of some of the curious folks and contraptions on display. These include a cameo from the beloved cyborg breakout star of *Forbidden Planet* (1956), Robbie the Robot; the time machine from the 1960 adaptation of the H. G. Wells novel; and Steven Spielberg (the movie's executive producer) circling around an ultramodern phone booth on a low-riding electric bike/wheelchair, looking at a monitor, with his leg in a cast. As usual, Dante loved filling his movies with pop culture references and included two in homage to Mr. Spielberg: a movie theater advertising a double bill of *A Boy's Life* and *Watch the Skies* (the working titles for *E.T.* and *Close Encounters*, respectively) on the marquee and gremlin leader Spike being spotted during the climactic scene hiding behind an E.T. doll on a department store shelf.

Although it does not appear in the opening credits as such, the original posters and advertisements for the movie proclaimed "Steven Spielberg presents" over the title.

"The Goonies 'R' Good Enough"

Music Video June, 1985

To coincide with the release of the Spielberg-produced adventure *The Goonies*, Cyndi Lauper released a music video (not recommended for those searching for subtlety) containing the song she wrote (with Stephen Broughton Lunt and Arthur Stead) for the movie. In the video, Cyndi finds her parents' gas station facing closure, and the villains responsible were played by several larger-than-life grapplers from the World Wrestling Federation (Captain Lou Albano, Rowdy Roddy Piper, and more). Lauper ends up uncovering a secret passageway in her house, where she finds a treasure map and encounters several of the young cast members from the film. As she's surrounded by pirates and other assorted weirdos on a rope bridge, the terrified singer shouts out, "Steven Spielberg! How do I get out of this one?" Watching the action on an editing monitor, Spielberg turns to the audience and starts to suggest "Well, the first thing you sho. . ." before realizing he's stuck for an answer.

This is another example of how Spielberg's name became the dominant one even on projects he did *not* direct. This is all the more curious since *The Goonies'* director, Richard Donner, was also the director of the Lauper video.

The song reached number ten on the *Billboard* charts in June of 1985.

The Tracey Ullman Show

Fox, November 5, 1989, 10:00 p.m. EST; Season 4, Episode 63, Segment 2: "The Gate"

Written by Marilyn Suzanne Miller. Directed by Ted Bessell.

Tracey Ullman's award-winning series allowed the British comic many an opportunity to show off her amazing knack at character comedy, playing a wide range of loopy and varied creations for a four-season run. One of the series' creators was Jerry Belson, who had assisted (uncredited) Steven Spielberg on his script for *Close Encounters of the Third Kind* and took sole credit as writer on Steven's 1989 release *Always*.

In the second segment of this episode (following one entitled "Two Time Losers"), Ullman played an unnamed lady, an ad agency art director, hoping to get through the front gate at Steven Spielberg's home, explaining to the fellow on the security intercom that she and the filmmaker had spoken on a plane ride from Chicago and that he gave her his address. The eager lady mentions how she bonded with the director over their love for Edward Hopper and Woody Woodpecker creator Walter Lantz; wowed him with impersonations of Julie Andrews, Diana Ross, and Minnie Ripperton; and insists she be able to see the famous man because they connected as people. "Doesn't Steven Spielberg have unexpected guests?" she wonders aloud. "I mean, isn't that what *E.T.* was all about?"

Having appealed to the moviemaker's humane side, the art director is delighted when the gates open and there stands Steven Spielberg in the flesh, delighted to recognize the lady from the plane ride. Reminding him of the song they sang during the flight, Spielberg and his guest break into the Sherman

Tracey Ullman has the audience meet her very special guest star, Steven Spielberg, at the finale of an episode of *The Tracey Ullman Show*.

Brothers' "It's a Small World" as they stroll up the (studio-manufactured) road to his home, hand in hand.

Easily the most charming on-camera "acting" appearance Spielberg has made, this sequence is then followed by a tag with Ullman asking the studio audience to give her special guest a hand. The director reappears to chat with his hostess, naively telling her, "Well, I don't normally do this sort of thing, but when I heard that Kurosawa, Bergman, and Fellini did the show, I couldn't say 'no.'" His glance at the audience following this misstatement is worth it alone.

So, yes, it's true. One of cinema's great filmmakers was once directed by the former costar of *That Girl*, Ted Bessell.

"Liberian Girl"

Music Video (1989)

In order to give his latest single—"Liberian Girl," from his hit album *Bad* (Epic Records)—a real kick, Michael Jackson filled the music video component with a plethora of friends and celebrities, some of them in blink-and-you-miss-'em cameos. The "plotline" had all of these famous folks waiting around on a sound-stage wondering exactly what they were expected to do and just where the missing Michael was, as the song (written by Mr. Jackson) played over the action (or, lack thereof).

Among those seen (some mouthing the song lyrics) were Paula Abdul, Amy Irving (at this point no longer married to Steven Spielberg), Olivia Newton-John, Jasmine Guy, Sherman Hemsley, Billy Dee Williams, Richard Dreyfuss (with his daughter, Emily), Lou Diamond Phillips, Danny Glover, and Michael's pet chimp, Bubbles. When a confused Whoopi Goldberg asks, "Who's directing this?" the camera zooms up to the name "Spielberg" on the back of a director's chair and then cuts to a frontal shot, pulling slowly away from Steven (wearing a Universal Studios tour hat) as he looks at his watch and then at the camera. He is later seen chatting with John Travolta and Quincy Jones (the song's producer, and Spielberg's producer on *The Color Purple*). At the conclusion, Jackson makes himself known at last, as he is lowered onto the set on a camera crane, leading one to get the impression that the singer himself was the director of the video, when in fact Jim Yukich handled the chores.

The song was issued as a single only for the overseas market.

Steven Spielberg Presents Tiny Toon Adventures: "New Character Day"

Season 1, Episode 61; February 20, 1991

Written and Directed by Eddie Fitzgerald.

At the beginning of this episode, series regulars Buster and Babs are holding auditions for new animated characters. First up is the eponymous star of the 1988 fantasy blockbuster *Who Framed Roger Rabbit*, who is begging for the job, as he needs "to keep my wife in glitter paint." Despite his pleas, he's dispensed with through a trap door. Roger's voice is not that of Charles Fleischer, who performed the job in the movie and subsequent shorts and videos, but an unrecognizable Steven Spielberg, making his first vocal cameo on the show.

Steven Spielberg Presents Tiny Toon Adventures: "Buster & Babs Go Hawaiian!"
Season 2, Episode 8; November 18, 1991

Directed by Art Leonardi. Written by Renee Carter, Sarah Creef, and Amy Crosby.

Frustrated by their lack of involvement in too many episodes, and especially their total absence in the new Hamton adventure, "Fléche de Lard," Buster and Babs burrow their way into Steven Spielberg's office, where, to the strains of "The Ride of the Valkyries," they find their show's producer playing a video game in which he appears to be zapping little Mickey Mouse hats as he cries, "Get out of here, you no good vermin!" Although caricatures of the Man in Charge had appeared throughout the various cartoon series he produced, this was the one time he actually agreed to provide his own voice rather than leave it up to someone else to imitate him.

In order to placate his unhappy stars, Spielberg gives them the script of this very episode we are watching, which he claims was written by a trio of eighth graders—which indeed it was. Renee Carter, Sarah Creef, and Amy Crosby, fans of the series from Waynesboro, Virginia, wrote their own script which managed to delight the producer, who declared it "too clever to turn down." The girls even got to appear in animated form in the episode, as did glimpses of Doc Brown from *Back to the Future*, Darth Vader (revealed to be George Lucas under his helmet); Jessica Rabbit's legs; Spielberg's production assistant (and eventual producer of *Saving Private Ryan*), Bonnie Curtis; and the two stars of Steven's upcoming new release, *Hook*, Robin Williams and Dustin Hoffman, in character as a Peter Pan and Captain Hook. Spielberg's office walls are adorned with posters of *E.T. the Extra-Terrestrial*, *Raiders of the Lost Ark*, *Always*, and one of his more recent producer credits, *Gremlins 2*.

Once Babs and Buster arrive in Hawaii (on a plane piloted by manic Montana Max and featuring Spielberg among its passengers, this time in an E.T. baseball cap), their exploits include a mistaken shark attack on the beach, which turns out to be the ever-annoying Elmyra, sporting a fake fin. The adventure ends with Buster and Babs being flung into the ocean because of a volcanic eruption, echoing the big finale of another Spielberg production, *Joe Versus the Volcano*. Buster is dissatisfied enough with the plotline to wonder: "Oh, what is *with* this story? It's like thirteen-year-olds wrote it!" But that's not the end of his collaboration with the Waynesboro Trio. Spielberg arrives at the climax, driving a golf cart with his three young protégés, to compliment the two bunnies ("You guys were great! What a wonderful show!") and announce to the aerophobic Buster that the girls have written another script, "Buster and Babs Go to Mars on a Rocket Ship."

Your Studio and You

1995

Prior to their breakthrough success with the foul-mouthed cartoon series *South Park*, Matt Stone and Trey Parker were hired to create a thoroughly irreverent tribute to Universal to be shown at a party marking the sale of the venerable studio to Canadian liquor company Seagram. Sending up the stilted and frequently hokey instructional videos of a bygone era, the fourteen-minute short was shot in black and white and filled with winking cameo appearances, including Demi Moore, Sylvester Stallone, director John Singleton, producer Brian Grazer, rapper Heavy D., Michael J. Fox, and Shelley Fabares, reminding viewers that she appeared in Elvis Presley's *Clambake* (!!).

Early in the presentation, the Universal tram is seen making its scheduled stop to allow the *Jaws* shark to jump out of the water, a staple of the tour, but an attraction the narrator—labeling it "old and stupid"—fears represents a stodgier era, one the studio must move on from. What gives the segment its "bite" (for lack of a better word) is that the tour guide on the tram is played by none other than the reason that mechanical shark is there in the first place, Steven Spielberg. "Look out! A shark! Here it comes! A shark is coming!" he shouts, trying in vain to get a rise out of the bored passengers. The narrator's query "How can we improve the studio?" (apart from adorning any available site, including the shark lake, with a porcelain deer statue) is followed by a glimpse of the *Jurassic Park* attraction then being constructed at the park.

Funny as Spielberg's sequence is, it can't complete with the sight of a cheerful Angela Lansbury applying a coat of paint to the *Psycho* house.

The Lost World: Jurassic Park

Universal, May 23, 1997

In one of the more obscure cameo appearances by a famous person in not only the Spielberg canon but in the entire history of cinema, the director actually *does* show up in his *Jurassic Park* sequel, fleetingly, although only the sort of folks who scrutinize movies frame by frame probably spotted him initially. In best Hitchcockian fashion, this guest appearance indicates that one cannot take things too seriously. In the movie's penultimate scene, after the action is over, Malcolm (Jeff Goldblum), Sarah (Julianne Moore), and Kelly (Vanessa Lee Chester) are sitting on the couch watching a CNN television report about the aftermath of the T-Rex's destruction of San Diego. Only there seems to be—if one looks closely at their reflection in the TV set—someone on the couch with them. A fellow resembling Steven Spielberg, sporting a beard, glasses, and a baseball cap, is there on the sofa enjoying popcorn with the others. Only he's not there when the camera cuts to the reverse angle of the tired adventures, two of whom, Sarah and Malcolm, are now asleep.

Vanilla Sky

Paramount, December 14, 2001

Director/Screenplay: Cameron Crowe

The life of a cocky and sinfully rich New York publishing magnate, David Aames (Tom Cruise), goes off the rails when he is disfigured in a car accident deliberately caused by a vengeful lover (Cameron Diaz). In order to show just how much David is "livin' the dream" and rubbing elbows with the elite, one of the guests at his birthday party is Steven Spielberg (in a baseball cap, of course), who embraces the man of the hour, affectionately telling him "Happy Birthday, you son of a bitch."

This convoluted drama (a remake of the Spanish film *Abre los Ojos/Open Your Eyes*) was made directly before Spielberg's first collaboration with Cruise, *Minority Report*, in which Steven returned the gesture by giving *Vanilla Sky*'s director, Cameron Crowe, a bit as a passenger reading a newspaper on a train and throwing a suspicious glance at Cruise while he's one the run.

Austin Powers in Goldmember

New Line Cinema, July 26, 2002

Director: Jay Roach. Screenplay: Mike Myers and Michael McCullers.

Comedian Mike Myers's gleefully silly send-up of the outrageous spy capers of the 1960s—those of James Bond specifically—had earned enough of a devoted following with the first two installments, *Austin Powers: International Man of Mystery* (1997) and *Austin Powers: The Spy Who Shagged Me* (1999), that several of the principal characters had become iconic in the minds of movie audiences by the turn of the millennium. These included the titular hero (Myers), a self-proclaimed ladies' man with bad teeth and an ultragroovy wardrobe, hopelessly stuck in the ways and attitudes of London's "Swinging '60s;" his bald-pated nemesis, the flamboyantly mannered, pinky-sucking Dr. Evil (also Myers), with his endlessly inept schemes for world domination; and Evil's pint-sized, lookalike minion, Mini-Me (Verne Troyer).

By the time the third (and last) chapter of the saga, *Austin Powers in Goldmember*, went before the camera, it wasn't hard to get some big names to get in on the fun and do some cheeky cameos. These included the man Powers proclaimed "the grooviest filmmaker in the history of cinema," Steven Spielberg, who popped up in the movie's opening scene as the guiding force behind a "biography" being filmed about the legendary supersleuth. Following a reenactment of an outlandish stunt, the onscreen Powers interpreter is revealed to be none other than Tom Cruise, while his leading lady, portraying the suggestively named Dixie Normous, is Gwyneth Paltrow. To add to the all-star mix, Kevin Spacey logs in as Dr. Evil with Danny DeVito as his sidekick, Mini-Me.

Hearing Spielberg's voice yell "cut!" after a take, we first see him turning around in his director's chair (marked with his name for those unaware) on the

Paramount backlot, asking Powers for his reaction to what he has just witnessed. Despite his "shag-a-delic!" enthusiasm, the secret agent has some reservations about the staging, but Spielberg one-ups him by holding up a faux Oscar statue and letting him know "My friend here thinks it's fine the way it is." Powers decides the picture still needs mojo and intends to show the director just what he means by indulging in an elaborate production number to his theme music (Quincy Jones's "Soul Bossa Nova"). To start off the dance, a stunt gymnast, dressed in Spielberg's same outfit, exits the scene hilariously by doing multiple flips off the set.

Myers adds additional guest bits to the show, including Jones himself, Britney Spears, Nathan Lane, news anchor Katie Couric, Ozzy Osbourne and family, Burt Bacharach, and John Travolta. According to director Jay Roach, Spielberg was the first "name" to sign up for this all-star party.

The end credits feature a mention for "Mr. Cruise, Ms. Paltrow and Mr. Spielberg's Hair by Mark Anthony Townsend," while the moviemaker is identified in the cast list simply as "Famous Director."

Paul

Universal, March 18, 2011

Directed by Greg Mottola. Written by Simon Pegg and Nick Frost.

So associated with aliens had Steven Spielberg become, on the basis of *Close Encounters* and *E.T.*, that actors Simon Pegg and Nick Frost pretty much combined the storylines of both films when they wrote their affectionate spoof, *Paul*, and then managed to enlist the director to be part of the fun.

Opening with more than a passing resemblance to *CE3K*, we see a lonely farm house in Moorcroft, Wyoming, not unlike Melinda Dillion's dwelling from Spielberg's 1977 film, special effects suggesting an alien presence hovering above, and a mysterious occurrence, this one happening to a dog named "Paul." Cutting to the present day, the main story follows two enthusiastic sci-fi nerds, Graeme Willy and Clive Gollings (Pegg and Frost), as they travel through the Southwest searching for famous UFO sites in their Winnebago, only to encounter something even better—a foul-mouthed extraterrestrial named Paul (voiced by Seth Rogen) who is on the run from government authorities and anxious to get back to his home planet after sixty years on Earth.

As Paul explains to his hosts that he has had tremendous influence on pop culture during his stay here, we are treated to a 1980 flashback of the alien chatting on the phone with Steven Spielberg (heard but not seen) and offering suggestions for an upcoming movie project. When Spielberg mentions that he wants the extraterrestrial in his film to have messianic powers, Paul wonders if the director might be open instead to the concept of "cellular revivification." Spielberg admits he doesn't know what that is, so Paul explains that it is a form of healing power, much like his own ability. Now hyped on the possibilities, Steven pictures the celluloid E.T. having a finger that lights up at the end. While a skeptical Paul thinks he should adhere to the adage "less is more," Spielberg knows better. "Hey, trust me," he says.

Further connections to the famous director and his works include a marquee showing *Duel* on a double bill with Dennis Hopper's *Easy Rider*; a fireworks cannon labeled "The Five Tones" from which emanates John Williams's unmistakable *Close Encounters* notes; Paul's request for Reece's Pieces (a la *E.T.*) when his hosts drop by a convenience store; and a climax taking place in the shadow of Devils Tower. Deviating off the alien theme, there is also a nod to *Jaws*, when government agent Haggard (Bill Hader) points his gun at Paul and barks "Smile, you son of a bitch!" echoing Roy Scheider's immortal send-off to the shark.

9

The Sound of Spielberg

The Important Use of Music in Steven Spielberg's Films, with a Special Nod to John Williams

T he collaboration between Steven Spielberg and composer John Williams has been one of the movies' most dedicated and lasting partnerships. When it came to scoring his very first motion picture, *The Sugarland Express*, Spielberg instantly thought of Williams, principally on the basis of the music he had written for Mark Rydell's 1969 movie *The Reivers*. Spielberg was thrilled with the results and declared Williams his go-to composer for every subsequent movie he would make, with three exceptions: *Twilight Zone: The Movie*, for which Jerry Goldsmith was hired to score each of the four segments, including Spielberg's chapter; *The Color Purple*, because one of the producers was composer Quincy Jones, and he had already signed on with the idea that he would be providing the musical sound to the film as well; and *Bridge of Spies*, which was simply a case of Williams not being available when the scoring job needed to be done, and Thomas Newman being hired in his place.

Beyond Williams's often soaring, sometimes classic themes, Spielberg has used a variety of established tunes, instrumentals, and new songs in varying ways that are worth notating and exploring the possible reason behind the selections, reflecting upon which scene or images they have been paired off with.

This chapter gives a listen to both Williams's background themes as well as the additional music used in each of Spielberg's movies, with the exception of *Twilight Zone*, which has nothing on hand worth noting beyond Goldsmith's underscoring.

The Sugarland Express

"Main Theme"

For his maiden voyage with Steven Spielberg, composer John Williams knew that the Texas setting required something with a folksy sound and came up with this effective theme, a mournful lament carried principally by harmonica (performed by noted jazz musician Toots Thielemans). It is heard at the start of the picture, shortly after Lou Jean (Goldie Hawn) gets off the bus and makes her way to the pre-release center. It is also heard as the end title cards rise to tell us about the fate of the principals and the credits commence, with Michael Sacks (as Officer Maxwell Slide) beautifully silhouetted against the water by Vilmos Zsigmond's shimmering cinematography.

"Living Together Alone"

To set the southern tone, this duet by Conway Twitty and Loretta Lynn (released in 1972) is heard in the visitors' yard at the pre-release center as Lou Jean makes her way through the cluster of cons and their families, the title credits still rolling. Although the opening line is all too fitting for Lou Jean and her husband Clovis's (William Atherton) situation ("I can't believe the life we live"), the song pertains to a broken marriage due to the husband carrying on with someone else.

"The Texian Boys"

Jazzed up to be heading over the border into Texas to join the mayhem of the Poplin pursuit, a Louisiana patrolman (Guich Koock) starts to sing to his fellow officer (Roger Ernest) over their police radios this variation on the 1840s song "Come All You Virginia Girls" (writers unknown). These lyrics warn the girls of their home state not to dabble with Texas boys, although in the film it's the Louisianans who help cause a major police car crack-up because of their interference.

"When My Blue Moon Turns to Gold Again"

Heard on the car radio as performed by Merle Haggard, the song is later sung in a fractured manner by fugitives Clovis and Lou Jean, as they near their destination of Sugarland. As with most casual radio listeners, the two don't exactly get all the words right, singing their own line, "I'll be back with you, home again," perhaps as a hopeful nod to their desire to be reunited with Baby Langston. The tune was first recorded by its composers, Wiley Walker and Gene Sullivan, in 1941.

"The Eyes of Texas" and "Yellow Rose of Texas"

Despite Captain Tanner's (Ben Johnson) wishes that the Poplins and their hostage (Michael Sacks) *not* enter the town of Rodrigo because innocent civilians might get hurt by the barrage of cars racing through, the self-serving fugitives aren't about the let the law influence them this late in the game. Lou Jean is eager to see the townspeople whom she is certain are just as anxious to see them, considering all the mindless adoration pouring their way so far. Turns out Rodrigo is celebrating the Fourth of July with a parade, and as the car caravan approaches, a high-school band is playing "The Eyes of Texas." This is most appropriate, as the eyes of Texas have indeed been riveted to the drama of the Poplin pursuit, which represents just about the only excitement around to fill the void of too many empty lives. Back in 1903, John Sinclair had added new lyrics to the already established folk tune "I've Been Working on the Railroad, "turning "The Eyes of Texas" into the fight song of the University of Texas. It had shown up previously in such movies as George Stevens's *Giant* and George Sidney's *Viva Las Vegas*. The band soon segues into another Lone Star State staple, "Yellow Rose of Texas" (writer unknown), also heard (most memorably) in *Giant*.

Jaws

"Theme from 'Jaws' [Main Title]"

With those unmistakable, ominous "bum-bum-bum-bum" notes, John Williams entered the realm of modern folklore with his main theme to *Jaws*, making it the go-to music for anyone wanting to conjure up menace or suspense. (It was later parodied by Williams and Spielberg themselves at the start of their 1979 collaboration *1941*, as well as added to the opening gag of the classic 1980 send-up *Airplane!*) With the ongoing success of the movie, it made perfect sense for MCA records to issue the instrumental track from the soundtrack LP as a single (the music, as heard in the single, is never played this long on screen), just to see if it might take off on the pop charts. Although it never climbed to any impressive position, it did reach number thirty-two the week of September 13, 1975, and stayed in the Top 40 for seven weeks total.

Quint (Robert Shaw) takes aim at his fearsome nemesis while Matt Hooper (Richard Dreyfuss) pilots the boat in *Jaws*.

Dickie Goodman, famous for his "break-in" records that featured dialogue interrupted by snatches of Top 40 tunes (he and his partner, Bill Buchanan first hit the airwaves doing this sort of thing in 1956, with their number three hit "The Flying Saucer, Parts 1 & II"), bested Williams in sales with his novelty record, "Mr. Jaws" (on the Cash label), reaching number four on the *Billboard* charts that very same week (September 13, 1975). Opening with Williams's theme and the line "We're here on the beach where a giant shark has just eaten a girl swimmer," an interviewer (Goodman) then proceeds to get feedback from the shark himself (i.e. the query "What did she say when you grabbed her?" is answered by the title phrase of Olivia Newton-John's "Please, Mister, Please."). Best enjoyed by kids.

Posing less competition that same year was a disco single, "Super Jaws," by a group called Seven Seas. This tune basically consisted of a pulsating beat interrupted every so often by the chorus alternately chanting "Jaws" or "Super Jaws." Presumably there was no need to list the lyrics on the back of the record sleeve.

"(You're) Having My Baby," "I Honestly Love You," and "The Muffin Man"

Despite Sheriff Brody's (Roy Scheider) better efforts, the Amity beach remains open, causing him to sit tensely and watch the water for signs of danger. Among the distracting sounds on the beach, coming from portable radios, are two number one hits from the summer of 1974: Paul Anka's "Having My Baby," hated by feminists everywhere, and Olivia Newton-John's easier to take "I Honestly Love You" (written by Peter Allen and Jeff Barry). Brody's younger son, Sean (Jay Mello), is also chiming in with his rendition of the traditional nursery standard "The Muffin Man" while playing in the sand, but all of these pieces of music are soon wiped out by the sound of John Williams's ominous main theme, as the camera prowls under the water toward poor Alex Kintner (Jeffrey Voorhees).

"Spanish Ladies" and "Show Me the Way to Go Home"

Being a man of the sea, Quint (Robert Shaw) is heard singing (on more than one occasion) the British naval tune "Spanish Ladies," which originated sometime around 1796. It is therefore fuzzy as to who its writers were.

When Quint starts to reprise the tune during the drunk scene in the *Orca* cabin, Hooper (Richard Dreyfuss) cuts in by singing "Show Me the Way to Go Home," which both his shipmates join him in. First heard back in 1925, the song's authorship was credited to Irving King, who was, in fact, two men, James Campbell and Reginald Connelly.

Close Encounters of the Third Kind

"Theme from 'Close Encounters of the Third Kind'"

Needing a five-tone signal that would be crucial to the plotline of Spielberg's alien contact epic, John Williams came up with something that became as iconic as his repeated *Jaws* notes. It therefore made sense to incorporate this motif into an instrumental piece and try it out as a single and see if it might make a dent on the radio airwaves. The 45 rpm (on the Arista label) did in fact do better on the charts than its Spielberg-related predecessor—given its revved-up instrumentation that was more commercially viable for radio play at the time—reaching number thirteen on January 21, 1978. (A few months earlier, Williams's single of "Theme from 'Star Wars'" hit number ten). The three-and-a-half-minute track included a playful reimagining of the film's back-and-forth interplay between the earthling scientific team and the mothership.

"Theme from 'Close Encounters'"

Discofied to reflect the times, Meco's rendering of the movie's theme (on Millennium records) went so far as to end with a recreation of Cary Guffey's memorable "goodbye" to the aliens. Although the same artist (whose full name was Meco Monardo) had gone right to the top with his take on "Star Wars Theme/ Cantina Band" back in the summer of 1977, John Williams won this time out on the chart wars. Meco only got as high as number twenty-five, on the very same date of Williams's highest positioning, January 21, 1978.

"She'll Be Coming 'Round the Mountain"

Not the most complex song, lyrically, and therefore often thought of as a children's tune, this traditional folk number is heard being whistled by the eccentric farmer (Roberts Blossom) who is waiting with his family for the appearance of the extraterrestrials. As they are positioned on the road by a bend, it is most appropriate, as the aliens do appear to be coming 'round a mountain.

The awesome mother ship arrival scene that provided the climax of *Close Encounters of the Third Kind* and dazzled audiences with a rousing alien-earthling rendition of John Williams's famous five-tone musical signal.

"The Square Song" and "Chances Are"

The aliens in the film are, no doubt, intrigued by Earthling music. When they first make their presence known at the house of Gillian Guiller (Melinda Dillon) and her son Barry, they set off several mechanical or electrical objects, including a phonograph which begins to play "The Square Song," a Joe Raposo composition from the children's television series *Sesame Street*, as performed by cast member Loretta Long.

Later, when the alien disruption sends Gillian's place into a real uproar, leading to Barry's abduction, the needle drops on an LP on a turntable, playing Johnny Mathis's classic 1957 rendition of "Chances Are," by Robert Allen (music) and Al Stillman (lyrics).

"Love Song of the Waterfall"

Country singer Slim Whitman's rendition of this tune (by Bob Nolan, Bernard Barnes, and Carl Winge), from his 1965 album of the same name, is barely heard, presumably coming from a radio playing in a toll booth as the alien ships, the police, and Roy race through the obstruction, without any of them paying the required twenty-five cent fare.

Whitman would later have a more severe impact on extraterrestrials, when he proved an earsore to the deadly invaders in Tim Burton's 1996 comedy *Mars Attacks!*

"Wish Upon a Star"

Steven Spielberg had turned to the unforgettable Academy Award-winning song (music by Leigh Harline and lyrics by Ned Washington) from Disney's 1940 classic *Pinocchio* as his inspiration while creating the various drafts of his film, fully intending to use Cliff Edwards's (who had voiced the role of Jiminy Cricket) rendition of it over the end credits. Following the October preview of *CE3K* at the Medallion Theater in Dallas, Texas, however, Spielberg realized that the song had the opposite effect than intended, pulling audiences right out of the wonder of the finale, making the story seem fanciful rather than possible. He had it replaced by John Williams's score. The tune *was* heard in the final cut, however, coming instrumentally from a Pinocchio music box seen in the Neary household, and did end up being heard in a wordless rendition at the climax after all, albeit only in the 1980 "Special Edition" re-release of the movie. When Spielberg recut the movie yet again, for a third version, that music was no longer part of the end titles. The "Special Edition" also featured some dialogue about Roy trying to psyche his family into going to the movies to see *Pinocchio*, which had been dropped the first time out.

1941

"In the Mood"

As expected, Spielberg's World War II comedy had its share of period music, including one of the definitive instrumental sounds of the era, "In the Mood" by Wingy Manone. Heard when we are first introduced to Wally Stephens (Bobby Di Cicco), who is flipping kitchen plates back in forth with fellow restaurant worker Dennis DeSoto (Perry Lang), the number serves to show us that Wally is adept at some fancy footwork, as he intends to enter a dance contest at the USO and win some money.

"Down by the Ohio" and "Daddy"

Up on the bandstand at the USO dance are three chirpy chorines referred to as the "Anderson Sisters." Lest the obvious reference to the Andrews Sisters, whose distinctive harmonies came to define the sound of the era perhaps more than any other vocalists, be missed, it is not the three actresses (Carol Culver, Marjorie Gaines, and Trish Garland) who are heard singing "Down on the Ohio" (and less audibly "Daddy") but the Andrews girls themselves, as their recordings of these numbers are mimed to. The former (a 1920 composition with music by Abe Olman and lyrics by Jack Yellen) was recorded by the Sisters in 1940. The siblings recorded Bobby Troup's "Daddy" in 1941, the same year Joan Davis and Jinx Falkenberg sang it in the Columbia feature *Two Latins from Manhattan.*

"Deep in the Heart of Texas"

Wild Bill Kelso's (John Belushi) frequently murmured "theme" song is Don Swander and June Hershey's "Deep in the Heart of Texas," which came to prominence that very year, 1941, per Perry Como's rendition on Decca Records.

"Swing, Swing, Swing"

Once again John Williams comes through with this exciting instrumental homage to the big-band era that sounds very much like the real thing. It is played (supposedly by Sal Stewart and His Serenaders) during the big jitterbug competition at the USO, which is further rocketed to life by Paul De Rolf's exuberant choreography.

"They All Laughed"

After they end up in Wild Bill's runaway sidecar, Stretch Sitarski (Treat Williams) and his relentless pursuer, Maxine Dexheimer (Wendie Jo Sperber), crash through various egg crates and other noisy props, after which the latter chimes in with the line "Who's got the last laugh now?" from the Gershwin Brothers' 1937 classic from the Fred Astaire-Ginger Rogers musical *Shall We Dance.*

"Baby Mine" and "When I See an Elephant Fly"

While it's never a good idea to include clips from a superior movie when your own project is curling up and dying onscreen, it was nevertheless a nice respite from the mayhem when footage from *Dumbo* was featured in General Stillwell's (Robert Stack) stopover at a Hollywood Boulevard theater. Heard and seen from the 1941 Disney cartoon were "Baby Mine," sung by Dumbo's doting mom (vocals by Betty Noyes) after her offspring has suffered abuse, and "When I See an Elephant Fly," memorably rendered by three crows (the voices of Cliff Edwards, Jim Carmichael, and the Hall Johnson Choir). The songs were by Oliver Wallace (music) and Ned Washington (lyrics).

"I'll Be Home for Christmas"

Strictly there to set the mood, Bing Crosby's version of Walter Kent (music) and Kim Gannon's (lyrics) evocative Yuletide promise is heard in the background as Macey Douglas (Jordan Brian) attempts to rescue Claude Crumm (Murray Hamilton) and Herbie Kazlminsky (Eddie Deezen) from their Ferris wheel outpost. Clearly a product of the war years and created to comfort those pining for the boys overseas, this song was, in fact, first recorded two years after the action taking place onscreen.

"By the Beautiful Sea"

Macey Douglas tries to switch on the Ferris wheel in order to rescue Claude and Herbie but accidentally turns on the entire amusement park, including the lights, rides, and music, which includes a calliope rendition of this classic Oceanside tune by Harry Carroll and Harold R. Atteridge, first heard in 1914. Now the Japanese sub has a clear target, which they assume is Hollywood.

"The March from *1941*"

Certainly one of the pluses of Spielberg's misbegotten production was the always dependable John Williams score, chief among the compositions being this rousing blast of patriotism, heard onscreen to underscore Wild Bill Kelso's scenes, and given a full rendering during the closing credits. It was good enough to make audiences feel that they'd just seen something a lot more fun than it actually was.

It was issued as an Arista single early in 1980 (with Williams's "Swing Swing Swing" on the flipside) but made no impact on the *Billboard* charts.

Raiders of the Lost Ark

"The Raiders March"

So rousing and irresistible was this piece of music by John Williams that it entered the public consciousness and became Indiana Jones's instantly recognizable theme

CAPTIVES OF THE EVIL ONE

Captives Marion (Karen Allen) and Indiana Jones (Harrison Ford) are smart enough to keep their eyes shut at the opening of the ark in this trading card depicting the supernatural climax of *Raiders of the Lost Ark*.

without even finding a place on the 1981 pop record charts. "The Raiders March," the last cut on Side B of the original Columbia Records soundtrack LP, would be heard again in each of the subsequent Indiana Jones adventures.

Despite the phenomenal success of the movie, the soundtrack album only peaked at number sixty-two on the *Billboard* charts, on August 8, 1981, before beginning its descent.

"Sir Joseph Porter's Song" and "A British Tar"

Indy's Arabian sidekick and faithful participant in archeological digs, Sallah (John Rhys-Davies), is clearly a fancier of the musicals of (W. S.) Gilbert and (Arthur) Sullivan. When Sallah and Indy (Harrison Ford) realize that their nemesis, Belloq, has miscalculated the height of the staff needed to pinpoint the location of the coveted ark, the former breaks into the famous opening lines ("I am the monarch of the sea") of the piece known as "Sir Joseph Porter's Song/When I Was a Lad I Served a Term" from *H.M.S. Pinafore*. He halts his musical revelry in order to save Indy from a poisoned date. Later, after Marion (Karen Allen) gives Sallah a kiss of thanks and farewell before she and Indy board the *Bantu Wind*, the delighted excavator sings the beginning of another *Pinafore* piece, "A British Tar."

E.T. the Extra-Terrestrial

"Theme from 'E.T. the Extra-Terrestrial'"

E.T.'s ethereal "theme" was another John Williams composition that lodged itself firmly into 1980s iconography, one reason being that it was the underscoring used for the movie's most indelible image, the gracefully lovely sight of Elliott (Henry Thomas) peddling his bicycle past the full moon, with his alien companion comfortably seated in a basket on the handlebars. Although MCA saw fit to release this music in November 1982 as a single (MCA 52072) under the name "Theme from 'E.T. the Extra-Terrestrial'" (backed by the track "Over the Moon"), record buyers were less interested than expected, and it failed to chart. The full MCA soundtrack album contained no track by this name. Instead, the music was heard on the tracks "E.T.'s Halloween," "Flying," and the fifteen-minute-plus wrap-up, "Adventure on Earth." The soundtrack LP peaked at number thirty-seven on the *Billboard* charts on August 28, 1982, and stayed there for another week before dropping.

Notable cash-ins at the time were a discofied "Dance to Themes from E.T." (also on MCA) performed, produced, and arranged by Walter Murphy, who had reached the number one spot back in 1976 with his instrumental "A Fifth of Beethoven." It was available as both a 7-inch single and an elongated 12-inch, but it did not chart. Nor did the electronic "Themes from E.T. Medley: Flying/Over the Moon" by the United Kingdom's Denny Randell and the Rockophonic Orchestra. (This featured a non-*E.T.* composition on the B-side, "Back to the Beginning.")

The sanctioned *E.T.* record that soon fell into oblivion was a forty-minute narrative of the story as told by pop superstar Michael Jackson, which simply went under the name *E.T. the Extra-Terrestrial*, with the familiar bicycle-moon image on the cover. Produced by Quincy Jones, the boxed packaging included a poster of Jackson very happily posed with the extraterrestrial star; a registration card to join the official E.T. fan club; and a twenty-page storybook. Added to the mix was a new song, "Someone in the Dark," with music by Rod Temperton (who wrote Jackson's smash hit single "Thriller") and lyrics by Oscar-winners Marilyn and Alan Bergman. Because MCA reneged on its agreement to *not* release the album or the song until *after* Jackson's *Thriller* (on Jackson's Epic Records label) was in the stores for the 1982 holiday season, it was withdrawn under threat of legal action and therefore became a collector's item. Jackson won one of his many Grammy Awards for the LP, which was named "Best Recording for Children" in 1984. It was through this collaboration that Quincy Jones first came into close contact with Steven Spielberg, thereby paving the way for *The Color Purple*.

The most popular song that has a connection to the movie was not featured on its soundtrack nor taken from any of John Williams's themes. "Heartlight," a reference to the visible glowing organ inside E.T. and his fellow extraterrestrials

E.T. spends a relaxing day at home in this trading card image from *E.T. the Extra-Terrestrial*.

was the title track from Neil Diamond's Columbia LP and was released as a single in September of 1982. Inspired by having seen Spielberg's movie together ("gonna take a ride across the moon" is one of its lyrics), Diamond wrote it along with Carole Bayer Sager and Burt Bacharach. It reached number five on the *Billboard* Hot 100 chart on October 2, 1982, and later down the line hit number one on the Adult Contemporary chart. The healthy sales more than made up for the $25,000 the trio was required to pay Universal Studios to avoid lawsuits of any sort.

"People Who Died," "Papa Oom Mow Mow," "Willie," "Twilight Zone Theme," and "Accidents Will Happen"

Pop songs are seldom intrusive when used in Spielberg moves, and this film is no exception. When we first meet the lead character, Elliott (Henry Thomas), he is anxiously trying to convince his older brother Michael (Robert McNaughton) and his friends to let him join them in a role-playing board game. The punk rock favorite "People Who Died," written and performed by author-musician Jim Carroll (later played by Leonardo DiCaprio in the 1995 bio film *The Basketball Diaries*), is barely heard in the background, coming from the radio.

When Elliott returns from collecting the pizza ordered by the boys, a song one of them (K. C. Martel) has requested by phone, "Papa Oom Mow Mow," is now emanating from the radio, just as Elliott first hears sounds from what will turn out to be his new extraterrestrial friend. Written by Al Frazier, John Harris, Carl White, and Turner Wilson Jr. (who comprised the pop group the Rivingtons, who first introduced the song in 1962), it was a cover version by the R&B group the Persuasions, heard on their 1977 album *Chirpin'*, which was used in the film.

Back in the house, a frantic Elliott tries to alert his mother (Dee Wallace) and his brother, while another tune, "Willie," by Jenifer Smith, is barely audible to the audience.

Figuring Elliott's claim that someone threw a baseball back to him from the shed is little more than a figment of the lad's imagination, one of the boys taunts him by singing the famous opening eight notes of Marius Constant's theme from *The Twilight Zone* (which would, of course, be heard in the next Steve Spielberg release, *Twilight Zone: The Movie*).

Later, when Michael returns home from school, before he confronts his brother about faking his illness, he is heard singing a few lines from "Accidents Will Happen," from Elvis Costello's 1979 album *Armed Forces*.

Indiana Jones and the Temple of Doom

"Anything Goes"

If indeed movies are supposed to take us by surprise on occasion, Spielberg and Lucas's follow-up to *Raiders of the Lost Ark* did just that, giving unsuspecting audiences one of the great "Is this really happening?" openings of the eighties, and of all time, for that matter. Action fans expecting some fisticuffs or physical bravado to kick off the new Indy epic instead were treated to leading lady Kate Capshaw

Entertainer Willie Scott (Kate Capshaw) lets her audience know that "Anything Goes" in the delightful opening production number from *Indiana Jones and the Temple of Doom*.

stepping out from behind a curtain in glittering attire and launching into a version of Cole Porter's classic song "Anything Goes" . . . in Mandarin Chinese. Therefore, "In olden days a glimpse of stocking/was looked on as something shocking/But now, God knows/Anything goes" became, approximately, "Yi wang si-i wa ye kan dao/Xin li bian yao la jing bao jin tian zhi dao/Anything goes." This was followed by an exuberant tap dance (choreographed by Danny Daniels, who'd done similar outstanding work on the 1981 Steve Martin musical *Pennies from Heaven*) by lines of chorus girls in the style of a sprightly, old-fashioned Hollywood musical of the era in which the movie took place, the mid-1930s, only with the benefit of Technicolor, something that was not used in abundance at that time.

Spielberg's delightful handling of the sequence made one long to see the great director take a crack at a full-scale musical, something he has frequently expressed interest in doing. During many an era when it would have been difficult to get the studios interested in such a property, Spielberg could have been one of the few directors to receive a green light. Alas, to date, he's never come through on his promise. "Anything Goes," therefore, remains his one traditional, full-scale contribution to the genre.

Porter's song had been introduced by Ethel Merman in the 1934 Broadway musical of the same name. The property had been adapted to films twice by Paramount: in 1936, with Merman singing an aborted version of the tune, and then again in 1956, when Mitzi Gaynor sang it.

The Color Purple

"Main Title"

Quincy Jones's main theme for the film, used initially to underscore the joyous image of young Celie (Deserta Jackson) and her beloved sister Nettie (Akousa Busia) skipping through the flowers and playing pat-a-cake, is nothing less than haunting. A gentle, lulling swoop gives way to an all-embracing sense of wonder, heartbreak, and deep longing all in one piece of music. It is heard just as effectively at the emotional reunion finale, leading into the end titles backed by the now-grown Celie (Whoopi Goldberg) and Nettie against a setting sun.

"Makidada"

The ditty sung by Celie and her sister Nettie while they perform pat-a-cake among the flowers at the movie's opening and closing sounds like a traditional chant but was, in fact, a new collaboration between Quincy Jones, fellow composer Rod Temperton, and the screenwriter, Menno Meyjes. The lyrics "You and me/Us never apart" perfectly capture the unbreakable bond between the girls. The title is Swahili for "little sister."

"The Dirty Dozens"

Wanting something authentic for the first tune Shug Avery is heard singing (Táta Vega providing the vocals for actress Margaret Avery to mime; it is later reprised, a cappela, as Shug encourages Celie to smile) at Harpo's juke joint, Quincy Jones selected this blues song, which first came to attention with Speckled Red's 1928 recording. Red (real name Rufus Perryman) and J. Mayo Williams were the songwriters. The title refers to the African-American tradition of trying to top one another with insults—the customary number swapped adding up to twelve. How early the original version of this song dates back before the record was made is unspecified, but the 1922 date of the action onscreen means it was most likely being used anachronistically.

"Miss Celie's Blues (Sister)"

Needing a knockout number for the important scene in which Shug Avery declares her affection for Celie by singing directly to her in Harpo's juke joint in front of an uncomfortable Mr.____ (Danny Glover), Quincy Jones called on the writer of Michael Jackson's best-selling "Thriller," Rod Temperton, and pop star Lionel Richie. Jones and Temperton came up with the melody, and all three worked on the lyrics. A splendid declaration of sisterhood and love between women ("gonna steal your stuff away, my sister"), it was considered good enough to release as a single (Qwest Records, 28754; backed by the instrumental track combination

"Celie Shaves Mr." and "Scarification Ceremony") but made no headway on the *Billboard* charts.

When it was nominated for an Oscar, it became the first song from a Steven Spielberg film to receive such a mention. Ironically, it lost to another tune written by Lionel Richie, "Say You, Say Me" (from *White Nights*), which had been a number one hit for the star.

"My Heart" and "Hot Lips"

During the scene in which Shug encourages Celie to dress up in her juke joint outfit, this first instrumental piece, performed by Louis Armstrong and his band, the Hot Five, is heard playing on the Victrola. Written by Armstrong's second wife, Lil, it was recorded in 1925.

The title of the second instrumental, a 1922 Paul Whiteman recording (written by Henry Busse, Henry Lange, and Lou Davis), is most appropriate, for it provides the underscoring for the key moment when Shug gives Celie her first romantic kiss.

Mr. _____ (Danny Glover) once again lets Celie (Whoopi Goldberg) feel his wrath in *The Color Purple*.

"The First Noel" and "O Come All Ye Faithful/Adeste Fideles"

This first traditional carol, origins unclear, underscores the forlorn Christmas of Sofia (Oprah Winfrey), back from prison and now working for foolish Miss Millie (Dana Ivey). It is heard on a phonograph record at the general store, where Celie quietly assists Sofia in collecting up the groceries, and then at Odessa's house, where Sofia meets her children again for the first time in years only to have to cut her visit short because of Millie's combination of automotive incompetence, racism, and overall selfishness.

The second carol—the composer's identity is open for debate—is also heard on a phonograph at Odessa's as Sofia experiences the ambiance of Christmas again.

"Scarification Chant"

In a tense and clever bit of crosscutting, the African ceremony that involves Young Adam (Jadili Johnson) having his skin cut with a knife is contrasted with Celie seriously contemplating finally cutting Mr._____ 's throat with the straight razor she is using to shave him. Fortunately, for Celie's sake, Shug stops her in time from the latter happening. Letta Mbulu provides the vocal in the piece written by Caiphus Semenya.

"Old Ship of Zion"

A bad man exits the earth not soon enough when Pa (who actually turns out to be Step-Pa; Leonard Jackson) finally dies and this tune (by Thomas A. Dorsey, the "father of black gospel music") is heard being sung as he lay in his coffin in church. Paying her respects, Celie meets Pa's new wife (Donna Buie), who explains that the old man expired on top of her.

"Maybe God Is Tryin' to Tell You Somethin'"

For a scene completely created from scratch and not featured in the original novel, Quincy Jones needed a composition that sounded like a traditional spiritual to be sung by the preacher's (John Patton Jr.) congregation. They are then joined by Shug Avery and her "sinners" from the nearby juke joint, as she leads them into the church, finally breaking the barriers between herself and the preacher, who turns out to be her father. The tune had been heard in fragmented form earlier when the preacher is sweeping up his church and is interrupted by Shug, who chimes in on a few lines, without moving the man of the cloth one iota.

This time Jones was joined in the writing of the song by Andrae Crouch (a gospel singer-producer who had worked with Táta Vega), David Del Sesto, and Bill Maxwell (who was the drummer with Crouch's group, the Disciples), with Vega again vocalizing for Margaret Avery.

"Heaven Belongs to You"

As Celie pretends to study her Bible while in fact reading another of Nettie's letters, this hymnal is being sung in church at the time. It was another composition by Andrae Crouch, this one in collaboration with his sister, Sandra.

Empire of the Sun

"Suo Gan"

A Welsh lullaby, the title of which translates into "lull song," this haunting piece of music (composer unknown) is heard during the opening moments of the film over the eerie sight of broken coffins floating in the Huangpu River. It continues to the Xujahui Catholic Church, where it is being sung by the lead character, Jim Graham, and his fellow choir members. It was impressive enough for Spielberg to find someone as talented as Christian Bale to carry the entire film; it would have been too much to ask that he also sing like a bird. Therefore, his solo on the piece is strictly a good miming job. The actual vocalist was twelve-year-old James Rainbird. The song was reprised by Jim at the prison camp, when he sees the Kamikaze pilots preparing for flight through the barbed wire fence and salutes them. Finally, it is heard on the soundtrack when Jim is spotted among the missing children by his parents. Its Welsh origins were fitting for young Bale, even if his singing required a "ghost," since he was, in fact, born in Wales.

Mazurka in A Minor, Op. 17 No. 4

A piece of this Frederic Chopin composition from 1833 is heard being played on the piano by Jim's mother (Emily Richard) while dad (Rupert Frazer) plays golf and Jim rides his bicycle, to show a typically civilized day in the Graham household before all hell breaks loose. When Jim returns to his house after his parents have escaped the city, he is falsely led to believe that his mother has returned when he hears the same piece playing from inside.

"God Rest Ye Merry Gentlemen" and "Good King Wenceslas"

Dr. Lockwood (Robert Stephens)—the ever-cheerful, seemingly ever-potted, and Santa outfit-clad host of the costume party the Grahams attend—greets them at the door with the first of these traditional Christmas carols. The same tune was later heard in Spielberg's *Hook* when the Banning family arrive at Granny Wendy's house.

Staying in the holiday spirit no matter how dire the situation, Dr. Lockwood is there to greet Jim later on, after he wakes up in the detention center, chiming in on the second traditional ditty.

"South of the Border," "These Foolish Things," and "A Nightingale Sang in Berkeley Square"

When Jim is taken to the secret shipboard hideaway of Frank (Joe Pantoliano) and his fellow scrounger, Basie (John Malkovich), these three tunes are heard on the radio in their makeshift quarters. Each recording, very fittingly, is by performers who became popular in England, thereby keeping the UK connection of the story.

The first (written by Jimmy Kennedy and Michael Carr for Gene Autry's 1939 movie of the same name) was a recording by Al Bowlly, a Mozambique-born jazz crooner who had his moment of UK popularity in the 1930s. He was gone by the

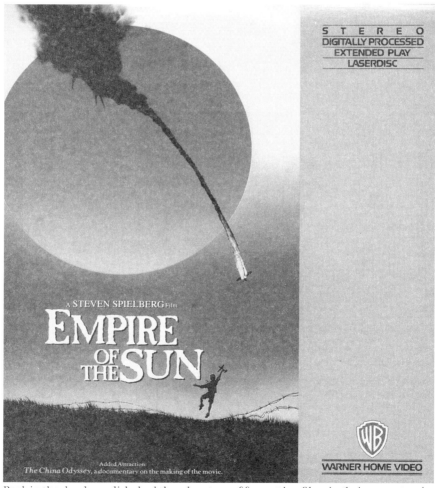

Back in the day, laser disks had the advantage of formatting films in their correct ratio. Here is the Warner Bros. Home Video release of *Empire of the Sun*.

time the events in the movie were happening, however, having been killed in a London air raid in April of 1941.

New Jersey-born Elizabeth Welch provided the vocals on the other two recordings, both with lyrics by Eric Marschwitz: "These Foolish Things" (music by Jack Strachey, from 1936) and "A Nightingale Sang in Berkeley Square" (music by Manning Sherwin, from 1940). Like Bowlly, Welch based most of her career in England.

"It's a Long, Long Way to Tipperary"

This 1912 British music hall favorite (written by Jack Judge and James "Harry" Williams) soon became equated with the First World War. A prisoner (Jack Dearlove) who appears to be losing his grip on reality because of his incarceration at Soochow is first heard singing it as his fellow captives rush eagerly for their potato rations, which are then cruelly knocked into the mud by a Japanese soldier. The same fellow reprises the number as the prisoners begin their long exodus from the camp. One assumes perhaps he is thinking back on his experiences in the previous war, when he was a soldier and not a POW.

"Exsultate Justi"

Arguably John Williams's most impressive contribution to the score is this exuberant choral anthem, adapted from Psalm 33. It is first heard near the end of the picture, when Jim returns to the abandoned prison camp, as he rides a bicycle and delights at a capsule of food supplies crashing through the roof of one of the dorms. Near crazed from his experience, he is liberated at last by the arrival of some American soldiers. The music is reprised twice during the closing credits, making for a rousing and very hopeful exit high.

Indiana Jones and the Last Crusade

"You're a Sweet Little Headache"

While in Venice, Indy (Harrison Ford) hears a phonograph playing Benny Goodman's recording of this tune (written by Leo Robin and Ralph Rainger) in Elsa's room. When Elsa (Alison Doody) pops out of the bathroom, she appears surprised that her room has been ransacked, the song apparently having covered over the noise. It turns out later that there was no such need, as the ransacking was a ruse, and Elsa is on the side of the enemy.

Goodman recorded the tune in 1938, a few months before the debut of the Bing Crosby film *Paris Honeymoon*, for which it was written. Like *Last Crusade*, *Honeymoon* was a Paramount release.

Always

"Garryowen"

No, not the announcer on *Rowan and Martin's Laugh-In*! "Garryowen" is the name of one of the most recognizable of march-step tunes, even for those not aware of what it's called. This Irish ditty was written sometime in the 1680s by an unknown composer and later became the theme of the 8th Cavalry Regiment. The name is a combination of the Irish words "Garrai" (garden) and "Eoin" (the name John). In the film, this is Pete's (Richard Dreyfuss) signature tune to whistle when he is flying, and it is first heard early on in the opening scene, when he suddenly realizes he is out of fuel and must glide in to the airport, or a "dead stick," as its referred in air traffic lingo. Later, while instructing Ted Baker (Brad Johnson) during one of his test run flights, Pete encourages him to relax, perhaps by using his technique of singing or whistling. Piping in on another whistled rendition of "Garryowen," he gets Ted to (subconsciously, of course) join him.

"Happy Birthday to You"

A few lines of the venerable tune by the Hill Sisters are sung by pilot Ted Baker as he arrives with balloons and a gift for Dorinda Durston (Holly Hunter), his job being to fly around such festive greetings to chosen recipients. An angry Dorinda is not impressed (it isn't her birthday, after all), shoving the gift box right back at him and cutting off his song.

"Nick of Time" (written and performed by Bonnie Raitt), "Boomerang Love" (written and performed by Jimmy Buffett), and "Give Me Your Heart" (written by Phil Marshall; performed by Denette Hoover and Sherwood Ball)

In a bar on base populated by the aerial firefighters, these three tunes are heard (ever so unobtrusively) in the background: as Pete tries to set the scene to celebrate what he believes to be Dorinda's birthday; as Pete is presented with a proposal by his fellow firefighter Al (John Goodman) to leave behind the dangerous work and become an instructor in Colorado; and when Pete and Dorinda toast to the two of them being together, always.

"Smoke Gets in Your Eyes"

In the same bar setting, Pete pretends to have forgotten that he and Dorinda have "their song" until he instructs the house band, played by real life musician-songwriter J. D. Souther and his group, to sing that very song, "Smoke Gets in Your Eyes." The couple dance a slow dance until they are interrupted by the other firefighters (notably Al, who displays some wild moves counter to the gentility of the tune) who are anxious to get in on some close physicality with the much-loved Dorinda. The fact that Pete does not follow through on the entire song with his partner is perhaps a foreboding of what will become their unfinished love story. Ironically, the man who will end up with Dorinda, Ted, is the one pilot denied his chance to dance with her.

Originally written by Jerome Kern and Otto Harbach for Tamara to sing in the 1933 Broadway musical *Roberta*, Souther's rendition of "Smoke" is clearly based on the arrangement that the Platters made famous in 1958 with their number one single. It is the Platters' version that shows up later in the movie in a key scene in which Dorinda and Ted are feeling romantic during a dinner she has thrown together for him. Once the song pops up on the tape they are dancing to, Dorinda suddenly cannot follow through and asks Ted if they can "finish this dance some other time." Instead, once he is gone, she puts on the very dress Pete had given her earlier in the film and dances to the song, seemingly alone, but with the now deceased Pete following her steps in one of the most gently melancholy of moments in any Spielberg film. (This same recording had shown up in a previous Richard Dreyfuss movie, *American Graffiti*.)

Although the title of this song turned out to be just too ideal in light of the firefighter milieu, it was not intended to be the key song in the relationship between the two leads. Steven Spielberg had wanted to use Irving Berlin's 1925 standard "Always." The composer decided against giving his blessing, claiming he had other plans for it in the future. Berlin died at age 101, three months before *Always* opened.

"The Toy Parade"

If you had just died and were in heaven on your way to meet Audrey Hepburn, what song would you whistle? For Pete, it's not his customary rendition of "Garryowen" but the theme from the fondly remembered 1950s family sitcom *Leave it to Beaver*. The instrumental tune actually had a name, "The Toy Parade," and was written by David Kahn.

"Matzoh Balls"

Al has really taken a shine to his new role as flight instructor and plays up his lofty position for all it's worth. Making his flunky (Michael Steve Jones) cart a boom box up to the top of the hill on which he is perched, Al commands his subordinate to tune the radio until he finds just the right song. It's this strange and silly jump blues number written and recorded in 1939 by Slim Gaillard, a jazz artist who specialized in gimmicky songs.

"Pennies from Heaven"

After Ted has dumped some flame retardant (egged on by prankster Pete) on an unsuspecting Al, he returns to base where Powerhouse (Keith David) and the other pilots are serenading him with a rendition of Arthur Johnston and John Burke's unforgettable title tune from the 1936 Bing Crosby musical of the same name. These guys are not only singing the lyric "make sure that your umbrella is upside down" but have brought along umbrellas to give the song some extra color. That extra color turns out to be red when a furious and encrusted Al pulls up covered from head to toe in reddish flame retardant.

"Cowboy Man" and "A Fool in Love"

Following his dismissal from flight training, a despondent Ted drowns his sorrows at a bar, where Rachel (Marg Helgenberger) attempts to flirt with him, much to the approval of Pete. Ted is too stuck on Dorinda to give Rachel the time of day. In the background these two numbers are heard, ever so slightly, the first written and performed by Lyle Lovett and the second a Michael Smotherman tune.

"Sweet Betsy from Pike"

Having failed to recognize Ted's impression of John Wayne (guessing it to be either James Stewart or Henry Fonda, much to the disbelief of not only Ted, but Pete, joining them afterlife style in the backseat of the car), Dorinda is now subjected to Ted's rendition of this 1858 ballad by John A. Stone, in Wayne's voice. A swerving school bus up ahead cuts him off, which is just as well, as he didn't seem too sure on the lyrics.

"Yakety Yak"

Not exactly adept at cooking, Dorinda frantically prepares a dinner for her date with Ted, bringing home takeout from a place called "Real Country Cookin'." This number one hit from 1958—the Coasters' most famous song ("Get all that garbage out of sight/Or you don't go out Friday night")—is heard throughout the sequence.

"Crazy Love"

Searching for an appropriate romantic number for their "date," Ted selects this 1970 Van Morrison song, much to the chagrin of Pete, who is trying to encourage him to use the *next* song on the tape, which, it turns out, is not such a great idea for Pete's aching heart.

Hook

"We Don't Wanna Grow Up," "When You're Alone," and "Pick 'em Up"

Having been adapted into a musical (successfully and not) on several occasions, *Peter Pan* came to be thought of by many as having singing be a built-in part of its storyline. Indeed, there were many times in J. M. Barrie's original work that the characters would break into brief songs or chants. They were out for fun, after all, and the wise among us know that there is great joy to be found in music. Steven Spielberg's take on the Pan legend ended up with three songs credited to John Williams, who worked in collaboration with Leslie Bricusse. Williams and Bricusse

Steven Spielberg watches a playback on the set of *Hook* with two of his stars, Julia Roberts and Robin Williams.

had a relationship that dated back to the 1960s and included such catchy tunes as the title song from *A Guide for the Married Man* (1967). Later down the line, they had come up with "Can You Read My Mind?"—the lovely little recitation for Margot Kidder to talk-sing while flying over Manhattan with Christopher Reeve in *Superman* (1978). Bricusse had already ventured to Neverland when he provided the songs (along with frequent partner Anthony Newley) for the 1976 *Hallmark Hall of Fame* version of the tale with Mia Farrow and Danny Kaye in the leads.

"We Don't Wanna Grow Up" was performed at the start of the movie as part of the grade school production of *Peter Pan* in which young Maggie Banning (Amber Scott) has been cast as Wendy and (following a long and curious tradition that dates back to the original Barrie play) a girl (Jewel Newlander Hubbard) is playing Peter. They are joined in awkward prepubescent fashion by the other youngsters in the cast, as Maggie's mother (Caroline Goodall) and brother (Charlie Korsmo) give the show their undivided attention, and Maggie's dad, Peter (Robin Williams), is more preoccupied with taking a phone call.

"When You're Alone" was the closest thing to a traditional musical performance, sung with much strain by Maggie as she stands wistfully by the pirate ship where she and her brother are being held captive, pining to return home. The start of the song is barely audible as Peter and hefty Lost Boy Thud Butt (Raushan Hammond) chat off in the distance by their treehouse encampment. Unlike "Somewhere Out There" from *An American Tail*, in which the cutesy kids' rendition of the number was offset by real vocalists reprising it during the closing credits,

"When You're Alone" received no such compensation. Despite this, it became the second song from a Spielberg film to earn an Oscar nomination, losing out to the title tune from Disney's *Beauty and the Beast*.

The third Williams-Bricusse composition, "Pick 'em Up," was actually more of a chant than a song ("Gotta lose a million pounds/get your fat butt off the ground") and is the rallying cry of the Lost Boys as they work to get the dispirited and overweight Peter into fighting shape to rescue his children and battle Captain Hook.

Another chant (that of "Hook! Hook! Hook!") was performed by Smee (Bob Hoskins) and the other pirates as they marched their way jubilantly on to the *Jolly Roger*, carrying the deadly prosthetic for their villainous captain upon a satin pillow. Underscored by Williams's exciting composition referred to on the Epic soundtrack as "Presenting the Hook," this sequence only emphasized the fact that *Hook* missed too many opportunities to go all-out in the musical comedy vein.

Jurassic Park

John Williams outdid himself with his score for Spielberg's blockbuster dinosaur adventure, providing not one but two great pieces of music that quite perfectly captured the spirit and excitement of one of the decade's most satisfying fantastical fun rides. The actual composition known as "Theme from 'Jurassic Park'" was a regal herald capturing, through its deliberate pacing, the ponderous thumping

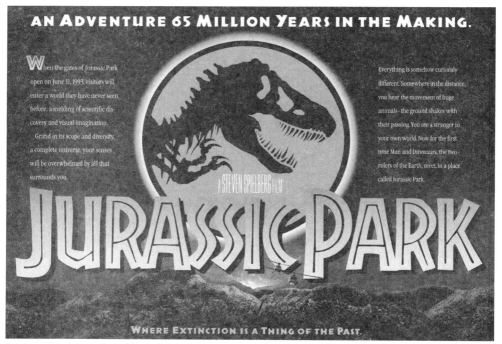

A magazine insert heralding the coming of *Jurassic Park*, with its memorable dinosaur logo and clever ad lines.

walk and majesty of a brachiosaurs. It was therefore appropriate that it made its most pronounced contribution to the movie in the scene where John Hammond shows off to the startled visitors his brachiosaurus, the first dinosaur to be seen in all its splendor in the story, the great beast craning up its neck to pluck leaves from a tree as Williams's music soars and becomes an essential comment on the dazzling wonder of the moment.

Equally thrilling was the theme first heard in the piece entitled "Journey to the Island" and signaled by Hammond's line "There it is," as the helicopter approaches the park itself and then drops through the valley onto its landing pad. This majestically trumpeted piece soared with the swoop of the helicopter ride suggesting the tremendous possibilities of something unusual and awesome about to happen, which indeed it did.

Both themes would be brushed off down the line for the sequels.

"Que Milagro Chaparrita"

There was only one bit of non-original underscoring in the picture, heard in San Jose, Costa Rica, when the shady "Dodgson" (Cameron Thor) arrives at an outdoor restaurant to meet with the slovenly Jurassic Park computer expert Dennis Nedry (Wayne Knight) and hand him a bag full of $750,000 so that he will steal for him some viable embryos from the lab. In the background, presumably coming from a radio and providing a flavorful atmosphere, is this tune by Dolores Ayala Olivares, performed by the Madacy Mariachi Band. The title translates roughly into "That Miraculous Little Girl."

Schindler's List

"Theme from Schindler's List"

John Williams's genius in being able to adapt his compositions to the style and setting of a movie is no more evident than his score here. In a story both of them liked to tell, Williams was so overwhelmed and humbled by Steven Spielberg's film when he first viewed it that he was certain this was one time his director should go looking elsewhere for a collaborator. Williams's suggestion that he get another composer was met by Spielberg's deadpan, "Yes, I know, but they're all dead." What Williams delivered was so moving and so right for the piece that it earned its place among the greatest of his scores, bringing him his fifth Academy Award in the process. At the Oscar ceremony he gave special thanks to Spielberg as "a seeming unending source of inspiration."

Most memorable in Williams's score is what is referred to simply as "Theme from 'Schindler's List,'" which somehow manages to both sound like a comforting lullaby and contain an almost unbearable sadness in its melody, conveying the shame and loss of the Holocaust. It is first heard over the image of hundreds of Jews crossing over the Pilsudski Bridge in Kraków to take up residence in the ghetto, a sad portent of worse to come. Later, it is effectively adapted for guitar as a grateful Regina Perlman (Bettina Kupfer) stands outside of Schindler's factory to see that Oskar Schindler (Liam Neeson) has managed to save her parents from the Plazkow camp, despite his protestations to the contrary. The most beautiful rendering of the piece underscores the most emotionally wrenching scene at the film's end, when Schindler is given the invaluable gift of an inscribed gold ring by his now-free workers and breaks down, ashamed he did not save more of them. Famed violinist Itzhak Perlman was enlisted to solo on the piece.

"Szomorú Vasárnap"

The title of Rezsö Seress's 1933 piece translates into "Gloomy Monday," but if that isn't depressing enough, it is also known by the name "The Hungarian Suicide Song." The tune is heard twice in the movie, first playing on the radio when we first see Oskar Schindler—or, rather, glimpses of Oskar Schindler—dressing to the nines for an evening out, his final addition to his outfit being his SS pin. Later, the music is heard being played by an onstage band when Oskar takes his visiting wife Emilie (Caroline Goodall) to a nightclub for some dancing. Since many have speculated that Seress wrote the song as a comment on the sorry state of Hungary and the encroaching situation in Germany, it is fitting that it has found a place here.

"Por una Cabeza"

This 1935 tango by Carlos Gardel (who is heard singing it as well) became well known enough to be used in films on several occasions, notably the American remake of *Scent of a Woman*, released only a year before *Schindler*. It creates the ideal atmosphere for the nightclub Schindler patronizes, as his strategy is a dance of sorts with Nazi party officials, winning them over to his side, creating a party vibe, and disarming men and women with his charm, easy way with liquor and money, and ability to sweet-talk the impressionable into believing he is behaving in *their* best interest, a theme that will run throughout the story.

"Die Holzauktion"

The party really gets going at the club, as we see two sprightly dancers in bowler hats entertaining the crowd to this song (the title of which translates into "The Wood Auction"), written sometime around 1890 by Otto Teich. The attire on the two women, smart jackets and tights, has a very Bob Fossesque feel to it, reminding one of his 1972 film of *Cabaret*.

"Mein Vater war ein Wandersmann"

We know that the wine has been pouring freely, as Schindler has now rallied the Nazis and their attentive dates to sing this undeniably catchy song, which translates into "My Father Was a Traveling Man" but is known by Americans as "The Happy Wanderer." Although there were variations on this tune around since the nineteenth century, the music for this one was written by Friedrich-Wilhelm Möller *after* World War II. No matter, the rousing chorus of "Faleri, falera/Faleri, Falera-ha-ha-ha-ha-ha" is hard to shake out of your head and can be interpreted as part of Schindler's brainwashing technique to get the SS officials on his side. To certain factions, this song is the equivalent of "99 Bottles of Beer on the Wall" for levels of annoyance, so perhaps a comment is being made on the Nazi's knack for torture.

"Auf der Heide blueht ein kleines Bluemelein"

Leave it to the Nazis to take a song that sounds perfectly harmless lyrically and turn it into something menacing. This military march, by Herms Niel, known commonly by the name "Erika," in reference to both the woman's name and the flower, is heard during the abrupt transition from the festivities in the nightclub to Kraków, where the SS troops march dominantly through the streets, a portent of the nightmare to come.

"La Capricieuse Opus 17"

With the esteemed Itzhak Perlman on violin, this Edward Elgar piece is heard over one of the comical scenes in the film, capturing Schindler's insatiable weakness for a nice looking woman, as he interviews secretaries to be his typist at his newly opened factory. The montage makes it clear that actual typing skills are somewhat immaterial.

"Meine Lippen, sie küssen so heiss"

Written by the composer most famous for *The Merry Widow*, Franz Lehar, this music from his 1933 operetta *Giuditta* is heard ever so briefly, being played on the piano at the party to celebrate the opening of Schindler's factory. There are no objections to the music by the Nazis in attendance, Lehar being a favorite of Hitler's, despite the fact that his wife had been Jewish before her conversion to Catholicism. So often the intolerant make their own rules as to who they will or won't hate.

"Oyf 'n Pripetsok"

In one of the boldest and most memorable strokes in Spielberg's depiction of the 1943 liquidation of the Kraków ghetto, he makes Oskar Schindler (and we the audience) focus most distinctly on a hapless little girl (played by three-year-old Oliwia Dabrowska) wandering through the carnage by allowing her red coat to be the only thing in color in the black-and-white surroundings. While she makes her way through the streets, this haunting piece by Mark Warschafsky is heard being sung by the Li-Ron Herzeliya Children's Choir of Tel-Aviv. Often sung in Jewish kindergartens, it tells the story of a rabbi teaching children the alphabet but is far more troubling than that, as the translated lyrics show: "When children, you will grow older/You will understand/How many tears lie in these letters/And how much crying." The nameless little girl is clearly experiencing the tears earlier than anticipated.

English Suite No. 2 in A Minor

During the brutal liquidation of the ghetto, one terrified man tries to stay out of the Nazis' sight by hiding within a piano but gives away his position by accidentally stepping on the keys as he exits. Following the inevitable gunshots, we hear this Bach piece being played on the instrument. The pianist is an SS soldier who appears oblivious to the discrepancy between this beautiful music and the slaughter about him. In the doorway, two other soldiers argue over who precisely is the composer: Bach or Mozart? One finally declares it to be Mozart. These being the sort of people who hope to run the world on brutality, even the most unversed in musicology can correctly assume that he is dead wrong.

"Tales from the Vienna Woods"

Partying at his villa perched high over the Plaszkow camp, Captain Amon Goeth (Ralph Fiennes) indulges in all the carnal pleasures he believes he is entitled too, which includes kissing every woman in sight, as he drunkenly does here. Being performed at this bacchanal is Johan Strauss II's evocative 1868 waltz.

Oskar Schindler (Liam Neeson) casts a spell over the revelers at a club as Carlos Gardel's "Por una Cabeza" provides the musical accompaniment in this scene from *Schindler's List*.

"Miłość ci wszystko wybaczy"

This Polish song by Henryk Wars and Julian Tuwim (introduced by Hank Ordonówna in the 1934 film *Szieg w masce*) is used during the crosscutting between three different scenes. It is first heard coming from the radio on Amon Goeth's balcony as the camp commander numbs himself with drink, tormented over his feelings for his Jewish housemaid, Helen Hirsch (Embeth Davidtz). Going down to the girl's basement quarters, he callously attempts to woo her with comments like "You're not even a person" and then proceeds to beat her as punishment for generating this desire in him. Meanwhile, the very same singer (Beata Rybotycka) heard on the radio is seen performing the song live, in a nightclub, for Schindler, who sits between SS officers Scherner (Andrzej Seweryn) and Toffel (Krzysztof Luft) and is eventually rewarded with a provocative kiss from the sultry chanteuse. This sequence is, in turn, intercut with the secret wedding in the Płaszów camp barracks between Rebecca Tannenbaum (Beata Nowak) and Josef Bau (Rami Hauberger).

It is fitting that the song translates into "Love Will Forgive You Everything," as the one real love going on here—between the imprisoned lovers—is the one that must be hidden. Goeth is too perversely corroded in his soul to be capable of love, let alone being forgiven for his actions. Oskar Schindler can certainly be forgiven for accepting another kiss from a woman who is not his wife, being shown affection by a girl who pointedly drifts right past his Nazi cohorts. But it can hardly be translated into love.

As so often is the case with bigotry, the Nazis appreciatively listen to the song, the music of which was composed by a Jew.

Moving to America after the war, Wars, altering his name to Henry Vars, ended up composing the title song for *Flipper* (!).

"To ostatnia niedziela"

Being feted on his birthday by colleagues, friends, and fellow Nazis, Schindler, true to form, makes sure every young lady at the party gets a kiss of appreciation. When a girl (Magdalena Dandourian) from the factory extends best wishes on behalf of the other workers, Schindler is too transfixed by her beauty to think of what he is doing when he gives her an extended smooch. A bit prolonged for comfort, it is not the length that unnerves certain party guests, but the fact that the young woman is Jewish. Quickly jumping in to cover the silence, the Rosner Brothers (Henry, on violin, played by Jacek Wójcicki; Leo, on accordion, by Piotr Polk) begin playing this noted Polish tune by Jerzy Petersburski, the title of which translates into "These Last Sundays" and which contains lines about lovers breaking up or parting. Perhaps the brothers realize if the Nazis have their way, Schindler will not be kissing any more Jewish girls in front of them again. Indeed, he is arrested for his behavior.

"Gute Nacht Mutter"

In a sequence that is almost too disturbing to bear witness to, the prisoners at the Plazskow labor camp are ordered to strip and parade themselves before the SS doctors for an "inspection" of sorts, to determine who is fit for work and who is too feeble or ill to continue being an asset to the Nazis and therefore doomed to perish. To provide a rather grotesque accompaniment to this terrible ritual, the Nazis play a gramophone record of Wilhelm Strienz's 1939 version of this sentimental song by German composer Walter Bochman and lyricist Erwin Lehnow, about a mother and son correspondence during the war. Strienz had become a favorite propaganda singer of the Nazis, performing on the radio and in films. The lyrics about the close bond between a parent and child are especially cruel in light of the Nazi's determination to destroy just such bonds.

"Mamataschi (Mommy Buy Me a Pony)"

Continuing to underscore their heinous acts with seemingly benign music, another recording is heard over the loudspeakers of the camp as the Jewish children are being ushered into trucks to be parted from their mothers. German cabaret singer Mimi Thoma, another favorite of the Third Reich, is heard singing this song about a child begging for a pony. The marching children of the camp innocently join in, suggesting they are familiar with the tune, which is meant to put them at ease and keep them ignorant of their fate.

"God Bless the Child"

So troubling have the circumstances become that Oskar Schindler can barely concentrate on making love to another beautiful woman. Leaving his latest nameless lady in the sack, Schindler stands contemplatively at the window as Billie Holiday's famous version of her own composition (written with Arthur Herzog Jr.) is heard. The lyrics remind us that those with money have lots of friends, as Schindler realizes he's got his share of cash and comes up with the heroic idea of buying his doomed factory workers from the Nazis.

"Yeroushalaim Shel Zahav (Jerusalem of Gold)"

In an audacious and moving transition, the freed Jews from Schindler's factory walk along in grateful happiness singing this song, the unofficial national anthem of Israel, about their desire to return to their homeland. Seen up to this point only in black and white, these characters then become their modern-day equivalents, in full color, as the song continues. The jump to the present makes it acceptable that Naomi Shemer's song wasn't around at the end of World War II, not having been written until 1967, as part of the celebration of Israel's nineteenth year of independence.

The Lost World: Jurassic Park

Piano Sonata No. 8 in C Minor, Op. 13 ("Pathétique") and Piano Sonata in A Minor, K. 310

Perhaps to show that John Hammond (Richard Attenborough) is a man of taste and refinement (when he's not genetically rebuilding dinosaurs), the above piano sonatas—the first by Beethoven, the latter by Mozart—are heard ever so faintly providing background music at his "creepy" Manhattan mansion to which Ian Malcolm (Jeff Goldblum) has been summoned. One assumes the pieces (performed by Jeno Jando) are coming from a stereo system of some sort.

"Tres Dias"

When the nastiest member of Roland Tembo's hunting party, Dieter Stark (Peter Stormare), decides during a break from trekking through the jungles that he is going to relieve himself elsewhere, he picks the wrong guy to tell. Carter (Thomas Rosales) has his headphones on and is listening to this Tomas Mendez song, as performed by Mariachi Los Camperos de Nati Cano. He is therefore oblivious to Stark's whereabouts, allowing the latter to be devoured by a persistent group of vicious "Compy" dinosaurs. Frankly, his demise was long overdue.

Fortunately, John Williams's soaring, stirring fanfare from the original film, present on such tracks from that movie's soundtrack as "Journey to the Island" and "Welcome to Jurassic Park," is heard during the final sequence of the dinosaurs thriving once again on the island and plays into the end titles.

Amistad

"Ya Weh"

Featured within the story are a series of West African chants of unknown origins that have been adapted for the movie by Sierra Leone historian Dr. Arthur Abraham and one of the film's producers, Debbie Allen. This particular song was heard being sung by the slaves aboard the *Amistad* after they have taken over the vessels, some of the women joyfully clapping in unison while they sing.

Andantino from Quartet No. 3 in G Major

Following their insurrection, Cinqué and the other slaves settle down for a long voyage home (or so they think), claiming their right to reside on deck after spending the trip over chained in the hold. In the fog of night, they are cautioned to be quiet as they hear the very unlikely sound of violins approaching. In a haunting moment, a ship passes by them, with a string quartet on board playing Giovanni Battista Viotti's lulling composition as the dining passengers wonder just who in hell is manning the other ship across the way, as silhouetted men, mostly shrouded

Cinqué (Djimon Hounsou) on his long-awaited voyage back home in *Amistad*.

in darkness, stare back at them. The juxtaposition between Cinqué and his fellow prisoners' ragged plight and the elegant evening sail seems almost surreal in its imbalance.

"Amazing Grace" and "I Love Thy Kingdom, Lord"

It appears that Cinqué and the other Africans have their share of supporters in America, only the prisoners don't quite interpret it that way. From behind bars, they see a group of nattily attired folks approach the prison and drop to their knees before singing a version of the traditional hymn. Cinqué's fellow prisoner Buakei (Derrick N. Ashong) decides that they must be entertainers, causing Cinqué to wonder, "But why do they look so miserable?" It's a wry comical moment to offset their bleak situation.

This religious group is later heard singing the second hymnal (music by Aaron Williams, with lyrics by Timothy Dwight) when Cinqué and his fellow captives insist on burying one of their men who has died, challenging the prison protocol.

"Dry Your Tears, Áfrika"

Requiring a rousing anthem to accompany the liberation of the Lomboko Slave Fortress and its eventual destruction by Captain Fitzgerald (Peter Firth) and his crew, John Williams took a 1967 poem by Ivorian writer Bernard Dadié, "Sèche Tes Pleurs," which was known in English as "Dry Your Tears, Áfrika," and set it to music. It was also translated from the original French lyrics into Mende, the language spoken by Cinqué and the other captives in the film. Sung by a chorus in so inspiring a fashion that it was also reprised in the closing credits, it certainly sent audiences out on an exulted high. It has been performed in concerts of Williams's music and remains one of his most thrilling and, unfortunately, least known film compositions.

Mezzo-soprano Pamela Dillard (who had been soloing during various choral pieces throughout the film) is heard singing a muted version of the piece over the haunting image of Cinqué standing majestically aboard ship as he returns home at last to Africa, as a title card informs us that all will not be as harmonious as he wants it to be.

Saving Private Ryan

"Solitude"

Although this Duke Ellington classic (known more commonly as "In My Solitude") tells of the suffering of lost love, its lyrics could just as easily apply to the despondency of being stuck in the middle of a war, dreaming of better days, "I sit in my chair/filled with despair/There's no one could be so sad." Private Mellish (Adam Goldberg) is heard murmuring the song softly to himself as he and his fellow soldiers continue their trek to find Private Ryan, sifting through a field of flowers, before the next hellish encounter with the enemy. We see the faces of some of the other men in deep thought, probably sharing that strange feeling of being among others and yet feeling absolutely alone.

"Tu es Partout" and "C'Était Une Historie D'Amour"

Amid the rubble of what's left of the French town of Ramelle, Captain Miller (Tom Hanks) and his squadron not only find Private Ryan (Matt Damon) but the serenity of music as well. A Victrola has somehow survived the beating the village has taken, and as the troops await the arrival of the German enemy they listen to France's most revered chanteuse, Edith Piaf, singing her 1941 recording of the tune "Tu Es Partout," which she wrote with Marguerite Monnot. This is an instance of a song not simply providing background but actually being commented on within the story. After Miller tells Ryan that it is Piaf whom they are hearing, Ryan wonders why she sounds so sad. Miller explains that according to the lyrics "Her lover left her, but she still sees his face everywhere she goes." (The song's title translates into "You're Everywhere.") The company's interpreter, Corporal Upham (Jeremy Davies), is very much taken by the song, trying to translate each line for his fellow soldiers and wanting them to feel it to the same degree that he does. Sgt. Horvath (Tom Sizemore), Pvt. Mellish, and Pvt. Reiben (Edward Burns) are less inclined to react with such naked appreciation and respond to Upham's enthusiasm with

Captain Miller (Tom Hanks) takes a moment away from his squad to reflect on the devastating situation in this scene from *Saving Private Ryan*.

just the sort of jokey cynicism and off-the-cuff dismissal to be expected within a group of non-coms possibly awaiting their own deaths.

The second melancholy Piaf number (by Henri Contet and Jean Jal; the title of which translates into "It Was a Love Story") is barely heard off in the distance as Ryan confesses to Miller that he somehow cannot see the faces of the three brothers he lost in battle. It is another lament of a lost love, which is only too perfect a comment on those whom Ryan has lost, and the wife Miller fears will lose him.

A.I. Artificial Intelligence

"The Garland Waltz"

Pyotr Ilyich Tchaikovsky's immortal waltz music from his 1890 ballet *The Sleeping Beauty* became even better known by twentieth-century movie audiences when it was featured in Walt Disney's 1959 animated feature *Sleeping Beauty*, with English lyrics by Sammy Fain and Jack Lawrence, and redubbed "Once Upon a Dream." In Spielberg's movie, Monica Swinton (France O'Connor) pipes the theme into her ten-year-old comatose son's incubation tube in hopes of reaching him, so there is a good chance the Disney version was her reason for the selection.

"I Only Have Eyes for You" (Harry Warren and Al Dubin), "Guys and Dolls" (Frank Loesser), and "Cheek to Cheek" (Irving Berlin)

For a robotic rent boy, Gigolo Joe (Jude Law) has great taste in music, at least as programmed into his system. As part of his seduction technique for his clients, Joe jerks his head to one side to play snatches of the above three tunes at different parts of the story. "I Only Have Eyes for You" has Dick Powell crooning from the 1934 Warner Bros. extravaganza *Dames*; "Guys and Dolls" features Stubby Kaye and Johnny Silver from the 1955 film adaptation of the Broadway hit of the same name; while "Cheek to Cheek" is performed by the inimitable Fred Astaire in one of his signature movies, *Top Hat* (1935).

"Dodo, l'enfant do"

This French lullaby (writer unknown) is sung by the FeMecha Nanny (Clara Bellar) who tries to comfort David (Haley Joel Osment) as they are being hoisted away in Lord Johnson-Johnson's balloon. The lyrics translate into such phrases as "the child will sleep quickly," which becomes more ominous considering they are being taken to the Flesh Fair.

"What About Us"

Needing a harsh sound for the gladiator-like atmosphere of the Flesh Fair sequence, Spielberg selected the industrial metal band Ministry to perform this tune (credited to group members Al Jourgensen, Paul Barker, and Max Brody, as well as Deborah Coon) onscreen, appearing on a stage in the arena. Barely audible in light of all the chaos and talking happening in the foreground, the song is a screech against oppression and conformity with lines like "You either kiss a lot of ass or tear the clock off the wall," but it's mostly there for background noise to give the scene the discordant and sinister feel it requires.

Der Rosenkavalier Suite, Op. 59

Stanley Kubrick had a preference for using established classical pieces or songs on the soundtracks of his movies; Steven Spielberg had a definite preference for John Williams's originals. Back when he was involved in the project, there was one moment in the film where Kubrick very specifically wanted to use classical music and that was for the entrance into Rouge City. The music in question was the waltz from the Richard Strauss's opera *Der Rosenkavalier*, so, in a nod to the late Kubrick's wishes, Williams incorporated it into his score as the car containing the accommodating teen drivers and their hitchhikers—David, Teddy, and Gigolo Joe—race over the bridge toward the "oral" tunnel.

Note: although the original soundtrack on Warner Bros. records contains two versions of the song "For Always" (performed by Lara Fabian, and then reprised by her and Josh Groban), with lyrics by Cynthia Weil and music by John Williams, it was not used in the completed film.

Minority Report

Symphony No. 8 in B Minor, D. 759, First Movement ("Unfinished") and Symphony No. 6 in B Minor, Op. 74 ("Pathétique")

As part of the procedure for determining the location of an upcoming killing, Pre-Crime Officer John Anderton (Tom Cruise) watches images loaded into a ball from the Pre-Cogs's visions. Using hand gestures not unlike those of a conductor, it is only fitting that Anderton's session is underscored by classical music. His composition of choice is Franz Schubert's Symphony No. 8, which became better known as the "Unfinished Symphony." Happily, John brings his joy of music home with him. As he enters his apartment from his transport bay, he lets his interactive tech system know that he's home, which instantly floods the apartment with the strains of Pitor Ilyich Tchaikovsky's Symphony No. 6.

"Pines and Oats"

This annoying commercial ditty is being sung directly to Anderton from the cereal box as he munches on the food, about to look at projected images of his late son. He can only take so much of Guy Moon and Bob Kurtz's tune before he tosses the box across the room.

"Jesus, Joy of Man's Desiring"

In a macabre, Phantom of the Opera-like touch, Pre-Crime's Department of Containment is run by Gideon (Tim Blake Nelson), who likes the play this Bach piece on his pipe organ, which he claims "relaxes the prisoners." The comatose prisoners happen to be entombed inside of creepy glass cylinders, making the idea of "relaxation" of any kind a moot point.

Menuet, from String Quartet in C Major, Op. 4 No. 1

Love of the classics extends to the creator of Pre-Crime, Dr. Iris Hineman (Lois Smith). When fugitive John Anderton, now on the run from his own organization, scales the wall of the Doctor's garden in hopes that she can help him, he is stung by her living vines. As she administers an antidote to the increasingly woozy officer, this gentle minuet by Joseph Haydn is heard playing in her greenhouse.

"Små grodorna"

This Swedish ditty (from unknown composers) is traditionally sung at midsummer as part of the maypole ritual. The title translates into "The Little Frogs." In the ratty doctor's office where Anderton had come to have his eyes swapped, the doc's (Peter Stormare) enthusiastic medical assistant, Miss Van Eyck (Caroline Lagerfelt) sings it in her native Swedish in anticipation of the operation. There is a reference in the lyrics to the frog having no ears, whereas Anderton will soon have no eyes.

John Anderton (Tom Cruise) knows Pre-Cog Agatha (Samantha Morton) holds the key to the murder he is predicted to commit in *Minority Report*.

"Bad Boys"

Confined in a dismal flophouse, waiting under bandages for his eyes to heal after an illegal operation, Anderton wakes up to rancid food and the strains of "Bad Boys." This 1987 song performed by a Jamaican reggae group called Inner Circle (and written by band member Ian Lewis) became the theme of the "reality" patrol series *Cops*, which is among the images playing on the large television screen in Anderton's shabby apartment.

"Solitude" and "Moon River"

There's hope for the future of retail, at least musically. When Anderton drops by a local Gap to pick up a more suitable set of clothes for his abducted Pre-Cog, Agatha (Samantha Morton), he is at first bombarded by personalized ads. However, once in the store, Billie Holiday's rendition of "Solitude" plays over the intercom system. It was written in 1934 by Duke Ellington, with lyrics by Eddie DeLange and Irving Mills, and was already used by Spielberg, four years earlier, in *Saving Private Ryan*.

When John is pursued by the Pre-Crime team into (presumably) a different mall, this time with Agatha along to give him helpful premonitions to elude the police, Henry Mancini's lovely music from the soundtrack of *Breakfast at Tiffany's*, playing the instrumental version of the classic song "Moon River," is heard.

Catch Me If You Can

"Catch Me If You Can" Theme

In a delightfully plucky mode, John Williams's title theme to the film gets things off to a rollicking start, using a progressive jazz sound, miles from the customary soaring anthems and fanfares usually associated with him. Played over Oliver Kuntzel's evocative title illustrations of stick figures and inching lines, there is a playful, sneaky staccato flavor to the piece that suggests the cat-and-mouse game of the storyline.

"To Tell the Truth"

Catch Me If You Can seizes the audience's attention instantly by opening with actual footage of Frank Abagnale Jr.'s 1977 appearance on the syndicated version of the venerable game show *To Tell the Truth*, interspersing clips of Leonardo DiCaprio and re-recorded dialogue along with the real deal. Heard playing over the scene is the wonderfully groovy theme song with the silly lyrics ("I'm blowing my cool right now/For you, to tell the truth") as the contestants are introduced. In the actual episode, the music was *not* played under the intros, but it was probably too hard to resist including it, simply to set the mood of the time. The music for the song was by Charles Fox, while those lyrics were the joint effort of Robert A. Israel and the show's producer, Paul Alter, only these two men being listed in the end credits.

More than any of Spielberg's other films, *Catch Me* features a whole slew of pop songs on the soundtrack to set the mood. Among them are:

"Embraceable You"

A happy moment in the Abagnale household takes place at Christmas, when Frank Jr. is seen dancing with his mother (Nathalie Baye) in the living room to the strains of Judy Garland's Decca recording of this Gershwin standard, which she had sung in her 1943 movie *Girl Crazy*. Frank Sr. (Christopher Walken) cuts in to show his son how a *real* smoothy can dance, Walken having done just that early in his Broadway theater career. Later, the same Garland recording is heard when Frank Jr. witnesses his fiancée's parents (Martin Sheen and Nancy Lenehan) swaying to it together in the kitchen. The song makes the transition from this scene to that of Frank Sr. sitting alone in his corner bar (presumably the tune is on the jukebox), it no longer being the happy memory it had once been.

"Put Your Head on My Shoulder"

If Judy brings the sunshine, the Lettermen bring the rain. It is their recording of Paul Anka's 1959 song that is playing when Frank Jr. returns home and stumbles upon the illicit rendezvous of his mother and her lover, Jack Barnes (James Brolin).

Since this sequence is supposed to be happening in 1964, it predates the actual Lettermen record, which was released in 1968.

"Body and Soul" and "I've Got the World on a String"

Frank Jr. invites his dad to a posh New York dining establishment (with chilled salad forks no less!) in order to bestow upon him the keys to a 1965 Cadillac DeVille, but the old man doesn't want to be helped and therefore admit defeat. Filling the background is jazzman Erroll Garner's skittering piano rendition of Johnny Green, Edward Heyman, Robert Sour, and Frank Eyton's 1930 song "Body and Soul." As Walken displays his range in a standout scene that no doubt ensured him his Oscar nomination for his performance, the background music switches over to Harold Arlen and Ted Koehler's "I've Got the World on a String."

"Take the A Train"

Frank Jr.'s pursuer is firmly established as a traditional, old-fashioned, by-the-books kind of guy, so his taste in music is not about to encompass the present day. This is evident from the fact that Billy Stayhorn's big band chestnut "Take the A Train" is playing on the radio as FBI agent Carl Hanratty (Tom Hanks) drives his unwanted assistants Tom Fox (Frank John Hughes) and Paul Morgan (Steve Eastin) through Hollywood, while hoping to trap their slippery prey.

"The Girl from Ipanema"

If you've got to include select numbers that exemplify the smooth and loose vibe of the decade, this bossa nova jazz track by saxophonist Stan Getz with vocals by Brazilian singer Astrud Gilberto certainly fits the bill. A 1964 hit (written by Antonio Carlos Jobim), it reached number five on the *Billboard* charts and ended up with the Grammy for Record of the Year. It is heard in the film as Hanratty and his team show up at the Tropicana Hotel to ask questions about a bum check, only to be pleasantly surprised when they learn Frank Abagnale is still on the premises.

"The Look of Love"

One of the great sultry sixties songs, this is heard during the scene in which a high class call girl (Jennifer Garner) makes herself very available to Frank in his hotel room, their fun contrasted with Carl spending the night waiting for his things to spin and dry at a laundromat. Probably too hard to resist for setting the mood, one could forgive the anachronism, since this tune was not yet around at the time, 1965, that the events were unfolding on screen. Burt Bacharach and Hal David wrote it for Dusty Springfield to sing in the outlandish James Bond spoof *Casino Royale* in 1967.

"Mele Kalikimaka"

Perhaps to show that Carl Hanratty just can't get with the times, even when it comes to his Christmas music, this kitschy number, recorded by Bing Crosby and the Andrews Sisters back in 1949 (written by Robert Alex Anderson), is heard playing on the radio when Frank calls the FBI agent on a lonely Christmas Eve night.

"He's So Fine"

Sitting in a café trying to figure out Frank's next move, Carl is inadvertently tipped off to some important information by a friendly waiter (Jeremy Howard). Having been introduced by Frank as "Barry Allen," the name, scribbled down on a pad by Carl, is spotted by the waiter, who figures Carl to be a fan of the comic book *The Flash*, insomuch as the hero is called Barry Allen. This leads Carl to conclude that his prey might be younger than he realizes. While this scene unfolds, the Chiffons'

Frank Abagnale Jr. (Leonardo DiCaprio) leads his bevy of lovely new stewardesses into the airport to the strains of Frank Sinatra's "Come Fly with Me" in *Catch Me If You Can*.

rendition of "He's So Fine," their 1963 Top 5 hit plays. Written by Ronald Mack, this is the song George Harrison would later wish he'd never heard.

"You Really Got Me"

At the hipster Riverbend Apartments in Atlanta, it's party time all the time. Frank, wearing his orange Italian knit shirt, is hosting such a bash while this 1964 Kinks hit (written by band member Ray Davies) is heard coming from Frank's reel-to-reel audio system.

"Un Poco Adagio" from Piano Concert No. II in D

Things get a bit more highfalutin over at the Strong estate, when Brenda (Amy Adams) brings Frank to meet her parents. Dinner, which includes Frank falling back on his dad's famous "two mice fell in a bucket of cream" analogy as a substitute for grace, is backed by a Joseph Haydn piece performed by the Norwegian Chamber Orchestra.

"Has Anybody Here Seen Kelly?"

In one of the film's most subtly charming moments, Frank is initially startled to see how seriously Brenda and her parents (Martin Sheen and Nancy Lenehan) take their viewing of the weekly variety series *Sing Along with Mitch*. Following Mitch Miller's lead and chiming in on the lyrics as they appear on the bottom of the TV screen, the three of them happily sing this tune by C. W. Murphy and Will Letters from the British music halls of days gone by (1908). Although Frank is bemused at first by this corny display of emotion, he himself is won over by the good spirits of the whole thing and the family bonding it represents, being more than a bit envious. In spite of himself, he joins the Strongs in the song. Although the series (1961–1964) had left the air by the time the events in the film were happening, it did pop back up on NBC during the summer of 1966.

"The Way You Look Tonight"

During the scene in which Frank Jr. finds his lonesome dad nursing drinks at his usual bar, having been forced to take a job as a mailman, the Lettermen's version of the 1936 Oscar-winning standard by Dorothy Fields and Jerome Kern (originally introduced by Fred Astaire) is now heard on the jukebox, once Judy Garland has finished singing "Embraceable You." Would it be a stretch to say the irony of Frank Sr. becoming a letter carrier is underscored by hearing the Lettermen? Probably.

"I'll Be Home for Christmas"

Another lonely Christmas, another call from Frank to Carl. While the latter is once again at the FBI office, Frank is nursing his sorrows in a bar. This wistful lament from World War II (written by Walter Kent, Kim Gannon, and Buck Ram, and already featured in Spielberg's *1941*) is heard on the radio, via the easy listening sounds of the Hollyridge Strings.

"I Can't Give You Anything but Love" and "I'm Shooting High"

Things are momentarily happy for Frank and Brenda as their wedding reception takes place in the backyard of the Strong family mansion. Ellis Hall (a protégé of Ray Charles) is heard singing from the bandstand Jimmy McHugh and Dorothy Fields's wonderful 1928 standard "I Can't Give You Anything but Love" before Carl Hanratty and his team show up and Frank once again flees. Although Ellis gets a close-up while singing the second song (this time McHugh collaborating with Ted Koehler), "I'm Shooting High" (first heard in 1936), most of this number is muffled by Frank trying to explain his predicament to his confused bride.

"Leaving on a Jet Plane"

For his latest scam, Frank auditions some lovely high school girls to be his personal "posse" of stewardesses. During the montage of auditions, one of the stews sings this 1966 song written by John Denver but made famous by Peter, Paul and Mary.

"Come Fly with Me"

Once the bevy of stewardesses has been selected, Spielberg gives us a sprightly image of Frank linking arms with his selected ladies as they approach the airport terminal, and the anthem of the airwaves—Frank Sinatra's peerless rendition of this 1957 Jimmy Van Heusen and Sammy Cahn tune—is heard.

"Peuple Fidèle" and "Les Anges Dans No Campagnes"

Christmas Eve, 1967, Montrichard. As Carl tracks Frank down to a printing office in this small French town, he walks past a church in the square from which comes the sounds of a chorus singing two notable carols, but with their French lyrics, of course. The first being the tune alternately known as "Adeste Fidelis" and "O Come all Ye Faithful," the latter the original name (it being French in origin) of what Americans think of as "Angels We Have Heard on High."

"The Christmas Song"

One last Yule tune is heard in the film after Frank makes his daring "toilet" escape from an airplane and hightails it to the new home where his mother now resides with her second husband. Looking through the window at what appears to be the perfect family holiday gathering he has longed to return to, Nat King Cole's immortal recording of Mel Tormé and Robert Wells's "The Christmas Song" (known by many through its opening line, "Chestnuts roasting on an open fire") is heard coming from within.

The Terminal

"The Tale of Viktor Navorski"

Going for an Eastern European sound with a clarinet the predominant instrument, John Williams gives the protagonist of Steven Spielberg's gentle comedy-drama the theme he deserves, a bouncy, slightly cheeky, but comforting piece that has a traveling sound, ironically, as Viktor Navorski (Tom Hanks) himself cannot go anywhere. It is first heard as Viktor goes through his ritual of washing and getting rejected by the immigration staff, and it plays most prominently during the closing credits, as each cast member and several behind-the-scenes principals offer their signatures, a nod to the plotline involving the signature of jazz musician Benny Golson.

"Strangers in the Night" and "Theme from 'A Summer Place'"

You'd think that a movie set almost entirely in an airport terminal would have *muzak* pouring out of its ears, but Steve Spielberg spares us that. In fact, it is the protagonist, Viktor Navorski who spares us. Sentenced to months making a "home" at lonely Gate 67, Viktor is ready to prepare his sleeping place and settle in, but not before he does something about the muzak wafting throughout the terminal sound speakers. The songs we hear are two of the immortal instrumental standards: Bert Kaempfert's "Strangers in the Night" (from the 1966 Universal comedy *A Man Could Get Killed*) and Max Steiner's "Theme from 'A Summer Place'" (from the 1959 Warner Bros. drama). The former is performed by a studio group known as Strings Unlimited, the latter by a similar prefab gathering called Starlite Orchestra. Finding the switch box, Viktor pulls the plug on the processed music.

"I Love New York"

As Viktor makes his most sincere effort to hand in the correct forms and give them to immigration employee Dolores Torres (Zoë Saldana), this ubiquitous tune (a catchphrase, really) that had served to promote New York as the ultimate tourist destination since 1977 is heard and glimpsed on a television screen hanging in the lounge area. Tony Randall gets the main spotlight in the ad, singing about a pepper in a grocery store, followed by flashes of the cast of *Bring in Da Noise, Bring in Da Funk*, the Rockettes, and others. Steve Karmen is the credited composer.

"The Glory of Love"

In the otherwise tuneless terminal, one song actually pops up as Viktor is trying to endure yet another meal of crackers and mustard in the food court. Blues singer Big Bill Broonzy's rendition of Bill Hill's 1936 standard is heard playing as Viktor mistakenly believes the airline stewardess with whom he is smitten, Amelia Warren

(Catherine Zeta-Jones), to be waving enthusiastically to him upon her return, when in fact it is her lover, Max (Michael Nouri), to whom she is signaling.

Krakozhia Anthem

When Peace comes at last to Krakozhia, Viktor is seen celebrating at a branch of Daily Grill with Mulroy (Chi McBride) and the patrons at the restaurant, singing the Krakozhian anthem atop a table with great enthusiasm and a drink in his hand. In so much as Krakozhia is a fictional country, the piece needed to be written for the movie. John Williams, of course, is behind the music, the theme having been heard earlier in the film on a television news report. The lyricist, however, receives no mention in the final credits.

"Killer Joe"

Receiving a temporary visa from Amelia, Viktor can at last travel into Manhattan and fulfill his dream: to meet jazz saxophonist Benny Golson and get his signature, therefore completing Viktor's father's project. The real Golson is on hand to perform his own tune, "Killer Joe," of which the beginning is heard as Viktor sits listening in the Lobby Lounge at a Ramada Inn on Lexington Avenue. Golson, seventy-five at the time the movie was filmed, was indeed in the famous photo that triggers Viktor's quest, a portrait of fifty-seven famous jazz musicians taken on August 12, 1958, in front of a brownstone at 17 East 126th Street in Harlem.

War of the Worlds

"Flatline"

In order to demonstrate that Ray's teen son Robbie (Justin Chatwin) is yet another one of those surly, uncommunicative, and self-entitled angry children of divorce that the cinema specializes in, the boy hides from the world by wearing his headphones and listening to this 2004 tune by the alternative rock band Aphasia. "Breathe in, don't flatline" is the oft repeated refrain. Band members Jeffrey Scott Harber, Jayce Alexander Basques, William Peng, and Drew DeHaven Hall are the credited writers.

"If I Ruled the World"

Desperate to cross the Hudson River to keep making their way north to Boston, Ray (Tom Cruise) and his family arrive at a ferry depot mobbed with people on the run from the aliens. In a bizarre touch, as the crowd files onto the boat, a loudspeaker plays Tony Bennett's version of this Cyril Ornadel-Leslie Bricusse tune from the 1963 West End musical *Pickwick*. Bennett recorded the song in 1965, the year the show came to Broadway, and made it part of the title of his LP: *If I Ruled*

A crashed plane in a New Jersey backyard? Ray Ferrier (Tom Cruise) observes the wreckage in this scene from *War of the Worlds*.

the World: Tony Bennett Sings for the Jet Set. This would have to be an example of sly Spielbergian humor, trying to calm the anxious citizens with easy listening and yet choosing the very number the aliens might relate to, had they Bennett LPs on their stereos in space. Right on cue, the tripod terrorists appear on the hill above, causing more widespread panic in another sequence staged magnificently by the director.

"Little Deuce Coupe" and "Hushabye Mountain"

Taking refuge from the rampaging spacemen in a farmhouse cellar already inhabited by nutty Harlan Ogilvy (Tim Robbins), Ray has trouble fulfilling his daughter Rachel's (Dakota Fanning) request to comfort her with either Brahms's "Lullaby" (which she refers to as "Lullaby and Goodnight") or "Hushabye Mountain." To placate her, he falls back on music more familiar to himself, the Beach Boys' "Little Deuce Coupe" (by Brian Wilson and Roger Christian; from the 1963 album of the same name). Later, when Ray realizes he has to dispose of their increasingly unhinged host, he wraps a blindfold around Rachel and asks her to sing the song he didn't know. She complies, giving her rendition of "Hushabye Mountain" (written by Richard B. and Robert M. Sherman for the 1968 movie musical *Chitty Chitty Bang Bang*) as her dad does the dirty deed in the next room.

Munich

"Remembering Munich"

John Williams begins the film with a haunting bit of original music (with lyrics and vocals by Lisbeth Scott) sung in Hebrew as the Universal and DreamWorks logos fade into the title and the night of the Munich massacre. From this point, Williams's frequent, pulsating, ominous theme takes over as the terrorists scale the fence and make their way to the apartment block and carry out one of the more shocking events of modern history. "Remembering Munich" is heard again, most startlingly, later in the story after Avner (Eric Bana) has moved to Brooklyn and what he hopes will be a peaceful existence. But the thoughts of the Munich massacre haunt him, and as he attempts to make love to his wife Daphna (Ayelet Zurer), the song plays on the soundtrack, as Spielberg crosscuts between their disturbed efforts to find pleasure with the senselessness of the slaughter.

"Hatikvah"

Following the murders of the Olympic athletes, a stunned Avner sits watching the news report on television of the bodies being returned to Israel, in preparation for the funeral. An instrumental version of the national anthem of Israel (which translates into "The Hope") plays from the television screen and over the reading of the names of the victims for a very stirring tribute to the fallen. The music derives from an Italian song by Giuseppe Cenci called "La Mantovana."

"Ain't No Sunshine"

Reconnecting with his friend Andreas (Moritz Bleibtreu) in order to get some information on Avner's terrorist targets, the two men and Andros's German girlfriend Yvonne (Meret Becker) sit around a grounded chandelier (a great visual touch) in a vast, darkened apartment, smoking grass as Yvonne expounds (in German) on the danger of free will. To further set the mood, Bill Withers's hit single (which had topped off at number three on the *Billboard* charts in 1971) is playing in the background. It's the song everyone remembers—the one where the vocalist sings "I know, I know, I know, I know . . ." repeatedly.

"My Girl"

Having successfully carried out their first revenge killing on Wael Zwaiter (Makram Khoury) in the lobby of his apartment building, Avner and his team meet at a plaza in Rome for some celebrating (or rejoicing, depending on the team member). Wafting over the plaza is the Temptations' first number one hit and signature tune, "My Girl," but not the familiar US version. The 1964 tune (written by group members Smokey Robinson and Ronald White) was later recorded by the group in Italian under the name "Solamente Lei" (Italian lyrics by Paolo Dossena) two years later.

"Clowns"

Posing as a journalist, Robert (Mathieu Kassovitz) gets access to the Paris apartment of the team's next target, Mahmoud Hamshari (Igal Naor), sneaking away to jot down the telephone serial number, allowing him and his fellow assassins to rig the instrument and place an explosive call at a later time. Just to emphasize the danger of their mission, Hamshari's daughter Amina (Mouna Soualem) enters the room to sit at the piano and practice this piece by Dmitri Kabalevsky.

"Papa Was a Rollin' Stone"

It's on to Cyprus and back to the Temptations, as Carl (Ciarán Hinds) and Steve (Daniel Craig) sit in a car awaiting the arrival of Hussein Abad al-Chir (Mostefa Djadjam), who will soon be dispatched with a bomb that has some jarring effects on the couple taking the hotel room next door. Steve is relaxed, but Carl is not, so after the former sings a few lines of the tune (written by Barrett Strong and Norman Whitfield), the latter tells Steve to shut up. The dates of the assassination are not clear, but this song had only just arrived at the top of the US *Billboard* charts in October of 1972.

"Black Magic Woman"

Against the wishes of their Moussad contact, Ephraim (Geoffrey Rush), Avner and his team head to Beirut, eager to wipe out three of the men responsible for the Munich attack in one fell swoop. As four rafts manned by Sayeret Matkal commandos make for the docks at night in order to team up with Avner and company, an anonymous band performs Santana's 1970 hit in Arabic. The gentle enjoyment of people dancing the night away to music creates an innocent background to the mayhem soon about to erupt. The sequence also adds a bizarre touch insomuch as select members of the commandos disrobe in order to disguise themselves as women.

"Des millions d'amoureux"

Meeting up once again in Paris with Louis (Mathieu Amalric), who has been giving him leads on his targets, Avner is invited to see "Papa," the head of this "secret" organization. As Louis's car pulls up we hear French singer Georgette Lemaire's 1969 rendition of this tune (by Franck Barcellini and Pascal Bilat) playing on the radio. The title translates into "Millions of Lovers," so there does not appear to be any statement being made on the action, just on Louis's taste in music.

"El Tahmilla," "Never on Sunday," and "Let's Stay Together"

Believing that Louis has secured them their own safe house for their Athens assignment, Avner and his team are shocked to find out that they must share their digs with four Palestinian members of the PLO. Avner and his men pass themselves off as a Basque terrorist group in order to hide their identity and keep the peace. Their differences are evident, however, when it comes to music. One Palestinian's decision to listen to the traditional Egyptian piece "El Tahmilla" on the radio is quickly quashed by Steve, who turns the dial over to hear some Greek music, although it's not just any Greek music but a song familiar to American movie fans: Melina Mercouri's rendition of Manos Hatzidakis's Oscar-winning "Never on Sunday" from the 1960 movie of the same name. Apparently, not a fan of the tune, or at least the Greek version, the Palestinian dials the radio back to "El Tahmilla" until Steve intervenes once again, this time choosing an American station that is playing Al Green's appropriately named 1971 number one hit, "Let's Stay Together." The tune continues its ironic statement as Avner and the Palestinian leader, Ali (Omar Metwally), argue over the Arab-Israeli conflict.

"Prelude to a Kiss" and "But Beautiful"

In the bar of the Hotel Europa in London, it seems at first that Avner has settled down for a moment of peace, but this is not that kind of film. One of Spielberg's most masterful touches is how he manages to maintain a feeling of dread and danger lurking around even the most seemingly harmless corner. Down the bar from Avner is a beautiful lady (the "Local Honey Trap" as he refers to her later) eager to get him upstairs and into bed. The music filling the bar is Stan Getz's

Robert (Mathieu Kassovitz) and Avner (Eric Bana) scope out the target for their next hit in this scene from *Munich*.

1951 recording of the Duke Ellington/Irving Gordon/Irving Mills composition from 1936 "Prelude to a Kiss." But this is *not* a prelude to a kiss as far as Avner is concerned, as he wisely rejects the tempting offer. Carl is not so fortunate and drifts into the bar and into the lair of a woman who turns out to be a Dutch assassin named Janette (Marie-Josée Croze). The song now playing, via Getz, is "But Beautiful," which Johnny Burke and Jimmy Van Heusen had written back in 1947 for Bing Crosby to sing in *Road to Rio*. Bing fared better that time out than Carl does here.

Indiana Jones and the Kingdom of the Crystal Skull

"Hound Dog," "Howdy Doody Theme," "Wake Up Little Susie," "Little Bitty Pretty One," and "Shake, Rattle, and Roll"

The 1957 setting for the fourth Indy adventure gave Steven Spielberg an opportunity to tap into the world of rock 'n' roll for part of the film's soundtrack. To this end, a number of familiar tunes that made the era what it was are on hand.

Elvis Presley's 1956 rendition of Jerry Leiber and Mike Stoller's "Hound Dog" is heard in the opening credit sequence, coming from the car radio as a group of thrill-seeking teens challenge what they assume are American soldiers to some daredevil driving. Being that they are really Russians and the plot's villains, they take them up on the challenge.

Looking for a place to hide out from the pursuing Russians, Indiana Jones (Harrison Ford) takes shelter in what he thinks at first to be a typically bland, prefab suburban neighborhood. What could be more all-American than a family lined up on the couch watching *Howdy Doody*? Only the family consists of mannequins, and this is a nuclear testing site about to be incinerated. The theme song (better known as "It's Howdy Doody Time"), coming from the television set, is real, however. It was an adaptation of the old vaudeville tune "Ta! Ra! Ra! Boom de Ay!" (original composer disputed) with new lyrics by the show's head writer Edward Kean. The star of the series, "Buffalo" Bob Smith, is given credit onscreen here despite Kean being the designated lyricist. The clip shown on the television set is in black and white, although the series was actually made available in color by this point in time. No doubt the government found it pointless to provide their fake family with a color set only to have it nuked.

Once Indy hooks up with young Mutt Williams (Shia LaBeouf), they sit at a typical 1950s teen hangout, a malt shop, where they discuss the disappearance of Professor Oxley and the legend of the kingdom of Akator. The background for this exposition is at first the Everly Brothers' most famous recording, "Wake Up Little Susie" (by Boudleaux and Felice Bryant), which hit the top of the charts that year in September. After a break for some dramatic John Williams music, another song is heard from the juke box, Bobby Day's "Little Bitty Pretty One." Although this was his own composition (credited under his real name, Robert Byrd) and he recorded a version that year with his band, the Satellites, the song reached the charts during the fall via Thurston Harris.

A family chase through the jungle, with Mutt Williams (Shia LaBeouf), Indiana Jones (Harrison Ford), and Marion Ravenwood (Karen Allen), in *Indiana Jones and the Kingdom of the Crystal Skull*.

Finally, once Mutt takes Indy for a feverish motorcycle chase through the streets of New Haven, one of the pioneering recordings of the genre, "Shake, Rattle, and Roll," by Bill Haley & His Comets, is heard on the soundtrack.

"A Solas," "Uri Balki, "and "Maja Galobuschka"

Once it's off to Peru, the fun period music stops. In Nazca, Indy and Mutt visit the mad house where Oxley had recently been an occupant, and they are shown his vacated but graffiti-ridden cell by a nun. In order to soothe the other occupants of the ward, a Victrola plays a record of "A Solas" by Juan Arvizu. Judging from the behavior of the inmates, it isn't working.

After Indy and Mutt are captured by the traitorous Mac (Ray Winstone) and his Russian cohorts and are taken up river to Ilha Aramaca, the villains cavort and dance around a bonfire to the strains of the traditional "Uri Balki." Because Professor Oxley (John Hurt) has pretty much lost his mind by this stage, he is first seen kicking up some dust with his captives during this sequence, although now the piece has changed to "Maja Galobuschka."

The Adventures of Tintin

While John Williams's music over the opening credits might bear too close a resemblance to his similar "sneaky" piece written to accompany the titles of *Catch Me If You Can*, there are many pleasures to be found in his score here. Appropriately rousing, it complements the motion-capture animation adventure perfectly. The exciting music to accompany Sir Francis Haddock's duel with the wicked Red Rackham, as the latter attempts to explode the ship with gunpowder is perhaps the score's highlight, heard on the soundtrack under the title "Red Rackham's Curse and the Treasure."

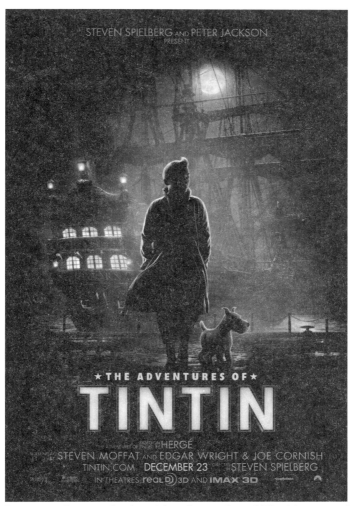

Some moody artwork advertising the coming of *The Adventures of Tintin* in 3D.

"Loch Lomond"

Outside of the original underscoring there are only a few opportunities for additional, traditional pieces. Our first sound of Captain Haddock coming from a porthole above a kidnapped Tintin is a famous song. Although it's quite hard to make out what in heaven's name the well-inebriated seaman is singing, it turns out to be the legendary Scottish folk tune from 1841. The song was selected for a very good reason, since, in the Hergé stories, Loch Lomond eventually became the boozy Haddock's whisky of choice.

Concert for Strings in F Major, R.V. 136 (Andante) and Rosina's Cavatina

There is a concert being held at the Sheik's palace, starring imperious opera grand dame Bianca Castafiore, known as "The Milanese Nightingale." When we are first introduced to the gathering audience and a glimpse of the Sheik's coveted ship model in its bulletproof glass case, Antonio Vivaldi's Concert for Strings in F Major is heard on the soundtrack, to set the elegant mood. As the Nightingale enters for her performance, Gioachino Rossini's instrumental introduction to "Rosina's Cavatina" from *The Barber of Seville* is played, but this does not lead to the aria itself.

"Ah, je veux vivre"

The aria being sung by Bianca is from Charles Gounod's *Roméo et Juliette* (libretto by Jules Barbier and Michel Carré), and it's not just there for atmosphere, to show off how cultured the filmmakers are or to make certain kids in the audience restless. Turns out the evil Professor Sakharine has made sure that the songbird will hit notes high enough to shatter the glass encasing the model ship he so fervently desires. And she does! So, Sakharine's falcon swoops in to snatch the desired scroll within the model, and the chase continues. The lady providing the high notes is celebrated soprano Renée Fleming. (It is worth noting that in the original Tintin adventures, Bianca's aria of choice is not this one but "The Jewel Song" from *Faust*.)

War Horse

"The Scarlet and the Blue"

This song ties the movie directly to the National Theatre production of Michael Morpurgo's book, as it was written for the stage version of the story by John Tams and Adrian Sutton. It is heard, in an abbreviated form, being sung by the villagers who have just enlisted for the Great War and have psyched themselves into believing they are marching off to something wonderful and victorious. The events about to unfold will show us that war is anything but.

"Roses of Picardy"

This tune, with music by Haydn Wood and lyrics by the very same fellow who had written "Danny Boy," Frederick E. Weatherly, became very popular among British soldiers during the First World War. It tells of an undying love, which perhaps served as an inspiration for men facing a possibly tragic future, and makes it very fitting to include here. It is celebrated Irish tenor John McCormack who is heard singing the song on a phonograph being played by Captain Nicholls (Tom Hiddleston) in the officers' study on the eve of a battle that will not turn out well for the British. Because the title card that follows this scene informs us that the year is 1914, the inclusion of this song is a bit off as far as accuracy is concerned. It was not published for another two years, while McCormick's recording did not come about until 1919, by which point the war was, thankfully, over.

"Blue Bonnets over the Border"

Albert (Jeremy Irvine) is geographically closer to his beloved horse Joey than he realizes when he is sent to the trenches in France, presumably fighting in the Battle of the Somme, although that famous altercation took place in 1916 and the title

A boy and his horse: Albert Narracott (Jeremy Irvine) shows his love for his beloved Joey in this scene from *War Horse*.

card here informs us that it is 1918. In any event, Albert and the other soldiers are ordered to climb out of their muddy, rat-infested trenches and run headlong into the battlefield and oncoming gunfire. The alternative to those turning back? Certain death. A bagpiper (Callum Armstrong) is there to inspire these nervous young fighters, although how often this tactic worked to instill heroics is open for debate. Perhaps more often than not it was used as a way of insuring the men ran from the trenches, to get away from the squealing noise of the instrument. Being played is a traditional Scottish piece, "Blue Bonnets over the Border," which was written about Bonnie Prince Charlie's 1745 march into England and did not refer to a lady's headgear but to a beret.

Lincoln

John Williams's score for this film is among his most subtle, from his gentle piano piece that underscores Lincoln's (Daniel Day-Lewis) horseback visit to the battlefield of Petersburg as he rides silently among the fallen, to his mournful trumpet elegy as Lincoln's devoted servant William Slade (Stephen McKinley Henderson) watches the President walk down the White House corridor in solitude, on his way to the theater, and into history.

"We are Coming, Father Abra'am"

Following his brief speech at a flag-raising, Lincoln is cheered on as the crowd sings this song, giving him a tremendous, almost religious stature in the eyes of his followers. James Sloan Gibbons's 1862 poem, written as a rallying cry to fight the Civil War ("we are coming, Father Abra'am, three hundred thousand more"), had been adapted to music by several composers, this one—Stephen Foster—being the most famous of his day.

Quintet No. 1 in B-Flat Major, K. 174

This Mozart piece provides the soothing backdrop as the Lincolns receive their guests at the White House Grand Reception of January 15, 1865. The music underscores the main body of the scene, in which Mrs. Lincoln (Sally Field) gives Chairman of the House Ways and Means Committee Thaddeus Stevens (Tommy Lee Jones) a piece of her mind about him nosing into her household accounts.

"Three Forks of Hell" and "Last of Sizemore"

Lobbyist W. N. Bilbo (James Spader) does his best to sway Congressman (and "The Postmaster of Millersburg, Ohio") Clay Hawkins (Walton Goggins) to vote in favor of the Thirteenth Amendment, but the nervous fellow has just been branded a traitor by the Democrats. He therefore leaves Bilbo feeling like the cause is lost as the lobbyist trails him relentlessly, out in the woods, reminding him that he'd

Daniel Day-Lewis in his Oscar-winning role as the sixteenth president in *Lincoln*.

already committed to the cause. The traditional banjo piece "Three Forks of Hell" (composer unknown) plays under the scene.

In the next scene, a worried Bilbo complains to Secretary of State Seward (David Strathairn) that efforts to secure votes have nearly gotten him killed, leading to one of the movie's comical moments, when Congressmen Harold Hollister (Michael Ruff) pulls a gun on Bilbo but fails to shoot him. Also underscoring for humorous effect, another banjo piece (also arranged by Jim Taylor and uncredited to a composer), "Last of Sizemore," is heard.

"O Nuit d'Amour!"

Having lost the fight to keep their oldest son Robert (Joseph Gordon-Levitt) from enlisting, Mary Lincoln throws further guilt on her husband by telling him he'd best make sure he gets the Thirteenth Amendment passed and thereby put an end to the war. As is too often the case in movies, this conversation goes on while the speakers are supposed to be giving their attention to the theatrical presentation in front of them, a version of *Faust* (by Charles Gounod, first performed in Paris six years before the events here). The singers portraying Faust and Marguerite are tenor John Bellemer and soprano Mary Dunleavy, respectively. Playing with our expectations, Spielberg makes this the one time in the movie we see the Lincolns sitting up in a theatre box, the famous assassination instead brilliantly dramatized via the reaction of their young son, Tad (Gulliver McGrath), sitting in his own presidential box at the time he hears the news.

"Battle Cry of Freedom"

The Thirteenth Amendment having been passed, the victors break into this song, one of the defining ones of the Civil War. The rousing number is picked up outside the Capitol and into the streets of Washington as Thaddeus Stevens make his way home to his waiting lover, his servant Lydia Smith (S. Epatha Merkerson), in the movie's great, late "reveal."

The song was written in 1862 by composer George Frederick Root, who was in favor of the Union and abolitionism (in contains the lyrics "and although they may be poor/not a man shall be a slave" which brings attention to economic disenfranchisement rather than race). It's opening line "Yes, we'll rally 'round the flag, boys" gave the song its other unofficial title and provided the title for Max Schulman's 1956 satirical novel *Rally 'Round the Flag, Boys!* and its 1958 film adaptation.

Overture to Egmont, Op. 84

While his parents attend the fatal presentation of *Our American Cousin* at Ford's Theater, their younger son, Tad, watches a more child-suitable *Aladdin and His Wonderful Lamp* at Grover's Theater several blocks to the west. His life will soon be shattered by the bad news, announced from the stage of the playhouse. The background scoring to the sword fighting scene onstage is a piece by Ludwig van Beethoven, although it was actually written to accompany a play called *Egmont*, by Johann von Goethe.

Bridge of Spies

Because illness made him unavailable, this marked the first time a Steven Spielberg movie hadn't been scored by John Williams in thirty years. Instead, another stalwart composer, Thomas Newman, filled in on this occasion. Newman's dad, the much-honored Alfred Newman, had been among the first to employ Williams in his early days of working in the motion picture industry. Williams returned the favor by allowing Thomas to do some orchestrating on his score for *Return of the Jedi*, thereby getting the younger Newman's Hollywood career off and running.

"Please Send Me Someone to Love"

The FBI having broken into Rudolf Abel's (Mark Rylance) apartment, they proceed to tear the place apart looking for clues to prove he's been spying for the Russians. Rudolf clearly needs someone on his side, which might be why, during the transition from this scene to the next, we hear jazz pianist Red Garland's version of Percy Mayfield's 1950 song. Turns out, in the following scene we first see Abel's savior, James Donovan (Tom Hanks), sitting in a lounge arguing about a case with another lawyer (Joshua Harto). The piano piece continues as if it's being played live right there in the lounge, although whether it's supposed to be Garland on piano is debatable.

"Nancy (With the Laughing Face)"

Famous for being recorded in 1944 by Frank Sinatra, in honor of his daughter Nancy (Frank's wife at the time was also named Nancy), this tune had a curious credit insomuch as Jimmy Van Heusen's lyricist on this occasion was comedian Phil Silvers. There was no particular tie-in to any of these people suggested by its use in the movie during the scene when Donovan, confronted by the C.I.A. agent who's been tailing him, Hoffman (Scott Shepherd), sits down to talk to him in a bar. The version heard, creating background for the scene, is not Sinatra's at all; rather, it is an instrumental not specific to the period and recorded by trombonist Bill Watrous long after the events being portrayed.

Concerto No. 2 for Piano and Orchestra, Op. 102

Here's a piece of music that is not merely used for underscoring but is actually commented on in the dialogue. Visiting his client once again in the prison detention room, Donovan sits with Abel pensively, listening to this piece by Dmitri Shostakovich playing on the radio. Donovan mentions the fact that the prison officials "checked the radio to make sure there was no transmitter in it." This suspicious nature cannot spoil Abel's enjoyment of the work of his fellow Russian, who was very much alive at the time of the real Abel's arrest. The composer had experienced his share of controversy from his country's government in his lifetime, including a period in which many of his works were banned, as they were perceived as having too much Western influence.

"77 Sunset Strip"

For those in the know, it is evident time has passed from the 1957 starting point of the film because the series for which this song was written did not premiere (on the ABC network) until the fall of the following year. The catchy title tune (by Mack David and Jerry Livingston) is heard while Donovan's eldest offspring, Carol (Eve Hewson), watches the program on the couch. Her leisure time is dangerously interrupted when gunshots blast through the window—an unnerving contrast to the more lighthearted capers that went on week to week on the Los Angeles-based detective series.

"My Romance" and "Unforgettable"

Poor Donovan just can't seem to get away from the ever-present Hoffman, who joins him in the restaurant at the West Berlin Hilton to find out if the swap between Abel and Airman Francis Gary Powers has been made. Filling the background are instrumental versions of Richard Rodgers and Lorenz Hart's "My Romance" (from the 1935 musical *Jumbo*) as performed by jazz pianist Dick Hyman, and Irving Gordon's 1951 tune "Unforgettable" made famous by Nat King Cole, but heard here as played by tenor saxophonist Hugh Brodie.

The BFG

"Piper's Maggot Jig" and "Il Barbiere Di Siviglia" Film Adaptation of the Cavatina

The first tune, a traditional piece (composer disputed) is heard coming from the corner pub down the street from Sophie's orphanage at the opening of the film. It's the kind of music you'd imagine a rowdy crowd of punters listening to in order to establish the scene, but what makes it unusual is the origin of this particular version. Rather than be recorded anew for Spielberg's film, the filmmaker instead paid tribute to his late friend and colleague, Stanley Kubrick, by lifting the music directly from the soundtrack of his 1975 period epic *Barry Lyndon*, as adapted by Leonard Rosenman.

He returns to the *Lyndon* soundtrack later in the movie when Sophie (Ruby Barnhill) and BFG (Mark Rylance) are dining at Buckingham Palace with the Queen. Heard playing over most of the scene is a genteel rendering of the Cavatina from Gioachino Rossini's classic opera, which we know in English as *The Barber of Seville*.

The BFG (Mark Rylance) entertains his tiny guest (Ruby Barnhill) in his cave dwelling in *The BFG*.

"Rule Britannia" and "Scotland the Brave"

The UK's naval anthem, music by Thomas Arne, is the fanfare used to introduce her majesty, Queen Elizabeth II (Penelope Wilton), as she and Sophie enter the ballroom and are followed cautiously by BFG, crawling down the corridor hoping not to wreck anything too valuable.

Later in the same scene, being told that BFG might enjoy some music with his meal, the Queen summons her bagpipers to pump and puff away at the most famous piece associated with the instrument, "Scotland the Brave."

10

Spielberg by the Numbers

How Spielberg's Films Have Performed at the Box Office

n light of how frequently the media and the public have emphasized the box office success of so many of his films, Steven Spielberg was heard to lament, "Part of me is afraid I will be remembered for the money my films have made, rather than the films themselves." This is a valid gripe, as there are those who think of the filmmaker first and foremost because he's made such a staggering amount of money in his lifetime, not only for the studios that have released his pictures but for himself as well.

The intention of this chapter is not to place money above achievement. I think what is remarkable about Spielberg's incredible run at world box offices is the fact that after proving himself early on and continuing to prove himself by being a director of both great artistry and commercial sense, his name became instrumental in getting studios to back difficult projects and, more importantly, to get audiences to pay to see things they might have been less inclined to patronize had they been done by others. Certainly *The Color Purple, Schindler's List,* and *Lincoln* are outstanding examples of this. The reason it's important that Steven Spielberg's movies have poured so much money into Hollywood's coffers, is because it meant that all kinds of risky properties he proposed got the greenlight out of admiration for his talents and the chance that profit could be made in the bargain. He's had an uncanny knack for connecting with public taste, perhaps greater than any other filmmaker.

Here are the figures on the thirty theatrical motion pictures Steven Spielberg has directed, concentrating principally on their North American box office returns. The charts indicate where exactly they placed each year, many of them near or at the top of the list. For those that did *not* come anywhere near the top of those charts, I thought it would be interesting to show a sampling of those motion pictures that did, for comparison.

The Sugarland Express

Universal. A Zanuck/Brown production. Color by Technicolor. Filmed in Panavision. Rated PG. 109 minutes.

Opened on Sunday, March 31, 1974, in New York City at Cinema II and the National Theater in Times Square. That Friday, April 5, the movie opened in the Los Angeles area at the Chinese Theatre in Hollywood (for a four-week run), the Bruin in Westwood, South Coast II in Costa Mesa, and drive-in theaters in Canoga Park and Anaheim; on the same day it also opened in Chicago at the Portage and Ford City I, among other nationwide theatres. First week gross at the National was $14,697 and $14,748 at Cinema II. Although the latter venue kept the film on for several more weeks, it was replaced at the National the very next week by *The Three Musketeers*, which had already premiered in select NY theaters on April 3.

Variety figures ending the week of April 10 showed the film making some $140,425 in rentals at eighteen tracked theatres, putting it at sixteenth place. Most venues across the country reported soft or mild returns. In the New York area, *Sugarland* broke wider to flagship theaters on May 3, 1974. As of May 8, *Variety* listed its total rental figure for the movie at $764,975. As it opened throughout the country at later dates in the course of the year, it would appear intermittently on *Variety's* box office chart. In November, Universal paired the film up with another Goldie Hawn feature from that same year, *The Girl from Petrovka*, which hadn't performed very well at the box office either.

With the January 8, 1975 issue, *Variety* listed the rental figures for all major movies release during 1974. *The Sugarland Express* was listed at $2,890,000, which was a portion of its unreported gross figure, which was often double the rental. It ranked at number

A girl with a great following... 600 troopers on her tail. And the rest of the country cheering her on.

A ZANUCK / BROWN Production

GOLDIE HAWN in

THE SUGARLAND EXPRESS

co-starring **BEN JOHNSON** MICHAEL SACKS · WILLIAM ATHERTON · Music by JOHN WILLIAMS · Screenplay by HAL BARWOOD & MATTHEW ROBBINS · Story by STEVEN SPIELBERG and HAL BARWOOD & MATTHEW ROBBINS · Directed by STEVEN SPIELBERG

PG PARENTAL GUIDANCE SUGGESTED Some material may not be suitable for pre-teenagers · Produced by RICHARD D. ZANUCK and DAVID BROWN A UNIVERSAL PICTURE · TECHNICOLOR® PANAVISION®

An alternate ad for *The Sugarland Express* allows William Atherton and Michael Sacks to receive some exposure with the film's star, Goldie Hawn.

fifty-one among 1974 releases. Future figures estimated the gross to be somewhere around $7 million.

A sure sign of box office disappointment was the fact that the film ended up debuting on television the very next year. NBC premiered it on their *Saturday Night at the Movies* series on November 8, 1975, while *Jaws* was still pulling in the crowds at cinemas. Not wanting to pass up their ultimate selling point, the *TV Guide* ad let viewers know that *The Sugarland Express* was "From the director of *Jaws*."

Budget: $3,000,000

Jaws

Universal. A Zanuck/Brown production. Filmed in Panavision. Color by Technicolor. Rated PG. 124 minutes.

The tremendous public response to *Jaws* was one of the greatest of all Hollywood success stories. At the time it was unusual for a major studio to debut an "A product" in so many theaters at once, but Universal knew it had a hot property on its hands that didn't need word-of-mouth anticipation to build interest and decided upon what was known in industry parlance as "saturation booking." People were clamoring to see the thriller from the get-go, but even its staunchest supporters had no idea just *how* anxiously awaited it was. Booked into 409 US theatres, the film opened on Friday, June 20, 1975. (The only other major studio release to debut that same week was Paramount's *Jacqueline Susann's Once Is Not Enough*, which launched in exclusive engagements, not wide.)

Bookings for Jaws took place at the following:

* Manhattan: UA Rivoli, Loew's Orpheum, Walter Reade's 34th Street East
* Brooklyn: Century's Kings Plaza North, UA Marlboro, Century's Rialto
* Bronx: UA Capri
* Queens: UA Astoria, UA Lefrak, Century's Prospect in Flushing

New Jersey (NY metropolitan area): *Bayville:* Berkeley Cinema #2; *S. Plainfield:* UA Cinema; *Hazlet:* UA Cinema #2; *Bricktown:* Tri-State's Circle Twin #2; *Montclair:* UA Claridge; *Hackensack:* UA Fox; *Fair Lawn:* UA Highway; *Jersey City:* General Cinema's Hudson Plaza #1; *Maplewood:* Triangle's Maplewood; *Parsippany:* General Cinema's Morris Hills Cinema #1; *Long Branch:* Movies #1; *Freehold:* Triangle's Pond Road Cinema; *Westfield:* UA Rialto; *Plainfield:* UA Plainfield Drive-In; *E. Brunswick:* UA Turnpike Cinema; *Wayne:* UA Wayne.

In the Los Angeles market, *Jaws* could be seen at: *Century City:* Plitt's Century Plaza #2; *Hollywood:* Pix; *Lakewood:* Lakewood Center #1; *Panorama City:* Americana Cinema 1&2; *West Covina:* Wescove #1; *Anaheim:* Brookhurst; *Costa Mesa:* Edward's Cinema; *Redondo Beach:* South Bay Cinema III; *La Habra:* Fashion Square #2; *Riverside:* UA Cinema #1; *Canoga Park:* Holiday Cinema; and drive-ins located in: Van Nuys, Paramount, Gardena, Culver City, La Puente, Long Beach, Buena Park, Ventura, Highland, Pasadena, and Oxnard.

According to *Variety*, the three-day opening weekend take was a "colossal" $7,061,513, with the breakdown being $2,063,892 for Friday, $2,475,172 on Saturday, and $2,522,449 on Sunday. In the NY metropolitan area, it did $1,003,531 in forty-six houses. Within its first week, *Jaws* had already made more money than *The Sugarland Express* had made during its entire run in US theaters.

After ten days the total take had reached $21,115,354. Clearly, this was unprecedented in the amount of public interest and was not the sort of film to make its money and go. *Jaws* fever had reached such a peak by the Fourth of July weekend that *Boxoffice* magazine reported near riots breaking out at a Raleigh, North Carolina, theater where patrons had to be turned away after having been given assurance that they would *not* be sold out of upcoming shows. The pivotal holiday weekend brought in an additional $6,443,138, helping to bring the total figure to $33,872,564 in the United States. Numbers for the New York area alone were $4,965,640 in seventeen days. At fifty-five theaters in Canada, the gross was $1,300,000 for the first week, breaking house records at all but two of the locations.

According to *Variety*, by mid- to late July the movie was now in 675 US and Canadian theaters for a three-day weekend (July 25–27) total of $6,150,000, bringing it to a thirty-eight-day total of $69,725,376. The LA figure in twenty-five houses was $4,718,161 in thirty-eight-days; $9,148,083 in the NY area in fifty-one houses. By this point it was clear that, should the business remain steady, *Jaws* stood a good chance of zooming right up to the top of the charts to become the highest-grossing motion picture of all time.

After fifty-nine days in release (increased to 954 houses), as of August 17, 1975, *Jaws* had broken through and passed the $100 million dollar mark, now lagging behind only three titles: *The Godfather, The Sound of Music,* and *Gone with the Wind*. In the pre-home video era, the desire to not only see *Jaws* but to *have* a copy prompted someone to steal the print from the Gopher Theatre in Minneapolis, one of many establishments where it had broken house records. The thieves, however, failed to notice they had left one reel behind. In further extreme news related to the movie, Ford City Cinema in Chicago reported a forty-five-year-old man succumbing to a heart attack while watching the thriller. Most of the surviving customers chose to stick around after the unfortunate patron was removed from the auditorium.

After eighty days, as of September 8, Universal could finally report that *Jaws* had broken the coveted all-time record, taking in $124,322,872 million in slightly less than 1,000 theaters, surpassing *The Godfather* and becoming the highest-grossing release of all time. For the same amount of days, the totals in the NY area at fifty houses were $13,915,483; for the LA area $7,195,193 at twenty to twenty-five houses; and $3,512 in Chicago at five spots. Not surprisingly, this meant it had held the top spot at the nation's box offices for twelve weeks straight,

A 1976 ad heralding the arrival of the new *Jaws* attraction at the Universal Studios Tour.

and counting. The impact and dominance of the movie on the nation's screens throughout the summer of 1975 became the stuff of legend and ended up tipping the scales down the line in favor of saturation booking for major film companies that wanted to score a similar bullseye. Eventually, Hollywood could seldom think in terms of this period being anything other than the season of the "blockbuster."

Success of this magnitude led to a merchandising bonanza, including those actually sanctioned by Universal Studios. A *Jaws* logo T-shirt sold some half-million units in eight weeks, and 100,000 beach towels were sold in the same amount of time. These were joined by shark's tooth gold charms and necklaces, inflatable sharks, blankets, hobby kits, rings, plastic water squirters, and inflatable, attachable fins. There was also an official *Jaws* game, which required players to remove pieces of "junk" from the shark with a gaff hook without the plastic creature snapping at you.

Jaws received its European debut on September 22 at the San Sebastian Film Festival. The movie was finally dislodged from the top spot on the *Variety* box office charts in America during the weekend of September 26, 1975, by the wide release of Woody Allen's comedy *Love and Death*. As of November 5, the US *Jaws* figure was $131.5 million, and the film brough in an additional $10 million from Canada.

In late November, Universal reported that the film had grossed $150,121,339 from 2,460 US and Canadian engagements in the twenty-three weeks since its premiere and was not showing signs yet of stopping. Come Christmastime and into the New Year, *Jaws* finally had its overseas openings in forty-four countries, encompassing 700 theaters. Because the title did not translate with the same meaning in most of the languages, Universal was obliged the slap various generic names on it. Among those were: *The White Shark* (Germany); *Shark* (Italy); *Teeth of the Sea* (France); and *Shark Summer* (Norway). After its December 6, 1975, opening in Japan, the movie broke all records in that country, taking in $1,068,005 in just two days. Within a week of its January 28, 1976 premiere in Paris, the movie grossed $1 million. Less than two months after its December 19, 1975, debut in Spain, it had broken that country's box office records by grossing $3,300,000. Because it brought in more than 3,000,000 patrons since its December 18, 1975, opening in West Germany, *Jaws* was given that country's Golden Screen Award.

When 1976 arrived, *Variety* announced that *Jaws* was the first movie to top the $100 million mark in rentals, landing at the top of the all-time list at $102,650,000. Worldwide rental figures reported on January 11, 1976, came in at $132 million, thereby passing, by a million, the record previously held by *The Godfather*. For its thirtieth week in the United States, as of the end of January, 1976, the domestic gross was now $160 million. Following the March 29, 1976, Academy Awards, where it came away with three wins, *Jaws* could be found playing in ninety-eight theaters in the New York metropolitan area, forty-one weeks after its initial opening.

As the ultimate indication of the movie's impact on pop culture, Universal made sure it became a part of its famous backlot-studio-tour attraction. Taking the already existing "Singapore Lake," which had been used to demonstrate "lighting and wave effects" to the tourists, and converting the Southeast Asian buildings on it to structures in the New England style that could pass themselves off as Amity,

Universal now had the setting for a *Jaws* attraction at its Universal City, California, location. Among the items dressing up the lake was a recreation of Quint's *Orca* fishing vessel. Tram riders were teased by a dorsal fin making its way through the lake—causing a dock to collapse, as in the film, and a lonely fisherman to be dragged into the drink—before the shark itself darted out of the water next to the passing tour vehicles. Opening on April 10, 1976, the attraction was an instant hit, was later recreated at Universal's Orlando and Japan locations, and became one of the most anticipated moments on the backlot tour.

As of May 10, 1976, *Screen International* reported that the movie had taken in $180 million at the domestic box office in forty-three weeks.

Budget: $10.5 million

Box office ranking among 1975 releases:

1. ***Jaws* (Universal)—$180,000,000**
2. *One Flew Over the Cuckoo's Nest* (UA)—$108,981,275
3. *Shampoo* (Columbia)—$49,407,734
4. *Dog Day Afternoon* (WB)—$46,665,856
5. *The Return of the Pink Panther* (UA)—$41,833,347

By the end of the decade, *Jaws* had been dethroned from the top of the box office charts by *Star Wars* but still maintained a lofty second place. Spielberg was, not surprisingly, the only director to have two movies in the Top 10.

Top 10 box office films of the 1970s in rental figures (according to *Variety*):

1. *Star Wars* (20th)—$193,500,000
2. ***Jaws* (Universal)—$129,549,325**
3. *Grease* (Paramount)—$96,300,000
4. *The Exorcist* (Warner Bros.)—$89,000,000
5. *The Godfather* (Paramount)—$88,275,000
6. *Superman* (Warner Bros.)—$82,800,000
7. ***Close Encounters of the Third Kind* (Columbia)—$82,750,000**
8. *The Sting* (Universal)—$78,212,000
9. *Saturday Night Fever* (Paramount)—$74,100,000
10. *National Lampoon's Animal House* (Universal)—$70,826,000

Close Encounters of the Third Kind

A Columbia presentation in association with EMI. A Julia Phillips and Michael Phillips production. Metrocolor. Panavision. Rated PG. 137 minutes.

Opening date: November 16, 1977, at the Ziegfeld Theatre in New York (breaking the house record in the first five days with a take of $121,125). The film would end up playing here for twenty-three weeks. Los Angeles opening: November 18, 1977, at the Cinerama Dome (breaking the house record in three days with $61,837). During the four-week period at these two theaters, *Close Encounters* took in $1,072, 536.

Nationwide release: December 14, 1977, at 270 US theaters. The first week at these theaters brought in $10,115,000. The movie added another 301 theaters the following week (for a total of 571) to bring in another $8 million for a $20 million total. When *Variety* published its list of Big Rental films of 1977 on January 4, 1978 *Close Encounters* was already the fourth-highest ranking 1977 release, after *Star Wars*, *Smokey and the Bandit*, and *The Deep*. For the holiday period covering December 14 through January 2, *Close Encounters* had taken in a total of $39.4 million. By April 17, 1978, the film had passed the coveted $100 million mark, having grossed $100,811,484. By late September, the figure was reported to be $120 million. Only

So big was *Close Encounters of the Third Kind* that it warranted a special Marvel Comics tie-in.

the unprecedented phenomenon of George Lucas's *Star Wars* kept Spielberg from once again having the highest-grossing release of the year.

Budget: $19.4 million

Box office ranking among 1977 releases:

1. *Star Wars* (20th)—$460,998,007
2. ***Close Encounters of the Third Kind* (Columbia)—$166,000,000**
3. *Saturday Night Fever* (Paramount)—$139,486,124
4. *Smokey and the Bandit* (Universal)—$126,737,428
5. *The Goodbye Girl* (WB)—$83,700,000

In 1980 Columbia reissued the film, advertised as *The Special Edition: Close Encounters of the Third Kind*, with newly filmed sequences and select scenes from the 1977 version now removed. The most heralded new sequence came at the end and showed the inside of the mother ship, which had been left to the imagination the first time out. Debuting in 663 theaters on August 1, *Variety* reported that it had taken in $6,614,157 in its first ten days of release.

1941

A Universal Pictures and Columbia Pictures presentation. Metrocolor. Panavision. Rated PG. 118 minutes.

Opening date: December 14, 1979, at 118 nationwide theaters; added additional houses during Christmas for 627 screens. (Note: The film was originally scheduled for a November 16, 1979, opening as a limited engagement on eight screens before being re-edited and rescheduled for a wider release.) Opened in New York at the Bay Cinema, Gemini II, Rivoli, and 86th Street Twin. By January 25, 1980, the film had vacated each of these houses. In Los Angeles its principal booking was at the Cinerama Dome in Hollywood. (The other wide release to open that day was Universal's Steve Martin comedy *The Jerk*.) Opening weekend brought in $3,617,254. The two-week total was $9,272,154. While failing to recoup its expensive cost in the United States, the movie did manage to take in some $60.7 million in total overseas box office grosses, which made up for its undernourished response here.

Budget $32 million

Box office ranking among 1979 releases:

1. *Kramer vs. Kramer* (Columbia)—$106,260,000
2. *The Amityville Horror* (AIP)—$86,432,000
3. *Rocky II* (UA)—$85,182,160
4. *Star Trek: The Motion Picture* (Paramount)—$82,258,456
5. *Alien* (20th)—$80,931,801

   • • •

21. *The Black Hole* (BV)—$35,841,901
22. *Starting Over* (Paramount) $35,649,012

23. *1941* (**Universal/Columbia**) **$34,175,000**
24. *. . . And Justice for All* (Columbia) $33,300,000
25. *Chapter Two* (Columbia) $30,000,000

Raiders of the Lost Ark

Paramount Pictures presents a Lucasfilm Ltd. production. Metrocolor. Panavision. Rated PG. 116 minutes.

Opening date: June 12, 1981, at 1,078 nationwide theaters. (Also opening in wide release on that day were Fox's Mel Brooks comedy *History of the World Part 1* and MGM's fantasy *Clash of the Titans*). The opening weekend gross for *Raiders* was $8,305,823 million (number one for the week), the ten-day gross $22,113,139. New York openings were at the Loew's Astor Plaza (where it had a twenty-three-week run), Coronet, 34th Street Showplace, and Orpheum 1. Los Angeles area openings included the Chinese Theatre in Hollywood (fifteen weeks at this location,

Indiana Jones (Harrison Ford) thinks he's found the solution to plucking a treasured idol from its pedestal in this scene from *Raiders of the Lost Ark*.

although it would actually return here later in the year, albeit in one of the smaller adjacent theaters) and the National in Westwood. Opened in London at the Empire Theatre on July 30, 1981, and three other venues for a weekend take of £71,105 (or $127,700 in US currency).

Although it was challenged in its second North American weekend by WB's *Superman II*, after its first fifty-two days in theaters, *Raiders* zoomed over its competition and became the highest-grossing movie of the summer, and, because no other films came close to its box office take, of the year. Unlike so many other titles in circulation that customarily dropped venues after their initial few weeks, *Raiders* added some 300 theaters the weekend of July 17 and rose back up to the number one position at the end of July. On August 19, 1981, *Variety* reported that the sixty-six-day total had leapt over the $100 million mark; after 111 days in release it surpassed *Grease* (1978) to become the highest-grossing title in Paramount Pictures' history. The film continued to stay in the US box office top ten well into December and (helped by adding 822 theaters) even managed to slip into the second-place slot during the Thanksgiving holiday, its twenty-fifth weekend in theaters. A year after its release, the film was still being exhibited, even landing a successful eleven-week run at the Cinerama Dome in Hollywood until it was obliged to vacate for *E.T. the Extra-Terrestrial* in June of 1982.

Budget: $18 million

Box office ranking among 1981 Releases:

1. **Raiders of the Lost Ark** (Paramount) $212,222,025
2. *On Golden Pond* (Univers al) $119,286,000
3. *Superman II* (WB) $108,186,000
4. *Arthur* (Orion/WB) $95,462,000
5. *Stripes* (Columbia) $72,179,00

E.T. the Extra-Terrestrial

Universal. Color by Technicolor. 115 minutes. Rated PG.

Opened on June 11, 1982, in 1,101 theaters. In New York it opened at the Movieland, Bay Cinema, and Loews New York Twin, and additional area theatres. Opened in Hollywood at the Cinerama Dome, as well as several area theaters. (That same day saw the release of Paramount's musical sequel *Grease 2* and Embassy Pictures' horror film *Humongous*.) The US opening weekend gross was $11,911,430, for a per-screen average of $10,818. The two-week gross was a spectacular $44,809,658, an industry record for that brief amount of time. With a $3-million-a-day average gross, this already indicated that the movie had tremendous word of mouth and was on its way to becoming one of the outstanding all-time grossers. Nobody could have predicted yet just *how* big it would get. With the Independence Day weekend it became quite evident that Universal had a growing phenomenon on its hands. *E.T.* grossed $17,254,946 that weekend at what had now increased to 1,323 theatres, the highest four-day gross in motion picture history. This meant it had already earned $86,920,785 in less than a month of release. When that month arrived, Universal announced that the film had already passed the $100 million mark, becoming the first ever to reach that position that rapidly.

As if to remind exhibitors that Steven Spielberg was some sort of king when it came to dominating the box office, Paramount reissued *Raiders of the Lost Ark* on 1,330 theaters the weekend of July 16, 1982, and it ended up in second place to *E.T.*, which continued to put all other summer competitors to shame. With an increase to 1,487 screens, *E.T.* had a weekend take of $12,826,160, triple the amount of *Raiders*'s weekend gross. By the end of July, *The Extra-Terrestrial* was only one slot below *Raiders* on the list of the all-time US film rental champs, coming in fifth place. The leaders were (1) *Star Wars* (20th); (2) *The Empire Strikes Back*

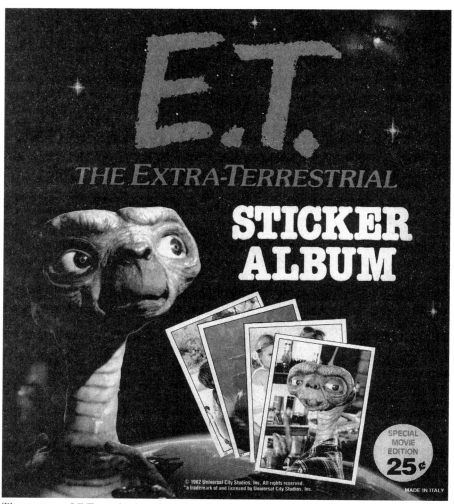

The success of *E.T.* resulted in an avalanche of merchandising, including this sticker book of images from the film.

(20th); and (3) *Jaws* (Universal). This meant that the top five films were all from either George Lucas or Steven Spielberg, or, in the case of *Raiders*, a collaboration of both.

E.T.'s six-week reign at number one came to a halt when another Universal release, an adaptation of the Broadway musical hit *The Best Little Whorehouse in Texas*, knocked it from the top spot for week number seven. The difference was not extreme, however, as *Whorehouse* made $11,874,268 and *E.T.* $11,089,490. The dethroning of the champ was only temporary, as the following week *E.T.* regained the top position, its total number of theaters now being 1,521, and its total gross $169,825,554 in fifty-two-days. After 66 days, *E.T. the Extra-Terrestrial* had cracked the $200 million mark in grosses and was second only to *Stars Wars* on *Variety*'s all-time film rental list.

The film continued a steady box office run throughout a relatively weak fall season and managed to slide right back into the number one slot over the extended Thanksgiving weekend, bringing in $4,083,604 at 1,180 theaters. By the following week (the first week of December), it hit another milestone, passing the $300 million mark and staying on top during an otherwise mild domestic box office period.

Late November openings in Australia, South Africa, and Singapore saw more records being broken. December brought openings in such other foreign markets as France, Japan, Spain, Italy, and West Germany.

E.T. received its London bow on December 9, 1982, at the Empire Leicester Square Theatre, with Prince Charles and Princess Diana, as well as Steven Spielberg, in attendance.

Back in the United States, 1982 ended with *E.T. the Extra-Terrestrial* having grossed $313,258,148 to date. During the Christmas holidays it was available on 911 screens, bringing in $2,814,148 that weekend period.

The weekend (February 18–20, 1983) after *E.T.* was honored with nine Oscar nominations, it could still boast of being on the list of the top ten box office grossers. It took in $2,106,254 at 725 screens in 256 days in wide release for a total of $337,456,254. As of March 25, 1983, its domestic box office total was $343,658,104, having picked up another half million dollars at the 315 screens on which it was still playing at that point.

In March of 1983 it was reported that *E.T.* had passed the 10 million admissions mark in Tokyo—the most for any motion picture to ever play in that country.

In May of 1983 the accounting firm of Laventhol & Horwath, in cooperation with *Variety*, took the all-time rental champs and adjusted them for inflation. This placed *E.T. the Extra-Terrestrial* in the number five spot, following (1) *Gone with the Wind*; (2) *Star Wars*; (3) *Jaws*; (4) *The Sound of Music*; and one spot ahead of *The Godfather*. That same month Universal announced that the movie would be taken out of circulation for a two-year period in anticipation of a major reissue; during that time there would be no video, cable, or any other ancillary media showings of the film.

On June 9, 1983, *E.T.* finally finished its fifty-two week run at the Movieland Theatre on Broadway in Manhattan. It had taken in more than $2 million at this site alone. It was replaced the following day by the Franco Nero-Anthony Quinn thriller *The Salamander.*

E.T. grossed $359 million domestically and $287 million overseas for a total of $646 million.

Budget: $10.5 million

Box office ranking among 1982 releases:

1. **E.T. the Extra-Terrestrial (Universal)—$359,197,037**
2. *Tootsie* (Columbia)—$177,200,000
3. *An Officer and a Gentleman* (Paramount)—$129,795,554
4. *Rocky III* (UA)—$124,146,987
5. *Porky's* (20th)—$105,492,483

Twilight Zone: The Movie

Warner Bros. Technicolor. Running time of film: 101 minutes. Running time of segment #2 (Spielberg's segment): 21 minutes. Rated PG.

Opened on June 24, 1983, on 1,275 screens. (Debuting that same day in wide release were Orion's pirate comedy *Yellowbeard* and 20th Century Fox's sequel *Porky's II: The Next Day.*) Los Angeles area theater bookings included the Chinese Theater in Hollywood and the National in Westwood. In New York, the film opened at the Sutton, New Yorker, Warner Twin, 34th Street East, and Coliseum Twin. The opening weekend gross was $6,614,366. For the follow-up Fourth of July weekend, the film was upped to 1,288 screens, where it took in $5,829,772 for a total of $16,197,870. After little more than a month in theaters, the screen count was down to 756 with a total sum of $27,012,861.

Budget: $10 million

Box office ranking among 1983 releases:

1. *Return of the Jedi* (20th)—$252,583,617
2. *Terms of Endearment* (Paramount)—$108,423,489
3. *Flashdance* (Paramount)—$92,921,203
4. *Trading Places* (Paramount)—$90,404,800
5. *WarGames* (MGM)—$79,567,667

• • •

23. *Snow White* (reissue) (Disney)—$30,100,000
24. *Never Cry Wolf* (Disney)—$29,600,000
25. **Twilight Zone: The Movie (WB)—$29,450,919**
26. *Easy Money* (Orion/WB)—$29,309,767
27. *High Road to China* (WB)—$28,445,927

Indiana Jones and the Temple of Doom

Paramount presents a Lucasfilm Ltd. Production. Deluxe color. Panavision. 118 minutes. Rated PG.

Opening date: May 23, 1984, at 1,685 nationwide screens. Two hundred and forty-three of these were 70 mm prints, making this the largest number of such prints ever for a motion picture's launch. Los Angeles theaters included the Chinese in Hollywood (all three screens) and the National in Westwood. New York included Loews Astor Plaza, Orpheum, and 34th Street Showcase. In its first six days of release, *Temple of Doom* grossed $42,267,345 million, topping the record set the previous year by Fox's *Return of the Jedi*, which had opened in 683

The Polydor soundtrack LP for the second Indiana Jones adventure.

fewer theaters. The second weekend take of $16.6 million brought the total to $68,124,122. After the weekend of June 15–17, the movie passed the $100 million mark, bringing the figure up to $103,487,041. By the end of July, having cut down the number of screens by about 630, the film's gross figure in the United States was $151,469,837. That just about matched the total foreign figure for the movie by the end of its run, $153,237,000. The combined worldwide grosses were a magnificent $333,107,271.

Budget: $28 million

Box office ranking among 1984 releases:

1. *Beverly Hills Cop* (Paramount)—$234,760,478
2. *Ghostbusters* (Columbia)—$229,242,989
3. **Indiana Jones and the Temple of Doom** (**Paramount**)—**$179,870,271**
4. *Gremlins* (WB)—$148,168,459
5. *The Karate Kid* (Columbia)—$90,815,558

The Color Purple

Warner Bros. Deluxe Color. Rated PG-13. 154 minutes.

Opened in New York on December 18, 1985, at the Beekman, Criterion Center, Loews 84th Street 6, and Art Greenwich Twin, and select area theaters. Premiered on December 18 at the Mann Plaza Theatre in Westwood and then opened wider on Friday, December 20, in the Los Angeles area, including the Chinese Theatre in Hollywood. Also on December 20, it opened at the Woods Theater in downtown Chicago and area theaters. The first weekend's theater count was 192, bringing in a total gross of $1,710,333. Over the following three weekends, with a slight expansion to 209 screens, the box office maintained a steady pace of over $3 million brought in each weekend. For the January 17, 1986, weekend, the movie increased its theater count to 561, bringing its box office gross up to $26,148,105. Following the February 5, 1986, announcement of the Oscar nominations, in which *The Color Purple* tied with *Out of Africa* with eleven each, the theater count nearly doubled to 1,109 screens. This brought the figure up to $45,889,128. During Oscar season, the-   movie kept up a very impressive showing, proving that it was a word-of-mouth hit, an audience favorite. The weekend after it managed to lose every one of its nominations, the movie still continued to strike a chord with audiences, its total up to $80,961,290, putting it one notch on that week's box office list *over* the Best Picture winner, *Out of Africa*. When it completed its theatrical run at the end of May of 1986, it stayed one position ahead of its competitor as the fourth highest-grossing movie released in 1985.

Budget: $15 million

Box office ranking among 1985 releases:

1. *Back to the Future* (Universal)—$210,609,762
2. *Rambo: First Blood Part II* (TriStar)—$150,415,432
3. *Rocky IV* (UA)—$127,873,716

Sisters Nettie (Akosua Busia) and Celie (Desreta Jackson) are cruelly separated by Mr. ____ (Danny Glover) in *The Color Purple*.

4. *The Color Purple* (**WB**)—**$94,175,854**
5. *Out of Africa* (Universal)—$87,071,205

Empire of the Sun

Warner Bros. Color by Technicolor. 153 minutes. Rated PG-13.

Opened on December 9, 1987, in Los Angeles at the Chinese Theater in Hollywood and the Mann National in Westwood; in New York at the National Twin, Regency, Beekman, 34th Street East, and Movieland 8th Street Triplex; wider release in select theaters on December 11, 1987. At 225 screens for its first weekend, the movie grossed $1,314,509 million, a per-screen average of $5,842. It expanded its number of screens to 673 on December 25, 1987, for $6,610,192 total. After twenty-six days of release, the gross was $12 million. As of January 13, 1988, the total gross was $14,574,903. As of March 2, 1988, *Empire* was down to 221 screens (following a jump to 536 in hopes of Oscar nominations) for a total of $20,778,000. *Empire of the Sun* was Spielberg's lowest-grossing film in the United States since *The Sugarland Express*. It ended up on the year's box office list only one position above the most critically disdained of the *Jaws* sequels.

Budget: $35 million

Box office ranking among 1987 releases:

1.   *Three Men and a Baby* (Disney)—$167,780,960
2.   *Fatal Attraction* (Paramount)—$156,645,693
3.   *Beverly Hills Cop II* (Paramount)—$153,665,036
4.   *Good Morning, Vietnam* (Disney)—$123,922,370
5.   *Moonstruck* (MGM)—$80,640,528

   • • •

51.   *Raising Arizona* (20th)—$22,847,564
52.   *Benji the Hunted* (Disney)—$22,257,624
53.   **Empire of the Sun (WB)—$22,238,696**
54.   *Jaws IV: The Revenge* (Universal)—$20,763,013
55.   *Hello Again* (Disney)—$20,419,446

Indiana Jones and the Last Crusade

Paramount Pictures presents a Lucasfilm Ltd. production. Deluxe. Panavision. Rated PG-13. 127 minutes.

Opening date: May 24, 1989, at 2,327 screens. Scored a record $11.2 million on Saturday, May 27, the best single day at the box office of any movie up to that time. (This was topped a month later by WB's *Batman* which took in $15.5 on its opening Saturday.) Additional records were set when *Last Crusade* grossed $46.9 million in its first six days. As of June 7, 1989, the figure had risen up to $77,141,769. After nineteen days in theaters, it had topped the $100 million mark, with $102.8 million. As of July 12, the gross was $158,469,476, but it was soon passed by *Batman* as the number one movie of the year.

Budget: $48 million

Box office ranking among 1989 releases:

1.   *Batman* (WB)—$251,188,924
2.   ***Indiana Jones and the Last Crusade* (Paramount)—$197,171,806**
3.   *Lethal Weapon 2* (WB)—$147,253,986
4.   *Look Who's Talking* (TriStar)—$140,088,813
5.   *Honey, I Shrunk the Kids* (Disney)—$130,724,172

Always

A Universal Pictures and United Artists presentation. Color by Deluxe. Rated PG. 122 minutes.

Opening date: December 22, 1989, at 1,016 screens. (Also debuting on that day was WB's action adventure *Tango & Cash* with Sylvester Stallone and Kurt Russell.) New York area screens included Bay Cinema, Beekman, Chelsea 4, Regency, National

The third Indiana Jones adventure, *The Last Crusade*, gave Steven Spielberg his first *Premiere* cover, which he shared with his star, Harrison Ford.

Twin, and Worldwide Cinema 6. Los Angeles area bookings included Monica 4, Universal City Cinemas, Cineplex Odeon Showcase, and Avco III. The gross for the first three days of release was $3.7 million. Adding seventy-four screens, the second weekend gross was $7,106,800, bringing the holiday season total to $14,292,780 as of January 3, 1990. Ending weekend of January 28, at thirty-eight days in release, the film had made $34,125,875, the number of screens having increased to 1,206.

Budget: $31 million

Box office ranking among 1989 releases:

27. *See No Evil, Hear No Evil* (TriStar)—$46,908,987
28. *Black Rain* (Paramount)—$46,212,055
29. **Always (Universal)—$43,858,790**
30. *K-9* (Universal)—$42,247,647
31. *Three Fugitives* (Disney)—$40,586,886

Hook

TriStar Pictures presents an Amblin Entertainment production. Deluxe/Technicolor. Panavision. Rated PG. 142 minutes.

Opening: December 11, 1991, at 2,254 nationwide screens. Its opening day take (including a Tuesday preview the night before) was $2.1 million. Opening weekend gross came in at $13.5 million for a total of $19,124,885 million, making it the number one film in the country. It retained this spot the second weekend for a cumulative gross of $30.7 million and remained the number one film throughout the 1991 holiday season. *Variety* reported on January 6 that *Hook* had grossed $82.5 million to date and that on January 27 it had passed the $100 million mark.

Budget: $70 million

Box office ranking among 1991 releases:

1. *Terminator 2: Judgment Day* (TriStar)—$204,843,345
2. *Robin Hood: Prince of Thieves* (WB)—$165,493,908
3. *Beauty and the Beast* (Disney)—$145,863,363
4. *The Silence of the Lambs* (Orion)—$130,742,922
5. *City Slickers* (Columbia)—$124,033,791
6. **Hook (TriStar)—$119,654,823**
7. *The Addams Family* (Paramount)—$113,502,426

Jurassic Park

Universal Pictures presents an Amblin Entertainment production. Color by Deluxe. Rated PG-13. 127 minutes.

Officially opened on June 11, 1993, on 3,800 screens, following Thursday evening June 10 "preview" showings. The combination of the Thursday showings and Friday premiere posted a record $18.5 million combined. Also entering the record books was the $18 million gross for the first Saturday alone. By the end of the weekend the film had shattered yet another record, taking in $48 million to top the record set the previous June with WB's *Batman Returns*.

After its second Saturday in cinemas (June 19), the film broke another record, becoming the movie to hit the $100 million mark faster than any other (topping WB's 1989 *Batman*). It would hold the number one spot for its first three weeks in release, relinquishing the crown to Paramount's *The Firm* for week four. It did not, however, stop its record breaking. By the end of the Independence Day weekend it now became the movie to reach the $200 million peak quicker than any previous releases. Mid-June openings in the rest of the world included $8.4 million made in Japan in just two days, $3 million in Mexico, and $7.4 million in the United Kingdom (where it opened on July 16 on 434 screens) in three days, paving the way for a world market domination as well.

Over the weekend of July 23–25, *Jurassic Park* passed *Jaws* on the All-Time Box Office charts, reaching a $270.7 million total. The weekend of August 6–8 saw it pass *Star Wars* to become the second highest-grossing movie in US history, after *E.T. the Extra-Terrestrial*. By the end of August it had broken yet another record, crossing the $300 million mark faster than any other movie had done. In Japan, *Jurassic* had already bested *E.T.*, where it could boast of rentals of $43 million, the highest ever in the country's history, two million more than the final total on *E.T.* By the fall of that year its Japanese gross was over $100 million.

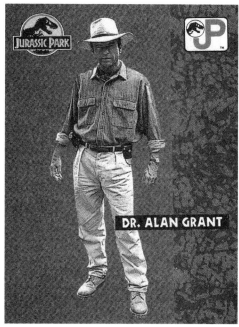

The Dr. Alan Grant *Jurassic Park* trading card, looking much like a wardrobe test for actor Sam Neill.

On October 5, 1993, *Jurassic Park* hit the absolute summit, at least as far as worldwide totals were concerned. With $704.7 million, this made it the highest-grossing motion picture in history, topping *E.T. the Extra-Terrestrial*'s worldwide gross of $701.4 million (combined from both its original 1982 run and its 1985 reissue). *Jurassic*'s overseas figure was $379 million at this point, versus *E.T.*'s $301.6 million. By year's end, the *Jurassic* foreign gross was over $500 million. On the domestic front, however, there was no thought of displacing *E.T.* from the throne just now. *E.T.* stood at a $399.8 million domestic total, and *Jurassic Park* still had too far to go to challenge that and was finally starting to slow down at the box office, meaning it would had to accept its second-place standing.

Budget: $60 million

Schindler's List

Universal Pictures presents an Amblin Entertainment production. Black and white (w/ color sequences) Rated R. 195 minutes.

The film had a special premiere on November 30, 1993, in Washington, D.C., with President Bill Clinton and First Lady Hillary Clinton in attendance, as well as Steven Spielberg, Liam Neeson, and Ben Kingsley on hand.

Opened on December 15, 1993, in twenty-five North American theaters. New York openings were at the Regency, First & 62nd Cinemas, and Chelsea Cinemas.

Los Angeles openings included the Avco Cinema in Westwood and the Beverly Connection 6. In its first five days in limited run, the movie brought in $860,000, a $24,000-per-screen average. On Christmas Day, the movie expanded to seventy-four theatres in thirty-three cities, bringing the second week total gross to $2.8 million; $17,233 per location. The film actually reached number ten on the nation's top box office list while only playing in seventy-six theaters, for a three week total of $6.2 million, a rise in screen average of $21,614 per screen. The movie stayed in the top ten with an expansion to 172 screens in early January. Increasing to 343

The original ad for Spielberg's critical and box office triumph, *Schindler's List*.

screens the weekend of January 21, the total six-week gross was now $19 million, with $9,930 average per location. (During *Schindler*'s first month in theaters, the undisputed box office champion was Fox's Robin Williams cross-dressing comedy *Mrs. Doubtfire*.)

The weekend of February 4–6, 1994, the total number of screens rose to 764 in anticipation of the February 9th announcement of the Oscar nominations, bringing the total gross to $29.3 million. At this point, the paperback movie tie-in of Thomas Keneally's original novel had hit the Best Seller charts, reaching number three as of February 3.

The movie, with twelve nominations, would maintain a steady box office pace over the weeks leading up to the Academy Awards. In the weekend directly before the March 21 Oscar ceremony, *Schindler* had expanded to 1,246 screens, where it took in another $4.3 million for a three-month total of $59.8 million. The weekend after the film won the coveted Academy Award for Best Picture, the number of screens was now 1,378, for a $5.7 million gross, a 31 percent box office increase, and a $68 million domestic total. On May 16, 1994, *Schindler's List* posted a weekend gross lower than $1 million for the first time since its premiere. It was still in the box office top ten, however, bringing in $91 million to date.

The film opened in London on February 18, 1994, on several screens (including the Empire in Leicester Square, the Trocadero in Piccadilly Circus, and the Screen on the Hill in Belsize Park), marking its European premiere. (Despite its late opening to the general public, the movie was deemed eligible for the 1993 BAFTAs, earning thirteen nominations.) The much-anticipated Germany opening took place on March 3, 1994; by the twenty-eighth day of that month, the film had grossed $6 million there, proving that a sizeable portion of the population was ready to experience a shameful reminder of their country's history. In the weeks following the Oscars, *Schindler* could boast of being the number one movie in Brussels, France, Germany, Holland, Italy, Japan, and the United Kingdom. As of June 21, *Variety* reported the gross in Germany alone was $38,350,509.

When it came time for its network television debut, incredibly, NBC agreed to show *Schindler's List* uninterrupted (sponsored by Ford) and with minimal cuts, on Sunday, February 23, 1997, between 7:30 and 11:00 p.m. EST, where it was seen by an estimated 65 million people. The broadcast was preceded by a taped message by Steven Spielberg cautioning viewers that the content might not be appropriate for a select younger demographic.

Budget: $22 million

Box office rankings among 1993 releases:

1. ***Jurassic Park* (Universal)—$346,250,210**
2. *Mrs. Doubtfire* (20th)—$219,195,243
3. *The Fugitive* (WB)—$183,875,760
4. *The Firm* (Paramount)—$158,348,367
5. *Sleepless in Seattle* (TriStar)—$126,680,884
6. *Indecent Proposal* (Paramount)—$106,614,059
7. *In the Line of Fire* (Columbia)—$102,314,823

8. *The Pelican Brief* (WB)—$100,768,056
9. **Schindler's List (Universal)—$96,065,768**
10. *Cliffhanger* (TriStar)—$84,049,211

The Lost World: Jurassic Park

Universal Pictures presents an Amblin Entertainment production. Color by Deluxe. Rated PG-13. 129 minutes.

Following Thursday night previews held on May 22, 1997, *The Lost World: Jurassic Park* opened the following day in 3,281 theatres, eventually encompassing 6,000 screens by the end of the weekend. At the finish of the Memorial Day weekend, the movie had taken in a record breaking $92.7 million in the United States and Canada, for a $28,262-per-screen average. The Sunday night take was $25.6 million, the best day of this period. Because the picture was available on so many screens in so many multiplexes it effectively negated the concept of waiting on long lines to see *the* hot film of the moment. It scored another record by becoming the first motion picture in history to reach $100 million at the box office after only six days, besting by a day the previous year's record holder in this department, *Independence Day* (20th). The following weekend's $32.6 million brought the total up to $140 million. After a month in theaters, the movie topped $200 million at the box office.

Budget: $73 million

Box office ranking among 1997 releases:

1. *Titanic* (Paramount)—$600,788,188
2. *Men in Black* (Columbia)—$250,690,539

Ian Malcolm (Jeff Goldblum), Eddie Carr (Richard Schiff) and Nick Van Owen (Vince Vaughn) are dazzled by some CGI Stegosauruses in this scene from *The Lost World: Jurassic Park*.

3. *The Lost World: Jurassic Park* (**Universal**)—**$229,086,679**
4. *Liar Liar* (Universal)—$181,410,615
5. *Air Force One* (Columbia)—$172,956,409

Amistad

A DreamWorks Pictures presentation in association with HBO Pictures. Technicolor. Rated R. 155 minutes.

Received a special premiere in Washington, D.C., on December 4, 1997, at the Warner Theater, with President Bill Clinton and First Lady Hillary Clinton in attendance. Steven Spielberg and stars Djimon Hounsou, Matthew McConaughey, Morgan Freeman, and Anthony Hopkins also attended.

Opened on Wednesday, December 10, 1997, in New York at the Lincoln Square and Coronet Cinema, and expanded on Friday, December 12 to 322 screens in limited release. For its first five days in release it took in $4.6 million for a $14,300-per-screen average. The screen count increased to 480 for the second weekend, bringing in $3.3 million for a $9.7 million total. On Christmas Day *Amistad* was upped to 712 theaters for a $5.1 million weekend gross and a $17.7 million total. For the New Year's 1998 weekend at 726 screens, the film grossed another $4.5 million for $26.7 million total. In anticipation of the Oscar nominations, the film expanded to 1,001 screens the weekend of January 16–18, which brought the total gross up to $35,032,339. By early February *Amistad* had earned $40,860,661 and then performed at a slower pace during Oscar season.

Budget: $36 million

Anthony Hopkins in his Oscar-nominated role as former President John Quincy Adams in *Amistad*.

Box office ranking among 1997 releases:

48. *Cop Land* (Miramax)—$44,862,187
49. *Nothing to Lose* (Disney)—$44,480,039
50. **Amistad (DreamWorks)—$44,229,441**
51. *Soul Food* (20th)—$43,700,855
52. *Wag the Dog* (New Line Cinema)—$43,061,945

Saving Private Ryan

DreamWorks Pictures and Paramount Pictures present an Amblin Entertainment production, in association with Mutual Film Company. Technicolor. Rated R. 169 minutes.

Opened on July 24, 1998, in 2,462 North American theaters. The first weekend's gross was $30,576,104, with a theater average of $12,414, putting it at the top of the charts. It remained there for a second weekend, with a gross of $23.3 million, for a $73 million total. Within its third weekend in theaters, in which it once again stayed at number one, *Ryan* had hopped over the $100 million mark. *Ryan* held the top spot for four weeks straight and continued at a steady pace throughout August, staying at more than 2,000 bookings until the end of September. It would finally drop out of the top ten in mid-October.

In anticipation of the Oscar nominations in February of 1999, the film returned to 1,027 screens and, following the February 12–15 weekend, managed to crack the $200 million mark. It was the fifth time a motion picture directed by

Sergeant Horvath (Tom Sizemore) and Captain Miller (Oscar-nominee Tom Hanks) about to lead their men into the hell of Omaha Beach in this scene from *Saving Private Ryan*.

Steven Spielberg would claim the top box office spot for its year. Over in England, where a good deal of it was shot, *Ryan* grossed $31,779,110; while in France, the movie's setting, the nearly as impressive figure was $26,760,936. Falling in between those was Germany (the movie's enemy at the time of the story), where it brought in $28,629,280. The combined grosses between the United States and the foreign market was a terrific $481,840,909.

Budget: $70 million

Box office ranking among 1998 releases:

1. **Saving Private Ryan (DreamWorks/Paramount)—$216,540,909**
2. *Armageddon* (Disney)—$201,578,182
3. *There's Something about Mary* (20th)—$176,484,651
4. *A Bug's Life* (Disney)—$162,798,565
5. *The Waterboy* (Disney)—$161,491,646

A.I. Artificial Intelligence

A DreamWorks Pictures and Warner Bros. Pictures presentation of an Amblin/Stanley Kubrick production. Technicolor. Rated PG-13. 146 minutes.

Opened on June 29, 2001, in 3,242 theaters. The film led the box office charts its first weekend, with a gross of $29,352,630. By the end of its second weekend (following the Independence Day holiday) it had nearly doubled that amount for $59,573,204. Dropping the number of theaters to 2,830 for weekend number four brought the total to $70,097,455. After that the film posted mild figures for the remainder of the summer. Over in England—where the filmmaker with whom this project had started, Stanley Kubrick, made his home for more than thirty years—the gross was $11,662,544.

Budget: $100 million

Box office ranking among 2001 releases:

1. *Harry Potter and the Sorcerer's Stone* (WB)—$317,575,550
2. *The Lord of the Rings: The Fellowship of the Ring* (New Line)—$313,364,114
3. *Shrek* (DreamWorks)—$267,665,011
4. *Monsters, Inc.* (Disney)—$255,873,250
5. *Rush Hour 2* (New Line Cinema)—$225,164,286

   • • •

26. *Atlantis: The Lost Empire* (Disney)—$84,056,472
27. *Jimmy Neutron: Boy Genius* (Paramount)—$80,936,232
28. **A.I. Artificial Intelligence (WB)—$78,616,689**
29. *Training Day* (WB)—$76,631,907
30. *Along Came a Spider* (Paramount)—$74,078,174

Minority Report

DreamWorks Pictures and Twentieth Century Fox present a Cruise/Wagner, Blue Tulip, Ronald Shusett/Gary Goldman production. Technicolor. Panavision. PG-13. 145 minutes.

Opened on June 21, 2002, on 3,001 North American screens. (Also opening in wide release that same day were the Disney cartoon *Lilo & Stitch* and Warner's basketball comedy *Juwanna Mann*.) *Minority* grossed $35,677,125 on its first weekend, giving it a marginal lead over *Lilo*. By mid-July it had passed over the $100 million mark and, as became the norm with widely-booked summer blockbusters, had pretty much made all its money and left the majority of its bookings by the time Labor Day arrived. *Minority Report* did superb business in Japan, bringing in $42,707,326. In the United Kingdom the gross was $31,388,860.
Budget: $102 million

Catch Me If You Can

DreamWorks Pictures presents a Kemp Company and Splendid Pictures production, a Parkes/MacDonald production. Technicolor. Rated PG-13. 141 minutes.

Opened on Wednesday, December 25, 2002, on 3,156 screens. Although Spielberg had many a film open in December as part of the end-of-the-year holiday season, this was the first of his titles to actually debut on Christmas Day. It was preceded in theaters, five days earlier, by another release starring Leonardo DiCaprio, Martin Scorsese's epic *Gangs of New York*. Although *Catch Me* was obliged to come in second place on its opening weekend to the second installment of the blockbuster *Lord of the Rings* trilogy, it still grossed a very impressive $48,646,930. By its third week in release, it had already swooped way past the $100 million mark and zipped past the year's other Spielberg release, *Minority Report*, by weekend number four.

Budget: $52 million

Box office rankings among 2002 releases:

1. *Spider-Man* (Columbia)—$403,706,375
2. *The Lord of the Rings: The Two Towers* (New Line)—$339,789,881
3. *Star Wars: Episode II: Attack of the Clones* (20th)—$302,191, 252

   . . .

10. *Chicago* (Miramax)—$170,687,518
11. **Catch Me If You Can (DreamWorks)—$164,615,351**
12. *Die Another Day* (MGM)—$160,942,139
13. *Scooby-Doo* (WB)—$153,294,164
14. *Lilo & Stitch* (Disney)—$145,794,338
15. *XXX* (Columbia)—$142,109,382
16. *The Santa Clause 2* (Disney)—$139,236,327

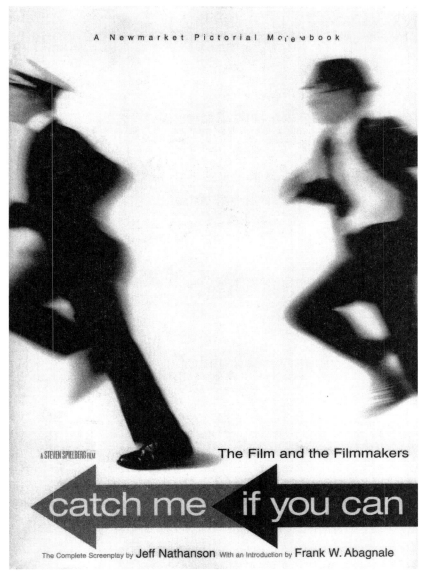

The published script for *Catch Me If You Can*, adorned with the deliberately blurry poster image that captured Carl Hanratty's (Tom Hanks) constant pursuit of Frank Abagnale Jr. (Leonard DiCaprio).

17. *Minority Report* (20th)—**$132,072,926**
18. *The Ring* (DreamWorks)—$129,128,133

The Terminal

DreamWorks Pictures presents a Parkes/MacDonald production. Technicolor. Rated PG-13. 128 minutes.

Opened on June 18, 2004. (The other two wide releases on that day were the Ben Stiller comedy *Dodgeball*, which topped the box office list that weekend, and the Jackie Chan remake of *Around the World in 80 Days*.) *Terminal* opened with $18.7 million for the first weekend. Its second weekend take was $13.9 million, for a $41,040,124 two-week total. Over the Fourth of July weekend the film scored another $10.2 million for a $56.7 million total.

Since there was no actual Krakozhia (where *The Terminal*'s protagonist hailed from), there weren't any box office figures to report from that country, but as far as the overseas market was concerned, the Japanese loved it, with the movie grossing $39,681,262 there.

Budget: $60 million

Box office ranking among 2004 releases:

1. *Shrek 2* (DreamWorks)—$441,226,247
2. *Spider-Man 2* (Columbia)—$373,585,825
3. *The Passion of the Christ* (Newmarket)—$370,274,604
4. *Meet the Fockers* (Universal)—$279,261,160
5. *The Incredibles* (Disney)—$261,441,092

   . . .

33. *Alien vs. Predator* (20th)—$80,282,231
34. *Man on Fire* (20th)—$77,911,774
35. **The Terminal (DreamWorks)—$77,872,883**
36. *Garfield: The Movie* (20th)—$75,369,589
37. *Ray* (Universal)—$75,333,600

War of the Worlds

DreamWorks Pictures and Paramount Pictures present an Amblin Entertainment/C/W production. Technicolor. Rated PG-13. 117 minutes.

Opened on Wednesday, June 29, 2005, in 3,908 locations. (The only other wide opening that same weekend was 20th's Martin Lawrence comedy *Rebound*, which debuted on July 1.) Opening day North American figures were $21.1 million. Encompassing the customarily lucrative Fourth of July holiday, the film ended up by the end of its first week with a $112.7 million total North American gross. The summer movie blockbuster scene had very much become a "hit and run" experience, with even the most popular moneymakers taking in the majority of their cash on the opening weekend on such a large number of screens. Paramount declared it the biggest opening ever for them and for star Tom Cruise, and, thanks to the amount of venues in which it was playing, *War* crossed the $100 million mark faster than had any previous Steven Spielberg movie. In overseas markets tallying seventy-eight countries, the picture took in an additional $102.5 million. The following weekend moved the film into second place (behind *Fantastic Four*) for a $165 million total to date. By its twenty-fourth day of release, *War of the Worlds* may have taken the inevitable summer slide from such a smash opening but had passed the $200 million mark in North America. The world market (it was *their* war too, after all) responded splendidly, with a magnificent $53,720,172 gross in Japan, $55,555,574 in the United Kingdom (H. G. Wells's home country), and $39,963,572 in France, to name the three largest. The cumulative worldwide box office was $591,745,540.

Budget: $132 million

Box office ranking among 2005 releases:

1. *Star Wars: Episode III – Revenge of the Sith* (20th)—$380,270,577
2. *Chronicles of Narnia: The Lion, the Witch and the Wardrobe* (Disney)—$291,710,957
3. *Harry Potter and the Goblet of Fire* (WB)—$290,013,036
4. ***War of the Worlds* (Paramount)—$234,280,354**
5. *King Kong* (Universal)—$218,080,025

Munich

A Universal Pictures and DreamWorks Pictures presentation. An Amblin Entertainment, Kennedy/Marshall, Barry Mendel production in association with Alliance Atlantis Communications. Technicolor. Rated R. 164 minutes.

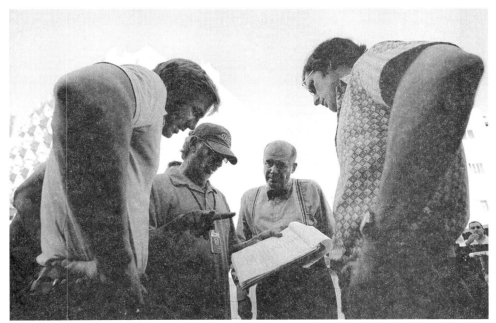

Steven Spielberg discusses a scene with three of his cast members, Daniel Craig, Hanns Zischler, and Eric Bana, on the set of *Munich*.

Opened on Friday, December 23, 2005, in limited release, on 532 screens. Opening weekend gross was $4,152,260. When the New Year arrived, the movie had taken in a total of $15,949,005. Two weeks later *Munich* expanded to 1,485 theaters for a weekend gross of $7,566,075 and a $25,350,740 total. By the time of the March 5, 2006, Academy Awards ceremony, where the movie competed as one of the Best Picture nominees, it had pretty much run its course at the box office, having taken in $46,113,190. Losing the trophy to *Crash* meant there was very little money made for the remainder of its run. In Israel (where it debuted on January 26, 2006), the final gross was $559,036, which put it below the figures in that country for Steven Spielberg's other recent release, *War of the Worlds*.

Budget: $70 million

Box office rankings among 2005 releases:

60. *Just Like Heaven* (DreamWorks)—$48,318,130
61. *The Skeleton Key* (Universal)—$47,907,715
62. **Munich (Universal)—$47,379,090**
63. *Kingdom of Heaven* (20th)—$47,398,413
64. *Boogeyman* (Screen Gems)—$46,752,382

Indiana Jones and the Kingdom of the Crystal Skull

Paramount Pictures presents a Lucasfilm Ltd. production. Deluxe color. Panavision. Rated: PG-13. 122 minutes.

Had its premiere at the Cannes Film Festival on Sunday, May 18, 2008. Opened in North America on May 22, 2008, on 4,260 screens. At the end of the five-day Memorial Day weekend, the film had taken in a huge $151 million in North America alone. It narrowly missed the all-time record, already set by *Pirates of the Caribbean: At World's End* in 2007. Meanwhile, having opened in theaters throughout the world, it could boast of having grossed a worldwide total of $311 million. Totals in Europe included $24 million in the United Kingdom and $14 million in France. By its second weekend, the $46 million it added meant the movie had already passed the $200 million mark in North America. The Fourth of July weekend (its seventh in theaters) brought its domestic total over $300 million. It ran neck and neck with *Iron Man* during this period, but the latter ended up with a marginally higher figure for the year.

Crystal Skull had the expected dynamite response overseas as well, bringing in $79,283,312 in the United Kingdom; $53,085,593 in Japan; $32,751,799 in Spain; and $41,114,044 in France, to name the four top countries.

Budget: $185 million

Box office ranking among 2008 releases:

1. *The Dark Knight* (WB)—$533,345,348
2. *Iron Man* (Paramount)—$318,412,101

3. *Indiana Jones and the Kingdom of the Crystal Skull* (**Paramount**)—$317,101,119
4. *Hancock* (Columbia)—$227,946,274
5. *WALL·E* (Disney)—$223,808,164

The Adventures of Tintin

Paramount Pictures and Columbia Pictures present in association with Hemisphere Media Capital, an Amblin Entertainment/Wingnut Films production, a Kennedy/Marshall production. Deluxe color. Panavision. 3D. Rated PG. 107 minutes.

Opened on Wednesday, December 21, 2011, on 3,087 screens. Following the Christmas weekend, the box office gross was $17,720,016, putting the movie in fifth place, three spots below one other wide release from that same week, Columbia's thriller *The Girl with the Dragon Tattoo*. As the New Year arrived, *Tintin* had taken in $51,400,450, landing it two notches below *War Horse*. If the domestic figures were below expectations, DreamWorks could find solace in the response overseas, where Hergé's hero was better known. This had prompted the decision to release the movie elsewhere in October before it opened in the United States. The eventual foreign gross was $296,402,120. France was responsible for the largest piece of that pie, scoring an astounding $53,970,688. In Hergé's native Belgium, the gross was $10,624,954. It was in these countries, as well as Switzerland, the United Kingdom (gross: $25,927,543), and the Netherlands, that *Tintin* had its first playdates, premiering on October 26, 2011, nearly two full months before the American opening. It also received a subtitle, *The Secret of the Unicorn*, deemed unnecessary on these shores.

Budget: $135 million

War Horse

DreamWorks Pictures and Reliance Entertainment present, an Amblin Entertainment/Kennedy/Marshall Company production. Distributed by Walt Disney Studios Motion Pictures. Deluxe color. Super 35 Widescreen. Rated PG-13. 147 minutes.

Opened on Sunday, December 25, 2011 in 2,376 theaters, ending up with $15 million in just two days of release. Once the first figures of the New Year were announced, it had made $43 million in a little more than a week. The following weekend of January 6–9, it passed over the $50 million mark, with $56.8 million total. Adding another seventy-three screens the following weekend brought the total up to $66,095,091. *War Horse* would end up marginally outpacing *Tintin* at American box offices. Its foreign gross was better than its domestic one, with a $97,700,000 total. Not surprisingly, considering its origins, the country in which it had the most appeal was the United Kingdom (where it opened on January 13, 2012), bringing in $29,572,235.

Budget $66 million

Box office rankings among 2011 releases:

1. *Harry Potter and the Deathly Hallows Part 2* (WB)—$381,00,000
2. *Transformers: Dark of the Moon* (Paramount)—$352,390,000
3. *Breaking Dawn Part 1* (Summit)—$281,290,000
4. *The Hangover Part II* (WB)—$253,470,000
5. *Pirates of the Caribbean: On Stranger Tides* (Disney)—$241,100,000

   . . .

39. *The Descendants* (Fox Searchlight)—$82,280,000
40. *Zookeeper* (Columbia)—$80,370,000
41. **War Horse (Disney/DreamWorks)—$79,890,000**
42. *Limitless* (Relativity Media)—$79,250,000
43. *Tower Heist* (Universal)—$78,100,000
44. **The Adventures of Tintin (Paramount)—$77,560,000**
45. *Contagion* (WB)—$75,660,000

Lincoln

A DreamWorks Pictures, Twentieth Century Fox, and Reliance Entertainment presentation in association with Participant Media and Dune Entertainment. Touchstone Pictures, distributed by Walt Disney Studios Motion Pictures. Deluxe color. Panavision. Rated PG-13. 150 minutes.

A solemn President Lincoln (Daniel Day-Lewis) scopes out the aftermath of the Battle at Petersburg in *Lincoln*.

Opened on November 9, 2012, in eleven theaters. In this small number of houses the film brought in nearly $1 million on its first weekend, with a per-screen average of $85,846. The following weekend, expanding to 1,775 screens brought the total up to $22,468,242. A wider opening for the Thanksgiving holidays to 2,018 screens proved that there was tremendous interest in the film as its box office leapt up to $62,840,796, a per-screen average of $12,724. The film climbed steadily, breaking the $100 million mark the weekend of December 14. The following weekend it expanded to its largest number of screens (2,293) the weekend before Christmas. At the finish of the holiday season, after the weekend of January 4–6, 2013, the total gross was $144,089,046. After receiving twelve Oscar nominations, the film returned to a larger number of screens, bringing the total to $152,600,253. The movie remained a steady performer throughout Oscar season, its weekend take only dropping below the $1 million mark as of February 22, 2013. It was the sort of gratifying box office success that almost restores one's faith in modern audiences.

Lincoln was more than Americana made strictly for American tastes, as it proved a strong draw in several countries, bringing in $13,264,838 in the United Kingdom (perhaps a testament not only to Spielberg and Mr. Lincoln himself but to that country's own Daniel Day-Lewis); $10,863,693 in France; $9,467,518 in Japan; and $8,304,392 in Spain.

Budget: $65 million

Box office ranking among 2012 releases:

1. *The Avengers* (Disney)—$623,357,910
2. *The Dark Knight Rises* (WB)—$448,139,099
3. *The Hunger Games* (Lionsgate)—$408,010,692
   • • •
11. *Dr. Seuss's The Lorax* (Universal)—$214,080,500
12. *Wreck-It Ralph* (Disney)—$189,422,889
13. **Lincoln (Disney/20th)—$182,207,973**
14. *Men in Black 3* (Columbia)—$179,020,854
15. *Django Unchained* (Weinstein Co.)—$162,805,434

Bridge of Spies

A DreamWorks Pictures, Fox 2000 Pictures, and Reliance Entertainment presentation, in association with Participant Media and TSG Entertainment, a co-production between Afterworks Limited and Studio Babelsberg, an Amblin Entertainment/Marc Platt production. Touchstone Pictures, distributed by Walt Disney Studios Motion Pictures. Color. Hawk Scope. Rated PG-13. 142 minutes.

Although the subject matter might lead one to believe that Disney wanted to open this slowly and nurture it along, those days were long gone for most studio product, and therefore the film opened wide at 2,811 theaters in North America on October 16, 2015. The first weekend gross was $15,371,203. Two weeks later another sixty-two screens were added, bringing the total up to $45,531,900. After

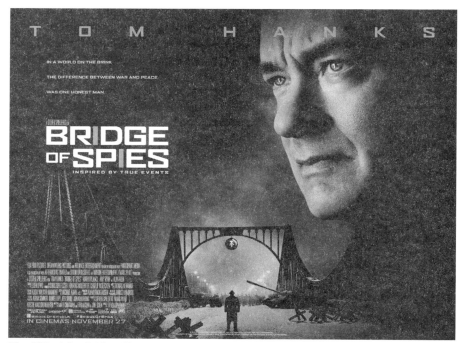

The UK ad for *Bridge of Spies*.

the Thanksgiving holidays, the movie diminished its number of venues considerably, by which point it had made $67,563,007. It was kept in circulation throughout "awards season" for the next three months. Overseas, *Bridge* had its best showing in Italy of all places, with a $12,123,245 gross, while the Russians, who were instrumental to the storyline, shelled out $2,058,944.

Budget: $40 million

Box office ranking among 2015 releases:

1. *Star Wars: The Force Awakens* (Disney)—$930,758,000
2. *Jurassic World* (Universal)—$651,728,000
3. *Avengers: Age of Ultron* (Disney)—$495,006,000
4. *Inside Out* (BV) —$356,419,000
5. *Furious 7* (Universal)—$351,033,000

  • • •

29. *Pixels* (Columbia)—$78,605,000
30. *The Intern* (WB)—$75,765,000
31. ***Bridge of Spies* (BV)—$72,314,000**
32. *Paul Blart: Mall Cop 2* (Columbia)—$70,710,000
33. *The Big Short* (Paramount)—$69,816,000

The BFG

A Disney, Amblin Entertainment, and Reliance Entertainment presentation, in association with Walden Media. Color. Panavision. 3D. Rated PG. 118 minutes.

Opened on July 1, 2016 on 3,357 screens. In the Los Angeles area it debuted at forty-six theaters including: Pacific's The Grove Stadium 14, Regal Cinema L.A. Live Stadium 14, Laemmle's NoHo 7, Century 8 North Hollywood, ArcLight Hollywood; in New York at: Loews Lincoln Square 13, Regal E-Walk Stadium 13, Loews 34th Street 14, and others.

At the end of the Independence Day weekend, the movie had taken in $22,716,809, putting it in fifth place among wide releases. The second weekend it had dropped down to the eighth position, bringing in $7,604,000 on an additional thirty-five screens for a total gross of $38,738,762. By its third week it was clear that interest in the movie was mild at best, and it lost some 1,210 screens, bringing in $3,747,000 for a $47,336,611 total. The fourth week found it on only 273 screens, with a soft $458,064 gross and a $52,146,349 total. By late August the figure was $54,319,626.

The BFG found a somewhat more enthusiastic response in England—the native country of the story's original author, Roald Dahl—following its July 22 opening there. It headed the top of the box office charts its first weekend, with a $6.97 million gross. Because people love to make competitive lists, it was reported that this was Spielberg's third-best three-day weekend opening in the United Kingdom, following *War of the Worlds* and *Indiana Jones and the Kingdom of the Crystal Skull.* The movie ended up with $35,837,674 there by summer's end. Australia followed suit with a healthy $11,408,251 after two months in release.

Budget: $140 million

Sophie (Ruby Barnhill) takes a ride on the shoulder of her new friend, BFG (Mark Rylance), in *The BFG.*

Box office ranking among 2016 Releases:

1. *Rogue One* (Disney)—$531,431,000
2. *Finding Dory* (Disney)—$486,295,000
3. *Captain America: Civil War* (BV)—$408,085,000
4. *The Secret Life of Pets* (Universal)—$368,040,000
5. *The Jungle Book* (BV)—$364,002,000

    . . .

56. *Fences* (Paramount)—$57,673,000
57. *Me Before You* (WB)—$56,246,000
58. ***The BFG* (Disney)—$55,484,000**
59. *Neighbors 2: Sorority Rising* (Universal)—$55,455,000
60. *Office Christmas Party* (Paramount)—$54,768,000

Bibliography

Abagnale, Frank W., and Stan Redding. *Catch Me If You Can*. New York: Broadway Books, 2002.

Aldiss, Brian. *Supertoys Last All Summer Long*. 1969. Reprint, featured in: *Adaptations: From Short Story to Big Screen*. New York: Three Rivers Press, 2005.

Awalt, Steven. *Steven Spielberg and Duel: The Making of a Film Career*. New York: Rowman & Littlefield, 2014.

Ballard, J. G. *Empire of the Sun*. London: Granada Publishing, 1985.

Barrie, J. M., and Maria Tatar. *The Annotated Peter Pan: Centennial Edition*. New York: W. W. Norton & Company, Inc., 2011.

Benchley, Peter. *Jaws*. New York: Doubleday, 1974.

Blake, Edith. *The Making of the Movie Jaws*. New York: Ballantine Books, 1975.

Brode, Douglas. *The Films of Steve Spielberg*. New York: Citadel Press, 2000.

Clement, Henry. *The Sugarland Express* (novelization). New York: Popular Library, 1974.

Crichton, Michael. *Jurassic Park*. New York: Ballantine Books, 1990.

———. *The Lost World*. New York: Ballantine Books, 1995.

Dahl, Roald. *The BFG*. New York: Puffin Books: 2015.

Dick, Philip K. *The Minority Report*. 1956. Reprint, featured in: *Adaptations: From Short Story to Big Screen*. New York: Three Rivers Press, 2005.

Donovan, James. *Strangers on a Bridge: The Case of Colonel Able and Francis Gary Powers*. 1964. Reprint: New York: Scribner Books, 2015.

Duncan, Jody. *The Making of The Lost World: Jurassic Park*. New York: Ballantine Books, 1997.

Erickson, Glenn, and Mary Ellen Trainor. *The Making of 1941*. New York: Ballantine Books, 1980.

Friedman, Josh, and David Koepp. *War of the Worlds: The Shooting Script*. New York: Newmarket Press, 2005.

Gale, Bob. *1941* (novelization). New York: Ballantine Books, 1979.

Goodwin, Doris Kearns. *Team of Rivals: The Political Genius of Abraham Lincoln*. New York: Simon & Schuster, 2005.

Guise, Chris. *The Art of The Adventures of Tintin*. New York: Harper Design, 2011.

Harrison, Stephanie (editor). *Adaptations: From Short Story to Big Screen*. New York: Three Rivers Press, 2005.

Hergé. *The Secret of the Unicorn*. New York: Little, Brown & Co., 1974.

———. *The Crab with the Golden Claws*. New York: Little, Brown & Co., 1974.

———. *Red Rackham's Treasure*. New York: Little, Brown & Co., 2011.

Huyck, Willard, and Gloria Katz. *Indiana Jones and the Temple of Doom: The Illustrated Screenplay*. New York: Ballantine Books, 1984.

Jonas, George. *Vengeance: The True Story of an Israel Counter-Terrorist Team*. New York: Simon & Schuster, 2005.

Kasdan, Lawrence. *Raiders of the Lost Ark: The Illustrated Screenplay*. New York: Ballantine Books, 1981.

Keneally, Thomas. *Schindler's List*. New York: Touchstone, 1982.

Kushner, Tony. *Lincoln: The Screenplay*. New York: Theatre Communications Group, 2012.

Matheson, Richard. *Duel: Three Terror Stories by Richard Matheson*. New York: Tor, 2003.

McBride, Joseph. *Steven Spielberg: A Biography, Second Edition*. Jackson, MS: University Press of Mississippi, 2010.

Morpurgo, Michael. *War Horse*. New York: Scholastic, Inc., 1982.

Morton, Ray. *Close Encounters of the Third Kind: The Making of Steven Spielberg's Classic Film*. New York: Applause Books, 2007.

Nathanson, Jeff. *Catch Me If You Can: The Film and the Filmmakers*. New York: Newmarket Press, 2002.

Owens, William A. *Black Mutiny: The Revolt on the Schooner Amistad*. 1953. Reprint: Baltimore: Black Classic Press, 1997.

Palowski, Franciszek, translation by Anna & Robert G. Ware. *The Making of Schindler's List: Behind the Scenes of an Epic Film*. Secaucus, NJ: Carol Publishing Group, 1998.

Reeves, Tony. *The Worldwide Guide to Movie Locations: The Ultimate Travel Guide to Film Sites Around the World* (Updated Edition). London: Titan Books, 2006.

Rinzler, J. W., and Laurent Bouzereau. *The Complete Making of Indiana Jones: The Definitive Story Behind All Four Films*. New York: Del Rey, 2008.

Rubel, David. *Lincoln: A Cinematic and Historical Companion*. New York: Disney Editions, 2013.

Sanello, Frank. *Spielberg: The Man, The Movies, The Mythology*. Dallas, TX: Taylor Publishing Company, 1996.

Serling, Rod. *The Season to Be Wary*. New York: Bantam Books, 1967.

Shay, Don, and Jody Duncan. *The Making of Jurassic Park*. New York: Ballantine Books, 1993.

Spielberg, Steven. *Close Encounters of the Third Kind* (novelization). New York: Delacorte Press, 1977.

Spielberg, Steven, and Melissa Mathison. *E.T. the Extra-Terrestrial: From Concept to Classic: The Illustrated Story of the Film and Filmmakers*. New York: Newmarket Press, 2002.

Spielberg, Steven (introduction). *War Horse: Pictorial Moviebook*. New York: Dey Street Books, 2011.

Stafford, Nick. *War Horse*. London: Faber and Faber, Ltd., 2007.

Struthers, Jane M., and Jan Harlan. *A.I. Artificial Intelligence: From Stanley Kubrick to Steven Spielberg: The Vision Behind the Film*. New York: Thames & Hudson, 2009.

Taylor, Matt. *Jaws: Memories from Martha's Vineyard*. Martha's Vineyard, MA: Moonrise Media, 2011.

Walker, Alice. *The Color Purple*. New York: Simon & Schuster, 1982.

Wells, H. G. *The War of the Worlds*. 1898. Reprint: New York: Bantam, 2003.

Index

ABC Movie of the Weekend, 93–95

A.I. Artificial Intelligence, 4, 13, 52–55, 145, 172, 186–188, 215, 221, 261, 268, 316–317, 367

A-List, The, 258

A-Team, The, 181

Abagnale, Frank, Jr. 57–59, 148–151, 319–322

Abel, Rudolf, 75–76, 166–168, 338–339

Abrams, J. J., 230

Ace Eli and Rodger of the Skies, 2, 170–171

Adams, Amy, 148, 323

Adams, John Quincy, 51–52, 142, 365

Adler, Charlie, 243

Adventures of Tintin, The, 14–15, 66–69, 160–161, 222, 223, 254, 333–334, 373

Akira Kurosawa's Dreams, 189

al-Chir, Hussein Abad, 64–65

Aladdin and His Wonderful Lamp, 338

Alaskey, Joe, 243–244

Albano, Captain Lou, 276

Aldiss, Brian, 52–53, 186

Aldrin, Buzz, 231

Alfred Hitchcock Hour, The, 19

Alfred Hitchcock Presents, 102, 241

All the Way, 259, 270–272

Allen, Debbie, 50, 313

Allen, Karen, 10, 117, 119–120, 159, 332

Allen, Nancy, 116, 190

Allen, Peter, 287

Allen, Robert, 289

Allen, Woody, 4, 346

Alter, Paul, 320

Alves, Joseph, Jr. 86, 109

Always, 7, 36–39, 131–132, 219, 253, 261, 279, 302–304, 358–360

Amalric, Mathieu, 157, 328

Amazing Stories, 6, 80, 90, 96, 100–103, 170, 177, 178–185, 199, 240–242, 245

Amazing Stories: "Alamo Jobe," 179

Amazing Stories: "The Amazing Falsworth," 180, 242

Amazing Stories: "Ben and Dorothy," 183

Amazing Stories: "Blue Man Down," 184

Amazing Stories: "The Doll," 242

Amazing Stories: "Fine Tuning," 180, 242

Amazing Stories: "Gather Ye Acorns," 182–183, 242

Amazing Stories: "Gershwin's Trunk," 242

Amazing Stories: "Ghost Train," 6, 100–101, 241

Amazing Stories: "Go to the Head of the Class," 242

Amazing Stories: "Grandpa's Ghost," 242

Amazing Stories: "The Greibble," 184

Amazing Stories: "Guilt Trip," 242

Amazing Stories: "Hell Toupee," 242

Amazing Stories: "The Main Attraction," 178–179

Amazing Stories: "Mirror, Mirror," 183, 242

Amazing Stories: "Miss Stardust," 242

Amazing Stories: "The Mission," 6, 101–103, 179, 182, 242

Amazing Stories: "Mr. Remote Control," 180–181

Amazing Stories: "Mummy Daddy," 179

Amazing Stories: "No Day at the Beach," 182

Amazing Stories: "Santa '85," 181

Amazing Stories: "Secret Cinema," 242

Amazing Stories: "The Sitter," 90

Amazing Stories: "Vanessa in the Garden," 6, 181–182, 222, 242

Amazing Stories: "The Wedding Ring," 184–242

Amazing Stories: "What If . . . ?," 80, 242

Amazing Stories: "Without Diana," 242

Amazing Stories: "You Gotta Believe Me," 184

"Amblin'," 2, 81

Ambrose, Stephen E., 253, 256

America's Millennium, 104
American Tail, An, 6, 197–198, 207, 305
American Tail: Fievel Goes West, An, 7, 198, 207–208
Amistad, 11, 15, 50–52, 141–143, 251, 313–315, 365–366
Amistad I (essays), 50
Amistad II (essays), 50
Anderson, Joe, 265
Anderson, Michael, 63
Anderson, Robert Alex, 322
Andrews Sisters, 290, 322
Animaniacs, see *Steven Spielberg Presents Animaniacs*
Animaniacs Sing-Along: Yakko's World, 247
Anka, Paul, 287, 320
Annie Hall, 4
Aphasia, 326
Apted, Michael, 191
Arachnophobia, 7, 206–207
Arlen, Harold, 321
Armageddon, 214
Armstrong, Callum, 336
Armstrong, Lil, 297
Armstrong, Louis, 297
Arnaz, Desi, 121, 180
Arne, Thomas, 341
Around the World in 80 Days (2004), 370
Arvizu, Juan, 332
Ashong, Derrick N., 314
Asner, Edward, 249
Astaire, Fred, 317, 323
Astin, John, 248
Astin, Sean, 177–178, 257
Atherton, William, 2, 107, 285, 343
Attal, Yvan, 155
Attenborough, Richard, 43–44, 134, 141, 313
Aubochon, Remi, 261
Auschwitz, 235–236
Austin Powers in Goldmember, 281–282
Avery, Margaret, 97, 126, 273, 296, 298
Aykroyd, Dan, 115, 125, 274, 275

BFG, The, 15–16, 77–79, 130, 168–169, 256, 340–341, 377–378
Bach, Johann Sebastian, 310, 319
Bacharach, Burt, 243, 321
Back to the Future, 5, 193–195, 203, 205
Back to the Future Part III, 7, 205

Back to the Future Part II, 7, 203
Backlinie, Susan, 108, 114
Bain, Barbara, 98
Bairstow, Scott, 252
Baker, Chris ("Fanghorn"), 145, 186
Baker, Rick, 214
Balaban, Bob, 112, 180, 242
Baldwin, Roger, 51–52, 142
Bale, Christian, 10, 34, 127, 299
Ball, Lucille, 121, 180
Ball, Sherwood, 302
Ballard, J. G. (James Graham), 33–36, 126–127
Baltes, Jameson, 185
Balto, 10, 211
Bana, Eric, 155, 328, 330, 371
Band of Brothers, 13, 15, 223, 253–255, 255, 259–260
Banderas, Antonio, 216–217, 220
Banks, Elizabeth, 148
Barber of Seville, The, 334
Barbier, Jules, 334
Barcellini, Franck, 329
Barker, Paul, 317
Barnes, Bernard, 289
Barney, Chuck, 251
Barnhill, Ruby, 169, 340, 377
Barrie, J. M., 39–40, 133, 304
Barry, Gene, 86–88, 154
Barry, Jeff, 287
Barry Lyndon, 340
Barrymore, Drew, 101, 122
Barrymore, Lionel, 38
Barsi, Judith, 201
Bartel, Paul, 242
Barwood, Hal, 2, 172, 174, 191
Basch, Bill, 218
Bashil, Summer, 267
Batman, 358, 360
Batman Returns, 360
batteries not included, 6, 199–200, 219
Bay, Michael, 225
Baye, Nathalie, 148, 320
Beach, Adam, 223
Beacham, Stephanie, 246
Beallor, June, 218
Beatles, The, 190
Beatty, Ned, 116
Beauty and the Beast, 306
Becker, Meret, 328

Beethoven, Ludwig van, 313, 334
Begelman, David, 172
Bell, Jamie, 160, 223
Bellamy, Ralph, 97
Bellar, Clara, 317
Belle, Camilla, 141
Bellemer, John, 337
Belson, Jerry, 174, 277
Belushi, John, 26, 114, 191–192,
    274–275
Benchley, Peter, 22–23, 25, 109
Benedict, Dirk, 181
Bennett, Harve, 251
Bennett, James, 123
Bennett, Jeff, 249
Bennett, Tony, 326–327
Benson, Lucille, 114
Benz, Julie, 256
Berenger, Tom, 257
Bergasse, Joshua, 265
Bergl, Emily, 256
Bergman, Alan, 293
Bergman, Marilyn, 293
Berle, Milton, 180
Berlin, Irving, 39, 303, 317
Berry, Halle, 268
Bessell, Ted, 278
Best Little Whorehouse in Texas, The, 353
Big Cartoonie Show, The, 252
Bigham, Will, 258
Bilat, Pascal, 329
Billingsley, Barbara, 181
Billy Bathgate, 134
Binder, Mike, 147
Bird, Brad, 179, 245
Bista, Henryk, 136
*Black Mutiny: The Revolt of the Schooner
    Amistad*, 50
Blackmun, Harry, 142
Blanchett, Cate, 157, 159
Bleibtreu, Moritz, 155, 328
Blossom, Roberts, 100–101, 288
Bluel, Richard, 92
Blues Brothers, The, 4, 274–275
Bluth, Don, 197, 207
Boam, Jeffrey, 128
Bochco, Steven, 19, 91
Bochman, Walter, 312
Bodie, Jane, 150
Body Heat, 191

Boehm, David, 38
Boehm, Leslie, 256
Bogdanovich, Peter, 171
Bond, Ward, 39
Borenstein, Max, 270
Borgnine, Ernest, 248
Borle, Christian, 265
Bosley, Tom, 82, 86
Bouzereau, Laurent, 266
Bowlly, Al, 300–301
Boxer, Amanda, 144
Boyer, Christopher, 165
Boyle, Lara Flynn, 219
Bradbury, Ray, 269
Bradford, Jesse, 223
Braga, Brannon, 263
Brahms, Johannes, 327
Branagh, Kenneth, 130
Brandis, Jonathan, 246
Brennan, Frederick Hazlitt, 38
Bricusse, Leslie, 304–306, 326
Bridge of Spies, 15, 75–76, 166–168, 203,
    269, 284, 338–339, 375–376
Bridges, Beau, 181–182, 257
Bridges, Jeff, 229–230
Bridges, Lloyd, 85, 204
Bridges of Madison County, The, 189, 222
Broadbent, Jim, 158
Brodie, Hugh, 339
Brody, Max, 317
Broken Silence, 255
Brolin, James, 84, 320
Brolin, Josh, 233, 257
Brooks, Mel, 350
Broonzy, Big Bill, 325
Brown, Blair, 191–192
Brown, David, 215
Brown, Georg Stanford, 6, 103, 242
Brown, James, 275
Broyles, William, Jr. 223
Bruce, Lorraine, 267
Bryant, Boudleaux, 331
Bryan, Felice, 331
Buffett, Jimmy, 237, 302
Buie, Donna, 298
Bull, 272
Burke, John, 303
Burke, Johnny, 331
Burnett, Mark, 258
Burns, Edward, 12, 269, 315

Burton, Steve, 252, 256
Burton, Tim, 245, 265, 289
Busia, Akousa, 296, 357
Busse, Henry, 297
Butler, Bill, 97
Byrd, Robert, 331

Caan, James, 115, 202
Cagney & Lacey, 6, 107, 242
Cahana, Alice Lok, 218
Cahn, Sammy, 324
Calloway, Cab, 275
Cambridge, Godfrey, 85–86
Cammin, Petra Maria, 167
Campbell, James, 287
Campbell, Martin, 217
Candy, John, 116
Cannom, Greg, 179
Cape Fear, 189
Capra, Frank, 238, 245
Capshaw, Jessica, 14, 257
Capshaw, Kate, 7, 13, 123–124, 275, 295
Carey, Michele, 98
Carmelo, Tonantzin, 257
Carney, Art, 114
Carr, Michael, 300
Carradine, Keith, 257
Carré, Michel, 334
Carroll, Jim, 294
Carson, John David, 92
Carter, Renee, 279
Carter, Rick, 145, 153, 163
Casper, 10, 210–211
Cassidy, Jack, 91
Castle, Nick, 41
Catch Me If You Can, 13, 57–59, 148–151,
     166, 269, 320–324, 368–369
Cattle Queen of Montana, 195
Cavett, Dick, 183
Cenci, Giuseppe, 328
Champs, 185
Charman, Matt, 75
Chatwin, Justin, 153, 326
Chester, Vanessa Lee, 280
Chicago, 221
Chiffons, The, 322
Child, Julia, 208
Chopin, Fredric, 299
Christian, Roger, 327
Chukhraj, Pavel, 255

Ciccolella, Jude, 152
Cinqué, 51–52, 141–143, 313–315
Clark, Bob, 181
Clarke, Arthur C., 186
Clash of the Titans, 350
Class of '61, 7, 245
Cleese, John, 208, 249
Clement, Jemaine, 169
Cline, Ernest, 15
Clinton, Bill, 104, 361, 365
Clinton, Hillary, 361, 365
Clooney, George, 11
Close, Eric, 256
Close Encounters of the Third Kind, 3–4,
     13, 17, 36, 100, 101, 110–113,
     146, 172–174, 180, 186, 208, 230,
     232, 247, 277, 282–283, 287–289,
     347–349
Clough, John Scott, 179
Clouse, Robert, 97
Coasters, The, 304
Cody, Diablo, 258
Coen Brothers (Joel and Ethan), 75,
     229–230
Cohen, Jeff, 178
Cohen, Jon, 55
Cohen, Lynn, 64, 156
Colby, Barbara, 91
Cole, Nat King, 324, 339
Coleman, Gary, 181
Collette, Toni, 258–259
Collins, Russell, 28
Color Purple, The, 6, 29–33, 97, 125–126,
     128, 221, 235, 242, 273, 278,
     284, 293, 296–299, 342,
     356–357
Color Purple, The (novel), 29–33
Columbo: "Murder by the Book," 2, 90–91
Columbus, Chris, 128, 177, 196, 205
Conan Doyle, Arthur, 196
Conn, Shelley, 263
Connally, Merrill L., 106
Connelly, Reginald, 287
Connery, Sean, 128–130, 150
Constant, Marius, 294
Contet, Henri, 316
Continental Divide, 4, 191–192
Conversation, The, 3
Cook, Rachael Leigh, 257
Cooke, Olivia, 16

Cooksey, Danny, 243
Coon, Deborah, 317
Coppola, Francis Ford, 3, 238
Cops, 319
Corbett, John, 259
Costello, Elvis, 294
Costner, Kevin, 102
Courtney, Joel, 230
Covey, James, 52
Cowboys & Aliens, 14, 231–232
Cowen, Mark, 255
Cox, Alan, 196
Cox, Ronny, 251
Coyote, Peter, 122
"Crab with the Golden Claws, The,"
    66–68
Craig, Daniel, 160, 232, 329, 371
Cranston, Bryan, 270–272
Crawford, Joan, 2, 18, 81–83
Creature from the Black Lagoon, The, 21
Creef, Sarah, 279
Cresson, James, 171
Crichton, Michael, 44–45, 48–50, 134,
    213
Crone, James Kenneth, 21–22, 106
Cronkite, Walter, 208
Cronyn, Hume, 199–200
Crosby, Amy, 279
Crosby, Bing, 291, 301, 303, 322, 331
Cross, David, 16
Cross, Joseph, 223–224
Crothers, Scatman, 28–29, 123
Crouch, Andrae, 298–299
Crouch, Sandra, 299
Crowe, Cameron, 146, 281
Croze, Marie-Josée, 157, 331
Cruise, Tom, 55, 62, 146, 270, 281–282,
    318–319, 326–327
Cunningham, Liam, 163
Curry, Tim, 249
Curtis, Richard, 70

D'Onofrio, Vincent, 214
Dabrowska, Oliwia, 137, 309
Dad, 7, 202–203
Dadié, Bernard, 314
Dahl, Roald, 77–79, 168, 377
Dale, James Badge, 259
Damon, Gabriel, 181
Damon, Matt, 143–144, 228, 315

*Dan Finnerty & the Dan Band: I Am
    Woman*, 257
Dandourian, Magdalena, 138, 311
Dangerous Woman, A, 189
Daniels, Danny, 295
Daniels, Jeff, 206
Danson, Ted, 202–203
Dante, Joe, 29, 180, 184, 198, 276
Darden, Severn, 87
Darling, Joan, 90
Das Boot, 117
Davenport, Jack, 265
Daviau, Allen, 101, 124
David, Hal, 321
David, Keith, 303
David, Mack, 339
Davidtz, Embeth, 139, 311
Davies, Jeremy, 144, 213, 315
Davies, Ray, 323
Davis, Lou, 297
Day, Bobby, 331
Day-Lewis, Daniel, 15, 163, 336, 337,
    374
Dayal, Manish, 235
Days of Remembrance: PastForward, 235
de Bont, Jan, 55
de Guzman, Michael, 183
Dearlove, Jack, 301
Death Becomes Her, 42
Deep, The, 348
Deep Impact, 11, 214–215
Deezen, Eddie, 114, 116, 190
DeHaan, Dane, 165
Del Sesto, David, 298
del Toro, Guillermo, 238
DeLange, Eddie, 319
Dennehy, Brian, 269
Dennis, Sandy, 96–97
Dent, Catherine, 256
Dent, Ila Fae, 21–22, 172
Dent, Robert, 21–22, 172
Denver, John, 324
Dern, Laura, 10, 43, 135, 219
DeVito, Danny, 184, 214, 242, 281
Di Cicco, Bobby, 190, 290
Diamond, Keith, 214
Diamond, Neil, 294
Diaz, Cameron, 281
DiCaprio, Leonardo, 57–58, 148–149,
    269, 294, 320, 322, 368–369

Dick, Philip K., 55, 57
Dick Tracy, 201
Diff'rent Strokes, 181
Dillard, Pamela, 315
Dillion, Melinda, 110, 289
Disney, Walt, 289, 315
Djadjam, Mostefa, 329
Dodgeball, 370
Dog's Purpose, A, 189
Don't Say No Until I Finish Talking: The Richard D. Zanuck Story, 265–266
Donahue, Heather, 256
Doniger, Walter, 85
Donner, Richard, 276
Donovan, James B., 75–76, 166–168
Doody, Alison, 129, 301
Dorsey, Thomas A., 298
Dossena, Paolo, 328
Doubt, 204
Dreyfuss, Richard, 10, 24, 36, 83, 109, 110–111, 131–132, 278, 286–287, 302–303
Driver, Adam, 164
Dubin, Al, 317
Duel, 2, 18–21, 80, 85, 93–96, 97, 105–106, 114, 248, 283
"Duel" (short story), 18–21
Duhamel, Josh, 239
Dukakis, Olympia, 203
Dumbo, 27, 115
Dunleavy, Mary, 337
Dunne, Irene, 36, 39
Durning, Charles, 184
Duvall, Robert, 215
Dwight, Timothy, 314

E.T. the Extra-Terrestrial, 5, 17, 28, 66, 77, 96, 101, 120–122, 124, 136, 170, 189, 230, 249, 250, 269, 276, 277, 279, 283, 292–294, 351–354, 361
Eagle Eye, 14, 226
Eastin, Steve, 320
Eastwood, Clint, 14, 181, 222–225, 228, 242, 265
Echevarria, Rene, 263
Eckstein, George, 19, 94
Ed Sullivan Show, The, 190
Eddison, Robert, 129
Edwards, Cliff, 291

Egmont, 338
Eick, David, 261
Ejiofor, Chiwetel, 51
Eleniak, Erika, 122
Elfman, Danny, 214
Elgar, Edward, 309
Elizabeth II, 69, 341
Ellington, Duke, 315, 331
Elliott, Denholm, 118, 128, 158
Elliott, Marianne, 69
Ellis, Kirk, 257
Elwes, Cary, 213
Empire of the Sun, 6, 33–36, 126–128, 299–301, 357–358
Empire of the Sun (novel), 33–36
Empire Strikes Back, The, 352
Erman, John, 171
Ernest, Roger, 285
"Escape to Nowhere," 1
Everly Brothers, 331
Explorers, 180
Extant, 268
"Eyes" (story), 17–18
Eyes Wide Shut, 187
Eyton, Frank, 321

Fabian, Lara, 317
Fabian, Miri, 137
Fain, Sammy, 316
Fairbanks, Douglas, 216
Falk, Peter, 91
Falling Skies, 261
Falvey, Justin, 259, 261, 262–263, 265–269, 272
Fame Is the Name of the Game, 86
Family Dog, 245
Fandango, 102, 184, 189
Fanning, Dakota, 153, 256, 327
Fantastic Four, 371
Fantastic Voyage, 198
Far Off Place, A, 189, 201
Farrell, Colin, 147
Fassbender, Michael, 254
Faust, 337
Favreau, Jon, 232
Feldman, Corey, 178
Ferdin, Pamela, 86
Ferrero, Martin, 134
Field, Sally, 15, 99, 163, 251, 336
Fields, Dorothy, 323–324

Fields, Verna, 109
Fiennes, Ralph, 136, 138
"Fighter Squadron," 1
Finding Oscar, 16, 238
Finkel, Dave, 259
Finnerty, Dan, 257
Firelight, 1
Firestone, Renée, 218
Firm, The, 360
Firth, Peter, 314
Fisher, Carrie, 41, 258, 275
Fisher, Mickey, 268
Five Came Back, 16, 237–238
Flags of Our Fathers, 14, 222–224, 270
Fleischer, Charles, 279
Fleischer, Richard, 198
Fleming, Renée, 334
Fleming, Victor, 38
Flintstones, The, 9, 208–210
Flintstones in Viva Rock Vegas, The, 189
Flippen, Keith, 147
Flipper, 311
Fonda, Henry, 304
Fonda, Olga, 233
Ford, Harrison, 10, 83, 101, 117–120,
        122, 123–125, 128–129, 157, 159,
        275, 292, 301, 331–332, 350, 359
Ford, John, 15, 99, 122, 238
Forrest Gump, 190
Fosse, Bob, 308
Foster, Stephen, 336
Four in One, 83, 85, 88
Fox, Charles, 320
Fox, Megan, 225
Fox, Michael J., 193, 195, 280
Franciosa, Tony, 86
*Francis Gary Powers: The True Story of the
        U2 Spy Incident*, 75
Frank, Darryl, 261–263, 265–270, 272
Frank, Scott, 55
Frankel, David, 255
Franklin, Aretha, 275
Franklin, Carl, 261
Franzoni, David, 50
Frazer, Rupert, 299
Frazier, Al, 294
Freakazoid!, see *Steven Spielberg Presents
        Freakazoid!*
Freeman, Joshua, 63

Freeman, Morgan, 51, 142, 215,
        265–266, 365
Freeman, Paul, 118
French, Daniel Chester, 231
Frewer, Matt, 256
Frost, Nick, 160, 282
Frye, E. Max, 253
Fryer, Robert, 171
Fuller, Samuel, 116
Fyre, Forest, 257

Gagnon, Pierce, 268
Gail, Max, 184
Gaillard, Slim, 303
Gale, Bob, 27, 114, 190, 193
Gambia, Fred, 117
Gangs of New York, 368
Gannon, Kim, 323
Gardel, Carlos, 308
Garland, Judy, 213, 320, 323
Garland, Patrick, 95
Garland, Red, 338
Garner, Erroll, 321
Garner, Jennifer, 148, 321
Garris, Mick, 199
Garwood, Norman, 133
Gavigan, Luke Hudson, 14
Gaynor, Mitzi, 295
Gebr, Jaroslav, 182
Geer, Will, 99
Geffen, David, 9, 189, 258
George Burns and Gracie Allen Show, The,
        180
Gershwin (George and Ira), 320
Gertz, Jami, 213
Getz, Stan, 321, 330
Ghostley, Alice, 171
Gibbons, James Sloan, 336
Gibson, Scott, 259
Gilberto, Astrud, 321
Gilchrist, Keir, 259
Gillberg, Swen, 233
Gingrich, Newt, 214
Giuditta, 309
Girl from Petrovka, The, 343
Girl with the Dragon Tattoo, The, 373
Glatter, Leslie Linka, 182
Gleason, Jackie, 114
Gleason, James, 38
Gleeson, Brendan, 145

Glover, Danny, 10, 125, 278, 296–297, 357
Glover, John, 205
Gluck, Griffin, 267
Godfather, The, 345–346, 353
Goeth, Amon, 46–47, 138, 310–311
Goethe, Johann von, 338
Goetzman, Gary, 255
Goggins, Walton, 336
Going, Joanna, 257
Goldberg, Adam, 144, 315
Goldberg, Marcel, 46
Goldberg, Whoopi, 126, 278, 296–297
Goldblum, Jeff, 43, 140, 280, 313, 364
Golden, Arthur, 220–221
Goldfinger, 150
Goldsmith, Jerry, 284
Golson, Benny, 325–326
Gone with the Wind, 121, 345, 353
Good, Meagan, 270
Goodall, Caroline, 305, 308
Goodman, Dickie, 287
Goodman, John, 10, 37, 131, 206–207, 209, 302
Goonies, The, 5, 177–178, 230, 276
"Goonies 'R' Good Enough, The," 276
Goorwitz (Garfield), Allen, 191
Gordon, Irving, 331, 339
Gordon-Levitt, Joseph, 164, 337
Gortsas, Demitri, 144
Gottlieb, Carl, 23–24, 97, 99, 170, 265, 273
Gounod, Charles, 68, 334, 337
Grais, Michael, 175–176
Grant, David Marshall, 265
Grazer, Brian, 232, 280
Grease, 351
Grease 2, 351
Great White Hope, The, 23
Green, Al, 330
Green, Johnny, 321
Greene, Graham, 257
Greengrass, Paul, 238
Greenwood, Bruce, 16, 265
Gregory, Natalie, 183
Gremlins, 5, 128, 177, 205, 275–276
Gremlins 2: The New Batch, 7, 205–206, 279
Gretsch, Joel, 256
Grier, David Alan, 248

Grier, Pam, 248
Groban, Josh, 317
Gross, Arye, 147
Grush, Stephen Louis, **266–267**
Guber, Peter, 29
Guest, Revel, 70
Guffey, Cary, 110, 288
Gulager, Clu, 89–90
Guy Named Joe, A, 36–39, **103**, **131**

Haas, Charlie, 205
Haas, Lukas, 101, 165
Haddock, Laura, 239
Hader, Bill, 283
Haggard, Merle, 285
Haggis, Paul, 223
Hagy, George, 107
Haid, Charles, 185
Haley, Bill (& His Comets), **332**
Haley, Jackie Earle, 165
Hall, Ellis, 324
Hall, Lee, 70
Hamill, Mark, 183, 248
Hamilton, George, 216
Hamilton, Murray, 114, 116
Hammond, Raushan, 305
Hamshari, Mahmoud, 63, 65, **329**
Hanks, Chet, 158
Hanks, Colin, 254
Hanks, Tom, 9–10, 12, 16, 59–61, **83**, 143–144, 148, 151–152, **158**, 166–167, 196–197, 204, **213**, **229**, 250, 253–254, 259, **261**, **315**, **316**, 321, 325, 338, 366, **369**, **376**
Hanna-Barbera, 209
Hannah, Liz, 16
Harbach, Otto, 39, 303
Hardy, Tom, 254
Harlan, Jan, 188
Harline, Leigh, 289
Harnell, Jess, 247
Harrington, Desmond, **256**
Harris, Ed, 262
Harris, Jared, 165
Harris, John, 294
Harris, Jonathan, 249
Harris, Mark, 237
Harrison, Tom, 179
Harry and the Hendersons, **189**
Hart, Jim V., 41

Hart, Lorenz, 339
Harto, Joshua, 338
Harvey, Alfred, 210
Harvey, Anthony, 196
Haskin, Byron, 61
Hastings, Peter, 252
Hatzidakis, Manos, 330
Hauberger, Rami, 311
Hawke, Ethan, 203
Hawkes, John, 165, 256
Hawks, Howard, 140
Hawn, Goldie, 2–3, 10, 106–107, 284, 343
Hay, John, 74
Haydn, Joseph, 318, 323
Hayes, Ira, 223
Hedren, Tippi, 251
Helgenberger, Marg, 38, 304
Helmet for My Pillow, 260
Henderson, Stephen McKinley, 336
Henley, Barry Shabaka, 152
Henriksen, Lance, 257
Hepburn, Audrey, 38, 131–132, 303
Hereafter, 14, 228–229
Hergé (Georges Remi), 66–68, 161, 334, 373
Herzog, Arthur, Jr. 312
Hewson, Eve, 339
Hiddleston, Tom, 161, 335
High Incident, 185–186
Hill, Arthur, 92
Hill, Bill, 325
Hill, John, 174
Hill Sisters, The, 302
Hilty, Megan, 265
Hinds, Ciarán, 155–156, 329
Hines, Gregory, 180
Hingle, Pat, 181
Hirsch, Helen, 47, 311
History of the World Part 1, 350
Hitchcock, Alfred, 226, 246
Hitched, 98–99
Hoffman, Dustin, 5, 8, 40–41, 99, 133–134, 243, 279
Hoffman, Philip Seymour, 213
Holbrook, Hal, 163
Holiday, Billie, 312
Hollyridge Strings, 324
Honey, I Shrunk the Kids, 201

Hook, 7, 39–42, 100, 132–134, 171, 299, 304–306, 360
Hooper, Tobe, 5, 175, 177, 242, 256
Hoover, Denette, 302
Hope, Leslie, 265
Hopkins, Anthony, 142, 216, 220, 239, 251, 365
Hopper, Dennis, 283
Horner, James, 198, 201
Hoskins, Bob, 40, 200, 211, 306
Hounsou, Djimon, 141, 314, 365
How to Make an American Quilt, 189
Howard, Jeremy, 149–150, 322
Howard, Ron, 232, 265
Howard, Susan, 98
Howdy Doody, 331
Howell, Tom (C. Thomas), 121
Hudis, Stephen, 88
Hudson, Rock, 91
Hughes, Frank John, 321
Hughes, Howard, 120, 145
Humongous, 351
Hundred-Foot Journey, The, 15, 235
Hunchback of Notre Dame, The, 127
Hunt, Helen, 212
Hunt, Marsha, 84
Hunter, Holly, 131, 302
Hurst, Ryan, 256
Hurt, John, 332
Hurt, William, 145
Hussey, Olivia, 248
Huston, John, 6, 238
Hutton, Jim, 89
Huyck, Willard, 123
Hyams, Peter, 180, 242
Hyman, Dick, 339
Hynek, J. Allen, 172

I Love Lucy, 180
I Wanna Hold Your Hand, 4, 189–191, 193
I'm Mad, 244
Idle, Eric, 248
In Dreams, 189
Ince, Thomas, 121
Independence Day, 364
Indiana Jones and the Kingdom of the Crystal Skull, 14, 42, 157–160, 226, 331–332, 372–373, 377
Indiana Jones and the Last Crusade, 7, 128–131, 158, 301, 358–359

Indiana Jones and the Temple of Doom, 5, 123–125, 178, 179, 196, 219, 275, 294–295, 355–356
Ingram, James, 198
Inner Circle, 319
Innerspace, 6, 128, 198
Into the West, 257
Invasion America, 251
Iron Man, 372
Ironside, Michael, 246
Irvine, Jeremy, 161–162, 335
Irving, Amy, 5–7, 10, 91, 101, 125, 201, 278
Irving, Richard, 91
Isabella, Queen, 142
Israel, Robert A., 320
It's a Wonderful Tiny Toons Christmas Special, 245
Itzin, Gregory, 165
Ivey, Dana, 126, 298

Jack the Giant Slayer, 79
Jackson, Desreta, 125, 296, 357
Jackson, Leonard, 125, 298
Jackson, Michael, 278, 293, 296
Jackson, Peter, 65, 160–161, 227
Jackson, Samuel L., 10, 135
Jal, Jean, 316
James, Colton, 141
Jasny, Vojtech, 255
Jaws, 3, 22–26, 36, 96, 97, 94, 95, 107–109, 110, 113, 136, 170, 215, 227, 249, 250, 265, 275, 280, 286–287, 344–347, 353, 357, 361
Jaws (novel), 22–26
Jaws, the Revenge, 183
Jaws 3-D, 109
Jaws 2, 23, 86
Jenney, Lucinda, 185
Jennings, Will, 201
Jerk, The, 349
Jijikine, Igor, 158–159
Jobim, Antonio Carlos, 321
Joe Versus the Volcano, 7, 203–204, 279
Johnson, Ben, 2, 107, 285
Johnson, Brad, 131, 302
Johnson, George Clayton, 28
Johnson, Jadili, 298
Johnson, Lyndon, 270
Johnson, Van, 37–38

Johnston, Joe, 219
Jonas, George, 63
Jones, Michael Steve, 303
Jones, Quincy, 29, 104, 278, 282, 293, 296, 298
Jones, Tommy Lee, 15, 161, 211, 217, 233, 336
Jonny Quest, 249, 251
Jordan, Jeremy, 265
Jordan, Will, 190
Jourgensen, Al, 317
Judge, Jack, 301
Jurassic Park, 4, 8–9, 42–45, 48, 134–136, 140–141, 187, 202, 208, 213, 219, 237, 245, 249, 251, 259, 263, 280, 306–307, 360–361
Jurassic Park (novel), 42–45
Jurassic Park III, 13, 218–219
Jurassic World, 15, 236–237
Juwanna Man, 368

Kabalevsky, Dmitri, 329
Kaempfert, Bert, 325
Kahn, David, 303
Kaminski, Janusz, 146
Karmen, Steve, 325
Kasdan, Lawrence, 191, 238
Kassovitz, Mathieu, 329–330
Katz, Gloria, 123
Katzenberg, Jeffrey, 9, 189
Kaye, Danny, 247
Kaye, Stubby, 317
Kean, Edward, 331
Kearns Goodwin, Doris, 72–74
Keckley, Elizabeth, 163
Keitel, Harvey, 181–182
Keith, David, 185
Kelley, Mikey, 251
Kemmerling, Warren, 112
Kenan, Gil, 222
Keneally, Thomas, 45–48, 363
Kennedy, Jimmy, 300
Kennedy, Kathleen, 4, 16, 69, 188, 189
Kent, Walter, 323
Kern, Jerome, 39, 303, 323
Kershner, Irvin, 242
Khoury, Makram, 155, 328
"Kick the Can" (TV episode), 27–29
Kidman, Nicole, 11
Kiley, Richard, 45, 82

King, Irving, 287
King, Martin Luther, 104
King, Stephen, 266
King Kong vs. Godzilla, 89
Kingsley, Ben, 10, 47, 137, 361
Kinks, The, 322
Knight, Wayne, 134, 251, 307
Knight Rider, 181
Knoxville, Johnny, 219
Koch, Alexander, 266
Koch, Sebastian, 167
Koehler, Ted, 321, 324
Koepp, David, 42, 48–50, 63, 141
Korsmo, Charlie, 40, 134, 305
Kassovitz, Mathieu, 156
Kozak, Harley Jane, 207
Kubrick, Christiane, 187
Kubrick, Stanley, 13, 53, 128, 186–188,
    213, 317, 340
Kuntzel, Oliver, 320
Kupfer, Bettina, 307
Kurtz, Bob, 318
Kushner, Tony, 73–74

Lacey, Ronald, 117
LaBeouf, Shia, 158, 225, 226, 331–332
Ladd, Alan, Jr. 173–174
Lagerfelt, Caroline, 318
LaMarche, Maurice, 243, 248, 252
Lamas, Lorenzo, 251
Land Before Time, The, 6, 201–202
Landau, Martin, 98–99
Lander, David, 116
Landis, John, 4, 27, 114, 274–275
Lang, Stephen, 263
Lange, Henry, 297
Lange, Jim, 181
Langella, Frank, 216, 272
Lansbury, Angela, 241, 280
Lantos, Tom, 218
Larson, Brie, 259
Lassick, Sydney, 181
Last Days, The, 11, 218
"Last Gunfight, The," 1
Latham, Louise, 87, 99
Lauper, Cyndi, 276
Laverne & Shirley, 115–116
Law, Jude, 54, 317
Lawrence, Jack, 316
Layne, Jerry, 116

Lean, David, 123
Leave It to Beaver, 181, 303
Leckie, Robert, 259
Lee, Christopher, 116
Lee, Michele, 244
Lefevre, Rachelle, 266
Legend of Zorro, The, 13, 217, 220
Lehar, Franz, 309
Lehnow, Erwin, 312
Leiber, Jerry, 331
Leland, David, 255
Lemaire, Georgette, 329
Lemkow, Tutte, 117
Lemmon, Jack, 202
Lenehan, Nancy, 320
Leo, Melissa, 272
Leonard, Terry (J.), 119, 191
LeRoy, David, 214
Let There Be Light, 238
Letscher, Matt, 216–217
Lettermen, The, 320–321, 323
Letters, Will, 323
Letters from Iwo Jima, 14, 222, 224–225
Letts, Tracy, 16
Levin, Zoe, 267
Levinson, Richard, 90, 98
Lewis, Damian, 253
Lewis, Huey, 195
Lewis, Ian, 319
Lewis, Jerry, 246
Li, Gong, 221
Li-Ron Herzeliya Children's Choir of
    Tel-Aviv, 309
Liberace, 177
"Liberian Girl," 278
Liboiron, Landon, 263
Liepold, Josef, 46
Lilo & Stitch, 368
Lincoln, 9, 15, 72–74, 99, 163–165, 224,
    231, 256, 270, 336–338, 342,
    374–375
Lincoln, Abraham, 72–74, 102,
    163–165, 374
Lincoln, Mary, 336–337
Lincoln, Robert, 74, 161, 337
Lincoln, Tad, 164, 337
Link, William, 91, 98
Linney, Laura, 245
Lipper, Ken, 218
Lipton, C. Carwood, 255

Lithgow, John, 242
Little Giants, 189
Little Rascals, The, 189
Livingston, Jerry, 339
Livingston, Ron, 253
Llewellyn Davies, Jack, 42
Lloyd, Christopher, 195, 205
Lloyd Webber, Andrew, 14
Locke, Sondra, 181
Loesser, Frank, 317
Loftin, Cary, 94
Loncraine, Richard, 253
Long, Matt, 266
Long, Shelley, 196
Lord of the Rings, The, 368
Lost Children of Berlin, The, 251
Lost World, The (novel), 44–45, 48–50
Lost World: Jurassic Park, The, 11, 42–43, 48–50, 140–141, 214, 219, 280, 313, 364–365
Love and Death, 346
Lovely Bones, The, 14, 227–228
Lovett, Lyle, 304
Lucas, George, 4, 5, 10, 117, 120, 123, 125, 128, 157, 210, 214, 275, 279, 353
Lucas, Josh, 245
Lucky 7, 266–267
Luedtke, Kurt, 45
Luft, Krzysztof, 311
Lunt, Stephen Broughton, 276
Lynn, Loretta, 285

MacDonald, Laurie, 214
Mack, Ronald, 323
Mackie, Anthony, 271–272
MacNeille, Tress, 243, 247
Macola, Beatrice, 137
Madacy Mariachi Band, 307
Madritsch, Julius, 46
Maitland, Sara, 186
Majors, Lee, 92
Malet, Arthur, 171
Malikyan, Kevork, 130
Malkovich, John, 34, 300
Maltin, Leonard, 206
Mancini, Henry, 319
Manheim, Camryn, 268
Mann, Barry, 198
Mann, Danny, 245

Mansour, Alana, 263
Mapother, William, 270
Marcus Welby, M.D., 83–85, 92, 171
Marcus Welby, M.D.: "The Daredevil Gesture," 2, 83–85
Mariachi Los Camperso de Nati Cano, 313
Mark of Zorro, The, 216
Marschwitz, Eric, 301
Marshall, Frank, 4, 69, 119, 125, 126, 176, 189, 206
Marshall, Garry, 248, 258
Marshall, Penny, 115
Marshall, Phil, 302
Marshall, Rob, 221
Marta, Jack A., 95
Martel, K. C., 121, 294
Martini, Maximilian, 144
Mary Poppins, 200–201
Mask, 193
Mask of Zorro, The, 11, 216–217
Massee, Michael, 51
Massey, Raymond, 85
Mastrosimone, William, 257
Masucci, Elizabeth, 269
Matheson, Tim, 116
Matheson, Murray, 28
Matheson, Richard, 18–20, 28, 93–95, 233, 242
Mathis, Johnny, 289
Mathison, Melissa, 28, 66, 77, 122, 170
Mauldin, Bill, 116
Maxwell, Bill, 298
Mayehoff, Eddie, 86
Mayfield, Percy, 338
Mazzello, Joseph, 135, 141, 259
Mbulu, Letta, 298
McBride, Chi, 326
McCarthy, Tom, 223
McClure, Marc, 190
McConaughey, Matthew, 51, 142, 365
McCormack, John, 335
McCulley, Johnston, 216
McDaniel, James, 256
McDonough, Neal, 146, 223, 254, 269
McDowall, Roddy, 82, 248
McDowell, Alex, 151–152
McG (Joseph McGinty Nichol), 257
McGavin, Darren, 96–97, 273
McGill, Bruce, 164

McGrath, Gulliver, 164, 337
McGraw, Phillip C., 272
McHugh, Jimmy, 324
McKean, Michael, 116, 248
McMahon, Ed, 181, 248
McMillan, Ronnie, 26
McNamara, J. Patrick, 116
McNaughton, Robert, 121–122, 294
McNeely, Jerry, 92
McNeil, Kate, 184
McNichol, Kristy, 251
McPhee, Katharine, 265
Means, Russell, 257
Meco (Monardo), 288
Medavoy, Mike, 41, 171
Mehta, Zubin, 14
Meir, Golda, 156
Melin, Maggie, 148
Mello, Jay, 287
Memoirs of a Geisha, 13, 220–221
Memphis Belle, 238
Men in Black, 11, 213–214
Men in Black 3, 15, 233–234
Men in Black II, 13, 219
Mendelsohn, Ben, 16
Mendez, Tomas, 313
Mercouri, Melina, 330
Merkerson, S. Epatha, 164, 338
Merman, Ethel, 295
Merriman, Ryan, 256
Messick, Don, 243
Messing, Debra, 265
Metwally, Omar, 155, 330
Meyjes, Menno, 29, 33, 102, 128, 242, 296
Mientus, Andy, 265
Mifune, Toshiro, 114
Milius, John, 27, 191
Miller, Dick, 190
Miller, George, 29
Miller, Mitch, 323
Miller, T. J., 16
Million Dollar Baby, 223
Mills, Irving, 319, 331
Mills, Hayley, 184
Milne, Matt, 162
Milner, Martin, 91
Milo, Candi, 243
Minion, Joseph, 183
Ministry, 317

Minority Report, 4, 13, 55–57, 146–147, 221, 254, 256, 269, 270, 281, 318–319, 368, 269
Minority Report (TV series), 270
"Minority Report, The" (story), 55–57
Mirren, Helen, 235
Modine, Matthew, 257
Molina, Alfred, 117
Moll, James, 218
Möller, Friedrich-Wilhelm, 308
Moment of Eclipse, The, 52
Monaghan, Michelle, 226
Mondo, Peggy, 89
Money Pit, The, 6, 196–197
Monnot, Marguerite, 315
Monroe, Marilyn, 264
Monster House, 14, 221–222
Moon, Guy, 318
Moore, Julianne, 49, 140, 226, 280
Moore, Michael (2nd unit), 119, 179
Moore, Michael (sound), 179
Morgan, Jeffrey Dean, 268
Morris, Kathryn, 147
Morrison, Van, 304
Morrow, Vic, 27
Morpurgo, Michael, 69–72, 334
Morshower, Glenn, 239
Morton, Samantha, 56, 146, 319
Mozart, Wolfgang, 310, 313, 336
Mrs. Doubtfire, 363
Mucchassi, Zaid, 64
Mullan, Peter, 161
Munich, 9, 13, 63–66, 155–157, 328–331, 371–372
Murder, She Wrote, 241–242
Murphy, C. W., 323
Murphy, Walter, 293
Murren, Dennis, 196, 198
Mustillo, Louis, 185
Myers, Mike, 281

NBC Mystery Movie, 91
NBC World Premiere, 91
Name of the Game, The: "LA 2017," 2, 83, 86–88
Nanayakkara, D. R., 123
Napier, John, 133
Nash, Erik, 233
Nasseri, Mehran Karimi, 59–61
Naor, Igal, 329

Nebbou, Mehdi, 156
Neeson, Liam, 10, 48, 137, 308, 310, 361
Neill, Sam, 10, 43, 135–136, 219, 361
Nelson, Barry, 38
Nelson, Tim Blake, 165, 318
Neuwirth, Bebe, 249
Newlander Hubbard, Jewel, 305
Newley, Anthony, 305
Newman, Alfred, 338
Newman, Susan Kendall, 190
Newman, Thomas, 284, 338
Newton-John, Olivia, 287
Niel, Herms, 309
Night Gallery, 85–86, 88, 91
Night Gallery: "Eyes," 2, 17–18, 80–83, 182
Night Gallery: "Make Me Laugh," 2, 83,
    85–86
Nimoy, Leonard, 231, 251
1941, 4, 26–27, 112–116, 119, 120, 133,
    178, 181, 188, 190, 275, 286,
    290–291, 324, 349–350
Ninomiya, Kazunari, 224
Noises Off, 189
Nolan, Bob, 289
Norris, Dean, 266
Northam, Jeremy, 142
Nouri, Michael, 326
Nowak, Beata, 311
Noyes, Betty, 291
Nutter, David, 255

O'Brien, Edmond, 87
O'Connor, Frances, 145, 187, 316
O'Mara, Jason, 263
O'Reilly, Bill, 231
O'Ross, Ed, 214
O'Rourke, Heather, 176
Oates, Warren, 114
Obama, Barack, 15, 231
Odenkirk, Bob, 16
Olivares, Dolores Ayala, 307
Olmos, Edward James, 104
On the Lot, 258
*Operation Over Flight: The U2 Spy Pilot
    Tells His Story for the First Time,* 75
Orandel, Cyril, 326
Oriolo, Joe, 210
Osment, Haley Joel, 54, 145, 187, 317
Otto, Miranda, 153
Our American Cousin, 338

Out of Africa, 45, 356
Owen, Clive, 245
*Owen Marshall: Counselor at Law: "Eulogy
    for a Wide Receiver,"* 2, 92–93
Owens, Michael, 229
Owens, William A., 50
Oyelowo, David, 165

Pace, Lee, 163
Pacific, The, 14–15, 259–261, **270**
Page, LaWanda, 181
Pal, George, 61–62
Pallana, Kumar, 152
Paltrow, Gwyneth, 281–282
Pantoliano, Joe, 300
Paquin, Anna, 142
Paranormal Activity, 265
Paris Honeymoon, 301
Parker, Trey, 280
Parkes, Walter F., 214
Parsons, Nancy, 181
Parton, Dolly, 14
Patton, John, Jr. 126, 298
Paul, 282–283
Paulsen, Rob, 247, 248, 252
Paulson, Sarah, 16
Paxton, Bill, 212
Paymer, David, 257
Peacemaker, The, 11
Peck, Bob, 135
Pegg, Simon, 16, 160, 254, **282**
Peli, Oren, 265
Peña, Elizabeth, 199
Peña, Michael, 252–253
Penn, Zak, 15
Pepper, Barry, 223, 229
Perlman, Itzak, 309
Perlman, Rhea, 184
Perry Mason, 148
Persuasions, The, 294
Peter Pan, 39–42, 133, 304
Peter, Paul and Mary, 324
Peters, Bernadette, 171, 247, **265**
Peters, Jon, 29
Petersburski, Jerzy, 311
Phillippe, Ryan, 223
Phillips, Anastassia, 267
Phillips, Julia, 110, 173–174
Phillips, Michael, 110, **173–174**
Phoenix, River, 130

Picardo, Robert, 198
Pickens, Slim, 116
Pinky and the Brain, see *Steven Spielberg Presents Pinky and the Brain*
Pinky and the Brain Christmas, A, 11, 250
Pinky, Elmira and the Brain, see *Steven Spielberg Presents Pinky, Elmira and the Brain*
Pinocchio, 289
Piper, Rowdy Roddy, 276
Pirates of the Caribbean: At World's End, 372
Plague of the Zombies, The, 183
Platters, The, 303
Plucky Duck Show, The, see *Steven Spielberg Presents The Plucky Duck Show*
Podeswa, Jeremy, 261
Pointer, Priscilla, 101
Polk, Piotr, 311
Polseres Vermelles, 267
Poltergeist, 5, 97, 101, 174–177, 222, 256
Porky's II: The Next Day, 354
Porter, Cole, 295
Portis, Charles, 229
Post, The, 16
Powell, Anthony, 275
Powell, Dick, 317
Power, Tyrone, 216
Powers, Francis Gary, 75–76, 167–168, 338
Powers, Shifty, 255
Pratt, Chris, 236–237
Preminger, Otto, 2
Prescription Murder, 91
Presley, Elvis, 331
Presnell, Harve, 223
Price for Peace, 256
Project Greenlight, 258
Pryor, Frederic, 75
Psychiatrist, The, 85
Psychiatrist, The: "Par for the Course," 2, 89–90
Psychiatrist, The: "The Private World of Martin Dalton," 2, 88–89
Public Morals, 269
Puenzo, Luis, 255
Pugh, Willard, 125
Purdy, Jolene, 266

Quan, Ke Huy, 123–124, 178, 275

Quiet Man, The, 122
Quinn, Bill, 28, 99, 123

Rabe, Lily, 269
Raiders of the Lost Ark, 4–5, 66, 96, 117–120, 123, 130, 158, 179, 191, 248, 279, 291–292, 294, 350–352
Rain Man, 201
Rainbird, James, 299
Rainger, Ralph, 301
Raitt, Bonnie, 302
Ram, Buck, 323
Ramirez, Oscar, 238
Randall, Tony, 206, 325
Randell, Denny, 293
Ransom for a Dead Man, 91
Rapaport, Larry, 257
Rapaport, Michael, 269
Raposo, Joe, 289
Ready Player One, 16
Reagan, Ronald, 195, 238
Real Steel, 14, 232–233
Rebeck, Theresa, 264
Rebound, 370
Red Band Society, 267–268
"Red Rackham's Treasure," 67–68
Redgrave, Vanessa, 215
Reeves (Eastwood), Scott, 223
Regan, Laura, 270
Reit, Seymour, 210
Reno, Kelly, 179
"Requiem for a Heavyweight," 18
Return of the Jedi, 355
Reuben, Gloria, 163
Reynolds, Burt, 242
Reynolds, Kevin, 184
Reynolds, Norman, 117
Rhys-Davies, John, 117–118, 128, 248
Ribisi, Giovanni, 144
Ricci, Christina, 211
Richard, Emily, 299
Richards, Ariana, 44, 135, 141
Richards, Evan, 28
Richie, Lionel, 296–297
Richter, William, 255
Ríos Montt, Efrain, 238
Rising: Rebuilding Ground Zero, 261–262
Riva, J. Michael, 178
River, The, 265
Rivingtons, The, 294

Roach, Jay, 272
Roach, Pat, 119
Robards, Sam, 145
Robbins, Matthew, 2, 172, 174, 179–191, 199
Robbins, Tim, 154, 183, 327
Roberta, 39, 303
Roberts, Julia, 42, 133, 243, 305
Robertson, Cliff, 171
Robin, Leo, 301
Robinson, Ann, 154
Robinson, Phil Alden, 255
Robinson, Smokey, 14, 328
Rodat, Robert, 261
Rogen, Seth, 282
Rodgers, Mark, 98
Rodgers, Richard, 339
Rogel, Randy, 247
Rogers, Ginger, 22
Rogers, Will, 168
Roller Coaster Rabbit, 201
Romeo et Juliette, 68, 334
Ronan, Saoirse, 227
Ronstadt, Linda, 198
Root, George Frederick, 338
Rosales, Thomas, 313
Rosemont, David A., 257
Rosengrant, John, 233
Rosenman, Leonard, 340
Ross, Diana, 201
Ross, Herbert, 196
Ross, Steve, 99
Rossini, Giaochino, 334, 340
Rourke, Mickey, 116
Rowe, Charlie, 267
Rowe, Nicholas, 196
Rudy, Reed, 185
Ruegger, Tom, 244, 247, 248, 250
Ruff, Michael, 165, 337
Rugg, Paul, 249
Rush, Geoffrey, 155, 329
Russel, Tony, 86
Ryan, Meg, 204
Rybotycka, Beata, 311
Rydell, Mark, 284
Rylance, Mark, 15–16, 83, 166, 169, 338, 340, 377

Sacks, Michael, 2, 285, 343
Sackler, Howard, 23

Sagal, Boris, 82
Sagalle, Jonathan, 136
Sager, Carole Bayer, 294
Saint James, Susan, 86, 91
Salamander, The, 354
Salameh, Ali Hassan, 64–65, 156
Saldana, Zoë, 325
Sale (Ross), Courtney, 99
Salomon, Mikael, 253, 261
Salter, Claudia, 171
Samuelson, Peter, 7
Sanford and Son, 181
Sands, Stark, 270
Santana, 329
Saturday Night at the Movies, 83
Saturday Night Live, 274
Savage, 2, 97, 98–99
Saving Private Ryan, 11–12, 15, 143–144, 182, 218, 223, 229, 238, 252, 253, 255, 261, 269, 279, 315–316, 319, 366–367
Sayle, Alexei, 128
Scent of a Woman, 308
Scheider, Roy, 10, 24, 108, 245–246, 247, 283, 287
Schenkkan, Robert, 259, 270, 272
Schickel, Richard, 252
Schiff, Richard, 50, 364
Schindler, Oskar, 45–48, 137–139, 307–312
Schindler's Ark (UK printing of novel), 45
Schindler's List, 9–10, 15, 45–48, 105, 136–139, 218, 250, 307–312, 342, 361–364
Schindler's List (novel), 45–48
Schnapp, Noel, 166
Schrader, Paul, 173–174
Schubert, Franz, 318
Scorsese, Martin, 183, 242, 368
Scotch Marmo, Malia, 41–42
Scott, Amber, 133, 305
Scott, Elliott, 124
Scott, Lisbeth, 328
Scott, Naomi, 263
Seale, Douglas, 181
seaQuest DSV, 8, 245–246, 247
seaQuest 2032, 245–246
Sease, Drew, 164
Season to Be Wary, The, 17
Secret of the Unicorn, The, 67–68

Seda, Jon, 259
Semenya, Caiphus, 298
Semper Fi, 252–253
Seneca, Joe, 183
Seress, Rezsö, 308
Serling, Rod, 2, 17–18, 80–83, 85–86, 248
Settle, Matthew, 257
Seven Seas, 287
Seward, William, 72–73, 337
Seweryn, Andrzej, 311
Shaiman, Marc, 264
Shakespeare in Love, 11
Shanley, John Patrick, 204
Shannon, Vicellous Reon, 252
Shaw, Robert, 108, 286–287
Shea, Eric, 171
Shear, Barry, 82
Sheen, Charlie, 182
Sheen, Martin, 320
Sheinberg, Sid, 1, 81, 98
Shemer, Naomi, 312
Shepherd, Scott, 166, 339
Sheridan, Tye, 15
Sherman, Richard B., 327
Sherman, Robert M., 327
Sherwin, Manning, 301
Shifflett, Michael, 165
Shining, The, 213
Shooting War, 252
Shostakovich, Dmitri, 339
Shrek, 189
Sidney, George, 286
Siemaszko, Casey, 102
Siemion, Adam, 137
Sikking, James, 251
Silvers, Phil, 339
Silvestri, Alan, 203
Simmons, Richard, 181
Sinatra, Frank, 150, 201, 322, 324, 339
Sinclair, John, 285
Sing Along with Mitch, 323
Singer, Bryan, 79
Singer, Josh, 16
Singleton, John, 280
Serkis, Andy, 160
Sizemore, Tom, 144, 315, 366
Skidoo, 2
Sledge, Eugene, 259
Sleeping Beauty, 316

Sloane, Barry, 269
Small Soldiers, 189
Smash, 264–265
Smith, "Buffalo" Bob, 331
Smith, Cecil, 87, 95
Smith, Dick, 203
Smith, Lois, 318
Smith, Jennifer, 294
Smith, Lois, 147
Smith, Maggie, 133–134
Smith, Will, 104, 214, 219, 233–234
"Smoke Gets in Your Eyes," 39
Smokey and the Bandit, 348
Smotherman, Michael, 304
Something Evil, 2, 96–97, 273
Sommer, Josef, 112
Sonnenfeld, Barry, 214
Soualem, Mouna, 329
Sound of Music, The, 247, 345, 353
South Park, 280
Souther, J. D., 302
Spacey, Kevin, 281
Spader, James, 165, 336
Special Edition: Close Encounters of the Third Kind, The, 4, 349
Speckled Red (Rufus Perryman), 296
Spell Your Name, 222
Spencer, Octavia, 267
Sperber, Wendie Jo, 190
Spielberg, Arnold, 1
Spielberg, Anne, 1, 90, 242
Spielberg, Destry, 11
Spielberg (Adler), Leah (Posner), 1, 16
Spielberg, Max, 5, 125, 203
Spielberg, Mikaela, 11
Spielberg, Nancy, 1
Spielberg, Sasha, 7
Spielberg, Sawyer, 7
Spielberg, Susan, 1
Spielberg, Theo, 7
Spooktacular New Adventures of Casper, The, 210
Spotlight, 224
Sprague, Chandler, 38
Springfield, Dusty, 321
Sssssss, 107
Stack, Robert, 27, 84, 115
Stadler, Joerg, 144
Stafford, Nick, 69–72
Stallone, Sylvester, 214, 280

Stanton, Edwin, 164
Star is Born, A, 213
Star Trek, 231, 251
Star Wars, 4, 117, 122, 243, 251, 349, 352, 353
Starlite Orchestra, 325
Starr, Mike, 185
Starski, Allan, 139
Stead, Arthur, 276
Steenburgen, Mary, 205
Steiner, Max, 325
Steinfeld, Hailee, 229–230
Stephens, Robert, 299
Stern, Tom, 223
Steven Spielberg Presents Animaniacs, 11, 246–247, 248, 250, 252
Steven Spielberg Presents Animaniacs: "Three Tenors and You're Out," 247
Steven Spielberg Presents Animaniacs: "Yakko's World," 247
Steven Spielberg Presents Freakazoid!, 11, 248, 249–250
Steven Spielberg Presents Freakazoid!: "The Freakazoid," 250
Steven Spielberg Presents Freakazoid!: "Freakazoid is History," 250
Steven Spielberg Presents Freakazoid!: "Next Time, Phone Ahead," 250
Steven Spielberg Presents Pinky and the Brain, 12, 248–249, 250, 252
Steven Spielberg Presents Pinky and the Brain: "Schpiel-borg 2000," 249
Steven Spielberg Presents Pinky, Elmira and the Brain, 13, 252
Steven Spielberg Presents The Plucky Duck Show, 7, 244
Steven Spielberg Presents The Plucky Duck Show: "The Return of Batduck," 244
Steven Spielberg Presents Tiny Toon Adventures, 7, 243–244, 252
Steven Spielberg Presents Tiny Toon Adventures: "Buster & Babs Go Hawaiian!," 243, 279
Steven Spielberg Presents Tiny Toon Adventures: "Cinemaniacs!," 243
Steven Spielberg Presents Tiny Toon Adventures: "Fox Trot," 244
Steven Spielberg Presents Tiny Toon Adventures: "KACME TV," 243
Steven Spielberg Presents Tiny Toon Adventures: "New Character Day," 278–279
Steven Spielberg Presents Tiny Toon Adventures: "A Quack in the Quark," 243
Steven Spielberg Presents Tiny Toon Adventures: "thirteensomething," 244
Stevens, George, 238, 286
Stevens, George, Jr. 104
Stevens, Thaddeus, 74, 163–165, 336, 338
Stewart, Douglas Day, 90
Stewart, James, 207, 304
Stifel, David, 146
Stiller, Ben, 370
Stillman, Al, 289
Stillwell, Joseph W., 27, 115
Stokes, J. B., 255
Stoller, Mike, 331
Stoltz, Eric, 193
Stone, Matt, 280
Stone, John A., 304
Stone, Oliver, 182
Stone, Richard, 247, 248, 250
Stoppard, Tom, 128
Stormare, Peter, 50, 57, 140, 313, 318
Story, Joseph, 142
Stowell, Austin, 167, 269
Strachey, Jack, 301
Strangers on a Bridge: The Case of Colonel Abel, 75
Strathairn, David, 337
Strauss, Richard, 317
Strauss II, Johan, 310
Streep, Meryl, 16, 235, 238
Strienz, Wilhelm, 312
Strings Unlimited, 325
Strohl, Rod, 255
Strokes of Genius, 5, 99–100
Strong, Barrett, 329
Strong, Phillip, 126
Studi, Wes, 257
Stuhlbarg, Michael, 16
Sugarland Express, The, 2, 21–22, 88, 98, 99, 106–107, 171–172, 179, 191, 199, 265–266, 284–286, 343–344, 357
Sullivan, Barry, 82–83, 87, 99

Sullivan, Ed, 190
Sullivan, Gene, 285
Summer, Cree, 243, 252
Super 8, 14, 230
Superman II, 351
"Super-Toys Last All Summer Long"
    (short story), 52, 186
Survivors of the Holocaust, 11, 250
Sutherland, Kiefer, 103
Sutton, Adrian, 334
Swarcz, Jeannot, 86
Sword of Gideon, 63
Syndicate, The, 267
Szász, János, 255

Taken, 13, 256–257
Tambor, Jeffrey, 248
Tams, John, 334
Tandy, Jessica, 199–200
Tango & Cash, 358
Taxi Driver, 173
Taylor, Danny Gordon, 233
Taylor, Jim, 337
Taylor, Mark L., 206
Tchaikovsky, Pyotr Ilyich, 316, 318
Team of Rivals: The Political Genius of
    Abraham Lincoln, 72–74
Teenage Mutant Ninja Turtles, 242
Teich, Otto, 308
Temperton, Rod, 293, 296
Temptations, The, 328
Terminal, The, 13, 59–61, 151–152, 166,
    325–326, 370
Terminal Man, The (book), 60
Terra Nova, 262–264
Texas Chain Saw Massacre, The, 176
Thielemans, Toots, 284
Thing from Another World, The, 172
Thinnes, Roy, 88
Thoma, Mimi, 312
Thomas, Henry, 10, 121, 189, 292, 294
Thomas, Jake, 145
Thor, Cameron, 307
Three Musketeers, The, 343
Thumbelina, 244
Timeless Call, A, 14
Tiny Toon Adventures, see *Steven Spielberg*
    Presents Tiny Toon Adventures
Tiny Toon Adventures: The Looney
    Beginning, 242

Tiny Toons' Night Ghoulery, 248
Tiny Toons Spring Break, 247
Titanic, 214
To, Tony, 255
To Tell the Truth, 320
To Wong Foo, Thanks for Everything, Julie
    Newmar, 189
Tonight Show, The, 181
Toonsylvania, 251
Tormé, Mel, 324
Townsend, Mark Anthony, 282
Townsend, Tammy, 253
Toy Story, 211
Tracey Ullman Show, The, 277–278
Tracy, Spencer, 36
Trail Mix-Up, 201
Trainor, Mary Ellen, 178
Transformers, 14, 225–226, 233
Transformers, The, 231
Transformers: Age of Extinction, 15, 234,
    239
Transformers: Dark of the Moon, 14, 230–231
Transformers: Revenge of the Fallen, 14,
    226–227
Transformers: The Last Knight, 16, 239
Travolta, John, 278, 282
Treadaway, Luke, 69
Trigger Effect, The, 189
Troyer, Verne, 281
True Grit, 14, 229–230
Truex, Ernest, 27
Truffaut, Francois, 112
Trumbo, Dalton, 38
Trumbull, Douglas, 112
Tucci, Stanley, 152, 227, 234, 239
Tummy Trouble, 201
Turner, Kathleen, 201
Turturro, John, 225, 239
Tuwim, Julian, 311
21 Hours in Munich, 63
Twilight Zone, The (TV series), 17, 19, 27,
    82, 179, 184, 233, 240–242, 294
Twilight Zone: The Movie, 5, 27–29, 99,
    114, 122–123, 154, 284, 294, 354
Twister, 11, 212–213
Twitty, Conway, 285

UFO Experience: A Scientific Inquiry, The,
    172
Ullman, Tracey, 277–278

Under the Dome, 266
Unfinished Journey, The, 104
United States of Tara, 258–259
Used Cars, 4, 190–191, 193

Van Heusen, Jimmy, 324, 331, 339
Van Nuys, Ed, 38
Van Patten, Tim, 259, 261
Van Sickel, Dale, 94
Vanilla Sky, 146, 281
Vaughn, Vince, 140, 364
Vega, Táta, 296, 298
*Vengeance: The True Story of the Israeli
     Counter-Terrorist Team*, 63
Ventimiglia, Milo, 269
Vernon, Jackie, 85
Victor, David, 84, 92
Victor, Mark, 175–176
Viotti, Giovanni Battista, 313
Visionary, The, 90
Visnjic, Goran, 268
Vivaldi, Antonio, 334
von Sydow, Max, 147
Voorhees, Jeffrey, 109, 287
Voyage to the Bottom of the Sea, 246

Wahlberg, Mark, 239
Wajda, Andrzej, 255
Walken, Christopher, 58, 150, 320–321
Walker, Alice, 29–33
Walker, Benjamin, 223
Walker, Wiley, 285
Wallace, Dee, 251, 269, 294
Waller, Leslie, 174
Waltons, The, 116
War Horse, 14–15, 69–72, 161–163,
     334–336, 373–374
War Horse (novel), 69–72
War Horse (play), 69–72
War of the Worlds, 13, 42, 61–63, 88, 105,
     153–155, 183, 232, 256, 261,
     326–327, 370–371, 377
War of the Worlds, The (novel), 61–63
War of the Worlds, The (1953 film), 61
Warden, Jack, 191
Warhol, Andy, 234
Warlock, Dick, 109
Warner, David, 249
Warren, Harry, 317
Warren, Marc, 253

Wars, Henryk (Henry Vars), 311
Warschafsky, Mark, 309
Warshofsky, David, 165
Warwick, Dionne, 214
Washington, Ned, 289
Watanabe, Ken, 221, 224
Waterston, Sam, 104, 183
Watkins, Michael, 253
Watrous, Bill, 339
Watson, Ian, 186
Wayne, John, 229, 304
*We Stand Alone Together: The Men of Easy
     Company*, 255
We're Back! A Dinosaur's Story, 9, 208
Weatherly, Frederick E., 335
Weatherly, Michael, 272
Weaver, Dennis, 10, 85, 91, 93–95, 105,
     114
Webb, Frank, 84
Weil, Cynthia, 198, 317
Welch, Elizabeth, 301
Welker, Frank (K.), 244, 249
Welles, Orson, 61–62, 153
Wells, H. G., 61–63, 153
Wells, Robert, 324
West Side Story, 246
Whispers, The, 268–269
Whitaker, Forest, 183
Whitaker, Johnny, 97
White, Carol, 294
White, Julie, 163
White, Ronald, 327
Whiteman, Paul, 297
Whitfield, Norman, 328
Whitford, Bradley, 16
Whitman, Slim, 289
Who Framed Roger Rabbit, 6, 200–201
Wilder, Billy, 196
Williams, Aaron, 314
Williams, Anson, 92
Williams, Esther, 38, 114, 133
Williams, Guy, 216
Williams, J. Mayo, 296
Williams, James "Harry," 301
Williams, JoBeth, 175
Williams, John, 10, 13, 104, 143, 219,
     284, 286–293, 301, 304, 306–
     307, 313–314, 317, 320, 325–326,
     328, 333, 336, 338
Williams, Richard, 201

Williams, Robin, 8, 133, 279, 305, 363
Wilson, Brian, 327
Wilson, Stuart, 216
Wilson, Thomas F., 205
Wilson, Turner, Jr. 294
Wilton, Penelope, 169, 341
Winfrey, Oprah, 126, 235, 243, 298
Winge, Carl, 289
Wingett, Bill, 255
Winston, Stan, 13, 134, 136, 140
Winstone, Ray, 157, 332
Winters, Richard, 255
With the Old Breed at Peleliu and Okinawa,
    260
Withers, Bill, 328
Wittman, Scott, 264
Wizan, Joe, 171
Wizard of Oz, The, 213
Wójcicki, Jacek, 311
Wong, BD, 237
Wood, Elijah, 215
Wood, Haydn, 335
Woods, Zach, 16
Wyle, Noah, 261
Wyler, William, 238

Wylie, Philip, 87

Yeoh, Michelle, 221
Yellowbeard, 354
Yost, Graham, 261
Young, Harrison, 144
Young, Robert, 84
Young, Stephen, 92
Young Sherlock Holmes, 6, 195–196
Your Studio and You, 280
Yukich, Jim, 278
Yune, Karl, 233

Zaillian, Steven, 45–48
Zano, Nick, 270
Zanuck, Harrison, 266
Zanuck, Richard D., 171, 215, 265–266
Zemeckis, Robert, 27, 42, 114, 178, 179,
    189–190, 191, 195, 200, 242
Zeta-Jones, Catherine, 216–217, 326
Zisblatt, Irene, 218
Zischler, Hanns, 155–156, 371
Zsigmond, Vilmos, 285
Zurer, Ayelet, 155, 328
Zwaiter, Wael, 63, 64, 155–156, 328

THE FAQ SERIES

AC/DC FAQ
by Susan Masino
Backbeat Books
9781480394506.............. $24.99

The Band FAQ
by Peter Aaron
Backbeat Books
9781617136139 ....$19.99

Baseball FAQ
by Tom DeMichael
Backbeat Books
9781617136061.............. $24.99

The Beach Boys FAQ
by Jon Stebbins
Backbeat Books
9780879309879 ....$22.99

The Beat Generation FAQ
by Rich Weidman
Backbeat Books
9781617136016 ....$19.99

Beer FAQ
by Jeff Cioletti
Backbeat Books
9781617136115 ....$24.99

Black Sabbath FAQ
by Martin Popoff
Backbeat Books
9780879309572...................$19.99

Bob Dylan FAQ
by Bruce Pollock
Backbeat Books
9781617136078 ....$19.99

Britcoms FAQ
by Dave Thompson
Applause Books
9781495018992 ....$19.99

Bruce Springsteen FAQ
by John D. Luerssen
Backbeat Books
9781617136939...................$22.99

**Buffy the Vampire
Slayer FAQ**
*by David Bushman and
Arthur Smith*
Applause Books
9781495064722...................$19.99

Cabaret FAQ
by June Sawyers
Applause Books
9781495051449...................$19.99

A Chorus Line FAQ
by Tom Rowan
Applause Books
9781480367548 ....$19.99

The Clash FAQ
by Gary J. Jucha
Backbeat Books
9781480364509 ....$19.99

The Doors FAQ
by Rich Weidman
Backbeat Books
9781617130175 ....$24.99

Dracula FAQ
by Bruce Scivally
Backbeat Books
9781617136009 ....$19.99

The Eagles FAQ
by Andrew Vaughan
Backbeat Books
9781480385412...................$24.99

Elvis Films FAQ
by Paul Simpson
Applause Books
9781557838582...................$24.99

Eric Clapton FAQ
by David Bowling
Backbeat Books
9781617134548 ....$22.99

Fab Four FAQ
*by Stuart Shea and
Robert Rodriguez*
Hal Leonard Books
9781423421382...................$19.99

Fab Four FAQ 2.0
by Robert Rodriguez
Backbeat Books
9780879309688...................$19.99

Film Noir FAQ
by David J. Hogan
Applause Books
9781557838551.......................$22.99

Football FAQ
by Dave Thompson
Backbeat Books
9781495007484 ....$24.99

Frank Zappa FAQ
by John Corcelli
Backbeat Books
9781617136030...................$19.99

Godzilla FAQ
by Brian Solomon
Applause Books
9781495045684 ....$19.99

The Grateful Dead FAQ
by Tony Sclafani
Backbeat Books
9781617130861.......................$24.99

Guns N' Roses FAQ
by Rich Weidman
Backbeat Books
9781495025884 ....$19.99

Haunted America FAQ
by Dave Thompson
Backbeat Books
9781480392625...................$19.99

Horror Films FAQ
by John Kenneth Muir
Applause Books
9781557839503 ....$22.99

Jack the Ripper FAQ
by Dave Thompson
Applause Books
9781495063084...................$19.99

Jimi Hendrix FAQ
by Gary J. Jucha
Backbeat Books
9781617130953.......................$22.99

Johnny Cash FAQ
by C. Eric Banister
Backbeat Books
9781480385405.............. $24.99

KISS FAQ
by Dale Sherman
Backbeat Books
9781617130915.......................$24.99

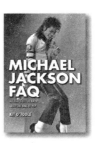

Led Zeppelin FAQ
by George Case
Backbeat Books
9781617130250 ....$22.99

Lucille Ball FAQ
*by James Sheridan
and Barry Monush*
Applause Books
9781617740824......................$19.99

MASH FAQ
by Dale Sherman
Applause Books
9781480355897......................$19.99

Michael Jackson FAQ
by Kit O'Toole
Backbeat Books
9781480371064 ....$19.99

Monty Python FAQ
*by Chris Barsanti, Brian Cogan,
and Jeff Massey*
Applause Books
9781495049439 ....$19.99

Morrissey FAQ
by D. McKinney
Backbeat Books
9781480394483..................$24.99

Neil Young FAQ
by Glen Boyd
Backbeat Books
9781617130373......................$19.99

Pearl Jam FAQ
*by Bernard M. Corbett and
Thomas Edward Harkins*
Backbeat Books
9781617136122 ....$19.99

Pink Floyd FAQ
by Stuart Shea
Backbeat Books
9780879309503..................$19.99

Pro Wrestling FAQ
by Brian Solomon
Backbeat Books
9781617135996......................$29.99

Prog Rock FAQ
by Will Romano
Backbeat Books
9781617135873 ....$24.99

Quentin Tarantino FAQ
by Dale Sherman
Applause Books
9781480355880 ....$24.99

Rent FAQ
by Tom Rowan
Applause Books
9781495051456......................$19.99

Robin Hood FAQ
by Dave Thompson
Applause Books
9781495048227 ....$19.99

**The Rocky Horror
Picture Show FAQ**
by Dave Thompson
Applause Books
9781495007477 ....$19.99

Rush FAQ
by Max Mobley
Backbeat Books
9781617134517 ....$19.99

Seinfeld FAQ
by Nicholas Nigro
Applause Books
9781557838575....................$24.99

Sherlock Holmes FAQ
by Dave Thompson
Applause Books
9781480331495....................$24.99

The Smiths FAQ
by John D. Luerssen
Backbeat Books
9781480394490..................$24.99

Soccer FAQ
by Dave Thompson
Backbeat Books
9781617135989......................$24.99

The Sound of Music FAQ
by Barry Monush
Applause Books
9781480360433..................$27.99

Star Wars FAQ
by Mark Clark
Applause Books
9781480360181....................$24.99

Steely Dan FAQ
by Anthony Robustelli
Backbeat Books
9781495025129 ....$19.99

Three Stooges FAQ
by David J. Hogan
Applause Books
9781557837882....................$22.99

TV Finales FAQ
*by Stephen Tropiano and
Holly Van Buren*
Applause Books
9781480391444 ....$19.99

The Twilight Zone FAQ
by Dave Thompson
Applause Books
9781480396180....................$19.99

Twin Peaks FAQ
*by David Bushman and
Arthur Smith*
Applause Books
9781495015861......................$19.99

UFO FAQ
by David J. Hogan
Backbeat Books
9781480393851 ....$19.99

Video Games FAQ
by Mark J.P. Wolf
Backbeat Books
9781617136306 ....$19.99

The X-Files FAQ
by John Kenneth Muir
Applause Books
9781480369740..................$24.99

HAL•LEONARD®
PERFORMING ARTS
PUBLISHING GROUP

FAQ.halleonardbooks.com